DANGEROUS Curves

Action Heroines, Gender, Fetishism, and Popular Culture

JEFFREY A. BROWN

University Press of Mississippi (Jackson

www.upress.state.ms.us

Designed by Peter D. Halverson

The University Press of Mississippi is a member of the Association of American University Presses.

Earlier versions of selected chapters appeared in the following publications and are reprinted here with permission: Chapter 1: "Gender and the Action Heroine: Hardbodies and the Point of No Return," *Cinema Journal* 35, no. 3 (1996); Chapter 2: "Gender, Sexuality, and the Bad Girls of Action" in *Action Chicks: Tough Girls in Contemporary Popular Culture*, Sherrie Inness editor, University of Pennsylvania Press (2004); Chapter 5: "If Looks Could Kill: Power, Revenge, and Stripper Movies" in *Reel Knockouts: Violent Women in Film*, Neal King and Martha McCaughey editors, University of Texas Press, (2001).

First printing 2011
∞
Library of Congress Cataloging-in-Publication Data

Brown, Jeffrey A., 1966–
  Dangerous curves : action heroines, gender, fetishism, and popular culture / Jeffrey A. Brown.
    p. cm.
  Includes bibliographical references and index.
  ISBN 978-1-60473-714-1 (cloth : alk. paper) — ISBN 978-1-60473-715-8 (ebook)
1. Women heroes in motion pictures. 2. Heroines in literature. 3. Comic books, strips, etc.—History and criticism. 4. Women in popular culture. I. Title.
PN1995.9.W6B76 2011
  305.4—dc22   2010029696

British Library Cataloging-in-Publication Data available

FOR *Anastasia*

CONTENTS

DANGEROUS CURVES

"WHERE ALL WOMEN WEAR SPANDEX AND KNOW KUNG FU"

For over forty years James Bond has reigned as the quintessential action hero. Whether it is the original Ian Fleming novels, the twenty-plus feature films (the most successful movie franchise of all time), the affiliated merchandise, the comic-strip incarnations, or even the video games, James Bond is a worldwide phenomenon and the prototype for modern heroes. As the promotional tag line for the Bond collectible videos declares: "Bond is the *original* action hero." It doesn't seem to matter if he is embodied by Sean Connery, George Lazenby, Roger Moore, Timothy Dalton, Pierce Brosnan, or Daniel Craig . . . Bond is every man's ideal self. And why not? The international intrigue, the gadgets, the sophisticated lifestyle, the cars, the license to kill, and, of course, the women.

Ever since Ursula Andress sauntered out of the ocean in a bikini in *Dr. No* (1963), the "Bond Girl," as she is officially known, has been as famous for her beauty and sexuality as Bond has been for his adventures. With none-too-subtle monikers like Pussy Galore and Holly Goodhead, the Bond Girl has always been an erotic accessory for Bond. If Bond is the man every male viewer wants to be, then the Bond Girl is the woman every male viewer wants to bed. But the bluntness of the traditionally patriarchal fantasy played out in each Bond movie runs the risk of seeming too anachronistic in this new millennium. Over the years the films' producers have struggled with the question of how to change the Bond Girl to reflect shifts in cultural values and gender politics without losing their core audience.

One answer was to hire Halle Berry for the role of Jinx in *Die Another Day* (2002). The casting of Berry seemed ideal; she is one of Hollywood's hottest actresses, the first African American woman to win an Academy Award as Best Actress, and is typically ranked in the popular press as one of the most

Stay linked to a world...

Where all women wear spandex and know kung fu.

Stay linked to movies.

Movielink
movielink.com

0.1. Print advertisement
for the Internet movie
database, Movielink.

beautiful women in the world. The character of Jinx is described as "a smart-mouthed, catsuit-clad American Spy every bit as indestructible as Agent 007 himself," and much of the publicity surrounding the film focused on the possibility that Berry as Jinx "may pull off something not even Andress did: She might steal the movie" (Svetkey 2002: 23). By retooling the Bond Girl as an action heroine in her own right—able to shoot, fight, and wisecrack her way through extravagant and dangerous scenarios—Berry's Jinx appeared to be the ideal solution for both Bond and MGM Studios. More than just offsetting the phallocentric nature of the Bond formula, Jinx had the potential to headline an action franchise of her own. In fact, MGM was so sure they had found the winning combination of a sexy and respected actress with a wide audience appeal—and a viable character designed for fast-paced adventures—that the studio initiated plans for a Jinx spinoff even before *Die Another Day* was released. Berry's Jinx was, in other words, an ideal chance for the studio to enter the growing, but as of yet, underexploited trend of action heroines.

As much as the *Die Another Day* producers enjoyed patting themselves on the back for creating "a totally new type of Bond Girl" (Svetkey 2002: 23), a Jinx-type character was hardly new to audiences. In fact, just one Bond film earlier, *Tomorrow Never Dies* (1997), included Michelle Yeoh as Chinese agent Wai Lin, who was, in almost every aspect, as much the action hero of the film as Bond. The crucial difference between Yeoh's Lin and Berry's Jinx seemed to be the studio's willingness to promote Jinx as more than just another Bond Girl. As a tough, self-reliant, and sexy adventuress, Jinx joins the ranks of action heroines who have infiltrated every facet of popular culture over the last few years.

In contemporary Western society the action heroine is everywhere. Recent big-budget Hollywood movies have seen the likes of Uma Thurman, Milla Jovovich, Kate Beckinsale, and Angelina Jolie shooting, slicing, and kicking their way through the *Kill Bill* (2003 and 2004*)*, *Resident Evil* (2001 and 2004), *Underworld* (2003 and 2006), and *Tomb Raider* (2003 and 2005) series respectively. As a recent print advertisement for the Internet movie database, Movielink, proclaimed: "Stay linked to a world where all women wear spandex and know kung fu" (Figure 0.1). Likewise, on television new heroines have met with phenomenal critical success and/or cult popularity on programs such as *Alias*, *Witchblade*, *Veronica Mars*, the new *Bionic Woman*, and *Terminator: The Sara Connor Chronicles*. Meanwhile their most recent small-screen predecessors, such as *Xena: Warrior Princess*, *Buffy the Vampire Slayer*, and *La Femme Nikita*, continue to thrive in reruns.

Even children's animated programming has joined the action heroine trend with *The Powerpuff Girls*, *Kim Possible*, *My Life as a Teenage Robot*, and *Atomic Betty*. In the world of computer games, the phenomenal popularity of Lara Croft in the *Tomb Raider* series has spawned countless other virtual heroines including Jennifer Tate in *Primal*, Vanessa Z. Schneider in *P.N.03*, and Nikki Connors in *Rogue Ops*. Contemporary literary heroines such as Sara Paretsky's V. I. Warshawski, Sue Grafton's Cordelia Gray, and Amanda Cross's Kate Fansler remain popular with adults. They have been joined on the bookshelves by a range of younger heroines aimed at the tween reading audience in series such as Francine Pascal's *Fearless*, Carrie Asai's *Samurai Girl*, and even the Olsen twins-endorsed *Mary-Kate and Ashley In Action*. Likewise, comic book superheroines have been revitalized in this era of omnipresent action genres with new versions of Wonder Woman, Batgirl, Catwoman, and Storm fighting it out shoulder-to-shoulder with their male counterparts, both within the stories and at the sales counter. After decades of playing the sidekick or the villainess, the new action heroine has come into her own. Jinx may have been a remarkably progressive step for the Bond franchise, but it was a step that had already been taken in many other popular action genres.

The modern action heroine has an interesting lineage. She is built upon the foundation of such diverse precedents as the female sleuths in the writings of Agatha Christie and Dorothy Sayers, the femme fatales of 1930s and 1940s film noir, the spunky tomboys of 1950s teen films, and the leather-clad mod heroines of 1960s television programs like *The Avengers* and *Honey West*. In the 1970s it was the vengeful heroine of blaxploitation films like *Coffy* (1973) and *Cleopatra Jones* (1973) and the sexy television detectives of *Charlie's Angels* and *Police Woman*. But to say the action heroine is a common fixture in contemporary popular culture does not mean she's become an incontestable figure. She is still rare enough that nearly every new heroine is treated in the entertainment press as either a harbinger of ass-kicking feminism or as yet another example of how excessive violence has taken hold of every facet of popular culture.

Action heroines seem to be heralded or denigrated in waves. For example, the 1991 release of *La Femme Nikita*, *The Silence of the Lambs*, *Terminator 2*, and *Thelma and Louise* touched off a wave of public debate about women entering the violent domain typically reserved for male heroes. Similarly, in 1997, publications as politically disparate as *Entertainment Weekly* and *Girlfriends* used the phenomenal success of *Xena: Warrior Princess* to profile a trend of tough, smart, and sexually ambiguous heroines on the small screen including the characters of Dana Scully on *The X-Files* and Captain Janeway of *Star Trek Voyager*. More recently, the extreme violence dished out by Uma Thurman's character, The Bride, in *Kill Bill* resulted in numerous profiles of supposedly post-feminist heroines from *Alias* to *The Powerpuff Girls* in such publications as the *New York Times* and the *Village Voice*. Each seemingly new wave of action heroines is documented in the popular press as a surprising new trend.

Reporters ask: "Does she represent a new standard of liberation?" "Does she represent actresses being accepted into the hallowed halls of film machismo?" "Does she represent the mainstreaming of lesbian desires?" "Does she represent new trends in leather fashion?" Her ambiguous nature means she can represent many different things to many different people. It also means she can become the poster-girl for whichever cultural fantasies and/or fears are currently in vogue. The action heroine is a lightning rod for public debate because she is such an in-your-face challenge to basic cultural assumptions about gender roles in real life and in fantasy.

The action heroine has also become a much-debated figure among cultural, media, and gender critics because she both problematizes and reinforces some of the most basic tenets of film studies and gender portrayal. Over the last decade, the literature on action heroines has become a fruitful growth industry. Initiated in part by the work of scholars like Yvonne Tasker (1993) and Susan Jeffords (1994) who took masculinity in 1980s action films as their launching point, and Carol Clover's (1993) work on the "Final Girl" of horror movies, a phenomenal amount of excellent research and speculation has been published about the narrative, social, and political implications of action heroines.

Book-length treatises like Tasker's follow-up, *Working Girls* (1998), Sherrie Inness' *Tough Girls* (2000), and Dawn Heinecken's *The Women Warriors of Television* (2003); and anthologies like McCaughey and King's *Reel Knockouts* (2001), Early and Kennedy's *Athena's Daughters* (2003), and Inness' *Action Chicks* (2004) have joined the numerous essays in film, media, and gender studies journals. The amount of studies produced about academic favorites like Buffy of television's *Buffy the Vampire Slayer*, and Ripley of the *Aliens* film series, is staggering. This book draws upon many of the research interests found in the past scholarship including the negotiation of gender roles in performance, violence, sexuality, and genre traditions. I also suggest some new directions that may help free the action heroine from the theoretical predictability in which she has become mired.

On the one hand, the most fundamental position argues, the modern action heroine is a far cry from the traditionally passive roles offered to women. She commands the narrative and controls her destiny, makes her own decisions, and fights her own battles. She is inquisitive and intelligent, physically and emotionally strong, and is clearly portrayed as a heroic ideal with which audience members identify. On the other hand, the action heroine perpetuates the ideal of female beauty and sexuality that has always been the primary cultural value of women in our society. Whether portrayed in live-action film and television by supermodels and centerfolds, in cartoons by anime-inspired wide-eyed preteen waifs, or stylized polygons and pixels in digital games, action heroines are conventionally beautiful, glamorous, and sexualized.

The contradictory nature of action heroines is understandable given the commercial imperatives of contemporary media forms. The audience for all forms of action has traditionally been considered exclusively male; thus, portraying action heroines as both tough and sexual, violent but desirable, allows producers to expand the basic range of action narratives and still cater to the more prurient interests of their key consumers. The problem, at its simplest, is that this double bind constructs these emerging roles for women as both a heroic subject and as a sexual object.

The unequal burden of sexuality faced by action heroines was evident in both the narrative and the promotional campaign for *Die Another Day*. Bond may be the sexual ideal—he may even be a sex object, but his desirability has never been the defining characteristic of his persona in the way it has been for the Bond Girls. For all the talk in the press about how great an actress Halle Berry is, and how tough the character of Jinx is, the dominant selling point for the film was the image of Berry in an orange bikini. To be fair, Jinx does fight, shoot, and toss around double entendres nearly on par with Bond . . . but her primary function is still to be fetishized by the camera. Every story that appeared about the film in print, on television, or on the Internet included photos of Berry/Jinx emerging from the surf in her bikini.

Differing standards for male and female action stars are evident in the DVD packaging of *Die Another Day*. The DVD contains a foldout cover that depicts Bond and Jinx in side-by-side stills from the film. But whereas Bond is dressed in a bulky black turtleneck sweater and trousers with his gun at the ready, Jinx is simply standing around in a seashore café clad in just her bikini, a diving knife slung provocatively across her hips. However progressive the role of Jinx is in the film, the juxtaposition of these two images makes clear the traditional gender dichotomy long existent in Hollywood. Here Bond is still marked as powerful and in control, his body is concealed and contained, he is ready for action, has a piercing gaze and his "weapon" is raised.

In contrast, Jinx is presented as an object to be looked at; her body is open to the viewers' pleasure. Her breasts, stomach, and hips are framed for emphasis by both the cut of the bikini and the focus of the photograph. Her facial expression may not be inviting, but the rest of the image is more pinup fantasy than heroic ideal. And whereas Bond's gun reinforces his power and authority in clearly phallic terms, Jinx's still sheathed knife is an almost humorously exaggerated example of fetishization, of phallic compensation for her apparent lack. If Jinx, like all action heroines, is no longer passive and powerless, she is still a long way from overcoming some of the most basic patriarchal and heterosexist conventions that persist in popular culture and continue to undermine the validity of heroic femininity. One step forward, two steps back.

The conflicted nature of action heroines in contemporary media is also reflected in the tension between her seemingly omnipresent image and her uneven success at the movies and in television ratings. If action genres are becoming "a world where all women wear spandex and know kung fu," as the Movielink ad asserts, it is still not yet a world where these women are equally popular with audiences. While Ellen Ripley and Sara Connor proved to be immensely popular in the late 1980s and early 1990s by assuming the role of muscular hard-body heroism made famous by such male icons of the genre as Arnold Schwarzenegger and Sylvester Stallone, their success has proven difficult to repeat. Other modern action heroines, such as Uma Thurman's The Bride from the *Kill Bill* movies (2003 and 2004), Kate Beckinsale's Selene from the *Underworld* films (2003 and 2006), and Jennifer Garner's Sydney Bristow from the television series *Alias* (2001–2006), have been huge triumphs. But more often than not, the action heroine has struggled to achieve blockbuster notoriety through the late 1990s and 2000s.

Despite the popularity and Academy Award-winning credentials of actresses like Angelina Jolie, Halle Berry, and Charlize Theron, their high-profile outings in *Tomb Raider: Cradle of Life* (2003), *Catwoman* (2004), and *Aeon Flux* (2005) met with disappointing returns. Widely circulated promotional images of the actresses in revealing leather outfits attracted a lot of attention but never translated to critical or box-office success. When Jennifer Garner's heavily promoted *Daredevil* (2003) spin-off *Electra* (2005) likewise bombed on its opening weekend, critics pondered the viability of action heroines en masse. *Entertainment Weekly*, for example, wondered: "Does Jennifer Garner's dud opening doom superchick flicks?" (Schwartz 2005). The apparent answer to this rhetorical question is a resounding "No!" While these failing films, and others including *Barb Wire* (1996), *The Long Kiss Goodnight* (1996), *Bloodrayne* (2005), *Ultraviolet* (2006), *Bandidas* (2006), and *Dead or Alive* (2007), may have proven to be box-office poison, Hollywood has continued to crank out action heroine vehicles.

By and large, action heroines have achieved much more critical and commercial success (not to mention devoted fan followings) in serialized formats. Whether on television, in novels, or in comic books, serialized heroines benefit from the ability of longer formats to fully develop and explore characters. Yet, even in feature films, the occasional success story—and the logical industry assumption that the primarily male audience for action genres will be attracted to sexy heroines—has overridden the action heroines' commercial weaknesses. That the thoroughly fetishized action heroine is a staple in popular culture despite her uneven returns is evidence she encapsulates specific cultural concerns and needs to be more fully explored.

My primary concern throughout the essays in this book is the awkward balance between the hope that action heroines embody radical cultural change in acceptable gender roles and the fear they have only solidified the eroticization of female characters. I certainly do not mean to imply that action heroines should be considered primarily as an "either/or" scenario. To understand these figures as simply *either* good and empowering—*or* as bad and disempowering, is to miss the complex range of issues their current popularity raises. The real importance of the action heroine is that she is not easily written off as "either/ or." She does muddy the waters of what we consider masculine and feminine, of desirable beauty and threatening sexuality, of subjectivity and objectivity, of powerful and powerless. Rather than replicating the simplistic binary logic that our society all too often resorts to for interpreting the world around us, the contestability of the action heroine challenges our basic assumptions and may force a new understanding of cultural norms.

Instead of one step forward and two steps back, it may be a matter of three steps sideways. Because the action heroine is a direct affront to notions of gender acceptability, she requires audiences to see her as more than just a woman—and conversely because her femininity is so visually stressed, she also forces audiences to see her as more than just a woman taking on a male role. Likewise, her performance of conflicting gender attributes are often matched by the carefully staged performance of traditionally fetishized female roles, thus bringing into question the naturalness of identity as a stable term. It also problematizes the very notion of fetishization in the sense of phallic compensation, unconventional sexual desires, and even as a form of commodification.

The term "action heroine" indicates the twin focuses of this book: genre and femininity. Action as a genre has become a dominant form of entertainment worldwide and is a mainstay of numerous media, including film, television, comic books, literature, and computer games. As a clearly defined genre, Action serves as a useful cultural text for analysis because it is structured around easily recognizable formulas and conventions. Thus, each new generic invention can be read as a marker of both a structural need to keep the genre fresh and as a sign of shifting cultural perceptions grounded in an existing visual rhetoric. Fundamental changes such as the gender of the lead characters indicates a twist in how the entire genre speaks to social needs and fantasies, as well as how gender is perceived through the lens of a specific narrative iconography.

It is the various ways femininity is reconfigured through the language of action genres that constitutes the central purpose of this book. By considering new roles of femininity within the context of contemporary Action, it is possible to come to a deeper understanding of a host of crucial issues women and men face in a persistently misogynistic world dominated by media images. Yet while the structural properties of a genre help provide a framework for analysis, it is still a polysemic frame open to a wide range of diverse and often conflicting possibilities.

The 2003 summer movie season provided a striking example of how women complicate the symbolic terrain of Action. Within weeks of each other, numerous action heroines appeared on the cover of various magazines to promote their films and TV series. The rash of cover stories is in itself standard entertainment industry promotion, but what was striking, however, was the similar iconography used in each of the cover images. *Wired* featured Jada Pinkett-Smith astride a motorcycle to link into the hype of her role as Niobe in *The Matrix Reloaded* (2003), the science fiction magazine *Cinescape* reproduced a still of Angelina Jolie as Lara Croft riding her motorcycle from *Tomb Raider: Cradle of Life* (2003), and Jennifer Garner of television's *Alias* graced the cover of *GQ*'s annual Hollywood issue posed in a short leather skirt on a motorcycle in the middle of the desert. On their own each of these images is merely meant to promote the actresses and their projects, but as a whole they represent a specific visual convention of the genre. These examples are just the tip of the proverbial iceberg when it comes to the odd pairing of heroines and motorcycles, and it is a theme I will return to throughout the book.

Sexy action heroines posed with powerful motorcycles are nothing new. Only a few years earlier the media was saturated with the image of Pamela Anderson dressed as a dominatrix and straddling her chopper for her first feature film, *Barb Wire* (1996). Likewise, Beyonce posed on a motorcycle while sporting a black bodystocking for the cover of *Movieline*'s music issue to promote her blaxploitation parody role as Foxy Cleopatra in *Austin Powers: Goldmember* (2002). In all, the list of modern action heroines with motorcycles as their ride is lengthy. The Bride races around Tokyo on her yellow street bike and matching leathers in *Kill Bill*; Trinity weaves through *The Matrix: Reloaded* on her motorcycle in her signature black leather and dark sunglasses; as Catwoman in the film of the same name (2004), Halle Berry also dons a slinky leather outfit to cruise city streets on a Ducati; Max, Jessica Alba's character in TV's *Dark Angel*, made her way around a post-apocalyptic Seattle on her customized motorcycle; the animated series for adults, *Striperella*, features its stripper/superheroine riding down evil-doers on her bike; in the comics, on television, and in the movies Batgirl has her Batcycle—even Shania Twain suited up in head-to-toe black leather to zoom around on a CGI supercycle for her award-winning, sci-fi-inspired music video "I'm Gonna Get You." Though motorcycles have traditionally been thought of as a masculine form of transportation in Western culture, the Action genre associates motorcycles with heroic women.

The simple convention of depicting action heroines on motorcycles raises certain questions, and consolidates certain issues that repeatedly surface in the following chapters. Symbolically the image of action heroines on motorcycles can be interpreted as a carefully orchestrated sign of liberation and empowerment. After all, the motorcycle has long represented freedom, mobility, and the open road in American culture. The modern equivalent of the cowboy's horse, the motorcycle can go almost anywhere—it is rugged, powerful, fast, and commands attention. It is the vehicle of choice for some of Hollywood's most iconic rebel heroes: Marlon Brando in *The Wild One* (1953), Elvis Presley in *Roustabout* (1964), and Steve McQueen in *The Great Escape* (1963).

It is also an obvious phallic symbol, suggesting that whoever has mastered the machine, male or female, has also mastered power, privilege, and individuality. Thus, it is the perfect vehicle for Lara Croft to race against her tough guy male partner in *Tomb Raider 2* to prove her superiority, or for the Bride to stalk her pampered, chauffeur-driven adversaries in *Kill Bill*. At this symbolic level, the motorcycle clarifies that the action heroine is a radically different female character—and the exact opposite of being passive, weak, and in need of saving. In fact, it allows the heroine to take on the role of the shining knight who rides in on the trusty steed to save the day—literally in films such as *The Matrix Reloaded*, *Barb Wire*, and *Resident Evil 2: Apocalypse* (2004). The motorcycle marks the action heroine as a tough, independent woman in control of herself and the situation, no matter how harrowing.

The motorcycle in Action genres is a fully loaded sign. So much so in fact that it may reveal itself to be nothing but a sign—sound and fury signifying nothing. Of the magazine examples noted above, it is curious that in three of them the motorcycle is nothing more than a convenient prop for a glamorous photograph. Niobe never actually rides a motorcycle in *The Matrix: Reloaded*—nor does Sydney Bristow in any of the episodes of *Alias* or Foxy Cleopatra in *Goldmember*. Coupled with the de rigueur leather tank tops, boots, and body stockings, the image of action heroines astride motorcycles is also a very traditional sign of fetishization. If the symbolic iconography of heroines on motorcycles suggests a parity, or even a superiority, with action heroes, it simultaneously suggests pinups of naked or bikini-clad babes draped over hot rods and choppers. In the context of fetishization, the action heroine becomes not the master of phallic power but a worshipper of it. It is a thin line between symbolizing empowerment and exploitation. (Chapter Five addresses a similar connotative shift that marks the difference between women who wield guns and those who are subservient to them.)

As fetishized objects, both the women and the motorcycles serve as objects of desire rather than as subjects of identification. They become something that is idealized and possessable, equivalent objects of adornment, and pornographic fantasy figures on offer to male viewers. The women are also reducible to the same level of commodification as the motorcycles, the implication being that both are available to be bought, sold, accessorized, and ridden by a male consumer. I will take up an extreme example of this in Chapter Five where the ability to control action women in computer games actually results in a melding of the female body and the motorcycle. That something as innocuous and conventional as the use of motorcycles can be so fraught with both positive and negative connotations for action heroines is indicative of just how complex the symbolic terrain can be. Despite the popular press's desires, there are no easy answers when it comes to developing new roles for women in the media.

Because our depiction of women in the media is so grounded in eroticism and objectification it is difficult to conceive of them in different terms. It would also be a mistake to consider new roles as clearly demarcated from the larger culture-wide system of fetishizing women. No matter how progressive action heroines may be, they still operate from within a system better prepared to exploit women's looks than celebrate their achievements. But it is the potential action heroines have to function as progressive role models, despite the cultural- and genre-derived fetishization, I want to argue throughout this book.

Chapter One, "Gender and the Action Heroine: Hardbodies and the *Point of No Return*," lays the groundwork for understanding these new roles as a renegotiation of gender. This essay, which originally appeared in *Cinema Journal*, addresses some of the early theoretical work on modern action heroines that focused on how the characters alternated between performing femininity and masculinity. Concentrating on films from the early 1990s wave of action heroism, I discuss such key characters as Ripley from *Aliens*, Sarah Connor from *Terminator 2: Judgment Day*, and Maggie from *Point of No Return*, the Hollywood remake of *La Femme Nikita*. In their own way, each of these heroines is an important reference point for understanding the ways in which action heroines reconfigure gender. Whereas Ripley and Connor have been credited with performing masculinity through their use of muscles and weapons, Maggie goes a step further and intentionally performs femininity to disguise the threat she poses. Whether action heroines are depicted as masculinized hardbodies or as soft, miniskirted ass-kickers, they ultimately challenge the assumption that gender and behavior are biologically determined.

Chapter Two, "Gender, Sexuality and Toughness: The Bad Girls of Action Film and Comic Books," continues the analysis of the action heroine's gender as a performance that undermines the usefulness of "masculine" and "feminine" as mutually exclusive categories. Concentrating primarily on the film *Barb Wire* (1996) and its roots in the genre of "Bad Girl" superhero comics, I argue that the type of hyper-sexualized action heroine embodied by Pamela Anderson does not alternate between masculine and feminine characterizations but rather combines traits associated with both gender categories. Like her equally tough and highly sexualized counterparts in the comics, Barb Wire is an object of fear and desire for young male consumers. Her cartoonish sexuality is combined with violence and fetishistic clothing that reveals the action heroine as akin to the fantasy figure of the dominatrix. Yet, rather than just a kinky stock character from the realms of S&M pornography, the action heroine can be understood as a dominatrix in that she wields both physical and social power thanks to her ability to combine masculinity and femininity in a single character. Even the most exploitative examples of action heroines can challenge traditional cultural beliefs about gender and sexuality.

The theme of action heroines personifying a threatening and disguised sexuality is further explored in Chapter Three, "Alias, Fetishism, and Pygmalion Fantasies." Focusing primarily on the TV series *Alias*, I argue that the use of femininity as a masquerade, a formulaic element that constitutes a central component of the series, successfully undermines specific fetishistic fantasy figures while simultaneously showcasing them. In every episode the heroine, Sydney Bristow, undertakes a mission that requires her to go undercover, usually assuming the role of a sexualized feminine character. Ostensibly, costuming Sydney (and Jennifer Garner, the ex-model turned award-winning actress who portrays her) in such aliases as prostitute, geisha, dominatrix, damsel-in-distress, Catholic school girl, southern belle, sexy businesswoman, sexy nurse, and so on—allows her to infiltrate top-secret male domains because the bad guys always underestimate her as "just a woman." While this use of fetish costuming is explicit in *Alias*, it exists in almost every representation of action heroines.

Whether it is the gothic skin-tight leathers worn by Kate Beckinsale in the *Underworld* (2003 and 2006) films, Angelina Jolie dressed as a dominatrix in *Mr. and Mrs. Smith* (2005), the four teen heroines of *D.E.B.S.* (2004) in their Catholic school-girl outfits, or Jessica Biel in leather pants and belly-shirt in *Blade Trinity* (2005), the action heroine is routinely costumed to cater to sexual fantasy. Perhaps more than any other action heroine though, Sydney Bristow of *Alias* is presented as a fully rounded character that merely uses her various masquerades to gain access to a traditionally masculine domain of intrigue, espionage, and power. Narratively, Sydney is surrounded by father figures who aid her in her adventures and ensure her sovereignty in the symbolic realm of paternal law enforcement. But, whereas Sydney may be master of her own identity and fate within the ongoing fiction of *Alias*, the authority credited to series' creator J. J. Abrams suggests that Sydney, and other action heroines, may also function as a type of masquerade for male writers, directors, and producers.

In addition to mobilizing sexual, ethnic, and commodity fetishism, the action heroine is subject to a more precise form of Pygmalion fetishism. Almost without exception, the action heroines' story involves seeking approval from her father, or making herself over in his heroic image. This cliché of the action heroine as "Daddy's girl" is mirrored by the real-world creation of, and sometimes obsession with, ass-kicking heroines by such noted creators as Abrams, James Cameron, Quentin Tarantino, Joss Whedon, and Jean-Luc Besson. Both within the narrative and extratextually, action heroines often serve as a way for male authority to revel in a form of threatening female sexuality, and to control it.

Chapter Four, "Play With Me: Sexy Cyborgs, Game Girls, and Digital Babes," strays from a strict focus on action heroines to consider how the female body has been displaced in recent films in favor of a completely idealized and commodified female form. This chapter expands the definition of action heroines to include certain heroic women of science fiction and computer gaming. Ever since Donna Haraway's essay "Cyborg Manifesto" was first published in 1991, the female cyborg has been a favorite of feminist film theory for her potential to destabilize traditional cultural categories and resist patriarchal authority. But, I argue, the typically hyper-sexualized body of the female cyborg presents her not as a subversive figure but as a phallic woman and a sexual commodity for men, both within the narrative and in the audience.

It is no coincidence that technology in human form is most often represented in science fiction by beautiful women. The use of sexy actresses on television like Jeri Ryan as the Borg 7 of 9 in *Star Trek: Voyager*, Lexa Doig as a virtual embodiment of the spaceship's systems in *Andromeda*, or Tricia Helfer as a Cylon in *Battlestar Galactica* manages to both sexualize technology and to dehumanize ideal female bodies. It is only a small step from the cyborg embodied by real-life beautiful women to the robotic pinups gracing the covers of *Heavy Metal* magazine, numerous North American and Japanese comic books, and the scantily clad heroines of various video games like *Tomb Raider* and *Bloodrayne*. The real body is replaced by a robotic, synthetic, or digitized version that acts as a chimera of female beauty—a body that can be manipulated and idealized to achieve a sense of physical perfection impossible for real women to duplicate. And while it may be a heroic female body, as it is in the game versions of Tomb Raider, Xena, Dark Angel, Alias, Buffy, Resident Evil, Catwoman, and so on, it is also a body devoid of subjectivity. The action heroine becomes nothing more than a stylized vessel for gamers to control.

The reworking of action and rape-revenge genre conventions constitutes the primary focus of Chapter Five, "If Looks Could Kill: Power, Revenge, and Stripper Movies." By focusing on such traditionally derided genres as erotic thrillers, straight-to-video action, and pornography that present strippers as defiant and self-rescuing heroines, I argue that the power of the male gaze is destabilized. Or, at least, that the privilege associated with the assumed right to look at exposed female bodies is destabilized in fiction. The fantasy on offer in these films is that even women who are fully open for male inspection actually wield more concrete power than the men doing the looking. Yet, while the notion that the women being looked at are really the ones in control of the situation fits well with the belief that women can be both heroines and sex objects, the economic and social reality is that female strippers have very little control. Ultimately, the fiction that women can find true strength by being alluring and sexually objectified operates as a distancing technique that allows men to consume women and their sexuality in the most conventional of gendered forms in a relatively guilt-free manner.

While the hyper-violent and the hyper-sexualized version of the modern action heroine dominates her representation in feature films, her cuter, kid-friendly younger sister has emerged as a mainstay in children's animated television programming. The teen and pre-teen action heroine of such popular kids shows as *Kim Possible*, *The Powerpuff Girls*, *Totally Spies*, *Atomic Betty*, *My Life as a Teenage Robot*, and *The Life and Times of Juniper Lee* become the focus of Chapter Six, "'She Can Do Anything!' The Action Heroine and the Modern (Post-Feminist) Girl." Though marketed to children, these programs and their like repeat many of the traditionally fetishistic themes of their older counterparts, albeit in a less obvious manner. These girl heroines have to balance saving the world with shopping for cute outfits and crushing on boys. Where the feature film action heroine explores the tenuous balance between sexualization and empowerment, the younger girl heroine version presents a glamorous form of "Girl Power" in a very physical sense.

The superpowers, athleticism, and overall toughness of these heroines lend a certain muscle to the message of post-feminism chic through girlishness and consumerism. The girlish action heroine provides young viewers with a more active image of girlhood without sacrificing traditional girlish concerns and behaviors. In other words, in addition to reinforcing the association of ass-kicking femininity with sexual fetishization, the trend of girl action heroines also clarifies the link between these roles and consumer fetishization. It is no coincidence that the title for the first book in the action-oriented *Spy Goddess* series for young readers is *Live and Let Shop* (a reference to the famous James Bond title *Live and Let Die*, which neatly shifts the emphasis from deadly action to empowerment through girls being tough and still spending time at the mall).

The modern action heroine is predominantly represented in the media as an ideal of feminine beauty that is almost exclusively Aryan. Despite the influential precedents of African American heroines who achieved a great deal of notoriety during the Blaxploitation era and the still-common presence of strong Asian women in kung fu films, almost all contemporary Hollywood versions of action heroines feature idealized white actresses. In Chapter Seven I concentrate on various superheroines of color currently popular in comic books to explore how strong female characters continue to be depicted according to concepts of Orientalism. Issues of ethnicity and skin color often take center stage in comics, and the more narrowly defined male-centered superhero genre allows the writers and artists to address racial issues in a very fundamental manner. Ethnically identified female characters like Misty Knight (African American), the most recent Batgirl (Asian), the current White Tiger (Latina), and Dust (Middle Eastern), are discussed in detail as representatives of a changing ethnic landscape within the comics. Yet for all the surface progression these superheroines of color stand for, they also represent Western culture's standard depiction of non-white women as exotic beauties overwritten by stereotypical racist and sexist conceptions of ethnicity.

The strong female heroes of horror film, the type famously described by Carol Clover as "Final Girls," are some of the most influential predecessors of the modern action heroine. This cross-genre link remains apparent in a number of action films and television shows that feature action heroines battling a stock horror monster. The vampire in particular is a common enemy of action heroines, or as in the case of the *Underworld* and *Bloodrayne* films, the heroine may even be a vampire herself. Chapter Eight, "Kinky Vampires and Sexy Action Heroines," builds off the association between vampires and action heroines to consider how each character type functions as a symbol of alternative sexual fantasies. Within the official Hollywood texts the action heroine is usually characterized as a fairly conservative sexual figure who ultimately confirms a hetero-normative ideal despite the excessively fetishized way she is depicted. But like the vampire before her whom she often fights against, the action heroine is also an easily co-opted symbol of polymorphous sexuality that facilitates a range of erotic fantasies including lesbian and sadomasochistic desires. This chapter addresses such iconic heroine series as *Buffy the Vampire Slayer* and *Xena: Warrior Princess* as examples of how both conventional and alternative sexual relations are depicted by the narratives and how they are embraced in alternative ways by fans.

Chapter Nine, "When the Action Heroine Looks," delves into the ways these heroines reconfigure the logic of power, privilege, and narrative authority associated with looking in media theory. Rather than simply being the subject of a male gaze (a concept that has maintained a prominent position in feminist theory dealing with visual depictions of women for over twenty-five years now), most action heroines have assumed an active gaze of their own. Despite attempts to punish the women for looking, as in horror or film noir, and to reduce to mere sex objects, as in almost all mainstream media depictions, these women investigate crimes, look at whatever or whomever they want to, safe in the knowledge that they can control whatever they may discover. The role of active female looking in various media forms has been a fundamental issue for understanding the female detective who has become a popular figure in film and television since the 1970s.

This chapter traces the development of the active female gaze from such key texts as *Cagney & Lacey* and *The Silence of the Lambs* through to more recent examples including *Twisted* and *Taking Lives*. While these detective heroines have gradually become stronger and more independent agents, their mastery of vision is still presented as a weak spot that keeps female characters tethered to a narrative position as potential victims and as sexualized objects of a threatening male gaze. The action heroine, a close sister of the detective heroine, assumes the active, investigatory gaze in a more successful manner that permits her to assert a complete mastery over the events within her narrative. Coupled with the heroines' assumption of an investigating gaze, this chapter also considers how action heroines in general rework the gaze as a glare. Whereas a gaze connotes an easily exercised, almost casual looking, the glare employed by action heroines implies an aggressive, angry, and knowing use of looking.

The concluding chapter, "Wondering About Wonder Woman: Action Heroines as Multi-Fetish," brings together all the disparate, and at times apparently conflicting, issues addressed in the book. The issues of sexuality, fetishization, gender role reworkings, masquerades, the importance of fictional fathers and male creators, consumption, girlishness, audience control, and all the rest, are considered in their entirety. My main concern is to demonstrate how these different themes work together to inform our overall cultural reading of action heroines as contestable figures.

To help unite how these issues operate at various levels and in competing ways, I will explore how the single character of Wonder Woman has been reconfigured in multiple forms in recent years, and discuss the difficulties that have plagued Hollywood's efforts to produce a live-action Wonder Woman feature film. As one of the most readily identifiable action heroines since her debut in the 1940s, Wonder Woman holds a unique place in contemporary popular culture as both a symbol of heroic feminism and a fetishized sex symbol. As a character that currently cuts across different mediums (comics, live-action films and television, animation, computer games, and even Internet pornography) and different theoretical issues (age, sexuality, male dominance, consumption, fetishization, and access to power), Wonder Woman illustrates how multiple understandings of a single action heroine can coexist and serve differing political and personal concerns.

In an attempt to deal with the complex depictions of action heroines in contemporary media, I have consciously adopted two specific strategies in the writing of this book. The first, and probably most obvious at this point, is that I have included as many visual examples as possible. The physical representation of these characters is a crucial component of how they are understood by audiences. The appearance of the actresses and the stylization of the illustrated characters are fundamental to their appeal. I feel it is important for readers to see the depictions for themselves whenever possible.

The highly sexualized visual representation of contemporary action heroines is a prominent aspect of how they are marketed and packaged for potential viewers/consumers. This eroticized promotional style is important because it marks the point where action heroines are offered up as objects for male consumption. The visual eroticization of this character type enhances their value as commodity fetishes in tandem with their sexual fetishization. Furthermore, because many of the issues I address are based on the look of the characters, how they are costumed, and how they are visually framed, I want readers to see if the images bear out my interpretation of them.

My second strategy is to reference many of the action heroines in multiple chapters. As commercial intertexts, action heroines do not exist in single formats, nor do they confront single theoretical concerns. By focusing on specific examples I do not want to lose sight of how these characters are interrelated or of how they all deal, in different degrees, with the various issues I discuss.

For example, though Sidney Bristow of *Alias* is the major example I use in Chapter Three because she clearly demonstrates Pygmalion themes and self-conscious masquerading, she is also an example of a heroine who assumes an active glare as discussed in Chapter Nine, of a character controlled by male computer gamers as considered in Chapter Four, as the type of muscular heroine as addressed in Chapter One, a dominatrix like the subjects of Chapter Two, and even as an animated heroine as in Chapter Six. In fact, most of the heroines cross over into almost every point of discussion, and I have tried to mention them where appropriate to avoid any false assumption that the heroines or the issues they represent can be neatly separated. As a character type, the contemporary action heroine is not restricted to a single medium. She has infiltrated every aspect of popular culture, from film and television to computer games, to comics and teen literature; thus, action heroines need to be considered beyond the confines of a single medium, or a single field of scholarly media studies.

1) GENDER AND THE ACTION HEROINE

Hardbodies and the Point of No Return

$\mathcal{A}$s one of the most dominant genres of popular cinema since the early 1980s, the action film has done much to construct the body of the male hero as spectacle. The well-displayed muscles of such heroic icons as Sylvester Stallone and Jean Claude Van Damme have worked within a narrative space that presents masculinity as an excessive, almost hysterical, performance. Indeed, the spectacle of the muscular male body has become the genre's central trademark, a feature that allowed Arnold Schwarzenegger to catapult from professional body builder to at one point the highest-paid movie star on the planet.

With their obvious emphasis on masculine ideals, action films in the 1980s seem to deny any blurring of gender boundaries: men are active, while women are present only to be rescued or to confirm the heterosexuality of the hero. Yvonne Tasker has described the action genre as "an almost exclusively male space, in which issues to do with sexuality and gendered identity can be worked out over the male body" (1993: 17). Yet as the genre evolved in the 1990s, women were increasingly placed at the center of these traditionally male-only films.

Building upon the success of the few '80s action films featuring female protagonists—most prominently Sigourney Weaver as Ripley in *Aliens* (1986)— the genre produced a number of narratives revolving around action heroines: *Blue Steel* (1990), *Silence of the Lambs* (1990), *Eve of Destruction* (1991), *V. I. Warshawski* (1991), *Thelma and Louise* (1991), *Aces: Iron Eagle III* (1991), and *Terminator 2: Judgment Day* (1991), as well as numerous straight-to-video works such as *Sweet Justice* (1993) and the Cynthia Rothrock martial arts videos. All of these works, and many others, revolve around heroines more than capable of defending themselves and vanquishing the bad guys. The development of the hardbody, hardware, hard-as-nails heroine who can take it—and give it—with the biggest and the baddest men of the action cinema indicates a growing acceptance of non-traditional roles for women and an awareness of the arbitrariness of gender traits.

The reaction of both the general public and film critics to these new action heroines has been remarkably varied. While *Aliens* and *Terminator 2* reaped huge profits at the box office and *Thelma and Louise* and *Silence of the Lambs* collected Academy Awards for best screenplay and best film respectively, other films featuring the new action heroine were commercial and critical failures. Beyond the mainstream movie audience, one would expect feminist-influenced film reviewers, who have been critical of Hollywood's depiction of women for years, to welcome these new roles with open arms—but this is not always the case. As many critics have pointed out, the image of heroines wielding guns and muscles can be conflated within the binary gender codes of the action cinema to render these women as symbolically male. This suspicion of gender cross-dressing is rooted in the feminist critique of patriarchy based on the "politics of the body" that emerged in the 1960s and 1970s.

Simply put, the feminist trope assumed what Susan Bordo has referred to as "an oppressor/oppressed model which theorizes men as possessing and wielding power over women—who are viewed correspondingly as themselves utterly powerless" (1993: 23). This binary structure situates men as active, women as passive—men as violent, women as having violence done to them. Thus, within this strict binary code the action heroine, who fights and kills on par with the men, confuses the boundaries and is seen by some critics as a gender transvestite. Occasionally the popular press has carried the argument that action heroines are, as the subtitle of a feature article in *Film Review* put it, "really only 'boys' in 'girls' clothing" (James 1992: 21). This notion of the hardbody heroine as a male impersonator has even been taken up within the pages of traditionally light women's fashion magazines. A recent issue of *Glamour* quotes Jeanine Basinger, the chair of film studies at Weslyan University, as saying, "Putting women in traditional male action roles, without changing their psychology, is just cinematic cross-dressing" (Johnson 1994: 153). The suspicion is that the action heroine is just a sheep in wolf's clothing, rather than a legitimate role for women.

This deterministic linkage of role and sex within the old feminist discourse is hampered by what many of the new feminist theorists charge is an overly simplified, pessimistic, dualistic, and paranoid view of cultural subordination. Many contemporary feminists have begun to challenge the underlying assumptions of the earlier feminist theory that women are powerless, cultural dopes. Recent feminist work has even gone so far as to find subversive and empowering aspects in women's use of cosmetic surgery (Davis, 1991) and makeup (Radner, 1989).

Influenced by deconstructionism, poststructuralism, and cultural studies, modern feminists often seek to explore the complex, multifaceted dimensions that are possible in the reading of every cultural act. At the root of these projects is the humanities' current emphasis on the constructedness of reality. Central to this new wave of gender studies is Judith Butler's work on the performative nature of gender. Butler's concept of gender as a learned set of characteristics that has assumed an air of naturalness, and her claim for the destabilizing effect of drag as gender parody, opens the door for a less deterministic reading of the action heroine. The modern action film has gone Butler's example of drag one further by repositioning destabilizing gender performances onto feminine bodies that are not easily read as merely humorous or sexually perverse.

The complexity of gender performance and Western culture's assumption of natural gender traits forms the narrative tension of the French action film *La Femme Nikita* (1991) and the Hollywood remake, *Point of No Return* (1993). After discussing the historical antecedents personified by the heroines of *Aliens* and *Terminator 2* and some of the preconceived cultural perceptions of the action heroine in general, I will turn to the case of *Point of No Return* to consider how it might be read as laying bare the artificiality of gender absolutism. In effect, the heroine of *Point of No Return* can be seen as a biological female who enacts femininity as a disguise for her symbolically masculine role—she is a double-cross-dresser.

While the natural distinction of male/female gender roles has been brought into question by other action heroines, most notably in *Aliens* and *Terminator 2*—only to be recovered by a heterosexual logic dictating that any woman who behaves in a manner so heavily coded as masculine must be a man in drag—*Point of No Return* reemploys a feminine masquerade to further emphasize the performative nature of gender roles. By considering how heroic females have been constructed as masculine within the male domain of the action film in general, and how this depiction has been further complicated in *Point of No Return* specifically, it becomes apparent that, whether intentionally or not, recent action films challenge both cinematic and cultural assumptions about what constitutes natural or proper female behavior.

In *Gender Trouble* (1990), Judith Butler investigates the performative nature of gender roles as they have been socially constructed within Western culture. Her goal is to provoke gender trouble by denaturalizing traditional gender categories grounded in biological determinism. Butler's theory of gender is twofold: a consideration of gender as performance and a claim for parody as the most effective means for undermining the current binary frame of gender. For Butler, gendered identities are not a reflection of one's authentic core self, but are a culturally coded effect of performance. Gender does not prescribe our performance, rather it is performance that ascribes our gender.

According to Butler's deconstruction of the traditional theory of mind/body and nature/culture dualism, there is no real and biologically determined self at the core of our being, only the mannerisms and gestures we have learned. Butler argues that bodily "acts, gestures, enactments, generally construed, are *performative* in the sense that the essence or identity that they otherwise purport to express are *fabrications* manufactured and sustained through corporeal signs and other discursive means. That the gendered body is performative suggests that it has no ontological status apart from the various acts which constitute its reality" (Butler 1990: 136). The body itself, Butler continues, is "not a 'being' but a variable boundary, a surface whose permeability is politically regulated, a signifying practice within a cultural field of gender hierarchy and compulsory heterosexuality" (139). Butler argues that there is no natural gender identity or even any form of androgyny that preexists socialization. A person is not born man or a woman, but rather *becomes* one. As Butler puts it: "Gender is the repeated stylization of the body, a set of repeated acts within a highly rigid regulatory frame that congeal over time to produce the appearance of substance, of a natural sort of being" (33).

Because this highly rigid regulatory frame is so ensconced as natural in Western culture, destabilizing traditional notions of gender is a difficult process that must seek to renegotiate terms that have gained the aura of "fact." Butler offers parody as a prime method of gender subversion, claiming that because there are no resources for subversion existing outside of the cultural system of gender identification, challenges to the natural or essential assumption of gender must arise from within the system—by parodying traditional gender conventions. Her most fundamental example of gender parody can be found in drag: "In imitating gender, drag implicitly reveals the imitative structure of gender itself—as well as its contingency" (137). Butler's theory of gender subversion sees drag as laying bare the artificiality of established conventions. As an obvious performance of gender not "naturally" linked to a biological "truth" of the performer, drag subverts and destabilizes gender essentialism from within the system. Rather than falling under the illusion of opting out of gender categories, drag makes do with the tools at hand. By using culturally recognizable gender traits, Butler argues, drag parodies the very notion of an original:

> To be more precise, it is a production which, in effect—that is, in its effect—postures as an imitation. This perpetual displacement constitutes a fluidity of identities that suggests an openness to resignification and recontextualization;

parodic proliferation deprives hegemonic culture and its critics of the claim to naturalized or essentialist gender identities. Although the gender meanings taken up in these parodic styles are clearly part of hegemonic, misogynist culture, they are nevertheless denaturalized and mobilized through their parodic recontextualization. As imitations which effectively displace the meaning of the original, they imitate the myth of originality itself. (Butler 1990: 138)

Butler's theory of gender parody as a destabilizing cultural act is intriguing, but her example of drag may not be as clear a challenge to the notion of naturalized or essentialist gender identities as she would have us believe. Her nod to parodic style as part of hegemonic, misogynist culture is never fully dealt with for its most obvious effect of reinscribing and naturalizing gender difference via the absurdity of cross-dressing. While cross-dressing and transvestism are a crucial point of gender blending, drag in its most common form as nightclub performance relies on the audience's recognition of the performer's underlying, or true, gender. Many of the drag's jokes, and the skill of the overall female impersonation, only make sense if viewers believe that the performer is a man. Rather than negating the concept of an original and natural gender, drag usually reinscribes essentialism by revealing gender transgression as ultimately humorous or tragic.

For me, the more confounding of hegemonic norms are the less burlesque forms of gender parody, forms that do not hint at an underlying real gender, forms that are not as easily marginalized by dominant perceptions. Butler briefly refers to "the sexual stylization of butch/femme identities" (137) as an alternative form of gender parody that has been criticized within feminist theory for its parallel of heterosexual relations. Although Butler gives the concept short shrift, I believe it is this type of parody that truly destabilizes gender norms. For the butch and the femme there is no underlying difference; their gender performance is never held up as cover for their real sex. Yet the destabilizing work of lesbian and gay gender performance is still strongly resisted in our culture. They are often discredited as freaks, hormonally imbalanced, psychologically unbalanced, or ungodly heathens. But unlike the drag's reliance on the humor of gender impersonation, and unlike the untolerated homosexual, the masculinized heterosexual woman reveals the arbitrariness of gender in a way that is not easily discounted.

Within cinema (which has done much to define gender- appropriate behavior in our culture) the modern action heroine confounds essentialism through her performance of traditionally masculine roles. Indeed, the common criticism that the action heroine is a man in drag can be read as an initial attempt to deny the arbitrariness of gender. Her performance, her narrative function, and her very body emphasize the artificiality of gender roles. But from a feminist perspective, the popular press's perception of action heroines as masculine is not as much a recognition of gender as performative, as it is limiting of legitimate, alternative female identities.

MASCULINE HEROINES

The gender-destabilizing work performed by the modern action heroine poses a direct challenge to one of the key perspectives of film theory over the last twenty-five years. The action heroine is an obvious contradiction to the woman-as-image theory typified by Laura Mulvey. For a long time after Mulvey's landmark essay, "Visual Pleasure and the Narrative Cinema" (1975), feminist film theory assumed an active male subjectivity and a passive female objectivity. Mulvey argued that "In a world ordered by sexual imbalance, pleasure in looking has been split between active/male and passive/female" (1975: 11). Classical cinema conventionally portrays man as the bearer of a voyeuristic gaze and woman as its object. Men, Mulvey goes on to argue, are the agents that propel the narrative, while women stop it—men act while women are passive.

For Mulvey, the sexual difference demarcated by the active/passive split marks the cinematic gaze as a masculine look that objectifies women as spectacles to be looked at. This masculine gaze of the camera forces female viewers to adopt either a narcissistic overidentification with women on the screen or a masochistic male point of view. But the modern action heroine is far from passive. She fights, she shoots, she kills, she solves the mysteries, and she rescues herself and others from dangerous situations. In short, she is in full command of the narrative—carrying the action in ways normally reserved for male protagonists.

Certainly the action heroine is often filmed to accentuate her body, but this new hardbody is not offered up as a mere sexual commodity. While the well-toned muscular female body is obviously an ideal in this age of physical fitness, it is presented in these films as first and foremost a functional body, a weapon. Even as the action-heroine hardbodies of the 1980s and early 1990s gave way to a more traditionally feminine and sexualized body by the late 1990s and into the 2000s, the emphasis on the strength and competence of these bodies remained. The cinematic gaze of the action film codes the heroine's body in the same way it does the muscular male hero's—as both object and subject. Where once stood silicone-injected breasts and delicate shoulders, now stands ripped pecs and striated delts. Her body does not exist solely to please men, it is a body designed to be functional.

This development of the hardbody heroine is a relatively recent phenomenon in a genre so closely associated with the larger-than-life male hero. Women in the action movies of the 1980s usually occupied the passive position described by Mulvey. They were loved ones in distress like Holly Gennaro (Bonnie Bedelia), the estranged wife of hero John McClane (Bruce Willis) who is held captive by terrorists in *Die Hard* (1988). Or they were expendable love interests like Rika Van Den Haas (Patsy Kensit), who is killed off after consummating her relationship with Martin Riggs (Mel Gibson), thus providing the necessary excuse for the hero's excessive violence in *Lethal Weapon 2* (1989). Or they were appended to the narrative to counter the subtext of homoerotic tension between the male partners, such as Gabriel Cash's (Kurt Russell) pursuit of Kiki (Terry Hatcher) in *Tango and Cash* (1989). Women were often removed from the narrative entirely in films like *First Blood* (1982), or at least from the bulk of the screen time in such prison films as *Lock Up* (1988) and *Death Warrant* (1990), or war films like *Uncommon Valour* (1983) and *Predator* (1987). In short, the female characters were almost never central to the narrative except as motivation for the hero's mission. Tasker describes these women as "An hysterical figure who needs to be rescued or protected, the heroine is often played for comedy" (1993: 16). All that was required of an actress was an innocently sexual appearance and a ready scream. This type of female role still exists today but is overshadowed by the new action heroine.

The prototype for the '90s action heroine, the one standout amongst women in '80s action movies, the first woman to make it into the boys' club—was Sigourney Weaver's Ripley in *Aliens* (1986). This sequel to Ridley Scott's horror/science fiction success *Alien* (1979) picks up with Ripley's emergence from hyper-sleep fifty-seven years after her defeat of the monstrous alien of the first film. Ripley soon finds herself accompanying a squad of Marines back to the planet that has since been colonized by humans. The Marine's encounter hordes of the aliens and find their weapons and methods useless against them.

Although just a civilian advisor, Ripley is forced to take over from the inexperienced Marine commander in an attempt to save the lives of the crew and Newt, a little girl who is the sole survivor of the colony. After numerous struggles, Ripley is the only one left to fight and must dramatically arm herself with oversized guns and a mechanical exoskeleton in order to vanquish the queen mother of the aliens. *Aliens* exchanged the horror conventions of its predecessor for those of the action genre and developed the already tough character of Ripley into the striking image of a muscular, gun-toting heroine who was alternately dubbed by the press "Fembo" and "Rambolina."

The association of Ripley with Rambo is not that far-fetched. *Aliens'* director and screenwriter, James Cameron, had previously penned *Rambo: First Blood Part II* (1985), and the similarity of the character's iconography in promotional stills was hard to miss. Both Rambo and Ripley were seen in numerous pictures wearing almost identical action hero uniforms: a muscle shirt, loads of ammunition, an oversized machine gun, and sweat dampened hair. Interestingly, where Rambo's stock promotional photo occasionally showed him carrying a bedraggled prisoner of war, Ripley's photo often showed her carrying the frightened little girl, Newt, who is central to the narrative of *Aliens*. That Ripley had more in common with the usual male action hero than the typical screaming woman was well noted by the press. In a feature article lauding *Aliens* as the summer's megahit, *Time* magazine wrote that:

> In action pictures, women are supposed to swoon or retreat to a safe corner (or, at best, praise the Lord and pass the ammunition) while the male lead protects them and defends Western civilization as we know it. In *Aliens*, it is the guys who are all out of action at the climax and Ripley who is in a death duel with evil. (Schickel 1986: 48)

In the original film, *Alien*, now considered a classic of the horror genre, Ripley's struggle against the horrific alien makes her a perfect example of what Carol Clover refers to as the Final Girl in slasher films. The Final Girl is the stock character who "not only fight(s) back but do(es) so with ferocity and even kill(s) the killer on their own, without help from the outside" (Clover 1992: 37). Strongly influenced by Butler's theory of gender as performance, Clover's fascinating essay goes on to argue that the Final Girl is clearly marked as a masculine character via her ability to survive agonizing trials, rise to the occasion, and defeat the monster with her own hands and cunning.

According to Clover, horror and rape-revenge films "operate on the basis of a one-sex body, the maleness or femaleness of which is performatively determined by the social gendering of the acts it undergoes or undertakes" (159). This fluidity of gender, Clover believes, is what allows the mostly male audience to identify with the heroism of the Final Girl. Despite Clover's excellent deconstruction of gender attributes in horror films, she finally undercuts the male audience's ability to identify with a female character by reading the Final Girl as a "congenial double for the adolescent male" (51). This cross sex doubling is seen as a way for adolescent males to vicariously partake in the masochistic pleasures of the horror film without risking their perceptions of male competence. Clover's identificatory twist, while intriguing, seems to discredit the male audience's capacity to cheer on a *woman as a woman* in a self-reliant role. In spite of her eventual retreat to a modified Mulveyian concept of viewer/gender identification, Clover does go a long way in describing the falsity of gender essentialism in contemporary film theory.

Cameron's transformation of the sequel into an action film repositioned Ripley's tough self-reliance as more than just another in the long line of horror's Final Girls. Ripley's heroism seemed to place her in the realm of the overtly masculine, to what Clover herself calls a "space-age female Rambo" (1992: 46). As the first mainstream action heroine, Ripley's blurring of gender boundaries seemed more problematic to the critics than to filmgoers. Uncertain of how to read the character, the cover of *Time* magazine featured an out-of-character Weaver in traditionally feminine make-up while the article refers to her as a "Rambette." Meanwhile, *Aliens'* producer Gale Anne Hurd was impressed with audiences' acceptance of Ripley's role and was quoted in the *San Francisco Examiner Datebook* observing, "I really appreciate the way audiences respond. They buy it. We don't get people, even rednecks, leaving the theatre saying 'That was stupid. No woman would do that.' You don't have to be a liberal ERA supporter to root for Ripley." The excessively masculine association of carrying over-sized guns, saving women, children, and inept soldiers, and generally kicking ass seems to necessitate a character's reading as overtly masculine by critics but not necessarily by the general public.

This perception of the action heroine who kicks ass as a man in drag was brought to the fore again in Cameron's smash hit *Terminator 2: Judgment Day* (1991). In this sequel to his own breakthrough success of 1984, *The Terminator*, Cameron scripts the character of Sarah Connor (Linda Hamilton) as the most extreme of his, as Richard Corliss put it in *Time*, "tough-as-kryptonite women" (Corliss 1991: 46). One of the most captivating images of the film, second only to the special effects shape-shifting of the liquid metal T2000, was Sarah Connors' new hardbody. Like Ripley before her, the visual image of Connors in *T2* explicitly identifies her with the archetypal Rambo persona. In this instance the symbolic cross-dressing is taken beyond the level of undershirts and oversized guns into the realm of the body itself as Hamilton's muscular appearance was the subject of much speculation about the ability of women to toughen up.

Hamilton's most recent work previous to *Terminator 2* was in the wistfully romantic television series *Beauty and the Beast*. In direct contrast to her role as "beauty," Hamilton physically refashioned her body to be more of the "beast" in *T2*. Her intense training routine was widely reported in promotional materials and the popular press. *Entertainment Weekly* reported that Hamilton worked with a personal trainer for more than three months prior to filming

T2—six days a week, running, biking, swimming, stair climbing, and hours a day in the weight room—as well as learning judo, military techniques, and weapons handling from an authentic Israeli commando.

A cover story in *New York* magazine about the new killer women of film describes Connor/Hamilton as "the power body—the arms and shoulders packed with muscle, the straight thick waist, the boy's hips, no ass, the bosom so small it doesn't require a bra . . . the arms have rivers of veins rising above the bulging muscle" (Baumgold 1991: 26). Sarah Connor, as played by Hamilton in *T2*, does not just perform masculinity via her aggressive role, she embodies it. The thick waist, boy's hips, no bosom—overlaid by combat boots and ammunition clips—worked for many critics to efface femininity altogether.

The Sarah who was a stereotypically weak woman in need of saving at the beginning of the first *Terminator* has, in effect, become a cold, deadly, unstoppable terminator herself. Susan Jeffords has argued convincingly that one of the central narrative devices of *T2* is inversion, particularly the exchange of roles that constructs the T1000 terminator (Arnold Schwarzenegger) as the caregiving female character while the muscular Sarah assumes the masculine, machine-like killer.

> This 'new' Sarah Connors looks like the mercenary she has trained to be through all the intervening years, wearing military fatigues, toting heavy weapons, and having a mission to perform. As final proof of her new hard character she even forgets to love her son . . . we are witness to how Sarah ignores her son for most of the film. The excuse, that she's concentrating on keeping him alive, puts her in direct competition for the Terminator's role, and body . . . And while she is focusing on being a super-soldier, the Terminator is working on being a better mom, listening to and playing with the son that Sarah hardly notices for all the weapons she's carrying. (Jeffords 1993: 249–50)

That the cyborg Schwarzenegger can be read as the more feminine role is an indication of how overdetermined our cultural notions of appropriate gender behavior are. *Terminator 2* is preoccupied with discrediting surface appearances as nothing is as it seems— the fluidity with which the T2000 shape-shifts is indicative of all the characters' manipulations of the discrepancies between image and identity. Certainly the film's gender negotiations were an innovative challenge to cultural expectations (any film that can construct Linda Hamilton as tougher and meaner than Arnold Schwarzenegger is bound to shock), but does it destabilize gender categories if Connor is decoded as a man in drag? While the film does illustrate the constructedness of gender, the critical reading of Connor as "male" facilitates the dominance of gender absolutism. Gender categories and appropriate behavior are retained in the face of obvious biological inconsistency. Rather than aggressiveness being deemed legitimate for women and compassion acceptable for men, both Sarah Connor and the T1000 are suspected of transvestism.

The tough, self-reliant action heroines personified by Ripley in *Aliens* and Sarah Connor in *Terminator 2* are described by Tasker as operating "within an image-world in which questions of gender identity are played out through, in particular, the masculinization of the female body" (1993: 139). This masculinization of the female body that is equated with the masculinization of the character's performed gender role is most visible through her possession of the most eminent of male icons: guns and muscles. The action heroine ostensibly commandeers these traditionally male signifiers in order to fulfill her narrative function. In the circular logic of gender/role identification, the character wields the guns and the muscles because of the role, and is identifiable in the heroic role because of the guns and muscles. The intimate linkage of these possessions in determining role classification for the action heroine is clear in the press' labeling them "hardware" (guns) and "hardbody" (muscles) heroines. The repetitive use of "hard" in describing the heroines emphasizes the removal of the "soft" (read: feminine) qualities. It also indicates the symbolic phallicization of the actress, the hard flesh of the body, and the hard barrel of the gun being usurped and appropriated from the male domain. Both guns and muscles can be seen to empower women in ways that have, until recently, been solely masculine.

The emerging popular discourse about the increasing use of guns by women as a means of defense and empowerment, both in real life and on the screen, is discussed by Kirsten Marthe Lentz. Lentz compares the conflicting feminist reception of guns marketed for women to the feminist pornography debates, or sex wars, of the 1980s. The pornography debates revolved around disagreement by feminists about the nature and extent of women's passive victimization. While the anti-porn side saw pornography as blatantly misogynistic and degrading to all women at all times, the anti-anti-porn side sought to understand how women could partake in pleasures of pornography by theorizing "a subject for whom victimhood, danger and pleasure exist in profoundly complicated ways" (Lentz 1993: 375). Thus, in the same ways that pornography could represent to some women a means of empowerment, modern women's "knowledge of, aptitude with and willingness to use guns affords a pleasure familiar to feminists: the female subject masters with utter competence a 'masculine' practise, attitude and/or domain" (Lentz 1993: 374). In other words, the action heroine who exhibits a mastery of guns represents a woman who has usurped a particularly phallic means of power. In *Aliens*, when Ripley unofficially takes over command of the Marines from an inept officer, one of the soldiers offers to "introduce [her] to a close personal friend of mine", his "M-41A pulse rifle, 10mm, with over and under 30mm pump-action grenade launcher." After quickly learning how to operate the "pulse rifle," she asks about another of the weapon's functions, and the corporal replies, "That's the grenade launcher . . . I don't think you want to mess with that," but Ripley insists: "You started this. Show me everything. I can handle myself."

The sexual implications of female gun use in contemporary cinema has not been ignored by filmmakers. The fetishistic qualities of women wielding such a heavily coded phallic symbol constitutes one of the major themes of feminist director Kathryn Bigelow's *Blue Steel* (1990). Throughout the film rookie cop Meghan Turner (Jamie Lee Curtis) is forced to negotiate her conflicting gender status as it is implicated in her relationships with guns and powerful men. The opening credits sequence is an obvious fetishizing display of Turner's weapon: in an extreme close-up, with vaguely erotic background music and stylistic blue lighting, the camera dwells on the contours, the shaft, and the hollows of her standard issue Smith & Wesson. This segues into Turner's (cross) dressing in her new police uniform as she narcissistically admires herself in the mirror. Her obvious enjoyment in dressing up and possessing the phallus is cut short, as it were, when she is reprimanded for killing a thief whose own weapon can not be found at the scene of the crime.

The gun in question was in fact stolen by Eugene Hunt (Ron Silver), a Wall Street trader mesmerized by the sight of Turner using her weapon. As Cora Kaplan has noted, "*Blue Steel*'s plot depends on a deadly serious running gag about the gun's fetishized meaning" (1993: 42). Men repeatedly question Turner's desire to be a cop—her alarming response is that "ever since I was a kid, I wanted to shoot people"—and in a thinly disguised Freudian rationale, we are witness to Eugene's obsession with Turner's possession of the phallus. Eugene carves Turner's name on bullets and begins indiscriminately shooting people in her name, thus placing her in a marginalized/suspect position amongst her fellow officers. And more directly, during a seduction scene (before Turner realizes his true identity) Eugene asks Turner to pull out her gun and hold it "with both hands." In the end Turner manages, albeit just barely, to repossess her gun, eliminate Eugene, and triumph over her abusive father, but the trials she is forced to endure are all brought about by her pleasurable appropriation of masculine power.

The second most emblematic sign of the action heroine's masculinized persona is the development of physical strength. In the context of numerous films, this strength is represented through the heroine's superior ability in martial arts. The extremely successful straight-to-video films featuring Cynthia Rothrock typify this sub-genre of kung fu movies.

More visually striking to Western audiences than the grace of martial arts is the muscled heroine. Richard Dyer points out in his study of the male pinup that "muscularity is the sign of power—natural, achieved, phallic" (1982: 68). Similarly, Susan Bordo has argued that "muscles have chiefly symbolized and continue to symbolize masculine power as physical strength, frequently operating as a means of coding the 'naturalness' of sexual difference" (1993: 193). The image of Sarah Connor's/Linda Hamilton's bulging biceps and striated shoulders in a black undershirt clearly mark her masculinization while simultaneously questioning the naturalness of muscles as markers of sexual difference. Likewise, Rachel McLish, a former champion bodybuilder, is repeatedly filmed in *Aces: Iron Eagles III* in ways that foreground her muscularity. The camera zooms in on McLish's flexing biceps once when she frees herself from iron shackles, and again when she overpowers one of the villains in an arm wrestle for his knife.

Indeed, while McLish co-stars with numerous men, she is the only one of the good guys to throw a punch. Muscularity is so essentially linked with the "natural" superiority of men in power relations that it semiotically overwhelms biological identity. The muscular woman is seen as a gender cross-dresser. Mirroring the critics' reading of the action heroine as a man-in-drag, Laurie Schulze's research of societal attitudes towards female bodybuilders found that "People who find female muscularity aesthetically unpleasurable often claim that these bodybuilders "look just like men," or are "trying to be men." Often too, there is the implication that female bodybuilders are lesbian" (Schulze 1990: 73). Extremely muscular women in action films are similarly equated with becoming symbolic males and/or lesbians. The threat of action heroines being too manly or possibly lesbian eventually led to an increased emphasis on the sexuality of heroines in later films.

Due to the homophobic nature of most mainstream audiences, many narratives overtly seek to establish the heterosexuality of action heroines by providing a nominal male love interest, or by, as in *Aliens* and *Terminator 2*, linking the action heroine to notions of a fierce maternal instinct. The lesbian innuendoes about the muscular/masculine woman are reserved for lesser and more expendable characters who are portrayed as butch. Corinna Everson, another champion bodybuilder who made her initial foray into action films in the Jean Claude Van Damme vehicle *Double Impact* (1992), played the villain's hired muscle. Everson's muscularity is juxtaposed with the voluptuousness of the hero's girlfriend. The distinction between Everson's bad/muscular body and the girlfriend's good/feminine body comes to a head when Everson corners the girl in a storage room and tries to force herself upon her sexually.

In the reductive logic of the film, Everson's character is necessarily lesbian because she is muscular, and muscular because she is lesbian. Ironically, at the showing of *Double Impact* I attended it was the muscular Everson who elicited shouts of approval from audience members, perhaps proving that the well-toned body is currently more of a female ideal than the voluptuous-but-weak body. It is interesting to hear how audiences respond upon first seeing such muscular women as Hamilton, McLish, and Everson. Rather than blatant wolf whistles, there is a sense of awe and respect (from both male and female viewers) for the hard-earned muscularity that stands so far removed from even the well-aerobicized Hollywood norm.

A more positively explored butch character is Private Vasquez (Jenette Goldstein) in *Aliens*. Vasquez is a woman even more blatantly coded as masculine than Ripley. Heavily muscled and with a crew cut, she has to deal with the criticism of the male Marines. In one notorious scene, Vasquez awakes from hyper-sleep and immediately begins doing pull-ups. One macho Marine looks at her and asks, "Have you ever been mistaken for a man?" to which she replies, "No, have you?" as she high-fives her buddy. The message of the joke is clear: masculinity is determined by one's ability to perform certain culturally recognizable traits, and conversely to fail to perform these traits adequately implies one can be seen as feminine. Vasquez's exaggerated masculinization works by comparison so as to lessen the gender-threatening aspects of Ripley's character, whom Vasquez initially refers to as "Snow White."

While the action heroine's heterosexuality is somewhat recovered by the narrative in order to escape any possibly offending lesbian implications, she is still read within the confines of gender attributes as symbolically male. The ability of women to function successfully in what is coded as a masculine role illustrates the socially constructed nature of that role. On one level gender is shown as a performative act, a bundle of traits, and not as a sex-specific absolute. Yet the argument advanced by some critics that these characters are simply "men in drag" undermines the revelatory possibilities of women assuming these roles.

If a female character seen as kicking ass must be read as masculine, then women are systematically denied as a gender capable of behaving in any way other than passive. *La Femme Nikita* and *Point of No Return* take women in action movies a step beyond by not assuming a masculine identity in kicking ass, but by remaining garbed in obvious signifiers of femininity. The audience's gender beliefs are more directly destabilized because the image of a petite,

pretty woman in a dress kicking ass denies the narrative logic that allows viewers to deride the heroine as a butch or as a woman trying to be a man.

FEMININITY AND THE ACTION HEROINE

Although *La Femme Nikita* was the original film, I will refer here to the American remake, *Point of No Return*, because it has garnered more attention with
the North American press and movie audiences due to its wider release. As a
remake *Point of No Return* was unusually faithful to the original, so in effect,
any reference to one film is a reference to both. Indeed, many of the reviews
noted, often critically, *Point of No Return*'s faithfulness to *La Femme Nikita*.
The *Wall Street Journal* claimed that "Almost nothing has been altered" (Salamon 1993: A12) in the conversion, while *Newsweek* agreed that "To call *Point
of No Return* a remake of the 1991 French pop fantasy *La Femme Nikita* isn't
adequate; carbon copy is more like it" (Ansen 1993: 65).

Point of No Return is the story of Maggie (Bridget Fonda), a drug-addicted
misfit sentenced to death for killing a police officer during a botched drug
theft from a corner store. Maggie's ferociousness while under arrest is noted
by the mysterious Bob (Gabriel Bryne) who works for the covert government
agency that arranges for her fake execution and subsequent initiation as an
elite assassin. Maggie undergoes months of strict physical and social retraining
in order to blend in with the high-class individuals she will be assigned to kill.
After earning her graduation from the agency by murdering a foreign digni-
tary, Maggie is relocated to Los Angeles where she meets and falls in love with
the innocent J. P. (Dermot Mulroney). But Maggie's attempts at a normal life
are undermined when the agency continues to assign her assassinations.

In a desperate effort to win her freedom, Maggie accepts an assignment
where she is promised that if she successfully pulls off this last big job she will
never be bothered again. Unfortunately the hit goes bad and the agency sends
in Victor the Cleaner (Harvey Keitel) to assist and then terminate her upon
completion of the assignment. Maggie manages to defeat the bad guys and
the Cleaner, but realizes she can never go back to her life with J. P. Instead,
Maggie allows the agency to assume she died in a car crash while she, battered
and bruised, walks off into the horizon to begin a new life.

The central plot device of *Point of No Return* resides in the Pygmalion-
like transformation of Maggie from, as the press release puts it, a "scruffy,
ferocious, drug-addicted misfit" to an "intelligent, curious, lovely woman of
elegance and refinement." Maggie's initial rugged aggressiveness is tantamount

to the action heroine's performance of masculinity. Maggie is physical and self-reliant, murdering without remorse—and capable of overcoming Bob and holding him hostage in an attempt to escape the agency in an early scene. This early Maggie is persistently violent and physically unkempt in old jeans and a man's undershirt—the same type of black undershirt worn by Sylvester Stallone in the *Rambo* series, Bruce Willis in *Die Hard*, and such muscular/masculine women as Linda Hamilton in *Terminator 2*, and Rachel McLish in *Aces: Iron Eagle III*.

This black undershirt that has become a standard costume of the genre is functional for its ability to reveal the hero's body. It is quite literally a muscle shirt, putting the hero or heroine's pumped-up body on display. The linkage within the action cinema of the black undershirt with the heroic male/muscular body is a key signifier of gender that facilitates the reading of the muscular heroine as masculine. The association of clothing with the social construction of body and gender identity, often examined by fashion theorists, is a formalized and explicit element of costume design for film. "The rules of costume and typage," Jane Gaines argues in her essay on costume and narrative, are "that the dress should place a character quickly and efficiently, identifying her in one symbolic sweep" (Gaines, 1990: 188). As a costume, the undershirt Maggie wears early in *Point of No Return* identifies her as a masculinized character—it supports her aggressive behavior, signifies her cross-dressing, and situates her in relation to previous men and women of the genre.

In an interesting example of *Point of No Return*'s play with gender and genre iconography, this heavily coded signifier of the black undershirt is incorporated into Maggie's initial feminine disguise. Her black cocktail dress appears in the film and in the promotional stills to be a frilly version of the undershirt. Arguably the most circulated image of the film was Fonda in the sleeveless black dress brandishing an oversized pistol. This image condenses the apparently conflicting signifiers of feminine and masculine iconography. The masculine undershirt is reconfigured as a feminine dress, and the feminine body is equipped with a masculine gun.

The destabilizing resonance of this image is echoed by the press's fascination with it. *Maclean's* main description of Maggie is "with a big gun and a killer miniskirt" (Chidley 1993: 43), *Newsweek* describes her "chic cocktail dress and semiautomatic fashion accessories" (Ansen 1993: 65), and the *New York Times* claims that Fonda herself fits in well with "the story's other basic ingredients: little black dress, great big gun" (Maslin 1993: C10). Audiences were likewise captivated by this unusual image—the review in the *Wall Street Journal* notes that "What the audience seems to respond to is the sight of a slight woman deftly handling big guns" (Salamon 1993: A12). This combination of signifiers denies an easy gender ascription. While other action heroines symbolically garbed themselves exclusively in masculine accoutrements, thus allowing their characters to be read as predominantly male, the use of obvious signs of femininity and masculinity in one image confounds the strict categorization of gender absolutism.

Much of Maggie's retraining for life as an assassin involves practical skills such as martial arts, weaponry, and marksmanship, yet it is increasingly apparent to her instructors that Maggie is more than adequately versed in these manly arts. Indeed, it is her unruly pleasure in these skills that sets her apart from the other, more complacent students. On the firing range Maggie is handed a gun and told, "You have two seconds per target. Shoot only the bad guys. Do not shoot the good guys." As the various targets pop up Maggie wantonly shoots them all, little old ladies and muggers alike. When the instructor asks her "What do you call that?" Maggie responds with "Fun."

The reckless glee with which Maggie performs and excels in physical combat worries her trainers. When she is called upon in martial arts class to try and strike the instructor, Maggie reluctantly participates by playfully exaggerating karate gestures. But when the instructor lowers his guard in an assumption she's not taking the exercise seriously, she breaks his nose with a single sucker-punch.

In these training scenes we glimpse Maggie's ability to exploit her opponent's perceptions of her as a weak female. While some reviewers found it "surprising that Fonda didn't pump up for the role" (Gleiberman 1993: 31) and others noted that "she's hardly an icon of physical menace in this era of iron-pumping maidens" (Ansen 1993: 65), it is this very lack of Maggie/Fonda's gender transgressive bodily signifiers that allows her to disarm her opponents. When she successfully passes as feminine, Maggie refigures gender-appropriate behavior by demonstrating that masculinity and femininity are not mutually exclusive identities. At the same time, Maggie destroys the audience's perceptions of biologically determined identity and role as determining biology. In other words—just because she looks like a woman does not mean she is one, and just because she acts like a man does not mean she is one.

The conscious manipulation of traditional perceptions of female characters as weak has become a standard convention in action heroine films. A quintessential example of this scenario is a scene from *Blade Trinity* (2004) that introduces the character of Abigail Whistler (Jessica Biel). A group of young street punks (who are actually vampires) menace some people in a subway station. They brazenly terrorize potential targets as they decide whom their ideal victim will be.

After rejecting an older woman and an overweight man as unappetizing, the punks spot a woman trudging along with her baby and a load of groceries and decide they have hit the jackpot. They follow her down to an empty subway platform, taunting her with creepy catcalls and jumping out at her from the shadows. Set up as a clear parallel to gang rape, the seemingly helpless Agigail struggles to escape as the young vampires descend upon her.

Two of the punks tear the baby away as two more force her to the ground: "Scream if this hurts, Chicka!" But the tables are quickly turned—their prey is no helpless female victim, and the baby is a doll rigged with an exploding garlic spray. Abigail easily kicks off her assailants, then whips off her dowdy overcoat to reveal her fit, action-ready body and pummels each punk with a series of perfect martial arts moves before staking them to dust.

In a complete reversal from victim to avenger, Abigail tells the last one to "Scream if this hurts, Chicka!" before stabbing him in the chest. By knowingly exploiting a perception of female weakness the action heroine routinely questions the validity of gender binaries and takes a distinct pleasure in reversing victim and avenger gender roles. Characters such as Maggie and Abigail are clearly presented as women who can feign vulnerability in order to best men in fights, and womanliness becomes just another tool for a strong and resourceful character.

While Maggie's training in masculine skills in *Point of No Return* is soon recognized as redundant, it becomes obvious Maggie is not as naturally adept in femininity. Maggie's training now focuses on teaching her how to behave as a lady, and Amanda (Anne Bancroft) is employed to instruct Maggie and the other women at the school in the acquisition of refined manners and sophistication. When Maggie struggles in her lessons, Amanda recognizes the problem and tells her, "What you need is balance, we must find your feminine side." Maggie is taught how to walk, talk, dress, and act as a lady, and we soon witness the physical and behavioral changes she undergoes.

Her straggly black hair becomes a well-coiffed blond, her skin clears up, her face is softened by subtle makeup, and her teeth are capped. She no longer swears, enunciates perfectly, her posture is good, and her manners delicate—she even dabbles in French. In short, Maggie is now the perfect image of a proper lady. This strategic need to school action heroines in the art of proper female performance is repeated in later films like *Ms. Congeniality* (2000) wherein a team of beauticians and etiquette specialists transform the crass and tomboyish FBI agent Gracie Hart (Sandra Bullock) into a beauty pageant contestant.

Time and again, action heroine stories reveal the artifice behind assumed gender roles. Moreover, Maggie's animalistic snarl has been replaced by a coquettish smile and her memorized feminine response to uncomfortable situations: "I never did mind about the little things." In a genre famous for tight-lipped Stallones and Eastwoods, Maggie's change in language is a subtle but fundamental gender performance. Her initial untamed behavior was reinforced by her casual use of profanity and her aggressive and prolific swearing clearly coded her as unfeminine. The distinction between masculine/foul and feminine/polite language in the gender binarism of the film is made clear when Bob asks, "Why do you talk so dirty, Maggie?" and she responds, "Why do you talk so faggy, Bob?" Despite his position of authority, Bob, in his Armani suits and soft-spoken elocution, is depicted as "softer" than Maggie. In the world of action films, to be mannered is to be feminine and to be feminine is to be perceived as weak.

Once Maggie's transformation is complete, Bob escorts her to an elegant Washington restaurant for what she thinks is a celebratory dinner, a coming out party for the newly fashioned debutante. Instead, Bob gives Maggie an oversized automatic pistol and tells her to execute a VIP and his bodyguard. She has no choice but to comply, so in a short cocktail dress and newly dyed and styled blond locks, Maggie catches the bodyguard unawares, killing him and his boss. She then shoots and fights her way past the remaining bodyguards to the washroom where Bob said she would find an escape window and a waiting car.

But Bob has lied—the window is bricked over and Maggie is thus forced to make her own way out of a restaurant full of men trying to kill her. In one telling moment as Maggie is caught in the washroom by another burly bodyguard, she raises her arms, feigning the role of a helpless female. The bodyguard lowers his gun, but Maggie immediately shoots him. This technique, encouraging her enemies to underestimate her, is foreshadowed in her fight with the martial arts instructor but in this instance it accentuates her play with gender roles. As viewers we are privileged in witnessing Maggie's fluid alternation from performing masculinity/aggressiveness to femininity/passiveness and back again. Prior to her being discovered in the washroom we see Maggie, the recent murderer, pounding her fists in frustration against the bricked-over window, but then when found completely changes her disposition to one of innocent helplessness—and just as quickly reverts to aggressiveness by blowing away the guard as soon as she sees her chance.

Throughout the film it is this image of a frail, pretty, slip of a girl that allows Maggie to catch her enemies off guard. The males arrogantly assume they have nothing to fear from such an obviously feminine character, and the presence of a young, thin, classically pretty Bridget Fonda in a sleeveless cocktail dress is at odds with the role of a ruthless killer. Maggie is the action genre's equivalent of Joan Riviere's famous patient described in her landmark essay "Womanliness as Masquerade," originally published in 1929. The patient was a successful female intellectual who would often revert to flirtation with men after addressing a male audience. She was, Riviere argued, compensating for her theft of masculinity by accentuating her feminine gestures. From this Riviere concluded that women who venture into male terrain might employ femininity as a masquerade.

> Womanliness therefore could be assumed and worn as a mask, both to hide the possession of masculinity and to avert the reprisals expected if she was found to possess it—much as the thief will turn out his pockets and ask to be searched to prove that he has not stolen the goods. (Riviere 1929: 38)

Riviere's analogy of the thief is particularly apt for thinking about *Point of No Return*. Like the thief, Maggie presents the image of innocence when caught in the restaurant washroom—appropriately, the men's washroom. To avoid the reprisals of behaving as a masculine assassin, Maggie turns out her gender pockets, offering her delicate femininity as proof that it was not her who stole the phallus. We plainly see Maggie's femininity as a masquerade she uses at her convenience to exploit traditional cultural perceptions of gender.

Since women as action heroines are seen as enacting masculinity, as stealing the phallus, *Point of No Return* complicates the gender issue by blatantly employing womanliness as a masquerade. Indeed, any beliefs about the naturalness of the mask are destroyed as we see the careful construction of a feminine identity created *for* Maggie. She is taught the clichés necessary for a convincing performance of femininity.

The same obvious construction of the mask can be seen in other popular Pygmalion-like films such as *Educating Rita* (1983) and *Pretty Woman* (1990), but in these films the performative nature of class is more central than that of gender. The depiction of most action heroines as masculinized challenges the viewers' perception of gender behavior but it is still present as a natural act. That is, the masculine heroine is shown to act in the way she does because it is her nature. In *Point of No Return* the heroine's masculinity is disguised by her feminine masquerade, further emphasizing the performative nature of gender roles. We witness the easy fluidity with which Maggie performs both masculinity and femininity. In this regard, a biological female is free to enact either, or both, the most stereotypical of masculine or feminine behavior.

AUDIENCES AND THE ACTION HEROINE

Point of No Return provides viewers with an example of masculine behavior that is not divorced from a feminine identity. The artificiality of both masculine and feminine roles is exposed through Maggie's obvious play with gender convention. The dual drag she performs is subversive, in Butler's sense, because it "implicitly reveals the imitative structure of gender itself" (1990: 137). We witness Maggie's manipulation of gender identity and see her using femininity as a masquerade as much as we see a woman performing as a man. The machinations of gender performance are laid bare. Yet as a dual drag, as a calculated performance of both femininity and masculinity, the role of Maggie is perhaps most illustrative of Butler's primary postmodernist claim that "gender is an identity tenuously constituted in time, instituted in an exterior space through a *stylized repetition of acts*" (140) [italics in original].

Maggie is a dual character who has mastered the stylistic gestures that amount to femininity and masculinity in Western culture. She can swear, punch, and shoot like a man . . . as easily as she can wear high heels, bat her eyes, and feign helplessness. Her casual alternation between, and combination of, the two styles destroys the notion of one state being more natural than the other. For Maggie there is no original—she is both and neither at the same time. While traditional performative drag of the male-to-female nightclub variety, relies on the viewer's implicit understanding that the performer's natural identity is masculine, *Point of No Return* shows that all layers of identity are performed, that there is no underlying natural state.

This subversion of cultural assumptions about gender in *Point of No Return* is rife with the potential of pleasurable, vicarious empowerment for female viewers. Here audiences are presented with a character overtly recognizable as female that consciously plays with gender performance. For Maggie, femininity becomes a means to empowerment rather than a hindrance to it—her play with gender roles becomes another weapon in her arsenal.

At the viewings of both *La Femme Nikita* and *Point of No Return*, I heard a noticeable amount of cheering and after-screening enjoyment by the female audience. Self-conscious shouts of "You show him, sister!" and "Wasn't that great when she . . ." were not uncommon. The positive response of female audience members eager to partake in the pleasures of the action cinema *may* be read as a subversive act that empowers women at the same time it exposes the performative nature of gender. Yet I would not argue that *Point of No Return* is a subversive act in itself.

As Susan Bordo points out in her critique of Judith Butler's theory, "Subversion of cultural assumptions (despite the claims of some deconstructionists) is not something that happens *in* a text or *to* a text. It is an event that takes place (or doesn't) in the reading of the text" (Bordo 1993: 292). *Point of No Return* facilitates subversive readings of gender but does not necessitate them. For example, many men seemed to understand the film as a feminist turn at the action genre that played with stereotypical cultural perceptions of gender, but others I spoke with simply saw Maggie's character as a way to incorporate some "tits and ass" into the action genre.

This sexist view is the dark side of the coin faced by films featuring action heroines. On an analytical level viewers may be willing to recognize how heroines like Ripley, Sarah Connor and Maggie problematize gender categorization, but Hollywood's (as well as the rest of our male-dominated culture) history of displaying the female form leaves a disturbing possibility that the action heroine can be seen as a fetishization of violence. "Are you ready for the Terminatrix?" asks *Newsweek* (Fleming 1993: 66). And it is just this type of playful diminutizing slippage between the heroine as a self-reliant character and a sexual object that undercuts the effectiveness of the more progressive aspects of mainstream popular cinema's negotiation of gender.

These drastically different readings contribute to the suspicions that leave feminist film critics teetering between praising and condemning the emergence of the action heroine. In their article "Hardware Heroines," Sue Botcherby and Rosie Garland cautiously ask, "Does the rise of the aggressive heroine really pose a threat to men or does she merely contribute to male fantasy via the eroticisation of hardware and violence?" (1991: 41). Yet, we must not forget that in its often comic-book presentation of the heroic body, action cinema is perhaps an equal-opportunity offender. The muscular male torso, loaded with guns and ammo, is paraded across the screen in fetishizing shots at least as often as the female form.

It also seems to me that the fear of the hardware heroine as an eroticization of guns and violence is to misread her role in the films. These heroines are not equivalent to the bikini-clad babes suggestively draped over gigantic guns on heavy metal album covers and James Bond paperbacks. This is not to deny the long history of Hollywood's exploitation of the female body, but the more progressive depictions of the action heroine place her at the same level of erotic portrayal as the male icons of the screen—as primarily subject and secondarily object.

Certainly the Hollywood studios cannot be given too much credit for advancing the cinematic image of women in this day and age where top actresses are often heard decrying the lack of decent roles for women. An article in *Entertainment Weekly* about the rise of actresses in upcoming action movies declared that the "studios aren't as concerned with striking a blow for feminism as they are in tapping into a lucrative market" (Hruska 1993: 7). In the same week *Newsweek* agreed that "the current search for female action stars is about profit, not political correctness" (Fleming 1993: 66). This market-driven response is the really hopeful sign of the general public's acceptance of, and desire for, aggressive female roles. It is an indication that women as well as men can partake in the pleasures of the action film, and that men do cheer for heroic female characters.

Here is where I think pessimistic readings like Carol Clover's miss the mark. Clover claims that to "applaud the Final Girl as a feminist development, as some reviews of *Aliens* have done with Ripley, is, in light of her figurative meaning [really a man], is a particularly grotesque expression of wishful thinking" (1992: 53). Clover's claim is based on her observation that the Final Girl in horror films does not have a cinematic equal in any male characters. The Final Girl is a substitute that allows the male viewer to vicariously experience an initial sense of powerlessness. But Clover is mistaken in her reading of *Aliens* as the same as its predecessor. *Aliens* is clearly viewed as an action movie and not a horror—and the action genre contains a plethora of male heroes the viewer can identify with, but male viewers openly choose to accept Ripley in a heroic role regardless of her biology. *Aliens* has gained somewhat of a cult status amongst the mostly male fans of action movies, and at more than one midnight screening I have seen legions of male viewers quote Ripley's best lines in sync with her and wholeheartedly cheer her on.

That the same viewers can identify with both a Ripley and a Rambo, a Maggie and a Martin Riggs *in the same way* suggests that viewer identification based on gender is a much more fluid practice than many critics will accept. Likewise, the enormously popular queen of the straight-to-video martial-arts movies, Cynthia Rothrock, claims: "I get lots of letters from young men. They say I make Jean Claude Van Damme look like a wimp" (Fleming 1993: 66). That young men choose Rothrock *over* Van Damme is an indication audiences are perhaps more open-minded toward gender acceptability issues than they are often given credit for. Despite the ambivalence of some critics to welcome the action heroine as a challenge to the notion of gender as biologically determined, the growth of cinematic images of women kicking ass helps push the envelope of culturally appropriate gender traits. The success of *La Femme Nikita* and *Point of No Return* indicates the emerging acceptance of feminine identities that encroach upon even the most masculine of domains.

2) GENDER, SEXUALITY, AND TOUGHNESS

The Bad Girls of Action Film and Comic Books

Gear magazine's review of the film *The Transporter* (2002) opens with the declaration that "director, writer and producer Luc Besson knows better than most how to make a beautiful woman even more beautiful: arm her to the teeth" (Dawson 2002: 27). This peculiar observation about a filmmaker best known for putting big guns in the hands of wide-eyed waifs in movies such as *La Femme Nikita* (1990), *The Professional* (1994), and *The Fifth Element* (1997) elucidates the problematic reception of tough women in action movies. When women are portrayed as tough in contemporary film, are they being allowed access to a position of empowerment, or are they merely further fetishized as dangerous sex objects? Even within feminist film theory the modern action heroine has emerged as an extremely fruitful but difficult character to interpret. On the one hand, she represents a potentially transgressive figure capable of expanding the popular perception of women's roles and abilities; on the other, she runs the risk of reinscribing strict gender binaries and of being nothing more than sexist window-dressing for the predominantly male audience.

A central concern for critics has been the common interpretation of the action heroine as simply enacting masculinity rather than providing legitimate examples of female heroism. This tendency to read action heroines as figurative males is crystallized in the now legendary figures of Lieutenant Ripley (Sigourney Weaver) from the *Aliens* series and Sarah Connor (Linda Hamilton) from the *Terminator* series. As muscular, gun-toting, ass-kicking characters it is easy to see why these women are readily identified as performers of masculinity. Together these two figures have informed not just the portrayal of subsequent action heroines in films including *The Real McCoy* (1993), *Bad Girls* (1994), *Cutthroat Island* (1995), *Charlie's Angels* (2000), *Tomb Raider* (2001), and *Resident Evil* (2002), but also many of the scholarly discussions about gender and action cinema and the commercial press's quick identification of the new heroines as masculine proxies. A preoccupation of feminist film scholarship in recent years has dealt with the cultural implications of identification and the shifting landscape of gender roles when women cross over into the traditionally masculine terrain of toughness. That several of the first scholars to address these new roles for women identified them as "figurative males" (Clover 1992), "masculinized female bodies" (Tasker 1993), and "Dirty Harriet[s]" (Kaplan 1993) has led to a misconception that action heroines are *only* enacting masculinity.

The foundational work on women in tough roles by the likes of Carol Clover, Yvonne Tasker, and Cora Kaplan effectively questions our cultural belief in gender absolutes by documenting the female characters' penchant for being just as tough as male characters. Their own work, and the subsequent wave of scholarship concerned with these new depictions of women, has approached these transgressive figures from a variety of perspectives. Film studies' ongoing fascination with Ripley from the *Alien* series is indicative of the range of interpretations that have been utilized. For example, Barbara Creed (1993) considers Ripley and the film in relation to concepts of the abject female body, Paula Graham (1994) discusses the lesbian implications of Ripley's persona, Janice Hocker Rushing (1995) interprets Ripley as a co-opted mythological archetype, and Elizabeth Hills (1999) reads her as a "Post-Woman" able to function in the middle space between binaries. The range of scholarly approaches applied to the figure of Ripley is indicative of the multiple ways strong female characters are interpreted both within critical circles and presumably by audience members. But, as Hills points out, any critique of a character grounded in her depiction as an atypical female is likely to become mired in a language of symbolic gender constructs.

It is perhaps inevitable that discussions of shifting gender roles in film would be ensnared in the logic of either masculine *or* feminine since this conceptual binary underscores our basic perception of the physical and behavioral differences between the sexes. One of the problems, as I see it, is that the strict categorization of traits as male or female dominating film theory ever since Laura Mulvey's "Visual Pleasure and the Narrative Cinema" was first published in 1975 means that any atypical portrayals tend to be interpreted as cinematic transvestism. The previous chapter explored the logic of the symbolic gender cross-dressing typically performed by action heroines and some of the possibilities these transgressive figures may hold for changing cultural perceptions about masculine and feminine norms.

This chapter underscores an alternative interpretation accounting for both the toughness and sexiness of action heroines that does not deny the engendered elements of these traits but incorporates them into a solitary figure effectively critiquing the very notion of stable gender identities. The action heroine does enact both masculinity and femininity, but rather than swapping a biological identity for a performative one, she personifies a unity of disparate traits in a single figure. She refutes any assumed belief in appropriate gender roles via an exaggerated use of those very roles.

Without doubt the macho female action heroine continues to dominate attempts to integrate female characters (or, more importantly, the popular female stars who play them) into the narrative center of the profitable action genre. But the hard-as-nails action heroine is only one of the more visible variants of the tough-girl type. In fact, Yvonne Tasker, whose seminal *Spectacular Bodies: Gender, Genre and Action Cinema* set much of the interest in action heroines in motion, devoted a great deal of discussion in her subsequent book, *Working Girls: Gender and Sexuality in Popular Cinema* (1998), to variations such as the tomboy (*Speed*, 1994), the feisty heroine (*The Abyss*, 1989), the protective mother (*Fatal Beauty*, 1987), the official female partner (*Broken Arrow*, 1996), the wife/partner (*True Lies*, 1994), and the female partner as racial Other (*Strange Days*, 1995). But it is the variation that Tasker spends the least amount of time discussing, the one she describes as "a fetishistic figure of fantasy derived from comic books and soft pornography involving an exaggerated statement of sexuality: performed quite precisely in the action/porn hybrid *Barb Wire* (1996) with Pamela Anderson" (1998: 69), that will be explored more fully in this chapter.

The "fetishistic figure of fantasy" Barb Wire and her ilk clearly represent are a difference in degree, not a difference in kind, from the other female characters who take center stage in the action genre. For all its faults, its campy performances, and over-the-top presentation of Anderson's body, *Barb Wire* reveals the adolescent fear and desire of female sexuality that is exercised through the figure of all action heroines. Moreover, with *Barb Wire* and the film's comic book origins we can discover, from a different angle, that the ascribed masculinity of the archetypal action heroines may have more to do with a controlled sexualization than cross-gender performance.

Rather than masculinized women, the action heroine most often functions within the symbolic realm of the dominatrix by both breaking down and exploiting the boundaries between the sexes. It is because of *Barb Wire*'s exaggerated sexuality, not despite it, that the film can make explicit the fetishistic nature of the action heroine's real toughness. At a fundamental level every action heroine, not just those explicitly sexualized, mobilizes the specter of the dominatrix. It may be most apparent when the heroine is portrayed by Pamela Anderson, Angelina Jolie, Jennifer Lopez, Lucy Liu, or any of the straight-to-video centerfold types, but it is also an important ingredient in what have been considered the more serious roles of Sigourney Weaver as Ripley and Linda Hamilton as Sarah Connor. My contention is that modern action heroines are transgressive characters not only because their toughness allows them to critique normative standards of femininity, but because their coexistent sexuality (epitomized in *Barb Wire*) simultaneously destabilizes the very concept of gender traits as mutually exclusive.

"SUCK MY DICK!"

The persistent interpretation of tough women in action films as figurative males is understandable given how clearly the role of action hero is defined as a masculine domain in contemporary Hollywood films. But while the action genre in the 1990s evolved to the point where the one-dimensional masculinity represented in the 1980s by the likes of Schwarzenegger and Stallone (and Willis and Van Damme and Lundgren and Seagal) is no longer bankable—their stoic, blue collar, white masculinity being supplanted by such non-white and often comedic stars as Wesley Snipes, Will Smith, and Jackie Chan—their archetypes remain the standard against which all subsequent action heroes are read. Thus, an easy point of reference for newspaper reviews and magazine articles is to liken even the cartoonishly sexualized Pamela Anderson to Stallone: the *Toronto Star* review dubbed her role Pambo (1996, May 9: E1); or Schwarzenegger: *Premiere* magazine ran a feature profile on Anderson entitled "The Lust Action Hero" (1996: 70).

Elizabeth Hills has complained that "[A]lthough these powerfully transgressive characters open up interesting questions about the fluidity of gendered identities and changing popular cinematic representations of women, action heroines are often described within feminist film theory as 'pseudo males' or as being not 'really' women." Hills goes on to argue:

> [O]ne of the reasons why action heroines have been difficult to conceptualize as heroic *female* characters is the binaristic logic of the theoretical models on which a number of feminist theorists have relied. For example, feminists working within the dominant model of psychoanalysis have had extremely limited spaces within which to discuss the transformative and transgressive potential of the action heroine. This is because psychoanalytic accounts which theorize sexual difference within the framework of linked binary oppositions (active male/passive female) necessarily position normative female subjectivity as passive or in terms of lack. From this perspective, active and aggressive women in the cinema can only be seen as phallic, unnatural or "figuratively male." (1999: 38)

The alternative Hills offers to the strict psychoanalytic gender binarism that codes active as exclusively male and passive as exclusively female is to interpret action heroines, particularly Ripley, according to Deleuze's notion of becoming. As the only character, male or female, who transcends her original state of being and cognitively adapt to an external threat, Ripley becomes a form of Post-Woman operating in the productive spaces between strict cultural formations. In essence Hills proposes that Ripley is best understood as moving beyond the restrictive gender dichotomy. She functions not in terms best understood as male or female but as a transcendent and progressive character. The alternative I suggest here is that the tough action heroine is a transgressive character not because she operates outside of gender restrictions but because she straddles both sides of the psychoanalytic gender divide. She is both subject and object, looker and looked at, ass-kicker and sex object.

Like Hills, my concern stems from the now habitual interpretation of action heroines as men in drag that limits the acceptability of toughness as a legitimately feminine characteristic. But I do want to stress that this concern does not mean I disagree with the interpretation of these heroines as enacting masculinity, merely that there are other factors that contribute to the appeal of the action heroine in her varied guises. In fact, the "figurative male" description of action heroines, which once seemed such a unique insight facilitated by film theory, now seems all too obvious in many movies.

As the genre has become increasingly self-reflexive, the gender dilemma represented by the action heroine has become more overt. Where the masculinization of Lieutenant Ripley and Sarah Connor was in service of their respective films' plots, the gender transgression of subsequent action heroines seems to *be* the plot. Both *The Long Kiss Goodnight* (1996) and *G.I. Jane* (1997) exemplify the self-conscious masculinization of their female protagonists. A brief review of these two films and their critical reception illustrates the lengths the filmmakers go to explore the rigidity of gendered roles and to position their heroines as intentionally transgressive, masculinized figures.

The Long Kiss Goodnight was the second attempt, after the notorious failure of *Cutthroat Island,* by then husband-and-wife team Renny Harlin and Geena Davis (the Pygmalion-like control exercised by male producers over their real-life love interest actresses is discussed in the next chapter) to establish Davis as a major action star. The binary gender codes at work in *The Long Kiss Goodnight* are central to the film's plot—Davis plays Samantha Caine, a stereotypical midwestern mother and schoolteacher afflicted with amnesia for eight years.

With the assistance of down-at-his-heels private eye Mitch Henessey (Samuel L. Jackson), Samantha discovers her old life as a Cold War–era government assassin and in the process, unwittingly becomes involved in fighting her old enemies, now allied with her former employer. They plan to blow up the bridge to Canada at Niagara Falls in a fake terrorist attack to secure more anti-terrorist funding from Congress. As Samantha gradually learns about her previous self, her true persona, Charly, reemerges. The transformation of sweet Samantha into ass-kicking Charly constitutes the central fantasy of the film and is clearly structured along traditional gender binaries. The self-discovery of *The Long Kiss Goodnight* is a literal stripping away of the feminine masquerade embodied by Samantha in favor of the underlying masculine character of Charly.

The film takes an obvious pleasure in juxtaposing Samantha's initial inno-cence and timidity with Charly's aggressive and violent personality. As Tasker puts it, "if Samantha is determined by motherhood, Charly is (over) deter-mined by an excess of phallic imagery" (1998: 87). Samantha is shown at the onset of the story as a loving mother to her daughter and as happily engaged to a sensitive man, but, this being an action film, audiences anticipate the demise of the sweet charade and revel in the character's increasingly violent abilities.

Though Samantha is initially surprised by her emerging skills—expert knife handling (which she humorously misinterprets as a sign that she was a chef) and instinctively assembling a high-powered rifle in mere seconds—the moth-erly disguise is soon abandoned all together. In a hyperbolically symbolic sce-nario her final (re)masculinization from Samantha into Charly occurs during a torture scene. Submerged in freezing water, Samantha/Charly retrieves a gun from the crotch of a drowned corpse and proceeds to kill her torturer. From this point forward the narrative revels in Charly's freed masculine behavior.

She physically transforms into Charly: she cuts her hair short and dyes it blond, wears harsh make-up, and trades in the dresses and sweaters for tight pants and a bullet-riddled leather jacket. Mitch watches awed, as Charly chain smokes and drinks, happily downing several shots of hard liquor and swearing like a trucker, or as Mitch tells her: "You used to be all 'Phooey, I burned the cookies,' now you walk into a bar and ten minutes later sailors come running out."

She is also more sexually aggressive, asking Mitch if he wants to fuck. Most importantly, Charly is repeatedly shown as the master of phallic power, out-shooting, out-fighting, and out-thinking the villains at every turn. The real plot of *The Long Kiss Goodnight* is not the anti-terrorist struggle, nor is it Samantha/Charly's efforts to save her daughter after she's kidnapped. The real plot is the gender negotiation of feminine Samantha into masculine Charly and then the final attempt at a reconciliation between the personas at film's end.

A year after the self-conscious gender exploration of *The Long Kiss Good-night*, Ridley Scott, who had already directed the landmark tough women film *Thelma & Louise*, also took the masculinization of a female hero as the main plot of his film *G.I. Jane*. Though more of a military basic training movie in the vein of *An Officer and a Gentleman* (1982) or *Heartbreak Ridge* (1986) than simply an action movie, *G.I. Jane* cast Demi Moore as Lieutenant Jordan O'Neil in the same masculinized mold as the quintessential action heroine. Capitalizing on real-life debates about women's expanding role in the military, *G.I. Jane* is the story of O'Neil's struggles to become the first female Navy SEAL. And, like *The Long Kiss Goodnight*, the convoluted plot of *G.I. Jane* seems secondary to the film's main purpose, which is to document the transformation of Moore's character into a masculine proxy.

The cover of *Sight and Sound* summed up the real importance of the film when it declared "Demi Moore Takes It Like a Man" (Williams 1996: 18). Though the overwrought surface message of the film is that women are perfectly capable of entering even the most masculine of military service, the implicit message is that she can only achieve success as a SEAL by putting her femininity behind her and capitulating to the symbolic realm of what Lauren Tucker and Alan Fried refer to as "techno masculinity" in their analysis of the film (1998: 165). A *Rocky*esque montage of training and self-transformation signals her resolve to make the grade on the same terms as her male comrades. Tucker and Fried point out:

> O'Neil's transformation is initially signaled by the loss of specific physical indicators of her femaleness, one of the most overt of which is her long hair. In a dramatic scene, she slowly and carefully cuts off her hair without the aid of the briefly-absent barber. Her intense personal training routine results in the loss of her period, and her body starts to take on a harder, more masculine look. (1998: 170)

Her more masculine appearance is matched by her mastery of masculine skills as she dominates such drill tests as the obstacle course and rifle assembly. Eventually O'Neil becomes the best and the most respected recruit in the class. Accepted by her peers as "one of them," O'Neil's masculine abilities are ultimately tested in a real combat situation where she manages to rescue first her commanding officer and then her whole platoon.

If their cumulative performances throughout the films do not make it clear enough that for these women to be tough they have to be masculinized, the triumphant moment for both Samantha/Charly in *The Long Kiss Goodnight* and for O'Neil in *G.I. Jane* is accompanied by the almost hysterically obvious, gender-transgressive challenge to "suck my dick!" Charly shouts "Suck my dick, every last one of you bastards!" while speeding an eighteen-wheel truck at her enemies amidst the explosions of the film's climactic battle. Like-wise, this becomes a catchphrase when, after being beaten and thrown to the ground in front of her fellow recruits during a mock training mission, O'Neil defiantly tells the Master Chief to "Suck my dick!" Signaling her resolve is still intact, O'Neil wins over her peers who cheer her bravado and taunt their Chief with a group chant of "Suck my dick!" In their essay about the gun as metaphorical masculinization in *G.I. Jane*, Tucker and Fried rightly observe that it is at this moment as "she basks in the cheers and acceptance of her fellow recruits, [that] O'Neil's transformation into a rugged, individualistic techno-male is complete" (1998: 172).

Where the appropriation of the phallus by past action heroines is illus-trated by masculine characteristics and symbolic accoutrements like guns, swords, and muscles, the heroines in *The Long Kiss Goodnight* and *G.I. Jane* go a step further and verbally declare their appropriation. Moreover, in moving from wielding phallic symbols to declaring possession of a phallus, both these characters not only further masculinize themselves, but more importantly—they feminize their adversaries. They openly reveal their position of assuming power and strength through the rhetoric of gendered terms.

"You do not have to be well versed in psychoanalysis to know that dick means power," wrote Linda Williams in her insightful discussion of Demi Moore's body upon the release of *G.I. Jane*, "the power towards which every-one, more or less unsuccessfully, aspires. To grasp the position from which 'dick' can be spoken and then to yell the word back at your assailant makes the speaker, whatever anatomy has destined them for, the better endowed" (1996: 20). The essence of the action heroine wielding masculinity is crystallized in the open challenge to "suck my dick" by both Samantha/Charly and O'Neil. By assuming male traits, they gain access to a form of power (both physical and social) that has been systematically denied to women, while simultane-ously demonstrating that the association of "maleness" with "power" is not innate but culturally defined since anyone can mobilize even the most basic of male privileges: the privilege to assert phallic authority through reference to an actual phallus.

"DON'T CALL ME BABE!"

While the traditional binaristic approach to sexual difference grounded in the active male/passive female split is still undeniably essential to the reading of such films as *The Long Kiss Goodnight* and *G.I. Jane*, it is certainly not the only way to explore the action heroine. "From this perspective [of binaristic logic],"

Hills points out, "active and aggressive women in the cinema can only be seen as phallic, unnatural or figuratively male" (1999: 39). Hills' own alternative approach is a consideration of Ripley from the *Alien* series as an adaptive, transformative, and alternative *feminine* figure. Yet even without rejecting the limitations of the "figurative male" thesis altogether, the array of types under the category of action heroine bring the concept of gender transgression into question.

Where the Rambo references to Sigourney Weaver's Ripley as "Fembo" and "Rambolina" seem warranted, the relatively tongue-in-cheek references to Pamela Anderson's Barb Wire as "Pambo" (made in both the *Toronto Star* and the *London Spectator*) underscore the absurdity of reading both Anderson and the Barb Wire character through the male action heroes lens. Though Barb Wire behaves in ways coded as masculine (she fights, shoots, talks, and drinks like the toughest of screen characters), it is ludicrous to think of her as a figurative male just because she acts tough. Despite her gun and bad attitude, it is near impossible to read Barb Wire as anything but a male fantasy when she always wears revealing leather corsets with her hair perfectly coiffed and her perfect make-up (Figure 2.1). The excessive presentation of Anderson's cartoonishly sexualized body seems on the surface to counter any transgressive potential the film might hope for. But it is exactly this over-fetishization of her sexuality and violent abilities that facilitates an understanding of all modern action heroines as questioning the naturalness of gender roles by enacting both femininity and masculinity simultaneously.

Barb Wire, the film, as many critics observed, is an odd mix of soft-core porn and action movie clichés. Though it was the first big-budget feature starring a well-known celebrity to employ this formula so blatantly, it is a common foundation for a whole sub-genre of straight-to-video films. Anderson as Barb Wire is essentially an actioned-up version of Humphrey Bogart's Rick in this gender-reversed remake of *Casablanca* (1942). Set in a future where America has become a chaotic military state, Anderson's Barb Wire is, as the promotional materials put it, "the sexiest, toughest woman in Steel Harbor" who will "use any dangerous weapon, including her body, to take what she wants."

Wire owns the most popular nightclub in town and moonlights as a bounty hunter. When her ex-lover shows up one night to ask for help smuggling a renowned scientist out of the United States, she initially refuses, but after repeated assaults by police and the Nazi-like military, Wire finds herself morally obligated to help smuggle the scientist out of the country. The final scene has Wire and the corrupt Chief of Police (who has had a last-minute change of heart) standing on a rain-slicked runway repeating the famous ending of

2.1. Pamela Anderson as Barb Wire.

Casablanca with an appropriate updating of the dialogue: "I think I'm falling in love," the Chief says, to which Wire retorts, "Get in line!" as the camera pans her leather-clad form one last time.

Even with the plot's liberal borrowing from such a film classic, *Barb Wire* is a far cry from *Casablanca*. The extended opening sequence of *Barb Wire* is typical of a heavy metal music video fantasy and sets the tone of sexploitation for the rest of the movie. Wire dances erotically in a skin-tight latex mini-dress as water is splashed over her body and numerous men hoot and holler (she is, conveniently, undercover as a stripper). Shot entirely in fragmented, slow-motion close-ups, the scene establishes Wire as a sexual icon. The message is clear: this body is in no way masculinized—it is to be looked at and desired.

More importantly, the culmination of the scene establishes Wire's body as not just something to be desired, but to be feared. One audience member becomes increasingly obnoxious, shouting for her to "take it all off" and "show us what you've got, babe!" In response, Wire fires off a stiletto-heeled shoe at him, piercing him between the eyes. She leaves the stage muttering, "If one more person calls me babe," which becomes a running joke and sets up Wire's catchphrase: "Don't call me babe."

The film's marketing clearly tried to spin the phrase as a pseudo-feminist tagline in the tradition of Dirty Harry's "Go ahead, make my day" and the Terminator's "I'll be back" or "Hasta la vista, baby." As the signature line of the film, "Don't call me babe" neatly crystallizes the fundamental conflict of Wire as action heroine. Despite the character's protest, the film is dependent on Anderson's status as the quintessential "babe" of the 1990s. Yet because she is supposed to be a tough action heroine, she quickly kills anyone who tries to position her as object rather than subject, anyone who dares to call her babe. Wire's body may be desirable, but as the promotional copy on the back of the DVD box says, it is also a dangerous weapon. Like nearly all of the action women who have come before and after *Barb Wire*, the film constantly struggles to find an appropriate way to sexualize and empower tough women.

Despite sharing some violent behavioral traits with previous action heroines, *Barb Wire* illustrates the impracticality of conceptualizing an action heroine as a figurative male. "Pambo" or not, her highly sexualized but also highly dangerous body is semiotically something altogether different. To grasp the full fetishistic appeal of the film, the comic book trend that gave birth to the character must be taken into account. The *Barb Wire* comic book series was published by Dark Horse Comics and was part of a larger industry trend known as the Bad Girl.

The Bad Girls label primarily refers to the highly sexualized nature of these female characters that dominated the struggling comics industry in the mid-nineties. In a blatant attempt to attract the attention of the mostly male adolescent comics consumer, publishers flooded the shelves with titles featuring leggy and buxom superheroines in revealing, skin-tight costumes. In addition to *Barb Wire*, series such as *Lady Death*, *Lady Rawhide*, *Razor*, *Avengelyne*, *Witchblade*, *Double Impact*, *Vogue*, and *Fatale* quickly became hot commodities.

The iconography was simple and central to their popularity—The covers depicted a scantily clad babe in a revealing pose and carrying a prominent weapon, usually a gun, sword, or whip. The cover of *Lady Rawhide* #1 (Figure 2.2) is a typical example of Bad Girl cover art, emphasizing both the sex kittenish bodies of the title heroines and their excessive weapons.

"For years," Rogers Cadenhead wrote in the leading comics fanzine, *Wizard*, "the conventional wisdom in comics has been that female characters can't succeed in their own books. After spirited efforts with protagonists like Wonder Woman and She-Hulk, companies resigned themselves to the fact that their largely male audience largely wants to read about large males" (1994: 42). The world of superhero comic books is still a bastion of adolescent power

2.2. *Lady Rawhide #1*, 1995.

fantasies, and images of hypermasculine men continue to dominate the colorful worlds where every wimpy Clark Kent or Peter Parker can become a Superman or a Spider-Man. It is a world where they magically transform into heroic and powerful beings that can handle any threatening situation with ease, and brute force becomes the solution for all of life's problems. The scenario for female characters likewise involves an increase of raw bodily power, but it also carries with it an increased erotic appeal.

Ironically, it was the growing emphasis on "large males" as subject matter that resulted in the emergence of the Bad Girl trend in the first place. Through the 1990s a shift within the comics industry to particularly stylistic artists as stars and the concomitant rise of several independent and creator-owned publishing companies resulted in an increasingly excessive representation of the male body. Hypermasculine characters are now routinely drawn with arms as big as couches and chests the size of mini-vans. The Bad Girl subgenre emerged as an offshoot of this hypermasculine shift. Scott Bukatman's description of these new female characters captures the absurdity of their depiction:

> The spectacle of the female body in these titles is so insistent, and the fetishism of breasts, thighs, and hair so complete, that the comics seem to dare you to say something about them that isn't just redundant. *Of course* the female form has absurdly exaggerated sexual characteristics; *of course* the costumes are skimpier than one could (or should) imagine; *of course* there's no visible way that these costumes could stay in place; *of course* these women represent simple adolescent masturbatory fantasies (with a healthy taste of the dominatrix). One might note that women participate more fully in battle than they once did. It's worth observing that they're now as powerful as their male counterparts. They no longer need protection; they are no longer victims or hostages or prizes. (1994: 112)

Many creators of these Bad Girl comics stress what Bukatman notes in his description: their characters are no longer damsels in distress waiting for a man to save them. They are typically as powerful, violent, skilled, smart, and self-assured as any of the male comic book counterparts. While this may indeed be a positive development, it is offset by the compensatory exaggerated feminine form, resulting in an odd combination of toughness and sexiness. At least on a symbolic level, the physical extremes that typify the Bad Girl (huge, gravity-defying breasts, mile-long legs, perpetually pouty lips, and perfectly coifed big hair) amount to an almost hysterical mask of femininity.

That these characters have exaggeratedly feminine bodies is not surprising given the superhero genre's preoccupation with the physical ideal. The interesting aspect is that in their sexualized hyperfeminine depiction they not only compensate for assuming traditionally masculine roles but combine the symbolic "manliness" of toughness with the most basic symbols of "womanliness." Like Barb Wire in the film version, and to a lesser extent all the other heroines of action cinema, these characters embody and enact both genders, ridiculing the very notion of a stable gender position. The progressive impact of action heroines is not that they can enact masculinity (Ripley and Connor) nor that they can be effectively masculinized (Samantha/Charly and O'Neil), it is that in every case they combine femininity and masculinity. The surface bodily differences that symbolize these characters as male or female are ultimately revealed as nothing but symbols. The excessive gender images exist only as a compensatory surface to the underlying theme that toughness does not need to be conceived as a gendered trait.

The complex combination of pouty fantasy woman and oversized weapons is part of a larger cultural system of fetishization within an iconography of pinups and soft porn. The fact that Bad Girls so often seem to be merely posing in skimpy costumes with weapons held ready like so many frames of stylized S&M porn reveals a central paradox of the action woman: she is required to be both active and static at the same time. Building on Richard Dyer's (1982) observations of the muscular male pinup, Tasker notes the tension in film between "an image built, designed for contemplation in static poses and the situation of such images within the context of action. By extension it is possible to understand the difficulties involved in putting the eroticised female image from pinup into 'action'; both she and the male bodybuilder are subject to display and to the need to 'pose'" (1998: 70).

Pamela Anderson is thus perfectly cast in *Barb Wire* since her star image is grounded in the popularity of her pinup career, especially her famous *Playboy* pictorials. At the same time this need to pose Anderson may hinder the narrative motion of the film, it does stress the important association between action women and photographic porn images. The Bad Girl comic book heroine is only the middle ground between the explicitly sexualized porn model and the ass-kicking Hollywood heroine. Other post–Barb Wire comic book (and animation, and video game) heroine film adaptations such as *Catwoman*, *Ultraviolet*, *Aeon Flux*, and *Tomb Raider* have struggled with the same difficulties of mobilizing characters whose popularity resides in large part in their success as static pinups. Still images of Halle Berry in her fetishistic Catwoman costume proved far more popular than the film itself. Not surprisingly, some examples reverse the *Barb Wire* trajectory, where a popular television/pinup/soft-porn star embodies an adolescent fantasy of comic book womanhood. The link between the three different media forms (Hollywood action movies, Bad Girl comics, and pornographic images) used to express a certain type of female sexuality is so fluid that some real-life women have become fictional comic book characters, so to speak. For example, B-movie Queen and former *Penthouse* "Pet of the Year" Julie Strain is now featured in *Heavy Metal* magazine as the cartoon heroine F.A.K.K.[2], and popular *Playboy* model Alley Baggett has become the subject of her own superhero comic book, *Alley Cat*.

The fetishization of these Bad Girls with guns, swords, and whips does not so much mark them as masculine as it marks them as dominatrixes, all part of a broader fetishizing of the female body. It is no coincidence that Pamela Anderson is clad in leather bondage wear throughout *Barb Wire*. Bukatman understates it when he refers to the Bad Girls as "simple adolescent masturbatory fantasies (with a healthy taste of the dominatrix)" (1994: 112).

There is more than just a "healthy taste of the dominatrix" going on here. These characters are first and foremost images of threatening female sexuality. Their bodies may be alluring to young male readers, but they are also, like Barb Wire/Pamela Anderson's body, "dangerous weapons." In a telling variation on the guns as phallic symbol cliché, a mob boss asks about Barb Wire at the start of the film by referring to her as the one with the "guns," meaning her large breasts. The highly sexualized female body is as capable of being coded as a weapon as it is a passive plaything. Moreover, this notion of the costumed heroine as a thinly veiled dominatrix is not new.

Even with Wonder Woman the analogy was obvious shortly after her creation in the early 1940s. In her miniskirt, armored bustier, and steel bracelets, she was the first in a long line of moderately fetishized heroines. Clearly her famous golden lasso has always been layered with implications of bondage: when men are bound with it, they must submit to her will. And, tellingly, if a man ever binds Wonder Woman with the lasso, she loses all of her powers. And certainly the Jungle Janes and the Phantom Ladies who appeared in 1950s comics owed as much to the popular bondage photos of Bettie Page as they did to their heroic male counterparts such as Superman and Batman. The half-naked Bad Girls filling the comic book pages of today look and act less like pinup cheesecake and more like hard-core mistresses of pain. In fact, while most of the publishers involved in the Bad Girl sub-genre publicly deny the fetishistic overtones of the characters by claiming it is all just good, clean, comic book fun, others have overtly recognized the dominatrix appeal of the characters (for example Jones and Jacob 1997).

It is important to recognize that these Bad Girl bodies are presented as dangerous not just because they can fight or shoot, but *because* they are alluring. Being able to fight and shoot may make them tough, but it is this toughness combined with overt sexuality that makes them dangerous in a way male characters can never be. Given the age of many comic book readers, it is not surprising that extremely attractive and aggressively sexual female characters who clearly embody a simplistic form of castration anxiety find some purchase.

Like Delilah cutting Sampson's hair to steal his legendary strength, many of today's Bad Girls can directly steal a man's power with just a touch or a kiss. Rogue, a hardbody Southern belle and a member of Marvel Comics' mutant team the X-Men, can steal a man's psyche by touching her flesh to his. Likewise, Broadway Comics' Fatale is described as a "powerful, good-looking woman born with the ability to absorb knowledge, skills and strength from other people, especially men, through physical contact." It is perhaps no small coincidence that for both Rogue and Fatale (and villainesses such as Poison Ivy from the Batman comics), the preferred method for stealing a man's strength through physical contact is to kiss him.

Where the superpowers of the comic book Bad Girls are less than subtle metaphors for the ability of female sexuality to drain a man of his phallic powers, the same fetishistic themes exist in action movie heroines. In the comics, people of either gender can fly, hurl automobiles, or bounce bullets off their chests. Likewise, in action movies people of either gender can fight, shoot, and blow things up. But in both genres only women can combine these tough skills with the threat of seduction. The Bad Girls of comics and the tough girls of action films combine threats traditionally engendered as either masculine (toughness) or feminine (seduction).

The film version of *Barb Wire* is grounded in these fetishistic elements of the Bad Girl comic books and even builds upon them where it sees fit in order to both exploit the appeal of Anderson's body and to position itself as a quintessential action movie. Scene after scene in the film juxtaposes Barb Wire's cartoonishly sexual appearance with her penchant for violence directed at the men who ogle her. The opening striptease where she incapacitates a man with her high heel is one clear example of her violent response to males who presume her sexuality is on display merely for the pleasure of their gaze.

In an extended scene that consolidates the fetishistic themes, Wire, dressed as a dominatrix in thigh-high leather boots, fishnet stockings, a leather bustier, and a dog collar, poses as a prostitute who "likes to play rough" to gain access to a highly secured apartment building. Once inside the apartment of the fat, sweating, leering man she has picked up as her trick, she suggests he change into something more comfortable (so she can check out how to break into the apartment next door where her bail-jumping bounty is holed up). The trick asks if he can change into something less comfortable instead, and Wire plays along. When he returns in a leather body suit she tells him he has been a bad boy, takes a paddle and cracks him across the back of the head so hard that he drops like a ton of bricks. Then, in a flurry of action Wire sets explosives and blows a hole in the wall, dashes through, beats up the bounty and handcuffs him to the bed. As two bodyguards burst into the room with guns blazing, she returns fire from behind an overturned table, then finishes both in hand-to-hand combat after they run out of bullets, grinding her stiletto heel into the groin of one before killing him for—calling her *babe*.

Scenes like the one described above may seem ludicrous in a live-action movie but it is true to the comic book source material. *Barb Wire* is a perfect combination of comic book Bad Girl and Hollywood action heroine thanks primarily to Pamela Anderson's famously extreme figure and some over-the-top action sequences. The film is a transparent representation of the fear and desire of women so consistently fetishized in the comics.

While Anderson's performance as a cartoonish dominatrix is indicative of modern Hollywood's ongoing practice of displaying the body as an erotic spectacle, it is not necessarily all that different from the more "respectable" action heroines. The sexualized themes of fear and desire so obvious and visually apparent throughout *Barb Wire* may in fact be essential to the complex appeal of other action heroines as well. Even the most systematically masculinized of cinematic action heroines incorporate conventional feminine sexual attractiveness to some degree. The casting alone is indicative of the film industry's attempts to present established sex symbols as tough heroines in the attempt to create a combination of sex and violence irresistible to action film fans. My point is that every action heroine is a combination of conventional sexual attractiveness and violent abilities—symbols of fear and desire. The sex symbol status of action heroine actresses is most obvious in the cases of Pamela Anderson, Demi Moore, Angelina Jolie, Jessica Biel, Jessica Alba, Halle Berry, and Milla Jovovich. But even Sigourney Weaver and Linda Hamilton have often been cast as sex objects in their roles outside of the *Alien* and *Terminator* series. While these characters may all enact masculinity, in their femininity/sexuality they also enact the principles of the dominatrix. The dominatrix-like qualities may be more apparent in *Barb Wire* than in more serious fare, but these qualities exist nonetheless.

I do not mean that all action heroines mobilize the dynamics of whip-wielding, leather-clad sexual sadists who punish men for pleasure (though even this extreme argument may be plausible). In fact, I think it is the overriding sexual implication of the term "dominatrix" that steered the discussion of action heroines in the exclusive direction of "figurative maleness" to begin with. Because the powerfully symbolic and marginalized sign of the dominatrix may superficially reduce these potentially groundbreaking characters to the level of mere sexual fetishes, it has rarely been addressed in relation to tough women in film. The connotations of "dominatrix" may be an acceptable derision for a Pamela Anderson movie within film studies circles, but not for Ridley Scott– or James Cameron–directed installments of the *Alien* series. But, I believe, the symbolic function of the dominatrix is at the root of all the images of tough women that populate action films, whether they are straight-to-video exploitation pictures or Academy Award–winning feature films. I mean "dominatrix" here not as a kinky subcultural fetish but as a complex symbol that combines and exploits power (both physical and social) along the axis of gender (both masculine and feminine).

Beyond its distractingly symbolic surface, the figure of the dominatrix is an icon that, as Thaïs E. Morgan points out, "uses the signs of masculinity to mock masculinity" (1989: 125). The really transgressive potential of the action heroine may be that, as with the dominatrix, she mocks masculinity as she enacts it. Rather than crossing gender boundaries, the dominatrix combines them in a playful, yet effective manner. While cross-dressing or performing the gender of the opposite sex is momentarily transgressive, it still reinscribes gendered traits as the norm, as gender specific, because they are presented as mutually exclusive. If the action heroine is a figurative male, the importance of signs such as muscles, self-reliance, competence, and control within the economy of masculinity is not really undermined but reinforced. But if the action heroine is read as a dominatrix, the exclusivity of gendered traits is truly brought into question because one set of gendered signs does not replace the other; instead, the boundaries are confounded *because* they are combined.

Both the dominatrix and the action heroine combine disparate signs: male and female, subject and object, powerful and powerless, pleasurable and punishing. At their most rudimentary, these combinatory figures may represent castration anxiety for male viewers, but at their most progressive they also demonstrate the frailty of binary opposite cultural categories. When a curvaceous Pamela Anderson or a waif-like Bridget Fonda (*Point of No Return, Kiss of the Dragon*), Milla Jovovich (*The Fifth Element, Resident Evil*) or a schoolgirlish Drew Barrymore (*Bad Girls, Charlie's Angels*) or the literal school girls of the film *D.E.B.S.* pick up guns and proceed to kick ass, the playfulness of manipulating traditional signs is hard to miss. Like the dominatrix, the action heroine "refuses the terms of the social contract of sexual difference" (Morgan 1989: 125). She does not just dress up as a male or simply enact masculinity. She dresses up as both male and female, enacting both masculinity and femininity. Thus she illustrates by example not only that gender is primarily a performance of culturally determined traits and conventions, but that these traits and conventions do not have to symbolize sexual difference. The signs of masculinity and femininity are not complete sets but individual pieces to be played with. "Suck my dick" and "don't call me babe" may seem antithetical, but, within the gender reworking logic of dominatrix semiotics, both catchphrases are appropriate for the same female character.

TELEVISION V.I.P.S

Given the amount of critical attention devoted to the action heroine, it is important to note that most of these films were box-office failures. Despite the enormous popularity of *Aliens* and *Terminator 2*, none of the other action heroine films mentioned in this chapter were even moderate successes. Some of them, including *Barb Wire*, *Cutthroat Island*, and *V. I. Warshawski*, are infamous flops. While the larger-than-life male action hero continues to dominate movie theatres worldwide, the action heroine struggles to gain a firmer foothold in feature films. Though the action heroine in her various guises is a progressive female character wrapped up in some obvious titillation for the predominately male audience of these genre films, perhaps the dominatrix overtones she embodies are still too unsettling for viewers within this realm of masculine fairy tales to accept en masse.

Yet, while the sexy action heroine has seldom found box office success at the movie theater, she has become a hit on television. Contemporary television programs such as *Xena: The Warrior Princess*, *Buffy the Vampire Slayer*, *La Femme Nikita*, *Dark Angel*, *Witchblade*, *Alias*, and *V.I.P.* have all built upon their initial cult appeal to become mainstream ratings giants. Taking their cue from the popularity of sexy but tough female characters, *Star Trek: Voyager* replaced the likes of Captains Kirk and Picard with the strong female Captain Janeway and the sexy but unemotional Borg engineer Seven of Nine. Moreover, *Star Trek: Enterprise* replaced Spock with a sexy Vulcan science officer in order to ensure its ratings competitiveness. The erotic appeal of this type of science fiction and robotic heroines is discussed further in Chapter Six.

These television tough women have received a great deal of attention from gender studies scholars in their own right (see, for example, Helford 2000, Wilcox and Lavery 2002, and Ogersby and Gough-Yates 2002). Though the appeal of TV heroines raises a variety of different issues, it is clear that the TV series are just as dependent on the sex appeal of the lead actresses as feature films are. Lucy Lawless (Xena), Sarah Michelle Gellar (Buffy), Peta Wilson (Nikita), and, of course, Pamela Anderson, who created and stars in *V.I.P.*, all represent modern ideals of female beauty and are routinely costumed in skimpy and skin-tight outfits. The dominatrix overtones of these living room action heroines may be toned down a little bit from their big screen counterparts, but they still exist. Clad in a leather and armor bustier, Xena may be the most easily identifiable as a dominatrix-influenced fantasy, but the sight of an adolescent Buffy dressed in club wear and high heels as she kicks and stabs ghoulies to death is not that far off the mark either. Nor does Pamela Anderson venture far from the terrain of Barb Wire each week on *V.I.P.* as her bodyguard character runs around Los Angeles in various bikinis and latex mini-dresses with a gleaming revolver in hand.

Despite the surface similarities between the sexy and tough action heroines of the big and small screens, two key differences facilitate a widespread popularity for the television characters. First, the serial format of television makes it easier to grasp the heroine as more than a mere fetish object for male viewers. They may be sex symbols, but they are sex symbols we come to know over time as fully rounded characters. This all-important character development is due to the serial format of television and a component rarely achieved within the roughly two-hour time limit of feature films. Second, the content restrictions of prime time television necessitate a certain degree of campiness, which softens the sexism and often gives the narratives a tongue-in-cheek quality, signaling that audiences should have fun with the fantasy.

A prime example of audiences embracing the campy aspects of the programs are the well-known legions of lesbian *Xena* fans who celebrate the close and potentially sexual relationship of Xena and her companion Gabrielle. Together, these two key elements distinguish television action heroines from film action heroines in a manner that allows women to embrace the characters without alienating male viewers. Nor is this an entirely new phenomenon. Women have always been able to identify with tough and sexy female characters on television even if the characters were intended by network executives as eye-candy for male viewers.

Whether it was Emma Peel and her leather cat-suit in *The Avengers* (see Andrae 1996) or "TV's Private Eyeful" Honey West (see D'Acci 1997) or even those queens of jiggle-TV, *Charlie's Angels* (see Fiske 1988), female viewers are capable of latching onto the strength at the core of characters rather than just focusing on their outer beauty. If television is any indication, perhaps the real liberating and stereotype-breaking potential of female characters in action roles is that they can assume positions of power while also being sex symbols. This has subversive potential because it mocks masculine presumptions and undeniably illustrates that even the most cartoonishly feminine of heroines can also be tough, self-reliant, and powerful.

3) *ALIAS*, FETISHISM, AND PYGMALION FANTASIES

*D*uring its first season the TV series *Alias* (2001–2006) enjoyed critical success, attracting a strong cult following. The lavishly produced show about a beautiful graduate student, Sydney Bristow, who leads a secret double life as a super spy for a clandestine organization, took longer to catch on with the mainstream audience however. In an effort to promote *Alias* to the wider viewing public, ABC ran a striking advertisement in the popular press that captured many of the show's key ingredients. "She's not just a secret agent," the copy teased beneath a blue-tinted close-up of star Jennifer Garner in a blonde wig and tight, low-cut latex dress, "she's a concealed weapon." The ad managed to highlight not just Garner's sex appeal and the basic secret agent premise of the show, but also the underlying concept that beneath all of Sydney Bristow's sexy aliases is an agent who is capable and deadly.

The promotion also hints at the series' reworking of gender iconography. Consider the not-so-subtle allusion to the poster for the quintessential action movie *Lethal Weapon* (1987) starring Mel Gibson and Danny Glover: "Two cops. Glover carries a weapon. . . . Gibson is one. He's the only L.A. cop registered as a Lethal Weapon." Gibson's iconic action hero Martin Riggs is so tough that he is equated with the ultimate phallic signifier, the gun. He is a weapon in that he embodies phallic masculinity. By extension, you do not have to have an extensive background in Freudian theory to wonder just what weapon is concealed under Sydney's dress. Like Riggs, her body is so lethal it is a weapon/gun. But, as a female weapon, the threat she poses is effectively concealed beneath fetishistic costuming. Clearly, many involved with the production of *Alias* knew that the series was bringing a type of phallic woman to prime-time television.

Under creator J. J. Abrams' direction, Sydney Bristow was a smart, resourceful, fearless and tough woman who always managed to outthink and outfight her adversaries, no matter how impossible the odds. Perhaps more than any other single action heroine to date, Bristow functions as a fetish object on multiple levels. Throughout its five-year run *Alias* crystallized many divergent ways that action heroines are fetishized in a manner that allows them to be both an empowering image of female strength and to be contained within the broader patriarchal logic of American popular culture. On the face of it, *Alias* (like *Xena: Warrior Princess* [1995–2001], *Buffy the Vampire Slayer* [1997–2003], *La Femme Nikita* [1997–2001], and other long-running action heroine TV series) is about a woman taking control of her life and assuming a position of power in a male-dominated world. But just under the surface is another story of masculinity in crisis—of patriarchy struggling to control and contain female sexuality.

Alias is ostensibly the long, complicated story of Sydney Bristow's adventures as an international super spy, but it is also about her relationships with family and coworkers, particularly her father. The show's pilot episode sets the tone for the fast-paced series with multiple deceptions and mysteries. We learn that Sydney has been hiding her double life as an agent for the shadowy espionage organization, SD-6. When Sydney reveals the truth about her clandestine occupation to her fiancé, SD-6 murders him in order to keep their existence a secret.

Outraged, Sydney lashes out at her employers, especially the ruthless head of SD-6, Arvin Sloane. She finds herself on the run from her own agency and quickly discovers that nothing in her life is as it seemed—SD-6 is not a division of the CIA as she believed, but instead a terrorist organization bent on world domination. And, even more shocking, Sydney discovers that her emotionally distant father, Jack Bristow (Victor Garber), is also an agent for SD-6 when he risks everything to help her. Sydney eventually approaches the real CIA and agrees to work for them as a double agent within SD-6 alongside her father, himself a CIA/SD-6 double agent.

At the core of the series is the evolving relationship between Sydney and her father, which is troubled by issues of trust, the reemergence of Sydney's mother as a Russian spy, the fact that Sloane may be her biological father, and her inter-agency romantic relationships. Over the years the alliances, the cast of characters, and government agencies may shift but the episodic formula remains consistent. Whether she is fighting terrorists, rescuing scientists, or recovering mystical Rimbaldi artifacts, every episode requires Sydney assume an alias to complete her mission. And, as the tone of the "She's not just a secret agent" ad suggests, each alias is a highly sexualized version of the fantasy female.

Though the extensive use of femininity as masquerade is crucial to *Alias'* narrative formula, I do not explore these masquerades simply as further examples of the action heroine's manipulation of gender as performance. Certainly Sydney's undercover roles as helpless secretary, naïve co-ed, French maid, prostitute, and so on, demonstrate for the viewer the arbitrary and constructed nature of womanliness in a manner perhaps even more obvious than in some films already discussed like *Blade: Trinity, Point of No Return,* and *The Long Kiss Goodnight.* Likewise, Sydney's abilities in hand-to-hand combat and the depiction of her athletic body can be seen as a direct descendent of cross-gender masculinity (or masculinity, as Yvonne Tasker refers to it) enacted by the heroines of *Aliens* and *Terminator 2.* And her feminine and masculine traits can position her as a dominatrix à la *Barb Wire* (more than once her undercover alias is an actual dominatrix), but in this chapter I wish to focus on how the action heroine, and Sydney Bristow specifically, is constructed and consumed as a fetish.

Both within the narrative and in the broader cultural consumption of the text, action heroines often meld together the properties of both sexual fetishism and commodity fetishism. It is this combination of fetishisms in the figure of the action heroine that reveals the depth of male anxiety associated with tough women. By shifting the focus of this chapter to the relation of action heroines to certain masculine roles, particularly the fictional fathers and the male creators, I do not want to bracket out the progressive nature of the characters for female fans or as improved images of strong women in the media. I do, however, want to address how these overtly fetishized images of active women also work to exploit and contain male fears of female sexuality in an era when masculine privilege is perceived by many men to be in decline.

THE ACTION HEROINE AS A SEXUAL OBJECT

In many ways the *Alias* "mild-mannered-all-American-girl-is-secretly-a-kick-ass-spy" premise is anything but original. This conventional fantasy is really just the grown-up version of superhero comics' adolescent wish-fulfillment where inside every powerless Clark Kent or Peter Parker (and by extension every stereotypical comics reader) is a Superman or Spider-Man. The appeal of this masculine fantasy in recent years has been hard to miss. Film versions of such classic wimp-to-warrior superheroes as *Superman* (2006), *Spider-Man* (2002, 2004, and 2007), *The X-Men* (2000, 2003, and 2006), and *Batman* (2005, 2008) have enjoyed enormous success. The basic fantasy has also served

as the premise for serious action films like *The Bourne Identity* series (2002, 2004, and 2007), where amnesiac spy Jason Bourne rediscovers his exceptional abilities, and *The Matrix* trilogy (1999 and 2003), where the average Neo discovers he is "The One" who will save all humankind from their virtual reality enslavement to machines. The fantasy empowerment is no less effective in comedies like *Bad Company* (2002), *Johnny English* (2003), or *Code Name: The Cleaner* (2007), where completely inept men still manage to be effective spies.

Young boys have found their inner James Bond in popular film and literary characters like Agent Cody Banks, Alex Rider, and (obviously) Young James Bond. And, perhaps the most successful example of this traditional male fantasy is poor, mistreated Harry Potter who discovers he is really a powerful wizard. Importantly, this power fantasy is no longer engendered as exclusively masculine. In addition to *Alias*, female characters have discovered their inner spy in properties as diverse as the feature films *The Long Kiss Goodnight* and *Resident Evil*, the cartoons *Totally Spies* and *Princess Natasha*, and the children's book series *Undercover Girl*, *Spy Goddess*, and *Jane Blonde*.

As we discussed in the previous chapter, an important component of this comics-based adolescent power fantasy is the character's hypersexualiztion. But, whereas for the men this means increased muscularity and sexual confidence, for women it means increased skills but also an exaggeration of obvious sexual signifiers. For example, in the first Spider-Man film, the key transformation scene shows Peter Parker waking up after being bitten by a radioactive spider to find his body more muscular and defined. But the romantic comedy *My Super Ex-Girlfriend* (2006) astutely demonstrates young G-Girl's transformation from nerd to superheroine by showing her braces flying off, her hair turning blonde, and her breasts swelling several cup sizes. A succinct metaphor for puberty, these superhero films imply that becoming a man means becoming powerful, but becoming a woman requires the additional burden of becoming a sex object. (I will return to this concomitant need to sexualize powerful *adolescent* females in Chapter Six.) What is obvious with all action heroines is that the fantasy of physical empowerment is inextricably associated within sexual idealism.

The association of tough action heroines with sexuality is clear not just in the fictional narratives, but also in how the entertainment industry positions the actresses relative to their roles. It is no coincidence that *Esquire* magazine declared first Angelina Jolie and then Jessica Biel to be the sexiest woman alive in the same years that they starred in, respectively, *Tomb Raider 2* and *Blade Trinity*. Nor that Halle Berry graced the cover of *People* magazine's "50 Most Beautiful People" issue the same year she starred in *Catwoman*. Or that both *Rolling Stone* and *GQ* featured cover stories about Jessica Alba as "America's sexiest starlet" upon the release of *The Fantastic Four* (2005) starring Alba as the Invisible Woman. Even teenage *Veronica Mars* star Kristen Bell was featured in lingerie on the cover of *Maxim*. Likewise, nearly all of the press coverage of *Alias* over the years concentrated on Garner's sex appeal—with erotic photos of Garner on dozens of magazine covers with headlines describing her as everything from "TV's Sexiest Spy" (*Entertainment Weekly*) and a "breakout sex symbol" (*Arena*) to the explicitly provocative "Sexy But Deadly" (*Esquire*) and "Just your average butt-kicking coed in leather" (*Rolling Stone*) (Figure 3.1).

The persistent emphasis within the genre and the media coverage of the character's/actress's beauty led Marc O'Day to use the term "action babe heroine" in his analysis of the trend. O'Day accurately describes the entertainment industry logic that demands action babe heroines must be represented by "an actress who is 'young' (usually in her twenties or early thirties), slim, shapely, often (though by no means exclusively) white, and marketed as of primarily (though not necessarily wholly) heterosexual orientation who repeatedly undergoes the celebrity makeover of the beauty and gossip industries" (205–6).

The emphasis on the beauty/sexuality of the characters and actresses facilitates their role as fantasy objects that viewers can either lust after or identify with (or both). O'Day refers to this as the "have me/be me" axis of desire.

This persistent association of empowered female bodies with an excessive sexual objectification reveals a modern reworking of male insecurities about women's sexuality and increased agency. Freud's original conception of fetishism as a result of unresolved castration anxiety is crucial to understanding the importance of action heroines as undeniably phallic women. "To put it plainly," Freud wrote, "the fetish is a substitute for the woman's (the mother's) penis that the little boy once believed in and . . . does not want to give up. . . . [F]or if a woman has been castrated, then his own possession of a penis was in danger" (1927: 147). To compensate for this perceived lack, the fetishist seeks to phallicize women. In other words, because the woman's lack represents the male's own possible castration (and the less literal implications of unknown or insatiable feminine sexual desires that may leave men powerless), individual men and patriarchal society in general have ascribed to women phallic substitutes, or fetishes. In this way, the eroticizing and idealizing of specific body parts (e.g., hair, legs, breasts) and/or the association of the female body with external erotic accoutrements (e.g., lingerie, whips, high heels) is an attempt to thwart male fears.

According to psychoanalysis, fetishism attempts to disavow the threat that the female lack poses to men. The range of techniques and symbols used to fetishize women means that, in Freudian terms, every sexually idealized female form is in essence a "phallic woman." In *Fantasies of Fetishism* (2002) Amanda Fernbach describes the classic psychoanalytic account of fetishism as "associated with conservative cultural fantasies about fixing women and producing idealized flawless icons of femininity. In these fantasies differences are eliminated and a single 'phallic' standard of beauty is erected" (23). The modern colloquial use of the term fetishism has become inextricably associated with the kinky extremes of sexuality. And, while I think it is important to maintain this popular link between fetishism and kink in our discussion of action heroines, I also want to explore the compensatory roots of these characters beyond their surface associations with a single type of fetishism.

For Freud, fetishism is an individual male's response to castration fears. And though an individual pathology, certain items that phallicize the female body are so widely shared that they approach a level of cultural symbolism. Whips, stilettos, thigh-high boots, corsets, authoritative uniforms, tight leather or spandex so clearly harden, constrain, and adorn the female form that the individual pathology of fetishism may appear to be a cultural pathology.

Jon Stratton insightfully describes the transition of fetishism from an individual pathology to an institutionalized cultural condition as the result of changes in consumption, industry, and public life from the mid-nineteenth century onwards. "[C]ultural fetishism," Stratton argues, "refers to the effect of the institutionalization of the difference between the individual man's penis and the cultural phallus which, in the light of his experience of the modern state, he comes to feel he should have." In other words, the modern consumer society creates an undeniable discrepancy between real men's experiences of phallic power and the state's expression of masculine privilege. Thus, Stratton argues, "The male experience of inadequacy is projected onto the female form which is produced as the key phallic fetish." For Stratton, who convincingly argues that this production of the female form as the key phallic fetish is the result of cultural and economic changes, sexual fetishism and commodity fetishism merge in contemporary patriarchal societies. Women and images of the female form are, both literally and figuratively, treated as consumables.

But, as Stratton points out, the persistent cultural fetishism of women creates a conflicting fantasy of women as both desirable and threatening. In order to symbolically exercise control over women and the threat of castration/disempowerment they represent, the female body is phallicized in one of two ways: passive or active.

> The fetishistic phallicisation of the female body has a dual effect on men's relations with women. The fetishistic context makes women both more sexually desired—their bodies appearing to acquire a heightened desirableness—and more feared—whilst simultaneously their bodies become the site of a fetishistic terror which compliments, but is quite different in origin from, the fear of castration provoked by recognition of women's 'lack' of a penis. The cultural overdetermination of cultural fetishism means that women may be constructed in two ideal-typical ways by men. First, and dominant, is the spectacle of the 'passive,' phallicised woman, the woman who appears compliantly to express, for men, the spectacle of the phallicised body. Second, there is the spectacle of the 'active', phallic woman who, from a male perspective, reworks the phallic power attributed to her into a spectacle which men experience as threatening to their own, already lacking, feeling of phallic power. (Stratton 2001: 144)

As diametrically opposed as "passive" and "active" might seem, they are both a form of fetishism designed to compensate for masculine feelings of inadequacy. Both forms of phallicization are indicative of male attempts to control and contain threatening female sexuality as a means to reinforce or validate their own masculinity. What this means is that, at a broad cultural level, the consumption of fetishized women (as pinups, as models, as housewives, as sexual fantasy figures of every type) reinforces for men their association with the institutionalized phallus that is the state/patriarchy.

It is the combination of passive and active phallicization in the figure of the action heroine as a means of compensating for male insecurities that I want to explore further; however, for the sake of clarity, I prefer to use the terms "fetishized passive" and "fetishized active" rather than "phallicized." In a strict psychoanalytic sense either form of fetishizing the female body provides symbolic substitutes for its perceived phallic lack. However, the term phallus is so closely intertwined with presumptions of power that aligning it with passivity, while not oxymoronic, does confuse the issue.

As Laplanche and Pontalis argue, the term "phallic woman" is often misused "in a loose way as a description of a woman with allegedly masculine character-traits—e.g., authoritarianism—even when it is not known what the underlying phantasies are" (1973: 312). This literal usage of the term "phallic woman" elides depictions of women that do not overtly wield power. The *fetishized active* woman is phallicized in both senses of the term (compensating for lack and possibly wielding power). The *fetishized passive* woman, on the other hand, is primarily sexualized only in a manner that compensates for her lack. By emphasizing both constructions as fetishization I want to highlight that each are strategies meant to exert masculine control over female sexualities.

FETISHIZED PASSIVE AND FETISHIZED ACTIVE

As the Stratton's quotation above makes clear, the dominant strategy used to assuage male fears of castration anxiety and female sexuality is to fetishize women as a spectacle of passivity. In our patriarchal society passivity has been defined as the norm for women, especially when it comes to their depiction as sex objects. Women have traditionally been conceptualized in our culture, particularly in mass-mediated sexual fantasies, as compliant bodies for men to look at and consume. In their analysis of female fetishism, Gamman and Makinen describe this association "between women's objectification and their lack of power within patriarchal discourse" (1995: 172–73) as a fundamental basis for much of feminist criticism. It is, for example, the founding principle for Mulvey's foundational theory of the male gaze and women's value in the cinema for their "to-be-looked-at-ness." Mulvey's original thesis also characterized the depiction of women in classic cinema as "masculinized" or phallicized through a variety of filming and costuming techniques that turn the women into visual fetishes that serve to allay male castration fears.

The action heroine, however, explores the concept of the fetishized passive woman in the media in a manner far more complicated than in traditional depictions. As I have argued earlier, Mary Anne Doane's concept of femininity as a masquerade and Butler's theory of gender as performance help to illustrate how the action heroine's use of conventional gender identities brings the naturalness of these sexual norms into question. But, as the wide range of masquerades, or aliases, assumed by Sydney Bristow over the course of the series makes clear: not all fetishized fantasies are equal. While action heroines may enact womanliness (in the general sense) as a cover, oftentimes the narratives depict the disguise as excessively passive, as almost vehemently disempowering. By using very specific fetishistic fantasies of women as disempowered, the portrayal of action heroines allows male consumers to enjoy the most rudimentary sexist fantasies of women while simultaneously distancing themselves from the misogynistic roots of those fantasies . . . if they so desire.

Many of the feminine identities Sydney assumes over the course of *Alias'* five-year run are tongue-in-cheek portrayals of disempowered fantasy roles. Sydney has gone undercover as such passively fetishized female types as a maid, a spoiled Daddy's girl, a Southern Belle, a secretary, a prostitute, a Catholic school girl, a Vegas show girl, a beach bunny, a groupie, a nurse, a Swedish tourist, and a trophy wife. In a similar manner, many of her disguises constitute a form of ethnic fetishism combined with passivity. Despite Sydney Bristow being Caucasian, she has at various times gone undercover as a Japanese geisha, an East Indian servant, a Spanish dancer, and a Chinese youth. Of course the narrative conceit of these roles is that viewers know Sydney will eventually throw off the disguise and kick some unsuspecting male's ass, but it does allow the series to present Garner visually as part of a disempowering scenario.

Other action heroines have explored similar passively fetishized roles to a lesser extent than *Alias'* protracted narrative permits, and these roles are often played for comedic effect. The Catholic school girl heroines of *D.E.B.S.*, the FBI agent as beauty pageant contestant and Vegas showgirl in *Ms. Congeniality* and its sequel, almost all of the undercover outfits worn by Charlie's Angels in both their TV and film incarnations, Buffy's original role as high school cheerleader, and *Heroes'* indestructible cheerleader all emphasize the humorous distance between powerless female identities and the tough women who may lie beneath. Yet, for all the pretense about placing heroines in these demeaning roles to point out their absurdity, these films and TV shows still benefit by offering viewers images of Hollywood sex symbols in the most rudimentary of fetishistic costumes. What all of these fetish culture clichés have in common is their reference to, or reenactment of, traditionally submissive roles for women.

To borrow a phrase from Valerie Steele's discussion of fetish fashion, these submissive fantasy figures exaggerate and play on "the power differential implicit in traditional gender stereotypes" (172). By mobilizing these roles of fetishized passive female figures, the action heroine may be critiquing inflated sexual fantasies but it also reinforces them by providing a narrative premise for them. Sexual fetishism in contemporary culture is first and foremost about erotic fantasy. In Freudian terms, the fetish is usually thought of as a particular object or thing that takes on an overblown significance because it compensates for fears about female lack. As Kaplan describes it: "The adult fetishist cannot introduce his penis into that temple of doom called a vagina without a fetish to ease the way" (1991: 54). But to focus merely on the specific fetish object, or cluster of objects, is to miss the necessary sexual scenario associated with it.

Robert Stoller has famously, and succinctly argued that "a fetish is a story masquerading as an object" (1985: 155). The exaggerated role-playing of the action heroine provides a version of the story to help animate the fetish. When Sydney Bristow dons a maid's uniform or a secretary outfit to momentarily play the role of a helpless female servant, she enacts an entire fantasy scenario of a beautiful woman fully at the service of more powerful men. The fetishized passive heroine enacts an erotically charged mis-en-scène of submissiveness. Despite knowing it is all an act so Sydney can dupe powerful men, we still see her being bossed around, ordered to change her lingerie or dance erotically, being openly leered at, and even groped by those men. There is certainly an immense pleasure experienced by most viewers at the moment she turns the tables and kicks their asses, but the joy of that comeuppance is premised on a more suspect pleasure associated with Sydney's performance of degradation.

Yes, this type of charade can and does function as a feminine masquerade, but it is also an exploration of the erotic relationship between those who wield power and those subject to it. However the larger narrative of each episode may undermine the veracity of these submissive roles, they are still premised on an understanding of women as subject to the sexual whims of patriarchy. And, as I'll explore more fully later in this chapter, the action heroine is never fully able to overcome the sexual control of men. Being fetishized passive may seem antithetical for the figure of the action heroine (and thus often humorous), but it is indicative of overarching themes of fetishism and control to which she is subject.

While the fetishized passive portrayal of the action heroine is always revealed as a narrative ruse, the same cannot be said for her depiction as a fetishized active ideal. Indeed, it is her ability to run, fight, shoot, drive, solve problems, and generally kick-ass that unites these women as atypical female characters in the first place. Though these narratives present this strong image as the real woman, it is no less a fantasy construction than is the uber-tough male action hero. It is the fetishized active heroine, her most common form, that best fits the literal usage of "phallic woman" as a description of "a woman with allegedly masculine character traits" (Laplanche and Pontalis 1973: 312).

As noted in earlier chapters, given our strict cultural categories that equate women with passivity and men with activity, there has been a marked tendency in the scholarly discussion of action heroines to interpret them as simply enacting masculinity. Certainly these characters act in ways our society usually reserves for men—and to see them as "men-in-drag" or "Rambolinas" or "Pambos" helps to bring into question the arbitrary nature of gender norms. But just as the images of these women mobilize vehemently disempowering fantasies when they are fetishized passive, the specific forms they tend to take on when they are fetishized active reveal an underlying pathology regarding strong women.

In the hyperbolic action genre women are never just strong, intelligent, and competent—they are impossibly gifted martial artists, superhumanly strong, and undefeatable with guns, swords, bows, and whips. They are also costumed and stylized to evoke very specific fetishistic fantasies of dominant and sexually threatening women. While male action heroes are depicted with a hysterical degree of emphasis on their muscular bodies (a phenomenon explored at length in the groundbreaking work of Tasker, Jeffords, and others), female action heroines are further eroticized in a standard of tight/revealing leathers and spandex. The kinky fetishistic costuming of action heroines raises questions that go beyond the reworking of gender norms. Whether it is the gothic skin-tight leathers worn by Seline in the *Underworld* films (2003 and 2006), the spandex diving suit worn by Lara Croft in *Tomb Raider 2*, the ripped leather bra and pants worn by Catwoman in her most recent live-action incarnation, the leather suits worn by Trinity in the *Matrix* films, the yellow leather biker outfit worn by the bride in *Kill Bill*, or the leather pants and belly-shirt worn by Abby Whistler in *Blade Trinity*, the action heroine is routinely costumed to cater to the very specific sexual fantasy of the dominant woman, or dominatrix.

Action heroines in comic books and video games are so routinely depicted in fetishistic costuming that it would be ridiculous to try listing examples. This symbolic cliché of the leather-clad action heroine is so common it even surfaces in such non-traditional genres as children's entertainment. In the banal kiddy flick, *Looney Tunes: Back in Action* (2003), for example, when the live-action pop star Dusty Tails (Heather Locklear) reveals she is really an international spy, she takes the time to change into a black rubber cat suit that elicits wolf whistles from the animated Daffy Duck. Likewise, in the computer-animated TV series *Jimmy Neutron: Boy Genius*, the recurring femme fatale, Beautiful Gorgeous, wears a similar form-fitting black rubber suit that causes the preadolescent male characters to fight over her ("Hubba, hubba, I think I'm in love," shouts one. "Will you be my Mommy?" pleads another disturbingly). At the risk of being repetitive, for women to be fetishized active means to be symbolically coded as excessively phallic and dangerously erotic dominant women.

While this use of fetishistic costuming is utilized in almost every representation of action heroines, it is explicitly presented as a masquerade in *Alias*. Sydney's overall portrayal as a tough action heroine—as a fetishized active character—is exaggerated even further through certain personas she takes on during her missions. She has gone undercover in such threatening and powerful fetishistic personas as a dominatrix, a demanding executive, a Soviet military officer, a stern scientist, a cowgirl, and alternately as a tough punk, goth, and hip-hop club-goer. The depiction of heroines as fetishized active clearly does a lot more than simply adorn her with symbols to compensate for her perceived lack. She also gives life to the story, or the fantasy scenario, that is a crucial element of fetishism.

Where the fetishized passive version alludes to a powerless fantasy woman, the fetishized active figure explores the erotic appeal of powerful women. In this guise viewers get to see Sydney ordering men about. She barks commands that they must follow or be punished, whether it is getting her a cup of coffee or crawling on hands and knees. The network's promotional department was well aware of Sydney's dominatrix-like appeal when it ran advertisements petitioning for Emmy awards. "For your Emmy consideration," the promotional ad declared alongside a photo of Sydney glowering at readers in a leather vest, "YOU tell her no." When fetishized active, the action heroine provides a very effective mis-en-scène of dominant female sexuality.

The concomitant relationship between the passive and the active fetishizing of Sydney Bristow demonstrates that the performance of each type reinforces the other. The action heroine's various guises facilitate a fantasy figure that cuts both ways—she can be both object and subject, passive and active, powerless and powerful. The strategy of presenting idealized Hollywood starlet bodies in skimpy and erotic costumes under the pretense of crafting empowered female characters allows the media to have their cake and eat it too.

Likewise, alternating between passive and active fetishization allows for a whole cornucopia of sexual scenarios to be acted out. The two divergent roles simultaneously expose the illusion of such heavily coded fantasies of powerless and powerful feminine identities and reinforces the fetishistic fantasies they are based on. To understand the erotic playacting of submissive positions, the willing performance of the role needs to be revealed and vice versa.

One narrative strategy often undertaken on *Alias* to achieve this effect is to quickly alternate between the two extremes. As early as the second episode "So it Begins," for example, is an undercover operation where Sydney first poses as a hotel maid (complete with blonde hair in pigtails and a traditional black and white aproned uniform) to gain access to a Russian mobster's room. Then, as soon as she discovers her partner is in danger in the hotel nightclub, she quickly changes into a rubber mini-dress (the same one used in the "concealed weapon" ad) and stilettos to rescue him by defeating a room full of bad guys in hand-to-hand combat. The immediate oscillation between the two fetishized roles underscores the erotic fantasy implied by both. The kinky nature of the submissive maid scenario is confirmed through the knowledge that it "is just an act," just as the physical threat of the sexualized woman can remain titillating despite, or because of, the knowledge that it too "is just an act."

Whereas the narrative of *Alias* tends to juxtapose Sydney's being fetishized passive and being fetishized active, media coverage of the program and its lead actress typically fused the dual fetishistic forms. Feature articles in the popular press always focused on what they described as Jennifer Garner's inherently sweet and innocent good looks and her ability to perfectly embody a strong and sexually aggressive heroine. *Rolling Stone* characterized her as a "double fetish" and likened her appeal to being spanked by a dominatrix while at Disneyland. Moreover, the visual representation of Sydney Bristow/Jennifer Garner in media coverage often combined both active and passive fetishism.

The cover of *GQ* magazine's 2003 Hollywood edition, for example, featured a highly stylized photograph of Garner in thigh-high boots, a miniskirt, and open leather vest astride a chopper. "Jennifer Garner revs it up," the accompanying copy declared, positioning the actress as aggressive while simultaneously offering her up as an erotic spectacle. The mock warning continued to suggest that the feature article, or perhaps Garner herself, "contains strong sexual content and thematic elements, adult language and other provocative things." As this cover makes clear, while Sydney Bristow may be a tough and in-control female, and Garner may be an award-winning actress with an ascending career, both the character and the actress are still situated within the larger cultural dynamic of fetishism. She (they) is first and foremost a sexual fetish constructed to fulfill the fantasies of viewers and a visual commodity fetish (like the accompanying motorcycle) to be bought and enjoyed by consumers.

ACTION HEROINES AND THE LAW OF THE FATHER

To this point I have considered the action heroine, Sydney Bristow in particular, as phallically fetishized in various ways in a relatively abstract manner via the patriarchal logic of our culture as enunciated in the media. While images of strong women in the media are a welcome and necessary step to effect any kind of change in stereotypical gender norms, the action heroine is not as close to throwing off the yoke of male control as she may first appear. Now I will discuss how the action heroine's story and her creation retain very specific elements of male control—not in the abstract sense of patriarchy (though that dominant cultural form still influences every aspect of gender representation), but in clear narrative terms.

Alias provides an especially in-depth example of three central themes of patriarchal control associated with action heroines. First is the relationship between the heroine and her father or clearly recognizable father figures. Second, and interrelated, is the relationship between the heroine and state-sanctioned institutions of patriarchal control such as the law, the military, and the government. And third is the relationship between the predominantly male creators of these fictional action heroines and the actresses who portray them.

The pivotal bond between Sydney and Jack Bristow on *Alias* is nothing new. In fact, the interplay between the action heroine and her father is one of the most tried and true conventions of the formula. In her overview of action heroine types, Yvonne Tasker notes that "the female hero may be represented as identified with the father, in search of authority and, sometimes reconciliation with authority" (69). The sometimes supportive, sometimes troubled connection the modern heroine has with her father and with authority is a crucial ingredient for considering how these women are situated in relation to patriarchy. Even a cursory listing of contemporary heroines reveals a preoccupation with the father/daughter dynamic regardless of the medium in which she appears.

Iconic teen sleuth Nancy Drew's father is District Attorney Carson Drew, just as television's Veronica Mars seems to have inherited her formidable detective skills from her proud father private investigator-cum-sheriff Keith Mars. In both the film *Out of Sight* (1998) and short-lived TV series *Karen Sisco*, U.S. Marshall Karen's chief advisor is her father, ex-FBI agent Marshall Sisco. Lara Croft's tomb-raiding adventures are a continuation of her father, Lord Richard Croft's, life work (played, interestingly, in the film version by Angelina Jolie's real-life father Jon Voight). Abby Whistler is inspired to hunt vampires in *Blade: Trinity* by her father Abraham. Batman may be Batgirl's figurative father, but she is also Barbara Gordon, daughter of Police Commissioner Gordon (the most recent comic book version of Batgirl, Cassandra Cain, has a far more complicated relationship with her father that I will return to later in this chapter).

The animated *Powerpuff Girls* are invented in a lab by their scientist "father" known simply as The Professor. Gaia Moore, the young heroine of Francine Pascal's immensely popular teen book series *Fearless*, has a complicated relationship with her CIA agent father. Even the short-lived TV adaptation of the comic book *Birds of Prey* was initially promoted featuring the character of the Huntress poised on a gargoyle in full dominatrix leathers with the byline "Batman's little girl is all grown up."

Suffice to say, the list goes on and on, especially if we broaden the term to include father figures and not just biological ones. It is also worth noting that in almost every case the action heroine's mother is non-existent. She is typically deceased, sometimes divorced, while other times her absence is not explained at all. Apparently the action heroine formula tellingly has very little use for matriarchal roles. It is the young woman's relationship with her father that matters most in this formula.

Daddy's Girl (2007) is Lisa Scottoline's best-selling novel in her Natalie "Nat" Greco series of legal thrillers. While the phrase "daddy's girl" carries with it connotations of infantilization, possessiveness, and parental favoritism, it is still an apt term to consider when discussing the father/daughter dynamic at the core of the action heroine narrative. That an increasing number of action heroines are young girls and how that relates to debates in feminism is an issue that I will take up in more detail in Chapter Six.

Though Sydney's personal and professional relationship with her father is often strained, it is still the dramatic core of *Alias*. The series begins, in part, with the shocking discovery that her seemingly boring and emotionally distant father is also a secret agent. And not just any secret agent, Jack Bristow is (in addition to being a double-agent) an extremely high-ranking international man of mystery with decades worth of experience, clandestine connections, secrets, and assassinations to his credit. For all of Sydney's abilities, she is still a novice compared to her father, and a junior to him in the chain of command.

Sydney's adventures may take center stage each week, but viewers are constantly made aware of Jack's superior knowledge and ruthless protection of his daughter. It is Jack's role as ranking officer and the voice of experience to assign Sydney many of her missions—and to teach her about the complexities of SD-6 and its cartel of related villains. That Jack doles out minimal and in-complete information to Sydney is both a narrative device to create suspense/foster mistrust and a means to establish his superior position.

It takes the entire first season, for example, for Sydney to uncover exactly what Jack's role was in the killing of her fiancé Danny in the first episode. Rather than just telling her that he tried to stop the assassination, his terse responses to Sydney's questions leave her wondering if he had pulled the trigger himself. Likewise, it takes pretty much the entire series for Jack to reveal to Sydney the true identity of her supposedly deceased mother, and all of the sordid aspects of betrayal involved in their relationship.

Though viewers often wonder if Jack is trustworthy, the series makes it clear that he ruthlessly protects his daughter as we witness his behind-the-scenes machinations to keep her safe. As the preeminent super spy he manipulates information, lies to superiors, tortures enemies, endures torture himself, and even kills to protect her. Catherine Tunnacliffe describes Jack Bristow as an ideal fantasy father "who kills, maims and puts his own life in jeopardy to save his adored child on a regular basis. Many parents say they'd kill for their kids, but Jack literally does so, and unhesitatingly puts his own life in jeopardy for Syd over and over" (2005: 36).

Jack "takes care of" anyone endangering Sydney's well-being, whether that means physically threatening them, assaulting them, or undermining their power within the agency. At one point he kills an arms dealer in cold blood just for making a disparaging sexual remark about Sydney. He also (appar-ently) murders her own mother when he discovers plans that implicate her in a planned assassination of their daughter. That Sydney herself is not always aware of the many ways her father safeguards her only serves to reinforce Jack's all-powerful paternal position.

What Jack Bristow represents as a father and an eminent secret agent is pa-triarchal authority writ large. Jack, like other action heroine fathers (some of whom I have listed above) who are police officers, FBI or CIA agents, sheriffs, district attorneys, judges, governors, generals, and so on, is an embodiment of state-sanctioned and institutionalized authority. Through her father, or father figures, the action heroine is made over in his image, and she is indoctrinated into the masculine realm of The Law. More than merely being masculinized through her aggressive behaviors, her muscular body, or her "manly" assump-tion of power, the action heroine becomes a dutiful subject and agent of pa-triarchal authority.

In her landmark work *The Powers of Horror* (1982), Julia Kristeva develops her theory about the role of the abject in the construction of cultural norms that seek to define and delineate the borders between order and that which lies beyond acceptability. Central to Kristeva's theory is the contrast between maternal authority and the law of the father. Kristeva argues that the semiotic process involved with an individual's contact with authority can be contrasted between the alignment of the abject (e.g., bodily wastes) with maternal authority and the association of proper social regulation with paternal law. "Maternal authority is the trustee of that mapping of the self's clean and proper body," writes Kristeva. "It is distinguished from paternal laws within which, with the phallic phase and acquisition of language, the destiny of man will take shape" (72).

Borrowing this language from Kristeva, the action heroine represents an exaggerated identification with the masculine domain of paternal laws. If, as Kristeva argues, we are all learning and relearning the cultural rules of maturation that involve negotiating the boundaries between the abject realm of the mother and the proper adoption of paternal social rules, then the action heroine demonstrates for viewers the desirability of mastering the law of the father. As the heroine develops skills, defeats the bad guys, and becomes an effective agent of law enforcement and social control, we experience a vicarious rush of confidence and power. We are aligned with the greater good despite any individual reservations or differing levels of identification we may have.

In a less metaphorical sense, the action heroine's role does not just secure a proper place within the Symbolic. Because the action genre almost exclusively deals with crime as its central narrative device, the action heroine's dogged pursuit of her enemies is a literal example of countering the abject. To enforce paternal law is to reject abject chaos. As Kristeva writes: "Any crime, because it draws attention to the fragility of the law, is abject, but the premeditated crime, cunning murder, hypocritical revenge are even more so because they heighten the display of such fragility. He who denies morality is not abject, there can be grandeur in amorality. . . . Abjection, on the other hand, is immoral, sinister, scheming and shady" (1982: 4).

As a crime fighter in either a very strict sense (e.g., Sydney Bristow CIA agent, Dana Scully FBI agent) or a very broad sense (e.g., Abby Whistler vampire hunter, Alice the zombie fighter in the *Resident Evil* films), the action heroine is clearly positioned as an agent of social order and paternal law. It is worth noting that when the heroine is not literally an agent of law enforcement, she often is even more involved in direct conflict with the abject. In her discussion of the abject in horror, Barbara Creed (1986) points out that many of the classic movie monsters embody the abject. Vampires, zombies, and werewolves all cross boundaries between the living and the dead in a manner that makes them particularly abject. This may explain the popularity of action heroines in films that venture into horror themes such as *Blade: Trinity*, the three *Resident Evil* films, the *Bloodrayne* movies, the *Underworld* series, *Skinwalkers*, (2007), and so on.

The association of the action heroine with a denial or refutation of the abject may also explain the close affinity between her and the Final Girl of horror films as discussed in detail by Carol Clover. In fact, Creed's primary example of how horror negotiates the abject feminine is *Alien*, the film that first introduces Lt. Ellen Ripley, the modern prototype of the action heroine. To shore up the borders between order and chaos, the action heroine must become an agent of authority—whether it is institutionalized state authority, or of a higher moral ground, is not as relevant as the fact that her actions are presented as in the service of communal good. That the action heroine often takes on this role under the direct tutelage of her father or father figure symbolically compounds the association between the law and paternity.

This emphasis on the action heroines' successful entry into the male domain of paternal law may help explain the curious absence of mothers. So concerned with the father/daughter relationship is the action heroine narrative that in addition to the mother's absence not even being noted in some cases (or the feminine not even needed for conception as in *The Powerpuff Girls*), the mother is sometimes simply shunted aside because she is a distraction to the story. The first season of *Veronica Mars*, for example, revolves in part around the mysterious disappearance of Veronica's mother. Veronica loves her mother and eventually tracks her down and brings her home.

Despite Veronica's attempt to restore her ideal nuclear family, she quickly discovers her mother is an out-of-control alcoholic, adulterer, liar, and thief. Her father, on the other hand, is consistently portrayed as loving, smart, morally upright, and protective. So preferable is Keith Mars in contrast to the mother, and so complete is the father/daughter bonding of the show, that within just a couple episodes the mother is of no interest and runs off once more . . . never to be mentioned again or missed by either Veronica or her father.

One of the most emotionally rewarding moments of the series is when a paternity test confirms that Keith is Veronica's biological father. This disregard for mothers, or, at times, outright hostility towards them, is not exclusive to action heroine narratives—it is prevalent in many facets of popular culture. In her book *Cinematernity* (1996), Lucy Fischer describes film criticism itself as prone to a type of "amnesia" about motherhood and maternal roles. But the manner in which the maternal is treated (or ignored) in these stories is noteworthy given their central theme of gender identity and such a clear desire to portray the feminine in a positive light.

In its semiotic association with the abject, the maternal can represent that which must be shunned in order to ascend to the realm of the father. In its extreme form, Barbara Creed has described the abject mother figure as the "monstrous-feminine" archetype so often found in horror film. Creed characterizes one aspect of the monstrous-feminine as the obsessive maternal figure (e.g., *Psycho*, *Carrie*, *The Birds*) who "[B]y refusing to relinquish her hold on her child, prevents it from taking up its proper place in relation to the Symbolic" (42). In contrast, the absent mother of the action heroine who either refuses or is unable to take hold of her daughter may force her into an over-identification with the Symbolic.

As *Alias* progresses, Sydney learns that the ideal mother she thought deceased was actually Irina Derevko (Lena Olin), an undercover Soviet spy who only married Jack to learn about a secret program code-named "Project Christmas"—and that she is alive and well and running an evil espionage cartel. Though her mother's loyalty and intentions are never made clear (and certainly shift throughout the course of the series), her failings as a mother help push Sydney and Jack closer together. The promotional campaign for season two bluntly stressed the action heroine's rejection of the maternal. "Like mother, like daughter? Like hell." So read the copy above a photo of Sydney and her mother, with Sydney wisely concealing a gun behind her back in the ad. "She always knew the job could kill her," the copy continues. "She didn't know her deadliest enemy would be her mother."

The action heroine's alignment with paternal law is further consolidated, albeit erotically, through some of the symbolic costumes she dons. At times, when Sydney's undercover operations fetishize her active, she is outfitted in uniforms that carry the weight of official and/or institutionalized systems of authority such as the military or the government. Uniforms as fetishistic costuming may sexualize the action heroine but they also ground her power within larger systems of paternal power. "Uniforms also frequently symbolize authority," points out Valerie Steele in her discussion of fetishistic clothing, "evoking fantasies of dominance and submission. Military and police uniforms, in particular, signify that the wearers are legally endowed with state-sanctioned power. By contrast, the maid's uniforms imply servility and a lack of power" (1997: 180).

When Sydney assumes the masquerade of a sexy General, a diplomat, a corporate executive, or even a scientist, her association with state-sanctioned power is crystallized. That the legitimate authority symbolized by these uniforms is undercut by the erotic implications of mere role-playing by an attractive woman further illustrates the undermining of action heroines as fetish objects. The erotic fantasy of a sexy woman in a traditionally male costume representing state-sanctioned power is perhaps most apparent in the opening scenes of *Blue Steel* where Megan Turner (Jamie Lee Curtis) first tries on her police uniform and takes an obvious pleasure in modeling it. In a more general and less explicitly eroticized sense, the depiction of Sydney as a CIA agent in well-tailored pantsuits (à la FBI agent Scully of *The X-Files* [1993–2002] or forensic anthropologist and FBI consultant Temperance Brennan of *Bones* [2005–present]) dresses her in the trappings of state-sanctioned law enforcement.

In *Female Masculinity* (1998) Judith Halberstam discusses how the image of "epic masculinity" embodied by characters like the archetypal James Bond can be understood as dependant on larger systems of patriarchal authority including "a vast subterranean network of secret government groups, well-funded scientists, the army, and an endless supply of both beautiful bad babes and beautiful good babes" (4). As an agent of patriarchal law, the action heroine is likewise able to access all the might of institutional authority afforded to eminently masculine characters like Bond. That she has to do so without giving up any of her status as one of the "beautiful good babes" indicates that her assumption into the realm of The Law may never be complete.

CREATING THE PERFECT MAN-MADE KILLING MACHINE

Implicit in this discussion of action heroines as fetishized passive and/or active, and as indoctrinated into the realm of paternal law, is the notion that these characters are made over by some masculine force. Whether we think of it as specific male characters such as Jack Bristow or broad patriarchal forces like the CIA or FBI, there is a sense that, despite all their strengths, these women are subject to the whims of male fantasy and control. The fairy tale-like opening of *Charlie's Angels* ("Once upon a time there were three little girls") may seem comical in retrospect, but it is a reminder that these women, like many of the heroines they precede, are rescued, trained, and now work for men ("Now they work for me. My name is Charlie.").

On many levels the action heroine is constructed by men. The most obvious is the recurring scenario of the strong woman-as-makeover story. In his analysis of the requisite beauty associated with what he refers to as the "action babe," Marc O'Day identifies the publicity and behind-the-scenes coverage of the actresses' exercise regime as an important factor in positioning them as heroines. It seems a necessary step in the press coverage to emphasize that beautiful Hollywood starlets like Angelina Jolie, Cameron Diaz, Halle Berry, and Kate Beckinsale are "willing to undergo what we can call 'the action makeover' to prepare her for the rigors of fights and stunts in the action babe spectacle" (O'Day 2004: 206).

The muscular makeover of Linda Hamilton's body for *Terminator 2* was cause for numerous newspaper and magazine features detailing the intensive regimen she endured to transform her from the soft body of the first film to the hard body heroine of the sequel. The reviews of *G.I. Jane* focused on the ways Demi Moore resculpted her famously sexy body for her role as the first female Navy Seal by undergoing real boot camp. The press coverage of *Alias* always mentions the extensive training Jennifer Garner undertook to prepare for her role as Sydney Bristow: 4:00 a.m. wake-up calls to meet with her trainers, constant martial arts instruction, marathon running sessions, pilates, weapons training, even language classes. Garner's training was so intense that she told British *GQ*: "I can tuck an elbow, drill a fist and do a roundhouse kick in my sleep" (Bhattacharya 2005: 232). Likewise, Uma Thurman underwent a grueling regime for *Kill Bill* just three months after giving birth: "she was sent for nine weeks' training with martial arts master Yuen Wo-Ping . . . Wu-shu style fighting, hand-to-hand combat combinations, eight types of kicks, flips on a wire, back flips, front-flips, weight training, cardio training, Japanese language practice . . . and other physical things" (Martin 2003: 126).

At an extratextual level, the actresses who portray action heroines are subject to a very physical makeover that inculcates them into a realm of physicality usually associated with masculinity. It is no coincidence that the army of personal trainers, martial arts instructors, and stunt coordinators who oversee these makeovers are typically male. These experts in physical activity help initiate the actresses into a particularly male domain and represent an official endorsement of the women as acceptably tough. They are, in a sense, the real-life gatekeepers of masculine standards.

Within the films, television programs, comic books, and novels featuring action heroines the makeover is often an important story element as well. In Chapter One I discussed the dual makeover that Maggie is subjected to in *Point of No Return* to train her in both the manly arts of fighting and shooting, and the womanly arts of beauty and proper manners. Likewise, the slow reacquisition of Samantha's espionage skills in *The Long Kiss Goodnight* discussed in Chapter two is tantamount to a makeover. In its simplest narrative form the makeover can be seen in the common training sequences or montages that signify the heroines' shift from helpless females to deadly femmes.

Just as the real-life training is usually overseen by men, the fictional instruction of the women is typically undertaken by a male mentor. In the western/action/comedy *Bandidas* (2006), for example, spoiled Mexican aristocrat Sara

(Salma Hayek) and farmer's daughter Maria (Penelope Cruz) must be taught how to shoot, throw knives, handle dynamite, and rob banks by the experienced outlaw Bill Buck (Sam Shepard) before they can avenge their fathers. And in *Kill Bill 2* we learn in flashbacks that The Bride, even after receiving training from Bill, also had to undergo extensive and degrading martial arts boot camp with the legendary master Pai Mei who teaches her the mystical "five-point-palm, exploding heart" technique she uses in the end to kill Bill.

A fascinating aspect of the man-made action heroine is the trend of having male characters turning young girls into programmed killing machines. One overarching plotline in *Alias* concerns a clandestine spy training agenda code-named Project Christmas. In season two viewers learned that Project Christmas was a black ops program developed by Jack Bristow in the 1970s designed to identify and train six-year-olds in various skills such as marksmanship, linguistics, and knowledge retention. After the training is complete, the children's memories are erased and they are returned to their families as unknowing sleeper agents. When Sydney discovers a variation of this program is being used throughout Europe and the Soviet Union, she investigates and discovers that her father subjected her to Project Christmas training, one reason she is such an accomplished agent as an adult—and why she was recruited to SD-6 in the first place.

The sadistic implications of training and programming little girls to be assassins are further explored in two contemporary comic book characters. Both the recent incarnation of Batgirl (DC Comics), and X-23 (Marvel Comics) feature characters literally bred to be killers. After the original Batgirl, Barbara Gordon, is confined to a wheelchair, DC Comics introduced the mysterious character of Cassandra Cain to take up the Batgirl mantle and aid Batman in his fight against crime. Despite being a pre-teen female, this new Batgirl is considered one of the deadliest fighters in comics, and perhaps the only person who could defeat Batman himself in hand-to-hand combat. Initially a mute character, Cassandra/Batgirl's history is slowly revealed—Batman discovers Cassandra was bought as an infant and raised to be a perfect assassin by the notoriously ruthless hit man Kane. Cassandra, we find out, was the most successful subject in Kane's experiments to train killers in silence so they could read the body language of opponents and anticipate their every move.

Likewise, Marvel Comics' X-23, aka Laura, is a pre-teen female clone of the popular and deadly male character Wolverine. A shadowy agency clones X-23 (the twenty-third attempt) in order to train a perfect assassin from infancy. In addition to her healing mutant factor and metal claws, X-23 is taught a range of martial arts and subjected to various abuses to mold her into an obedient killing machine. The Project Christmas storyline of *Alias* and the comic book heroines Batgirl and X-23 are clear examples of the fictionalized Pygmalion scenario associated with action heroines.

The interrelated premise of young heroines bred or trained by father figures/patriarchal institutions, and of being the most successful result in a long line of experiments, are fairly common themes in the action heroine formula. The young girl River in *Serenity* (2005) is manufactured in a lab to be a deadly fighter, Violet is a medically enhanced assassin in *Ultraviolet* (2006), and Max of TV's *Dark Angel* is the result of experiments in genetic engineering. Buffy is merely the most recent vampire slayer overseen by the Watcher's Council, likewise Sara Pezzini of *Witchblade* is only the most recent woman to wield the magical gauntlet that turns her into a living weapon, the seemingly reincarnated Ripley of *Alien 4* discovers she is only the most successful result of numerous attempts to clone the original Ripley's DNA, and Halle Berry's Catwoman learns she is just the latest in a long line of catwomen.

Over the course of the *Resident Evil* films we discover that the zombie asskicking heroine Alice (Mila Jovovich) has been genetically altered and subsequently cloned by the scientist for the ruthless Umbrella Corporation. The third film, *Resident Evil: Extinction* (2007), concludes with Alice about to activate an entire army of her own clones to assist in hunting down the heads of the Corporation. Whether the fictionalized Pygmalion narrative is blatantly obvious as in the Project Christmas, Batgirl, and X-23 type—or more generally implied through training sequences and fatherly mentoring—the action heroine is presented as a product of male design.

Whether the action heroine is indoctrinated into the realm of the father and paternal law, trained in deadly arts by male experts, fetishized by patriarchy in general, or even made over into glamorous beauty queens by men, there is an element of the Pygmalion to the relationship. In *Female Perversions* (1991) Louis Kaplan describes the male's Pygmalion-like makeover of women into an ideal of femininity as a preeminent example of fetishism. Though Kaplan is concerned with the fashion industry, her description has parallels to the various makeovers action heroines are subjected to. "Our modern day Pygmalion," writes Kaplan, "enjoys nothing so much as taking an unformed girl and transforming her into a highly valued, sexually exciting woman—the ideal phallic woman he wishes he could be" (263).

Within the action heroine narratives we routinely see men of authority taking unformed girls and transforming them into highly valued and sexually exciting killing machines. They are certainly ideal phallic women, whether fetishized active or passive, and do wield their power in a manner that suggests a fulfillment of the male's own wish for perfection. Jack Bristow is visibly proud of his daughter's ability to kick ass, as is Keith Mars of his daughter Veronica's ability to solve crimes. Even Bill (David Carradine) in *Kill Bill 2* is proud of his lover/protégé, the Bride, when she bests him in combat. The male creators/ fathers of both Batgirl and X-23 are simultaneously proud and envious of their "daughters'" ability as flawless killers. In most cases the student surpasses the instructor, the action heroine becomes the better fighter, the physically stronger, or the smarter detective that the father wishes he could have been.

The Pygmalion fetishization that occurs within the diagesis of the film or television series reveals a preoccupation with the media's control of female images. But this fictional Pygmalion scenario is mirrored by the real-life dynamic whereby male creators exercise a great deal of control over the construction of the female characters—a control that, at times, has very disturbing undertones. As a longtime writer and teacher of gender and popular culture, I always found it surprising that, while action heroines in film and television (and comics and video games) are the most visible portrayals of progressive female types, rarely are they created by women themselves.

The recognition Kathryn Bigelow has received in scholarly writings about action heroines has always seemed unequal to her lack of success as a director. Even her most interesting film dealing with women in action narratives, *Blue Steel*, received little attention by the public when it was released, and has all but been forgotten by everyone except academic critics. Instead, the action heroine is very closely aligned with male auteurs. The success of *Alias* may have rested primarily with the appeal of Jennifer Garner in the lead role, but the genius of the series was always credited to its male creator, J. J. Abrams, who was portrayed in the press as the omniscient puppeteer pulling Sydney Bristow's strings. An early *Entertainment Weekly* feature on the series described Abrams as "*Alias*' 35-year-old creator/executive producer/writer/director/theme music composer/opening credits designer" (Snierson 2002: 26) who transformed Jennifer Garner into his ideal fantasy figure of a super-heroine.

"I thought there was unlimited potential with Jennifer, like she could do anything," Abrams explained. "She played a nerd in *Pearl Harbor*. When she was on *Felicity*, she was the nerdy girl with glasses, the composer, the brain. . . . But I felt she was Clark Kent. And I was dying to see her rip those glasses off and fly. It's like 'Who is she going to be?'"(Snierson 2002: 28). Whereas in the Pygmalion fable the artist sculpts and brings to life his ideal of the most beautiful woman, the *Alias* version casts Abrams as Pygmalion playing out an additional adolescent/comic book fantasy. "Who is she going to be?" Whoever Abrams wants her to be—which is, apparently, a sexy, role-playing, fetishized, ass-kicking version of Superman. Galatea with a layer of the dominatrix.

The notion that the idealized action heroine is a fantasy image of women brought to life by a male artist is not exclusive to *Alias*. Numerous other high-profile action heroines are seen as the brain-children of male creators with exceptional gifts. It does not take a diehard fan or cineaste to know that Joss Whedon was responsible for *Buffy the Vampire Slayer* and the character of River in *Serenity*; that the bride in *Kill Bill* was the creation of Quentin Tarantino; that Lt. Ripley's strongest outing in the *Aliens*, Sarah Connor in *Terminator 2*, and Max in *Dark Angel* all came from James Cameron; that Luc Besson specializes in kick-ass women in *La Femme Nikita*, *The Fifth Element*, *The Messenger*, and *Transporter 2*. Likewise, though perhaps less famously, we can add to the list Rob Thomas as the creative force behind *Veronica Mars*, Len Wiseman as the writer/director of the *Underworld* films starring Kate Beckinsale as Seline, Aaron Spelling as the uber-producer behind the original *Charlie's Angels*, Craig McCracken as the artist/producer/director who created *The Powerpuff Girls*, and so on. In fact, almost every action heroine in film and television is a direct product of a male creator.

On the few occasions women are the central creative force behind action heroines the formula is typically more comedic in tone, such as in the Salma Hayek–produced *Bandidas*, the Sandra Bullock–produced *Ms. Congeniality* movies, the Drew Barrymore–produced *Charlie's Angels* films, or the Angela Robinson–written and directed *D.E.B.S.* As I have attempted to clarify throughout this book, the strong image of femininity embodied by the modern action heroine is first and foremost a progressive step in the history of women's images in the popular media, a welcome challenge to restrictive and outdated gender norms, and a much-needed figure to expand the possibilities of audience identifications. But the progressive possibilities of these roles are tempered when we also consider *who* may be creating them, and more importantly, *why* they take the specifically sexualized forms they do. The preponderance of male creators suggests a deeper and more systemic level of male control over women.

There are, of course, examples of successful and serious female-created action heroines as well. And as women become a stronger creative force in television and film, we can begin to expect more strong female characters that challenge stereotypes. But when women are the primary creative force behind the characters, their representation tends to take on a different focus.

The most successful female-created heroines in contemporary popular culture exist on the printed page, and an enormous number of literary heroines created by women clutter the bestseller lists. From children's literature series like *Undercover Girl* (Christine Harris) and *Jane Blonde* (Jill Marshall), to teen series like *Samurai Girl* (Carrie Asai) and *Fearless* (Francine Pascal), to such fan-favorite series characters as Stephanie Plum (Janet Evanovich), Evan Delaney (Meg Gardiner), Kinsey Millhone (Sue Grafton), Parrish Plessis

(Marianne de Pierres), and Jane Rizzoli (Tess Gerritsen), the action heroine has proven a bankable character at the bookstore. Even Harlequin Books hopped on the tough female investigator bandwagon for a while with its Silhouette Bombshell imprint.

As Linda Mizejewski points out in *Hardboiled & High Heeled* (2004), part of the success of these literary heroines with female readers may lay in the fact that they are not visual portrayals. The reader is freer to imagine the character based only on the verbal description of her appearance. And, while the literary heroine is still usually described as beautiful, the medium is less restrictive than the typical Hollywood portrayal of beautiful. Cover art and promotional illustrations occasionally provide a specific visual representation of the books' heroines, but even this is often avoided by featuring images either devoid of a human figure or of only "teasing parts" of the heroine visible. Instead of depicting the heroine as embodied by a sex-symbol actress or model, Mizejewski argues that the close association of female authors with their characters facilitates an association between the images of the various writers and the way their characters may appear. Patricia Cornwell, for example, is depicted in the press as a real-life version of her heroine, Kay Scarpetta.

Visually associating the fictional heroine with the female author rather than an actress or model is a shrewd tactic the literary genre utilizes to avoid the common fetishization of women prevalent in other popular media forms. Yet even in literature there are exceptions. For example, the press coverage of model-turned-author Tara Moss' mystery novels carries on the association of the writer with her main character, but because Moss is still young and beautiful the pictures that accompany print book reviews feature her in lingerie or sexy dresses and carrying a gun. That some of Moss' sexy pictorial book reviews appear in men's magazines like *Maxim* and *Stuff* makes it clear that the conventional wisdom still calls for strong female characters must be thoroughly fetishized in order to sell them to men.

To say that men have control over women in the entertainment industry is nothing new. Male producers and directors in particular have long been associated with the "casting couch" scenario and of using their power to turn struggling actresses into stars to curry sexual favors. Titillating scandals of this nature have been a mainstay in Hollywood from Fatty Arbuckle and Charlie Chaplin to Roman Polanski and Woody Allen and beyond. Alfred Hitchcock's works have often been interpreted in relation to the sexually sadistic way he treated his lead actresses. Taking into account the long history of this particularly unequal gender relationship in Hollywood raises certain questions about the male-constructed action heroine. At her core, is she just another image of the fetishized woman made for the consumption of men?

This show business cliché certainly haunts the visual representation of supposedly strong women. For example, when supermodel Cindy Crawford was cast in a co-starring role for the action film *Fair Game* (1995), the movie magazine *Premiere* featured Crawford on its cover in a revealing mini-dress and brandishing a pistol. The erotic nature of the image is made all the more creepy by the shadowy presence of the film's producer Joel Silver seated behind her in dark sunglasses. Though the movie was a notorious failure, the *Premiere* cover is a poignant reminder that even action heroines are fundamentally sexual fantasies made by men for other men.

In referring to the dynamic between male creators and the figure of the action heroine as a type of Pygmalion scenario, and by mentioning the legacy of the "casting couch" in Hollywood, I do not mean to imply a sexual relationship necessarily exists between directors and the actresses. It is worth noting, however, that James Cameron and his *Terminator 2* star Linda Hamilton shared a long-term relationship, that Luc Besson was married to Milla Jovovich who played various action heroines in his films *The Fifth Element* and *The Messenger* (Jovovich then married her *Resident Evil* director Paul Anderson), that Len Wiseman married Kate Beckinsale during production of *Underworld*, and that the press widely reported that Uma Thurman and her husband divorced amid rumors she'd had an affair with her *Kill Bill* director Quentin Tarantino. Certainly not all of the director/action actress relationships are determined by such a direct sexual Pygmalionism.

There is a huge symbolic difference between the *Variety* cover for *Alias* and the *Premiere* cover for *Fair Game*. On the *Variety* cover Garner and Abrams pose side-by-side with matching black clothes, each with their arms crossed in a comfortable stance. The Abrams/Garner image clearly implies a more equal and less sexually charged dynamic than the Silver/Crawford image suggests. It is also worth noting that several of the male directors most famous for creating strong heroines are gay—though any shift in the creator's sexual orientation does not negate the general Pygmalion nature of the relationship. In fact, when Louise Kaplan refers to the Pygmalion-like makeover of women as a type of fetishism, she originally meant it in the context of gay men transforming women within the world of fashion.

Quentin Tarantino likens his relationship to Uma Thurman as one of an artist and his muse. In a cover story entitled "The Goddess and the Geek: Inside Quentin's Obsession with Uma," (Figure 3.2) Tarantino told *Rolling Stone* magazine:

"It's just this cool connection that happened while we were doing Pulp Fiction," Tarantino explained about his obsession of Uma Thurman. "I mean, von

Sternberg had Marlene Dietrich, Hitchcock had Ingrid Bergman, Andre Techine had Catherine Deneuve. It's a special bond that I'm proud to have, and hopefully, one day, people will reference me and Uma like they do the others. But the thing about it is, it just kind of is, and there are certain things I don't really want to understand subtexturally. I just want it to be and do. (Hedegaard 2004: 42)

But to be a muse is merely to inspire creativity. The relationship of directors to actresses is one not just of inspiration but also control. Like all directors, those most closely associated with action heroines dictate everything from what to say, to how to move, and what to wear within the fictional film's world. And though Tarantino may not "really want to understand it subtexturally" [*sic*], clearly a degree of sadistic fetishization is at work in most male-directed action heroine films.

The *Rolling Stone* article reported that "during the shooting of the *Kill Bill* movies, Tarantino liked to put Uma through hell on the set" (48). "He's always having me tied up or shot," Thurman told the magazine, which quoted a conversation with David Carradine, who plays Bill, where Thurman complained, "Why does Quentin do these things to me? He's always cutting me up, and getting me covered in mud, and having me tied up and shot in the face with a shotgun. What the hell is this shit? I mean, he says he loves me, but what kind of love is that?" (48). Likewise, *Entertainment Weekly* wrote that no director has ever enjoyed "bloodying up beautiful actresses" more (Schilling 2004: 32). The piece further quotes Thurman on how Tarantino treats her: "Me in the dirt, with blood everywhere is his favorite thing in the world. He wants to rough me up every day. He wants to see me mad" (32). While most comments of this sort tend toward promotional hype, they are indicative of the degree and control male directors exercise over their actresses.

Explicit themes of masculinity controlling or indoctrinating women occur at multiple levels within action heroine narratives. Whether it is patriarchal in general or specific male characters is beside the point. That men almost exclusively author these characters suggests an attempt to fashion strong women according to particular fantasies of what the ideally fetishized woman should be. Does this fact necessarily negate the action heroine's progressive nature? Certainly not.

Nor do I imply that Abrams, Tarantino, Cameron, Beeson, Whedon, and the like play out symbolic resolutions to their personal problems with women or their own insecurities as men. This may be a possibility, but that is topic for their therapists. Even with the autonomy granted to Hollywood auteurs such as these, the entertainment industry is still an industry. Hundreds of people are involved with the production of these characters, and the fantasy has to

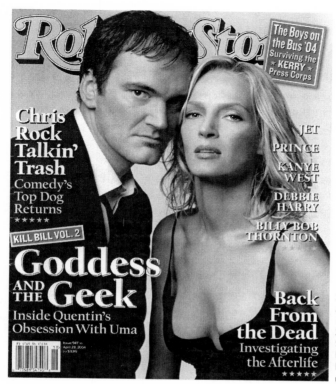

3.2. Cover photo by Albert Watson from *Rolling Stone*, April 29, 2004. © Rolling Stone LLC 2004. All Rights Reserved. Reprinted by permission.

appeal to a large segment of the population in order to sell tickets. My point is that in addition to being fetishized in a Freudian sense to neutralize the threat posed by the female body, the action heroine is also a commodity fetish in the Marxist sense. She is a commercial property to be bought and sold at the theater, on DVD, merchandising, related novelizations, computer games, and so on.

If the action heroine is read at face value as just a progressive step in the representation of women in the media, we run the risk of ignoring the larger industrial factors involved in her creation. To take the action heroine on her own merit alone is to fall for the system of disavowal that is at work in her sexual and economic fetishization. In her groundbreaking analysis of hardcore pornography, Linda Williams insightfully notes:

> Although Marx and Freud define their fetishes very differently, they both share a common will to expose the processes by which individuals fall victim to an illusory belief in the exalted value of certain (fetish) objects. Thus both writers

pose the illusion of the fetish object's intrinsic value against their own greater knowledge of the social-economic or psychic conditions that construct that illusion. (Williams 1989: 104)

While the sexual fetishism functions to compensate for the female's perceived lack, it also disavows the extensive cultural mechanisms involved in eroticizing the female form. Similarly, commodity fetishism disavows the human labor, or the means of production, involved in creating the commodity. The risk is that if we disavow the human labor that creates action heroines as a commodity we lose sight of the fact that, above all else, these characters are male-constructed fantasies. They may be empowering feminine roles, they may be opening up new terrain for actresses and female viewers alike, and they may broaden our society's perception of women's abilities—but they are also (primarily) commodities/images made by men for men.

A constant undercurrent of the action heroine narrative is one of men controlling women, or at the very least a specific image of women. For all the fiction of these characters controlling their own lives and besting men physically, they also represent the reality that men are still in power. In an era where women have made great strides in the real world and seemingly threaten patriarchal norms at every turn, the action heroine is a comforting fantasy that even the strongest of women are still available for male sexual pleasure.

In conclusion I relate an example of how the male fantasy of controlling women is explicitly marketed for consumers (a theme I will return to in more detail in the following chapter). To promote a computer game version of *Alias* to the predominantly male gaming market, retailers distributed demos with the tagline "Now YOU can take control of Jennifer Garner!" The implications of this marketing strategy are clear. Male consumers of this game are not being offered the chance to be super-spy Sydney Bristow, but to control her. And, disturbingly—not just the character but the real-life actress who portrays her.

Rather than a threatening image of a powerful woman, she becomes a plaything for consumers. Even the guys sitting at home in front of their gaming consoles are still man enough to control this woman.

4) "PLAY WITH ME"

Sexy Cyborgs, Game Girls, and Digital Babes

*O*f the myriad ways action heroines are fetishized in popular culture, one of the most telling is the manner in which this type of female character is figured in relation to technology. In general, images of women in western culture have been so thoroughly fetishized that it has become an unquestioned norm. Almost every depiction of women in the media transforms them into living dolls. The standard glamorous presentation of actresses and models with perfect faces and hair, thin bodies and augmented breasts, sexy clothing, and provocative poses reinforces the standard objectification of women for male pleasure at every turn.

The modern action heroine is a key, if extreme, example of fetishization as an attempt to control and contain the threat of female sexuality. But, in trying to control this threat, many of our cultural anxieties about strong women are laid bare. In this chapter I argue that the action heroine is often specifically fetishized as a technological figure in order to justify a complete eradication of her subjectivity. Moreover, I will explore how even excessive objectification reveals more about male insecurities in an environment of changing gender relations than it does about popular culture's ability to control women. Of particular concern here is the way some action heroines are conceived as erotic cyborgs, sexualized video game characters, or CGI fantasy figures. When the action heroine intersects with technology, her fetishization as pure object is brought to the fore in a manner that both reinforces and reveals our culture's ongoing efforts to construct ideal femininity as a commodifiable form readily available for sexual consumption.

Japanese visual artist Mariko Mori's photograph entitled "Play With Me" confronts some of the issues about the troubled relationship men often have with idealized images of women that are at the heart of this chapter. In the photo Mori presents herself as a real-life Anime babe in the doorway of a

93

Tokyo video and gaming store. In a white wig with long ponytails, dressed in a spandex and metallic superheroine and cyborg-like costume with pronounced breast plates, a miniskirt and over-the-knee boots, Mori looks every bit like the idealized image of young heroines made popular in such Anime as *Sailor Moon*, *Ghost in the Shell*, and so many others (which have found an ever-increasing fan base among western males in recent years). The irony of the image and its "Play With Me" title is that the men seem to be avoiding this fantasy object come to life.

The implication is that the men are more interested in the commercial products in the store—they would rather play with the fictional characters than the real woman. At an intuitive level, the lack of attention Mori receives from these men seems unbelievable. I would write this photograph off as selectively chosen for the purposes of social/feminist commentary if I had not witnessed this type of avoidance in other contexts. Mori's piece reminds me of a scene I observed while attending the Chicago Comic Convention doing research for another book (Brown 2001). At the time, *Penthouse* magazine was launching a line of superhero comics featuring costumed heroines participating in gratuitous sexual adventures that fans often dream of (if fan fiction is an indication of underlying fantasies).

To promote the titles, *Penthouse* had sent one of their centerfold models to sign autographs. When I noticed a group of young men peering around the corner to look at the model instead of approaching her, I asked her what was going on. She complained that this was a common occurrence at the promotional stops and that many men were simply afraid of talking with her. Elsewhere at the convention dozens of models worked the promotional booths dressed in skimpy superheroine costumes to the delight of male visitors. The *Penthouse* model's dilemma seemed to stem from the fact that she was dressed in normal clothes—she appeared too real and thus intimidating. The practice of utilizing real-life models dressed as sexy heroines to promote comics and video games at conventions is an issue I will return to later. What Mori's photograph, and my own experience, suggests is that many men may prefer their fetishized women safely contained on film or the printed page.

Marketing action heroines caters to the fantasy of safely consuming and objectifying sexualized images of heroic women. Advertisements for DVDs starring Jennifer Garner as Elektra, for example, featured images of her in a revealing costume with the tag "Buy the DVD and stare all you want!" to promote *Daredevil* (2003), and "Don't let anything stand between you and her special features" to promote *Elektra* (2005). That even the blind Daredevil appears to be staring at Elektra in the first image also makes the ad a hysterical ode to the persistent privileging of the male gaze and reinforces the presentation of action heroines as valuable primarily for their beauty. That action heroines are subjected to this dominant mode of representation is not surprising since almost all depictions of women in the media construct femininity according to their sexual desirability. This theme is restated throughout this book in various ways. Tied into this overarching theme is the manner in which this type of objectification can be taken to literal extremes that can reduce even strong, active heroines to the status of mere material objects.

SEXY CYBORGS

The most literal fetishization of femininity as pure phallic object occurs with the figure of the cyborg woman in science fiction and action genres. Whether the combination of machine and human is represented as fully robotic (as is the case in films ranging from *Metropolis* (1927) to *The Stepford Wives* (1975) to *Terminator 3: Rise of the Machines* (2003), or a melding of flesh and technology (as is the case in television series like *The Bionic Woman* and *Star Trek: Voyager*), the machine woman embodies a technological fantasy very different from that expressed when the figure is gendered masculine.

In Donna Haraway's landmark essay, "A Manifesto for Cyborgs" (1985), she optimistically proposed that the concept of cyborgs represented new and progressive possibilities for reconfiguring gender. Haraway argued that cyborgs could exceed the boundaries inherent between humanity and mechanization, that the very concept could undermine the hegemonic premise of what she referred to as "organistic" science, and that as a sui generis and gender-free figure it could challenge cultural preoccupations with master narratives and myths of origin. Unfortunately, as it is envisioned in popular culture, the cyborg usually reinforces traditional gender distinctions.

"Instead of creating a space outside gender, or at least having a complicated relation to sexuality," Despina Kakoudaki points out in contrast to Haraway, "Male cyborgs are represented as invincible (see *Terminator* films), whereas female cyborgs are mostly sexy and sexually exploited" (2000: 166). In countless media representations the cyborg continues to be gendered in a manner that very clearly armors the male version and sexualizes the female form. Similarly, Mary Ann Doane notes that despite the progressive gender possibilities that can be explored in science fiction, visual representations of cyborgs typically combine anxieties about sexuality and technology into a single threatening form:

> Although it is certainly true that in the case of some contemporary science fiction writers—particularly feminist authors—technology makes possible the

destabilization of sexual identity as a category, there has also been a curious but fairly insistent history of representations of technology that work to fortify—sometimes desperately—conventional understandings of the feminine. A certain anxiety concerning the technological is often allayed by a displacement of this anxiety onto the figure of the woman or the idea of the feminine. This is certainly the case in cinema. . . . It is striking to note how often it is the woman who becomes the model of the perfect machine. (Doane 1999: 20–21)

As the model of the perfect machine (and more recently as the ideal virtual figure), the female cyborg, or more accurately gynoid, unites the twin Others of technology and woman into a single commodifiable form, and the technology-based action heroine becomes the perfect fetish object. Or, as Stratton remarks: "The gynoid is a more complete phallic fetish than a woman could ever be" (2001: 209). Any suggestion of a real woman is displaced by an idealized weapon/body, the ultimate phallic object.

The sexualized depiction of gynoids in science fiction and action film, television, comics, animation, and video games is, on the one hand, typical of the way popular culture fetishizes women in general. While visual science fiction occasionally challenges conceptions about feminine beauty, it usually panders to the more lurid expectations of male fans. Modern science fiction women are usually portrayed more in the ass-kicking action heroine mode than the erotic damsels-in-distress version popular in the pulp magazines of the 1930s and 1940s, but she is still as sexy as ever—witness the dozens of fan-run websites dedicated to cataloging the beautiful women of science fiction.

Likewise, the mainstream press reinforces and capitalizes on the fetishism of these women. Glossy science fiction magazines run regular cover stories (with photos) ranking the most erotic females in the genre. For instance, *Sci-Fi*, the official magazine of the SyFy Channel, does an annual feature on the twenty-five sexiest women in Sci-Fi; *Dreamwatch* runs cover stories like "The Ten Women who Shook Sci-Fi: From Buffy to Xena, Sci-Fi's Greatest Female Icons are Revealed!" and; *SFX* listed "The 69 Sexiest Aliens: They're HOT, Jim, but not as we know it!" Even *TV Guide* did a special collectors issue with eight different covers about "The Sexiest Stars in the Universe." Each cover featured a different character and offered "Cosmic close-ups with the actresses who put the sigh in sci-fi."

Not to be outdone, men's magazines have turned actresses like Jolene Blalock, who played a sexy Vulcan science officer on *Star Trek: Enterprise*, and Tricia Helfer, who played a sexy cyborg on *Battlestar Galactica*, into regular cover models. The active framing of these actresses as fetish objects is clear in the suggestive descriptions of them. Blalock is described as a "Science Vixen"

(*Maxim*), a "Vulcan Vixen" (*Ramp*), and a "Star Trek Siren!" (*Loaded*). Scantily clad cover images of Helfer likewise claim "We'd betray planet Earth for her, and you would too" (*Maxim*), "Lust in Space! Set your phasers to stunning!" (*Stuff*), and "Battlestar Galactica's Tricia Helfer Sheds her Cylon Suit" (*Playboy*). And the American version of *FHM* pulled out all the stops to feature nine different bikini-clad heroines on the cover of its "Space Babe Bonanza!" issue. Far from challenging gender norms, the representation and marketing of women in contemporary Science Fiction solidifies their value as sex objects.

On the other hand, because these science fiction stories deal with futuristic societies and alien races, they can present progressive tales about shifting gender relations. Female characters can, and do, command Federation starships, serve as ruthless military operatives, and command scientific research stations. It is within this conflicted context that gynoids are sometimes called upon to balance overt sexualization with liberal thinking about gender relations. By self-consciously ascribing gender to what is ostensibly a mechanical object, the narratives can periodically enact a range of cultural concerns about appropriate gender norms and physical ideals.

One of the most popular and most-realized cyborg characters is Seven of Nine from the *Star Trek: Voyager* TV series. Seven is an interesting case because the Voyager crew "rescues" her from the alien Borg collective and removes her cybernetic implants (except for a few fashionable pieces around her eyes and hands), but her psychological and social orientation remains more Borg-like than human—and much of the series deals with her resistance to becoming human. More to the point, Mia Consalvo has argued that, for Seven, "Redeveloping her humanity is accomplished through the appropriate gendering of her body and herself" (2004: 185). As a human/machine hybrid, Seven is presented as unemotional, brusque, physically strong, and technologically brilliant. In short, her demeanor is coded as decidedly masculine. In stark contrast to her cold, business-like manner, however, Seven's appearance firmly places her within the pantheon of sexy cyborgs and sci-fi babes. Consalvo notes the conflict between the visual representation of Seven and the narrative's emphasis on challenging traditionally gendered behaviors:

Although Seven is clearly shown as unwilling to gender her behavior in a feminine way, her appearance works against this unwillingness and undermines her claims to an ungendered existence. The character is dressed in a skin-tight jumpsuit, has long blonde hair and fair skin. She wears high-heeled boots, and has a thin body and large breasts. Whether she consciously enacts gender or not, her body is a marker, delineating precisely what gender she "should" become. (2004: 186)

Over the course of the series, Seven does learn to perform femininity in a manner more in line with her physical appearance as a desirable woman (she exhibits a more sensitive inter-personal style and even wears an occasional dress). Despite being undeniably presented as the sexiest member of the crew (or perhaps because of it), Seven is an interesting, and rare, instance of utilizing cyborgs to question the naturalness of gender norms.

The sexualized technological woman of contemporary science fiction and action media is only the most recent incarnation of a theme prevalent for centuries. The most obvious precedents in art, literature, and oral traditions date back at least to Greek legends of Pygmalion, which recount the story of an artist who sculpts such a perfect rendition of womanhood that he falls in love with his own masterpiece even before it magically comes to life. Likewise, the industrial revolution inspired a number of works (both in the high and low arts), such as *L'Eve future* (1886), *The Benumbed Woman* (1899), and *Helen O'Loy* (1938) that explored the fantasy of man-made mechanical women that were undeniable improvements on their flawed real-life counterparts.

Even the surrealist movement's idealization of female mannequins professed a belief that gynoids could embody ideal femininity in a manner that real women never could. Both Andreas Huyssen (1986) and Jon Stratton (2001) provide thorough discussions of how these earlier robotic and inanimate female forms were used to explore male fantasies and fears. From the latter half of the twentieth century onward, the gynoid has become a common figure used in fiction to craft tales ranging from domestic comedies (*My Living Doll*, 1964–1965) to feminist horror films (*The Stepford Wives*, 1975) to romantic comedies (*Mannequin*, 1987) to Disney children's television movies (*Life-Size*, 2000). The gynoid is also a staple of science fiction literature, and has featured prominently in numerous television series from the original *Star Trek* to the recent *Battlestar Galactica*. Whatever the variety of formats, the modern gynoid is always presented as a sexually desirable, perfect woman.

Cinematically, it was Fritz Lang's enormously influential *Metropolis* that set the standard for portraying the gynoid as a sexually alluring but threatening character. Set in a futuristic society, the film is a cautionary tale about the class struggle between the industrial and political elite who rule from on high and the dehumanized workers toiling beneath the city's surface to keep the great machines operating. *Metropolis* is a remarkable feat of political critique that is also framed as a love story about Freder, the privileged son of Johann Fredersen, the Master of Metropolis, and Maria the saintly working-class heroine who preaches compassion and social harmony.

But the film's most memorable character is the gynoid duplicate of Maria created by the scientist Rotwang at the behest of Fredersen, which he uses to incite the workers so that he can carry out a retaliatory strike against them. Once the robotic gynoid is made over to look exactly like the real Maria to pass for human, she becomes a mechanical vamp whose striptease performance incites wealthy men to riot and encourages the workers to mount a full-scale rebellion. The resulting chaos all but destroys the metropolis and the workers' underground city alike. The mobs then turn on the mechanical Maria, and only discover she is a gynoid when they burn her at the stake and her human visage melts away. In the end, Freder and the real Maria finally bridge the gap between the two classes and bring a hope for a more utopian future. Or, as the film puts it: the heart finally succeeds as the mediator between the brain and the hand.

In his fascinating chapter "The Vamp and the Machine: Fritz Lang's Metropolis" (1988), Andreas Huyssen delves into many of the crucial issues inherent in the use of robotic women that continue to be a concern with more recent representations of gynoids and virtual women. Huyssen's central concern is the question of why "male fantasies about women and sexuality are interlaced with visions of technology in the film" (202). By considering *Metropolis* in its historical context, Huyssen argues that in addition to the political climate of Weimar Germany in which the film was produced, the twin threats of technology and female sexuality that are united in the figure of the gynoid Maria were both marked as an unstabling otherness that instigated male anxiety and reinforced an urge to dominate and control. Huyssen points out that prior to the post-Industrial Revolution era robots and cyborgs were equally conceived as male or female, and were typically portrayed as a testament to the genius of mechanical invention. "Historically, then," Huyssen notes, "we can conclude that as soon as the machine came to be perceived as a demonic inexplicable threat and as a harbinger of chaos and destruction . . . writers began to imagine the *Maschinenmensch* as a woman" (203). Just as machines were initially designed to serve men and fulfill their desires, so too was the socially constructed female expected to serve men. The threat posed by both technology and women is that they have exceeded man's ability to control them. This issue of control is, according to Huyssen, the central fantasy of the film:

> The context of the film makes it clear that in every respect, it is male domination and control which are at stake: control of the real Maria who . . . represents a threat to the world of high technology and its system of psychic and sexual repression; domination of the woman-robot by Rotwang who orders his creature to perform certain tasks; control of the labour process by the Master of Metropolis who plans to replace inherently uncontrollable living labor by robots; and, finally control of the workers actions through Fredersen's cunning use of the machine-woman, the false Maria. (205)

The threat of female sexuality initially posed by Maria (it is Freder's instant infatuation with her when she intrudes upon him that sets the story in motion) is fully displaced onto the mechanical Maria who embodies a lurid fantasy of sexuality run amok. It is the melding of machinery and Maria's image that mobilizes male fears of female insatiability and the destructive/castrating potential of active female sexuality. The film ultimately excises the mechanical vamp, who brings destruction and causes both high-class and working men alike to lose control, by publicly destroying her.

What *Metropolis* establishes, above all else, is the conception of the machine-woman as a sexual and threatening entity. This conflation of female sexuality as a threat reinforced by the mechanical strength and uncaring nature of gynoids can still be seen in contemporary films ranging from the serious (in *Eve of Destruction* [1990] the sexy gynoid Eve 8 goes on a murderous rampage and is equipped with a nuclear bomb where her uterus should be) to the comedic (in *Austin Powers* [1997] the hero is attacked by lingerie-clad, sex-kittenish Fembots that fire bullets from their nipples). In the comics, superheroines (and villainesses) have been illustrated as sexy gynoids for years. Among these superheroine cyborgs are Jocasta from *The Avengers*, Indigo from *The Outsiders*, and Void from *WildC.A.T.s*.

The comics have had an equal share of stylized male cyborgs as well, such as Colossus from *The X-Men* and Red Tornado from the *Justice League of America*, but as Scott Bukatman (1998) has noted, the male versions may have ideal bodies but they are not as explicitly depicted as desirable. "Void," Bukataman observes, "has the liquid metal sheen of the Silver Surfer and *Terminator 2*'s T-1000, but they never looked quite so *naked*" (65). As an example of the unequal burden of sexuality evidenced among comic book cyborgs, it is worth pointing out that when Marvel comics recently updated the character of Vision, they changed the robot from a male to a female.

For decades the male Vision was a member of Marvel's premier team The Avengers and, clad in a standard superhero costume (cape and all), was used Pinocchio-like to explore issues of morality and humanity. The newer, female version of the Vision has yet to be "fleshed" out as a character but she is drawn as a pure erotic object. "My body is exquisitely designed for two things. Communication and propulsion," she informs a scientist/superhero who is attracted to her. But this seems a little more than disingenuous—she is essentially a nude robotic figure, whose curvy metal frame is fashioned like a contemporary pornographic version of the robotic Maria, complete with pseudo thigh-high boots and D-cup breastplates. In short, she looks more like one of the artist Soyarama's robotic pinups than an advanced alien system designed for communication and propulsion.

Chapter Four touched on some of the ways that action cinema eroticizes the female form by visually associating women with guns. Guns are obvious phallic symbols and when wielded by sexy action heroines they clearly signify phallic compensation. The use of guns by beautiful women eroticizes violence, but it also cements the fetishistic representation of women and reinforces the underlying themes of castration anxiety at play in the genre. When the action heroine is reinterpreted as a powerful gynoid—as the physical embodiment of both a sexy female figure and a weapon of mass destruction—the theme of strong women as potentially castrating threats is taken to a ludicrous extreme. *Eve of Destruction* eschews any pretense to subtlety when the cyborg Eve bites off a misogynist's penis when he calls her a bitch.

That the sexy technological action heroine is in large part an eroticized gun is made excruciatingly clear in some cases. The Engineer, one of the main superhero characters in the popular comic book *The Authority*, for example, is a female scientist whose curvy body is infused with nano-technology. She becomes a living machine who can interact or control any technology in the universe and is illustrated as a naked silver beauty who can transform her limbs into any gun imaginable. Similarly, in the *Planet Terror* half of the Rodriguez/Tarantino tribute to B movies *Grind House* (2007), Rose McGowan plays Cherry Darling, a Go-Go dancer with a machine gun leg. The humorously phallic leg is a gift from her bad-ass boyfriend who attaches it in a mockingly erotic scene. As half sex-kitten, half machine gun, Cherry blasts away monsters and would-be rapists alike, and eventually becomes the high priestess of a post-apocalyptic new world. Though *Planet Terror* may be a parody of 1970s B movies it still carries on the tradition of phallic women as desirable and threatening.

That the gynoid is always depicted as desirable despite being a living weapon hints at the depths of her value as a fetish. Whether completely robotic or a combination of living flesh and machine parts, the gynoid is typically depicted as the perfect combination of sex and violence. In his discussion of fully artificial women, Stratton insightfully argues that the heightened libidinal charge of these fetishized figures is derived from the male fantasy of the ideal woman as pure sexual object:

> Manufactured by men, the production of the gynoid literalises the fetishistic reconstruction of the female body. However, the female body has an existence prior to its taking-up within the fetishistic structure, and where the female body is inhabited by a 'woman' capable of resistance to her fetishistic interpellation, the gynoid is able to occupy more fully the role of libidinised phallic fetish. As an oftentimes indistinguishable or even 'improved upon' substitute for a woman,

the gynoid retains the sexual quality as a 'woman' of being an object of heterosexual male desire whilst, in addition, being the site of an overdetermining
fetishistic desire. From around the middle of the nineteenth century gynoids
are preferred, and are both more desired and more feared, than the women for
whom they substitute. (Stratton 2001: 210)

Whereas the fetishizing of real women always carries with it the shadow of
their own underlying subjectivity, the gynoid comes closer to being a complete phallic fetish. The narrative fantasy is that she has no autonomy, no
purpose, no goals, no desires of her own. She is an ideal figure because she is
constructed simply and wholly to satisfy her male creators. She is, to put it
crudely, the perfect fuck-doll. She exists to satisfy male sexual fantasies without any of the drawbacks that accompany real women. You know, undesirable
things like wanting their own needs met, having their own opinions or, God
forbid, not being satisfied sexually. Though Stratton is talking about entirely
artificial women, there is more than a hint of this fantasy still in play with
modern gynoids even if they are only technologically enhanced real women.
That many sexy cyborg narratives do ultimately threaten men only illustrates
just how deep a psychological threat women pose to masculinity.

The pornographic scenario that constructs gynoids as high-tech fuck-dolls
is part of the core fantasy inherent in every representation of the machine
woman. Rotwang originally created the gynoid in *Metropolis* with the intention of making her in the image of Fredersen's deceased wife, whom both men
loved. Even the Bride in *The Bride of Frankenstein* (1935) was constructed for
the sole purpose of providing a mate for the monster. The landmark film *Blade
Runner* (1982) epitomizes the gendered use of cyborgs—male versions perform
heavy labor, and females, referred to as "pleasure models," perform sex.

More recently, gynoids have been depicted as explicit fuck-dolls in films
like *Virtuosity* (1995), where a computer programmer goes home each night to
his virtual girlfriend Sheila, and in *Serenity* (2005) where a reclusive techno-
geek lives with his love-bot "wife" Lenore. Perhaps the most explicit depiction
of the gynoid as fuck-doll, and one that makes a direct connection between
action heroines and fetishistic fantasies, is the Buffybot in the fifth season of
Buffy the Vampire Slayer. Commissioned by Buffy's sometimes enemy/some-
times ally the roguish vampire Spike, the Buffybot is an exact replica of Buffy.
Spike is in love with Buffy but she spurns his affections, so he turns to her
robotic doppleganger, which is programmed to worship him and do anything
he desires. The Buffybot gleefully submits to all of Spike's sexual demands,
playing out scenarios where he defeats her in combat as a precursor to intercourse, and uttering, "Oooh Spike, you *are* the big bad!" during sex.

The Buffybot looks just like the real Buffy but will never reject Spike or make him feel he isn't man enough to win her. From Spike's point of view, the Buffybot is clearly the "improved upon substitute for the real woman" Stratton mentions above. When the Buffybot is first revealed to him by its creator, Spike appreciatively remarks that "some say its better than the real thing." When the real Buffy (whom Spike refers to sarcastically as "the not so pleasant one") finds out about the Buffybot and what Spike has been doing with her, she is understandably outraged at the violation. By the end of the episode, the Buffybot is destroyed and the real Buffy chastises Spike, telling him that "it wasn't even real. That robot was gross and obscene!"

What makes the Buffybot and other artificial females an "improved upon substitute for the real woman" or "better than the real thing" is that she exists as pure object. In the fantasy scenario of the man-made woman, subjectivity is preserved as a masculine privilege. In Chapter Three I discussed the Pygmalion-like implications inherent in so many action heroine narratives wherein powerful women are trained or created by male institutions or father figures—and extratextually by male directors/creators. This trope is taken to its logical extreme with gynoids who are literally made by men for men.

Though this construction is often framed as an arrogant god-like aspiration, it's also a metaphor for male objectification and commodification of women in general. The beautiful robotic woman made for male pleasures epitomizes the common conception of femininity in our culture as a standardized, consumable, and indeed replaceable form. As a completely objectified figure, the gynoid is akin to the assembly-line conception of women that Marshall McLuhan describes in *The Mechanical Bride* (1967) where the interfusion of sex and technology envisions femininity as a replaceable part. From the advertisements and chorus lines that McLuhan analyzes, to Busby Berkley musicals (see Phelan 2000), to beauty pageants (see Garland-Thompson 1998), to fashion photography (see Laennec 1988), to cosmetic surgery (see Bordo 1993), modern conceptions of a perfectible female form have been interlaced with the industrial logic that women can be shaped and disciplined to conform to a male-defined standard of beauty.

This mechanized and repeatable ideal is evident in the sequential nature of many contemporary gynoids, where numeric lineage is often incorporated into their very names. The sexy Borg/human hybrid on *Star Trek: Voyager* is Seven of Nine. The vengeful Eve 8 of *Eve of Destruction* is so named because she was the eighth attempt at creating a cyborg weapon. Jenny, from the cartoon *My Life as a Teenage Robot*, is also known as X-J9, the ninth in a line of teen girl robots. In the comics, X-23 is the twenty-third attempt to clone Wolverine, the original "Weapon X." And in the recent *Battlestar Galactica* the evil Cylons have been revisioned in human form, most centrally as the seductive cyborg simply known as Six.

For all the posturing about cyborgs as a narrative device to facilitate mediations about morality and the true meaning of humanity, the female cyborg is also a convenient trope to erase female subjectivity. The problem with this fantasy of ideal female bodies devoid of subjectivity is that even in fiction it is difficult to fully suppress feminine agency. Time and again, these stories witness a return of the repressed.

The unchecked sexuality of the robot Maria leads to chaos. The Bride of Frankenstein violently refuses to mate with the Monster and has to be destroyed along with him. The real Buffy returns to dismantle the Buffybot and tell off Spike. Eve 8 goes on a murderous spree against men, specifically those who wronged her human counterpart/creator. Thus, while these tales enact an ultimate fetishizing of the female body, they also demonstrate the depths of our cultural and misogynistic fears. Though this particular fantasy seeks to contain the perceived threat women pose by literally turning them into consumable and possessable objects, it simultaneously denies the possibility that femininity can be contained. This is what makes so many of these tales not just science fiction but horror stories for men. In the rare case where femininity can be contained, as in *The Stepford Wives*, they are more specifically horror stories for women.

VIRTUAL BABES

Where sexy cyborg stories try, but often fail, to completely eradicate female subjectivity by recasting women as literal objects, recently a more effective effort to erase female subjectivity through the use of virtual women has emerged. As society's technological fascination with the mechanical has given way to the digital, so too has the ideal of femininity represented by the female cyborg been increasingly displaced by the flawless virtual babe. And so the dawn of the new millennium introduced a bevy of computer-generated cyber-babes who became popular media personalities.

Glasgow Records had a series of hit songs and videos with their virtual pop star T-Babe, as did the Japanese/Korean virtual singer Diki (aka DK-96). In the UK, the green-haired virtual babe Ananova, reportedly an amalgamation of the best features from Posh Spice, Kylie Minogue, and Carol Vorderman, became a popular newscaster. And, in perhaps the next logical step in the modeling industry's attempts to find the perfect woman, the Elite Modeling Agency launched its virtual model Webbie Tookay in 2000. Like the perfectly sculpted gynoid devoid of any subjectivity of her own, Elite's head, John Casa-blancas, praised Webbie over flesh-and-blood models because she: "will never complain about long hours, she'll never add a pound or get some idiot boy-friend who will mess up her career, and she never talks back" (Gebler Davies 2000: 30). Some say its better than the real thing, indeed. And, of course, there's Lara Croft, the phenomenally popular virtual game girl and preemi-nent cyber sex symbol. We will deal with Lara in more detail soon as she is especially important to the discussion—not just for her virtuality but because she is a key link between virtual babes and the figure of the contemporary ac-tion heroine.

Like painting and photography before it, the idealization of the female form is a favorite subject for digital illustrators working with static images. In the pursuit of the perfect female visage, computer artists have moved beyond the time-honored traditions of airbrushing and digitally enhancing photo-graphs of real women. The entirely computer-illustrated woman has become an artistic genre of its own.

The coffee table art book company Taschen even canonized the practice with the publication of *Digital Beauties* in 2003 (Wiedemann). Featuring the work of over a hundred (predominantly male) computer artists, the *Digital Beauties* "portraits" demonstrate the alliance between computer animation and the pinup/pornographic tradition. Despite the book's claims, and the medium's goal—computer animation's attempt to create lifelike and realistic images—the virtual women of this sort are excessively fetishized as sci-fi and fantasy babes who oscillate between dominatrix personas and passive sex kit-tens. Ranging from cute anime-inspired schoolgirls to hardcore S&M layouts, the vanguard of computer illustration, as presented in *Digital Beauties*, carries on the media's dominant tradition of presenting "ideal" women as erotic and threatening spectacles.

With artist portfolio titles like "Teenagers' Sexy Dreams," "Digital Femme Fatales," "Super Hot Virtual Babes," and "Bikini Girls with Machine Guns," it is clear this brand of computer illustration is dominated by images that makes Pamela Anderson strapped into her leather corset in *Barb Wire* tame by comparison. Not surprisingly, many images in the book resemble erotic game girls inspired by Lara Croft. Taking their cue from Taschen, the editors of the gaming magazine *Play* have published a series of newsstand specials titled "Girls of Gaming" that features nothing but glossy pinups of the sexiest female computer game characters.

While CGI characters have also become commonplace in modern cinema, we have yet to experience the virtual actor or synthespian that can pass for human in the manner that Barbara Creed has questioned in her article, "The

Cyberstar: Digital Pleasures and the end of the Unconscious" (2002). To date, CGI characters integrated into live-action films are demarcated as fantastical beings such as Gollum, Scooby-Doo, King Kong, Spider-Man, and The Hulk. What Creed questions is the ability of lifelike computer-generated performers to elicit audience identification because the "cyberstar is not subject to the same experiences as the living star, experiences such as mothering, oedipal anxiety, hunger, loss, ecstasy, desire, death. . . . In short, the synthespian does not have an Unconscious" (2002: 132). This lack of an Unconscious that Creed sees as an impediment to audience identification is also a further link between the fantasy of the gynoid as the perfect woman devoid of her own identity and the cyber babe as an actualization of a female figure that can be completely controlled by male consumers. It is not just the association with technology that makes the virtual babe the new millennium's successor to the sexy cyborg, but the underlying fantasy of control and containment.

Though CGI characters have yet to pass convincingly for human, it is telling that the only Hollywood feature film to directly address the issue of cyberstars, so far, focuses on the creation of a sexy woman. Andrew Niccol's 2002 film *Simone* is a modern Pygmalion story about a struggling director, Viktor Taransky (Al Pacino), who finds success when he casts the entirely computer-generated Simone (played by real-life model Rachel Roberts) as his leading lady. Taransky fools the world into believing that Simone is a real person and because she is so "perfect," she becomes a worldwide multimedia phenomenon with commercial endorsements, magazine covers, hit records, and eventually even a marriage to Taransky and a child of their own, Chip.

Simone echoes the themes of such notable films as *Laura* (1944) and *Rebecca* (1940) where the specter of beautiful but absent women, all the more ideal because they exist primarily in the imagination of the male leads, haunt the heroes who love them. In many ways, however, the story of this fictional virtual babe follows the same pattern as the sexy cyborgs narratives. At first she is the perfect fantasy woman willing and able to do anything Taransky desires, but as her popularity escalates she seems to take on a life of her own—a life beyond the control of her Pygmalion, who at one point tries to destroy Simone for being an unappreciative "bitch." Even here, with a nonexistent woman, the repressed returns to undo the male creator's fantasy of controlling women.

Still, *Simone* tells a story wherein Creed's concern that cyberstars can never attain the stature of real performers is moot. Simone is adored by millions (and even wins a Best Actress Oscar) and the film clearly implies this is possible because stars, especially sexy female ones, are already artificially constructed fantasies. It is no surprise that this film is focused on using technology to create a beautiful woman since so much of our media already strives to create women as ideal fantasy figures. The image of the ideal woman does not need an Unconscious, the film tells us, because they are even more ideal without one. Where fictional parables like *Simone* may grant virtual women some sense of agency, some sense of their own identity, real virtual women as they exist now in other media forms more fully cater to male desires of complete control.

Current technological limitations have restricted large-scale use of virtual women as feature characters in contemporary film and television, but no such limitations exist in the related world of video games. In the multimedia and synergistic marketing environment that constitutes modern popular culture it is worth noting that revenues for the gaming industry now surpass those of film and television. Video games, and more importantly the virtual characters or avatars that star in the games, have become a very profitable commodity. Rather than compete with the gaming industry, Hollywood has joined forces with game producers in order to promote their properties and to share in the royalties derived from licensing their characters for use in games.

Given the game industry's reliance on the dominant "first-person-shooter" format, action movies and television series have proven the easiest and most successful properties to adapt. It is now standard practice for a new video game to be released in conjunction with every major action film. With the premiere of each Harry Potter, Spider-Man, or James Bond film there is an officially licensed game that allows users to play the movie.

This interdependent relationship between Hollywood and the gaming industry has encouraged and profited from images of sexy virtual action heroines. Some game heroines have been popular enough to warrant their own feature films, such as the *Tomb Raider* (2001, 2003) and *Resident Evil* films (2002, 2004 and 2007), as well as *Final Fantasy* (2001), *Bloodrayne* (2006), and *Dead or Alive* (2007). Conversely, filmic action heroines are routinely transformed into successful game characters—sometimes the games actually turned out to be far more popular and profitable than the films, as was the case with the games based on the feature film versions of *Catwoman* (2004) and *Aeon Flux* (2005). Like their big screen counterparts, TV action heroines have also enjoyed an enormous amount of success as game characters. For example, the live-action heroines from series including *Xena: Warrior Princess*, *Buffy the Vampire Slayer*, *Alias*, and *Dark Angel*, as well as animated heroines from programs like *Kim Possible*, *The Powerpuff Girls*, and *My Life as a Teenage Robot*, have all spun-off into best-selling games.

The incredible popularity of Lara Croft from the *Tomb Raider* series is the most obvious example of how digital heroines inform our cultural perception of action heroines. Lara Croft was an instant success when the first installment of *Tomb Raider* was released by Eidos in 1996. As one of the first adventure games to feature a female character, Eidos took a huge risk since the dominant perception was that the overwhelmingly male gaming audience would balk at the prospect of playing a first-person shooter platform with a female avatar. But any industry concerns were quickly put to rest as the game racked up record sales figures and Lara herself became a popular culture phenomenon.

Lara Croft's ascent dovetailed nicely with the mid-1990s wave of Girl Power rhetoric, and her highly stylized and sexualized image fostered attention far beyond that of the gaming world. Within a year and a half of the game's initial release, Lara Croft was featured on the cover of over fifty magazines, many of which had little or nothing to do with game culture. She appeared on tour with super-group U2 via digital backdrop, modeled Gucci dresses, recorded a hit single, profiled in countless newspaper articles, featured on T-shirts and posters, inspired a series of action figures, and hundreds of devoted websites.

The Lara phenomenon eventually resulted in her own comic book series and two Hollywood feature films starring A-list actress Angelina Jolie. By most accounts, the incredible popularity of Lara Croft is due as much (if not more so) to her idealized image as it is to the quality of the game. Described as "[E]qual parts Pamela Anderson and Indiana Jones with a dash of *La Femme Nikita*," *Newsweek* dubbed her "the perfect fantasy girl for the digital generation" (Croal and Hughes 1997: 33). The success of Lara Croft as a multimedia action heroine and as a digital fantasy girl brings to the fore the complex relationship between male viewers and tough female characters.

Given Lara Croft's exaggerated sexual form it is no surprise that most of the writings about her, both popular and academic, begin by discussing how clearly she epitomizes male fantasies about ideal women. Helen W. Kennedy, for example, points out "Lara's status as an object of sexual desire, a factor which the marketing/advertising of *Tomb Raider* was keen to reinforce" (2002: 2). Taking the point even further, Anne-Marie Schleiner argues in "Does Lara Croft Wear Fake Polygons?" that "Lara Croft is seen as the monstrous off-spring of science: an idealized, eternally young female automaton, a malleable, well-trained techno-puppet created by and for the male gaze" (2001: 222). In addition to stressing Lara's visual fetishization, Schleiner's remark is a reminder that Lara Croft is an artificial construction made by and for men in a manner akin to the fantasy of the sexy cyborg, of which she is a direct descendant.

Much like the sexy cyborgs, and similar to the live-action heroines discussed in Chapter Three, Lara Croft was originally conceived in true Pygmalion fashion by game designer Toby Gard to be his ideal woman. In an interview with *The Face*, Gard mentions that "Lara was designed to be a tough, self-reliant, intelligent woman. She confounds all the sexist clichés apart from the fact that she's got an unbelievable figure. Strong, independent women are the perfect fantasy girls—the untouchable is always the most desirable" (*The Face* 1997: 24). Carrying the Pygmalion analogy to its logical conclusion, Gard later told *USA Today* that his departure from Eidos, and thus the corporately owned Lara Croft, in order to have more control over the characters he invents was "similar to losing a love," since "you're not really allowed to go near her" (Snider 2001). Gard's professional estrangement from Lara Croft is typical of the legal and industrial distancing of authors from fictional characters that is standard practice in contemporary media culture (for an interesting discussion of the impact of this in relation to Lara Croft, see Mikula 2003). But it is also a reminder that no matter how much Lara Croft may seem to take on a life of her own, she was initially just a commercial "techo-puppet" created to fulfill male fantasies.

Certainly Lara's hypersexual appearance is an important part of her popularity. The digital Lara has appeared on numerous "Hottest Women" lists in men's magazines, as have the flesh and blood models and actresses who have embodied her at conventions, for promotional photo-shoots, and in feature films. What is really interesting, though, is not just that she is another example of how stringently fetishized the female form is in popular culture (the ideally sexualized female body is part and parcel of every modern action heroine after all), but that this particular body type has proven so successful in a realm that carries issues of viewer identification to an entirely different level.

In traditional film studies audience identification has long been a key issue because it is an essential concept for understanding how narratives and cinematic techniques can influence viewers' belief systems. The basic assumption is that viewers are persuaded to adopt a film's ideological perspective because they are set up to identify with specific characters. Through a range of formal techniques, such as filming the action from the hero's point of view or including voice-over commentary from the hero, viewers are sutured into the narrative, and thus the ideological, perspective favored by the film. And, as we have discussed in earlier chapters, gender has become the most dominant trope for aligning viewer identification. As Mulvey's original template structured it, cinema facilitates an identification with the dominant male gaze, or the masculine subject position, while the on-screen woman is predominantly presented as mere object.

A great deal of theory has explored and advanced this original premise over the years, but the rigid gender alignment of the concept still holds sway. In both the scholarly literature and the entertainment industry, the belief that men identify with male characters and women with female ones is a key principle. The ideological work of identification is so effective because being aligned with the ego ideal on the screen is perhaps the greatest pleasure most of us derive from popular movies. For most men, and many women too, it is fun to fantasize we are as smart, dashing and heroic as James Bond or Indiana Jones for a couple of hours.

This pleasure in identification with the heroic is also one of the primary reasons the action heroine is an intriguing figure because she complicates not just our cultural standards of who can be conceived as heroic, but of how gender specificity can be nullified. If women are occupying the traditionally masculine position as hero and subject what does this do to male identification? The big question is this: *can men identify with characters like Ellen Ripley, The Bride, and Sydney Bristow?* And what does this mean for changing ideas about gender and power in our society?

Far less consideration has been given to player identification in video games. Studies on player identification with game characters primarily argue that because players control the characters, they automatically form a close identification with their avatars. Unlike passive observers of movies, game players take charge of the figure on the screen and dictate what they do. Identification in games is associated with the interactive nature of the experience.

As Jansz and Martis put it in their analysis of gender identification with gaming characters: "Many video games enable their players to enact identities in the most literal sense of the word. Gamers can actually 'be' their characters in a playful virtual reality" (2007: 142). So fundamental is the assumption that players figuratively become their gaming characters, the advertisements for all three games based on the most recent film adaptations of *Spider-Man* (2002), *The Hulk* (2003), and *Batman* (2005) used the tag line "Be Spider-Man," "Be the Hulk," and "Be the Batman." The game version of *Superman* (2006) took this 'be' the character approach as well, and even gave their website the simple designation of "besuperman.com."

The logical assumption that video game players develop a close identification with the on-screen avatars helped shape the type of adventure games that would dominate the market. Since the primary audience for games is males between the ages of fifteen and thirty, the majority of first-person shooter games opted for macho male characters such as Duke Nukem (self-titled series) or Mr. 47 (*Hitman* series) to facilitate player identification along gender lines. The conventional industry thinking was that males would never accept a game that required them to play as a female character. This belief meant that Lara Croft was a huge risk for Core Design. Histories of the game report that a possible male protagonist for *Tomb Raider* was preferred by the marketing department due to fears that a female character would automatically undermine sales.

The unprecedented success of Lara Croft challenges some of the most basic assumptions about same sex gender identification. If sales are any indication, the target male audience has no problem with "being" a female character. *Tomb Raider's* use of a strong female protagonist has also been credited with attracting female users to the world of action games, though most industry accounts say women still constitute a small minority of the gaming market.

That men enthusiastically accepted playing as Lara led some critics to consider the game as tantamount to a transgendering experience. Schleiner, for example, argues that "gender roles are broken down, allowing young boys and men who constitute the majority of *Tomb Raider* players to experiment with 'wearing' a feminine identity, echoing the phenomenon of gender crossing in Internet chat rooms and MUDs" (2001: 223). Kennedy likewise points out that "through having to play *Tomb Raider* as Lara, a male player is transgendered" (2002: 6), and that this relationship is akin to a new form of queer identity. At first glance, the willingness of male players to assume a female character is a potential indication of more fluid movement between identification with masculine and feminine subjects than ever before. But, of course, there is much more going on with Lara Croft (and the cyber-babes who followed her) than simple cross-gender identification.

Rather than considering male users transgendered, it may be more accurate to think of their experience as an easy oscillation between identifying with Lara Croft's masculine characteristics and objectifying her feminine form. Carol J. Clover (1992) has famously described how specific behaviors commonly found in horror movies are engendered as either masculine or feminine regardless of the biological sex of the character that exhibits these qualities. Within horror, Clover argues, incidents of abject fear (screaming, cowering, fainting) are engendered feminine, while triumphant self-rescue (killing the monster on one's own) is engendered masculine. That these behaviors are understood so clearly in our culture facilitates male viewers' identification with the female heroine, or Final Girl, and a distancing from any cowardly male figures.

Similarly, games like *Tomb Raider* capitalize on the binary logic of our society that continues to engender adventuring as masculine and erotic spectacle as feminine. Male players can thus identify with Lara's masculine attributes as she runs, leaps, shoots, and fights her way across exotic landscapes without any direct challenge to their own sense of identity as males. Moreover, they can freely objectify Lara when the game is not in an action sequence, when she is clearly engendered as a feminine erotic spectacle. In this manner, male players do not really have to identify with a female character since what they experience through Lara are masculine attributes. They can also neatly sidestep the awkwardness of eroticizing a masculinized figure, because when Lara is static she is thoroughly engendered feminine.

While the identification with Lara when she operates in a manner engendered masculine brings the player closer to her, objectification of her when she is visually engendered as feminine provides a comfortable distance between the gamer and the erotic figure. As film theorists like Christian Metz (1975) and Mary Ann Doane (1982) have established, the voyeur requires a certain distance or gap between himself and the object in order to experience the fetishistic scenario of visually consuming the female figure being spied upon. The oscillation between identifying with and objectifying Lara, between closeness and distance, works to reinforce traditional gender relations rather than challenge them.

Lara Croft's hyper-sexual appearance positions her as an object of visual pleasure for male players in close proximity to being a subject of identification. As Maja Mikula asks: "Is this target audience—the young men who take on the character of Lara to play—primarily being invited to take sexual pleasure from *looking* at her? Or to enjoy the pleasures of *being* her?" (2003: 80). The question of this balance between the pleasures of looking at Lara and being her, between the character as object and subject, is a crucial one for considering the appeal of the action heroine in all her representations. The most obvious answer is that the excessive fetishization of Lara Croft is conducted as a form of backlash.

The emphasis on Lara's breasts and buttocks within the game (technically *Tomb Raider* is a third-person shooter format that importantly lets players see the character—not just see through her eyes as is common with male first-person games) and the marketing of her as a digital sex symbol clearly position her as an ideal sex object despite her masculine adventures. Moreover, the eroticization of her by her male fans can (and has) been interpreted as a type of sexist compensation for the dissonance players may feel about identifying with a female character. The most widely recognized of these practices is the infamous Nude Raider patch that allows players to reconfigure Lara as a naked character. Alongside official promotional images of Lara in bikinis and revealing gowns, there are numerous unofficial images of Lara nude on the web, and even sites offering "videos" of her performing stripteases.

The sum effect is much like the fetishistic costuming of live-action heroines and the erotic layouts of the actresses in men's magazines, all of which compensate for male identification with threatening female characters. According to Kennedy: "the desperate re-encoding of Lara as 'sex object'—on the part of male players—may arise from an anxiety over the fact that these experiences *are* mediated by a female character and thus signify an attempt to deny any empathy/identification with Lara" (2002: 4). This type of fetishization can comfort male viewers/players by reinforcing the fantasy that these women are sexually available to them or, at the very least, that their heterosexual masculinity is not in doubt.

As the title of Helen W. Kennedy's essay, "Lara Croft: Feminist Icon or Cyberbimbo?" suggests, this question about the balance between Lara as a subject of identification or an object of pleasure is at the core of most of the serious writings about *Tomb Raider*. Mike Ward's article "Being Lara Croft, or, We are All Sci Fi" (2000), which appeared in the online journal Popmatters.com, lays bare some of the conflicting impulses at work in Lara's sexually charged relationship with male players. Ward's personal take on Lara as both an erotic object and a point of player identification begins with his troubled reaction to a promotional image of Lara Weller, one of a series of official models employed to embody Lara Croft in photographs and at personal appearances.

For Ward the image of Weller dressed in Croft's trademark combat boots, tan shorts, and skintight latex tank top is troubling because she is posed staring directly at the camera/viewer with her guns drawn. The paradox that Ward rightly points out is that the virtual Lara Croft never returns the viewer/player's gaze. As a virtual character controlled by the player, Lara is oblivious to her objectification. The real-life Lara Weller, on the other hand, confronts the viewer head on.

What makes Ward uneasy is that "Weller's Lara is sexual spectacle at the same time that she embodies rage against the spectacle. She appears pissed that someone is looking and offers to pay back the sexual gaze, not with sexual dominance, but simple annihilation" (1). According to Ward the subjectivity expressed in this image of Weller as Croft is disruptive because it challenges the perfect objectification of the character as an ideal figure available to be consumed and incorporated through the eyes of the player. The distance between Lara Croft and the player is collapsed, thus making it difficult for gamers to play as Lara without truly becoming her. Ward argues that this objectifying distance is necessary for players to ground their own subjectivity in her virtual actions.

Ward is well aware of the problematic balance between players' sexual desire for the digital Lara Croft and their identification with her while playing the game. In a sense, by playing as Lara, men can become their own sex object. As Ward puts it: "And even if she incorporates my banality, my ordinariness, still, she's beautiful. The player's gaze is a strange closed circle of the desiring look and the beautiful, powerful exhibition. In fact, the look and the exhibition are one and the same, bound into a single narcissistic contract safer and more symmetrical than anything Leopold von Sacher-Masoch was ever able to dream up" (3). Mastery of Lara becomes self-mastery as players learn to act, move, and shoot in a seamless symmetry with a character that they also desire.

As the reference to Sacher-Masoch makes clear, there is a potentially sadistic element to this relationship wherein men can completely control and become one with the object of their own lust. "Eventually, when the cntl, alt, ins, and end keys become second nature," Ward argues there is a vanquishing of self-doubt and technical frustrations. Once Lara is mastered "[T]here are no more impasses, only a fluid, reflex connection, a virtuosity that seems to put Lara and the player both in the same body, so that it's no longer clear which is the origin of her performances." In Ward's scenario Lara is the perfect sexual fetish because she can become completely consumed and controlled by the male player. She is the perfect object with no subjectivity beyond that which is provided for her by the male controller. She is the ultimate Galatea who not only looks like the perfect woman, but will never question or refuse her master.

Both Kennedy and Allyson D. Polsky (2001) have understandably taken issue with Ward's article because it emphasizes, and even seems to revel in, the rudimentary pleasure heterosexual men can take in Lara so long as she remains a mute and oblivious object. "This pleasure," Kennedy notes, "is only disrupted when she is made flesh in the form of Lara Weller who *can* look back, and through this can express a subjectivity outside of this phantasmic circle" (2002: 5). Certainly it is disturbing to be so blatantly confronted with the possibility that male gamers can, and perhaps do, prefer their active heroines as sexual objects without any hint of subjectivity. Kennedy is also concerned that by focusing on Lara as a male fantasy object, discussions of her potential for female or queer fantasy and identification may be foreclosed.

Indeed, Lara does hold the potential to mobilize a wide range of alternative relationships, but given the dominant male market for the game (likewise, for action characters in film and television) it is important to come to terms with some of the more prevalent scenarios despite how disturbing they may be. Polsky also reacts strongly to Ward's essay and describes it as "both disturbingly misogynist and incessantly heterosexist. In Lara, Ward seems to be looking for the digital equivalent of a blow-up porno doll" (2001: 11). Polsky's likening Lara to a blow-up porno doll is a particularly apt description, and one that can certainly be applied well beyond the confines of *Tomb Raider*.

The inherent theme of virtual babes as sexually available to male gamers, as having no more agency to resist or judge men than a blow-up doll does, is exactly the dynamic that Mariko Mori's self-portrait as a cyborg/digital babe "Play With Me" questions. Rather than simply "play as me" or "be me" (Be

Spider-Man, Be the Batman, Be Superman, etc.) that is associated with male characters, the flirtatious "Play With Me" stresses the erotic implications that always exist when a predominantly male audience is invited to partake in games where they can do anything they want with a female character. The joke of Mori's photograph is that she may look like the ideal fetish object but, like Lara Weller as an angry Lara Croft, she is real and thus carries the potential of voicing her own subjectivity. Male insecurities and fears can be laid bare when they are confronted with the real thing.

Virtual babes performed by real women bring to mind the big-talking guys who are afraid to approach beautiful women for fear of being shot down, or the men who suddenly turn timid when female performers talk to them in strip clubs. I'm also reminded of a piece on Howard Stern's morning radio show several years ago when Stern and his male cohorts decided to compare measurements of their erect penises, but when a visiting porn star took them into a back room to help arouse them, each man failed to become hard because they were fearful of her aggressiveness and apprehensive about being judged by such an experienced woman (they were only able to complete the contest when another visitor, a less sexual, average woman offered her services to arouse them). "Be careful what you wish for" may be the message of both Mori's art and Weller's impersonation of Croft, but it is a theme we see elsewhere in popular culture when masculinity is confronted with a sense of subjectivity in women presumed to be mere objects.

The fear Mike Ward expresses over the confrontational subjectivity implied in the promotional image of Lara Weller as Lara Croft may help explain the peculiar relationship that exists between fans and the costumed models, or "Booth Babes," who dress up as heroines for conventions and other promotional purposes. As described at the start of this chapter, male fans often exhibit a certain tension when confronted with beautiful women clad as sexy fictional characters. They alternate between fearing them, or at least being embarrassingly uncomfortable in their presence, and crowding close to gawk or take their picture. There is a discrepancy between a completely passive and readily objectifiable digital image of a buxom gun-wielding babe and a real woman, who is already in possession of her own thoughts, her own judgments, her own subjectivity. This difference can be disconcerting for fans that have already invested in a close and perhaps personal relationship with a character.

Whereas the photograph of Weller did too much to convey a sense of her/Croft's own presence, most promotional models and Booth Babes are instructed to be as mute and compliant as possible—as interchangeable approximations of a fantasy figure. The use of interchangeable women, pretty faces, and curvy bodies devoid of their own selves to embody specific fictional characters makes real the notion of assembly-line beauty. Weller herself was the fifth of nine official Lara models, so far, employed by Eidos to pose for promotional photographs. And while many Lara Croft fan web sites include galleries dedicated to each official models, Eidos has been careful to maintain the fantasy of Lara Croft as a blank slate. When the second official Lara Croft model, Rhona Mitra, made a splash in the media in the late 1990s by expressing her own opinions about the character and other issues, Eidos quickly replaced her with multiple and less-talkative models, thus squashing any fantasy-destroying sense of female subjectivity.

This preference for Lara Croft as a blank slate may be one of the reasons the feature film versions failed to achieve the box office success Paramount Studios anticipated. *Lara Croft: Tomb Raider* (2001) brought in roughly 130 million at the domestic box office, so the movie was hardly a failure, but with production costs reported to be near 115 million, along with a massive advertising budget, the film was not a resounding success either, and generally perceived as a disappointment. Reviews proved mostly negative and it never achieved the summer blockbuster status studios need to recoup their costs on such expensive properties. A record-breaking opening weekend followed by a sharp decline in attendance meant that negative word of mouth prevailed, and even devoted Lara Croft fans did not return for repeat viewings.

When the second film, *Lara Croft: Cradle of Life* (2003), was released viewers stayed away in droves, despite the sequel receiving marginally better reviews. With *Cradle of Life* raking in only sixty-five million domestically (it cost approximately ninety-five million to produce) it would seem the movie franchise is dead. A problem for fans may have been that as a scripted character in the movie Lara exhibits an autonomy that is absent in the game. The filmic Lara does what she wants (or at least what the director wants) and is beyond the control of viewers.

Another reason Lara's transition to live action was less than successful could be because in casting a real actress the character is automatically conceived as less of a pure object. That the actress in question is Angelina Jolie, an outspoken, controversial, Academy Award–winning performer means that Lara is now anything but a blank slate. As popular and beautiful as Jolie is, as much as she is routinely objectified as a sex symbol and as an identifiable persona she is undeniably imbued with a subjectivity of her own. Jolie is famous for her romantic liaisons, her humanitarian work, her numerous adoptions—in short, as skilled an actress as she may be, Jolie's recognizability as a celebrity is in direct conflict with a gaming character whose popularity is based in large part on her lack of self.

Lara on the big screen is no longer a figure in which fans can anchor their own subjectivity, and she can not be controlled and/or manipulated as she is in the game. Interestingly, there is talk that Paramount may revive the franchise for a third film but without Jolie, choosing instead to go with an unknown for the lead—presumably an actress that filmgoers have no preconceived notions about. Someone who's a blank slate.

PLAYING WITH ACTION HEROINES

As with the sexy cyborgs and gynoids that predated the modern virtual babe, the fundamental issue is still the all-important male fantasy of control over women, something all the game critics mentioned in this discussion agree upon. Ward's argument is based on the notion that controlling Lara Croft is evidence of self-mastery. Maja Mikula stresses the pleasures available to male gamers through control: "For these male players, it is obvious that at least part of the pleasure of playing this game involved 'controlling' a female character as feisty and attractive as Lara" (2003: 81). Contemplating the transgendering possibilities of men "being" Lara, Kennedy ultimately surmises: "It seems much more likely that the pleasures of playing as Lara are more concerned with mastery and control of a body coded as female within a safe and un-threatening context" (2002: 7).

Polsky similarly argues that Lara and other female avatars created by, and for, men "are likely to be nothing more than an extension of a masculinist will to power, reflective of a desire to produce, control, and contain the other" (2001: 7). And Schleiner discusses the possibility that boys and men may be inspired to dispense with relations with real women altogether in favor of the "easily controlled virtual female bots" (2001: 223) found in games like *Tomb Raider*. This critical emphasis on the underlying male fantasy of controlling women is crucial for understanding how even the most active of strong women in the media are still hampered by a dominant and misogynistic desire to position women as mere objects for male pleasure and consumption.

By controlling female characters as "feisty" and threatening as Lara Croft and other action heroines, by negating their assumption of subjectivity, male consumers can still enjoy a heterosexual and discriminatory fantasy of gender relations. This does not mean that other and more progressive readings of active heroines do not exist. Female and queer pleasures of identification with strong ass-kicking women are an undeniable part of their appeal, as is cross-gender identification accepting of changing female roles and less sexist stereotypes.

But there is still a very real reason to be concerned with how aggressive female characters are marketed and interpreted by a majority of the audience. Even a casual consideration of how game girls and other action heroines are promoted reveals how producers of these characters encourage and bank on the appeal of their core sexual fantasy as objects to be controlled by men. The ironic "Play With Me" come on of Mori's photograph became the seductive offering of "Play me . . . ," for example, in gaming and men's magazine advertisements for the erotic computer game *Riana Rouge*, starring the fetish-garbed and gun-wielding likeness of Playboy Playmate Gillian Bonner. Other games such as Playstation's *Kinetica* have gone so far as to morph digital women into sexy motorcycles that players can control, and metaphorically "ride," with promotional lines like "G-string Meets G-force" and "Zero to Sixty in 36-24-36." Even the game for Xena: Warrior Princess, a character that Sherrie A. Inness (1999) describes as the most progressive heroine to date: "a far tougher image of womanhood than we would have seen on television even ten years ago" (180), was marketed with the challenge "Are You MAN Enough to Control the Princess Warrior?" and the immediate promise that "When You Experience *Xena: Warrior Princess*, You Are!"

Perhaps the most disturbing example of this prevailing persistent fantasy of controlling a threatening female character are the promotions announcing the release of the popular game based on the television series *Alias*. In the tamer of the two ads an image of Jennifer Garner, who plays Sydney Bristow in the show, is flanked by two digital versions of the character, one dressed in a metallic miniskirt with no side panels and a loose halter top, the other in tight black leggings and a matching tummy-baring shirt. The copy describes her simply as a "Stealth Bombshell," succinctly uniting both the character's sexuality and threat potential. The other ad features the series' signature image of Bristow in a red wig with the declaration: "Play It Now! *Alias*, Now YOU can take control of JENNIFER GARNER!" Direct and unsettling, this ad promises not only that you can control the character but that by doing so you can actually control Jennifer Garner. This linguistic slippage between the character and the sex symbol who portrays her clarifies the fantasy. As a quintessential action heroine she may be sexy, she may be tough, she may be strong, she may be able to kick ass, but both the character and the real woman are available for your pleasure and control.

In a very real sense this incredibly competent action heroine, now reconfigured as a digital babe with guns, is reduced to a purely controllable and consumable sex object. As Polsky described Ward's envisioning of Lara Croft as "the digital equivalent of a blow-up porno doll," and as sexy cyborgs were described earlier in this chapter in the same way, the marketing of the *Alias* game positions Bristow/Garner as available for whatever puerile fantasy male players may desire. The scenario is not really that far off from the one behind such successful interactive porn series such as "Virtual Sex With . . ." and "My Plaything," in which famous porn stars directly address viewers who control everything from camera angles, to sexual positions, to the woman's responses. The distance from "Play It Now!" to "Play With Me" to "Play Me" to "My Plaything" is not that far in the digital world. Unfortunately, however, the fantasy of playing with these women is very far from the empowering fantasy of "Be Superman."

The sexy cyborgs of science fiction and the virtual babes of contemporary games are just two ways modern action heroines are characterized in the media. Like all action heroines, these character types combine sexuality and violence—they are beautiful but deadly, clad in skimpy outfits but able to best legions of men. And, like other action heroines, the sexy cyborg and the virtual babe occupy a conflicted symbolic terrain in popular culture as they combine stereotypical features of both masculinity and femininity, subjectivity and objectification. What these two interrelated figures make clear is that male desires to control threatening women are an underlying principle of how action heroines are constructed and consumed. The Pygmalion-like fantasy of creating the perfect woman who can fulfill her creator's desires is brought into the twenty-first century. And where the fictional narratives about gynoids perpetuate fears about these powerful robotic women turning on their makers—a return of the repressed—the virtual game babes are created to be completely compliant. Only when the virtual characters are reenacted by real women is there any hint that they may resist objectification.

The idea of controlling the perfect woman expressed in cyborg fictions is realized in the world of gaming, and controlling characters like Lara Croft can even be transferred from her corporate creator to the individual players of the game. This fantasy of male control over strong but beautiful women that is raised with the sexy cyborg and realized with the game babe reveals an important facet of the appeal of action heroines in general. For all the dangers that she poses, the action heroine is also reassuringly under male control and is available to men as their imaginary plaything.

5) IF LOOKS COULD KILL

Power, Revenge, and Stripper Movies

*T*here is an ancient legend of the infamous "Dance of Desire" performed by Ishtar, the Sumerian goddess of love, sex, and war. As a reward for successful battles and generous patronage at her temples (where sacred cult prostitution was practiced), Ishtar would, on exceptionally great occasions, take human form as the most beautiful young woman in all the land. In this guise she would perform her dance of desire for a select audience of sacred kings and the most powerful warriors. Accompanied by music heretofore heard only by the gods, Ishtar would twirl and float with such grace that each man believed she was dancing only for him. The audience was entranced as she shed more and more of her outer garments until, finally, she danced naked before them, a wonder to behold. It was said Ishtar's dance was so mesmerizing that after seeing it no man would ever desire to see anything else. Indeed, it *was* the last thing they would ever witness since all the men were so overcome by passion and lust that they died a blissful death, each humbled at the feet of such pleasure.

It is perhaps no surprise that by 1993 the fabled Ishtar would appear in a literary award-winning graphic novel, Neil Gaiman's *The Sandman: Brief Lives* (1993), as a stripper. It was bound to happen sooner or later. The legend of Ishtar's dance of desire, loaded as it is with issues of erotic performance, scopophilia, fetishism, and ultimately death, is a perfect metaphor for the dynamics of modern striptease. Or rather, I should say it is the perfect metaphor for the dynamics of modern striptease as it is portrayed in contemporary films. From *The Blue Angel* (1930) to *Striptease* (1996) the filmic presentation of strippers has always been a particularly rich point for analyzing the role of the cinematic gaze in relation to gender and issues of power.

In this chapter I consider striptease as a symbolic act of gender and power negotiation played out as a very clear formula in a spate of recent stripper movies. Moreover, since the story of these films is very close to the rape-revenge formula suggested by such scholars as Carol Clover (1992) and Peter Lehman (1993b), I hope to show how the shift in the films' focus from horror to eroticism allows a different reading of gender and empowerment—a reading whereby the avenging women are not reduced to the symbolic position of proxies for the male viewers, as mere "men in drag." And finally I want to touch on the discrepancy between the negotiation of power on the screen and the problems of those negotiations in real life.

More than any other narrative subject, stripper movies—or, as the French have dubbed them, "le cinema du strip"—lay bare (no pun intended) the most traditional relationship of the sexes and perhaps the most discussed dynamic in cinema studies: men watch and do, women are watched and done to. Strippers, both on film and in real life, are a quintessential example of Mulvey's famous concept of feminine value as "to-be-looked-at-ness." "In their traditionally exhibitionist role," writes Mulvey, "women are simultaneously looked at and displayed, with their appearance coded for strong visual and erotic impact so that they can be said to connote *to-be-looked-at-ness*" (1975: 27).

Mulvey goes on to point out that "the woman displayed has functioned on two levels: as erotic object for the characters within the story, and as erotic object for the spectator within the auditorium, with a shifting tension between the looks on either side of the screen. For instance, the device of the showgirl [or even more obviously, the stripper] allows the two looks to be unified technically without any apparent break in the diegesis" (1975: 27). According to Mulvey, and the legions of critics who have subsequently built upon her groundbreaking work, women's role as the object of the cinematic gaze is tied into a complex range of patriarchal motivations and disempowering film conventions. What I am most interested in here, though, is the character of the stripper who is employed as the ultimate object of a sadistic male gaze but whose to-be-looked-at-ness is also used as a way to advance the plot at the same time it stops the narrative—and how these films confound the traditional logic of voyeurism both within the narrative and for the male viewer in the real audience. In other words, the power of the masculine gaze is renegotiated in stripper movies to reveal the underlying control exercised by the object of the gaze—the fetishistic sadism of the look is exposed as ultimately masochistic.

Though it is getting more than its fair share of screen time in modern cinema, this concept of true power residing with the object of the gaze, which is almost exclusively a woman, is not a new idea. It is at least as old as the legend of Ishtar's dance. It is an archetypal myth, a morality tale warning about the deadly consequences of being entranced by desire. Long before straight-to-video thrillers cornered the market on seductive killer babes, the deadly dancer was a staple of literature and legend. Lilith, Judith, Circe, the Sirens, the Fates, Medusa, Cleopatra, Delilah, Mata Hari, Lolita—the list is lengthy and constitutes a "who's who" of castration anxiety. Consider, for example, the likes of Oscar Wilde's play *Salome* (1893), based on the legend of King Herod's sexually alluring stepdaughter who so captivated him that he offered to give her anything she wanted if only she would dance for him. Salome performs a striptease, the dance of the seven veils, but in turn she demands the head of John the Baptist delivered to her on a platter. Though he loathes the task and knows it will prove his undoing, Herod delivers John's head unto Salome. Another classic example of the archetype is Victor Hugo's portrayal of Esmerelda, the gypsy dancing girl whose beauty throws an entire city into turmoil in *The Hunchback of Notre Dame* (1831). Hugo's famous description of Gringoire's first vision of Esmerelda is revealing:

> In a wide space left clear between the crowd and the fire, a young girl was dancing.
>
> But was it a young girl, or a fairy, or an angel? Gringoire, skeptical philosopher and ironical poet that he was, could not at first decide, so deeply was he fascinated by this dazzling vision.
>
> She was not tall, but her slender lightsomeness made her appear so. Her complexion was dark, but one guessed that by daylight it would have been the beautiful golden tint of Andalusian and Roman women. Her small feet, too, were Andalusian, for they seemed at once tight yet comfortable in her dainty shoes. She pirouetted on an old Persian carpet, spread carelessly under her feet. Each time she twirled, her radiant face and her large black eyes seemed to glow for you alone. In the circle all mouths were agape and all eyes staring.
>
> She danced to a Basque tambourine which she tinkled above her head, thus displaying her lovely arms. She wore a golden bodice tightly laced about her delicate body, exposing her beautiful shoulders. Below her wasp waist billowed a multicolored skirt, which, in the whirling dance, gave momentary glimpses of her finely shaped legs. With all this, and her black hair and sparkling eyes, she seemed like something more than human.
>
> "In truth," thought Gringoire, "it is a salamander—a nymph—a goddess—a bacchante of Mount Maenalus!"
>
> At that moment one of the braids of this "salamander's" hair loosened, and a thong of yellow leather that had bound it fell to the ground.
>
> "Oh no!" said he. "It's a gypsy!" All the illusion faded.

Hugo's description is doubly revealing because not only does it entail the mesmerization of the exotic dance that will drive men to fatal feats of passion, but it also demonstrates the falsity of the goddess illusion so willingly embraced by male viewers. All of these almost mythic themes—exoticism, seductive dances, worship, an underlying disappointment, and the male viewer's downfall or death—are given new life in contemporary stripper movies, and their reemergence facilitates a different understanding of gender and power in a contemporary context.

Strong female characters have gained tremendous ground in popular culture. Whether in Hollywood action films like *Aliens* (1986) and *Terminator 2: Judgment Day* (1991), or foreign films such as France's *La Femme Nikita* (1991), India's *Pratighat/Retribution* (1988), or Hong Kong's numerous films like *The Heroic Trio* (1992) and *Robotrix* (1993). On television *Xena: Warrior Princess* was the highest-rated program during its run. Likewise, the MTV cartoon *Aeon Flux*, about a futuristic female mercenary with dominatrix leanings, has developed a huge cult following, as has *Tomb Raider*, a computer game starring a scantily clad female Indiana Jones-type. As a sub-set of this strong women theme, the stripper movies I will discuss here fall into the category of avenging women. And, like the rape-revenge films discussed by Clover and Lehman, the stripper movies are almost exclusively the domain of the lower genres, namely straight-to-video thrillers and pornography. Even the big-budget versions *Striptease* and *Showgirls* (1995) seem like nothing more than expensive—and laughable—versions of their top shelf predecessors including *Stripteaser* (1995), *Stripped to Kill* (1987) and *Stripped to Kill II* (1989), *Midnight Tease* (1994) and *Midnight Tease II* (1995), *Dance With Death* (1993), *Sunset Strip* (1993), *Angel of Destruction* (1993), *Lapdancer* (1996), *Lap Dancing* (1995), *Cover Me* (1996), *Blonde Justice* (1994) and *Blonde Justice II* (1995).

The plots of these stripper movies are very similar to the rape-revenge films, but with a few significant changes. In the most formulaic of the rape-revenge films—e.g., *I Spit on Your Grave* (1977), *Ms. 45* (1981), *Eyes of a Stranger* (1981)—the plot, at its most basic level, is that a harmless and innocent young woman is repeatedly harassed and then violently raped by one or more men, the system fails to do anything about the attack, and so she is forced to take matters into her own hands and kill the man, or men, usually in a very dramatic and poetic fashion. The stripper movie plots are generally some variation of this: a wholesome stripper (we know she is wholesome because she refuses to do drugs or turn tricks) is stalked by an unknown psycho/fan who has become obsessed with her, or the strippers from a particular club are being killed off one by one. The male authorities ignore the stripper's pleas for help because they think she must be a slut who willingly invites sexual predators—the exception is the disgruntled female cop (or journalist, or private detective, or a dead stripper's sister) who joins forces with the stripper(s) and/or goes undercover as a stripper thus becoming a victim herself until she, or they, manage to kill the psycho by film's end. This is not to say that all stripper movies follow this story line of *dance, be stalked, kill stalker*—they are a sub-set of films with strippers as their central focus. Other notable films like *Gypsy* (1962), *Portrait of a Stripper* (1979), *The Stripper* (1963), and *The Blue Angel*, deal with strippers in a different manner, though many of the themes of obsession and disrespect are consistent.

In her analysis of gender and horror movies, Carol Clover details the complex machinations of gender performance and audience identification across a wide range of sub-genres including rape-revenge films. A key element in Clover's argument is her reading of female heroines as symbolic proxies for the male viewer. The heroine, or the "Final Girl" as Clover calls her, is symbolically positioned as androgynous—she always has a boy's name, she abstains from any sexual activity, etc.—and through her actions—demonstrating mental and physical self-reliance, killing the rapist(s)—she enacts masculinity, which enables male viewers to identify with her originally disempowered position and to enjoy her revenge. As Clover puts it:

> [T]he willingness of the slasher film to re-represent the traditionally male hero as an anatomical female suggests that at least one traditionally heroic act, triumphant self-rescue, is no longer strictly gendered masculine. The rape-revenge film is a similar case, only more so; it is not just triumphant self-rescue in the final moments of the film that the woman achieves, but calculated, lengthy, and violent revenge of a sort that would do Rambo proud. (Paradoxically, it is the experience of being brutally raped that makes a "man" of a woman.) What I am suggesting, once again, is that rape-revenge films too operate on the basis of a one-sex body, the maleness or femaleness of which is performatively determined by the social gendering of the acts it undergoes or undertakes. (Clover 1992: 159)

Likewise, Peter Lehman's discussion of rape-revenge films claims that, on at least one symbolic level, the sub-genre clearly "suggests that these avenging women are really men" (1993b: 111). While both Clover's and Lehman's arguments are much more complex than I have space to go into here, the point I would question is the suggestion that because women defeat the villain on their own they somehow represent men in drag. For a more detailed Freudian criticism of this point see Creed, who writes "because the heroine is represented as resourceful, intelligent and dangerous it does not follow that she should be seen as a pseudo man" (1993: 127). In fact, in the case of stripper revenge, which is very similar to slasher and rape-revenge, the undeniability of the central character's femaleness is absolutely essential to the story. When the strippers who are so clearly marked as women and as sexual spectacles take up arms against their assailants they are not enacting masculinity, indeed the accumulated emphasis on their being women denies the possibility of reading them as men. What they are doing is exercising power over the men, both physical and visual/sexual power, in a manner that at least semiotically validates the possibility of female on-screen heroics.

The central storyline of stripper revenge films is almost exactly the same as that found in the rape-revenge narratives Clover and Lehman analyze. The woman is terrorized by a misogynistic male psychotic and when no one else is able or willing to help her she must take matters into her own hands with a "triumphant self-rescue in the final moments of the film." The distinguishing feature between the two formulas is the increased emphasis on the protagonist of the stripper revenge film as an explicitly erotic spectacle.

This crucial shift in occupation draws attention to the limitations of the "men-in-drag" thesis that has been so liberally applied to resourceful and independent female characters in recent years. To describe tough female characters as performing masculinity to the point of becoming "men-in-drag" undercuts the stereotype-shattering potential of these figures. By casting the heroine as a stripper the films can fully exploit the naked display of the female body and to code it as desirable perfection—as quintessentially womanly. Specifically, I am concerned with the discrepancy between the gender semantics of the theory and what the audiences may see and understand of the narrative as it is intended.

As the above quotation from Clover mentions, the symbolic transvestism of strong female characters operates on the basis of a one-sex body. The problem is that the one-sex body is a historical concept Clover borrows from Lacquer that is completely at odds with the physical presentation of these heroines and the perceptions of modern audiences. Representationally, the masculinization of the modern heroine may make more sense with action heroines like Sarah Connor in *Terminator 2* and Ripley in the *Alien* series who embody masculinity through their muscular appearance.

But the stripper revenge films empower a completely different type of female body. The protagonist's body in these films is first and foremost curvaceous and sexualized. While still hardbodies, they are muscular not in the bulging biceps and rippling veins manner of the bodybuilder, but rather in the perfectly toned and proportioned manner of the aerobics queen—usually with breast implants thrown in to further emphasize the sexual nature of the body. The sexualized body of the stripper heroine that is always abundantly shown naked and dancing (or in the case of the *Blonde Justice* films, actually having sex) is meant to be understood by audiences, and in fact is, as ideally female despite whatever strong actions she may take to protect herself from harm. In the stripper revenge films (and most other films with strong female leads) the heroine's body is so heavily coded as feminine that it overrides the masculine connotations of "triumphant self-rescue." In other words, rather than being masculinized by performing traits such as self-reliance and toughness, these films—as exploitive as they are—argue that such traits are accessible to "heroes" of either gender.

Like the rape-revenge genre, stripper films are most closely identified with low-budget straight-to-video thrillers, but they have on occasion appeared in every form from mega-budget Hollywood productions to XXX-rated pornographic videos. The rape-revenge formula has been played out in mainstream movies such as Clint Eastwood's *Sudden Impact* (1983) and, in its own way, the Academy Award–winning *The Accused* (1988), through its many B-movie incarnations, and even as hard-core pornography with the likes of *Naked Vengeance* (1985). Likewise, stripper movies have ranged from the failed mainstream film *Striptease* (for which Demi Moore received the highest salary ever paid to an actress: twelve million dollars—or six million a breast, as many critics joked) through the many straight-to-video versions, to pornographic videos like the *Blonde Justice* series. Because the films are generally the domain of the low-budget thriller their story is more direct, and often more inventive and revealing than pseudo-serious movies. The stripper revenge movies cut directly to the core and deal specifically with gender issues in a rather blatant way. As with most cinematic genres that transcend their original niche, the core of the formulaic story remains consistent.

Dance With Death is typical of the straight-to-video stripper movie. Strippers at "The Bottom Line" club in Los Angeles are being gruesomely murdered one by one. No one really seems to care—not the police, the club's owner, or the press. No one, that is, except for Kelly Crosby, an aspiring investigative journalist who has to convince her sexist boss to let her report on the story. Kelly goes undercover as a stripper and quickly meets the usual cast of characters and suspects: Art, the sleazy club owner; J.D., the horny M.C. who constantly tries to date the dancers; Henry, the nerdy knife-wielder who always sits in "perverts' row" but never tips; Jodie, the tough-as-nails lesbian dancer; and a variety of friendly stripper cohorts. Along the way Kelly also meets undercover detective Matt Shaugnessy, the rogue cop who actually shows an interest in the case.

More strippers are killed as Kelly and Matt review the long list of suspects, which, it turns out, includes Kelly's boss who had been dating one of the first women murdered. As Kelly immerses herself further into the stripper lifestyle she and Matt develop feelings for each other. Matt shoots Henry the pervert, while trying to arrest him and then insists that Kelly give up stripping even though she still suspects her boss. Matt then shoots her boss, but as he comforts Kelly she notices the stone for Matt's ring is missing—the same stone she found in the palm of Jodie's dead hand a few scenes earlier.

"You're just a whore like all the rest!" yells Matt when he realizes he's been found out. He chases a terrified Kelly to a nearby warehouse when she finally decides to fight back. And fight back she does—she trips him with a telephone line, pummels him with a two-by-four, stabs him with his own knife, breaks his jaw with a lead pipe, and ultimately douses him in gasoline and sets him on fire.

No one said these movies were subtle.

Although *Striptease*, based on the best-selling book by Carl Hiaasen, was a major Hollywood production, its central narrative themes are direct descendants of the film's straight-to-video predecessors. Toned down for mainstream audiences, *Striptease* is the story of Erin Grant who is forced to take work as a dancer at "The Eager Beaver" club to raise money for her upcoming custody battle with her deadbeat ex-husband. She quickly becomes the club's star attraction and develops a loyal following. In fact, Erin so captivates the men that when an overly aroused patron jumps on stage to hug her, a U.S. congressman, David Dilbeck, rushes to her rescue by breaking a champagne bottle over the guy's head.

In an interesting twist, *Striptease* exchanges the usual psycho for the loony congressman who subsequently becomes so obsessed with Erin—he instructs an aide to steal lint from her dryer to have sex with—he threatens Erin's attempts to regain custody of her daughter, and orchestrates the murder of her most devoted fan. A lone cop and a mentally unbalanced bouncer are Erin's only allies against the congressman and her abusive ex-husband, Daryl, who begins to stalk her. Frustrated by the lack of respect her case gets because she is "just a stripper," Erin takes matters into her own hands by kidnapping her daughter and manipulating the congressman, first at gunpoint and then through seduction, to confess all his crimes while she tape-records them. *Striptease* bombed at the box office, but has performed remarkably well in home video, suggesting that that venue is where these narratives are meant to reside.

One film definitely meant for home consumption is the "Adult Couples" video, *Blonde Justice*. Despite being a pornographic movie *Blonde Justice* (and *Blonde Justice 2*, which is really a *part two* rather than a sequel) incorporates a great deal of plot compared to other hard-core movies. In fact, I agree with

Linda Williams' (1989) excellent analytical history of pornographic film that to dismiss them as nothing more than flimsy narratives designed to link sex scenes together is to miss much of the complex meanings and pleasures on offer in pornography.

In *Blonde Justice*, Dominique, the feature dancer at an upscale strip club, is being terrorized by what she assumes is a crazed fan who sends her threatening letters. On the advice of Cora, Dominique's dancing partner and only friend at the club, she calls the police wanting protection; unfortunately she's told to call back after she's *really* been attacked, and is laughed off as just another whore looking for attention. Fortunately for Dominique, a female cop named Karen McClousky, who is in her supervisor's office complaining about his ordering her to wear a miniskirt to serve drinks to police V.I.P.s, overhears the call and volunteers her protection services. Despite Dominique's initial hesitation—she was looking for "a big strong cop"—she agrees to Karen's offer after she roughs up an obnoxious fan and chases the stalker through a back alley.

Between sex scenes—including one with Dominique and Karen that culminates in Karen giving the dancer a gun of her own,—several men and women are considered as suspects and then quickly eliminated. In the end it turns out the psycho is Giles, Cora's boyfriend who is both jealous of Cora's physical relationship with Dominique and who wants Cora to replace Dominique as the real star attraction. Ironically, in the last scene Giles shoots what he thinks is Dominique, but it turns out to be Cora in a blonde wig and a borrowed dress. Dominique discovers Giles over the body and just before he can kill her too, Karen bursts into the room and arrests him. *Blonde Justice* was apparently successful enough to spawn two more sequels, neither one of which had anything to do with stalked strippers or avenging women.

Like Ishtar, Salome and Esmerelda before them, the female protagonists of these stripper movies are beautiful women fetishized to an extreme, both for the male audience within the film's diegesis and for the target male audience of movie-goers/video renters. The interesting thing about the narrative pattern is that the fetishization of these women is so obviously and directly linked to the punishment of the male voyeur and the vindication of the female object. The fetishization of women in the cinema is not new, it is at the core of their "to-be-looked-at-ness," and that this fetishization is carried to extremes in stripper movies is hardly surprising.

The catalyst for the entire plot is men's obsessive looking at women on display. It is, at least on the surface, the traditional power relationship between the sexes cut to its most basic elements, but rather than portraying the voyeur as the bearer of power, the one in control, he is shown as pathetic. After just one look at Erin in *Striptease*, Congressman Dilbeck declares she is ". . . an angel. An angel of pure delight!" Others, like the drooling males in *Dance With Death*, *Blonde Justice*, *Stripped to Kill*, and *Midnight Tease II*, are shown as slack-jawed idiots who either lose all control or simply stare in awe at the dancers. Though this reversal of cinema studies' conventional wisdom about exactly who bears the power in relations of men looking at women is a staple of stripper movies, we can see clear examples of it emerging in more mainstream films.

The notorious interrogation scene in *Basic Instinct* (1992), the film that made Sharon Stone a star, is a prime example. When Catherine Tramell is brought in for questioning by the police she is supposed to be the one on the hot seat as a team of male detectives grill her. Instead Catherine remains calm and collected while the men are reduced to sweaty, blabbering fools after she briefly uncrosses her legs and they get a glimpse of her pantyless crotch. More directly, Von Sternberg's *The Blue Angel* was the epitome and inspiration for this motif of the male's ruinous obsession with a showgirl. In this classic film, Lola Frohlich's (Marlene Dietrich) erotic performance so captivates a morally and socially upstanding professor, Immanuel Rath (Emil Jannings), that he marries her and turns into such an obsessed fool that by the end of the film he is literally left a clown and a laughing stock.

The Blue Angel also set the standard for accentuating the props used in erotic performance to heighten the fetishization of the woman as an object of the look. In her top hat and lingerie, exposed garter belts and black stockings, cane, and seductive performance, Dietrich as Lola personifies the fetishized woman. In fact, Gaylyn Studlar (1988) has documented this relationship between Von Sternberg, Dietrich, and the aesthetic elements of their films as revealing a masochistic impulse of overwhelming proportions. The props of striptease are common fetishes made explicitly obvious through their inclusion in the erotic performance. They are the "furs, the fans, the gloves, the feathers, the fishnet stockings" that Roland Barthes described as costumes designed to reveal "nakedness as a *natural* vesture of woman" (Barthes 1957: 92).

The explicit erotic performance of striptease personifies Mulvey's description of the fetishistic pleasure of the male gaze. Mulvey's supposition is firmly grounded in Freudian theory that posits that the erotic display of women is influenced by the male viewer's horrific boyhood discovery of his mother's lack of a penis. Seeking to disavow that lack, that difference, the boy/man projects onto the erotic image symbolic replacements for the missing penis. Thus a high heel shoe, or a leather bustier, or any other fetish, comes to represent a symbolic phallic adornment. With striptease the dance is a ritualized spectacle performed for male scopophilic interests whereby the ultimate revelation both exposes what is not there—evidencing the absence of a penis—and eroticizes the female body itself as a phallic substitute. The plethora of fetish objects that accompany striptease as phallic compensation—and the ultimate fetishization of the female body—is an almost hysterically extreme example of the general principles of female representation in contemporary film.

What is interesting about the dynamics of fetishization in the cinematic sense is that it is supposed to function as a nullifier of the threat of castration supposedly posed by the female body. As Mulvey put it: "Woman as representation signifies castration, inducing voyeuristic or fetishistic mechanisms to circumvent her threat" (1975: 25). However, the complex processes of fetishization in stripper movies do not nullify castration anxiety but instead enhance it. Ignoring, for the moment, the overall narrative structure of the films we should consider the symbolically loaded image of women with guns on offer in these films.

The previous chapter addressed the semiotic importance of guns as phallic symbols when employed by women in contemporary action movies. There I was concerned with the characters' use of guns as an ingredient of gender performance, in other words, as a semiotic device used in films like *Aliens* and *Terminator 2* to align the female leads with a clearly masculinized subject position. I argued there, as I do here, that to read these characters as merely "men in drag" because they appropriate certain props and behaviors traditionally associated with masculinity is too simplistic and rigid an interpretation of gender norms. The image of women with guns in stripper movies operates within a different symbolic system. While the figure of a muscular Linda Hamilton with an oversized gun in *Terminator 2* enhanced her position as a "masculinized" hero, the combination of guns and strippers, who are clearly marked as sexual spectacles, does more to eroticize the gun than to masculinize the woman.

This image of eroticized wielding of weapons is a rather loaded semiotic device. The symbolic use of guns in stripper movies encapsulates the male viewer's conflicted perception of the fetish in a much more direct manner than do horror or action movies, or any other narrative that emphasizes avenging women. In this case the fetish, the phallic woman, is clearly revealed as a fantasy that is both desired and feared. The imagery exposes this complex relationship through its often very rudimentary symbolism.

The video box cover for *Dance With Death* (Figure 5.1), for example, is a clear illustration of phallic symbolism. It depicts a beautiful, busty blonde clad in a skimpy red bikini embracing a gun larger than she is. The model's expression is one of pure pleasure as she caresses the barrel of the massive pistol, the implications obvious. The woman (who is not an actress in the film)

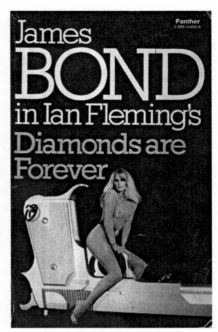

5.1. *Dance with Death* video box cover.   5.2. *Diamonds Are Forever* paperback cover.

is displayed in the throes of phallic worship, reduced to a stock caricature of pornography: the all-accepting woman desperately wanting the (viewer's) phallus. The image is reminiscent of the famous series of paperback covers used in the 1970s for Ian Fleming's James Bond novels wherein each book featured a glamorous woman riding or lounging on a larger-than-life revolver (Figure 5.2).

In their analysis of James Bond as a cultural icon Bennett and Woollacott (1987) point out: "In depicting one or more exotically but scantily clad women placed astride a large golden gun, the covers of this period clearly cue, as the central concern of the novels, the subordination of women to the regime of the phallus" (59). I believe the same can obviously be said for the cover image of *Dance With Death*, as it clearly symbolizes the male fantasy of women subordinated to the regime of the phallus. But unlike the James Bond stories that feature a hero who literally embodies masculinity and phallic power, stripper movies—including *Dance With Death*—ultimately deliver conflicting messages of women *not* subordinated by the phallus.

While the poster iconography may depict the eroticized woman as subordinated to the phallus, the film narratives deal with the woman's gradual

mastery of (phallic) power. They are not disempowered as the object of a fetishizing male gaze, nor are they passive damsels in distress; these women exert
power over males first through their control of the men's looks and secondly
through their ultimate victory over those who seek to terrorize them. It comes
as no surprise that when these women defeat the villains in the final scene they
usually do so at gunpoint or with another phallic substitute such as a spear,
knife, or two-by-four.

So while at one level these films cater to male voyeurism in their excessive
striptease scenes, they also reveal the darker implications of male scopophilia,
namely they enact the threat of castration anxiety that necessitates their being
fetishized in the first place. In other words, these films accentuate the desire
and fear embodied in the voyeur's gaze of the female body. Jon Stratton's description of the dual implications of scopophilia is useful for our understanding of the dynamics at work in the stripper movies:

> [The] fetishistic phallicisation of the female body has a dual effect on men's
> relations with women. The fetishistic context makes women both more sexually
> desired—their bodies appearing to acquire a heightened desirableness—and
> more feared—whilst simultaneously their bodies become the site of a fetishistic
> terror which complements, but is quite different in origin from, the fear of cas-
> tration provoked by the recognition of women's 'lack' of a penis. The cultural
> overdetermination of cultural fetishism means that women may be constructed
> in two ideal-typical ways by men. First, and dominant, is the spectacle of the
> 'passive', phallicised woman, the woman who appears compliantly to express,
> for men, the spectacle of the phallicised body. Second, there is the spectacle
> of the 'active', phallic woman who, from a male perspective, reworks the phallic
> power attributed to her into a spectacle which men experience as threatening to
> their own, already lacking, feeling of phallic power. (Stratton 2001: 144)

Stripper movie heroines transcend the two ideal ways fetishism constructs
women for men. They appear to be the "passive" phallicized woman who
exists merely for the viewing pleasure of the male audience, but they are also
the "active" phallic woman who threatens, and in fact conquers, male phallic
power.

The most interesting twist about stripper movies is that the main female
characters are a device for combining the two fetishized ideals of women—
passive and active—thus revealing how the apparent passivity is also the source
of activity, the source, and the threat of power male fantasy plays into. These
are obviously fetishized women and, by extension, are also phallic women, but
unlike other genres that highlight avenging women, stripper movies ascribe

the women's true power as the very quality that at first glance seems to disempower them. In other words, their seductive desirability is the real weapon, the phallic symbolism of the guns is just an external marker of the "activity" that can result from their inherent power. The real threat to male observers is not that these women take on the qualities of masculinity in defense of themselves and as a result of their objectification, it is the castrating power they wield as seductive objects.

A fitting metaphor for this form of desirability as a castrating threat is most clearly expressed in the sub-genre of vampire stripper movies. Though most of them are B-Movies, or pretend to be, films such as *Vamp* (1986), *Dance of the Damned* (1988), *From Dusk till Dawn* (1995), *Bordello of Blood* (1996), *Night Shade* (1996), and *Club Vampire* (1997) all feature vampires who perform as strippers in order to seduce their prey. It's hard to think of a more apt metaphor for the threat of castrating power strippers pose than that of vampirism. The female vamps literally suck the energy and the life out of their enraptured, willing male victims—victims who initially thought they were in control because they were the bearers of the look.

The duality of these phallic women as fetishized objects representing both activity and passivity is played out on another level in the villain's dual perception of the strippers. Harkening back to the age-old stereotypes that position women as either saints or sinners, as virgins or sluts, the male psycho's motivation usually lies in what he sees as a disappointment. In *The Hunchback of Notre Dame* the illusion fades for Gringoire when he discovers Esmerelda is a gypsy, whereas in contemporary films the image is destroyed when the obsessed man discovers the stripper is not a chaste angel dancing only for him. In *Striptease* Congressman Dilbeck describes Erin as "an angel of pure delight, she's so pure and clean . . . not like the rest of these whores." Likewise, in *Dance With Death*, when Matt turns on Kelly he declares: "I thought you were special, but you're just a whore like all the others." Within the diegesis of the film the obsessive male voyeur initially perceives the woman as the ultimate passive object of desire. It is only when he discovers that the dancer is also an active phallic woman, particularly when she is sexually active with someone other than the psycho, that the dissonance drives the man to murderous actions. It is the discrepancy between the fantasy of the woman as passive, as saint, as accepting of only the viewer, and the reality of the woman's power and autonomy over her own sexuality that forms the crux of motivation for these stories.

The morality tale played out within these stripper movies is really quite simple. On the one hand it is a tale of castration anxiety that warns about the

dangers of giving oneself fully to the seductive illusion of the beautiful dancers; on the other hand it is a tale of powerful avenging women and a lesson in
female subjectivity. Within the films it is clear what the male voyeur's source
of pleasure is and how that relates to his ultimate downfall. Time and again,
the male character who idolizes the erotic spectacle of the stripper to the point
of obsession is driven to criminal and psychotic behavior when he realizes she
is not the perfect, all-accepting female of his fantasies.

What these films usually try to stress is that the strippers are merely enacting a stage persona of pornographic fantasy. This convention of trying to
show that female strippers are "not just sex objects" may seem tenuous, but it
is typical of Hollywood's attempts to market exploitation as empowerment. In
essence, these films repeatedly offer a voyeuristic fantasy and then condemn
the fictional voyeur. What is less clear is the complex layers of pleasure these
movies offer to external male viewers, either in the theater or in front of the
DVD player. The stripper revenge movies do not operate for male viewers in
the way Mulvey and others have described mainstream films as working to
nullify the threat posed by phallic women. The woman is not clearly brought
back under the patriarchal system by the end of the film, rather her actions
reveal the uselessness and the dangerous sexism inherent in the system.

Nor do these films conform to the "guys in drag" thesis at the root of
the theories about the popularity of rape-revenge films for male viewers. Lest
there be any misunderstanding, I agree with much of Clover and Lehman's
readings of rape-revenge films, but the complex gender performances in those
movies that facilitate the Final Girls as masculinized proxies for male viewers are not found in the stripper revenge movies. The strippers never enact
masculinity—they may appropriate such phallic symbols as guns and knives,
they may behave in an active, traditionally "masculine" manner defending
themselves and killing the villains without male help—but their female sexuality is foregrounded to such an extent that it is near impossible to confuse
these women with "men in drag." Moreover, their undeniably female identity
is necessary for the story to work. If they are not firmly established as desirable
women then all plot motivation is lost, as are the very pleasures of looking
that appeal to both the men within the film and those without. What, then,
is at the root of these films' popularity with male audiences?

The most obvious answer is laughably simple: "Naked babes, dude! Lots of
naked babes!" And I do not want to make the mistake of denying that the primary appeal of these films, for heterosexual men anyway, is that they provide
a form of masturbatory pleasure. The million-dollar advertising campaigns
for *Striptease* and *Showgirls* certainly pandered to male libidos as the primary
audience for the films. Nor is it surprising that both these films enjoyed more

success as video rentals than their original theatrical run. It is no coincidence that, like hardcore pornography, these erotic thrillers cater to solitary home viewing. It would be ridiculous to underestimate the lure for heterosexual men of seeing Demi Moore (*Striptease*) or Salma Hayek (*From Dusk till Dawn*) naked.

Though I have generally stressed the narrative plot of the films so far, it is important to remember that these films do present a great deal of eroticized female nudity. I would not want to skip over this undeniable fact for the sake of a purely theoretical analysis. Perhaps many men do use these films strictly as masturbatory aids, focusing only on the moments of erotic display and otherwise ignoring the plot and the ultimate punishment that the story consistently visits upon the voyeur—but even if this were the case it does not account for the repetitive nature of the formula. Why would the films always disparage the characters who most closely resemble the viewers?

Even with the *Blonde Justice* films, which are hard-core pornography, there are clues that the pleasures available to men are more complex than the simple equation of voyeurism equals pleasure. As the promotional copy for *Blonde Justice* quoted before makes explicit, what the viewer takes into his own hands when watching the film is up to him—the promise is that the film will be so arousing that the viewer will not be able to resist masturbation. But as pornography, *Blonde Justice* is unusual. Susan Bordo has argued that the traditional critic's perception of porn as the ultimate "objectification of women" is not entirely accurate. Rather, Bordo argues, a certain female subjectivity is necessary for the fantasy, a subjectivity that allows the illusion that the women will be totally open to sex with the male viewer but in such a way that their voracious appetite for sex will always validate the male in ways that real women do not. Bordo surmises, quite correctly I think, that:

What is desired, and what much heterosexual pornography provides, is a world in which women are indeed in a state of continual readiness and desire for sex, but one in which female desire is incapable of "emasculating" the male by judging or rejecting him, by overwhelming him, or by expecting something from him that he cannot (or fears he cannot) provide. What is desired is a sexual encounter that does not put manhood at risk in any way—neither through female indifference to the male (leaving *him* feeling sexually "too much," exposed, ashamed) nor through "too much" independent, unpredictable desire, will, or need on the woman's part (eliciting anxieties that he will be unable to satisfy *her*). In pornography women are indeed voracious, yet at the same time completely satisfied by anything the male has to give and non-needful of that which he cannot give. (Bordo 1993: 707–8)

Yet, in *Blonde Justice*, the female lead does not conform to this basic acceptance of the male that would seem to be at the root of the male viewer's
pleasure. In fact, Dominique, the central character, is extremely active sexually, but only with other women. She rejects all male advances and makes no
effort to hide her belief that all males are idiots. In one telling scene near the
beginning of the first installment of the series, Giles (who turns out to be the
stalker) walks in on his girlfriend Cora having sex with Dominique in their
dressing room. Giles asks if he can come in but Dominique snaps at him:
"Fuck, no! Can't you see we're busy? Now get the hell out of here!" Hardly
the response of a character "incapable of emasculating" the male. The fact
that this scene runs directly parallel with the action in another dressing room
where two strippers have been joined by the male manager only emphasizes
that the typical pornographic response would have been to happily invite the
male in for a menage-a-trois.

On another level, this uncharacteristic rejection of the male in *Blonde Justice* is compounded for the viewer if he realizes the actress playing Dominique
is Janine Lindemulder—and it is likely this may be the case as she is currently the most popular starlet in the industry—who has a legendary "no
guys" clause in her contract (see Hudis 1997). Thus, both within the film and
perhaps through viewers' extratextual knowledge about the star, there is a
distinct variation on the supposition that the pornographic pleasure on offer
is an all-accepting one. And if the direct, privileged, voyeuristic pleasure can
be rendered problematic in a hard-core video, then what would seem to be
the most obvious pleasures of the less-explicit stripper movies might also be
more complex. Rather than the all-accepting sex object, these rejecting and
emasculating strippers have something of the dominatrix about them—this is
made clear in the cover art for *Blonde Justice 2* (Figure 5.3).

Although Dominique (you can be certain this name was not chosen at
random) never appears as a dominatrix in the film, the poster shows Janine
in leather lingerie and stiletto heels and seductively grasping a whip. Here
the shift away from the mixed symbolism that implied the strippers were
both passive and active phallic women is complete—there is no doubting
the nature of the erotic pleasure derived from looking at these women. It is a
pleasure that gives up power; in other words, part of the pleasure of the gaze
manifested in these narratives is masochistic rather than sadistic.

In suggesting that for male viewers much of the pleasure derived from
this particular form of phallic woman is, in a sense, masochistic, I agree with
Gaylyn Studlar's argument that masochism may be as much at the root of
the cinematic gaze as sadism is. Criticizing feminist film theory of the 1970s
and 1980s for subscribing too narrowly to the idea that images of women are

5.3. *Blonde Justice 2* movie poster.

always subjected to a sadistic, controlling masculine gaze, Studlar pointed out that the "theory of masochistic desire challenges the notion that male scopic pleasure must center around control—never identification with or submission to the female" (1985: 778). Moreover, Studlar argued that because of their political agenda theories of the sadistic gaze fall short of their logical conclusion that "would necessitate pairing masochism, the passive submission to the object, with fetishistic scopophilia" (783). Or as Rodowick (1982) put it before Studlar: "Mulvey cannot admit that the masculine look contains passive elements and can signify *submission to* rather than *possession of* the female" (7–9).

As avenging women these stripper movies align, narratively and symbolically, with masochistic impulses and in doing so they make explicit the association between the illusion of "possession of" and the fantasy of "submission to." Just as the character of the stripper transcends the positions of both passive and active phallic woman, so the visual pleasures available to male viewers transcend both looking at and submitting to. Where the voyeur within the diegesis of the film is driven to murderous impulses when his sadistic fantasy of possessing the ideal woman is frustrated, the voyeur in the theater or the living room is safely afforded the same fantasy of possession *and* the subsequent masochism of submission.

Another possibility for the popularity of these films, one that is not premised as directly on psychoanalysis, is that the narrative structure allows the male viewer to have his cake and eat it too. That is to say, he can look at the women as sexual spectacles but can also distance himself from the "bad" viewer within the film. The men in the films are always characterized as sleazy and obnoxious, or nerdy and perverted. Their point of view may be a necessary excuse to display often gratuitous portions of female flesh but their obsession with the display is characterized as so unwholesome that male viewers can look down upon the men in the film.

This device runs parallel to what Lehman describes in rape-revenge films where the "sexual desire these men have for the women must, in other words, be made to seem as far removed as possible from the male viewer's similar desire for her" (1993b: 112). The films' nods to feminism may be merely tokenism—for example, when Dominique tells Karen, "I don't get a chance to meet many strong women like you" in the middle of a pornographic video it feels rather dubious—but in this era of political correctness, pretensions of being more liberated viewers may be just the saving grace needed for male audience members. In fact, it is amazing how many straight-to-video erotic thrillers openly take voyeurism as their subject matter.

In addition to strippers, these videos have an inordinate number of models, photographers, filmmakers, and private eyes as main characters who spend their time either observing beautiful women or being beautiful women under observation. This apparent preoccupation with the morality and the dangers associated with looking in low-budget films is perhaps an interesting way in which this genre thinks out loud about itself, and it deserves more attention than I can afford it here. Within stripper movies, as with erotic thrillers in general, male viewers can scorn the leering psychotics at the same time that they themselves are caught looking, and align themselves through the narrative conventions with the female protagonist.

The narrative message of stripper movies is clear, at least in a self-serving, superficial post-feminist sort of way: ultimately the women exercise power over the men who look at them. But while this may be a common scenario, its relevance to real life seems suspect at best. These films, like all films, operate in the realm of the symbolic rather than the realistic.

I do not want to be misunderstood here—I am *not* anti-pornography, I am not against women exploiting their sexual power over men for economic or more personal reasons. I do believe women are capable of producing and enjoying their own meanings and pleasures in a multitude of ways that conform, challenge, and subvert societal norms. What I *do* stress is that the reality of gender and economic politics for women who work in striptease is more complex and problematic than it is on the screen. The films encapsulate systemic misogyny within a few symbolic male characters who are ridiculed as ineffective lechers or portrayed as violent psychopaths eventually killed off by the heroines—a message that is perhaps as comforting to male viewers as it is to female ones. If only it were that simple in real life.

"The feminist line is, strippers are victims," Camille Paglia told *Penthouse* magazine, who obviously has a vested interest in promoting extreme postfeminist views. "But women are far from that," Paglia continues. "Women *rule*: they are in total control . . . men in strip clubs are completely cowed" (Wells 1994: 57). I do not disagree with Paglia. I have been in strip clubs—men are, for the most part, scared of the women and their open display of sexuality. The women are in control of their interaction with customers, many of whom are so frightened they don't even know where to look. But I would not go so far as to say this means women rule.

The immediate interaction may grant all the symbolic power to the individual dancer, but this interesting revisioning of gender and power relations vis-a-vis the dynamics of looking should not blind us to the underlying system of control, the realm where real power is held, and usually held by men. For example, at approximately the same time Camille Paglia made her comments, reinforced by a range of stripper movies and pseudo-journalistic/autobiographical books like *Ivy League Stripper* and *Nine Lives* that proudly describe strippers as powerful women in complete control of their working world, Toronto was embroiled in a dispute between judges and strip club owners on one side and dancers on the other.

The ongoing dispute began in Toronto on February 10, 1994, when an Ontario Provincial Court judge ruled the managers of an uptown club, Cheaters Tavern, were not breaking any laws by offering lap dancing in their establishment. The judge claimed that due to changes in laws concerned with pornography, lap dancing now fell within contemporary community standards of tolerance, which is the constitutional measure of obscenity and indecency. In his judgment he outlined the following dancer behaviors as innocuous if performed by a woman of legal age and with a valid, government-issued striptease license: a) being nude except for wearing an open shirt or blouse; b) fondling her own breasts, buttock, thighs, and genitals while close to the customer; c) sitting on a customer's lap and grinding her bare buttocks into his lap; d) sitting on a customer's lap, reaching into his crotch, and apparently masturbating the customer; e) permitting the customer to touch and fondle her breasts, buttocks, thighs, and genitals; f) permitting the customer to kiss, lick, and suck their breasts; g) permitting what appeared to be cunnilingus.

Within days Toronto "gained the dubious distinction of becoming the lap-dancing capital of North America" (Chidley 1995: 35). The ruling also made for interesting press as pundits argued about the pros and cons of changing moralities, though it was not until a few weeks later that somebody asked the dancers what they thought. Most of them were not happy with the changes—sure, they could make a lot more money but they had less control. This wasn't dancing, they argued, this was prostitution.

The club owners were forcing the women to do lap dances despite protests about being groped and, many claimed, sexually assaulted. Several dancers tried to form a union to lobby the politicians and to provide some form of job security in the face of club owners who said "You lap dance or you don't dance at all," and who reportedly began importing desperate Asian women willing to do almost anything for a dollar a dance. So far the club owners are winning.

The dancers? Well, they have trouble getting the public to even take them seriously.

Interestingly enough, these real-life dancers' loss of power occurred when the dynamics of striptease changed from looking to touching. With the visual barrier broken, the issue of power and control is altered. When it is just a look, control and subjectivity can be found on either side of the interaction, but with touching, fondling, and servicing there is no room for illusion: the male patrons are clearly in control, and more importantly, the male club owners are in control of the women's bodies, economically, physically, and mentally.

As one dancer said: "You know, I used to like it when it was table dancing, when there was no touching. But you don't see any happy faces anymore. None of us is happy anymore. Back when it was table dancing I use to have these fantasies about being really sexual in my real world. But now I can't do that. The touching really depresses me" (Bhabra 1995: 52).

When push comes to shove for dancers in real life there is no easy solution, no single drooling villain they can stomp with a stiletto heel. In contrast, stripper revenge movies offer an idealized version of feminine power derived from mastery of the look. It's a good starting point and perhaps encouraging that at least in *fiction* our culture is beginning to recognize the consequences of misogyny and to accept women as heroes as women—but this does not necessarily mean things are changing yet in the real world.

6) "SHE CAN DO ANYTHING!"

The Action Heroine and the Modern (Post-Feminist) Girl

*O*ver the last fifteen years the television landscape has undergone dramatic changes. Most notably the increased number of channels available through basic cable packages and premium digital and satellite services has culminated in specialty channels and an increased need for content. The phenomenal success of such youth-oriented networks in the United States as Nickelodeon, The Cartoon Network, and The Disney Channel is credited with ushering in a new age of serial animation more sophisticated and diverse than ever before.

As a result of this boom, and in an effort to reach as many young viewers as possible, many popular girl action heroines have emerged. Whereas Saturday morning action cartoons of previous generations primarily targeted young boys, modern programming is far more likely to feature strong female characters side-by-side with boyish adventurers. The token inclusion of Wonder Woman as a member of *The Super Friends* in the 1970s and the He-Man spin-off *She-Ra: Princess of Power* in the 1980s has given way to a new breed of animated girl heroines in the late 1990s and 2000s.

Today's young viewers (and older fans of animation) enjoy the exploits of girl heroines with increased roles in team-based shows like *Justice League Unlimited, Teen Titans,* and *The Kids Next Door,* and in starring roles in series like *The Powerpuff Girls, Kim Possible, Totally Spies, Atomic Betty, My Life as a Teenage Robot, Princess Natasha,* and *The Life and Times of Juniper Lee.* In addition to television, there has been a notable increase in young heroines in literary series. *Nancy Drew* has remained a viable enough property to warrant new books and a feature film *Nancy Drew* (2007), and new series such as *Fearless, Undercover Girl, Spy Goddess,* and *Jane Blonde* have also proven immensely popular with young readers. Add to this the teen heroines of *Buffy the Vampire Slayer, Dark Angel, D.E.B.S.,* and *Veronica Mars* and you have an undeniable trend in popular culture: the young girl as action heroine.

The girl action heroine who has become a mainstay in youth-oriented television and literature in the new millennium encompasses a wide range of character types and appeals to an equally wide range of audiences. Some of these characters, such as The Powerpuff Girls, Atomic Betty, and Jane Blonde are grade-school age, while others are high-schoolers such as Kim Possible, Juniper Lee, Jenny X-9 of *My Life as a Teenage Robot*, and the three heroines of *Totally Spies*. Others like the live-action Buffy and Veronica Mars have aged from their initial high school settings to college. In Francine Pascal's popular book series *Fearless* (forty books and counting) the tough heroine Gaia Moore, who was born without the gene that would allow her to register fear, has developed from an ass-kicking high schooler, through university, and on to a career as an FBI agent.

Moreover, their personas as action heroines run the gamut of action types, including secret agents, vampire and monster slayers, super-powered avengers, genetic anomalies, intergalactic guardians, and even robots. What these young heroines have in common are their exceptional abilities at fighting, intelligence, beauty—and a sense of humor. Even in their more serious moments, these girls manage to have some fun while beating up bad guys or blasting alien invaders.

They also manage to balance saving the world with typically girlish pleasures such as shopping at the mall and pining after hunky boys. Kim Possible, for example, finds a perfect equilibrium between being head cheerleader and her globe-trotting missions against super villains. Or, as critical favorite Buffy famously declared: "I want to date, and shop, and hang out, and go to school, and save the world from unspeakable demons. You know . . . I want to do girly stuff."

The emphasis on youth in these contemporary heroines, both in their depiction as young girls and in marketing them to young female consumers, marks a significant change in how action heroines are conceived and perceived in the contemporary media environment. In this chapter I will focus on the young action heroine as a result and reflection of the cultural shift from second- to third-wave feminism. For better or worse, the girl action heroine represents a type of post-feminist character who operates in a world where earlier feminist concerns are seen as outdated. This is an era in which the media embraces a rhetoric that declares girls are unquestionably empowered. Girls can be anything they want, and they can do anything they want.

It is no coincidence that the tag line for Disney's *Kim Possible*, "She can do anything!" is taken directly from contemporary slogans about post-feminist girl power. And while this popularized declaration of girl's power does provide some needed positive role models for young consumers, it also glosses over some of the very real challenges women still face in our society. The girl action heroine allows us to consider the tensions between second- and third-wave feminism. The success of these heroines where so many previous ones failed to catch on illustrates the appeal of post-feminist sensibilities that embrace such girl culture pleasures as fashion, beauty, consumerism, and crushes. But their popularity also demonstrates the cultural machinations that reduce female empowerment to a superficial level that ignores larger concerns about politics, race, community, and misogyny.

THE WOMEN'S MOVEMENT

Since the 1960s and 1970s action heroines have shared an uneasy relationship with feminism, particularly on television. At first glance, strong female characters in the media would seem to be an ideal representation of second-wave feminist goals. And for many women (and young girls of the time) the few available heroines were welcome fantasies. Such early and campy figures as Batgirl, Honey West, and Emma Peel were popular heroines (see D'Acci 1997, Miller 1997) who paved the way for icons of strong women in the 1970s.

Featuring an image of Wonder Woman from the comics on the first cover of the feminist magazine *Ms.* in 1972 seemed perfectly logical. "We were looking for a cover story for its first regular issue," recalls Gloria Steinem, and since she and numerous other editors at the magazine "had been rescued by Wonder Woman in their childhoods, we decided to rescue Wonder Woman in return . . . [she] appeared in all her original glory, striding through city streets like a colossus, stopping planes and bombs with one hand and rescuing buildings with the other" (Steinem 1995: 15). Similarly, the increased presence of feminism in the 1970s saw a rise in heroic women on network television. Programs like *Police Woman* (1974–1978), *Charlie's Angels* (1976–1981), *Wonder Woman* (1976–1979), and *The Bionic Woman* (1976–1978) all featured heroines who could solve crimes and defeat bad guys without the help of men. These shows all owed much of their success to a mainstreaming of feminist issues, and demonstrated at least a superficial affiliation with second-wave politics.

When the Angels go undercover in a men's club to stop a killer, for example, they can worry without irony that "You know, I just had this horrible image of Gloria Steinem drumming us out of the corps for not solving this case!" (quoted in Gough-Yates 2001: 89). Rather than damsels in distress or dangerous femme fatales, these televised characters were heroines in their own right. They could shoot, fight, solve crimes, and in the case of *Wonder Woman* and *The Bionic Woman*, even lift cars or run faster than trains. In short, they could more than hold their own with men, whether it was by defeating male villains or showing up their male colleagues. And perhaps most importantly they held their own in the ratings alongside such male-dominated action series as *Kojak*, *Mannix*, *The Six Million Dollar Man*, and *The Incredible Hulk*.

Unfortunately these iconic action heroines of the 1970s were also key figures in the trend of jiggle TV. The popularity of *Charlie's Angels* had as much or more to do with the sex appeal of Farrah Fawcett, Jaclyn Smith, and Kate Jackson (and later Cheryl Ladd and others) as it did with their ability to fight crime. Likewise, the super-strength and heroic feats of Wonder Woman were offset by the erotic presentation of the series star (and former Miss World beauty queen) Lynda Carter in a costume which, though taken directly from the comics, seemed designed to display her legs and cleavage to maximum effect. These women were as much Daisy Duke and Chrissy Snow as they were Starsky and Hutch.

For most critics, these sexy heroines of the 1970s were at best watered-down versions of second-wave ideology and at worst a demeaning backlash against feminist rhetoric and political goals. The overriding emphasis on the characters' sexuality has been largely interpreted as nullifying their ability to enact feminist progress and as a means for patriarchy to absorb the threat feminism posed to the prevailing status quo (see Higashi 1980, Schwichtenberg 1981, Fiske 1989, Inness 1999, or Bradley 1998). Lorraine Gamman, for example, dismissed *Police Woman* and *Charlie's Angels*, arguing that "the idea of female power was equated with a fantasy of glamour (rather than violence). The potentially progressive representation of female strength is negated by the idealization of femininity" (1998: 10).

Gough-Yates sums up the critical perspective on *Charlie's Angels* as one in which "the perceived threat to the existing social order from the women's movement is seen as being absorbed by money-hungry television executives—notions of women's "independence" being recuperated through a sexual objectification of "liberated" heroines" (83). The commercial genre demands of television in the 1970s meant that the Angels were first and foremost presented as sex objects, and for many viewers it was difficult to believe these women were truly liberated when their images were so massively circulated as bikini-clad pinups. After all, the cultural impact of *Charlie's Angels* was as notable for introducing the Farrah flip hairstyle as it was for breaking new ground in the battle of the sexes.

Still, the extreme popularity of these 1970s action heroines and their enduring popularity within the public imagination suggests that something more was going on for viewers than just gratuitous jiggle TV. These shows were also very popular with women and young girls for more than the mere lifestyle fantasy they offered (though that was also of prime importance). In *Where the Girls Are: Growing Up Female with the Mass Media* (1994), Susan J. Douglas recognizes the conflicted nature of programs like *Charlie's Angels*, *The Bionic Woman*, and *Wonder Woman*. Overall, Douglas argues, the "pop culture versions of the liberated woman were meant, it seems in retrospect, to be a compromise between the demands of feminists and the resistance of antifeminists. But they were also a powerful tool for managing an extremely threatening, even revolutionary, social movement" (194).

But Douglas also acknowledges her own pleasure as a young feminist when watching *Charlie's Angels*: "[W]hen I first saw the show, I was as outraged as other feminists over its objectification of women and its celebration of patriarchy through the use of invisible Charlie's instructing voice. But you know what? I watched it regularly, and not just for work. At the same time that I hated it, I loved it. Unlike *Police Woman*, this show did something that I certainly wasn't supposed to admit, then or now: it gave me pleasure" (212).

Despite the over-the-top sexualization of the heroines, these programs, and *Charlie's Angels* in particular, did portray the characters as liberated and resourceful, they worked in cooperation with other women, and for the betterment of less fortunate women, and they did it all despite the sexism that surrounded them. Ultimately, Douglas argues the genius of *Charlie's Angels* is that it pulls off a perfect balance between the forces of feminism and antifeminism. On one level the show is clearly a low point in the media's tradition of objectifying beautiful women for the viewer's pleasure. But on another level, even feminists could view beyond the obvious sexism and enjoy the exciting stories of career women taking the law, and their lives, into their own hands.

In her insightful article "Angels in Chains?" (2005), Anna Gough-Yates explores this tension between the dominant criticism of *Charlie's Angels* as a potent cultural backlash against feminism and the pleasures the program offered to female viewers hungry for images of liberated women. Gough-Yates attributes the commercial success of *Charlie's Angels* to its ability to capitalize on the concept of lifestyle feminism that was becoming increasingly popular during the mid-1970s. As some of the political concerns of second-wave feminism (such as equal pay for equal work, a right to one's own sexuality, and the importance of female solidarity) gained a cultural foothold in the media, *Charlie's Angels* provided viewers an opportunity to reflect on and make a personal connection with the rhetoric of feminism.

Of particular importance for Gough-Yates was the popularized notion of the "single woman lifestyle" associated with Steinem, the media-friendly face of feminism, and the sexually liberated philosophy put forth by Helen Gurley Brown in *Sex and the Single Girl* (1962) that was revised and reprinted in the early 1970s and eventually provided the editorial foundation for *Cosmopolitan* magazine, the self-proclaimed bible for the single girl. It is within this historical context that Gough-Yates describes *Charlie's Angels* as engaging "with shifting discourses around feminism and the lifestyles of single women in a meaningful (albeit commercially oriented) way" (96). Thus, despite the show's depoliticizing of feminist discourses and excessive glamorization of active, confident, and independent women, it nevertheless "offered pleasurable glimpses of female solidarity and strength for women audiences as they formulate their cultural identities in the wake of the momentous social and political impact of the women's movement" (97). In fact, Gough-Yates argues that the program's decline in popularity (and eventual nostalgic resurrection) was not due to a decline in quality but to further changes in the image of liberated women that made the lifestyle feminism of *Charlie's Angels* seem outdated.

GIRL POWER

In the 1980s and early 1990s the glamorous strong woman was displaced by an increased preference for muscular and masculinized heroines in film (see Chapter One) typified by Ellen Ripley in *Aliens* and Sarah Connor in *Terminator 2*, and on television by the big shoulder-padded and business-like assertive women of nighttime soaps like *Dallas* and *Dynasty*. Overall, as Susan Faludi describes in *Backlash: The Undeclared War Against American Women* (1991), the popular culture of the 1980s and early 1990s resituated women according to standards of ideal femininity that saw them as passive sex objects more than as liberated subjects. The most notable exception, and a favorite of feminist media critics, was the groundbreaking police show *Cagney and Lacey* (see Gamman 1989, or D'Acci 1994). More recently, however, strong women have returned to television with a vengeance.

In addition to many action heroine series mentioned throughout this book, contemporary prime-time television has featured dozens of confident and capable female investigators on shows such as *Crossing Jordan*, *Cold Case*, *Angela's Eyes*, *Bones*, *The Closer*, and on ensemble shows like the *CSI* and *Law & Order* franchises (see Mizejewski 2005). These characters are all smart, strong, beautiful, and (mostly) equal to their male colleagues. The actresses' requisite model good looks and the standard professional pant-suit uniform moves them away from the blatant sexism of the jiggle TV era at the same time it avoids overly masculinizing them.

These investigative characters are also clearly depicted as full-grown women, ranging from their twenties to their forties, and while they may chase down crooks and throw a punch or two, their skills lay primarily in their analytical abilities (many of them are forensic doctors or expert criminal profilers, after all). The most prevalent *action* heroines on television today—those who swing from helicopters, do back-flips, and subdue villains with martial arts—are depicted as girls and are typically targeted at a younger viewership. In broad strokes, this shift from (pseudo?) liberated wonder *women* in the 1970s to action *girls* in the 2000s reflects the shift in feminism from the second-wave *women's* movement to third-wave feminism's preference for an ideology of *girl* power.

Contemporary third-wave feminism was instigated primarily by the Riot Grrrl movement of the early to mid-1990s and by the negative perception of second-wave politics as out-dated, dogmatic, and essentialist. For the young women who came of age in the 1990s, and for those coming of age in the 2000s, the world was/is a different place and they have grown up reaping the benefits of earlier feminist struggles. Third-wave feminism developed in a cultural and political climate where young women felt freer to explore their own gendered identities and their position within society. Growing out of real-life experiences, especially within the realm of popular culture, young critics and scholars exuberantly embraced and espoused what they saw as their own generation's understanding of feminism.

A number of influential works including Rebecca Walker's landmark article "Becoming the Third Wave" (1992) and anthologies like *Third Wave Agenda: Being Feminist, Doing Feminism* (Heywood and Drake 1997), *Catching a Wave: Reclaiming Feminism for the 21st Century* (Dicker and Piepmeier 2003), *Manifesta: Young Women, Feminism, and the Future* (Baumgardner and Richards 2000), and *Third Wave Feminism: A Critical Exploration* gave voice to the loose ideologies of the third-wave perspective and the perceived need for feminism to evolve to suit the needs of younger women in a postmodern and late capitalism period (Gillis, Howie, and Munford 2004). In these and countless other critical works, young women wrote about their experiences growing up as the daughters of second-wave feminists and their attempts to navigate and renegotiate their existence in a media-saturated culture. An exact definition of third-wave politics is rarely agreed upon, but a clear sense has emerged that in addition to carrying on a general struggle against misogyny and violence against women, this younger generation of feminism is differentiated by embracing popular culture and focusing on individual choice, consumerism, sexual freedom, cultural diversity, personal empowerment, and an ironic sensibility.

Unfortunately, despite the enthusiastic and innovative reworking of a feminist agenda undertaken by proponents of the third wave, this new trend was quickly watered down and appropriated within the realm of popular culture as a mere marketing slogan of Girl Power. With youth as one of the key ingredients of the movement and the reclaiming of traditionally girly pleasures as subversive and liberating, the third wave almost immediately segued into a notion of Post-Feminism. The politically minded and aggressive trend of Riot Grrrl bands was superseded by the ever-present image of the glamorous and playfully empowered Spice Girls who claimed "Girl Power" as their catch phrase, and the likes of Britney Spears singing "Hit me baby one more time" while dancing in a revealing Catholic schoolgirl outfit.

The mass-marketed concept of Girl Power is premised on the assumption that young women live in a post-feminist age—an era where gender inequalities have been overcome and feminism is no longer needed because girls are free to do whatever they please. Thus, under the guise of Girl Power, young women are encouraged to believe that anything they choose to do, from going shopping to dressing sexy to exposing themselves on video for *Girls Gone Wild* (Pitcher 2006), is a source of empowerment and a means for exercising their individual rights. The efficacy of Girl Power as both a source of liberation and as a rational for blatant sexism has been rightly criticized by such landmark feminists as Germaine Greer (2000) and Angela McRobbie (2004). As Rebecca Munford put it in the aptly entitled "Wake Up and Smell the Lipgloss": "[M]any feminist critics have been quick to position 'girl power' and its 'bad girl' icons as a form of popularized postfeminism—a depoliticized product of 'backlash' rhetoric" (2006: 142). Even within the pages of the popular magazine *Bitch* (often credited as a key player in the third-wave movement) articles have lambasted the media's co-option of the phrase:

> Girl Power reduces the theoretical complexity of feminism to a cheery slogan ("GIRLS KICK ASS!"); it represents the ultimate commodification of empowerment; it reinforces the simplistic conception of feminism as being, at heart, "all about choices." But most of all, it grabbed the rhetoric from one of the most potentially powerful, yet woefully misunderstood, feminist uprisings of my generation, discarded every ounce of political heft, and reduced it to cheap iron-on letters on a baby T. (Fudge 2006: 155)

Whatever the original intention of Girl Power was, it has become, under the direction of Madison Avenue, a rationale for a renewed sexualization of young women and a means to discredit feminism in general.

The marketing co-option of the Girl Power concept from the mid-1990s on synchronized well with the post-feminist enthusiasm for consumption and the media's recognition of young girls as a very important and affluent demographic. Young girls, for example, were credited with making *Titanic* the highest-grossing film of all time thanks to repeated viewings and their idolization of Leonardo DiCaprio. By the early 2000s the appeal of young actresses and singers for children, tweens, and teens was impossible to ignore. Moreover, the youth trend in popular culture was clearly engendered feminine. When *Vanity Fair* ran a cover story in 2003 about the rise of teen and tween stars it featured only the new female actresses (including such mega-powers as the Olsen Twins, Hillary Duff, and Lindsey Lohan) on its cover. Some young male performers were included in the story, but as the cover proudly boasted: "No Way! Nine girl teen stars on the cover and 19 more inside? *Way!*" It is at this cultural moment where postfeminism, Girl Power marketing, and the recognition of girls as an important consumer group have coalesced that young girl action heroines have come to the forefront.

The young girl action heroine category admittedly covers a wide range of film and television figures. However, whether they are animated heroines geared towards children like *The Powerpuff Girls* and *Atomic Betty*, or live-action noirish teen sleuths or vampire hunters aimed at teen and young adult viewers like Veronica Mars or Buffy, they all intersect with the larger cultural notion of Girl Power. Likewise, as discussed in detail in Chapter Three, even the adult heroines of TV series like *Alias* and movies like *Tomb Raider* can be considered girlish in relation to their fathers and patriarchal systems of authority.

In the *Sight & Sound* review of *Tomb Raider* Kate Stables astutely points out that the film neatly sidesteps any real threat the heroine may pose "by positioning Lara firmly as a *girl*, not a woman. From the tip of her schoolgirl plait to her army boots, she is a luscious tomboy" (2001: 20; italics in the original). The issues of power and agency at play within the action genre fit perfectly with the "girls can do anything" ethos of Girl Power, and helps frame these heroines as embodiments of that ethos. "Girl Power has infiltrated the action genre," writes Susan Hopkins in her overview of contemporary media images of empowered girls. "After decades of feminist critique, media images of weak women are finally losing currency. The helpless heroine has been replaced by the new stereotype of an ambitious dynamic tough girl seeking self-advancement and self-actualisation. The new girl action hero knows what she wants—and is willing and able to *fight* for it" (2002: 108).

While I appreciate Hopkins' optimistic perspective on girl heroines as a progressive new stereotype, the close association of these heroines with Girl Power rhetoric means that what exactly it is she knows "she wants" needs to be better understood. My concern is that in addition to all the positive and progressive behaviors modeled by these characters, what exactly is the message about femininity they teach? Can the young girl action heroine be more than just a Girl Power marketing concept that reduces female empowerment to a bundle of sexy images and catchphrases? Is she just a part of the backlash that helps contain a threatening cultural change, or can she be an instigator of changing gender norms?

While there are no easy answers to these questions, the general concerns surrounding Girl Power and postfeminism indicate a need to contextualize the young girl action heroine in relation to broader notions of feminism. Angela McRobbie (2004) insightfully points out that the emphasis on the tropes of freedom and choice associated with young women in contemporary late-capitalist culture functions as a very specific postmodern backlash against feminism and effectively negates any earlier achievements. McRobbie argues that "postfeminism actively draws on and invokes feminism as that which can be taken into account in order to suggest that equality is achieved, in order to install a whole repertoire of meanings which emphasize that it is no longer needed, a spent force" (4). Moreover, she notes that the denunciation of feminism coexists "with the visibility of a gendered, generational fault line, where young women are championed as a metaphor for social change" (6).

According to McRobbie's interpretation the media, and popular culture more generally, speaks to young women in an ironic manner that positions them as knowing insiders who live in a world beyond traditional sexism and the "seemingly tyrannical regime of feminist puritanism" (8). I will return to the role of irony, postmodernism, and camp aesthetics in more detail later in this chapter to consider how these specific tropes inform the reading of girl action heroines. But in general, McRobbie sees contemporary culture "taking feminism into account" as a strategy that characterizes feminism as a ridiculous and overly reactionary relic.

This is a post-feminist world now, the Girl Power logic implies, where women have the right to embrace the most stereotypical of girlish pleasures if they wish. And it is the truly liberated woman/girl who chooses to wear "Porn Star" T-shirts, is hip enough to attend strip shows, and to tart herself up to attract sexual attention. The real danger that McRobbie is concerned with is that despite her supposed freedom, young girls are "called upon to be silent, to withhold critique in order to count as a modern, sophisticated girl" (9). This particularly succinct criticism of postfeminism brings to the fore many of the concerns about how supposedly progressive roles for women function to undermine the truth about real sexual relations and power struggles in contemporary society.

As quintessential post-feminist characters it is not surprising that many of the young girl action heroines occasionally "take feminism into account" in a very direct manner. The Cartoon Network's phenomenally popular *The Powerpuff Girls* (1998–2004) is a fast-paced animated series (and a subsequent feature film in 2002) featuring three adorable kindergarten girls who fight crime in the city of Townsville. Created in a lab by their father "The Professor" when he combined sugar, spice, and everything nice (and accidentally chemical X), Blossom, Bubbles, and Buttercup are super-powered innocents who always manage to, as their promotional tagline puts it, "Save the world before bedtime!" Yet even in this humorous cartoon meant primarily for pre- and grade-school-aged children, feminism is taken into account in order to dismiss it in favor of a more contemporary and reasonable understanding of gender relations.

In the first season episode "Equal Fights," the girls encounter Femme Fatale, who is stealing all the Susan B. Anthony coins in Townsville. Clad in a skintight costume decorated with the astrological symbol for woman and using similarly themed weapons, Femme Fatale declares: "I'm going to rob this burg blind and there is nothing you macho meatheads can do about it!" When the Powerpuff Girls first apprehend her, she convinces them that they are not appreciated by men. "Female superheroes aren't nearly as revered as male superheroes," she claims. "Sure they are," counter the girls. "There's Supergirl, Batgirl." But Femme Fatale points out that those examples are "merely extensions of their male counterparts." When Wonder Woman is the only real female superhero the girls can come up with, they decide Femme Fatale is right and let her go as a sign of feminist sisterhood. Femme Fatale goes on an uninterrupted crime spree and the girls are shown as budding feminazis who bully the boys on the playground, refuse to clean their room when the Professor asks, and yell at the Mayor when he calls them to fight crime.

Eventually their teacher and the Mayor's assistant Ms. Bellum (who is always shown in the series only from the neck down, as an exaggeratedly curvaceous body) intervene and explain the error of the girl's immature brand of feminist thinking. "There is injustice in the world," they tell the girls, "and that's why we have you to protect the rights of everyone." The Powerpuff Girls smarten up and capture Femme Fatale while lecturing her about Susan B. Anthony who insisted on equal rights for everyone. The message is clear, even for pre-schoolers: the man-hating rhetoric of earlier feminism is just a self-serving excuse for women. Real Girl Power comes in the shape of the super-powerful girls who live in a world of gender equality.

More recently the TV series *Veronica Mars*, featuring Kristen Bell as the titular teen sleuth who ingeniously solves crimes ranging from dog-nappings to murder and rape, took feminism into account in just as direct a manner as the Powerpuff Girls. As Veronica transitioned from the California high school setting of her first two seasons to her local college, the show contrasted the cute, sassy, and eminently competent approach of its heroine with that of a group of militant campus feminists. In a story line spread out over the first half of the season, Veronica is in pursuit of a serial rapist at Hearst College who drugs his victims and shaves their heads as part of his assault. The local police and campus security have proven completely inept so Veronica makes the apprehension of the rapist her top priority, especially after one of her friends is assaulted and she feels personally responsible.

The case clearly divides the student body with many of the men—the fraternities and the editors of a campus humor magazine in particular—making light of the rape epidemic, and many of the women are understandably outraged, most visibly the feminists known as the Lilith House women. While many of the men's callousness is blatantly sexist and boorish, the series also, unfortunately, depicts the feminists as overly militant and reactionary as they harass the Dean to close down the fraternities, stage Take Back the Night Rallies, and chastise drunk female students they escort home from parties as part of a safe-ride-home program. At one point they even fake a rape of one of their members to gain support.

As one reviewer argues, "[T]he Lilith House denizens are relentlessly portrayed as dour, shrill, unreasonable, judgmental, and vindictive—in other words, as feminazis: humorless haters of men, of women who wear makeup, and of any intimation of fun in general" (Fudge 2007: 15). In contrast, cute, blond, and funny Veronica is repeatedly shown as the "real" feminist smart and resourceful enough to catch the rapists (it is actually two men working together) on her own. Who needs rallies and the Lilith women's misplaced anger when one truly liberated coed can save the day?

As the two examples above make clear, the young girl action heroine is very consciously aligned with postfeminism as a more enlightened alternative to what is characterized as outdated self-serving or man-hating feminism. Even when the contrasted feminists are roughly the same age, as in the *Veronica Mars* example, the more militant second-wave version is depicted as woefully out-of-date. In addition, the emphasis on youth with these new heroines makes explicit the larger generational fault line McRobbie describes "where young women are championed as a metaphor for social change" (2004: 6).

This generational fault line is at the core of much of the tension between second-wave feminism and third-wave/postfeminism. Since many initial proponents of the third wave wrote about their experiences growing up as the daughters of feminists, critics have often metaphorically framed the shift in ideology as a disjuncture between mothers and daughters. Building on Germiane Greer's concern about "the propaganda machine now aimed at our daughters" (2000), Munford emphasizes the "trope of mother-daughter conflict" (2006: 143) as the central disjuncture between generations of feminists.

Kathleen Rowe Karlyn (2003) uses this metaphor effectively in her analysis of the revisionist slasher film *Scream* (1996) to explore the importance of third-wave ideology for young girls coming of age in a politically conservative and popular culture-saturated environment. Rowe Karlyn sees the mother/daughter metaphor as important because it addresses "a nexus of cultural representations that 'erases' mothers into a broader political order that erases history or historical consciousness" (4). As we discussed in Chapter Three, the action heroine genre is complicit in the erasure of mothers in general. At a broader level Rowe Karlyn also considers the mother/daughter dynamic as a useful tool for conceptualizing women's relations across time. "Not all of us are mothers," she reasons, "but we all have mothers. And we all have a stake in the future of girls and young women, whether we see them as our daughters or not" (4).

This preoccupation with the mother/daughter dynamic in feminism is also a particularly apt metaphor for looking at the young girl action heroine. Leaving aside the muscular and masculinized heroine of the late 1980s and early 1990s, the contemporary girl action heroine has been positioned in the media as a descendant of the televised heroines of the 1970s. Within the genre lineage today's young heroines are the metaphorical daughters of earlier female action icons like Wonder Woman, Emma Peel, and the Bionic Woman. Susan Hopkins (2002) refers to these early characters as the "Camp Mothers" of modern Girl Power heroines. The continuing cultural resonance of these older characters and their influence on the genre is one reason so many of them have been revamped with varying degrees of success.

Emma Peel reappeared in the disastrous feature film version of *The Avengers* (1998) with a pre–*Kill Bill* Uma Thurman donning an array of fetishistic costumes. The new *Bionic Woman* came and went in the fall of 2007, and plans for a big-budget Wonder Woman movie have been in the works for years (I discuss the difficulties associated with this film project in the concluding chapter). And, perhaps most tellingly, the 1970s women of television's *Charlie's Angels* were revisioned via a "girlier, post-feminist aesthetic" (Stables 2001: 20) in the blockbuster film *Charlie's Angels* (2000).

What the "girlier, post-feminist aesthetic" of *Charlie's Angels*, and its sequel *Charlie's Angels: Full Throttle* (2003), reveals is a preference in post-feminism for playfully recontextualizing or undermining outdated conceptions of femininity. By skipping over the more serious phase of action heroism typified by Ripley and Connors in the *Aliens* and *Terminator* series respectively, the new Angels Dylan, Natalie, and Alex (played by Drew Barrymore, Cameron Diaz, and Lucy Liu), present female empowerment as primarily a fun-loving, campy strategy. Regardless of how straight-faced shows like *Charlie's Angels* were in the 1970s, they are now repositioned and reformatted in reruns as excessively campy pleasures.

In her intriguing discussion of the film and its relation to the original television series, Jacinda Read (2004) argues that the notion of camp is crucial to understanding the ironic position of the movie, particularly the way it renders traditional femininity as an excessive ruse. Read points out that the framing of the series in reruns "explicitly encourages ironic/campy readings of the show and, by extension, the film itself, making it hard to read the show or the film's self-conscious referencing of its conventions 'straight'" (211). The campy pleasures associated with action heroines is crucial in understanding how they can be progressive images for young women while simultaneously dismissive of female strength.

Whether earlier televised heroines were intended to be campy, as was the case with Emma Peel and Wonder Woman, or straight action-adventure series such as *Charlie's Angels* and *The Bionic Woman*, from a contemporary viewpoint their campiness has become their defining characteristic. The unintentionally silly plots, stiff acting, and the excessive emphasis on the heroines' beauty undermined their potential to embody truly tough new images of women. Both Susan Douglas and Sherrie Innes have criticized these 1970s series as ultimately presenting women who are, to use Inness' phrase, only "pseudo-tough." On the surface they may have been just as strong as the men but the campy aesthetic and the insistent hyper-sexualization of the actresses implies that these dangerous women are still merely sex objects.

According to Douglas and Inness, the fantastic storylines assured viewers that this type of strong woman did not exist in reality. The consistent use of masquerade likewise suggested that the heroines' strength was also just a narrative ruse, and most importantly, the shows confirmed the stereotype that women should strive to be sexually attractive to men. The camp accoutrements of action heroines established in the 1960s and 1970s have carried over into more contemporary examples.

There is a world of difference between intentionally campy heroines found on TV series like *Xena: Warrior Princess*, *V.I.P.*, *She Spies* (2002), and *Snoops* (1991–2000) and films like *D.E.B.S.*, and the unintentionally campy women of films like *Elektra* and *Catwoman*. Yet, while the intentionally campy versions benefit from a protective layer of irony and self-mocking stories, they, like the unintentionally campy heroines, still illustrate the absurdity of the women's heroic feats and the excessive fetishizing of the characters' bodies.

For many critics, the frequent tendency to align action heroines with camp aesthetics reinforces the ultimately misogynistic implications of the genre.

The notion of camp, fun, and irony as a political strategy for post-feminism—and as an avenue for pleasurable consumption for young women—is a point of contention with critics of modern action heroines and the ideology of Girl Power in general. In a post-structuralist world flooded with post-modern media forms, there is a legitimate concern that by focusing on the superficial and the campy, young women may be seduced by the mere illusion of strong women. It is easy for girls to feel a vicarious sense of empowerment when they are inundated by images of women kicking men's asses and uttering lines like: "I am woman hear me roar" (Catwoman) and "I'm gonna rock your world!" (Atomic Betty). But, we can ask, how can this equate to a truly radical shift when such aggressive posturing is bound up with images of women in skimpy latex costumes, micro-minis, and leather bustiers?

As mentioned earlier, critics like McRobbie and Fudge argue that this superficial post-feminist rhetoric marks a broader cultural trend that makes young women unwitting participants in their own exploitation. As Fudge surmises: "Girl Power tricks us all into believing that girls are naturally powerful and therefore ignores the many ways their power is contingent on adhering to cultural expectations of female behavior" (2006: 160). Similarly Christina Lucia Stasia argues in relation to contemporary action heroines: "While her brash femininity and tough girl antics are resonant with third wave 'Girlie' culture, the new female action hero reifies third wave feminism into slick visuals and girl power sound bites . . . offer[ing] girls the encouragement to do anything without providing them with the knowledge or tools to do so" (2005: 180–81).

The danger is that young women may buy into the fantasy that they, like fictional action heroines, really do live in a world where women have achieved equality and can do anything. As Stasia summarizes, the new breed of action heroines provides "attitudinal feminist heroes who spout feminist rhetoric and kick ass, but who neither acknowledge that oppression exists at an institutional level, nor that its forms are diverse" (181). While this is a very real problem, there is still hope that these texts can speak to their audience of young women in a way that challenges sexist ideologies and can foster a legitimate sense of female progress.

In fact, the post-feminist emphasis on fun and the campy aesthetics associated with so many "girlie" action heroines may facilitate a progressive and self-aware interpretation. Hopkins (2002) argues that this exaggerated style of female empowerment lies at the core, not just of the fun of Girl Power texts,

6.1. *D.E.B.S.* © 2005 Screen Gems, Inc. All Rights Reserved. Courtesy of Screen Gems.

but of young women's abilities to negotiate a personal sense of self-awareness as females in a predominantly sexist world. Where the women of Lilith House, from the *Veronica Mars* example cited above, can be dismissively characterized as stereotypical "humorless haters of men" and against "any intimation of fun in general," the program does offer Veronica as a witty and strong character who also mocks vapid sorority girls, the self-important and ineffectual Sheriff's department, and sexist frat boys. The real fun of a show like *Veronica Mars* is due in large part to the fact that it can criticize and trump both individuals and institutions that typically devalue women. That Veronica herself is cute, sexy, witty, and intelligent makes it clear for viewers that being a feminist and challenging the status quo does not mean forgoing the pleasures they derive from conforming to societal norms of attractiveness.

In her analysis of the campy revisionism in *Charlie's Angels*, Jacinda Read astutely argues that the film's caricature of traditional female roles and its tongue-in-cheek examples of excessively fetishized women reveal a succinct critique of media images at the same time it addresses the difficulties of balancing feminist desires with aspirations for romance and domesticity (2004: 215). Likewise, Kathleen Rowe Karlyn (2003) discusses *Scream* as a valuable film that speaks to young women in a humorously self-aware tone that addresses pertinent issues about virginity, media awareness, sisterhood, and motherhood. Rather than dismissing the often campy and fun tone of girl action heroine narratives as mere "sound and fury signifying nothing," we can perhaps see it as a discursive strategy whereby even the youngest of consumers are permitted to think through issues relevant to their emerging conceptions of themselves as women.

The cult film *D.E.B.S.* (2004), for example, is an intentionally campy story about young girls at a super secret spy academy in pursuit of Lucy Diamond, a beautiful criminal mastermind. At first glance *D.E.B.S.*, directed by Angela Robinson, is merely a light-hearted spoof of James Bond-style films, but it also addresses concerns of self-worth in a manner that few more serious films do. The four titular adolescents are clearly constructed in the post-feminist girly action heroine mode—though they are lethal spies in training for an elite covert agency, the D.E.B.S. are humorously depicted as exceedingly fetishized private school girls in dangerously short plaid miniskirts and tight tops. As the film's promotional tagline joked: "They're crime fighting hotties with killer bodies" (Figure 6.1). The film is pure farce, with the girls coveting their target's sweater while on a stakeout dangling from a restaurant's rafters on swings, losing their guns in the dirty laundry pile, and sweetly flirting with some of the bad guys.

But, in addition to mocking the Hollywood tendency to sexualize young women through their ridiculous costumes, *D.E.B.S.* also makes fun of numerous female stereotypes, promotes the need for girls to support each other, embraces lesbian longings, and champions the importance of young women being true to themselves. As a self-aware film scripted and directed by an African American lesbian feminist, *D.E.B.S.* avoids the criticism that post-feminism in general, and action heroines in particular, are exclusively white and heterosexual. For example, Stasia argues "the new female action hero is derivative of early third wave feminist theory—individualistic, almost always white, middle-class and straight" (2005: 181). Even though they are drawn as broad caricatures, the D.E.B.S. girls counter all of these categories. The leader of the D.E.B.S. is Max, a bossy overachieving African American; the second in command is Amy, the "perfect" blonde agent who really just wants to go to art school. Rounding out the squad are Dominique, a French-Asian beatnik who is also a sex maniac, and Janet, the youngest girl who is sweet and frilly but naïve.

Despite being a light-hearted comedy, *D.E.B.S.* is in many regards one of the most progressive films to come out of Hollywood in recent years. In *D.E.B.S.*, her first feature film, writer/director Angela Robinson manages to craft a fun parody of both spy movies and romantic comedies. The lesbian love story at the core of the film plays with all of the conventions found in typical heterosexual romantic comedies and ultimately presents an endearing message about accepting everyone's romantic inclinations. As an openly lesbian African American filmmaker, Robinson is able to present a different political perspective without seeming too political. As popular culture producers like Robinson are increasingly able to bring different perspectives to mainstream entertainments we begin to see other ways action heroines can be used to question the naturalness of the heretofore predominant depictions of gender, ethnicity, and sexuality.

The central story of the film is about the forbidden romance that develops between Amy—literally the D.E.B.S. academy's poster child—and their arch-nemesis, Lucy Diamond. Sparks immediately fly between the two young women when they first meet at gunpoint. Amy has just broken up with her FBI trainee boyfriend and Lucy is fresh from a disastrous blind date with a Russian female assassin (who only kills so she can pay for her dance lessons). The villainous Lucy courts Amy by abducting her and staging bank robberies to get her attention. Amy resists at first, both because she is reluctant to pursue a lesbian relationship and because Lucy is the D.E.B.S.' number-one enemy, but she eventually decides to follow her heart.

Amy is portrayed as a confused girl, trying to do what others expect of her and at a loss as to what she should do with her life. In the end, despite all of the pressure on her by the agency and her boyfriend to be straight and pursue a career as a spy, Amy, with the encouragement and blessing of the other girls in her squad, runs off with Lucy to live happily ever after (and go to art school in Spain). Despite being a campy and frivolous post-feminist film, *D.E.B.S.* is, at its core, an endearing lesson about girls making their own choices, taking control of their own lives and sexuality, and supporting each other. *D.E.B.S.* may be an extreme example given its clear sexual politics and savvy play with stereotypes, but it does illustrate that even the silliest instances of post-feminist girl action heroines can present messages of importance to viewers. Rather than simply assuming these stories reinforce misogynistic norms under a guise of vacuous Girl Power imagery, these texts are capable of speaking to young women about important issues in their own world. That the messages of these texts are articulated in a language that is fun and sexy indicates that the young consumers of today, the metaphorical daughters of feminism, speak and are spoken to in a manner that suits their popular culture savvy mind-set. They are not their mother's action heroines.

While the generational conflict between second-wave and third-wave feminism, and its popular presentation as post-feminism, can be usefully described as the tension of the mother-daughter dynamic metaphorically, the reality may actually be further displaced than a single generation. Despite being symbolically positioned as girls, the heroines of films like the *Charlie's Angels* and *Lara Croft* franchises are quite a bit older (the actresses were all in their mid to late thirties at the time) than the majority of the young girl heroine characters in high school or younger. The increasing difference in age between second-wave feminists and the children/teenagers who make up the primary audience for Girl Power products in the 2000s indicates a further generational shift. If proponents of the third wave were the daughters of second wavers, the children/teenagers reflected in the girlish action heroines whose adventures are set in grade schools and high schools are more likely to be the granddaughters of feminism.

In this ever-changing media environment, many of the popular culture elements that third wavers embraced have disappeared. The Riot Grrrl music scene has given way to Disney-sponsored bubble-gum pop princesses. If girls know Courtney Love today, it is as a drug-addled punch line, not as a musician who vocally challenged male standards. Likewise, culturally significant TV series like *Roseanne* and *Ally McBeal* are unknown to women in their teens or younger—if they do recognize them it is as quaint reruns from an earlier time alongside innocuous programs like *Full House* and *Family Matters*. Even the *Spice Girls* and *Britney Spears* are better known as mothers than singers now. For that matter, even *Buffy the Vampire Slayer*, which ceased production in 2003, is a relic. It pains me to admit that when I mention Buffy to my university students as an example of female heroism, many of them just give me blank stares. In her discussion of third-wave ideology losing its cultural resonance, Frankie Gamber correctly observes that:

> Younger women who have come into their feminism recently might have only been in elementary school during the Thomas-Hill hearings, herded out of the room by their parents before they could overhear any talk of pubic hairs or Long Dong Silver. They were probably watching Nickelodeon instead of *La Femme Nikita*, more apt to drop the names of the *Rugrats* than know the characters in *Xena: Warrior Princess*. (Gamber 2007: 44)

My point is not just that the generational metaphor needs to expand from a concern over the mother/daughter dynamic to include granddaughters, but that while the slogan of Girl Power has remained, even the most rudimentary media examples of feminism have shifted.

While I do not think it is fair to expect children's programming to present nuanced visions of empowered girls, I do believe that even the simplest girl action heroines have the potential to illustrate progressive gender norms. After all, even if the younger women who are awakening to feminism that Gamber describes were watching Nickelodeon instead of *La Femme Nikita* and *Xena: Warrior Princess*, they may have still learned "radically" different lessons about what it means to be a girl than their mothers or older sisters did.

Sarah Banet-Weiser argues, for example, that through such animated programs as *The Wild Thornberries*, *Rocket Power*, and *As Told By Ginger* Nickelodeon did not "simply exploit the commercial market of girl power; the network is also a significant *producer* of girl power culture" (2004: 120). Nickelodeon and other kid-oriented networks like The Disney Channel and Cartoon Network have continued to produce Girl Power–influenced programming with an explicitly action heroine bent through such animated shows as *The Powerpuff Girls*, *Kim Possible*, *Atomic Betty*, *My Life as a Teenage Robot*, and *The Life and Times of Juniper Lee*. While individual episodes may "take feminism into account," such as *The Powerpuff Girls* "Equal Fights" example described earlier—and they may express platitudes of empowerment without providing specific tools for fighting systemic sexism, it does not necessarily mean that they do not also offer even the youngest viewers a positive model of girlhood and a burgeoning sense of feminist issues.

Rather than dismissing older generations of women out of hand, the girl action heroine can also express a need for young girls to appreciate their mothers—and even their grandmothers. Disney's *Kim Possible*, for example, is a humorous adventure cartoon marketed to children. Kim is a popular high school cheerleader and a globetrotting adventurer who routinely saves the world with a little help from her dweebish sidekick, Ron Stoppable. And while Kim may be the epitome of a Girl Power–derived heroine—she is pretty, smart, funny, tough, and (as her promotional material always declares) can do anything—the series also reminds her (and viewers) that there is a lot to be learned from female elders.

Though not as adventurous as Kim, her mother is still depicted as a competent, loving, and strong woman. In addition to being a supportive parent, Mrs. Dr. P (as Kim's friends call her) is one of the world's foremost brain surgeons. In the episode "Mother's Day," Kim and Mrs. Dr. P pledge to spend the day together despite their busy schedules. When Mrs. Dr. P is called in to perform emergency neurosurgery Kim tags along and watches her mother in action. "I had no idea how major your job is. I mean it's, it's . . . well, it's brain surgery!" Kim marvels. "Aaaah, you were a big help in there, Kimmie," her mother responds, "and you didn't faint once."

Later her mother joins Kim on a mission to thwart her evil nemesis Drakken from unleashing a monster. Kim takes the lead in the action sequences aboard a runaway train, but Mrs. Dr. P impresses her with her athletic abilities and eventually saves the day by using her surgical dexterity to rewire a complicated power source, and freeing them from a trap with her handy laser scalpel. "You rock, Mom!" says Kim. Clearly, Kim Possible does not discredit her mother for sometimes being uncool or embarrassing her in front of her friends. Her mother is a source of inspiration for Kim and a woman she admires.

But *Kim Possible*'s recognition of older women as strong characters in their own right does not stop with her mother. In a season two episode, "The Golden Years," Kim learns that her paternal grandmother, Nana Possible, is much more than a sweater-knitting senior. When the entire Possible clan travels to Florida to help Nana move into a senior's center, Kim initially clashes with her overprotective grandmother. Nana chastises Kim for wearing a revealing midriff top, asks her if she has gotten through her going-on-missions "phase," and credits her fighting bad guys as natural teenage rebellion. But when Kim is forced to fight her Nana (who is under the mind control of the evil Drakken), she is surprised to find out that when she was younger Nana Possible "trained with the Shaolin monks to perfect the ancient art of Peng Lang Chuang kung fu." Moreover, Drakken informs her that Nana then "became a top aviatrix and was the first woman to successfully complete the navy's underwater demolition training program." When Nana eventually helps Kim defeat the villains in hand-to-hand combat, Kim proudly boasts that exceptionally heroic women "run in the family!"

As a daughter and granddaughter of feminists, Kim Possible demonstrates an acceptance and pride in the achievements of older women. If Kim Possible performs a Girl Power–influenced version of post-feminism for young viewers, it does so in a manner that recognizes the importance of earlier generations of women, and none too subtly suggests that all girls should respect and learn from the accomplishments of second wavers. By humorously populating Kim's lineage with exceptionally strong female characters (in a time-traveling episode she learns that even her great-great-great-grandmother was a feminist), the series acknowledges that Kim's current ability to "do anything" owes a lot to the hard work of the women before her, rather than simply living in a world magically free of gender restrictions.

As the *Kim Possible* examples suggest, contemporary stories about young girl action heroines often strive to balance their hip, post-feminist style with an awareness of their female predecessors. The fact that these characters are typically portrayed as adolescents or younger leaves a bit more room for older female figures to appear, and learning from their elders is an effective plot de-vice. These younger action heroines also avoid the tendency in post-feminism of being overly individualistic and pitting girls against each other rather than demonstrating a need for women to be supportive and encouraging of one another. The rogues gallery of villains faced by young girl heroines may be as likely to include an equal measure of male and female evil-doers, and they may be confronted with jealous and petty "mean girls" in their personal lives, but the narratives balance these negative portrayals with heartfelt depictions of devoted female friendships. For example, Kim Possible may routinely battle Drakken's super-powered henchwoman Shego, and she may have to overcome the schemes of her cheerleading rival Bonnie, but she also develops a close and comforting bond with her non-adventuring friend Monique.

Likewise, Jenny (aka X-J9), the female cyborg of *My Life as a Teenage Robot*, struggles with the nasty popular girls at her high school but she has a loving and helpful relationship with her "sisters," earlier, flawed versions of herself (robots X-J1 through X-J8) created by her scientist "mother." One of Veronica Mars' closest friends and helpers is Max, a female computer wunderkind. The Powerpuff Girls often demonstrate that they work best as a team, as do the three flighty but competent heroines Alex, Clover, and Sam of *Totally Spies*. Perhaps most obviously, Buffy's famous "Scooby gang" includes her Wiccan best friend Willow, her sister Dawn, and her social rival-turned-friend Cord-elia. In fact, as Patricia Pender (2006) has argued, the final season of *Buffy* can be read as a prolonged call for young women to unite in the face of mi-sogyny as Buffy assembles an army of girls to defeat the ultimate villain simply known as The First Evil. On a structural level, the narrative device of multiple heroines on programs like these (also *Charmed*, *She Spies*, *V.I.P.*, *Birds of Prey*, *Charlie's Angels*, *D.E.B.S.*, etc.) functions according to the convention Carol Dole (1998) identifies as "splitting," wherein the requisite heroic abilities are spread out among different female characters. But at a symbolic level, this for-mat champions the value of professional and personal relationships between women.

THE IMPORTANCE OF BEING YOUNG

Given the recent cultural attention to Girl Power as a sizable trend it is not surprising that the action genre has latched on to this type of character as a means to reach young audiences. The girlie action heroine seems a perfect fit with post-feminist ideals in that she can save the day and still make time to go to the mall. Stereotypically girlish pursuits and heroic adventures are no longer presented as incongruous. A popular poster for Kim Possible depicts the heroine in her two key costumes and proudly declares "Cheerleader by day. Crime stopper by night." Thus the girlie action heroine seamlessly unites different fantasies in a single figure.

Despite the shortcomings of post-feminism (and there are many), one positive result is a plethora of progressive role models. But the emphasis on youth in these television series, movies, books, and comics raises questions about why *girls* might be the ideal action heroine of the new millennium. Whereas the action heroines of 1970s television and the hardbodied heroines of the 1980s and early 1990s were clearly mature women, the modern action heroine is consistently depicted as girlish. This is clearly the case with the adolescent and childhood heroines discussed in this chapter, but even the full-grown women of the new *Charlie's Angels*, *Tomb Raider*, *Alias*, and so on are presented as girlish in many ways.

The persistence of this character type suggests more issues may be involved culturally than the obvious symbolic one McRobbie identifies as "young women are championed as a metaphor for social change" (2004: 6). This obsession with youth is due in large part to the entertainment industry's well-recognized bias for young and beautiful actresses. But, with so many of the girlie action heroines positioned as high school age or younger—and with so many of them marketed to children—the preoccupation with youth suggests other possibilities as well. In addition to working through issues of feminism, identity, and changing gender roles, the girlie and post-feminist action heroine crystallizes late-capitalist consumerist ideals and troubled notions of adolescent sexuality in the media.

Lest we forget, much of the impetus for Girl Power and its enunciation through the increasingly popular figure of the young girl action heroine came from the cultural recognition of young women as a potent consumer group. Fiscal strength and a passion for consuming has been closely aligned with young women in contemporary Western society and has been repackaged in popular culture as a form of empowerment in and of itself. As a post-feminist figure the action girl combines her heroic adventures with the more clearly feminine-defined joy of shopping, particularly for cute clothes. Oftentimes these two seemingly separate realms are joined in a single adventure, as when a trip to the mall for Juniper Lee turns into a battle with reanimated Viking ghosts terrorizing the stores. Or Kim Possible's quest to find a new signature style when her mission clothes are inexplicably discontinued.

While the young heroine's preoccupation with shopping and fashion may be humorous and even indicative of feminine frivolity (as when the D.E.B.S. are more concerned with where the villainess may have gotten her sweater than with capturing her), it also suggests that heroism and girly pleasures are not mutually exclusive. Rather than being depicted as a figurative male, as many of the quintessential action women of the recent past have been described, the young action heroine is consciously portrayed as ideally and conventionally feminine. This strategy serves the dual purpose of reinforcing heterosexual male interest in the characters as appropriate objects of fascination, and of figuring them as unthreatening subjects of identification for young female viewers. This preoccupation with consumption also serves the commercial industry's need to promote purchasing as a natural and pleasurable girlish activity. Rather than implying that young women should be concerned only with more important things than shopping, these narratives (produced by such multimedia conglomerates as Disney, Nickelodeon, and The Cartoon Network) suggest that consumption need not be sacrificed in order to do great things.

Since many of these programs are aimed at children (and older devoted fans of cult television shows), the young girl action heroine is also an ideal figure for reinforcing and promoting extratextual consumption among audience members. Like most contemporary media properties, these heroines exist as commercial intertexts wherein the character herself becomes an ideal consumable. Most obviously, animated characters like The Powerpuff Girls, Kim Possible, Atomic Betty, and Princess Natasha can be mass-marketed through ancillary licensing deals far beyond any merchandising possibilities available to more mature characters like Ellen Ripley or Sarah Connor. All of these young heroines have emerged as Girl Power–branded powerhouses through toys, clothing lines, music compilations, candies, posters, lunch boxes, jewelry, video games, stationery, and so on. The related merchandising deals for *The Powerpuff Girls* and *Kim Possible* alone number in the hundreds.

In writing about the merchandising of *The Powerpuff Girls*, Joy Van Fuqua (2002) notes the tension inherent between the series' message of female empowerment and the implication that what the show's young female viewers do best is buy stuff. "In spite of the program's content, which represents girlhood as power-*ful* rather than power-*less*," Van Fuqua argues, "the commercial intertexts tend to reframe this power in terms of consumerism" (216). While this extratextual message may be problematic to some degree, it does not undermine the positive attributes made available to young female fans by both the show and the related merchandise. After all, the consumption associated with *The Powerpuff Girls* may be gendered feminine in its marketing approach, but it really is not any different than the parallel marketing of characters like Batman and Spider-Man to young boys.

Like boys, even pre-school girls can now play with action figures and wear T-shirts adorned with their favorite heroic characters. What these extensive merchandising lines demonstrate is not simply that young girls are important only as consumers, but that strong female characters can be as commercially successful as male characters. In a media environment where bankability ensures cultural recognition, longevity, and imitation, the young girl action heroine is the best bet for establishing a model of strong feminine types.

More troubling of the young girl as action heroine is the degree to which she exists within a larger genre that excessively fetishizes the female form, and this book details the various ways the action heroine is routinely fetishized. From casting, to filming techniques, to the association of violence with sexuality, to dominatrix-influenced costuming—action heroines are a primary example of how the media continues to fetishize women for predominantly male viewing pleasure. And while such kid-oriented animated shows as *The Powerpuff Girls*, *Atomic Betty*, *My Life as a Teenage Robot*, and *Kim Possible* may seem light years away from the image of Pamela Anderson, Jennifer Garner, or Angelina Jolie dressed as dominatrixes in *Barb Wire*, *Alias*, and *Mr. & Mrs. Smith*, respectively, they are really just at the kid-friendly end of the fetishization spectrum.

They still sport leather boots, miniskirts, and belly-baring midriffs—and many of the villainesses they encounter appear in full fetish gear. Their live-action teenage counterparts take the fetishization of girlie heroines even further. Both Sarah Michelle Gellar and Jessica Alba were treated in the popular press as full-blown sex objects even though they played teenagers on *Buffy* and *Dark Angel*. For example, on strikingly similar *Entertainment Weekly* covers, both women posed in revealing black tank tops (still the dominant action hero and heroine uniform) with the cover copy coyly suggesting that readers could sink their teeth into Gellar—and that "Lips! Hips! Superpowers!" make Alba "Sci-Fi's Siren for the Next Generation." Despite playing adolescent heroines, Gellar and Alba were freely sexualized the same way the magazine promoted the quintessential sex object and former Playboy playmate Pamela Anderson for her role as an action heroine in *V.I.P.*: "Bullets! Bombs! Bras! Pamela Anderson Lee Racks Ups Ratings in TV's New Cult Hit 'V.I.P.'" Even Kristen Bell, who played the super-smart teen sleuth Veronica Mars was featured in lingerie on the cover of *Maxim* with the declaration: "We Surrender to TV's Hottest P.I.!"

This sexualization of the young girl action heroine is not surprising given our society's long-standing tradition of eroticizing adolescent female bodies. The current emphasis on youth and adolescent sex symbols in popular culture has created a media landscape where titillating images of young women is an unquestioned norm. This is an era, after all, where "Girls Gone Wild" is an accepted image of adolescent women, and where the notion of Lolita has changed from a metaphor for girls preyed upon by pedophiles to a sexy moniker for underage seductresses.

When the eroticization of young women is coupled with the accoutrements of threatening sexuality that is the standard iconography of mature action heroines, it raises questions about why the shift to younger heroines has become so popular within the action genre. As we discussed in earlier chapters, the fetishization of full-grown action heroines functions in part to eroticize the women and their bodies as a means to contain the threat these powerful women pose to men and patriarchy by accentuating their importance as sex objects. Increased emphasis on youthful action heroines allows the genre to further undermine the symbolic threat posed by images of women/girls who can kick ass as well as, or better than, men.

In general, the fetishization of adolescent and pre-adolescent girls can be attributed in part to the fact that they are not yet fully sexualized women. Jon Stratton argues that historically the fetishization of young girls developed as a consequence of male insecurities in the face of adult sexualities. "In a cultural order dominated by the male body," writes Stratton from a Freudian perspective, "the body of the pubescent girl is beginning to mark her as Other. Yet, as a pubescent girl, she is still experienced as safe because her body does not yet carry fully those mature female markers which signify her phallic lack" (2001: 37). In this regard, while the young girl action heroine is gender-coded as more girlie than tomboy, she is not fully a woman either. She may be eroticized but the threat of her sex is not yet wholly realized. The young girl action heroine may be fetishized but, by virtue of her age, is not completely phallicized and thus threatening.

The overall girlishness of the contemporary action heroine allows these characters to be sexually appealing to male viewers without implicitly challenging patriarchal standards. Jacinda Read's analysis of the modern *Charlie's Angels* film as a post-feminist text points out that the narrative's final displacement of the heroines' desires for heterosexual romance with a curiosity for the paternal figure of Charlie functions to erase any dangers they represent in the realm of adult sexuality. "In this way," Read summarizes, "it could be argued that the film recuperates the threat posed by the violent woman by positioning her as a girl-child rather than as a woman" (2004: 223).

By stressing the youthfulness of these post-feminist heroines either literally or figuratively as "girls," the narratives can have their cake and eat it too. As girls, the heroines can play out the most extreme fantasies of heroism in a liminal realm, and yet they may put aside such behavior as simply youthful rebellion. As Read puts it: "[T]he girlie identity—dependent as it is on not growing up—can offer only a temporary reconciliation of femininity and violence" (225). There is a clear implication that these active "girls" may grow up and settle down into proper female roles.

Indeed, as Stasisa (2004) points out in her discussion of *Tomb Raider*, at the film's end Lara Croft embraces her proper role as "Lady Croft" by donning a more traditionally feminine white dress. Likewise, the final moments of the series *Alias* shows Sydney retiring to an idyllic fantasy of marital bliss and motherhood. In this regard, the young girl action heroine may be an extremely palatable figure of strong femininity because it is free from the demands of adult responsibilities. It can depict challenging images of powerful girls without challenging cultural expectations of women that are still bound up with notions of nurturing mothers and/or sexual availability for men.

7) "EXOTIC BEAUTIES"

Ethnicity and Comic Book Superheroines

*T*have been an avid fan of superhero comic books my entire life, so it came as no surprise to anyone who knew me when I wrote *Black Superheroes, Milestone Comics and Their Fans* (2001) in order to explore the intersections of masculinity, ethnicity, fandom, and spandex-clad superheroes. That book focused on the presentation of African American heroes created by the then fledgling Milestone Media Inc. and how fans interpreted the characters and issues of masculinity according to genre conventions and conceptions of ethnicity. Because superhero comics have always been primarily about men and created for men, it seemed natural to use them to focus almost exclusively on themes of masculinity. But superhero comic books also feature a great number of superheroines and reveal a lot about the way our popular culture constructs and understands women.

Chapter Three addressed the symbolic and fetishistic aspects of comic book superheroines as they relate to the larger impact of action heroines in film and television but it did not factor in the issue of the superheroine's ethnicity. Even a cursory look at contemporary comic books reveals a significant increase in superheroines of color. DC Comics and Marvel, the *Big Two* of comics publishers, have produced such notable ethnically identified heroines as the Latina characters Arana, White Tiger, Fire, and Tarantula; the African American or African heroines Storm, Vixen, Onyx, Steel 2.0, Thunder, Lady Hawk, Misty Knight; the Asian Psylocke, Colleen Wing, Katana, and the most recent Batgirl; the Native North American Rainmaker, Dawnstar, and the most recent Shaman; and even the unprecedented Middle-Eastern superheroine Dust.

As non-Caucasian characters, these costumed heroines have added a great deal to the cultural diversity of mainstream comics. At their worst, these ethnically identifiable female characters reveal the long-standing tradition of exoticizing the female Other in popular culture. Yet, at their best, these superheroines are also used to question and problematize the racist and sexist stereotypes associated with specific ethnicities.

ORIENTALISM AND FEMININITY

As a particularly American art form it is no surprise that superhero comic books' approach to minority characters is thoroughly grounded in stereotypes and conceptions of what Edward Said famously referred to as Orientalism (1979). Influenced by Michel Foucault's theories about the nexus of knowledge and power, and Antonio Gramsci's concept of hegemony, Said argued that Western culture has a vested interest in defining itself in opposition to the East. But, as Said went to great pains to argue, the West's conception of the East is rooted in a self-serving colonialist fantasy of the Orient as a mysterious and exotic locale filled with primitive natives, a collective fiction that justifies the Western world's domination of non-Western nations and people.

Historically the fantasy image of the Orient was institutionalized through such mechanisms as travel guides, accounts of early explorers, journalists, foreign policy briefs, art, and literature. In contemporary times, despite an increased awareness about the diverse cultures that actually constitute the fictionalized Orient, the practice of Orientalism still thrives in such media as film, television, music, advertising, literature, and of course comic books. Still complicit in the concept of Orientalism is the characterization of non-Western people in stereotypical modes that reduce them to stock images of exotic Others.

Because the mythical Orient encompasses all non-Western cultures, and by extension all non-White peoples, ethnicities as diverse as African, Hispanic, Middle-Eastern, Far-Eastern, Mediterranean, and Asian are conceived primarily according to stereotypes. Among the more obvious (and often contradictory) stereotypes are uncivilized, devious, religiously fundamental, violent, immoral, excessively sexual and excessively bodily. The persistence and continued influence of Orientalism as a belief system for defining, knowing, and controlling the non-Western world and its people still dominates official foreign policies and racist attitudes.

While the Orientalist fantasy has resulted in very specific negative stereotypes and effects for both men and women categorized as Others, my primary concern here is how Orientalism continues to characterize women as exotic fetishes. The colonial and imperial practices that gave rise to Orientalism in the first place were always conceived in phallocentric terms that positioned the West as masculine conquerors and the Orient as a mysterious feminine Other to be controlled and occupied. This metaphorical gendering and sexualization of the Orient remains a dominant conception in popular culture.

Discussing colonial-themed films, Ella Shohat argues that: "The exposed, barren land and the blazing sands, furthermore, metaphorize the exposed, unrepressed 'hot' passion and uncensored emotions of the Orient, in short, as the world of the out-of-control id" (1997: 32). Moreover, this projection of the Orient as "hot" and "sexual" is encapsulated in the image of the ethnic woman, the veiled or the lustful woman, whose mysterious presence literalizes Freud's conception of the unknowable feminine as a "dark continent." Thus to know the Orient is to possess the exotic feminine, and vice versa. "It is this process of exposing the female Other, of literally denuding her," Shohat continues, "which comes to allegorize the Western masculinist power of possession, that she, as a metaphor for her land, becomes available for Western penetration and knowledge" (32–33).

This metaphorical conception of the feminine Other as hot, sexy, mysterious, and conquerable remains an important factor in how ethnically identified women are understood in the West even when the context is completely divorced from foreign lands. As feminist and ethnic studies scholars such as Anne McClintock (1995), bell hooks (1992), Patricia Hill Collins (2004), Diane Negra (2001), and Celine Parrenas Shimizu (2007) have demonstrated in their work, the power of exoticism is still a dominant trope played out on the body of the female Other, especially in visual mediums, in a manner that reduces her to a racially charged sex object and a readily consumable body. This burden of racial and sexual stereotyping coalesces well in the fantasy figure of the ethnic superheroine who is constructed as a locus of fetishization.

The specter of Orientalism and Colonialist-influenced beliefs is intimately intertwined with almost every media representation of non-Whites in contemporary popular culture. In particular, women of color are consistently marketed and consumed as more bodily, more sexual, and more mysterious than their Caucasian counterparts. In short, ethnically identified women are routinely overwritten by cultural stereotypes and expectations of exotic Otherness, and all the sexual fantasies that implies.

The persistent fetishization of ethnic women in the media is often presented as a type of celebration of ethnic diversity and appreciation, but in truth it never strays far from the racist and sexist origins of timeworn stereotypes. Whether it is the cultural fascination with Jennifer Lopez's and Beyonce's ethnic booties, Salma Hayek's and Penelope Cruz's hot Latina sexuality, or Lucy Lui's and Kelly Hu's Asian dominatrix Dragon Lady roles, the association between race and predetermined models of exoticism continue to shape our cultural perception of ethnic women. Perhaps the most egregious example of fetishizing ethnic women as exotic Others in recent years came from the newsstand special edition series of *Playboy* simply entitled *Exotic Beauties*. In response to criticism that the Playboy brand perpetuates the narrowly defined blonde and blue-eyed California type of female beauty as the pinnacle of ideal sexuality, the editors decided that to offset the relative lack of racial diversity in their magazine they would simply produce special pictorial-only issues dedicated to sexy women of color. Though this strategy is tantamount to visual segregation, Playboy promoted it as a special celebration of ethnic women, or, as the cover of the second issue declared: "Hot Girls with a Spicy Kick!" In the first issue the editorial premise for the series reads as a clear enunciation of fetishizing the female Other without even a hint of irony. In the brief rationale entitled "Exotic is Erotic" the executive editor writes:

> To describe something as exotic conjures up visions of mystery and excitement—a step outside the norm or an adventure beyond our comfort zone. We travel to exotic destinations, dine on exotic foods and drool over exotic cars. And then there are the women, whose physical makeup and ethnic background deem them as exotic. We find beauty and sensuality in the richness of their skin, the shape of their eyes, the texture of their hair and even the cadence of their names. In this our first *Exotic Beauties*, we take you to places and introduce you to ladies who evoke a romance and mystery that stirs our imagination. (Cohen 2002: 3)

In one quick swoop all non-white women are lumped together as exotic Others who are mysterious and exciting, physically different but in a sexy way, and are symbolically equated with foreign lands, spicy foods, and even cars—the ultimate fantasy commodity for men to possess and "drive"—well, the ultimate commodity except for the women themselves, the editorial implies.

As romanticized as the *Playboy* description of exoticism is, finding "beauty and sensuality in the richness of their skin," it does illustrate that the link between skin color as a signifier of ethnicity and eroticism still holds considerable sway. In superhero comic books color has always been an important component even if it has been treated separately from skin color as a signifier of ethnicity. After all, color has been one of the primary designations involved in the symbolic naming of characters from the very inception of the genre.

Superhero names tend to fall into one of four conventionally totemic categories. First are the names that emphasize the remarkable stature of the hero or heroine such as Superman, Wonder Woman, Captain Marvel, Ultra-Man, Power Girl, Mr. Fantastic, and so on. Second there are the names that align a character with animalistic totems such as Batman, Spider-Man, Hawkman,

Wolverine, Animal Man, etc. Third are the figures whose names clarify the heroes' powers in association with certain natural elements such as Aquaman, Iron-Man, Lightning Lad, and Storm. The fourth, and most curious, naming convention involves a color designation that has no relevance to either the heroes' powers nor their skin color such as Green Arrow, Red Arrow, Blue Beatle, Green Lantern, Black Canary, Black Widow, Silver Samurai, The Scarlet Witch, etc., etc.

For these characters color serves simply as a, well . . . colorful means to jazz up their costumes and theme their weapons. The only time when color is used as part of a superheroes' name to address their race was with the various characters produced during the blaxploitation era of comics including Black Panther, Black Lightning, and Black Goliath. While these names were an attempt to tap into the Black Power zeitgeist of the times, the direct reference to skin color also highlights the absurdity of singling out these characters based on their ethnicity, and makes it clear that white heroes were considered the unmarked norm.

As a form of science fiction, superhero comics have always incorporated skin colors without directly addressing the issue of racial inequality. In the world of superhero fantasy characters have never been limited to the racially identified skin tones found in reality. The presence of purple-, orange, and green-skinned characters allowed the comics industry to delude itself for decades that superheroes were beyond the real-world concerns about skin color. The absurdity of this situation was the basis for the now famous scene in *Green Lantern/Green Arrow #76* (1970) where an elderly black man asks the heroes: "I been readin' about you. How you work for the blue skins . . . and how on a planet someplace you helped out the orange skins . . . and you done considerable for the purple skins! Only there's skins you never bothered with. The black skins! I want to know . . . how come!"

This exchange set the two heroes off on a legendary quest to address a variety of social injustices that were especially topical at the time. But as the genre has moved on over the decades with few, but significant, new heroes of color, a noticeable tendency to create even more characters with fantastical skin tones continues. Current popular heroes and villains include the green-skinned Martian Manhunter, Ms. Martian, Beast Boy, Brainiac 5, Jade, She-Hulk, and of course The Hulk (who has also been grey and red in recent years); the orange-skinned Starfire, Arisia, and Soranik Natu, the blue-skinned Mystique, Nightcrawler, Shadow Lass, Forerunner, Blue Devil, the purple Indra, Laira, and The Purple Man, the red-skinned Hellboy and Kid Devil, and the silver-skinned Colossus, Mercury, Bulleteer, and Silver Surfer. While all these heroes and villains are "of color," they are all illustrated with decidedly

Caucasian features—their skin tones essentially functioning as a variation of the skintight colorful costumes superheroes have always worn.

Though white characters have always dominated superhero comics, their "whiteness" has rarely been an issue. This is not to say that white has never been a thematic issue in representational strategies. The color white has figured prominently in some superhero costumes and as a total absence of skin pigment usually used with ghostly characters like Deadman, Lady Death, Ghost, or The Spectre. Most noticeably though, excessive whiteness is used to accentuate the fetishization of specific superheroines. The blonde, blue-eyed American ideal in the vein of Supergirl is taken to an extreme in such white-costumed heroines as Power Girl, Dream Girl, and Emma Frost (formerly The White Queen).

These heroines, and their ilk, are routinely illustrated as almost blindingly white pinups. Their white hair and skimpy white costumes construct them as pinnacles of Aryan beauty. Their physical idealization combined with their Uber-whiteness makes these heroines the comic book equivalents of the "angelically glowing white woman" of film and photography that Richard Dyer describes in his book *White* (1997). Dyer argues that specific lighting techniques have been used to imbue white people with a beatific glow, an otherworldly aura that implies an inherent superiority over darker-skinned races. White women in particular tend to be depicted as glowing, as lit from within, as a means to suggest racial superiority. "The white woman as angel was in these contexts," Dyer argues, "both the symbol of white virtuousness and the last word in the claim that what made whites special as a race was their non-physical, spiritual, indeed ethereal qualities" (127).

While all superheroines are fetishized in the comics, the radiant whiteness associated with Power Girl, Dream Girl, and Emma Frost implies that their idealization is intertwined with their paleness. The heavy eroticization of these female characters, clad as they are in costumes that are really nothing more than white swim suits and lingerie, may not stand as a symbol of white virtuousness but their magical glow, their luminosity, does subliminally construct them as ethereal beauties and angelic images of white womanhood. Of course other superheroines who are brunettes or redheads or even ethnic Others are just as thoroughly fetishized but they are not as often lit from within in the same manner, as if by a divine light.

Explicit references to racial relations rarely occur in mainstream comics. In a fictional universe populated by superpowered beings, aliens, ancient gods, and mythical creatures, traditional ethnicities seem rather mundane. For the most part race and racial tensions are ignored, giving the impression that most of the characters (and certainly all of the heroes) have overcome racism.

Moreover, the fantastical range of beings that make up the comics world allow the medium to recast racism metaphorically.

The most obvious case of this is the Marvel universe's use of discrimination against mutants as a proxy for a variety of different real-world problems, including racism, sexism, classism, and homophobia. Government-sponsored Sentinels and religious Purifiers trying to eliminate the "mutant threat" take the place of real-life institutionalized and systemic discriminations, and every cry of "Damn muties!" is easy to understand as a variation on any number of derogatory slurs. When superhero comics do address racism directly they usually veer towards simple but optimistic scenarios. For example, when DC Comics ran a series of stories where their most important heroes interacted with indigenous superbeings from other nations in 2000, the message was a positive one about accepting cultural diversity. Unfortunately, the stories also involved a colonial logic such that when the heroes of Mexico who first rebuke Superman's help eventually come to respect his unselfish heroism, his noblesse oblige, and pledge their allegiance to him.

To point out that all modern comic book women are extremely fetishized is almost redundant. Nearly every female character in comics is illustrated as an adolescent fantasy of the perfect woman. Visually superhero comics are about perfect bodies, both male and female, with the costumes and the action designed to show off rippling muscles and heaving bosoms. But where the male characters are presented as ideals of identification for the mostly male readership, the women are displayed as sex objects, albeit ones that can deflect bullets and throw cars around.

Michael Chabon, the Pulitzer Prize–winning author of *The Amazing Adventures of Kavalier & Clay* (2001), has recently written, "Boobs were a big part—literally—of the female superhero package. Almost every superwoman, apart from the explicitly adolescent characters like the original Supergirl or the X-Men's Kitty Pryde, came equipped as if by the nature of the job with a superheroic rack. Furthermore, the usual way of a female-superhero costume was to advertise the breasts of its wearer by means of décolletage, a cleavage cutout, a pair of metal Valkyrie cones, a bustier. . . . Today's female costumed characters tend to sport breasts so enormous that their ability to simply get up and walk, let alone kick telekinetic ass, would appear to be their most marvelous and improbable talent" (Chabon 2008: 198 and 201).

Likewise, in his discussion of postmodern comic book bodies, Scott Bukatman (1994) describes the highly exaggerated female form that came to dominate the genre in the early 1990s and still persists today. "The spectacle of the female body in these titles is so insistent, and the fetishism of breasts, thighs, and hair so complete," Bukatman argues, "that the comics seem to dare you to say something about them that isn't just redundant. *Of course* the female form has absurdly exaggerated sexual characteristics; *of course* the costumes are skimpier than one could (or should) imagine; *of course* there's no visible way that these costumes could stay in place; *of course* these women represent simple adolescent masturbatory fantasies (with a healthy taste of the dominatrix)" (Bukatman 1994: 112). Elsewhere, I have discussed the excessive fetishization of comic book superheroines as it relates to issues of gender performance and dominatrix fantasies (see Brown 2004). In essence, despite all their powers and heroic acts, the modern superheroine is first and foremost a scantily clad and extremely curvaceous sexual ideal.

Bukatman does point out that in addition to their fetishization, contemporary superheroines have at least been elevated beyond the cliché of merely being damsels in distress. "One might note that women participate more fully in battle than they once did. It's worth observing that they're now as powerful as their male counterparts" (112). Yet despite being stronger and more capable in battle than ever before and possessing superpowers that rival or exceed those of their male counterparts, comic book heroines are still treated as second-class citizens in the world of superherodom. The inherent misogyny of the male-dominated comic book industry has been highly criticized of late for not just the eroticization of superheroines but also for the relatively unequal violence they are subjected to.

Much of the current wave of criticism centers around what female comics writer Gail Simone dubbed the "women-in-refrigerators syndrome" after a 1994 *Green Lantern* story arc where the body of the hero's mutilated girlfriend is discovered in his fridge. Simone and some of her industry colleagues put together a list of major female characters that had been killed, mutilated, and depowered. As Simone told *Bitch* magazine, the list "was shockingly long, and almost no one in the already small pool of valid superheroines escaped the wave of gynocentric violence" (Cochran 2007: 23). Yes, male heroes can die as well but they tend to die heroically and are often commemorated and/ or magically brought back from the dead on a regular basis.

The women, on the other hand, are more likely to be casually, but irreparably, wounded such as when Barbara Gordon's (the original Batgirl) spine was shattered by the Joker just for fun and has been restricted to a wheelchair for over a decade now. Or, as with the more recent death of Stephanie Brown who momentarily became the first (within the DC Universe's regular continuity) female Robin, the violence against women is often overtly sexualized. In 2004 Stephanie/Robin was bound and tortured by the villain Black Mask over several issues and ultimately killed when he ran her through with a power-drill. Stephanie's gruesome death had only a small impact on the story line, and almost no impact on Batman (he had, after all, told her to stay out of it), but fans have become outraged at the clearly misogynistic violence of the act and the industry's disregard for the character. Numerous protests were launched, including at least one website, Girl-Wonder.org, calling for better treatment of characters like Stephanie Brown, and at the very least a memorial for her in the Batcave, which is the standard canonization for Bat-characters who fall in battle. DC Comics has repeatedly insisted there are no plans for a fictional memorial.

The twin yokes of racial Otherness and fetishized femininity are essential to any consideration of ethnically identified women in popular culture. Within superhero comics women of color are doubly fetishized as both female and Other. Indeed, because women in the comics are already so heavily fetishized as sex objects, the added layer of exoticism involved in the portrayal of ethnic superheroines seems redundant. Still, the issue of racial stereotyping as "exotic beauties," to borrow the phrase from *Playboy*, plays an important role with the new wave of ethnic superheroines.

Though superheroines of almost every ethnicity and nationality now exist in the comics either as feature players or members of super-teams, I want to focus in the remainder of this chapter on a few specific ethnic heroines who have been especially popular during the last few years. The African American Misty Knight; the Asian Batgirl, Cassandra Cain; the Latina White Tiger, Angela del Toro; and the Middle-Eastern Dust, Sooraya Qadir all reveal the various ways that ethnicity and femininity are doubly fetishized in the comics at the same time the characters are important for incorporating cultural diversity into the genre. Each of these characters deals with issues of racism and sexism in a manner that challenges the conventional whiteness of the genre but also reinforces stereotypes about exotic beauties as hypersexual. While white superheroines are clearly fetishized as sexual ideals as well, the inscription of hypersexuality coupled with ethnicity perpetuates specific cultural stereotypes of exotic Otherness. As Celine Parrenas Shimizu describes:

> Hypersexuality is the inscription of pathological or non-normative sexuality as if it were a natural characteristic, one that is directly linked to a particular raced and gendered ontology. A Western fantasy of a perverse subject position for racial and gendered subjects in popular representation, the production of hypersexuality directly contrasts with normal or standard white male sexuality. . . . [T]his phenomenon powerfully ascribes the sexuality of nonwhite others as aberrant. While hypersexuality is a "fiction" that ultimately fails to capture the sexual subjectivities of raced and gendered subjects as a "factual" or coherent group, the differences between normal and abnormal classifications have values: right

versus wrong, knowable versus unknowable, acceptable versus unacceptable, and familiar versus different. (Parrenas Shimizu 2007: 31)

The excessively fetishistic representation of ethnic superheroines may be questioned through some of the characters addressed here but ultimately is utilized to solidify a conception of exotic beauties as relatively perverse sex objects for the predominantly white male readership.

MODERN ETHNIC SUPERHEROINES

African American superheroines have been one of the most widely represented ethnic groups in recent comics. Perhaps the most famous is the African born Storm from the X-Men books, but she has been joined by the likes of Rocket from the now-defunct *Icon* series, Vixen from the various Justice League titles, as well as such lower-profile characters as Onyx, Steel 2.0, Tesla Strong, XS, and Ladyhawk. In 2005 Marvel Comics revamped one of its most popular blaxploitation-era characters, Misty Knight, who, along with her Asian partner Colleen Wing, starred in the best-selling mini-series *Daughters of the Dragon: Samurai Bullets* and currently headlines the *Heroes for Hire* series. Despite being revamped for the new millennium, the portrayal of Misty Knight in *Samurai Bullets* is still heavily influenced by her blaxploitation origins.

In the story Misty and Colleen now run Nightwing Restorations, a bonding company that specializes in posting bail for, and frequently having to recapture, superpowered criminals. Through a series of mishaps, the Daughters of the Dragon find themselves entangled in a struggle over a mysterious microchip stolen from the ruthless supervillainess Ricadonna that is set to be sold to the highest bidder and will lead to the total destruction of all the world's computer systems. Armed with her bad attitude, guns, and a powerful cybernetic arm, Misty and the samurai-trained Colleen manage to defeat literally hundreds of bad guys and of course save the day.

Throughout *Samurai Bullets* Misty is depicted as a strong-willed woman who speaks her mind and is as concerned with the financial rewards of her job as she is with doing the morally right thing. By the end of the story Misty defeats Ricadonna, a far superior fighter, through shear stubbornness and basic street fighting. Overall, Misty is clearly presented as a smart and powerful heroine not to be messed with. But visually Misty is intentionally overloaded with reminders of her blaxploitation past. Most obviously she sports an unusually large 1970s style afro (large enough for several of the other characters to comment on) and carries a ghetto-blaster playing Curtis Mayfield's *Superfly* theme on one of her adventures.

Less ironically, Misty also conforms to the hypersexualized characterization of blaxploitation heroines made famous by the likes of Pam Grier and Tamara Dobson. Misty's sexual attractiveness is put on display for readers early on when her naked body is glimpsed in the shower over the course of two full pages. And immediately after leaving the shower Misty engages in her first solo fight with the privileged white villainess Ricadonna while clad only in a skimpy bathrobe, which conveniently affords lots of leg and cleavage shots. "Can I get dressed or are we gonna do this bareback?" Misty asks, but in true comic book (and blaxploitation) style the near-naked brawl starts anyway. "Bareback it is then," Misty concedes.

After losing this initial fight, during which Ricadonna cuts off Misty's cybernetic arm (which is replaced by a newer and more powerful version), Misty's anger takes over and she turns the case into a personal quest for revenge. Almost immediately, and without any narrative purpose, Misty marches off to meet her professional acquaintance Danny Rand, aka the magically enhanced martial artist Iron Fist, for some rough and dirty sex simply to "blow off some steam." Though the act is not depicted (thanks primarily to comics code restrictions), the aftermath is shown and it is clear the encounter was aggressive—headboards and lamps are broken—and as Misty dresses Danny lies spent in the broken bed, declaring "I think I need an I.V. drip and some pancakes."

This scene has no bearing on the story except to mark Misty's assertive and animalistic hypersexuality. Rarely, if ever, do white superheroines hook up for random sexual encounters just to "blow off some steam." Villainesses of every color might have kinky casual sex, and white heroines do have liaisons, though usually within the confines of a committed relationship with a fellow hero, but with an African American character the writers had no problem with depicting her sexual appetites as wanton. In contrast with the more chaste sexual encounters of white women in mainstream comics (no matter how visually fetishized they are), Misty's sexuality carries with it the burden of the hypersexual Other. Despite still being clearly positioned as the hero of the story, this type of depiction also situates the ethnic superheroine as a bearer of transgressive sexuality.

Daughter of the Dragon: Samurai Bullets focuses far more on Misty and her sexuality than on that of her partner, Colleen Wing, despite her being a superheroine of color as well. Colleen's sexuality is also coded as excessive but is pretty much limited in this particular story to several lesbian overtures made by the villainess, and to some non-too-subtle flirtations with her sparring partner, the American Samurai, who she distracts at one point by exposing her breasts with a coy, "Magical, aren't they?" It is worth noting that both Iron

Fist and the American Samurai are white male heroes with mystical ties to the Orient but who represent a racial fantasy of being seduced by the aggressive sexuality of these exotic beauties.

In addition to being a reminder of the interrelatedness of blaxploitation and kung fu films historically, the inclusion of Colleen Wing is also an indication Asian women have been fairly well represented within the superhero genre since the 1970s. In large part this is because Asian women are easy to associate with any range of martial arts and because they have a long history of being fetishized sex objects as either passive Lotus Blossom types or, more apropos of the comics, as seductive Dragon Ladies (a term derived from the classic villainess Lai Choi San, the Dragon Lady, from Milton Caniff's popular *Terry and the Pirates* newspaper strip of the 1930s). Colleen Wing is Japanese with samurai training, as is Katanna of the *Batman and The Outsiders* series. Psylocke of the X-Men, who was originally a white British aristocrat, was transformed in the 1990s into a Japanese ninja with telekenetic abilities. Miho is a Japanese assassin who protects the working girls of *Sin City*. And the mysterious Lady Shiva is considered the greatest master of all the martial arts in the DC universe. Numerous other Asian heroines have superpowers unrelated to martial arts, such as Jubilation Lee who shoots fireworks from her fingers, Surge who controls electricity, Swift who has wings and super speed, Grace Choi who wields super strength and is invulnerable, the shrinking Wasp, and the fire-powered Sunfire. One of the most prominent Asian superheroines in the 2000s has been Cassandra Cain, the daughter of Lady Shiva, who became the most recent character to assume the mantle of Batgirl.

Cassandra Cain is a complex character featured in her own series for several years and who now appears in a variety of super-team books. Initially Batman recruited the mute Cassandra for the role of Batgirl due to her exceptional martial arts skills. As her backstory unfolds readers learned that Cassandra was raised by the world's preeminent assassin, David Cain, in complete silence so that she would be able to read body language thus allowing her to know what her opponents will do before they even move.

Cain taught her every deadly skill known to man in the hopes of molding a perfect killing machine. But the preadolescent Cassandra leaves Cain when she begins to question the morality of her fate. Batman's subsequent mentoring of Cassandra takes on the tones of a philosophical quest to unleash her inherent potential for good despite her horrendous origins. Interestingly, Cassandra's Asian identity is rarely mentioned in the books, though it does seem to go hand-in-hand with her martial arts skills. Cassandra's racial identity is treated more implicitly than explicitly. Her costume design actually conceals her entire body so that while in her guise as Batgirl her ethnicity is completely unapparent. What is problematic is Cassandra's eventual fall from grace as she accepts her fate as Lady Shiva's daughter becoming an arch villain, the leader of the infamous League of Assassins, at the conclusion of her own seventy-three-issue series. While many fans were outraged when DC Comics turned Cassandra into a villainess, it does gel with notions of Asian women as not just mysterious and exotic but also as deceitful and dangerous. That Cassandra's turn to villainy is linked with her mother, the sexy and deadly modern Dragon Lady, implicitly aligns her ethnic heritage and her gender with the most negative connotations of Orientalism.

Before her embrace of the dark side, Cassandra's sexuality, like her ethnicity, is rarely emphasized. As an early adolescent her romantic encounters are limited to chaste flirtations with the young white male heroes Superboy and Robin. Still, as a costumed superheroine and an exotic Other, this Batgirl is fetishized even if she is not sexually active. Her version of the Batgirl costume is straight out of an S&M fantasy . . . head to toe skin-tight black leather, with even her eyes and mouth openings stitched over. Despite being garbed in an iconically kinky fashion, and having suggestions of the Asian schoolgirl fantasy in her secret identity, the *Batgirl* series often sought to address the inherent sexualization of comic book women.

For example, in issue #39 Cassandra is cajoled by Barbara Gordon (the now crippled ex-Batgirl) into wearing a bikini while aboard a cruise ship. Cassandra reluctantly wears the bikini but is immediately offended and angered by the way men treat her, especially an out-of-costume Superboy, because she can read their body language and knows that they are all thinking about her sexually. Furthermore, in *Batgirl* #45 Cassandra borrows Barbara's old costume after she describes how much fun she used to have as Batgirl and how exciting and empowering she found it when men fawned over her. But when Cassandra decides to fight crime in the old costume she finds it impractical (she trips in the high heels) and disconcerting that instead of being afraid of her, muggers quip: "Hey there, cutie . . . wanna play?" Even Robin is dangerously distracted when she comes to his aid in battling an entire mob, as he rambles on: "I—uh . . . nice costume. It—uh—it really suits you! In fact, I can't believe I never noticed it before, but you are one very hot—POW!"

Cassandra's status as an adolescent may mean that the writers can't depict her sexuality as gratuitously as with older characters, but she is still clearly fetishized. In the world of comics the adolescent superheroine is a trope that allows creators to have their cheesecake and tease about it too. Interestingly, a similar scene occurred with Marvel's teenage Latina superheroine Arana, Anya Corazon, when she shops for an appropriate costume and is depicted in various fetishized outfits parodying everything from Supergirl to *Kill Bill.*

The two-page spread permits Anya to address both the writers' and readers' fetishistic expectations, asking "Okay, which one of you has issues?" when she is dressed in a Sailor Moon schoolgirl outfit, and asking "You guys know I'm only fifteen, right?" when she is garbed as Wonder Woman. Being a teenage superheroine may mean these characters can't be depicted within the narrative as wantonly as their more mature counterparts, but as exotic Others they are still subject to visual fetishization.

The visual conventions of sexy superheroine costuming trumps not just characters' underage status, it also would seem to supersede even well-intentioned efforts to represent cultural and religious differences regarding bodily display. In 2002 Marvel added the unprecedented teen heroine Dust, Sooraya Qadir, a Sunni Muslim and an ex-slave from Afghanistan, to its ranks of international mutant good guys within the pages of the *New X-Men*. As her super-moniker suggests, Sooraya has the ability to turn her body into sand in order to fit through small spaces or rip the skin from her enemy's bodies with the ferocity of the most powerful sandstorm. Sooraya is unique in mainstream comics not only because she is an Afghani Muslim heroine introduced intentionally to raise issues of cultural awareness in a post-9/11 world, but also because she is depicted as eschewing flashy superhero costuming in favor of wearing her traditional burqa (the comics refer to it as a burqa but as many fans and critics have indicated, it is really a niqab).

The culturally and religiously distinct burqa she wears is at first consideration a bold and progressive move for Dust's creators to make since its very purpose is anathema to the fetishistic conventions of superhero costuming. A burqa (or niqab) is designed to conceal a woman's body and to mark her publicly as the property of a man. Sooraya wears her burqa willingly even after she relocates to America, as she tells her mother in *New X-Men: Hellions* #2: "I never wore it because of the Taliban, mother. I like the modesty and protection it affords me from the eyes of men." Unfortunately, however, the visual conventions of superhero comics dictated that Dust/Sooraya is still depicted as eroticized despite her professing that her costume affords her modesty and protection from the eyes of men.

As the cover image reveals, Sooraya's burqa may veil her body but her curves are still apparent. Sometimes her burqa is illustrated as a skin-tight wrap so readers can clearly see the outline of her breasts, buttocks, and legs. At other times she is depicted in private moments without her burqa, dressed in just her underwear so that readers are well aware that she is still sexy despite her religious and cultural conservatism. Writing about Orientalism in film, Ella Shohat notes that: "The Orient as a metaphor for sexuality is encapsulated by the recurring figure of the veiled woman. The inaccessibility of the veiled woman, mirroring the mystery of the Orient itself, requires a process of Western unveiling for comprehension. Veiled women in Orientalist paintings, photographs, and film expose flesh, ironically, more than they conceal it" (1997: 32). Thus, while the inclusion of a burqa-wearing Afghani Muslim teen superheroine is an amazingly progressive step, her visual depiction is still rooted in Western conceptions of exotic Orientalism that reposition her as a mysterious and tempting sexual object.

Arana may have been heralded as the first Latina heroine to headline her own series at one of the Big Two comics companies (see McGrath 2007), but her title was unfortunately short-lived. Other Latina superheroines exist in more secondary roles such as the Brazilian Fire, Beatriz da Costa, who occasionally works with the Justice League—and The Tarantula, Catalina Flores, who appeared as a reckless and seductive vigilante in the pages of *Nightwing* but turned to villainy within a few short issues. The Tarantula's hypersexuality was depicted as so essential to her character that at one point she rapes the dazed and confused white hero Nightwing (a former Robin) on a rooftop after he is injured by an explosion. Still others have broken traditional barriers such as the lesbian ex–Gotham City police officer Renee Montoya who became the new conspiracy-minded heroine known as The Question in the DC universe.

In 2006 Marvel reintroduced the character of the White Tiger in the form of Angela Del Toro, a former FBI agent. In this revamped version of the White Tiger (or La Tigresa Blanca, as she is also known) Angela is a novice superheroine who has inherited a magical amulet that enhances her martial arts skills from her uncle Hector Ayala, the original White Tiger. While this version of the White Tiger usually appears as a secondary character in a variety of Marvel books, she was featured in her own mini-series, "A Hero's Compulsion," written by the award-winning novelist Tamora Pierce. The series chronicles Angela's initiation into the world of superheroics and her first adventure battling a cabal of Yakuza crime lords, gunrunners, and several superpowered villains.

Like all superheroines, especially those that are doubly fetishized as exotic Others, the series goes to great pains to emphasize that Angela's White Tiger is as much a sex object as she is a heroine. When she tries on her formfitting white leather costume for the first time Angela wonders if it isn't a little over the top. But Spider-Man, who is included in this scene for no particular narrative reason other than to verify Angela's desirability, lustfully asks: "Can I have one of those for my wife?" Angela shrugs off his initial comments saying: "I don't know if I want to be a costume." To which Spider-Man adds, "But I want you to be a costume." At least Angela is forthright enough to tell Spider-

Man to leave and that next time only a male eunuch can come costume-shopping with her.

Moreover, when she first confronts some bad guys in her costume they greet her with flirtations: "You're an Angel—fallen from heaven, right?" and "I'm feelin' lucky, baby!" And when she breaks up a gun purchase in broad daylight, men from a nearby apartment building take pictures of her and scream from their windows: "Baby . . . I'm in love!" "All costumes should be hot like you, mamma!" and "You gonna protect us full-time, beautiful?" Even the headlines in the paper the next day focus more on White Tiger's looks than her heroism, writing "Normally we at THE BUGLE don't like Costumes—but in your case, baby, we'll make an exception! This hard-fighting, gun-totin' hot tamale was seen beating the stuffing out of a bunch of gang punks near the Bronx Zoo—when she wasn't blinding them with her skintight outfit that hugs her curves in all the right places." Definitely not the kind of public reaction or press that Superman or Captain America ever had to deal with.

The story goes to great lengths to remind readers that Angela is more than just a "hot tamale." She is repeatedly shown as brave, smart, and an exceptional fighter. Likewise, her ethnicity is framed as a positive attribute characterized primarily by close ties with her extended family and a sense of pride she shares with her brothers and cousins, all of whom are involved in law enforcement in some way—and of course her desire to live up to her uncle's iconic status as a Hispanic hero. The series does not exactly ignore racism, but it deflects it onto other more superheroic forms of bigotry such as anti-mutant sentiments (when she beats up some muggers they mistakenly call her a "damn mutie," to which she responds: "You have the right not to utter racial, ethnic, or *genetic* slurs") and the series is set amid a Marvel-wide story line about a government-imposed "Superhero Registration Act" with clear parallels to racial profiling and terrorist witch-hunts in the real world, leading Angela to comment: "Great. I was born in the Bronx—but if I put on a costume, I still have to get a Green Card."

An interesting twist in the case of Angela being a superheroine of color is that she is, thematically at least, a *White* Tiger. All the covers in the series are predominately white-on-white watercolors. Visually these images are similar to the excessively white depictions of blond and blue-eyed heroines like Power Girl, Dream Girl, and Emma Frost discussed earlier. And while Angela Del Toro is clearly portrayed as an exotic beauty rather than an Aryan type of beauty, these covers do confound Dyer's point about images of the "angelically glowing white woman" as a semiotic device implying that "what made whites special as a race was their non-physical, spiritual, indeed ethereal qualities" (127). In her secret identity name, come-ons by thugs, and the near glowing cover illustrations, there is an intention to align this exotic beauty with angelicness. Sure, a chance meeting in a café with Emma Frost, aka the White Queen, ends with Emma cattily saying "and I must say, white is *not* your color," but by the end of the series the reader knows it is. The series concludes with Angela embracing her superheroine identity as she leaps across rooftops and declares: "Nobody who wants to hurt my people gets past the White Tiger."

The twin yokes of gender and racial fetishization that make up the ethnic superheroine may yet prove to be more daunting than any fictional super villain. Certainly the superheroines I discussed here are still burdened with tropes of hypersexuality that are as much a part of their persona as are any exceptional skills or powers. But these new heroines are also more than just mere exotic beauties. Their increased presence in the superhero genre and their popularity with readers regardless of ethnicity hold great promise.

Though they may not confront issues of racial discrimination or sexism head-on, they do raise them as factors that women and various ethnic groups have to deal with on a daily basis. Change in cultural perceptions is always slow to come, particularly in a medium and a genre like superhero comics so thoroughly grounded in established visual conventions and fantastical stories. But change is happening, and the rise of female and ethnic characters—and female and ethnic writers—are driving a wedge into the white male pantheon of comic book superheroes. Now if they could just do it without skintight leather outfits. . . .

8) KINKY VAMPIRES AND ACTION HEROINES

$\mathcal{A}$s several of the preceding chapters have outlined, the diverse lineage of the action heroine unites and builds upon a variety of fetishistic representations of women. Narratively and visually the contemporary heroine intersects with conventions derived from (but not limited to) such diverse sources as 1970s jiggle-television, 1980s hard-bodied heroines, female detectives, femme fatales, video games, comic books, and pornography. Yet, perhaps the most significant influence on modern action heroines is not the larger, male-dominated action genre but her origins within late twentieth-century horror films.

In particular the character of the Final Girl that Clover so influentially identifies as the mainstay of slasher films exerts a direct influence on the action heroines themselves and their scholarly interpretation. In addition to taking up the heroic and gender-bending persona of the Final Girl, many of the action heroine stories I discussed thus far have also retained the horror films' preoccupation with vampires as mythical monsters in need of slaying. With the vampire's accumulative symbolism in popular culture as not just monstrous but also excessively sexual it is perhaps no surprise they figure so prominently in association with action heroines, whose very nature is entwined with their fetishization. The action heroine/vampire fantasy overlap in such notable examples as *Underworld* and *Underworld Evolution, Bloodrayne* and *Bloodrayne 2, Blade Trinity, Rise* (2008), and *Ultraviolet,* the continued cult status of Vampirella in comic books, the enormously popular Anita Blake book series, and of course TV's *Buffy the Vampire Slayer.*

The continued association of action heroines with vampires allows the fictions to stress issues of sexuality that can be at once transgressive, progressive, exploitative, and perverse. The action heroine tales that intermingle with the highly erotic realm of vampire stories brings to the surface many themes of sexuality that underlie the figure of the action heroine in general. The action heroine/vampire crossover clarifies the action heroines' flirtations with non-traditional options for female sexuality in an era of third-wave feminist sensibilities, yet still reaffirms conventional conceptions of proper female sexuality as a desirable norm for women. Despite the inevitable containment of female sexuality demonstrated in the official texts, the very possibility of alternative sexual desires represented by action heroines lies at the heart of the genre and the appeal of these characters for many viewers, thus contributing to their iconic and fetishistic presence in popular culture.

Even before the vampire became a dominant figure in modern popular culture, he (and on very rare occasions, she) was a sexually charged figure. The symbolism of legends, folklore, and campfire stories about vampires who attacked their victims in the night to drain them of their blood has long been interpreted as a sexual metaphor. Likewise, the erotic suggestions of paintings such as Henry Fuseli's *The Nightmare* (1781), Georg Kininger's *The Dream of Elenaor* (c. 1795), and Edvard Munch's *Vampire* (1895) are difficult to overlook. Folklorists like Bruno Bettleheim saw the vampire as a parable of sexual initiation. Early psychoanalysts such as Ernest Jones (1951) understood the vampire as a masturbatory adolescent fantasy:

> The explanation of these phantasies is surely not hard. A nightly visit from a beautiful or frightful being, who first exhausts the sleeper with passionate embraces and then withdraws from him a vital fluid; all this can point only to a natural and common process, namely to nocturnal emissions accompanied with dreams of a more or less erotic nature. In the unconscious mind blood is commonly an equivalent for semen. (Jones 1951: 33)

Literary and cultural critics have long argued that the enduring popularity of Bram Stoker's *Dracula* (1897) is based less on the novel's literary merit than its thinly veiled sexual content (see for example Twitchell 1985 and Jones 2002). The erotic overtones of Stoker's novel remained in place and were exaggerated as the story of Dracula was adapted to the stage and then to countless films from Universal's classic 1931 version and its many progeny, through Hammer studio's campy sexploitation outings in the 1960s and 1970s, to Francis Ford Coppola's blockbuster *Bram Stoker's Dracula* (1992), and Wes Craven's updated *Dracula 2000* (2000). The vampire remains an incredibly popular figure in contemporary novels, comics, films, and television in large part because, as James Twitchell observes: "He is no longer a figure of demonic terror; he has become an eidolon of sexual horror" (110).

That vampires are sexually charged figures is such a commonplace understanding nowadays that to point it out seems almost redundant. What is of interest here is that the vampire represents not just sex, but a form of sexuality that is unconventional, transgressive, overwhelming, dangerous, and perverse. From Gothic literature to modern Goths, the vampire has held a certain appeal because his sexuality is outside the norm but still coded as attractive. Traditional intercourse has almost no place in vampire lore. This is a creature with an obvious oral fixation that is easily symbolic of not just kissing but also fellatio and cunnilingus, both of which were considered exotic and taboo until relatively recently. He can reproduce through seduction but without traditional intercourse.

His, or her, victims may typically be of the opposite gender but not always. The possibility of same-sex liaisons has long made the vampire a popular icon with gay and lesbian viewers. Indeed, a number of scholars have focused on the importance of lesbianism within vampire films from *Dracula's Daughter* (1936), to *The Hunger* (1983), to *Rise* (2008). For example, both Bonnie Zimmerman (1984) and Andrew Tudor (1989) have influentially argued that the sexually aggressive and sexually ambiguous female vampire can be understood as an expression of cultural fears about lesbians and feminism.

Likewise, vampire fictions can represent a form of sadomasochistic sexuality with its intermingling of eroticism and violence, an emphasis on dominant and submissive relationships, and sartorially through its preoccupation with fetishistic costuming from high-fashion to leather bondage wear. It is within this terrain of unconventional sexuality that the association between vampires and action heroines makes sense. Like vampires, action heroines are untraditional but highly erotic figures. The action heroine stories and iconography facilitate unconventional fantasies of aggressive female sexuality and same-sex desires.

LEATHER AND LACE
Sadomasochism and Action Heroines

The colloquial contrast of leather and lace as a euphemism for rough versus soft sexuality is appropo when it comes to action heroines. Unlike the soft, lacy sexuality traditionally associated with ideal femininity, the leather- (and spandex-) wearing action heroine clearly symbolizes her transgressive nature as a tough, hard, active female figure. And, as I stressed in Chapter Two, the leather costuming that is standard action heroine garb just as clearly alludes to the stock figure of the dominatrix from sadomasochistic fantasies.

Whether the action heroine explicitly enacts the role of the dominatrix as is the case with Angelina Jolie in *Mr. and Mrs. Smith*, or Jennifer Garner in episodes of *Alias*, or implicitly as with Pamela Anderson in *Barb Wire* or Halle Berry in *Catwoman*, the specter of sadomasochism is always present. While the extreme S/M styling of action heroines is on one hand simply another example of popular culture's typical fetishization of women, it is also, on the other, a specific form of fetishization that brings at least the trappings of the sadomasochistic lifestyle to the foreground. The now common image of action heroines in tight leather bodices and bodysuits has contributed to a broader cultural awareness of fetish culture and is part of what McNair (2002) identifies as a larger trend of the acceptable "pornification" of our visual landscape.

Conversely, the fetish subculture has embraced the action heroine as a specific ideal. Ever since Michelle Pfeiffer graced the cover of the fetish magazine «*O*» in her leather Catwoman outfit in 1992, countless other fetish publications have run regular features about sexy action heroines. Action heroine costumes are now as likely to be worn by participants at fetish balls as they are by paid models and devoted "cos-play" fans (costumed role-playing) at comic book and gaming conventions. Hundreds of photo-layouts in magazines and on the Internet feature professional fetish models like Masuimi Max and Bianca Beauchamp in action heroine outfits. And, blurring the line between fetish subculture and mainstream popular culture, revealing action heroine costumes have become standard Halloween fare available in specialty stores and Wal-Marts alike. Like the vampire, the action heroine has been embraced by many as a symbol of non-traditional eroticism and may represent a mainstream acceptance of unconventional sexual practices.

As atypical female characters and a version of the unruly woman, the action heroine represents the possibility of championing unconventional sexualities. In addition to the fetishistic costuming as a symbol of kinky sexuality, the narratives often include scenes that illustrate the heroine enjoys her sexual power and the sexual threat she poses—indeed, she often claims to feel empowered by walking on the wild side. As an example, both the Michelle Pfeiffer Catwoman from *Batman Returns* and the Halle Berry version from *Catwoman* are transformed from passive office workers to whip-wielding adventurers once they don their costumes.

The awakening of sexuality and power that accompanies the transformation of plain Janes into action heroines (see similar scenes exist in films ranging from hardcore actioners like *The Long Kiss Goodnight* to goofy romantic comedies such as *My Super Ex-Girlfriend*) is very similar to the clichéd transformations of passive female victims transformed into vampires. As Creed observes about vampire films: "It is interesting to note that frequently female victims shed their state of languid torpor and emerge from their ordeal filled with an active, predatory desire" (1993: 62–63). But for all the kinky costumes and innuendo surrounding both Catwomen and numerous other action heroines who experience an onset of sexual prowess, their sadomasochistic overtones are ultimately revealed as a ruse with the women reestablished as good girls. Even the comics come closer to fully realizing the fetishistic implications of the characters than the films do.

While the action heroine may look like the ultimate S/M fantasy figure, her sexual relations within the official narratives are usually depicted as very traditional. Sure there is a lot of physical sparring between the heroines and their romantic partners that often amounts to foreplay—slamming each other against walls and throwing punches before finally falling into bed. But the actual liaison is almost always tender. When Seline, the skintight leather-clad vampire death dealer from the *Underworld* films, for example, finally puts down her knives to consummate her relationship with her vampire/werewolf hybrid boyfriend in the second film, it is presented as a soft and tender moment between caring lovers rather than the aggressive copulation viewers might have expected given the mise-en-scène of the story line. The same can be said for the filmic love scenes involving Lara Croft, Elektra, Trinity, Sydney Bristow, and any other host of action heroines.

In her work on *Buffy the Vampire Slayer* Elyce Rae Helford's observation that "perversity such as s/m sexuality is the kind of 'fun' Buffy neither needs or enjoys" (2002: 34) seems equally true for all heroines. In the rare instances when action heroines seem ready to act upon the erotic feelings aroused by violence, the narratives can quickly diffuse the consummation of their unconventional desires. For example, in the first episode of the television series *Burn Notice*, which follows the exploits of the blacklisted spy Michael Westen, his former lover Fiona, who is a petite ex-IRA gun-runner with a barely contained homicidal streak, he flatly rejects her sexual proposition as inappropriate. After Fiona disarms and savagely beats a thug who has pulled a gun on them, she tries to drag Michael upstairs for sex, but he declines: "Violence is foreplay for you, Fiona, but not for me. We should just call it a night." Thus, even if the action woman wants rough sex, her partner may function to police the boundaries of appropriate primetime or PG-13 sexual relations.

This failure to carry through on the promise of kinky sex has apparently not dampened the action heroines' popularity within the fetish subculture. But, as Carol Siegel has lamented, this failure to fully explore alternative models of sexual relationships that embrace female sadism and male masochism may be a missed opportunity to expand the boundaries of what acceptable female sexuality can be. In her fascinating article "Female Heterosexual Sadism" (2007) Siegel contrasts the landmark television series *Buffy the Vampire Slayer* with the *Anita Blake Vampire Hunter* series of novels written by Laurell

K. Hamilton to explore "why feminism, now in its third wave as a movement, cannot seem to accept the expression of female sexual sadism within consensual heterosexual relationships as potentially consonant with our political goals" (58). Siegel details how the dominant logic of feminism, as established in the second-wave era, continues to align heterosexual identities and desires according to a binaristic model wherein sadism is associated with masculinity exclusively, and masochism with femininity as a de facto result of enculturated sexist relations.

Debates still rage within gender studies about the liberatory potential of nontraditional gender identifications and the effect they can have on shifting perceptions about sexual relationships. Certainly gay and lesbian studies have done much to challenge the rigidity of dominant conceptions of sexual subject positions, as have considerations of the importance of male masochism to heterosexual fantasies and much of feminism's third-wave writings that champion women's choices of both traditional and alternative sexual identities. But, as Siegel points out, much of feminism still considers any embrace of heterosexual female masochism as a logical result of typical gender inequalities, and any instances of heterosexual female sadism as a "false consciousness" capitulation to perverse male desires. Indeed, this argument over whether or not women can truly experience their own sexual desires despite this central heterosexual paradox can be seen as fundamental to the debates between second and third wavers and popular post-feminist ideology described in Chapter Six.

If this new millennium is an era when women "can do anything," to borrow a phrase from *Kim Possible*, why is heterosexual female sadism not one of the possibilities? The excessively violent and sexualized action heroine would seem a likely figure for popular culture to work through the isssues of radically different female sexual identities. Yet, for all her independence and aggressiveness, the action heroine's sexuality within the diegesis of the stories is most often neatly contained within the parameters of normal sexual relations. This is not to say that viewers always accept these conventional sexual representations as definitive.

Like the vampire she so often fights, the action heroine is symbolically polymorphous enough in her sexuality that she is easily reconfigured to suit alternative fantasies, an idea I will return to later. A great deal of Siegel's argument about the media's failure to explore heterosexual female sadism is based on the various ways Buffy's sexuality is consistently regulated over the course of the series' seven-year run. Siegel observes: "*Buffy the Vampire Slayer* follows a pattern similar to that of the sex-regulating feminism that became majoritist in the second wave" (73). In other words, Buffy's sexuality is carefully regulated to conform to safely liberal conventions of ideal heterosexual female identifications of proper feminine roles. Despite Buffy's flirtations with alternative sexual desires, the series ultimately confirms that she is a good girl who shuns deviance. Two storylines in particular are worth discussing in detail for the way they demonstrate Buffy's rejection of dark desires: her relationship with Faith, another slayer who is depicted as an out-of-control Bad Girl; and her relationship with the villainous vampire Spike who becomes an ally/lover.

The character of Faith was written into the *Buffy* series in season three by the program's creator Joss Whedon as a means to explore the dark side of slaying. As numerous Buffy scholars have argued, Faith is very self-consciously utilized as Buffy's dark doppelganger (see for example Jowett 2005, Helford 2002, Hollows 2000, Tjardes 2003). While Buffy slays vampires because it is her responsibility, Faith seems to enjoy the power. Where Buffy attends school, Faith is a dropout. Where Buffy fights to protect humans above all else, Faith sees them as weaker beings that just get in the way—and shows little remorse when she kills a human by mistake. And most important to this discussion, where Buffy only engages in sex within the confines of monogamous long-term heterosexual romances, Faith approaches sex vigorously and with a variety of casual partners.

In contrast to Faith, Buffy is presented as a pinnacle of cute, white, middle-class femininity despite her exceptional powers, her role as a slayer, and her sexual desirability. As Hollows points out, Buffy's version of femininity is "privileged over other forms of feminine identity that have been labeled as 'deviant' or 'dangerous,' identities that have usually been identified with black and white working-class women" (2000: 31). Buffy's status as a Good Girl is predicated not just on her moral position as a slayer, it is closely aligned with her conformity to the standards of acceptable and proper feminine attitudes.

While the series does an interesting job of illustrating how integral Buffy's social and class standing is to her status as the Good slayer, it also relies on Faith's unbridled sexuality as the principle sign of the essential difference between the two women. In her detailed discussion of Faith as a preeminent Bad Girl, Jowett argues: "Faith's femininity is sexualized, focused on her cleavage and glossy pout, and she is described by Willow as a 'cleavagy slut-bomb.' Her negotiation of a gendered identity contrasts sharply with Buffy's more demure version of femininity" (2005: 85). Faith allows the writers to explore the association implicit in the series between violence and sexuality.

With Buffy the link between her violent occupation and her sexuality is safely deflected onto monogamous loving relationships with strong active men such as Angel, the vampire with a soul, and Riley, a black-ops military man who specializes in killing demons. The kinky aspects of Buffy's sexuality are carefully bracketed out. Not so with Faith. After a particularly rousing episode of vampire-killing Faith declares, much to Buffy's surprise, "Isn't it funny how slaying just makes you hungry and horny?" Faith embraces her appetites be it food or sex (both traditional markers of Otherness and unruly women). Faith is a Bad Girl within the logic of the series specifically because she does not control herself in the matters of violence and sex.

For Faith sex and violence are fun and interchangeable. Just as her slaying of vampires is not really about the larger goal of saving mankind, her sexual encounters are not about developing deep bonds. Justine Larbalestier describes Faith as a "bad girl precisely because she falls down on the male side of the equation, wanting sex, not intimacy" (2002: 218). Moreover, Jowett correctly observes that "Faith is presented as lacking the sense of responsibility and morality that Buffy and the other good girls display" (2005: 86). As a character equal in power to Buffy and with the same heroic calling to slay vampires but without conventional restrictions, Faith initially had the feminist potential to challenge the patriarchal norms of compulsory feminine sexuality that are usually reconfirmed by modern action heroines. But by casting Faith as a villainous Bad Girl unsuitable to assume the role of the slayer, the series managed to explore the link between slaying and sex only to deny it as perverse and cast it aside in favor of Buffy's Good Girl demeanor.

The most succinct vilification of Faith's attitudes and mirroring of the two slayers occurred in the season four fan-favorite episode "Who Are You?" wherein Buffy and Faith magically switch bodies which allowed the writers to contrast the essential differences between the characters and confirm that it is their core moralities that make Buffy better than Faith. One of Faith's first acts when she discovers herself in Buffy's body is to take a sensuous bath. This autoerotic bath is described by Kaveney as "a form of perverse love-making" (2003: 71) and marks not just Faith's alignment with personal sexual gratification but also represents her desires to experience Buffy's body sexually. Faith's preoccupation with unconventional sexuality continues beyond this initial scene of self-exploration and displaced lesbian longings as she teases the lovelorn Spike with Buffy's body and then engages in rough sex with Buffy's boyfriend Riley. Much to Riley's surprise Faith, in Buffy's body but with uncharacteristically sexy clothing, slinks across the bed and suggestively taunts him: "Am I a bad girl? Do you want to hurt me?" But Riley's reaction to Faith's version of sex is hesitant and clarifies his preference for the more respectable Buffy.

Faith as Buffy also mocks the heroine's moralistic approach to slaying by repeatedly mimicking her refusal to do certain things simply because "it's *wrong*." As both Jowett and Schudt (2003) point out, Faith's deadpan repetition of this phrase signals her awareness of the arbitrary nature of right and wrong and her willingness to ignore cultural standards of correct behavior. Ultimately, the episode teaches that Faith's perspectives on sex and slaying are wrong, a lesson that Faith herself begrudgingly comprehends. This realization only fuels Faith's hatred of Buffy's innate superiority and contributes to her own self-loathing.

By the end of the episode Faith tries to kill the real Buffy who inhabits her body as a means to take Buffy's place and to punish herself. Jowett correctly observes that by this point Faith has been forced to internalize the "conventional judgments of society" (88) as she lashes out at Buffy-as-Faith, screaming "You're nothing! You're disgusting! A useless, murdering bitch! You're *nothing!*" Buffy is, of course, victorious and the two are returned to their original bodies.

In subsequent episodes Faith's bad attitude and her self-loathing lead her to become a major villainess. But eventually Faith accepts responsibility for her actions, does her time, and repents. It is only when she "chooses to accept the law and take her place within ordered (patriarchal) society" (Jowett, 88) that the series allows her a form of redemption and returns her to the side of good. Faith's unconventional and aggressive persona, especially in regards to sex, allows the series to substantiate Buffy's Good Girl status as the correct identity for the modern action heroine.

Still, Buffy's status as a Good Girl as presented in her sexual relationships is also not without problems of its own. While the series emphasizes the heroine's pursuit of monogamous heterosexual relationships it also "endorses the traditional message that where sex is concerned young women and men can only be deadly enemies because of the incommensurability of their desires" (Siegel 2007: 81). Each of Buffy's three main love interests reinforce the idea that sex and violence cannot coexist in an acceptable manner.

Buffy's first lover, Angel, loses his soul after having sex with Buffy and reverts to his monstrous persona as Angelus. Riley feels inconsequential next to Buffy's power and is rejected by her when she discovers he has frequented vampire prostitutes seeking out a consoling high from having his blood sucked, an act she finds perverse and disgusting. But it is Buffy's third lover, Spike, who motivates the most transgressive and potentially subversive relationship in the show.

Spike is a vicious vampire who has killed several slayers in the past. Clad in black leathers, with dyed blond hair, and a sarcastic punkish attitude, Spike is the ultimate bad boy—an undead Johnny Rotten. Initially one of Buffy's archenemies, Spike eventually falls in love with Buffy (disturbingly enough to have a robot love-doll built in her image—see Chapter Four) and becomes one of her strongest allies once he is implanted with a microchip that painfully prohibits him from hurting humans. In a shocking twist in the sixth season, Spike becomes Buffy's clandestine lover after she is brought back from the dead.

Despite Spike's long-standing sexual interest in Buffy, his new status as one of the good guys—and the character's popularity with fans—the sexual liaisons between Spike and Buffy are depicted as anything but romantic. *Buffy's* sixth season was darker in tone than any before it. The atmosphere of despair is set primarily by Buffy herself who is angry that her friends used magic to summon her soul back from beyond the grave. Her allies thought they were rescuing her but she eventually reveals that she was happy in a heavenly state and wished she had remained there. And Buffy feels she "came back wrong"— something just did not seem right about being among the living again after working so hard to save the world.

Buffy's feelings of isolation and despondency lead her to degrading sexual trysts with Spike where they argue and fuck in back alleys and seedy bars. Buffy suffers from a clear sense of shame over her encounters with Spike, and her physical surrender to him is joyless and masochistic, with an almost addictive sense of self-punishment. Siegel's frustration with the Buffy/Spike relationship is due to how thoroughly it is coded as disgusting. Here is a situation where an icon of alternative femininity could portray unconventional sexual desires as not just acceptable but erotic and empowering. Why shouldn't a woman who fights demons indulge in a mildly kinky relationship with a desirable and consenting vampire?

The series, like so many other action heroine narratives, refuses to follow through with the unconventional sexualities that the costumes and mise-en-scènes suggest because it is so firmly grounded in the ideology that conventional heteronormative relationships are the only acceptable possibility. Eventually Buffy realizes how revolting she finds her liaisons with Spike to be and rejects him outright. Tellingly, it is only when she refuses to continue her sadomasochistic affair that she can connect with him on an emotional level. According to Siegel:

> Her response is to suppress, with great effort, the lust she feels. Ultimately she is able to love him because, in accordance with conservative ideology that reads sexual activity outside procreative monogamy as anti-romantic, she has rid herself of all predatory erotic feelings and killed his desire to act on his. Because in the Buffyverse gender is always either masculine or feminine, and masculinity is always locked by sex into a destructive opposition to femininity, they can only feel affection for each other in the ungendered space of asexuality. (2007: 83)

To really be a hero, the series implies, the action heroine must be a good girl sexually, regardless of how kinky the principle of the narrative may be at heart.

In contrast to the perpetuation of traditional sexual norms that takes place with Buffy, and, one might add, almost all other action heroines, Siegel offers the 'Anita Blake: Vampire Hunter series by Laurell K. Hamilton. In these novels, which have a tremendous following, Anita embraces alternative sexualities including lesbian and sadomasochistic relationships as desirable and fulfilling. With each succeeding book, she partakes in more and more untraditional sexualities and learns to accept and enjoy her various sexual activities because they feed her magical powers which in turn allows her to save others.

Siegel argues that the Anita Blake mythology closely resembles the ideology of sex radical third-wavers "in that it insists that women's sexual gratification is important, perhaps even necessary, to the preservation of the human race. But Hamilton goes beyond even this feminist sex radicalism by positing absolute female pleasure as predicated on absolute sexual power" (86). While the Buffyverse is akin to some dominant second-wave rhetoric that sees "little difference between casual sex and rape, or between consensual S/M play and the eroticization of murder" (84), Siegel regards Anita's stories as a wish-fulfilling fantasy world "in which women's pursuit of untrammeled sexual power is always rewarded [and] represents another sort of feminism, the kind that allows us to relax our vigilance and fall into pleasure" (87).

The enormous popularity of the Anita Blake books with female readers suggests that the supposed sexual deviance of the heroine has a larger appeal than Hollywood would seem to accept. The mainstream action heroine plays off the possibility of kinky pleasures but almost always reasserts that heroines are good girls through and through because they ultimately conform to traditional notions of female sexuality as exclusively heterosexual, monogamous, and tender. But, like the sexually ambiguous vampire, the erotic possibilities suggested by the tough, leather-clad action heroine opens the door to a range of alternative fantasies.

Siegel is right to observe that the action heroine usually rejects the kinky promise she seems to physically embody, but this rejection may have more to do with the conventions of most heroic narratives than with a calculated need to suppress alternative sexual identities. Despite her unconventional gendered persona, the action heroine is almost exclusively cast in the traditional heroic position of protecting humanity, of enforcing cultural rules about property rights, and the value of human life (as patriarchally defined as these rules may be). In Barbara Creed's terms the action heroine can be seen as a guardian not just against kink, but against abjection in general.

In her landmark essay "Horror and the Monstrous-Feminine: An Imaginary Abjection," Creed argues that horror films function symbolically to expose and ultimately expunge elements culturally inscribed as abject. The grotesque motifs of horror are clearly depicted as abject (blood, vomit, ooze, vampires, zombies, werewolves, etc.) because they trouble the borders between clean and unclean, good and evil, human and inhuman, life and death. The purpose of horror then is to police these borders.

"Although the specific nature of the border changes from film to film," Creed clarifies, "the function of the monstrous remains the same: to bring about an encounter between the symbolic order and that which threatens its stability" (40). Moreover, Creed details how the monstrous and the abject are engendered as feminine in horror films in as much as they are depicted as within the domain of maternal semiotic authority rather than the realm of paternal symbolic law. In Chapter Three I discussed the action heroine as a figure predominantly associated with literal and symbolic fathers who stand as representatives of institutionalized paternal law enforcement. As such, action heroines take on the role of maintaining law and order in their quest to defeat enemies who threaten a stable and law abiding society. When these enemies are also stock monsters from horror such as the vampires we have discussed here, or even zombies (the *Resident Evil* films), the action heroines' role as a guardian against abjection is compounded. Her purpose as an agent of paternal law means that she must defend the status quo *and* reestablish the symbolic order in the face of abjection. And, because unconventional sexualities are still categorized within dominant institutions as threatening to order, as abject, the action heroine also unfortunately functions to suppress alternative sexual identities.

In Creed's larger study of abjection and femininity in horror films, *The Monstrous-Feminine: Film, Feminism, Psychoanalysis* (1993), she addresses the issue of lesbian vampires more specifically. Creed argues "the female vampire is monstrous—and also attractive- precisely because she does threaten to undermine the formal and highly symbolic relations of men and women essential to the continuation of patriarchal society" (61). Female vampires in horror films, whether explicitly or implicitly lesbian, enact a form of aggressive sexuality rarely seen in female characters that challenges traditional ideas about gender relations. The only other notable female seductresses common in film (outside pornography) are the femme fatales of film noir whose similarly threatening and monstrous sexuality is neatly marked as unusually predatory in their depiction as "vamps."

For Creed the female vampire embodies abjection because "she disrupts identity and order; driven by her lust for blood, she does not respect the

8.1. *Underworld* © 2003 Subterranean Productions LLC. All Rights Reserved. Courtesy of Screen Gems.

dictates of the law which sets down the rules of proper sexual conduct" (61). But action is a very different genre from horror despite many shared motifs. Horror is meant to be frightening and disruptive to cultural norms even if it ultimately manages to reestablish the status quo however precariously.

The central purpose of action, on the other hand, is to deliver a vicarious thrill ride but more importantly it is also about protecting and solidifying the rules of society, including those of sexual conduct. Thus, even when the action heroine is a vampire, as in the *Underworld* and *Bloodrayne* films, she does not embody abjection as much as law and order. Both Seline and Rayne may be sexy, leather-wearing vampires (Figure 8.1), and Rayne may even entertain some lesbian flirtations, but their narrative purpose as heroines marks them as guardians *against* abjection rather than subversive agents *of* abjection.

Though Creed's concern is exclusively with horror films, her primary example of the film *Alien* also illuminates the importance of conventionally attractive action heroines as part of the reassuring fantasy of rejecting the abject. Creed argues that *Alien* is rife with symbols of a terrifying and lethal phallic mother (the alien ship, the alien itself, and the humans' own Mother ship/computer) that tap into a primal fear of abjection and the monstrous-feminine. But for all of the film's emphasis on the monstrous-feminine it also gives us Lt. Ellen Ripley as a prototypical action heroine, one who bridges the gap between horror's Final Girl and the modern kick-ass heroine. Ripley functions as a feminine agent of order against the abjection represented by the monstrous-feminine of the phallic mother. In particular, Creed sees Ripley's attractiveness as an essential contrast:

> Compared to the horrific sight of the alien as fetish object of the monstrous-feminine, Ripley's body is pleasurable and reassuring to look at. She signifies the "acceptable" form and shape of woman. In a sense the monstrousness of woman, represented by Mother as betrayer (the computer/life-support system) and Mother as the uncontrollable, generative, cannibalistic mother (the alien), is controlled through the display of woman as reassuring and pleasurable sign. (62–63)

Though Ripley's sexuality is not explicitly part of the reassurance she offers via her "acceptable" form, this argument does suggest that the post-*Alien* action heroine's conventional sex appeal is an integral part of her ability to symbolically safeguard against abjection. As an agent of symbolic order and paternal law the modern action heroine can only be conceived as sexually conservative.

Still, within the official texts of the dominant Hollywood version of the action heroine the hint of sadomasochistic sex is a facet that can barely be contained. The stories always end up portraying the heroines' sexual desires as traditional, but the ever present kinky costuming and scenarios are so visually striking that it is difficult for the conclusions to completely erase the underlying non-traditional fantasies. When Sydney Bristow, or Barb Wire, or Catwoman, or Mrs. Smith or any other action heroines slap around their sexually aroused enemies while dressed as dominatrixes the erotic implications are too clear to be simply undone by later clarifying that the women were not really turned on by the situation. At times even the characters have to wryly recognize the kinky setup, such as in the first *Underworld* film when the well-armed and leather bodysuit-clad Seline chains a submissive Michael to a chair in case he turns into a werewolf.

Television's *Buffy the Vampire Slayer* was well aware of its flirtations with BDSM themes and routinely joked about the importance of "safe words," of who was going to be a "top" and who a "bottom," and even had Angel tease Buffy with the observation: "You know what I just can't believe? All of our time together and we never tried chains." And, on rare occasions, even Hollywood films indulged in soft S/M dalliances with action heroines, as in *Bloodrayne* when the vampire/human hybrid Rayne forces herself on her would-be human captor Sebastian and has a passionate quickie with him pinned against the bars of her cell as she mounts him vertically by suspending herself from the iron bars. After their aggressive sexual encounter no relationship develops between Rayne and Sebastian aside from a few coy glances. Their leather-clad, dungeon tryst is portrayed as nothing more than an acceptance of animalistic passion and a rough sexual release. Even though the narratives may go to great lengths to position the heroines as sexually conservative good girls in the end, the polysemic nature of the action heroine's sexual representation facilitates a range of possible alternative interpretations.

Siegel argues convincingly that the sexual logic of *Buffy the Vampire Slayer* remains anchored in conservative feminist and cultural conceptions of gender, and that the Anita Blake series is a rarer representation of female action heroism because it imagines "female sadism as other than evil or pathological" and thus "breathtakingly refreshes old concepts of gendered sexuality" (58). And while action heroine narratives in general officially insist that the characters are essentially good girls when it comes to their sexuality, that does not mean that their ability to represent alternative sexual identities should be disregarded. The action heroine's status as a non-traditional female character type who takes center stage in a predominantly male genre means she is transgressive by her very nature. The modern heroine is physically tough, adept with a range of weapons, and smart enough to defeat all adversaries. Yet she is also conventionally attractive enough to offset any perceptions of trading in her femininity in deference to assuming a traditionally masculine role.

Because she is an unconventional figure combining disparately gendered traits, and because her behavior and heavily fetishized appearance are so beyond our cultural norms, the action heroine remains sexually polysemic enough to cater to a variety of audience desires. Though the sexual deviance of the action heroine may fall short of being explicit, and thus culturally validated and widely accepted, the barely contained subtextual implications provide a great deal of fodder for challenging dominant heterosexual and patriarchal standards. For critics, both academic and from special interest groups, the clear problem is that so long as alternative sexualities remain at the level of subtext the legitimacy of differing sexual identities also remains sub—forever under the surface of social acceptability, forever a shadowy Other to dominant fantasies.

While I agree that this marginalization of alternative sexual identities hinders progressive cultural change, I believe that the action heroine can still serve as a harbinger of shifting perceptions of sexual identity. Buffy's refusal to follow her kinky premise through to its logical conclusion may be a disappointment to Siegel and her desire for a positive model of sadomasochistic sexualities, but the series has legions of followers who enjoy Buffy's exploits precisely because they can be so easily read through a queer or S/M perspective. The appeal of the action heroine, like the vampire before her and whom she often fights (or is), lies in great part with her polysemic sexuality. Far from being a blank slate onto which different fantasies can be projected, the action heroine clearly leans toward radical sexual interpretations.

As I have outlined in earlier chapters, the action heroine's aggressive physical nature and her visual fetishization raises the issue of masculine masochistic pleasures. As Neale 1983, Silverman 1992, and even myself (Brown 2002) have argued, masochism has long been a part of identificatory fantasies offered to male viewers in movies. The willing adoption of a vulnerable masculine position, as temporary as it may be, is a crucial part of the heroic male fantasy. James Bond, Rambo, Indiana Jones, Martin Riggs, and their like have to be tortured in order to emerge as true heroes (for an extended discussion see both Tasker 1993, and Jeffords 1993). And even though these moments of vulnerability function to reinforce the male hero's hard-body status, the prevalence and visual emphasis of these scenes that ask audiences to identify with the hero's vulnerability brings into question the traditional gendered dichotomy between powerful and powerless.

When this fantasy of even momentary male vulnerability is coupled with images of female dominance, the entire scenario brings to the fore the non-too-subtle appeal of possible male sexual submission to the action heroine. For many male (and female) viewers the popularity of action heroines may reside, not in identifying with her empowerment, but with her victims' disempowerment. This would certainly seem to be the case with the fetish subculture enthusiasts who idolize various action heroines. The majority of fan fiction and fan art devoted to action heroines also reinforces this possibility. Whatever the texts' official position may be about the heroines' sexuality, viewers can literally rewrite it to suit their own needs.

ACTION HEROINE AS LESBIAN ICON

Perhaps even more widely accepted and practiced than the interpretation of the action heroine as an icon of sexual dominance and submission is her status as a symbol of lesbian fantasies. There is a rich and well-documented tradition among lesbians for identifying with and idolizing tough female characters. Wonder Woman, the first superheroine, has been an icon of not just feminist but also lesbian possibilities since her very inception in 1941. As a princess from an all-female island of fierce Amazon warriors whose early exploits involved a group of enthusiastic young female followers, Wonder Woman was always ripe for a queer interpretation. Perhaps not coincidentally she was also one of the first action heroines who overtly dallied in sadomasochistic scenarios thanks to the emphasis placed on her magic lasso and metal bracelets, not to mention her propensity for being bound in every adventure.

Questions about Wonder Woman's sexuality titillate fans to this day, and she remains a common symbol among lesbians. Over the years other tough women have emerged in popular culture and likewise appealed to lesbian audiences. Among the most notable action heroines adopted by lesbian fans are Pam Grier's blaxploitation characters, Charlie's Angels, the Bionic Woman, Cagney and Lacey, Ellen Ripley, and Sarah Connor. But the most famous example is Xena and her sidekick Gabrielle from the campy television series *Xena: Warrior Princess* that achieved worldwide notoriety in the 1990s.

Over the course of its six-year run *Xena: Warrior Princess* grew from a cult hit to a cultural phenomenon. The series charted the exploits of Xena, an undefeatable warrior fighting for justice in a quest for penance to make up for earlier misdeeds as a ruthless conqueror—and Gabrielle, a more peace-loving bard who follows Xena in her adventures and to escape her boring existence and arranged marriage to a man she does not love. The series' incredible popularity brought significant attention from both the popular and academic press. Xena's strength, skills, sense of humor, and unapologetic demeanor positioned her as a welcome corrective to decades of female media characterizations. The program, and the increasing public awareness of its devoted lesbian followers, became a focal point of debates about feminism, gender struggles, queer politics, and lesbian representation.

Xena: Warrior Princess was equally popular among viewers young and old, male and female, queer and straight. In her article about the show and its importance as a polysemic text open to queer interpretations, Elyce Rae Helford points out: "Feminists and lesbians, gay, bisexual and transsexual activists applaud the series for its strong woman-identified and ambiguously sexualized female hero" (2001: 135). Xena's status as an unconventional woman and an untempered action heroine opened up the series to a range of possible readings depending on viewers' subject positions and interpretive desires. Most famously *Xena: Warrior Princess* exemplified the way that lesbian audiences can exert an active queer reading of strong female characters.

Once the show became a widespread phenomenon newspapers reported Xena's popularity with lesbian viewers and "Xena Nights" at lesbian bars where women would gather to watch the show among fellow fans, some of whom would even show up dressed as their favorite characters. Central to the program's appeal to lesbians was not just her assertiveness and physical attractiveness, but the core relationship between Xena and her companion Gabrielle. While queer viewers have long been drawn to fictions about close relationships between same-sex characters (debates about Batman and Robin continue), *Xena: Warrior Princess* contained far more elements that opened it up to, and even invited, a queer reading than anything before it. As Helford summarizes: "Much is available within the program to enable . . . such a reading. In a number of episodes, Xena and Gabrielle share intimate experiences; they sleep on the same blanket or take a bath together, for example. They also engage in displays of affection, such as hugs, kisses, and shared tears. And they exchange ambiguous dialogue, including sexual innuendo and *double entendre*, as well as overt and direct declarations of love" (2001: 139).

Officially the show's producers kept the heroines' sexuality ambiguous. Both Xena and Gabrielle had relationships with men at various times, but as Helford and others have exhaustively documented there are also countless scenes that hint a sexual relationship exists between the women. The producers reportedly even increased the sexual tension between the characters after they became aware of just how dedicated a lesbian following had developed. One producer, Liz Friedman, went so far in an interview with the queer magazine *The Advocate* as to claim that she thought Xena and Gabrielle as "a perfect little butch-femme couple." By coyly sidestepping any direct pronouncements about the heroines' sexual orientations, the series managed to avoid alienating any particular audience groups. Still, the program's popularity with lesbian viewers, which continued long after the series ended, demonstrates the importance of action heroines as possible emblems for different sexual fantasies.

Helford argues that the butch-femme dynamic represented by Xena and Gabrielle is at the heart of the series' lesbian coding. Xena is taller, darker, harder in body and attitude than Gabrielle who is contrastingly blonder, noticeably petite, gentler, and more emotional. Though marked as a butchy character, Xena is still visually coded as attractive by any conventional standards with long hair, a voluptuous figure, and a rather revealing warrior costume, complete with a miniskirt and cleavage-baring breastplates. Xena, and especially her relationship with Gabrielle, remains a high point in the action heroine's explicit alignment with lesbian desires. Xena's harder, butchier components have been replaced by excessive sexual fetishization with most of the action heroines who have followed her, as has the muscularity of late-1980s heroines like Sarah Connor and Ellen Ripley.

In a sense the butch-femme aspects that were neatly divided between Xena and Gabrielle have been collapsed onto a single figure in more recent outings. Thus the supremely tough, leather-clad heroine Seline in the *Underworld* films is embodied by Kate Beckinsale, a petite, almost fragile-looking actress. Likewise the no-nonsense assassin Fox in *Wanted* (2008) is played by the legendarily sexy Angelina Jolie whose body is so thin as to seem implausible (appearing even more fragile than in either the *Tomb Raider* movies or *Mr. and Mrs. Smith*). That contemporary action heroine actresses are routinely drawn from the ranks of ex-models (Milla Jovovich, Rhona Mitra, Pamela Anderson, Natassia Malthe, etc.) or actresses known foremost as sex symbols (Halle Berry, Uma Thurman, Jennifer Garner, Kiera Knightly, etc.) ensures that any connotations of butchiness are offset by their status as undeniable feminine ideals. Much like Creed's description of Ripley's pleasurable body in *Alien* as a symbolic counter to the abject monstrous-feminine, more recent petite heroines signify a reassuring rejection of a possible butch persona.

Moreover, where *Xena: Warrior Princess* facilitated, even encouraged, lesbian possibilities, the action heroines who have emerged in her wake seem to avoid an ambiguous sexuality—and rarely does the modern action heroine even flirt with other women. Not that individual scenes of same-sex attractions have been eradicated: fans are quick to point out the lethal lesbian kiss between Elektra and the villainous Typhoid Mary amidst a battle in *Elektra* and Rayne's attraction to different women in *Bloodrayne*, for example. But, to my knowledge, *D.E.B.S.* is the only case of a post-Xena action heroine narrative to emphasize the characters' explicit lesbian identities, and *D.E.B.S.* never achieved more than cult status. Despite *D.E.B.S.* lack of mainstream success, the film does suggest that action heroines as a character type can be adapted to alternative sexual desires and that the struggles between heroines and villains, or villainesses, can be tantamount to sexual tension.

Moreover, several superheroines in comic books are openly lesbian such as the Amazonian Grace, the lightning-powered Thunder, and the new Batwoman who appear in *The Outsiders*, the title of the series doubling perhaps as an unfortunate comment about their status. But comic books remain the domain of a very specific subculture and is perhaps a medium more open to experimentation because of this. It is interesting to note that after *Buffy the*

Vampire Slayer TV series ended the stories continued on in comic books written by Joss Whedon, and it is here that Buffy herself eventually entered into a lesbian relationship. But direct connotations of lesbianism remain almost nonexistent within the mainstream narratives of the modern action heroine who is predominantly heterosexualized.

Still, as decades of research into fan communities have shown, audiences are adept at rewriting the official texts to fit their own desires. The unconventional nature of action heroines and the fantasies of their possible different sexualities may be officially rejected, but that does not mean they cannot serve a symbolic purpose within certain fan communities. Just as the vampire has long been interpreted as a sign of polymorphous sexuality, so too is the action heroine.

In addition to the prevalence of action heroine costuming being incorporated in the fetish subculture, explicit sexual stories and artwork featuring the heroines abound on the Internet. A staggering amount of fan fiction (or fan-fic) can be found that's devoted to action heroines from TV series like *Alias*, *Dark Angel*, and *Terminator: The Sarah Connor Chronicles*, and movies such as *Kill Bill*, *Underworld*, and *Resident Evil*. And it is in these fan-authored fictions where enthusiasts play out all the non-conventional sexual scenarios they desire involving action heroines, free as they are from the restrictions of network Standards and Practices censors and Film Ratings Boards explicitly charged with toning down sexualities interpreted as deviant in the mainstream media.

Even Siegel, despite her frustration with the official narrative stance taken by *Buffy the Vampire Slayer* towards sadomasochistic relationships, notes the plethora of online stories carrying the Buffy/Spike premise through to a more fulfilling conclusion. In fact, Buffy fans have been particularly productive when it comes to fan fiction challenging traditional gender roles and sexualities. Not surprisingly, a number of excellent scholarly studies of Buffy fan-fic focusing on such issues as incest (Busse 2002), masculinity and queer desires (McCracken 2007 and Keft-Kennedy 2008), female objectification (Middleton 2007), fetishism (Saxey 2001), male masochism (Alexander 2004), and lesbian BDSM (Isaksson 2009) have been written.

Where the canonical *Buffy* TV narrative shied away from liberatory alternate sexualities explored through the Spike/Buffy sadomasochistic relationship and the Faith/Buffy lesbian tensions in favor of keeping the series' titular heroine firmly ensconced in the socially acceptable category of "good girl," various adult-oriented threads of *Buffy* fan-fic presented the relationships as pleasurable, fulfilling, and even empowering. In her comprehensive statistical "The Fandom Project," Mary Kirby-Diaz (2005/2006) notes that the Spike/

Buffy relationship is the most popular fan-fic topic in the Buffyverse. The Spike/Buffy fans (or "Spuffies" as they are called) are described by Kirby-Diaz as not "expecting or believing in idealized love," rather they "like the passion and chemistry between the characters" (261).

Most of the Spike/Buffy stories build on the TV series' sadomasochistic themes and carry the scenarios through to graphic descriptions of the characters' rough sexual encounters. In some stories Spike is dominant, in others Buffy is dominant, and in some they alternate master and slave positions in their sexual play. In their explicitness, these fan-fics bring the action heroine into a realm of sexual possibilities that could never be realized in prime-time television or feature film.

This type of fan-fic, particularly common among Buffy fans, is referred to as "kink-fic," which Alexander describes as borrowing "its staging and its equipment from real-world BDSM practices. It commonly involves ingredients such as chains, whips, paddles, strap-ons, gags, and restraints, and invariably belongs to the more pornographic end of the fan-fiction register, although stories may vary in intensity and focus" (2009: 1). Popular Spike/Buffy kink-fic stories like "Love's Slave," "A Puppy Named Spike," and "A Whip of One's Own" represent more than just some fans' erotic fantasies for the characters, they represent an idealization of alternative sexual relations wherein BDSM practices between an action heroine and her lover result in an acceptance and recognition of the potential efficacy of non-normative female sexual identities. "The Buffyverse," Alexander concludes in her analysis of heterosexual kink-fic, "provides an ultimately 'female positive' space for the safe expression of female subjection as well as female dominance" (10).

Similarly, the heteronormative sexual identities ascribed to the action heroine in her official texts is confounded in queer fan-fic in general, and in kink-fic specifically. Numerous kink-fic stories about *Alias*, for example, feature Sydney Bristow torturing/being tortured by her evil opposite Lauren Reed as a prelude to a sexual encounter that occasionally ends with them falling in love and running away together to live a life of happy BDSM play. Likewise, several kink-fic stories feature Sarah Connor of the *Terminator* series exploring sadomasochistic lesbian/gynoid sex with the eroticized teen cyborg Cameron.

Buffy fan-fic also contains what Linda Rust calls "a large number of female/female pairings," as might be expected from a show with "an abundance of strong female characters" (2). There are literally hundreds of stories devoted to the sapphic combinations of Buffy, Willow, Cordelia, Tara, Dawn, and Faith in twosomes, threesomes, foursomes, and more. But, as Malin Isaksson points out in her analysis of queer Buffy femslash: "The female pairing par

excellence is Buffy/Faith" (1). While many of the Buffy/Faith stories detail
their lesbian and BDSM relations in a manner akin to the canonical television
series' approach that ultimately positions Buffy as a "good girl" who needs to
be seduced, tricked, or forced into sex with Faith's "bad girl," just as many es-
chew those conventional mores and characterize Buffy as an eager participant
or even initiator.

Thus, in fan fiction at least, action heroines like Buffy are not constrained
by traditional heteronormative standards. Fans can, and do, use these heroines as a vehicle to think about sexuality in non-prescriptive ways. The persistence of alternative narratives envisioning Buffy and Faith as a viable, and
often kinky, couple demonstrate the possibilities inherent in action heroines
for challenging rigid sexual identities. Moreover, as Isaksson concludes, "the
Buffy/Faith fictions question [such] cultural assumptions about what women
want from sexually explicit material designed to produce sexual arousal" (16).
Physically strong, sexually attractive, and sexually active heroines seem to serve
an important function of facilitating alternative fantasies.

While action heroine fan fiction and art on the Internet covers an enormous
range of sexual fantasies, the relatively anonymous production and consumption of these pieces makes it difficult to say with any certainty exactly whose
fantasies these are. The same-sex scenarios could be as much an expression of
the clichéd heterosexual male fascination with pseudo-lesbianism as it is of
homosexual female desires to interpret the action heroine as "really" lesbian.
And this may be moot since the stories and art may appeal to audiences from
any range of subject positions regardless of the fan writer/artist's original fetish
goal. The authenticity of the modern action heroine's importance to lesbian
viewers is, however, clearly substantiated by the attention she receives in the
lesbian-specific press.

The popular lesbian magazine *Girlfriends*, for example, routinely covers
nearly every new instance of action heroinism. Specific movies like *D.E.B.S.*
and TV shows like *Buffy the Vampire Slayer* have been heralded by the magazine as progressive steps in the mainstreaming of lesbian identities. Moreover,
Girlfriends runs regular cover stories about action "superheroines" in films
like *Charlie's Angels*, *Tomb Raider*, *The Matrix*, and so on. That none of these
"Superheroines of Summer," as *Girlfriends* calls them, are explicitly lesbian
is beside the point. The magazine typically argues that these kick-ass female
characters are ideal candidates for lesbian fandom because they are strong,
independent women whose desirability cuts across the artificial boundaries
between hetero and homosexuality. The popularity of modern action heroines
for lesbian audiences suggests that whatever sexual identity may be officially
encoded by the studios is essentially irrelevant. These characters can, and do,

speak to viewers' sexual (and political) fantasies in ways that exceed any intended meaning.

The continuing iconic status of action heroines for lesbians is also reinforced through the star personalities of many of the actresses who assume the roles. The ambiguous sex symbol status of Angelina Jolie, who has often alluded to her own bisexuality, lends itself to the polymorphous sexual interpretations of her action heroine roles in such films as the *Tomb Raider, Mr. and Mrs. Smith*, and *Wanted*. Jolie's bisexuality and her embrace of her lesbian following helps to facilitate a reading of her action roles as possibly lesbian. Likewise, the barely closeted Jodie Foster's apparent lesbianism becomes an important ingredient to interpreting her more cerebral action roles in films like *The Silence of the Lambs* and *The Brave One*. More directly, some actresses who are openly lesbian have substantiated the association between action heroines and homosexuality for fans. Kristan Lokken and Michelle Rodriguez have managed to synergize their real-life lesbian status by playing sexually ambiguous characters with lead action roles in *Terminator 3, Painkiller Jane, Bloodrayne*, and *Resident Evil*. The fact that Lokken and Rodriguez became a real couple after meeting on the set of *Bloodrayne* lends a certain validity to the practice of reading action heroines through a queer lens.

While the modern action heroine may be primarily situated as a traditionally heterosexualized character who reinforces cultural norms about proper female sexuality as monogamous, tender, and straight, she is also easily reinterpreted as a fantasy of polymorphous sexuality. Where the sexual transgressions of cinematic vampires have become clichéd, the action heroine's nontraditional persona has emerged as a challenge to conventional sexual norms. In a sense the action heroine has become the vampire of the twenty-first century.

Her unique standing as a highly sexualized figure who courts alternative fantasies allows the action heroine to challenge sexual norms as much as reinforce them. Because she is such a striking and powerful sexual being, the action heroine can be many things to many people. She can symbolize sadomasochistic sexuality, lesbian sexuality, bisexuality—pretty much any type of sexuality that audiences can imagine. No matter how conventionally her sexuality may be officially depicted the action heroine can shoot, kick, or rip open a wide crack in our culture's conception of what female sexual identities are.

9) WHEN THE ACTION HEROINE LOOKS

$\mathcal{O}$ne of the most anticipated new television series of 2007 was NBC's updated version of the *Bionic Woman*. Starring Michelle Ryan in the titular role as Jaime Sommers, a cybernetically enhanced bartender-cum-secret-agent-action heroine. The new *Bionic Woman* touches on many of the important action heroine themes explored in earlier chapters. As a darker revisioning of the original 1970s series starring Lindsay Wagner, the remake is a direct descendant of second-wave-era feminism's popular media representation: Sommers is presented as a primarily gynoid character constructed Pygmalion-like by her scientist/fiancé. The series' creation is credited in the press to producer David Eick, also the creative force behind the recent *Battlestar Galactica* (which likewise features a sexy cyborg). Michelle Ryan/Jaime Sommers was heavily marketed as a fetishized beauty (a *TV Guide* cover declared: "Faster! Stronger! Sexier! Jaime's back in fall's butt-kicking new hit!").

In addition to making the new Jaime faster, stronger, and sexier, one of the most intriguing updates was her robotic eye. Enhanced vision was reserved in the 1970s for *The Six Million Dollar Man*, Jaime's fictional predecessor. The original bionic woman had to make do with a bionic ear and the somewhat reduced ability to listen in on a villain's plans. By 2007 though, the producers decided to skip the bionic male prototype altogether and to grant Jaime enhanced vision (thanks in no small part to the independent success of action heroines in film and TV in the intervening years). This new bionic eye was heavily stressed in the promos that featured various close-ups of Ryan and the green digital lens of her right eye. This bionic woman can see farther and better than any man. She can see in the dark, she can see in different spectrums, she can see at different speeds, she can even record what she sees. In short, she has the dominant and the privileged point of view that is matched with her forthright quest for knowledge.

As this emphasis on the new Jaime's bionic eye suggests, the contemporary action heroine represents a privileged and progressive model of female vision in film and television. While these heroines are depicted as physically beautiful and excessively eroticized, they also manage to command the most dominant point of view within the narrative. They are "lookers" in both senses of the word.

The role of vision is one of the foundational tropes in film studies in relation to issues of gender and power. In short, the ability to see clearly in cinema is equated with power. Traditionally, the dominant visual perspective has been aligned with masculinity. Not just as a sexualized "male gaze" employed to freely look at female characters, but as a male-aligned ability to see what others do not—to decipher the truth, to control the narrative through controlling what others see. Conversely, when the woman looks in film she often fails to see properly, if at all. And if she does see the forbidden or uncover hidden truths, she has traditionally been punished.

Since women are fundamentally constructed as the object of the look, their visual transgression, their desire to see and know, has been systematically coded as meddling in dangerous situations better left to icons of patriarchal authority. But the modern action heroine represents one of the few truly progressive possibilities for female vision. Despite Hollywood's economic imperatives that continue to underscore the sexual desirability of strong heroines as an object of visual pleasure for male characters and audience members alike, when the action heroine looks she does so without fear of recriminations. Where earlier female characters and heroines in other genres failed to fully assume a phallic, investigative, and knowledgeable gaze, action heroines have succeeded and refuse to accept the masochistic implications of female looking.

GENDER AND THE RELATIVE DANGERS OF LOOKING

As Laura Mulvey (1975), Christian Metz (1975), John Ellis (1982) and others have argued, the pleasure of looking without being seen is one of the primary fantasies of film itself. Audiences are positioned as perfect voyeurs with an nearly omniscient viewpoint. We always know at least as much as the protagonist, and quite often even more, because we are sutured (as Metz describes it) into alignment with the hero's position. The conventional structure of looking facilitates an identification with the hero and invites us to enjoy what is usually "his" command of the narrative. A clear example of this from recent action films, and one that emphasizes the power of looking as preeminently masculine, occurs in the second Jason Bourne film, *The Bourne Supremacy*

(2004), and was recontextualized in the subsequent *The Bourne Ultimatum* (2007).

When the amnesiac assassin Bourne (Matt Damon) is hunted by his former clandestine government agency, he turns the tables on them and ruthlessly pursues information regarding his lost identity. Bourne calls Pamela Landy (Joan Allen), the agent in charge of finding him, and tells her he will meet only with Nicky (Julia Stiles), a minor character from the first film (*The Bourne Identity* 2001). When Landy stalls in an attempt to get the upper hand on Bourne by asking, "What if I can't find her?" Bourne shocks her when he says, "It's easy, she's standing right next to you."

Landy and the entire control center are thrown into a panic when they realize Bourne is watching them through his riflescope—and the audience is overjoyed with this demonstration of, and identification with, visual one-upmanship. Bourne's visual supremacy contrasts with a supposedly powerful female character, and he repeats variations of it throughout the film and its sequel, demonstrating his control of the gaze versus both the men and the women who pursue him. The naturalized implication is clear: heroic male characters are subjects of the investigative gaze, not its object.

The de facto gendering of looking in cinema is so naturalized that it is rarely questioned. Horror is perhaps the genre that most directly addresses the masculine privilege associated with looking and the feminine dangers of being looked at—or worse, of women trying to assume the gaze. In her landmark essay "When the Woman Looks" (1984), Linda Williams discusses the repercussions faced by women in horror films when they dare to look. In classic horror movies, for example, heroines are routinely punished and victimized when they try to look at the monsters. Whereas heroic male characters look for the monsters in order to vanquish them, women experience abject terror when they see the monster.

The woman's look in classic horror often leads to helplessness; all she can do is scream or turn away, hiding her eyes from the unbearable sight. In fact, according to Williams, the women in classic horror are so ineffectual as active lookers that the heroine's active and curious look typically results in a "trance-like passivity that allows him to master her through *her* look" (18). These women lack the safe voyeuristic distance inherent in the cinematic male's look that allows the men to reveal, control, and eventually slay the monster. Horror may be one of the few classic film genres to explore the possibilities of women looking, but it does so only to expose the female gaze as ineffectual and dangerous.

As Williams argues, a large part of the horror of the female look in these films is the recognition of affinity between the woman and the monster: "The female look—a look given preeminent position in the horror film—shares the male fear of the monster's freakishness, but also recognizes the sense in which this freakishness is similar to her own difference. For she too has been constituted as an exhibitionist-object by the desiring look of the male" (21). This recognition of similarity in difference is a potentially subversive acknowledgement of the power and potency of non-phallic sexuality. As Williams concludes, it is "[P]recisely because this (female) look is so threatening to male power, it is violently punished" (24). As a reflection of persistent misogynistic cultural standards, the ability to look in film and other media forms is a symbol of masculine power. To look implies a right to knowledge, a right that has traditionally been gendered male.

While the physical punishment associated with women who attempt to look is explicit in horror films, it is no less evident in other classical genres. The highly sexualized and villainous femme fatale of film noir challenges the masculine presumption of looking. She dares to assume a powerful position— to pursue her own pleasures and desires, to assume her own right to look, and to manipulate the male gaze for her own purposes. The femme fatale ruthlessly and manipulatively goes after whatever she wants, whether it is money (*The Maltese Falcon*, 1941; *Double Indemnity*, 1944), a successful career (*Mildred Pierce*, 1945; *Sunset Boulevard*, 1950), or just freedom from an oppressive relationship (*The Postman Always Rings Twice*, 1946; *Gilda*, 1946). But, by the film's end, she is thoroughly punished for her transgressive behavior.

The overt sexuality and ambition of the femme fatale places her in stark contrast with the token good women of the films who are passive and supportive of men. It also frames her demise, her punishment for assuming and manipulating the gaze, as a moral imperative. As Janey Place has argued, the "ideological operation of the myth (the absolute necessity of controlling the strong, sexual woman) is thus achieved by first demonstrating her dangerous power and its frightening results, then destroying it" (1978: 45). The disastrous fates that befall women who dare to look are likewise found in the melodramas and other movies from the 1930s to the 1950s loosely lumped together as "Women's Films." Even in these movies, which focused on female characters and were designed to appeal to female viewers, the woman's look was deemed punishable. In films such as *Gaslight* (1944), *Suspicion* (1941), and *Rebecca* (1940), the heroine's attempts to unravel the mysteries in her home and marriage result in violence and mental anguish, often inflicted by her own husband. As Mary Ann Doane has remarked in her discussion of the Woman's Film: "The woman's exercise of an active investigating gaze can only be simultaneous with her own victimization" (1984: 72). The woman's active and inquisitive look has a long history in cinema of being framed as a masochistic undertaking.

Indeed, the dominant, controlling look utilized in film and television is so thoroughly engendered as masculine that film studies often refer to it as phallic regardless of who is doing the actual looking. In *Men, Women, and Chainsaws: Gender in the Modern Horror Film* (1992), Carol Clover thoroughly dismantles the rigid alignment assumed between characters' biological sex and the gender of behavioral patterns. In Clover's analysis of modern horror films, women might not be as likely to be punished for looking as they were during horror's classical period, but the engendered attributes of looking remain stable.

In her analysis of eyes and the power of looking, for example, Clover argues (primarily through her discussion of the meta-horror film *Peeping Tom*, 1960) that horror contrasts the "assaultive gaze" that is gendered masculine with the "reactive gaze," which is gendered feminine. For Clover, the assaultive gaze, and the camera itself, is an act of phallic cruelty, while the reactive gaze is a feminine and masochistic position. To be the object of looking, to be in the feminine position in modern horror is to be bruised, scarred, terrified, and ultimately killed. Part of the vicarious thrill offered by horror, then, is a masochistic pleasure derived from being aligned (at least momentarily) with a disempowered and feminine position regardless of the audience members' biological sex. There is still, however, a close association drawn between the maleness of powerful looking and the femaleness/victimization of being looked at.

FEMALE INVESTIGATORS AND PRIVATE EYES

The success of female-centered detective and action series on television in the 1970s gave rise to new possibilities for women to succeed as active lookers in the media. While such pioneering programs as *Police Woman*, *Charlie's Angels*, *Wonder Woman*, and *The Bionic Woman* (discussed in Chapter Six) were burdened with an overemphasis on the erotic spectacle of the lead actresses, the shows did initiate a new and popular character type: the investigating woman. In the 1980s and 1990s the female private eye became (and remains) a familiar and very popular figure on the bookshelves. Led by successful paperback series authored by the likes of Sue Grafton, Patricia Cornwall, Sara Paretsky, and Janet Evanovich, the literary heroine has managed to carve out a substantial presence in detective fiction. Given the different fiscal imperatives of the publishing industry and its ability to cater to niche audiences, it is perhaps not surprising that some of the most interesting and progressive female characters to date are restricted to the printed page (for a detailed discussion of literary heroines see Walton and Jones [1999], or Mizejewski [2004]).

The higher financial commitments required for Hollywood has restricted the film industry's willingness to rethink traditional representations. Though the visual medium has been slower to develop new roles for women as active lookers, the female investigator still emerged more prominently in the 1980s and 1990s. The success of television series like *Cagney & Lacey* (1982–1988) and feature films like *The Silence of the Lambs* (1991) helped to establish female characters as capable investigators in their own right. But where these award-winning heroines managed to co-opt or rethink the cinematic gaze as a feminine (and feminist) right to look, many other female investigators struggled with the problematic balance between looking and being looked at.

Cagney & Lacey is perhaps the most thorough and challenging effort to position the investigative gaze as a legitimate subject position for female characters. Created by Barbara Avedon and Barbara Corday, the series featured Christine Cagney (Sharon Gless) and Mary-Beth Lacey (Tyne Daly) as competent and caring New York City police detectives who focused on crimes that often conveniently intersected with issues of particular concern to women such as abortion rights, prostitution, and domestic abuse. The feminist-inspired themes of the series have made it a popular subject of academic inquiry. For example, Christine Gledhill (1988) discusses the show as a form of textual negotiation over meaning between the producers and its predominantly female fans. Similarly, Julie D'Acci (1994) presents an extended analysis of how *Cagney & Lacey* acts as a form of mediated public discourse on the problem of defining femininity.

Throughout the series' run there was an explicit emphasis on the women establishing and maintaining their investigative abilities—their right to look. Cagney and Lacey were supportive of each other and they were, for the most part, accepted as equals by many of their male co-workers. The program was a conscious attempt to critique the dominant structures of the male gaze. In her essay "Watching the Detectives: The Enigma of the Female Gaze" (1989), Lorraine Gamman argues that "Cagney and Lacey are not simply passive objects; they 'speak' female desire. *They look back*. These central characters maintain autonomy and independent initiative throughout the series. They do this by pointing out to colleagues (and viewers) in a witty and amusing way why the male gaze is sexist" (16; italics in original). Though these heroines did routinely deal with sexism and both personal and professional problems, they were never presented primarily as objects for male viewing pleasures, nor were they punished in any sense for their own looking.

The feature film *The Silence of the Lambs* stands out, like *Cagney & Lacey* before it, as a critical feminist favorite for its conscientious presentation of female agency and the female gaze. The film repeatedly contrasts Clarice

Starling's (Jodie Foster) marginalization as both an FBI trainee and a woman working with an all-male task force with her undeniable competence as an investigator. While camera angles emphasize her diminutive stature relative to male characters, and her legitimacy as an agent is questioned by male authority figures, Clarice still manages to assert her presence as part of the investigative team and to put together the clues provided by Hannibal Lecter allowing her to find the serial killer, "Buffalo Bill," on her own.

Clarice is never overtly sexualized, though her potential vulnerability is stressed. When Clarice first questions Lecter in the prison's psych ward she is subjected to a barrage of vulgar, verbal sexual assaults by other patients but is still able to remain professional and gather the information she needs. Since Clarice is a trainee, she spends much of the film learning how to see as an investigator. Her FBI supervisor Jack Crawford officially trains her, helping her develop a psychological profile of the killer and to read the clues left on a dead body. She is unofficially tutored by Lecter whose deranged riddles and taunts help Clarice to see and understand the bizarre motivation of Buffalo Bill's actions.

Her investigation climaxes when Clarice figures out the location of the killer on her own while the rest of the task force chases a false lead. In a harrowing and memorable scene that crystallizes the female investigator's potential victimization from a dominant and punishing male look, Buffalo Bill stalks a frightened Clarice through his pitch-black house—he sees her perfectly through a pair of night vision goggles while she gropes helplessly in the darkness. The scene is filmed from Buffalo Bill's point of view so the audience sees/feels Clarice's vulnerability as the killer gets close enough to stroke her hair as she struggles to locate him. But just as he is about to kill her, Clarice hears the click of his gun and shoots him instead. While all the trappings of being punished for looking are apparent, she is able to resist that fate and triumph over this serial killer of women.

For the most part *The Silence of the Lambs* has been lauded in both academic literature and the popular press as a progressive representation of female subjectivity and for characterizing Clarice as a strong feminist figure. Even Jodie Foster, in her Academy Award acceptance speech for Best Actress, described the win as particularly gratifying because Clarice was "such an incredibly strong and beautiful feminist hero." But for all its positive attributes, other critics have pointed out the lingering vestiges of inequality that plague Clarice.

Walton and Jones, for example, note that from the very first scenes: "Rather than being a victim, Clarice is quite literally an agent, though she is, it becomes clear, a subordinated agent-in-training" (1999: 229). But, as Walton and Jones go on to recognize, Clarice's subordinate status within the FBI and her physical vulnerability allow the film to "raise important questions about female agency in the institutional site within the film (the FBI) and in the generic site of the film (the thriller-police procedural)" (1999: 231). Similarly, Linda Mizejewski's discussion of *The Silence of the Lambs* takes into account the various ways Demme's film version actually undermines the character of Clarice in contrast to the way she was presented in the Thomas Harris' novel.

In the film she is presented as more of an outsider and a novice with little or no social support within the FBI, and her exceptional skills as a sniper and the all-around best agent at the academy are not even referenced. Mizejewski also notes that Anthony Hopkins' terrifying and somewhat campy portrayal of Hannibal Lecter helped make the film as much his story as it is Clarice's. It is a credit to Foster's performance that Clarice still conveys a strong and independent presence in the film despite being disempowered more than she was in the novel, and much of Clarice's appeal may come from her marginalized position within the FBI.

According to Mizejewski, Clarice has a special meaning for many viewers precisely because she is a "female outsider determined to rescue the woman poised as Buffalo Bill's next victim. Women reviewers often praised *The Silence of the Lambs* as a feminist film, pointing out its triumphant storyline of a woman rescuing another woman" (176). The phenomenal success of *The Silence of the Lambs* and its ability to present a female character that remains strong and insightful despite emphasizing her status as a feminine outsider and an investigative novice marked it as one of the rare occasions in crime thrillers where the heroine is allowed to be truly heroic.

Where *Cagney & Lacey* and *The Silence of the Lambs* succeeded for the most part in crafting popular narratives where the lead heroines occupied a position as the subject of an active gaze rather than its object, the majority of post-1970s film and television depictions of investigating women have not fared as well. Female detectives have increased in number over the last two decades, but they are still, more often than not, burdened with explicit objectification. In film in particular, the merger of crime narratives with erotic thrillers has led to a standard conception of female investigators as a central component of the sexual spectacle. While the heroine may nominally be the looking subject, she is also importantly the object of investigation.

Yvonne Tasker has set forth an accurate schema for modern investigating women wherein female "protagonists and characters can be understood as located across three sites or realms within crime genres: the active, knowledgeable (or at least inquiring) space of the investigator, that of the criminal/object of investigation, and that of the victim of the crime" (1998: 92). Often the female detective occupies all three positions simultaneously. Tasker's analysis of such early 1990s films as *Impulse* (1990), *Blue Steel* (1990), and *Bodily Harm* (1994) reveals a pattern that involves "an exploration of the sexuality of the female investigators alongside, and complexly entwined with, the central case itself" (93). While the lead female character may be officially charged with tracking down a killer, the dominant narrative focus is on her sexuality and how her potentially dangerous personal desires intersect with the killer's. The melding together of crime stories, modern noir, police procedurals, and erotic thrillers has led to a conventional narrative pattern where the female investigator is as much an object of the investigative gaze as is the serial killer—a pattern that fits well with Hollywood's insistent dependence on casting only established sex symbols in lead female roles.

Much like the classic horror movies that Williams discussed, the contemporary thriller equates the female who looks with the monster, most typically recast as a serial killer. While there may not be a recognition of affinity between the two based on their shared position as "an exhibitionist-object of the desiring male gaze," there is a clear lack of distance between the investigator and the investigated—between the hunter and the hunted. The most conventional narrative device used to frame the female investigator as an object of the male gaze, to position her sexual desires as dangerous, and to clarify the closeness between her and the serial killer, is to have them involved in a sexual relationship.

In addition to the early 1990s films that Tasker focused on, this scenario has remained a common device in more recent films such as *Twisted* (2004) and *Taking Lives* (2004). In *Twisted* Jessica Shepard (Ashley Judd) is a detective with the San Francisco Police Department who has just received a significant promotion for her work in capturing a serial killer. Along with her new partner, Mike Delmarco (Andy Garcia), Shepard is assigned to a murder case where the victim is a man with whom she recently shared a one-night stand. Jessica is initially portrayed as a strong and exceptionally observant detective but as the story unfolds her competency and her sanity quickly seem to unravel. Jessica is haunted by the scandalous death of her parents.

Her father, himself an SFPD cop, apparently went on a murder spree that culminated with killing Jessica's adulterous mother and then himself. Raised by her father's ex-partner, John Mills (Samuel L. Jackson), the current Chief of Police, Jessica is an exceptional investigator, but she deals with her demons and personal doubts by drinking and picking up strange men in seedy bars for anonymous sex. When a second victim Jessica slept with washes up in the harbor, her male colleagues start to belittle her promiscuity and her status as an investigator. The case soon becomes as much about her sexual behavior as it is about the murders. After a long day of investigation even Jessica notes that every clue leads only to herself.

Jessica's problems are further compounded by violent outbursts and nightly blackouts apparently induced by her heavy drinking. She literally loses her ability to see anything and begins to question her own actions. Each morning she wakes with unexplainable cuts and bruises, and then discovers that yet another man whom she slept with was murdered by the particularly brutal serial killer. Her affairs with the four dead men and her inability to account for her whereabouts, make her the prime suspect, and even Jessica comes to believe that she must be a psychotic murder like her father.

When her mentor, Mills, explains that she is not blacking-out but has instead been repeatedly drugged with rohypnol (a date-rape drug), the two confront her partner, Delmarco, who has exhibited a creepy sexual attraction to her. It is only in the final moments of the film, when Jessica sees Mills drug Delmarco and begin framing his suicide, that she realizes it was Mills all along. When she tries to arrest him he strikes her down and reveals that he was the one who killed her parents due to her mother's infidelities and her father's unwillingness to do anything about it. In the end, she manages to relay his confession to other officers over her cell phone and shoots him just before he can finish Delmarco off. Jessica may survive and be cleared of the crimes, but she is still left emotionally shattered and humiliated. As a female investigator she repeatedly fails to see almost anything but her own demoralization and the deadly results of her promiscuity.

While the sex life of Special Agent Illeana Scott (Angelina Jolie) is not as thoroughly explored in *Taking Lives* as Shepard's is in *Twisted*, her sexual relationship with the killer is a crucial plot point and provides much of the psychological and erotic tension of the film. Scott is an insightful and intuitive FBI profiler brought in to help investigate a mysterious murder in Montreal that she quickly identifies as the work of a serial killer who assumes the identities of his victims. Somewhat eccentric in her approach to get inside the killer's psyche (she lies down in the pit where the first victim was discovered and in the bed of the prime suspect), Scott's help is initially resisted by the male investigators, but she does seem to have a privileged vision.

She looks at the body and finds clues that even the medical examiner missed, she finds evidence hidden in the victim's apartment the male detectives overlooked, and she deduces connections between different missing person's reports going back two decades. When a local art dealer, Costa (Ethan Hawke), is identified as a witness and a potential victim, Agent Scott first suspects him but then gradually finds herself attracted to him. After Scott and the police witness the man they think is the killer die in a car chase, she gives in to her feelings and spends a passionate night with Costa. The following morning she discovers Costa is the real serial killer but fails to apprehend him. She is an emotional wreck, fired from the FBI, and even assaulted by one of the officers who blames her sleeping with the killer for his partner being shot. Despite her superiority as a detective and her resistance to sexual innuendoes from male officers (she even wears a fake wedding ring to discourage unwanted advances), the film ultimately associates her sexual desires with compromising the investigation and aligns her with the monstrous, psychopathic killer.

The final scenes of *Taking Lives*, however, are set eight months after Costa made his escape, and show a very pregnant Scott living on her own in an isolated Pennsylvania farm house. Costa shows up and says he has been watching her for months and now wants to take his place as her husband and father of the twins she is carrying. When Scott refuses him, he taunts her and reveals he has confiscated all of the weapons that she had hidden around the house in anticipation of his arrival. They struggle, and he stabs her pregnant belly with a pair of gardening scissors. But to his (and the audience's) surprise she pulls them out of her stomach and kills him with them.

As he lies dying, she reveals that her "pregnancy" is just padding and all her activities for months had been a performance for him. "Everything you saw," she yells at him, "was what I wanted you to see!" In the end, the film seeks to reestablish the privilege of her vision over his, and while this may seem a triumphant finale, it can never completely recant how thoroughly and easily she was duped earlier. Scott's vision may have finally won out, but only after her ability to actively look had been undermined and she had been victimized by her own inadequate sexual discretion.

As *Twisted* and *Taking Lives* illustrate, the female investigator in twenty-first-century feature films still occupies the tripartite positions of subject of investigation, object of investigation, and potential victim. And the emphasis on serial killers as the embodiment of evil in crime narratives facilitates a tension wherein the female investigator is always the potential final victim. The case often becomes as much about saving one's own life as it is about saving innocents. These films, and others such as *Copycat* (1995), *Kiss the Girls* (1997), *The Bone Collector* (1999), *The Cell* (2000), *Murder by Numbers* (2002), and *Perfect Stranger* (2007), are all structured around the foreshadowing of the female investigator's position as the killer's ultimate victim.

The modern heroine may be a successful active looker, but she is still punished for looking. She does triumph in the final moments but there is often the sense her victory will forever be tainted by her vulnerability. The female investigator's intimate relationship with the killer and her status as a woman in a genre where women are predominantly coded as victims of male violence make her plight exponentially more dangerous than it would be for a male character. Her look may be an active one in that she sees clues and tracks the killer successfully, but she also sees unspeakable physical acts perpetrated against (most typically) female victims, and by implication, her own possible fate. To continue looking, to continue her pursuit in the face of this knowledge, is a masochistic quest.

In her discussion of slasher films, Carol Clover describes the anticipatory and seriatim structure of serial killer plots as evidence of masochistic identification. Like the Final Girl of horror, the investigator in pursuit of a serial killer "*sees* his or her fate in advance as it is visited on the person or persons ahead in line—impalement, flaying and castration in the 'execution' fantasy, and all manner of stabbing, drilling, and slicing in the slasher film" (1992: 219). Clover recognizes the masochistic visions at play in this type of scenario as identical to those that Reik observes in the sexual fantasies of his masochistic patient who "identifies with one of the victims, usually not the one who is just being castrated but with the next, who is compelled to look on at the execution of his companion. The patient shares every intensive affect of this victim, feels his terror and anxiety with all the physical sensations since he imagines that he will himself experience the same fate in a few moments" (Reik 1981: 42).

For Clover, this parallel fantasy supports her contention that horror audiences derive their vicarious pleasures in large part through adopting a feminine masochistic form of identification. The viewer's masochistic fantasy is saved from its logical and fatalistic conclusion in horror "through an eleventh-hour reversal, longer or shorter and more or less sadistic, and thus delivers the spectator back into the status quo" (Clover 1992: 222). But in the more realist genres of thrillers and police procedurals where female investigators pursue serial killers, the seriatim masochistic progression is at least as much about constructing the heroine as a potential victim, figuratively and sometimes literally punishing her for looking, as it is about facilitating audience identification. And because crime fiction is less fantastical than horror, the female investigator's eleventh-hour reversal that allows her to kill the killer never really permits her, or the viewer, a complete escape from masochism—a full return to the status quo.

Women as subjects of an investigating gaze have fared somewhat better on television in recent years. This may be due to the long history of TV as a feminine-identified medium, the potential of a weekly serial format to develop more fully rounded characters, and/or the greater presence of women as producers of television programming. Mizejewski notes: "Television series are actually more flexible than movies because television has the ability to develop a character and even make changes within one season to accommodate audience responses. So television has been relatively adventurous about portraying professional woman investigators, even during the 1970s, long before Hollywood did so" (2004: 10).

The TV female investigator may have been thoroughly packaged as a pinup in the 1970s, and continues to endure a heavy dose of sexualization today, but her consistent presence has helped establish a model of active female subjectivity. As Mizejewski describes it, "[T]elevision is exactly the place where we see how forcefully the female investigator has become part of our cultural 'central casting,' gradually infiltrating the all-boys crime shows" (11). In any case, female investigators on contemporary television are far more likely to exercise their right to look without being reduced to the sexualized object of the male gaze or the victim of the killer's look.

The wider range of possibilities for women as lookers on television even extends to the type of females who can assume an authoritative and knowledgeable vision. Older heroines like Jessica Fletcher (Angela Lansbury) from the long-running series *Murder She Wrote* (1984–1996) and Jane Tennison (Helen Mirren) from the popular BBC mini-series' *Prime Suspect* are practically unimaginable in feature films. Still, given that the American television industry operates under the same presumption as Hollywood film that lead actresses must always be exceptionally beautiful no matter what the role, there is a marked tendency to fetishize the lead character's looks even if her appearance is not a central plot point.

The stars of such popular female investigator series as *Profiler* (1996–2000), *Crossing Jordan* (2001–2007), *Cold Case* (2003–current), *The Closer* (2005–current), *Angela's Eyes* (2006), *Saving Grace* (2007–current), and *Women's Murder Club* (2007–2008) are all conventionally attractive women. The promotional campaigns for these series tend to emphasize both the female investigator's competence and her attractiveness—her explicit position as a subject of the investigation and as an object of the viewer's gaze. An advertisement for *Crossing Jordan* describes Jill Hennessy's character: "Medical Examiner Dr. Jordan Cavanaugh. Smart. Sexy. Refuses to play by the rules." A similar ad for the short-lived series *Karen Sisco* (2003–2004) starring Carla Gugino (based on the character made famous by Jennifer Lopez in the film *Out of Sight*, 1998) classifies her : "Smart. Sexy. Lethal. Just another girl looking for her man." So while these television heroines may not be as explicitly objectified by the gaze as big-screen female investigators tend to be, they still have to be smart and sexy.

In addition to a consistent emphasis on the beauty and sexiness of the smart female investigator in contemporary TV series, other conventions may undercut the singular authority of her visual perspective. One of the most common is the use of the buddy-cop formula to pair female investigators with male partners. Shows like *The X-Files* (1993–2002), *Mysterious Ways* (2000–2002), *Bones* (2005–current), and *Chuck* (2007–current) all feature strong female investigators who usually take a back seat to the primary male character. That most of these shows either explicitly or implicitly flirted with the romantic tensions inherent in male-female partnering did not help the women stand out as investigators on their own merit.

These contemporary male-partnered female investigators are less bound by the romantic premise that underlaid such early series as *Hart to Hart* (1979–1984), *Remington Steele* (1982–1987), and *Moonlighting* (1985–1989) but the suggestion of romantic coupling still exists as a way to recuperate her within a traditional heterosexual dynamic. As the modern progenitor of the formula, *The X-Files* also set the pattern whereas despite Scully's competence as both an FBI agent and a medical doctor, her vision was consistently devalued in comparison to Mulder's. Much to the frustration of fans, Scully simply failed to see important events. She was always looking the other way when supernatural creatures and aliens came into view.

Similarly, the female investigator is often one of the lesser, but also important, members of a male-led investigative team in popular television police procedural franchises such as *CSI* (2000–current), *CSI: Miami* (2002–current), *CSI: New York* (2004–current), *Law & Order* (1990–2010), *Law & Order: Special Victims Unit* (1999–current), *Law & Order: Criminal Intent* (2001–current), and *NCIS* (2003–current). There is also a tendency to align the efficacy of the female investigator's vision with a traditional assumption about women's intuition. While Special Agent Illeana Scott in *Taking Lives* lies down in the position previously occupied by the deceased in an attempt to identify with them, some television heroines have a more explicit way to communicate with the dead over the course of their investigations. Both of the popular shows *Medium* (2005–current) and *Ghost Whisperer* (2005–current) feature lead female characters with a supernatural ability to see and speak with the dead. Their privileged vision is associated with femininity as a touchy-feely perspective rather than a more rigid scientific approach to crime-solving.

Despite some major advances, when the woman who looks in film and television is an investigator, her relationship to that look is still problematic. There has been a marked tendency over the last thirty or so years to punish female characters who assume an active investigative gaze. Even when the women emerge victorious it is often at a great cost to their personal and professional well-being. And while the cinematic cliché of making the heroine's sexuality part of the investigation remains common, there have been gradual changes.

In her analysis of women detective movies of the 1990s, Linda Mizejewski notes the gradual upturn: "By the end of the decade, Jennifer Lopez in *Out of Sight* (1998) played a federal marshal with a snappy wardrobe and no apologies" (2004: 141). Mizejewski credits this improvement over the female detective who is all too often thoroughly assaulted and degraded to the rise of the action heroine as a Hollywood staple. "It was possible because a new kind of character was emerging in Hollywood, the action heroine," argues Mizejewski, "first cousin of the woman detective and popular enough to draw a market and an audience. In *Out of Sight*, Lopez doesn't need to explode through giant plate-glass windows or somersault out of burning cars. But when she's threatened by some mouthy testosterone, she whips a blackjack out of her designer handbag and makes the guy very, very sorry" (141). Thanks to the influence of the action heroine in modern Hollywood, the female investigator finally has the potential to actively look without fear of reprisals. That this progression has been slow to come to fruition is evidenced by the post-*Out of Sight* films that are still far more influenced by the narrative and visual conventions of the thriller (e.g., *Murder By Numbers*, 2002; *Twisted*, 2004; *Taking Lives*, 2004) than they are by the ass-kicking figure of the action heroine.

ACTIVE LOOKING AND THE DENIAL OF MASOCHISM

It is with the action heroine, that "first cousin of the woman detective," that female characters in film and television can fully exercise an active, powerful investigative gaze without being victimized by a concomitant masochistic form of punishment. While the emergence of heroic women in the action genre most obviously places female characters at the center of a narrative form that champions spectacle over detective reasoning, the ability of action heroines to see effectively is also an essential part of the formula. For all the back-flips, gunplay, and choreographed martial arts sequences, the heroine's capacity to control and command the look is critical. Action is defined by its frenetic sense of movement and over-the-top special effects, but the basic formula is always essentially a souped-up mystery. The action hero or heroine needs to find and defeat the all-powerful bad guy, locate the magical whatzzit, or foil the villain's plans for world domination. Like the detective and mystery genres, action requires investigation, deduction, and the accumulation of

knowledge. In short, seeing is as important to the plot as fight sequences are
to the spectacle.

There is a visual accentuation of the action heroine's eyes within the genre
because the steely glare signifies confident subjectivity and a commanding
presence. Like the *Bionic Woman* ads, the posters and stills used to promote
action heroine stories often focus on her eyes as well as her heavily fetishized
body. For example all the teaser posters for the feature films *Elektra* (2005),
Aeon Flux (2005), *Bloodrayne* (2006), and *Underworld: Evolution* (2006)
stressed the heroine's eyes. Within the films the camera often calls attention to
the primacy of the action heroine's look and the threatening gaze she wields.

An hyperbolic example of this occurs in *Kill Bill 2* when the Bride stands on
a cliff and glares angrily into the distance, the camera zooms in and out on her
eyes for an extended period while the music builds to a dramatic and cheesy
crescendo. Or, as with the opening sequence in each of the three *Resident
Evil* films, the heroine's vision is quickly established as the dominant point of
view through an extreme close up of Alice's eye jerking open as she abruptly
regains consciousness. Unlike in horror films, these eyes are not frightened,
they are angry; they are not vulnerable, they are threatening, and they never
have trouble comprehending what they see.

By stressing the efficacy of the action heroine's vision in this chapter I do
not mean to imply that they are not also thoroughly presented as objects of
the male gaze. As I have outlined throughout this book, action heroines are
first and foremost fetishistic fantasy women. Their beauty and sexual desirability are key parts of the character type and constitute the basis for marketing campaigns. The likelihood that a largely heterosexual male audience that
favors action flicks will pay to see sex symbols like Halle Berry, Milla Jovovich,
Charlize Theron, Kate Beckinsale, and Angelina Jolie in tight leather costumes
helps to justify the enormous budgets required to produce these films. And
within the diagesis of the stories the heroines are excessively fetishized and
treated as erotic spectacles by both male characters and the camera.

It is the precarious balance between subjectivity and objectivity, between
looking and being looked at, which positions the action heroine as such a
fascinating and complex character. This contrast between two extreme possibilities is apparent with the *Elektra* "Don't let anything stand between you
and her special features" ad discussed in Chapter Six, and the "Looks *can* kill"
poster for the feature film. In the first case Jennifer Garner is displayed in her
crimson bustier as an erotic ideal for men to look at, in the second the focus is
on her eye and her weapon, with the double entendre clarifying that it is *her*
look that can kill. To focus on the comically exaggerated fetishization alone
would miss the fact that the narratives never victimize the heroines through

their sexualization. Despite being more clearly fetishized and treated as objects of a male gaze than thriller heroines are, the action heroine is never merely that which is looked at. Nor is she punished for turning the visual tables on male characters.

As a fetishized visual object, the action heroine is more in line with the femme fatale of film noir than the helpless heroines of classic horror or the victimized female investigators of contemporary thrillers. Like the femme fatale, the action heroine exploits the male characters that ogle her, using her sexual allure to seduce, trick, and disarm men. But unlike the femme fatale who is ultimately punished for her sexual transgressions, the action heroine always emerges victorious. Whether it is simply unbuttoning her blouse to reveal more cleavage, or out-and-out seducing male characters, the action heroine easily manages to use men's lust for her against them. The ruse of flirting with armed men in order to defeat them is so routine that there is a clear message within the genre that any man who treats the action heroine as merely a sex object will himself be punished.

This form of feminine masquerade as a helpless sex kitten provides the foundation for *Alias* and is at the heart of some of the more comedic films like *Ms. Congeniality* and *Charlie's Angels*. In a season two episode of *Alias*, for example, Sydney Bristow pretends to be a high-class, whip-wielding prostitute in order to get information from a slovenly terrorist kingpin aboard his private jet. The episode opens with Sydney slowly strutting down a hallway in black lingerie to the pounding beat of AC/DC's "Back in Black." The villain and his bodyguard watch her appreciatively, then the villain orders her to change into red lingerie. After repeating the erotic scene again clad in red, the villain dismisses the guard and tries to embrace Sydney on the bed. She quickly chokes him and knocks him unconscious after mockingly asking, "What was wrong with the black one? You think it's comfortable wearing clothes like this?" She then steals the intel she needs, trounces the other bad guys, and parachutes off the plane.

Of course this type of scenario means that audiences still witness the heroine in an excessively eroticized manner that may not be fully compensated for by the eventual punishment she dishes out to the fictional exploiter. The balance between the extratextual sexualization of the actresses/heroines and the narratives of reversal means that the characters are still rooted in a position of being both object and subject. But the intent at least conveys a warning that these women can and will strike back if men try to position them as simply objects of a desiring gaze. Narratively, the look does not punish action heroines, but the action heroine does punish the looker.

The convention of having female agents go undercover as prostitutes is nothing new, nor is it exclusive to action heroines. In fact, it is a frequently used device in modern crime thrillers as a convenient way to eroticize heroines and to confirm their difficult position as females within the male-dominated world of law enforcement. Yvonne Tasker observes: "The recurrent depiction of women officers working undercover as prostitutes represents a trope that signals her problematic location within the force (it is invariably a subject of comment) at the same time as it functions as a fairly straightforward voyeuristic strategy for showcasing the body of the star/performer" (1998: 94). When police women are assigned to go undercover as street prostitutes it is a stark reminder that despite their official sanction as agents of the law, they are still erotic commodities (still "working girls" as Tasker puts it), and only one step removed from being the victims of sexualized violence.

While the action heroine undercover as a prostitute is similarly presented in fetishistic clothing, the more fantastic scenarios within the action genre allow a very different spin. Rather than the more realistic streetwalker cover utilized in crime thrillers, the action heroine is far more likely to go undercover as a dominatrix. Chapter Two addressed the pivotal scene in *Barb Wire* where Pamela Anderson impersonates a dominatrix and how that particular fantasy figure may be a useful metaphor for understanding action heroines as a complex combination of masculine and feminine traits rather than a symbolic gender cross-dresser. Other action heroines such as Sydney Bristow in *Alias* and Angelina Jolie's Mrs. Smith in *Mr. & Mrs. Smith* (2005) have likewise pretended to be leather-clad dominatrixes in order to gain access to their intended targets.

The difference between going undercover as a street-level prostitute and as a high-end dominatrix may be one of degree, but it is an important symbolic shift. The female investigator in crime thrillers is placed in a relatively powerless and degrading position, while the action heroine assumes an aggressive and domineering persona despite still being, ostensibly, a sexual commodity. The fantasy of strength and independence inherent in the figure of the action heroine allows her to resist being even momentarily victimized as a sexual object.

The action heroine story likewise refuses to treat her voluntary sexual relationships with men as a means to question her autonomy or her ability to carry out her mission. The cliché of marginalizing the female investigator's legitimacy by having her unknowingly sleep with the enemy (or at least aligning her sexual desires with his psychotic violence), plays out in a very different manner in action films. In a variation on the theme, the action heroine is often portrayed as either having a current or past sexual relationship with the villain.

In the case of *The Long Kiss Goodnight* not only had Samantha slept with the terrorist, Tim, she also mothered his child. Likewise, The Bride in the *Kill Bill* films is out to revenge herself against her former lover and employer, Bill, who is also the father of her child. In *Underworld* the vampire warrior Selene turns against her ex-lover, Kraven, the leader of their coven who has betrayed their entire species. Rather than being at a disadvantage because of these relationships with the bad guys, the action heroine manages to rebuke her lover and kill him without the almost crippling emotional breakdown experienced by the female investigator. Samantha enthusiastically guns down her ex-lover while simultaneously thwarting his terrorist attack and saving her daughter. The Bride can calmly slay Bill with the mysterious five fingers of death move. And Selene fights back against Kraven killing dozens of his men, destroying his plans, and revealing his betrayal to everyone in their coven.

In *Tomb Raider 2: The Cradle of Life*, Lara Croft makes her core autonomy explicitly clear to her mercenary lover. After a night of passion she handcuffs him to a chair so he cannot follow her. When he says she is leaving him behind because she loves him and would be unable to kill him, Lara retorts that she is leaving him because she *could* kill him (and she eventually does). For the action heroine sex—even with the enemy—is not an occasion for vulnerability but an opportunity to reassert her autonomy and dominance.

The action heroine occasionally reclaims power, dominance, and control from male challengers quite directly. Just prior to the explosive finale in *The Long Kiss Goodnight*, the recovering amnesiac Samantha is about to be locked in a freezer with her daughter and left to die by the villain (and her ex-lover), Tim. One of Tim's skills is his ability to know when people are lying by looking into their eyes. So when Samantha tells him "You're going to die screaming, and I'm going to watch," as he is about to close the door, he laughs at her until she challenges him to look her in the eye to see if she is lying. When Samantha's eyes confirm her confidence, the villain is unnerved and quickly rushes away. Of course, she escapes and carries through on her promise to kill him viciously.

The heroines of the new *Bionic Woman* and *Resident Evil: Extinction* each reclaim their visual control from males even more literally. One downside to Jaime Sommers' bionic eye is that her male handlers at the Burkit Agency can see whatever she sees through their computer link-up. Jaime is understandably upset by this invasion of her privacy, especially when her nemesis, Sarah Corvis (an earlier bionic woman gone rogue), sarcastically tells her, "Those Berkut guys look at you in the shower you know. And don't even get me started on how objectifying this whole 'Bionic Woman' thing is. They don't tell you anything. That's why you and me, we need to stick together, maybe form a union." But with Sarah's help Jaime learns she can override the system in her eye and turn off their access. When her boss complains, Jaime simply tells him that things are going to be done her way or not at all.

Likewise, in the third *Resident Evil* film the villainous men of the Umbrella Corporation that created and cloned the genetically enhanced heroine Alice, are able to access her brain, seeing what she sees and shutting her down completely. But through her strength of will Alice manages to reactivate herself and reject their commands. When they lose control of her the last thing they see through their computers is Alice descending upon them. Their attempt to control her vision only makes them witness to their own deaths.

The action heroine's mastery of the look, and her control over what she sees, is depicted in a very obvious way in both *Bionic Woman* and *Resident Evil: Extinction*. While the struggle to assert the primacy of the action heroine's look may not always be so literal, it is still at the core of the narrative. She is the one who has to investigate the crimes and piece together the clues, she has to uncover the secrets and discover the bad guys. Ultimately, it is her desire to know the truth that drives the plot. Her ability to look great and kick ass may provide the lion's share of the visceral thrills, but it is her curiosity that provides the story. And in the case of action heroines, curiosity never kills the cat.

The action heroine's adventure elevates her active looking to the level of an epistemological quest. Not coincidentally, the mystery inherent in most action heroine stories involves some form of self-discovery. Alice in the *Resident Evil* films is not just out to kill zombies and save the world, but to find out what the Umbrella Corporation did to her. Sydney Bristow in *Alias* has a wide range of adventures but the overall arc of the series was based on her attempt to decipher why she appears to be the key to ancient prophecies. Samantha in *The Long Kiss Goodnight* wants to recover her lost memories and find out who she was before her amnesia. Patience Philips in *Catwoman* fights crime with her newly endowed supernatural skills, but she also wants to find out what caused her to change and how it happened. In the feature film version of *Aeon Flux*, Aeon uncovers the mystery behind not just the totalitarian government but also behind her own creation.

Where the crime thriller tends to make the female investigator's sexuality an integral part of the criminal investigation, the action genre often makes the heroine's origin or sense of being part of the quest. Both strategies may be a way to position the woman herself as an enigma, as has long been a tradition in popular narratives. But with the action heroine the riddle to be untangled is tantamount to self-discovery or self-actualization as a form of empowerment rather than a way to perpetuate female sexuality as an unknowable threat to masculinity.

The eminently successful active and investigating look of the action heroine allows her not just to "see" but to "know" what is happening. In her later work, *Fetishism and Curiosity* (1996), Laura Mulvey rethinks the feminist possibilities inherent in the myth of Pandora's box in a manner that stresses the importance of a feminine desire to know. The myth of Pandora's box—like the story of Eve, the first woman to tempt man with forbidden knowledge—has traditionally been regarded as a misogynistic fable that casts woman as an alluring seductress whose beauty disguises her underlying threat to mankind. The box metaphorically represents the hidden and barely contained threat of female otherness coded as pain, suffering, and despair. Mulvey, however, argues that "Pandora's gesture of looking into the forbidden space, the literal figuration of curiosity as looking in, becomes a figure for the desire to know rather than the desire to see, an epistemophilia. If the box represents the 'unspeakable' of femininity, her curiosity appears as a desire to uncover the secrets of the very figuration she represents" (59).

In Mulvey's reconsideration of the myth, Pandora's curiosity has the potential to be a parable of a feminine desire to discover the truth about femininity itself. "The female figure not only is driven by transgressive curiosity, to open the box," Mulvey argues, "but is able to look at the supposed horror of those aspects of the female body that are repressed under patriarchal culture. It is here that the myth, otherwise from its very beginnings truly a symptom of misogyny, can find a point of transformation" (61).

This transformation from feminine curiosity as representative of mankind's downfall to a self-reflexive quest to discover hidden truths about oneself (and by extension of femininity) is enacted by the figure of the action heroine. While the heroines of classic horror and melodrama, the femme fatales of film noir, and the female investigators of most crime thrillers are typically punished for actively looking in much the same way that Pandora and Eve were, the action heroine represents a female figure that can look without accepting punishment. In the larger sense, the action heroine is able to solve not just the mystery of any given specific crime but of her own origins, her own meaning within a broader symbolic system. Many of the action heroine's adventures are intricately bound up with a quest for self-discovery. For example, both the *Underworld* and *Tomb Raider* films and their sequels illustrate how the heroine's mission can ultimately be read as a successful epistemophilial quest.

The *Underworld* films are stylish and frenetic tales about a centuries-old battle waged between sexy, goth-styled vampires and brutish werewolves. The story's heroine is Selene (Kate Beckinsale), a fetishy, leather-clad vampire who is a member of the Death Dealers, an elite group of lycan hunters—but in the first film, Selene is much more than just an effective killing machine. When Selene sees several lycans she is hunting target a specific human, Michael Corvin (Scott Speedman), she becomes curious and starts investigating why they are interested in this seemingly random human. When the leader of her coven, her ex-lover Kraven, orders her to leave the matter alone she refuses and continues to explore the mystery.

Selene discovers that Michael Corvin is a descendant of Alexander Corvinus, the legendary figure who sired twin sons, the first vampire and the first lycan, and that Lucien, the leader of the lycans, is out to turn Michael into a hybrid vampire/werewolf to help eradicate all of their enemies. In the course of rescuing Michael, Selene also discovers that Kraven has been conspiring with the lycans to overthrow his own kind. In her pursuit of answers, Selene awakens Viktor, one of the vampire elders who is a father figure to her since he turned her into a vampire centuries ago—after lycans supposedly killed her entire family. In the climactic battle between the vampires and the lycans, Selene also discovers that it was Viktor who started the blood feud when he had his own daughter killed rather than let her bear the child of her lycan lover, Lucien. And, more importantly for Selene's epistemophilial quest, she finds out that it was Viktor himself, not the lycans, who brutally slaughtered her parents and little sisters.

When Michael, in full hybrid form, is about to be killed by Viktor, Selene rushes into the fray both to save Michael and to avenge her family's death (and by extension her own origins as a vampire). In one majestic leap Selene slices Viktor's head in half before landing coolly on the other side of the cavernous room in which they were fighting. Not only does Selene perform an active and investigative gaze successfully to solve the initial mystery of Michael's importance, she also completes a pattern of self-discovery that reveals her own origins *and* is able to accept the truth about herself and to enact decisive retribution on behalf of her fallen loved ones.

The sequel, *Underworld: Evolution*, picks up where the first film left off, with Selene and Michael on the run from both the lycans and the vampires. She reasons that their best hope for survival is to awaken the original vampire elder Marcus Corvinus and explain that her slaying of Viktor was just. But Marcus does not care, he only wants to free his brother William, the original lycan, who was imprisoned centuries earlier by Viktor. Marcus attacks Selene and Michael and tries to steal a medallion from them that can be used to open William's tomb. In their quest to figure out what is going on, Selene and Michael visit Andreas Tanis, the exiled official historian of the covens. When

Selene informs Tanis that she killed Viktor, he notes, "So you've learned the truth." And in a metaphoric nod to her epistemophilia, her active and investigative gaze, he admiringly adds, "Your eyes are finally open."

Selene, it turns out, is the key to finding William because her father was the blacksmith who constructed the prison chamber whose location is hidden within her childhood memories. After Michael is apparently killed by Marcus, Selene gains additional powers and sets out to destroy both Marcus and William before their combined powers lead to the end of all humankind. In the end Selene finds the brothers, slays Marcus (a revived Michael defeats William), and creates a new and more promising world for both vampires and lycans. In *Underworld: Evolution*, Selene is more than just an ass-kicking babe and an eminently successful active looker, she discovers not just her own origins as a vampire but those of all vampires and lycans. Moreover, she is able to reclaim her own agency in the process.

Like the *Underworld* films, the *Tomb Raider* movies illustrate the action heroine's epistemophilia while simultaneously refusing to be placed in a masochistic position. *Tomb Raider 2: The Cradle of Life* is an especially clear example of how the action heroine exercises an active, investigative look and a feminine desire to know. Moreover, because the plot of *Tomb Raider 2* revolves around a quest to discover the mythical Pandora's box itself, the film repositions the figure of the fetishized woman from that which unleashes pain and suffering into the world, to the one person who can resist temptation and thus save the world.

In the film, *Lara Croft: Tomb Raider*, Angelina Jolie plays the titular heroine who had already become a worldwide phenomenon through an extremely popular series of video games and related merchandising (see Chapter Seven). This initial big-screen adventure saw wealthy relic hunter and adventuress Lady Lara Croft searching for a mysterious talisman that gives its possessor the ability to control time. Lara is in a race to find the object before the villainous coalition called the Illuminati can retrieve it and use it for their own nefarious ends. Lara's adventure is also a means to connect with her own origins as she must follow the clues left for her by her deceased father (played in the film by Jolie's real-life dad Jon Voight), who had first discovered the ancient device.

As with most action heroine tales, the first *Tomb Raider* film granted Lara the dominant visual perspective as she alone is able to see how to connect the clues, recover the artifact, and use it to her advantage. In addition to defeating dozens of men, first intellectually and then physically, in combat, Lara also triumphs over her corrupt lover, Alex West, a less scrupulous relic hunter. The second film echoes many of the same themes but shifts the focus away from Lara's desire to know in general and in relation to her personal past, to concern itself with the origin of pain and suffering on an apocalyptic scale.

Tomb Raider 2: The Cradle of Life begins with Lara discovering the lost treasures of Alexander the Great in an underwater tomb. Lara is ambushed in the tomb by merciless rival treasure hunters who kill her assistants, steal a mysterious glowing orb that she has recovered, and then leave her for dead. Later, back at her English estate, representatives from MI-6 inform Lara that the orb is actually a map which can reveal the location of the fabled Pandora's box, and that it was stolen for the evil scientist Jonathan Reiss who specializes in creating lethal viruses for terrorists.

Lara reasons that the legendary box contains the ultimate plague, anti-life in its most primordial form, which Reiss will unleash upon the world, thus killing billions. She agrees to regain the orb and keep the box from Reiss if they will release commando/gun-runner Terry Sheridan—her former lover—from a maximum security prison in Siberia. Lara wants Sheridan released into her custody not because she has feelings for him, but because she needs his terrorist connections to locate the orb quickly.

She thus teams up with Sheridan for much of the film but has explicit permission to kill him should he step out of line. Lara and Sheridan battle numerous bad guys throughout Asia and eventually steal back the orb. She then leaves Sheridan behind and figures out how to activate the orb so that she alone can see where Alexander the Great has hidden the box. Lara goes to a mountain in Africa, the cradle of life, to safeguard the box. But before she can recover it Reiss and his army of mercenaries show up (with Lara's two faithful assistants as hostages), and Reiss follows her into the underground chamber where the box floats in a pool of black acid formed by the tears Pandora cried when she looked into the box. As Lara and Reiss battle over the box, Sheridan joins them and shoots Reiss, who falls into the acid.

With the crisis averted, Lara thanks Sheridan for his help and they share a passionate kiss. Lara is ready to leave the cradle of life but Sheridan retrieves Pandora's box from the pool and starts to pack it to take with them. He figures the box, and the plague it contains, is worth unimaginable wealth and insists it is their right to capitalize on it together. Lara is not even tempted—she knows the catastrophic deaths that will occur if the box is opened and refuses to let him leave with it.

"You're not walking out of here with that box," Lara sternly declares as she stands between him and the only way out. "It could kill millions of innocent people." Sheridan does not care about the pain and suffering that might befall others and tells her, "You don't have it in you to stop me!" He strikes Lara to the ground but she gets to her feet and refuses to let him pass. Sheridan argues that Lara loves him and that she could never choose her morals and beliefs over him. When she steadfastly refuses to budge he draws his gun to kill her, but Lara manages to fatally shoot him first.

Loving a man who turns villainous does not indicate a weakness in Lara; in fact, her ability to stay true to her own ideals demonstrates for viewers that she and her sexuality are not one and the same. She unwaveringly and violently refuses to assume a masochistic position within the narrative. Her desire for knowledge is not her undoing but her strength. Tellingly, the film closes with a refiguring of the popular myth of Pandora's box when Lara, a woman whose life mission is to discover and retrieve lost artifacts, simply straightens the lid of the box and returns it to its original hiding place. She may have a passion for discovery, for seeing the truth of things, but she also has the fortitude to look away when she knows that to look would be masochistic to herself and could bring harm to others.

The action heroine in contemporary popular culture is a complex and often contradictory figure. She is a strong female character type but, as her critics like to point out, her strength and subjectivity are often undermined by the way she is visually portrayed as a fetishistic fantasy figure. Yet, the narratives consistently manage to have their (cheese) cake and eat it too. The exaggerated presentation of action heroines as objects of a male gaze does not translate within the narrative to a loss of their own visual superiority. More than any other female figure in film or television, the action heroine is in full command of an active and investigative gaze.

The exceptional fighting abilities she possesses as a prerequisite for heroism within action genres does mean that she can triumph physically as well as intellectually over her adversaries. It also means that she can actively refuse to be punished within the narrative for assuming the right to look. When the action heroine looks, she does not see the horror of her own otherness, nor the negative consequences of her own sexual desires. When the action heroine looks, she sees the truth behind all the subterfuge. She is also able to see and know the truth about herself. Perhaps the most positive aspect of the contemporary action heroine is not her superficial ability to kick ass, nor the challenge she represents to traditional perceptions of gender appropriate behavior, but her ability to "see" and "know" without having to accept a masochistic position.

WONDERING ABOUT WONDER WOMAN

Action Heroines as Multi-Fetish

*L*ive-action superhero movies came into their own in the early 2000s, thanks in large part to the incredible advances made in CGI technology, which allowed an almost seamless merger of special effects, digital characters, and living actors. The phenomenal big-screen success of films based on such recognizable comic book properties as Spider-Man, The X-Men, Batman, Daredevil, The Fantastic Four, Iron Man and Superman has inspired Hollywood studios to rush dozens of adaptations into production. Other big name characters like Green Lantern and The Flash will soon be released. Even lesser known comic book series have become extremely profitable movies, including *Sin City, Constantine*, and *300*. And while some comic book superheroines such as Catwoman and Elektra have headlined their own films, they were unfortunate failures, as were the television series based on the comic book superheroines in *Birds of Prey* and *Painkiller Jane*. The disappointing adaptations of these superheroines means that the feature film version of comicdom's oldest and most recognizable superheroine, Wonder Woman, has been put on the back burner.

In 2006 Warner Brothers was anxious to bring the legendary Amazon to life, even releasing a teaser poster to build excitement. The ad simply stated: "Experience the Wonder" alongside an illustration by fan favorite artist Adam Hughes. That only Wonder Woman's hair, chest, and one clenched fist adorned with her trademark bullet-deflecting bracelet were visible proved to be prophetic since the movie, like the image of the heroine herself, never materialized. Given Wonder Woman's pedigree as one of DC Comic's big three characters (along with Superman and Batman), her immense cultural recognition well beyond the narrow confines of comic fandom, the lingering popularity and nostalgia of the 1970s television series featuring Linda Carter, and the fact that Joss Whedon (the man behind *Buffy The Vampire Slayer*) was signed on to write and direct, the film had every indication of becoming a profitable franchise. But production delays and studio fears about the bankability of action heroines meant the apparent demise of big-screen hopes for Wonder Woman.

According to numerous film magazines and science fiction–related Internet sites the Wonder Woman film, which is a property of uber-producer Joel Silver, has been kicking around since early in 2002. The project has had numerous big-name directors attached to it at various times and Silver has commissioned several scripts. There has also been an enormous amount of speculation among fans as to which actress could best portray the Amazonian princess—nearly every brunette in Hollywood has been rumored to be interested in the role at one time or another.

According to *The Hollywood Reporter*, Whedon came on board in 2005 and was paid $2–3 million to develop his own take on the character. But in February 2007 Whedon broke the news that the studio was no longer moving forward with the project. "I had a take on the film that, well, nobody liked," Whedon announced on the Whedonesque.com fan Web site. "Hey, not that complicated," Whedon assured fans, "let me stress first that everybody at the studio and Silver Pictures were cool and professional. We just saw different movies, and at the price range this kind of movie hangs in, that's never going to work. Non-sympatico. It happens all the time. I don't think that any of us expected it to this time, but it did."

The studio's hesitancy to move forward with the Wonder Woman feature seems to be rooted in pure economics. After all, action heroines have had a checkered past at the box office. Just two years earlier an editorial in *Entertainment Weekly* had questioned the future of "superchick flicks" on economic grounds after *Elektra* fizzled on its opening weekend. "A spin-off of 2003's *Daredevil* in which (Jennifer) Garner plays a merciless assassin," *EW* reported, "the movie opened last weekend in fifth place with a limp $14.8 million— about a third of *Daredevil*'s debut, and also less than Halle Berry's much ridiculed, DC Comics-based *Catwoman*" (Scwartz 2005: 20). As the editorial went on to speculate, the failure of *Elektra* and *Catwoman* is difficult to reconcile with the financial success of the *Tomb Raider* and *Aliens* series but it does suggest that the uneven fiscal returns makes action heroines a risky genre for Hollywood. The fact studios are unwilling to take a risk with a character as prominent in popular culture as Wonder Woman does not bode well for the future of action heroines in general.

That the Wonder Woman movie failed to materialize is an indication of the troubled status of action heroines in contemporary media culture. Despite her slow increase in number, despite the remarkable fan devotion she inspires, and despite the substantial profits she sometimes generates, the action heroine continues to struggle with mass acceptance. As one of the earliest and most famous heroic females in popular culture, Wonder Woman epitomizes the conflicted status of action heroines. Her evolution and her contemporary status also reflects many of the themes explored throughout this book.

Like all action heroines Wonder Woman is overburdened as both a symbol of feminist agency in a genre rooted in masculine power fantasies and as a sexual fetish in visually oriented mediums that continue to present women as erotic ideals above all else. She is also a product of male creators and a corporate property subject to an economy where women are still perceived as more valuable as sexual commodities than as media consumers. But Wonder Woman, like many of the fictional heroines she inspired, has also managed to become a symbol for audiences, young girls and older fans alike, of female strength. She has emerged as a popular feminist icon and subversively as a symbol of lesbian identity. Wonder Woman represents the troubled cultural position of action heroines as contestable figures. She is a symbol of many things at once. And while many of the fantasies that surround Wonder Woman are conflicting and contradictory, they may also help explain at a broad cultural level why the action heroine is one of the most intriguing, progressive, and disputed signs of changing gender norms in popular culture.

BALANCING FEMALE EMPOWERMENT AND FETISHIZATION

Wonder Woman's status as an archetypal action heroine is due in equal parts to her being the first major female superhero character and the fact that she was conceived independent of a male character. Other superheroines are mostly knock-offs of successful male heroes such as Superman's cousin Supergirl, Batman's protégé Batgirl, and Hawkman's wife Hawkgirl. Wonder Woman made her original appearance in the comics in 1941 in a short story within the pages of *All Star Comics* #8 and proved an immediate success. Within months she became the lead character in her own self-titled series.

The story of her origins, both fictional and corporate, is well known, retold in countless histories of the medium: Wonder Woman is the bravest and most skilled warrior from an island of Amazons who chooses to leave her idyllic matriarchal paradise in order to help fight injustice in man's world. In reality Wonder Woman was conceived by the psychologist William Moulton Marston at the request of publisher M. C. Gaines after Marston publicly criticized the burgeoning comic book industry. Writing under the pseudonym of Charles Moulton, Marston imagined Wonder Woman as a strong but tender female character who could offset the decidedly masculine tone of the comics industry. As Marston wrote in 1944, his goal with Wonder Woman was to create a character who could be "tender, submissive, peaceloving as good women are," and armed with "all the strength of a Superman plus all the allure of a good and beautiful woman" (Marston 1944: 42–43). From her very beginning then, Wonder Woman has struggled with the symbolic burden of conforming to a masculine genre's fantasy of physical strength and the cultural preeminence of female beauty.

Since her inception the character of Wonder Woman has struggled with being both an eroticized fetish object and a progressive symbol of female empowerment contemporary heroines continue to face in all media forms. Marston has been described as an early feminist for insisting that Wonder Woman should always be portrayed as equal in strength to any male superheroes, and her adventures were always as exciting as the male heroes with Wonder Woman able to outfight and outwit any adversaries. Marston even went so far as to regularly reverse the clichéd gender scenario by having Wonder Woman repeatedly come to the rescue of Major Steve Trevor, who functioned in the stories in a manner similar to Lois Lane in the Superman books.

Wonder Woman is often credited with establishing an archetype of superheroinism and with attracting a substantial number of young female readers to comics, all without alienating the core audience of male fans. Of course the fact that Wonder Woman was illustrated as exceptionally attractive and clad in first a short skirt, and then tight shorts and a bustier, helped make her palatable to the boys and WWII servicemen who constituted the bulk of the comics reading market in the 1940s. The sexually charged and revealing nature of her costume set a standard for all action heroine costumes to follow.

The most obvious (and most often discussed) fetishistic aspect of Wonder Woman was the frequent use of bondage in her stories. A central part of the Wonder Woman mythos constructed by Marston was that she would become powerless if bound by a man. The creators never failed to exploit this Achilles heel and managed to craft scenarios where Wonder Woman would be tied up in every issue. But comics historians have argued that the device of placing Wonder Woman in bondage was not explicitly kinky because even the male heroes of the period were often captured and in need of assistance. As Trina Robbins argues in *The Great Women Super Heroes*: "[T]he fact is that in comics from the 1940s, if the heroes weren't getting tied up so that they could escape from their bonds, their girlfriends were getting tied up so that they could be rescued by the heroes" (Robbins 1996: 12–13). But none of the male characters were created with bondage as one of their core weaknesses.

And, as other comics historians and Marston biographers have document-ed, Marston (who wrote all the Wonder Woman stories until his death in 1947) intentionally used Wonder Woman to express his personal beliefs about the positive aspects of sexual submission (see for example Daniels 1995, or Bunn 1997). In his personal life Marston was a proponent of non-traditional sexual practices and openly lived with two female spouses. His belief in bond-age as an effective means to discover truth carried over into his other life's work: the invention of the lie detector.

Despite the rather explicit eroticization of Wonder Woman, she contin-ued to be an important icon of heroism for young women throughout the 1940s and 1950s. After Dr. Fredric Wertham singled out Wonder Woman for her sadomasochistic stories and possible lesbian undertones in his infa-mous book, *The Seduction of the Innocent* (1954), and the subsequent Senate Hearings on Juvenile Delinquency, her adventures became far tamer and less popular. Wonder Woman struggled to maintain her market share during the 1960s, but was rediscovered by both second-wave feminists and the general public in the 1970s. As was mentioned in Chapter Six, Wonder Woman was celebrated as an icon of feminine strength on the cover of the inaugural issue of *Ms. Magazine* because she was one of the few popular culture figures all of the contributing editors remembered positively from their youth. And at the same time that *Ms. Magazine* declared "Wonder Woman for President!" the campy television series *Wonder Woman* featured a highly sexualized version of the character as embodied by Lynda Carter.

The fact that a single character could simultaneously epitomize both fe-male strength and sexual objectification some thirty years after her creation is remarkable. In the cyclical lineage of action heroines, this repopularized mo-ment of Wonder Woman in the 1970s would eventually inspire the kick-ass women of modern film and television. With Wonder Woman as the archetype of action heroines in popular culture it is no surprise that fetishization has remained one of the most obvious character traits in the depiction of active women given that she was conceived within a genre catering to masculine fan-tasies and adolescent fears of female sexuality. This fear and desire for beautiful women that has always been clear with Wonder Woman appears to be one of the reasons contemporary action heroines continue not just to be fetishized but to struggle for mainstream acceptance. As *Charlie's Angels* screenwriter John August speculated to *Entertainment Weekly* about the box office struggles of "superchick flics": "Studios think all teenage boys want to see a beautiful girl kicking ass. But teenage boys are also kind of terrified of women, so the sexuality drives them away" (Schwartz 2005: 28).

By the mid-2000s Wonder Woman's iconic image in the media landscape continued to struggle, like most action heroines, with the conflicting nature of being both a symbol of female empowerment and a sexual fetish. Within the comic book pages of her own self-titled series and various DC Comics team books such as *Justice League of America* and *Justice League Unlimited*, Wonder Woman has experienced a resurgence in popularity of late. The *Wonder Woman* title was rebooted in 2007 and saw a marked increase in sales. Interestingly, this revamped *Wonder Woman* received a great deal of praise both within the comics industry and from the mainstream press for being written by such notable female creators as novelist Jodi Picoult and comics veteran Gail Simone. It should be noted, however, that the shift to female writers does not necessarily mean the character's sexual appeal was toned down.

As a *Newsweek* article titled "Holy Hot Flash, Batman! Make room in the boys' club, Caped Crusader. After 66 years, a woman takes over Wonder Woman" (Yarbroff 2008) makes clear, Wonder Woman's sexuality is too important a feature to dismiss. The article mentions that Jodi Picoult's requests to make Wonder Woman's costume more practical were dismissed by the powers that be at DC Comics. The closest Picoult came to addressing the issue was to write a scene in one issue where a patron in a bar wonders how the heroine manages to "fight crime in a freaking bikini." More to the point Gail Simone believes that Wonder Woman "has always been a strong female character," and that she "doesn't plan to insert a feminist agenda to the strip or tone down the superhero's overt sexiness. Part of her appeal," Simone says, "is that she makes your eyes pop out of your head" (Yarbroff: 59).

In addition to her numerous appearances in ongoing comic book series, 2007 saw Wonder Woman celebrated by DC Comics in a number of special collections and commemorative books. Michael L. Fleisher's *Encyclopedia of Comic Book Heroes: Wonder Woman* was updated and reprinted, a retrospective of some of the most important Wonder Woman tales were featured in *Wonder Woman: The Greatest Stories Ever Told*, and she took center stage as comicdom's most popular heroine in the coffee table book *DC Comic's Covergirls* (Louise Simonson). The contestable status of Wonder Woman as a strong character and as fantasy pinup figure is apparent in the way she is depicted in the *Wonder Woman: The Greatest Stories Ever Told* and the *DC Comic's Covergirls* books, which sit side-by-side on store shelves. In *The Greatest Stories Ever Told* Wonder Woman is shown as a powerful figure of justice across the decades, able to defeat the forces of evil and sexism single-handedly through both her powers (which rival Superman's) and her intellect. But in *DC Comics Covergirls* the emphasis is on her striking beauty and her always eroticized physical form.

In *Covergirls* Wonder Woman is described as powerful, but the images stress her fetishistic appeal—posed in semi-pornographic stances, bondage scenarios, and/or being targeted by non-too-subtle phallic missiles. The cover illustrations alone speak volumes about the inherent conflict of Wonder Woman. *The Greatest Stories Ever Told* features a fairly life-like illustration of Wonder Woman by Alex Ross that emphasizes her steely glare and strong build. The *Covergirls* image is derived from an earlier comic book cover illustrated by Adam Hughes, best known for his sexual depiction of comic women, and shows a modern, idealized, and more voluptuous version of the Amazon gasping at an earlier and more chaste illustration of herself. Another cover for the *Covergirls* book featuring art by Ross is available, but sold far fewer copies. Wonder Woman, it would seem, is still characterized as both one of the "Greatest" comic book superheroes and as the medium's premier "Covergirl."

Wonder Woman's status as a somewhat kitschy symbol for feminist ideals also remains intact in contemporary popular culture. In 2007, while Wonder Woman was featured in both *The Greatest Stories Ever Told* and the *Covergirls* books for comics fans, she was also featured again on the cover of *Ms. Magazine* for their thirty-fifth-anniversary issue. She was also prominent in an array of lighthearted self-help books in 2007 that addressed issues ranging from coping in the workplace to dealing with personal relationships. The publication of such books as *So You're Not Wonder Woman?: How Your Super Power Can Change Your Life* by Melanie Wilson, *What Would Wonder Woman Do?: An Amazon's Guide to the Working World* by Jennifer Traig and Suzan Colon, *I'm Not Wonder Woman: But God Made Me Wonderful* by Sheila Walsh, and *I Married Wonder Woman . . . Now What?: A Superhero's Guide for Leading and Loving the 'Proverbs 31' Wife* by Jess Maccallum kept the popular culture cachet of Wonder Woman as a symbol of female strength alive and well.

Wonder Woman's continued popularity means that the character has a presence in contemporary popular culture well beyond the printed page. As a property of the media conglomerate Time-Warner, Wonder Woman is the subject of substantial commercialization. Wonder Woman's image is available on a countless variety of T-shirts, underwear, pajamas, notebooks, nightlights, hats, mugs, calendars, and so on. Because of her longevity, Wonder Woman merchandise is marketed to older fans and young consumers alike. She is equally popular with middle-aged feminists (such as myself) and little girls (such as my five-year-old daughter) who know the character primarily from her presence on the Cartoon Network's animated television series *Justice League Unlimited*. As a parent I am glad that my daughter has a Wonder

Woman lamp and poster in her bedroom, as well as several Wonder Woman action figures to play with. She even has a motorized Wonder Woman figure that hangs from her ceiling and flies around in circles.

Action heroines like Wonder Woman, Kim Possible, The Powerpuff Girls, and Princess Natasha allow young girls entrance to an imaginative world of play where they can identify with the heroic adventures of female characters. As Sherrie Inness notes: "The increase in female action figures suggests that women are gaining a new access to heroic roles, which formerly have predominantly been the providence of men" (2004: 78). For decades girls have been limited to the beauty- and consumption-obsessed likes of Barbie and Polly Pocket, while active and heroic character toys were reserved only for boys. With the increased presence of action heroines in popular culture, girls now have "dolls" that can do so much more than change their clothes or go shopping.

While the Wonder Woman merchandise geared toward young girls facilitates fantasies of heroic identification, many items target older consumers that clearly shift the meaning of the character into the realm of sexual fantasy. The Wonder Woman action figures meant for children to play with are primarily sculpted in the manner of the innocent retro style based on the *Justice League Unlimited* cartoon. But there is no denying that even these toy versions of kid-oriented action heroines are presented as conventionally attractive. The compensatory sexualization of strong female figures is at work in even the most innocent cases. As Inness makes clear: "[T]he makers of female action figures struggle to balance beauty and sex appeal with toughness" (2004: 83). Moreover, these children's toys, which are initially priced in the ten-dollar range, are joined on the shelves by figures that skew older (and pricier) that embody Wonder Woman as a more erotic spectacle.

Many of these older-aimed "toys" are released as collectables and seem to have the core adolescent male comic-buying audience in mind. These limited edition figures are not meant as toys to be played with, instead they position Wonder Woman as a static and sexually charged figure. Some, such as the series of mini-statues modeled on the erotic artwork of Adam Hughes, clearly portray her more as an erotic spectacle than a heroic woman. It should, perhaps, come as no surprise that in many comic book stores these busts of superheroines are sold alongside action figures of porn starlets. This multiplicity of competing Wonder Women, from strong role model for young girls to erotic fantasy for older male consumers, reflects the multiple meanings inherent in the reception of all action heroines. Like all of the modern heroines discussed throughout this book, Wonder Woman can be, and is, understood as alternately a model of female strength, a performance of masculinity, a dominatrix, a feminist avenger, a post-feminist Girl Power avatar, an example of feminine masquerade, a product of male creators, and/or a successfully active looker. And, like all the heroines who followed her, Wonder Woman is a contestable figure because she embodies all of these conflicting attributes simultaneously.

The consistent difficulty with understanding Wonder Woman or any other heroine as primarily a progressive step in female representation is our cultural preference for the visual when it comes to women in the media. Because women have been so thoroughly fetishized as erotic spectacles, the image tends to outweigh the actions when heroines are costumed to emphasize their physical form. The dominant perception of Wonder Woman remains one of sexual fantasy regardless of how heroic her adventures are, and this is made explicit in the popular Halloween costumes widely available today. Marketed to young women alongside such staples as sexy witch, sexy schoolgirl, and sexy catgirl, the Wonder Woman costume is primarily about becoming an erotic fantasy figure that attracts men, rather than playfully identifying with an image of strength (as seems to be the case with superhero costumes marketed to men).

If the Internet is any indication, the Wonder Woman Halloween costume is an extremely pervasive sexual fantasy. Dozens of sites are devoted to cataloging photographs of amateurs, actresses, and professional models dressed in the Wonder Woman Halloween costume. Like all action heroines, Wonder Woman is so thoroughly conceived within the sexual logic that strong female characters must also be beautiful that her strength can easily be overshadowed by the fantasy of her as a dominatrix, an erotic spectacle, and as a sexual commodity for men. Within the sexually charged economy of contemporary Halloween costumes for women it is no surprise that alongside the fetish-derived costumes of Wonder Woman (and French Maids, and Naughty Nurses) are erotic costumes based on the heroines from *Kill Bill*, *Catwoman*, *Tomb Raider*, *The Matrix*, *Underworld*, and *Buffy the Vampire Slayer*.

This insistence on strong female characters as sexual fantasy figures is taken to an extreme in the phenomenon of superheroine photomanipulations. A popular Photoshop version of fan art, superheroine photomanipulations are altered photographs, primarily of nude centerfolds, that digitally draw superheroine costumes onto images of erotically posed women. I first became aware of this type of fan art when I saw an advertisement in a Chicago newspaper for a local nightclub's Halloween party. The ad (Figure 10.1) encouraged potential partygoers to "Flaunt Your True Colors. Come Dressed as Your Favorite Super Hero." Dominating the ad was an image of an erotically posed porn starlet with a Supergirl costume digitally painted onto her curvaceous body. This was obviously not an invitation for women to dress up as their favorite heroic role model, but to vamp themselves up in a superheroine-themed costume. I soon discovered that this image of a hypersexualized Supergirl was only the tip of the iceberg when it comes to fans creating erotic images by combining real-life centerfolds and fictional heroines. Of course Wonder Woman is one of the most popular subjects for the superheroine photomanipulation treatment, but she joins almost every comic book heroine and villainess imaginable.

The dominant forms of fan art and fan fiction (especially slash) have been discussed by critics like Bacon-Smith (1991), Lewis (1991), Jenkins (1992), Hills (2002), and Rhiannon (2005) as a strategy by which fans poach from media texts in order to explore narrative possibilities beyond the confines of the official text. This particular sub-genre of fan art similarly gives expression to unspoken fantasies that the fans feel lie just beneath the surface of the official texts. In the case of superheroine photomanipulations the fantasy in play is fairly obviously a further step in eroticizing powerful female characters. Here the erotic suggestion of the superheroine costumes is made explicit. The implicit threat of the superpowered woman is neutralized by depicting her as just another passive sex object. While the occasional image of a popular actress is used in the art, the reliance on centerfolds aligns superheroines with the stock fantasy of the perfect woman aroused and welcoming of the male gaze. That the costumes are drawn onto the image of a naked woman, effectively covering up an already excessively sexualized body, indicates just how fetishistically charged skintight superheroine outfits are.

By layering a superheroine costume over a nude centerfold, these photomanipulations foreground the erotic link between the active and passive fetishization of action heroines detailed in Chapter Three. The centerfold epitomizes the fetishized passive phallic woman—by redressing her in a superheroine costume, which contrastingly typifies the fetishized active phallic woman, the fan art manages to merge both fetishisms into a single image. In a very literal sense, superheroine photomanipulations then perform the symbolic consolidation of, and compensation for, the two contrasting ideologies at play in the figure of the action heroine who is both sexually attractive and threatening.

Whereas a character like Sydney Bristow in *Alias* can alternate between masquerading as passive and active phallic women, the superheroine phototmanipulations fuse these roles into a single figure. In other words, if fetishism exists because, as Kaplan puts it, the "fetishist cannot introduce his penis into that temple of doom called a vagina without a fetish to ease the way" (1991: 263), the superheroine photomanipulation doubles the degree of comforting objectification. This fetishistic doubling may be more explicit in photomanipulations but it also crystallizes the erotic appeal of action heroines for many

10.2. Advertisement in a Chicago newspaper for a local nightclub's Halloween party.

fans. Her threatening toughness may be erotic in and of itself, but it does not negate the more traditional fantasy of passive objectification with which it is intimately intertwined. What this practice does negate is the fact that these strong superheroine characters can also represent new and progressive roles for women. Likewise, when modern action heroines are primarily presented and consumed as sex symbols, the progressive possibilities of the role are overshadowed or erased completely.

THE FUTURE OF ACTION HEROINES

So if a character as enduring and admired as Wonder Woman faces seemingly insurmountable challenges in being turned into a feature film what does that imply about the future of action heroines in popular culture? And, if Wonder Woman has struggled with representing female empowerment and overt fetishization concurrently in every era and in every media form, what hope do modern action heroines have for escaping this conflicting and nullifying combination? What, in short, does the future hold for action heroines? These are important questions with no easy answers.

Despite the media's wary approach to action heroines as financially viable characters, and despite the mixed criticisms they have endured for being perceived as too manly or too sexualized, the action heroine seems here to stay. The 2008/2009 television season saw the launch of three new action heroine series. The *Bionic Woman* and *Terminator: The Sarah Connor Chronicles* series premiered to excellent ratings but then quickly fell out of favor with mass audiences. Slightly more promising was Joss Whedon's newest show *Dollhouse*, featuring Eliza Dushku as a superpowered secret agent. Moreover, the recent feature films *Wanted* (2008), *Doomsday* (2008), and *Whiteout* (2009) delivered strong action heroine roles for Angelina Jolie, Rhona Mitra, and Kate Beckinsale respectively. Likewise, an updated version of *Barbarella* is in production, as are new installments of the *Tomb Raider, Underworld*, and *Resident Evil* franchises. While none of these examples move away from the Hollywood imperative to eroticize heroines, they do demonstrate a continued interest in developing kick-ass roles for women. In one form or another the action heroine will continue to challenge outdated cultural perceptions about gender-appropriate behavior and model new attitudes about female agency and strength.

It would also be a mistake to assume that the failure to produce the Wonder Woman feature film is due entirely to the character's unbankable association with previous action heroines. The action film genre as a whole has struggled in the new millennium. Since the genre's heyday in the late 1980s and early 1990s, action has labored to maintain its undisputed dominance over the box office. No reliable male stars have emerged to succeed Arnold Schwarzenegger, Sylvester Stallone, Bruce Willis, and Harrison Ford. New hopefuls like Vin Diesel and The Rock have proven no more reliable in action films than their female counterparts.

The unpredictable market for action movies in the 2000s is one reason the studios concentrate on big-budget adaptations of pre-sold characters such as Spider-Man and Batman in the first place. Similarly, Hollywood has looked back to the 1980s for some of its most profitable films in recent years with new installments of the *Die Hard, Teenage Mutant Ninja Turtles, Rambo*, and *Indiana Jones* series. The commercial failure of recent action heroine vehicles may be due more to the questionable status of the action genre in general than to the gender of the lead characters.

The simplest answer to why action heroines have faltered at the box office is that the films featuring ass-kicking women have been lacking in quality. More often than not action heroine flicks seem content to pin their hopes for success on the sexual attractiveness of the lead character. It is difficult to overlook that many of the films place a far greater emphasis on the visual fetishization of the sex symbol stars than they do on good scripts. The leather-clad or wife-beater wearing heroine armed to the teeth is such a cliché that films like *Barb Wire, Catwoman, Aeon Flux, Elektra, Ultraviolet*, and *Bloodrayne* offer little else to viewers other than the sexual spectacle of a beautiful woman doing backflips, throwing punches, and firing weapons. As entertainment critics and movie reviewers have pointed out, the few action heroines who have achieved undisputed popularity, such as Ellen Ripley of *Aliens*, Sarah Connor of *Terminator 2*, and The Bride of the *Kill Bill* films, were all featured in well-written and directed movies.

That most action heroine films choose to focus on the look of the heroine rather than quality stories is unfortunate given that many of the most notable flops have starred award-winning actresses. While audiences and critics may not expect much more than a visually appealing package from films featuring centerfolds and models-turned-actresses like Pamela Anderson, Milla Jovovich, and Kristanna Loken, it is disparaging that Academy Award- and Emmy-winning actresses like Angelina Jolie, Halle Berry, Charlize Theron, and Jennifer Garner have been cast in action heroine roles that focus more on their sexuality than their acting abilities. Both Halle Berry and Charlize Theron went from winning Oscars for best actress in *Monster's Ball* (2001) and *Monster* (2002) to receiving Razzies (the anti-Oscars awarded for especially bad performances) in *Catwoman* and *Aeon Flux*. As the article "Superheroines Fly into Glass Ceiling: Women Warriors Don't Draw Big Crowds or Box Office" from *Advertising Age* argues: "Some Hollywood watchers say that [their box office failures] may have more to do with the way the characters are translated to movies than with audiences' reluctance to accept strong females in butt-kicking roles" (Stanley 2005: 2). The hypersexualization of action heroines at the expense of decent storytelling may prove a bigger obstacle than any monster or super-villain.

In any event, it seems unlikely Hollywood will abandon the excessive fetishization of action heroines any time soon. Because the sexualization of female characters in popular culture is still regarded as their primary appeal to audiences, especially the typically male audience that is assumed for all action genres, it is difficult to imagine that the strength and competence of heroines will ever outshine their erotic presentation. For example, the April 2008 *Sci Fi Magazine* published a special issue focusing on strong female characters and new television series. But instead of stressing the heroism of the characters, the headline "TV's Hot New Superwomen, Secret Agents, Cyborgs & More," and the internal glam photos of the characters reveal that, as always, these women are valued primarily for their sex appeal. So despite the marked increase of legitimate female superheroines, secret agents, and monster slayers on American network television during the 2008/2009 season, whatever media attention they get positions them as pinups more than heroes.

Even the well-reviewed, though short-lived, series *Terminator: The Sarah Connor Chronicles*, which features the deadly serious Lena Headly as the titular heroine, includes a sexy teenage female cyborg, Cameron, as a sidekick.

While the show is nominally about the dogged heroism of Sarah Connor and her efforts to save both her son and the future of all humanity, the beautiful cyborg was an essential ingredient in the program's marketing campaign and its immediate popularity. Cameron, as played by Summer Glau whose previous work includes the role of an ass-kicking teen babe in Joss Whedon's *Serenity*, carries the burden of fetishization in the series. She is at once an adolescent sex symbol, an eroticized cyborg, a figurative dominatrix, a phallic woman, and a superpowered heroine. The *Sci Fi* feature dubbed her "the new hot 'bot,'" and glowingly declared: "Few petite actresses can beat up a room full of big, tough guys with the grace and smoothness of movement that former dancer Glau does . . . there can be no doubt that Glau is, literally, a badass RoboBabe."

Yet despite the series' emphasis on the Cameron terminator's beauty, she is also a complex character who shares an intricate and well-told narrative. Cameron's complexity as a character manages to overshadow her more superficial fetishistic appeal. There is hope that quality television programs and films (and novels, comic books, and video games) featuring action heroines may yet position strong female characters as more than cheesecake no matter how fetishized they may be. Perhaps the new crop of action heroines who appear over the next few years will prove popular enough to jump-start a Wonder Woman feature film after all.

WORKS CITED

Alexander, Jenny. 2004. "A Vampire Is Being Beaten: De Sade Through the Looking Glass." *Slayage* 15.

Andrae, Thomas. 1996. "Television's First Feminist: *The Avengers* and Female Spectatorship." *Discourse* 18, no. 3: 112–36.

Ansen, David. 1993. "Devil or Charlie's Angel? A Flashy French Film Gets an American Translation." *Newsweek*, March 29.

Banet-Weiser, Sarah. 2004. "Girls Rule! Gender, Feminism, and Nickelodeon," *Critical Studies in Media Communication* 21, no. 2: 119–39.

Barr, Marleen S. ed. 2000. *Future Females, The Next Generation: New Voices and Velocities in Feminist Science Fiction Criticism*, New York: Rowman & Littlefield.

Barthes, Roland. 1957. *Mythologies*. Glasgow: Palladin Books.

Baumgardner, Jennifer, and Amy Richards. 2000. *Manifesta: Young Women, Feminism, and the Future*. New York: Farrar, Strauss and Giroux.

Baumgold, Julie. 1991. "Killer Women: Here Come the Hardbodies." *New York*, July 29.

Beltran, Mary C. 2002. "The Hollywood Latina Body as Site of Social Struggle: Media Constructions of Stardom and Jennifer Lopez's 'Cross-over Butt.'" *Quarterly Review of Film and Video* 19: 71–86.

Bennett, Tony, and Janet Woollacott. 1987. *Bond and Beyond: The Political Career of a Popular Hero*. New York: Methuen Inc.

Bhabra, H. S. 1995. "Ten Dollars a Dance." *Toronto Life*, May.

Bhattacharya, Sanjiv. 2005. "Fatale Attraction." British *GQ*, no. 189.

Bordo, Susan. 1993. *Unbearable Weight: Feminism, Western Culture and the Body*, Los Angeles: University of California Press.

————. 1993. "Reading the Male Body." *Michigan Quarterly Review* 32, no. 4.

Botcherby, Sue, and Rosie Garland. 1991. "Hardware Heroines." *Trouble and Strife* 21.

Bradley, Patricia. 1998. "Mass Communication and the Shaping of US Feminism." In *News, Gender and Power*, edited by Cynthia Carter, Gill Branston, and Stuart Allan. New York: Routledge.

Brown, Jeffrey A. 1996. "Gender and the Action Heroine: Hardbodies and the *Point of No Return*." *Cinema Journal* 35, no. 3, 52–71.

————. 2001. *Black Superheroes: Milestone Comics and Their Fans*. Jackson: University of Mississippi Press.

————. 2002. "The Tortures of Mel Gibson: Masochism and the Sexy Male Body." *Men and Masculinities* 5, no. 2: 123–43.

————. 2004. "Gender, Sexuality and the Bad Girls of Action." In *Action Chicks: Tough Girls in Contemporary Popular Culture*, edited by Sherrie Inness. Philadelphia: University of Pennsylvania Press.

Bukatman, Scott. 1994. "X-Bodies (The Torment of the Mutant Superhero)." In *Uncontrollable Bodies: Testimonies of Identity and Culture*, edited by Rodney Sappington and Tyler Stallings. Seattle: Bay Press.

Busse, Kristina. 2002. "Crossing the Final Taboo: Family, Sexuality, and Incest in the Buffyverse." In *Fighting the Forces: What's at Stake in Buffy the Vampire Slayer*, edited by Rhonda V. Wilcox and David Lavery. Lanham, MD: Rowman & Littlefield.

Butler, Judith. 1990. *Gender Trouble: Feminism and the Subversion of Identity*. New York: Routledge.

Cadenhead, Roger. 1994. "Bad Girls: Who Says Female Characters Don't Sell? Don't Tell That to These Women or Their Creators." *Wizard: The Guide to Comics*, no. 38: 42–47.

Chabon, Michael. 2008. "Designing Women." *Details Magazine* 26, no. 6: 196–201.

Chidley, Joe. 1993. "Killer in a Miniskirt: A Bad Girl Becomes a Lethal Lady." *MacLean's*, March 29.

————. 1995. "A No to Dirty Dancing." *MacLean's*, July 7.

Clover, Carol. 1992. *Men, Women, and Chainsaws: Gender in the Modern Horror Film*. Princeton: Princeton University Press.

Cochran, Shannon. 2007. "The Cold Shoulder: Saving Superheroines from Comic Book Violence." *Bitch*, no. 35: 23–26.

Collins, Patricia Hill. 2004. *Black Sexual Politics: African Americans, Gender, and the New Racism*, Routledge: New York.

Consalvo, Mia. 2004. "Borg Babes, Drones, and the Collective: Reading Gender and the Body in *Star Trek*." *Women's Studies in Communication* 27, no. 2.

Corliss, Richard. 1991. "Half a Terrific Terminator," *Time*, July 8.

Creed, Barbara. 1986. "Horror and the Monstrous-Feminine: An Imaginary Abjection." *Screen* 27, no. 1.

————. 1993. *The Monstrous-Feminine: Film, Feminism, Psychoanalysis*, New York: Routledge.

————. 2002. "The Cyberstar: Digital Pleasures and the End of the Unconscious." in *The Film Cultures Reader*, edited by Graeme Turner. New York: Routledge.

Croal, N'Gai, and Jane Hughes. 1997. "Lara Croft, the Bit Girl: How a Game Star Became a '90s Icon," *Newsweek*, November 10.

D'Acci, Julie. 1994. *Defining Women: Television and the Case of Cagney & Lacey*. Chapel Hill: University of North Carolina Press.

————. 1997. "Nobody's Woman? *Honey West* and the New Sexuality." In *The Revolution Wasn't Televised: Sixties Television and Social Conflict*, edited by Lyn Spigel and Michael Curtin. New York: Routledge, 73–93.

Davis, Kathy. 1991. "Remaking the She-Devil: A Critical Look at Feminist Approaches to Beauty." *Hypatia* 6, no. 2.

Dawson, Luke. 2002. "Armed and Dangerous: Hong Kong's Shu Qi Keeps Cool under Fire." *Gear*, September: 27.

Dicker, Rory, and Alison Piepmeier. 2003. *Catching a Wave: Reclaiming Feminism for the 21st Century.* Boston: Northeastern University Press.

Doane, Mary Ann. 1984. "The Woman's Film: Possession and Address." In *Re-Vision: Essays in Feminist Film Criticism*, edited by Mary Ann Doane, Patricia Mellencamp, and Linda Williams. Frederick, MD: University Publications of America.

———. 1999. "Technophilia: Technology, Representation, and the Feminine." In *Cybersexualities: A Reader on Feminist Theory Cyborgs and Cyberspace*, edited by Jenny Wolmark. Edinburgh: Edinburgh University Press.

Douglas, Susan J. 1994. *Where the Girls Are: Growing Up Female with the Mass Media.* London: Penguin.

Dyer, Richard. 1982. "Don't Look Now." *Screen* 23, no. 3–4: 61–73; reprinted in *The Sexual Subject: A* Screen *Reader in Sexuality*. New York: Routledge, 1992.

———. 1997. *White.* Routledge: New York.

Early, Francis H., and Kathleen Kennedy. 2003. *Athena's Daughters: Television's New Women Warriors.* New York: Syracuse University Press.

Ellis, John. 1982. *Visible Fictions: Cinema, Television, Video.* Boston: Routledge and Keegan Paul.

Faludi, Susan. 1991. *Backlash: The Undeclared War Against American Women.* New York: Crown Books.

Fernbach, Amanda. 2002. *Fantasies of Fetishism: From Decadence to the Post-Human.* New Brunswick, NJ: Rutgers University Press.

Fischer, Lucy. 1996. *Cinematernity: Film, Motherhood, Genre.* Princeton: Princeton University Press.

Fiske, John. 1988. *Television Culture.* London: Metheun.

Fleming, Charles. 1993. "That's Why the Lady Is a Champ: Women in Action Roles." *Newsweek*, June 7.

Freud, S. 1927. "Fetishism." Reprinted in *The Standard Edition of the Complete Psychological Works of Sigmund Freud, Volume XXI (1927–1931).* London: Hogarth Press.

Fudge, Rachel. 2006. "Girl, Unreconstructed: Why Girl Power Is Bad for Feminism." In *Bitch Fest*, edited by Lisa Jervis and Andi Zeisler. New York: Farrar, Strauss and Giroux.

Fudge, Rachel, and Juliana Tringali. 2007. "*Veronica Mars* and Its Feminist Stereotypes." *Bitch*, no. 35: 15.

Gaiman, Neal. 1993. *The Sandman: Brief Lives.* DC Comics. New York: Vertigo.

Gaines, Jane. 1990. "Costume and Narrative: How Dress Tells the Woman's Story." In *Fabrications: Costume and the Female Body*, edited by Jane Gaines and Charlotte Herzog. New York: Routledge.

Gamber, Frankie. 2007. "Wave Lengths." *Bitch*, No. 35: 42–47, 94.

Gamman, Lorraine, and Margaret Marshment, eds. 1989. *The Female Gaze: Women as Viewers of Popular Culture*. Seattle: Real Comet Press.

Gamman, Lorraine. 1989. "Watching the Detectives: The Enigma of the Female Gaze." In *The Female Gaze: Women as Viewers of Popular Culture*, edited by Lorraine Gamman and Margaret Marshment. Seattle: Real Comet Press.

Gamman, Lorraine, and Merja Makinen. 1995. *Female Fetishism*. New York: NYU Press.

Garland-Thompson, Rosemarie. 1998. "The Beauty and the Freak." *Michigan Quarterly Review* 37, no. 3.

Gebler Davies, Clancy. 2000. "Elite Unveils Cyber-Supermodel." *New Statesman*, May 21: 30.

Gillis, Stacey, Gillian Howie, and Rebecca Munford. 2004. *Third Wave Feminism: A Critical Exploration*. New York: Palgrave Macmillan.

Gledhill, Christine. 1988. "Pleasurable Negotiations." In *Female Spectators: Looking at Film and Television*, edited by E. Deidre Pribram. New York: Verso.

Gleiberman, Owen. 1993. "Gun Crazy." *Entertainment Weekly*, April 2.

Gough-Yates, Anna. 2001. "Angels in Chains?: Feminism, Femininity, and Consumer Culture in *Charlie's Angels*." In *Action TV: Tough-Guys, Smooth Operators, and Foxy Chicks*, edited by Bill Ogersby and Anna Gough-Yates. New York: Routledge.

Graham, Paula. 1994. "Looking Lesbian: Amazons and Aliens in Science Fiction Cinema." In *The Good, The Bad, and The Gorgeous: Popular Culture's Romance with Lesbianism*, edited by Diane Hammer and Belinda Budge. San Francisco: Pandora. 196–217.

Greer, Germaine. 2000. *The Whole Woman*. New York: A. A. Knopf.

Halberstam, Judith. 1998. *Female Masculinity*. Durham: Duke University Press.

Hammer, Diane, and Belinda Budge, eds. 1994. *The Good, The Bad, and The Gorgeous: Popular Culture's Romance with Lesbianism*. San Francisco: Pandora.

Haraway, Donna. 1985. "A Manifesto for Cyborgs: Science, Technology, and Socialist Feminism in the 1980s." *Socialist Review* 80: 65–108.

Hedegaard, Erik. 2004. "The Goddess and the Geek: Inside Quentin's Obsession with Uma." *Rolling Stone*, April 29.

Heinecken, Dawn. 2003. *The Women Warriors of Television: A Feminist Cultural Analysis of the New Female Body in Popular Media*. New York: Peter Lang Publishing.

Helford, Elyce Rae, ed. 2000. *Fantasy Girls: Gender in the New Universe of Science Fiction and Fantasy Television*. New York: Rowman & Littlefied.

Helford, Elyce Rae. 2002. "My Emotions Give Me Power": The Containment of Girls' Anger in Buffy." In *Fighting the Forces: What's at Stake in Buffy the Vampire Slayer*, edited by Rhonda V. Wilcox and David Lavery. Lanham, MD: Rowman & Littlefield.

Heywood, Leslie, and Jennifer Drake. 1997. *Third Wave Agenda: Being Feminist, Doing Feminism*. Minneapolis: University of Minnesota Press.

Higashi, Sumiko. 1980. "'Hold It!' Women in Television Adventure Series." *Journal of Popular Television and Film*, Autumn.

Hills, Elizabeth. 1999. "From 'Figurative Males' to Action Heroines: Further Thoughts on Active Women in the Cinema." *Screen* 40, no. 1: 38–50.

hooks, bell. 1992. *Black Looks: Race and Representation*. Boston: South End Press.

Hopkins, Susan. 2002. *Girl Heroes: The New Force in Popular Culture*. Melbourne, Australia: Pluto Press.

Hruska, Bronwen. 1993. "Make Her Day: Hollywood's Leading Ladies Are Getting in on the Action Genre." *Entertainment Weekly*, June 11.

Hudis, Mark. 1997. "The Sex Worker Next Door." *Gentleman's Quarterly* 67, no. 8.

Huyssen, Andreas. 1986. *After the Great Divide: Modernism, Mass Culture, Postmodernism*. Bloomington: Indiana University Press.

Inness, Sherrie A. 1999. *Tough Girls: Women Warriors and Wonder Women in Popular Culture*. Philadelphia: University of Pennsylvania Press.

Inness, Sherrie A., ed. 2004. *Action Chicks: New Images of Tough Women in Popular Culture*. New York: Palgrave-MacMillan.

Isaksson, Malin. 2009. "Buffy/Faith Adult Femslash: Queer Porn with a Plot." *Slayage* 28: 1–23.

James, Richard. 1992. "Women of Substance." *Film Review*, January.

Jansz, Jereon, and Raynel G. Martis. 2007. "The Lara Phenomenon: Powerful Female Characters in Video Games." *Sex Roles* 56: 141–48.

Jeffords, Susan. 1993. "Can Masculinity Be Terminated?" In *Screening the Male: Exploring Masculinities in Hollywood Cinema*, edited by Steve Cohan and Inna Rae Hark. New York: Routledge.

Johnson, Mandy. 1994. "Women as Action Heroes: Is Violence a Positive Direction for Females?" *Glamour*, March.

Jones, Darryl. 2002. *Horror: A Thematic History in Fiction and Film*. London: Arnold.

Jones, Ernest. 1951. *On the Nightmare*. New York: Liveright.

Jones, Gerard, and Will Jacobs. 1997. *The Comic Book Heroes: The First History of Modern Comic Books from the Silver Age to the Present*. New York: Prima Publishing.

Jowett, Lorna. 2005. *Sex and the Slayer: A Gender Studies Primer for the Buffy Fan*. Middletown, CT: Wesleyan University Press.

Kakoudaki, Despina. 2000. "Pinup and Cyborg: Exaggerated Gender and Artificial Intelligence." In *Future Females, The Next Generation: New Voices and Velocities in Feminist Science Fiction Criticism*, edited by Marleen S. Barr. New York: Rowman & Littlefield.

Kaplan, Cora. 1993. "Dirty Harriet/*Blue Steel*: Feminist Theory Goes to Hollywood." *Discourse* 16, no. 1: 50–70.

Kaplan, Louise. 1991. *Female Perversions: The Temptations of Emma Bovary*. New York: Doubleday.

Karlyn, Kathleen Rowe. 2003. "*Scream*, Popular Culture, and Feminism's Third Wave: 'I'm Not My Mother.'" *Genders Online Journal* 38.

Keft-Kennedy, Virginia. 2009. "Fantasising Masculinity in *Buffyverse* Slash Ficton: Sexuality, Violence, and the Vampire." *Nordic Journal of English Studies* 7, no. 1: 49–80.

Kennedy, Helen W. 2002. "Lara Croft: Feminist Icon or Cyberbimbo? On the Limits of Textual Analysis." *Game Studies* 2, no. 2.

Kirby-Diaz, Mary. 2005/2006. "The Fandom Project." *International Journal of the Humanities* 3, no. 4: 257–65.

Kristeva, Julia. 1982. *Powers of Horror: An Essay on Abjection*. New York: Columbia University Press.

Lacquer, Thomas Walter. 1990. *Making Sex: Body and Gender from the Greeks*. Cambridge: Harvard University Press.

Laennec, Christine Moneera. 1997. "The "Assembly-Line Love Goddess": Women and the Machine Aesthetic in Fashion Photography, 1918–1940." In *Bodily Discursions: Genders, Representations, Technologies*, edited by Deborah S. Wilson and Christine Moneera Laennec. Albany: State University of New York Press.

Laplanche, Jean, and J. B. Potalis. 1973. *The Language of Psycho-Analysis*. Translated by Donald Nicholson-Smith. New York: Norton Publishing.

Larbalestier, Justine. 2002. "Buffy's Mary Sue Is Jonathan: Buffy Acknowledges the Fans." In *Fighting the Forces: What's at Stake in Buffy the Vampire Slayer*, edited by Rhonda V. Wilcox and David Lavery. Lanham, MD: Rowman & Littlefield.

Lehman, Peter. 1993. "Don't Blame This on a Girl: Female Rape-Revenge Films." In *Screening the Male: Exploring Masculinities in Hollywood Cinema*, edited by Steve Cohan and Inna Rae Hark. New York: Routledge.

Lentz, Kirsten Marthe. 1993. "The Popular Pleasures of Female Revenge (or Rage Bursting in a Blaze of Gunfire)." *Cultural Studies* 7, no. 3.

Mallan, Kerry. 2003. "Hitting Below the Belt: Action Femininity and Representations of Female Subjectivity." In *Youth Cultures: Texts, Images, and Identities*, edited by Kerry Mallan and Sharyn Pearce. Westport, CT: Praeger.

Mallan, Kerry, and Sharyn Pearce, eds. 2003. *Youth Cultures: Texts, Images, and Identities*. Westport, CT: Praeger.

Martin, Michael. 2003. "Princess Bride." *Arena*, November.

Maslin, Janet. 1993. "Again the Black Dress and the Assassin in It." *New York Times*, March 19.

McCaughey, Martha, and Neal King, eds. 2001. *Reel Knockouts: Violent Women in the Movies*. Austin: University of Texas Press.

McClintock, Anne. 1995. *Imperial Leather: Race, Gender, and Sexuality in the Colonial Contest*. New York: Routledge.

McCracken, Allison. 2007. "At Stake." In *Undead TV: Essays on Buffy the Vampire Slayer*, edited by Elana Levine and Lisa Parks. Durham: Duke University Press.

McGrath, Karen. 2007. "Gender, Race, and Latina Identity: An Examination of Marvel Comics' *Amazing Fantasy* and *Arana*." *Atlantic Journal of Communication* 15, no. 4: 268–83.

McNair, Brian. 2002. *Striptease Culture: Sex, Media and the Democratisation of Desire*. London: Routledge Press.

McRobbie, Angela. 2004. "Notes on Postfeminism and Popular Culture: Bridget Jones and the New Gender Regime." In *All About the Girl: Culture, Power, and Identity*, edited by Anita Harris. New York, Routledge.

Metz, Christian. 1975. *The Imaginary Signifier: Psychoanalysis and the Cinema*. Reprinted in 1982. Translated by Celia Britton. Bloomington: Indiana University Press.

Middleton, Jason. 2007. "Buffy as Femme Fatale." In *Undead TV: Essays on Buffy the Vampire Slayer*, edited by Elana Levine and Lisa Parks. Durham: Duke University Press.

Mikula, Maja. 2003. "Gender and Videogames: The Political Valency of Lara Croft." *Continuum: Journal of Media and Cultural Studies* 17, no. 1: 79–87.

Miller, Toby. 1997. *The Avengers*. London: BFI Publishing.

Mizejwski, Linda. 2004. *Hardboiled and High Heeled: The Woman Detective in Popular Culture*. New York: Routledge.

Morgan, Thais E. 1989. "A Whip of One's Own: Dominatrix Pornography and the Construction of a Post-modern (Female) Subjectivity." *The American Journal of Semiotics* 6, no. 4: 109–36.

Mulvey, Laura. 1975. "Visual Pleasure and Narrative Cinema." *Screen* 16, no. 3: 6–18.

———. 1996. *Fetishism and Curiosity*. Bloomington: Indiana University Press.

Munford, Rebecca. 2004. "'Wake Up and Smell the Lipgloss': Gender, Generation, and the (A)politics of Girl Power." In *Third Wave Feminism: A Critical Exploration*, edited by Stacy Gillis and Gillian Howie. New York: Palgrave-MacMillan Press.

Negra, Diane. 2001. *Off-White Hollywood: American Culture and Ethnic Female Stardom*. New York: Routledge.

O'Day, Marc. 2004. "Beauty in Motion: Gender, Spectacle, and Action Babe Cinema." In *Action and Adventure Cinema*, edited by Yvonne Tasker. New York: Routledge.

Ogersby, Bill, and Anna Gough-Yates, eds. 2002. *Action TV: Tough Guys, Smooth Operators, and Foxy Chicks*. New York: Routledge.

O'Neill, Kristen. 1996. "Lust Action Hero." *Premiere Magazine*, May: 70–75, 99.

Palmiotti, Jimmy, and Justin Gray. 2006. *Daughters of the Dragon: Samurai Bullets*. New York: Marvel Comics.

Pender, Patricia. 2004. "'Kicking Ass Is Comfort Food': Buffy as Third Wave Feminist Icon." In *Third Wave Feminism: A Critical Exploration*, edited by Stacy Gillis and Gillian Howie. New York: Palgrave-MacMillan Press.

Phelan, Lyn. 2000. "Artificial Women and Male Subjectivity in *42nd Street* and *Bride of Frankenstein*." *Screen* 41, no. 2.

Pierce, Tamora, and Timothy Liebe. 2006. *White Tiger: A Hero's Compulsion*. New York: Marvel Comics.

Pitcher, Karen C. 2006. "The Staging of Agency in *Girls Gone Wild*." *Critical Studies in Media Communication* 23, no. 3.

Place, Janey. 1978. "Women in Film Noir." In *Women in Film Noir*, edited by E. Ann Kaplan. London: British Film Institute.

Polsky, Allyson D. 2001. "Skins, Patches, and Plug-ins: Becoming Woman in the New Gaming Culture." *Genders Online Journal* 34.

Radner, H. 1989. "'This time's for me': Making Up and Feminine Practice." *Cultural Studies* 3, no. 3.

Read, Jacinda. 2000. *The New Avengers: Feminism, Femininity and the Rape-Revenge Cycle*. New York: Manchester University Press.

———. 2004. "'Once upon a time there were three little girls . . .': Girls, Violence, and *Charlie's Angels*." In *New Hollywood Violence*, edited by Steven J. Schneider. New York: Manchester University Press.

Reik, Theodor. 1981. *Masochism in Modern Man*. New York: Grove Press.

Riviere, Joan. 1929. "Womanliness as Masquerade." Reprinted in 1989 in *Formations of Fantasy*, edited by Victor Burgin, James Donald, and Cora Kaplan. London: Routledge.

Rodowick, D. N. 1982. "The Difficulty of Difference." *Wide Angle* 5, no. 1.

Rowe-Karlyn, Kathleen. 2003. "*Scream*, Popular Culture, and Feminism's Third Wave." *Genders Online Journal* 38.

Rushing, Janice Hocker. 1995. "Evolution of 'The New Frontier' in *Alien* and *Aliens*: Patriarchal Co-optation of the Feminine Archetype." In *Screening the Sacred: Religion, Myth, and Ideology in Popular American Film*, edited by Joel W. Martin and Conrad E. Ostwalt Jr. San Francisco: Westview Press. 94–118.

Said, Edward. 1979. *Orientalism*. New York: Random House.

Salamon, Julie. 1993. "Film: Hollywood Copycats Do It Again." *Wall Street Journal*, April 1.

Sardar, Ziadudin, and Sean Cubitt, eds., 2002. *Aliens R Us: The Other in Science Fiction Cinema*. London: Pluto Press.

Savran, David. 1998. *Taking It Like a Man: White Masculinity, Masochism, and Contemporary American Culture*. Princeton: Princeton University Press.

Saxey, Esther. 2001. "Staking a Claim: The Series and Its Slash Fan-Fiction." In *Reading the Vampire Slayer: The Unofficial Critical Companion to Buffy and Angel*, edited by Roz Kaveney. London: Tauris Parke.

Schickel, Richard. 1986. "Help! They're Back!: *Aliens* Storms in as This Summer's Megahit." *Time*, July 28.

Schilling, Mary Kaye. 2004. "The Second Coming." *Entertainment Weekly*, April 16.

Schleiner, Anne-Marie. 2001. "Does Lara Croft Wear Fake Polygons? Gender and Gender Role Subversion in Computer Adventure Games." *Leonardo* 34, no. 3: 221–26.

Schulze, Laurie. 1990. "On the Muscle." In *Fabrications: Costume and the Female Body*, edited by Jane Gaines and Charlotte Herzog. New York: Routledge.

Schwartz, Missy. 2005. "Elektracuted: Does Jennifer Garner's Dud Opening Doom Superchick Flicks?" *Entertainment Weekly*, January 28: 20.

Schwichtenberg, Cathy. 1981. "A Patriarchal Voice in Heaven." *Jump Cut* 24/25.

Shimizu, Celine Parrenas. 2007. *The Hypersexuality of Race: Performing Asian/American Women on Screen and Scene*. Durham: Duke University Press.

Shohat, Ella. 1997. "Gender and Culture of Empire: Toward a Feminist Ethnography of the Cinema." In *Visions of the East: Orientalism in Film*, edited by Mathew Bernstein and Gaylyn Studlar. New Brunswick, NJ: Rutgers University Press.

Siegel, Carol. 2007. "Female Heterosexual Sadism: The Final Feminist Taboo in Buffy the Vampire Slayer and the Anita Blake Vampire Hunter Series." In *Third Wave Feminism and Television: Jane Puts It in a Box*, edited by Merri Lisa Johnson. New York: Palgrave Macmillan.

Silverman, Kaja. 1992. *Male Subjectivity at the Margins*. New York: Routledge.

Smith, Matthew J. 2001. "The Tyranny of the Melting Pot Metaphor: Wonder Woman as the Americanized Immigrant." In *Comics and Ideology*, edited by Matthew P. McAllister, Edward H. Sewell Jr., and Ian Gordon. New York: P. Lang.

Snierson, Dan. 2002. "Secrets and Spies." *Entertainment Weekly*, March 8.

Stables, Kate, 2001. "Run Lara Run." *Sight and Sound* 11, no. 8: 18–20.

Stasia, Cristina Lucia. 2004. "Wham! Bam! Thank You Ma'am!: The New Public/Private Female Action Hero." In *Third Wave Feminism: A Critical Exploration*, edited by Stacy Gillis and Gillian Howie. New York: Palgrave-MacMillan Press.

Steele, Valerie. 1997. *Fetish: Fashion, Sex & Power*. New York: Oxford University Press.

Stoller, Robert. 1985. *Observing the Erotic Imagination*. New Haven: Yale University Press.

Stratton, Jon. 2001. *The Desirable Body: Cultural Fetishism and the Erotics of Consumption*. Urbana: University of Illinois Press.

Studlar, Gaylyn. 1988. *In the Realm of Pleasure: Von Sternberg, Dietrich, and the Masochistic Aesthetic*. Urbana: University of Illinois Press.

———. 1992. "Masochism and the Perverse Pleasures of the Cinema." In *Film Theory and Criticism: Introductory Readings*, edited by Geralf Mast, Marshall Cohen, and Leo Brady. New York: Oxford University Press.

Svetkey, Benjamin. 2002. "To Die For: How James Bond Met His Match." *Entertainment Weekly*, November 29.

Taft, Jessica K. 2004. "Girl Power Politics: Pop-Culture Barriers and Organizational Resistance." In *All About the Girl: Culture, Power, and Identity*, edited by Anita Harris. New York: Routledge.

Tasker, Yvonne. 1993. *Spectacular Bodies: Gender, Genre, and Action Cinema*. New York: Routledge.

———. 1998. *Working Girls: Gender and Sexuality in Popular Culture*. New York: Routledge.

Tjardes, Sue. 2003. "'If You're Not Enjoying It, You're Doing Something Wrong': Textual and Viewer Constructions of Faith, the Vampire Slayer." In *Athena's Daughters: Television's New Women Warriors*, edited by Frances Early and Kathleen Kennedy. Syracuse, NY: Syracuse University Press.

Tucker, Lauren, and Alan Fried. 1998. "Do You Have a Permit for That? The Gun as a Metaphor for the Transformation of G.I. Jane into G.I. Dick." In *Bang Bang, Shoot Shoot! Essays on Guns and Popular Culture*, edited by Murray Pomerance and John Sakeris. Toronto: Simon & Schuster Press. 165–74.

Tudor, Andrew. 1989. *Monsters and Mad Scientists: A Cultural History of the Horror Movie*. New York: Blackwell.

Tunnacliffe, Catharine. 2005. "Daddy Knows Best." In *Alias Assumed: Sex, Lies, and SD-6*, edited by Kevin Weisman. Dallas: Benbella Books.

Twitchell, James B. 1985. *Dreadful Pleasures: An Anatomy of Modern Horror*. New York: Oxford University Press.

Van Fuqua, Joy. 2003. "What Are Those Little Girls Made Of?: *The Powerpuff Girls* and Consumer Culture." In *Prime Time Animation: Television Animation and American Culture*, edited by Carol A. Stabile and Mark Harrison. New York: Routledge.

Walker, Rebecca. 1992. "Becoming the Third Wave." *Ms. Magazine*, January/February: 39–41.

Walton, Priscilla L., and Manina Jones. 1999. *Detective Agency: Women Rewriting the Hard-Boiled Tradition*. Berkeley: University of California Press.

Ward, Mike. 2000. "Being Lara Croft, or, We Are All Sci Fi." *popmatters*.

Weidemann, Julius. 2003. *Digital Beauties: 2D and 3D CG Digital Models*. New York: Taschen.

Wells, Melanie. 1994. "Woman as Goddess: Camille Paglia Tours Strip Clubs." *Penthouse: The International Magazine for Men*, October.

Wilcox, Rhonda V., and David Lavery, eds. 2002. *Fighting the Forces: What's at Stake in Buffy the Vampire Slayer*. New York: Rowman & Littlefield.

Williams, Linda. 1984. "When the Woman Looks." In *Re-Vision: Essays in Feminist Film Criticism*, edited by Mary Ann Doane, Patricia Mellencamp, and Linda Williams. Frederick, MD: University Publications of America.

———. 1989. *Hard Core: Power, Pleasure, and the Frenzy of the Visible*. Berkeley: University of California Press.

———. 1996. "Demi Moore Takes It Like a Man: Body Talk." *Sight & Sound* 7, no. 11: 18–21.

Yabroff, Jennie. 2008. "Holy Hot Flash, Batman!" *Newsweek*, January 14: 59.

Zimmerman, Bonnie. 1984. "Daughters of Darkness: The Lesbian Vampire on Film." Reprinted in 1996 in *The Dread of Difference: Gender and the Horror Film*, edited by Barry Keith Grant. Austin: University of Texas Press.

INDEX

CABRINI COLLEGE
610 KING OF PRUSSIA ROAD
RADNOR, pa 19087-3699

DEMCO

In memory of uncle Ron, my best writing instructor

-and-

In gratitude to my husband Barry for his constant
support and encouragement

Table of Contents

CHAPTER 7:
INTERNET ISSUES REGARDING TRADEMARKS

APPENDICES

ABOUT THE AUTHOR

Linda A. Tancs has extensive experience as a transactional attorney in both corporate and private practice, concentrating in intellectual property, entertainment, information technology, e-commerce, and general business matters. Ms. Tancs holds a Juris Doctor degree, with honors, from Seton Hall University School of Law in Newark, New Jersey and is admitted to practice in several jurisdictions in the United States, as well as internationally.

Ms. Tancs managed the worldwide trademark portfolio of leading industrial and consumer products companies and regularly counseled in-house attorneys, executives, and small business owners on trademark, trade dress, advertising, domain name issues, and product packaging. She has also held leadership positions in bar associations, taught legal courses at two colleges, and has authored several articles for legal periodicals and general interest magazines.

Ms. Tancs operates her own consulting practice in the field of brand identification and management. She is also certified as a coach in the fields of personal, executive, and organizational coaching by New York University and works with both lawyers and non-lawyers to meet their personal and professional goals.

INTRODUCTION

This Almanac explores the mechanics of registering, maintaining, and enforcing trademark rights. Trademark rights can be obtained on a state, federal, or international level. The book will emphasize the process for registering a mark with the U.S. Patent and Trademark Office (PTO). As of 2007, nearly 395,000 trademark applications were filed with the PTO.

The reader will be introduced to the nature and functions of intellectual property law as it relates to trademarks. Intellectual property law is an evolving body of law that seeks to create a fair balance between the privilege to enter markets and compete and the privilege to realize the full value of one's own goods and services without unfair competition. Through this Almanac, the reader will gain an understanding of: the types of trademarks; how to protect and use a trademark; how to complete a trademark application; pre- and post-registration procedures of the PTO; how to monetize trademark assets; infringement issues such as likelihood of confusion, dilution, and counterfeiting; and the intersection of trademarks and e-commerce.

The appendices, together with the bibliography and recommended reading, provide readers of this Almanac with relevant statutes and other information to further the reader's knowledge of the matters discussed in this Almanac. The glossary contains a summary of key terms defined throughout the Almanac.

The information presented in this book is intended for general information purposes only and does not constitute the provision of legal services or advice. If such services or advice are required, the assistance of an appropriate professional should be sought.

CHAPTER 1:
THE NATURE AND FUNCTION OF
A TRADEMARK

WHAT IS A TRADEMARK?

A trademark is a word(s), name, symbol, or device (or a combination of these elements) that identifies and distinguishes one merchant's *goods* from those of others. A service mark likewise may consist of a word(s), name, symbol, or device but identifies and distinguishes one merchant's *services* from those of others. Of course, a merchant may designate both goods and services under a single mark. In that case, the mark is both a trademark and a service mark. Service marks are sometimes referred to as trademarks, and this Almanac will refer to both trademarks and service marks collectively as trademarks unless the context requires otherwise. Trademarks are commonly referred to colloquially as brands, brand names, or labels.

A trademark may also be in the nature of a collective or certification mark. For instance, collective *membership* marks are used by members of a group to denote their membership in the group (such as the designation CPA for members of the Society of Chartered Public Accountants); whereas, *collective* marks (such as the Automobile Club of America) are marks owned by a parent organization and used by its members to apply to their own goods or services. Likewise, a certification mark is used by others and certifies a mode of manufacture, quality, or some other characteristic of a good or service (such as the "UL Listed" designation granted by Underwriters Laboratories to those meeting the certification requirements). Sometimes, a trade or business name can also function as a trademark (such as IBM).

As any consumer knows, trademarks take many forms. Trademarks can be comprised of a single word (like NIKE or McDonald's); letters (ABC, NBC and CBS); numbers (7-Eleven); slogans (JUST DO IT); color (pink insulation); sound (the NBC chimes); and even scent (strawberry scent on a toothbrush). Product features such as shape or packaging, commonly referred to as trade dress, can also be protectable as a trademark so long as the feature is not integral to the functioning of the product.

Appendix 1, "Definition of Trademark, Service Mark, Certification Mark, and Collective Mark," of this Almanac provides the definition of a trademark, a service mark, collective and collective membership marks, and certification marks as found in the federal law governing trademarks, commonly known as the Lanham Act.

THE PURPOSE OF A TRADEMARK

The identifying and distinguishing functions of a trademark mean that an identifying word, phrase, symbol, or device that purports to be a trademark must be distinctive. Thus if a mark is not distinctive, it cannot identify for the consumer the origin of the goods or services to which it is applied in such a way as to distinguish one merchant's goods or services from another. However, it is important to note that a consumer need not know the name of the merchant using the trademark for the mark to function as an indicator of source; trademark rights attach when consumers recognize that a good or service to which the mark is applied comes from a certain source. For instance, a consumer of French's® mustard knows that a certain distinct source produces the product; it is not necessary that the consumer know that the source is a unit of the company Reckitt Benckiser.

Trademarks also suggest to consumers that they can expect a certain level of quality to be associated with the product or service. In fact, the requirement for quality control is such an integral part of the use and maintenance of a trademark that failure to exercise such control can result in abandonment of the mark and loss of trademark rights. Quality control will be discussed in greater detail in the section entitled "Licensing" in Chapter 5, "Monetizing Trademarks," of this Almanac.

WHERE TO PROTECT A TRADEMARK

Depending on the actual or intended geographical scope of use of the mark, a merchant may elect to file for protection of it nationally, internationally or locally. The owner of a U.S. federal trademark registration generally enjoys nationwide, superior rights to use of the mark on the goods or services claimed in the registration. Dissimilarly, state or local trademark protection is limited to the zone of commerce in which the merchant does business using the mark. Because federal trademark rights attach to marks used in interstate commerce (as discussed in detail in Chapter 3, "The PTO Trademark Application Process," of this Almanac), some merchants may be limited by the nature of their business to pursuing trademark rights locally. Other businesses with global interests are likely to pursue international protection of their marks, as explained in Chapter 4, "International Applications," of this Almanac.

Appendix 2, "State Trademark Offices," of this Almanac contains a list of state trademark offices.

THE STRENGTH OF A MARK

Not every word, symbol, or device is capable of functioning as a trademark— that is, as a source identifier. Some indicators are, by their very nature, incapable of functioning in a trademark sense. For example, generic terms are never capable of being appropriated exclusively by any one trader in the marketplace. According to case law, a term is generic if the general consuming public would not discern it as an indication of source. Such terms include *store*, *food*, and *t-shirt*. Sometimes, a trademarked word or phrase becomes such a common part of our vernacular that it becomes generic. In fact, words such as *aspirin*, *escalator*, and *thermos* once enjoyed trademark protection. Avoiding genericness will be discussed in more detail later in this chapter.

Whereas a generic indicator is not capable of distinctiveness, other kinds of indicators are inherently distinctive or capable of becoming so. Inherently distinctive marks are the strongest types of marks and are most easily registrable. Marks that are arbitrary, fanciful or suggestive fit this category. Arbitrary marks bear no descriptive relationship to the goods or services with which they are associated. Examples of arbitrary marks include Dutch Boy® paints and Blue Diamond® nuts. Fanciful marks likewise bear no connection to their products or services and are, as the term suggests, coined or conjured. Fanciful marks include Kodak® film and Reebok® sneakers. Somewhat less distinctive on the power scale are suggestive marks. As the name implies, suggestive marks bear some resemblance to the associated product or service but, nevertheless, require some additional mental leap to make the connection and are thus distinctive, such as Coppertone® suntan products or Roach Motel® insect bait.

Identifiers that do not fall into the above categories are not inherently distinctive. As a result, to serve the trademark function of distinctiveness, these identifiers must be capable of acquiring such distinctiveness over time. Acquired distinctiveness is often referred to as "secondary meaning." Secondary meaning is often established by evidence showing the use of the mark over a lengthy period of time (e.g., substantially exclusive and continuous use for at least five years), specific dollar sales under the mark, advertising figures, consumer or dealer statements of recognition of the mark, and any other evidence that establishes the distinctiveness of the mark as an indicator of source.

Marks that are "merely descriptive" are examples of identifiers requiring secondary meaning to be registrable because such marks incorporate a characteristic or quality of the product or service they represent and therefore do not require a mental leap on the part of the consumer to determine the nature of the product or service. Once it can be demonstrated that a merely descriptive mark is recognizable by consumers as denoting a single specific source for the product or service, then the mark will be deemed to have acquired secondary meaning and will be registrable. Merely descriptive marks include Computerland® computer stores and Chapstick® lip balm.

Similarly, other kinds of descriptive marks may have the capacity to become distinctive and therefore registrable, such as deceptively misdescriptive terms, geographically descriptive terms, and surnames. Deceptively misdescriptive terms misdescribe the features or attributes of the product or service in such a way that consumers may believe the misdescription. In other words, the terms used to describe the product or service do not actually pertain to that product or service but consumers may believe it to be so. Examples of deceptively misdescriptive marks that became distinctive are Glass Wax® polish and English Leather® toiletries.

Locations can also be deceptively misdescriptive—that is, geographically deceptively misdescriptive. However, such a mark is generally unregistrable because, as of 1993, Congress barred the registration of geographically deceptively misdescriptive marks. Therefore, only marks that could be shown to have acquired secondary meaning prior to 1993 could potentially be registered.

Other geographic issues concern using a mark to describe a region or country where goods affixed with the mark are produced, known as a geographical indication. Geographical indications are distinguishable from geographically descriptive marks. If the primary significance of the geographic indication is to name the place where the goods are produced, then the mark is primarily geographically descriptive, and secondary meaning must be shown to register the mark. On the contrary, geographical indications are a creature of the World Trade

Organization's Agreement on Trade-Related Aspects of Intellectual Property Rights (TRIPS). The TRIPS Agreement defines a geographical indication as "indications which identify a good as originating in the territory of a Member, or a region of locality in that territory, where a given quality, reputation or other characteristic of the good is essentially attributable to its geographic origin." Thus, a geographical indication not only names the region where a good is produced but also links that location with a characteristic or quality of the good. Examples of U.S. geographical indications are "Idaho Potatoes," "Vidalia Onions," and "Washington State Apples."

Surnames reflect another category of indicators that do not enjoy trademark protection absent a showing of secondary meaning. Even with such a showing, however, in the interests of equity it is possible for a commonly-shared surname to be used by parties other than the one who may possess trademark rights.

Finally, some proposed marks are never registrable according to the Lanham Act. Examples of unregistrable material include immoral or scandalous marks, the use of national symbols or insignia of a governmental authority, the use of a portrait or likeness of a living individual (except with written consent), and any mark which resembles a previously registered mark and is likely to cause confusion, or to cause mistake, or to deceive consumers as to the source or origin of the respective marks. This concept of likelihood of confusion is discussed further throughout this Almanac. Another proscribed form of mark is a deceptive mark, which should be distinguished from a deceptively misdescriptive mark that is registrable upon a showing that the term has secondary meaning in the marketplace.

Appendix 3, "Impermissible Marks," of this Almanac contains a list of impermissible marks as set forth in the Lanham Act.

HOW TO DISPLAY AND USE A MARK

Marks are commonly displayed using one of the following accompanying symbols: tm, sm, or ®. The use of "tm" (for *trademark*) or "sm" (for *service mark*) commonly denotes a mark that is not registered at the PTO. These designations may also be used, regardless whether application has been made for trademark registration at the federal or state level, simply to alert third parties to a claim of trademark rights in the matter which precedes it.

Owners of federally-registered marks are entitled to use the ® symbol although some registrants continue to use the "tm" or "sm" symbol even after the mark has registered. The preferred practice is to use the ® symbol in close proximity to the mark once it has registered with the PTO. In fact, a trademark registrant may be unable to recover profits or money damages in an infringement action if the ® symbol is not being used or if the defendant was not otherwise notified of the registration. It is also important to note that the ® symbol must not be used prior to the mark being registered with the PTO as fines can be imposed on the trademark owner who falsely indicates that a mark is federally registered.

The ® symbol is recognized almost universally to connote trademark registration of the accompanying mark. However, the display of the ® symbol can be problematic if used in a country where registration has not been secured. For instance, in some Asian countries, fines and imprisonment may be imposed against an owner who uses the symbol to signify a registration that has not been obtained there. In other countries, such as New Zealand, it is permissible to indicate that use of the symbol refers to a registration granted in another country. Omission of the symbol altogether could be deemed a failure to convey to the purchasing public that a trademark was intended, as one trademark claimant in the Benelux territory (Belgium, the Netherlands, and Luxembourg) discovered. Therefore, care must be taken by the trademark owner to ensure that the proper notice of trademark rights is displayed in countries where the goods or services affixed with the mark are provided.

Correct usage of a mark is just as important as its display. Trademarks are technically adjectives and therefore should always modify a noun. For example, it is appropriate to refer to a Sony product such as a television as a Sony® television and not simply as a Sony. Similarly, a trademark should never be used as a verb, such as "to Xerox a document." Rather, the correct terminology is to copy a document on a Xerox® copier. Also, trademarks should not be used as possessives (Sony's), in plural form, or hyphenated (Sony-like), unless the registration has been obtained in that format. Another potential misuse of a trademark is to combine two or more marks back-to-back because a trademark should be capable of standing alone. Incorrect usage, particularly the rendering of a trademark as a noun, can lead to genericness and a loss of trademark rights.

Marks are also often highlighted in textual materials such as advertising to distinguish them from common words. For instance, a trademark may be capitalized, italicized, used in bold print, or set off in some other distinctive way to enhance its visual appeal, which increases the likelihood that consumers will come to recognize the mark as distinctive of a certain merchant's goods or services. In some instances, a mark incorporates a type style, color, or logo, providing an added visual stimulus. Whatever the type or style of mark, it is important to treat its usage in all marketing and informational materials consistently to maintain effectiveness.

CHAPTER 2:
TYPES OF APPLICATIONS AND REGISTRATIONS

ABOUT THE PTO

As indicated in Chapter 1, "The Nature and Function of a Trademark," of this Almanac, trademark owners seeking nationwide, superior rights to use their marks file their applications for registration at the PTO. The PTO, established over 200 years ago, is an agency of the United States Department of Commerce located in Alexandria, Virginia. Its staff examines and issues (if found to be registrable) both patents and trademarks. Among its activities, the PTO administers the federal laws governing trademarks (to be discussed further in Chapter 3, "The PTO Trademark Application Process," of this Almanac) and advises the Secretary of Commerce, the President and the administration on intellectual property protection and trade.

TYPES OF APPLICATIONS GENERALLY

A trademark applicant has many decisions to make regarding the nature of the application to file, such as whether the mark will be applied to one class of goods or services (i.e., a single-class application) or multiple classes of goods or services (i.e., a multiple-class application). Another decision involves the selection of what is known as the filing basis for the application. There are five filing bases for a U.S. application: (i) a foreign application exists, applying the mark to the same goods or services as the intended U.S. application; (ii) a foreign registration exists with respect to the mark intended in the U.S.; (iii) the mark is being used in commerce; (iv) a bona fide intent exists to use the mark in commerce; or (v) there is a request for extension of trademark rights protection in the United States arising under the Madrid Protocol (which will be addressed in Chapter 4, "International Applications," of this Almanac).

In rare instances, concurrent use may be the basis of the application because the mark is in use by one or more unrelated third parties.

Single-Class and Multiple-Class Applications

A single-class application lists only one class of goods or services to which the trademark relates. Conversely, a multiple-class (combined) application lists two or more classes of goods or services. The selection of goods and services for applications will be discussed in more detail in the section entitled "A Description of Goods and/or Services in Chapter 3, "The PTO Trademark Application Process," of this Almanac.

Applications Based on Foreign Rights

Excluding the Madrid Protocol rights discussed later in this Almanac, an application based on a claim of foreign rights arises from a foreign application (§ 44(d) of the Lanham Act) or a foreign registration (§ 44(e) of the Act). Applications of either type are filed by foreign applicants seeking trademark protection in the United States. If the foreign applicant's trademark has not yet matured into registration outside the United States, then the applicant will file an application based on § 44(d), and that application will be given a filing date consistent with the date of filing in the country of origin provided that the U.S. application is filed within six months following the original filing by an entity residing in a country adhering to the Paris Convention. The Paris Convention for the Protection of Industrial Property is an international treaty first established in 1883, offering reciprocal rights of intellectual property protection to nations that adhere to the treaty. Under the Convention, any trademark application filed in a signatory nation within six months following the initial filing is entitled to claim a right of priority—that is, the applicant can claim the original filing date in all subsequent applications filed in member countries during the six-month window. Convention priority is likewise available to U.S. trademark applicants seeking to perfect rights overseas in member countries. In any case, the benefits of foreign registration are available to all applicants outside the six-month window, but priority will be lost—that is, the filing date of the foreign application will be the date that the application is received by the foreign intellectual property office rather than the filing date of the earlier application. Foreign applicants already possessing a foreign registration can file an application in the United States based on the foreign registration under § 44(e) by supplying a copy of the registration (translated into English, if applicable).

Appendix 4, "Signatories to the Paris Convention," of this Almanac contains a list of signatories to the Paris Convention. International considerations for U.S.-domiciled trademark owners will be discussed further in Chapter 4, "International Applications," of this Almanac.

Use or Intent-to-Use Based Applications

Most U.S. applicants base their application on either (i) actual use of the mark in commerce or (ii) a bona fide intent to use the mark in commerce. The latter type of application, commonly referred to as an ITU, was made an additional basis for filing an application upon enactment of the Trademark Law Revision Act of 1988 (TLRA). Congress's rationale for allowing trademark owners to apply for registration for marks that are not yet used in commerce was in part based on recognition that sometimes adoption of a mark will be contingent on the outcome of market testing or product research. As a result, TLRA provided applicants with the option to claim a bona fide, or good faith, intent to use a mark. Interestingly, in the Act of 1870, the first trademark statute, a similar provision was found to be unconstitutional and later attempts to weave ITU rights into trademark law were likewise foiled until the enactment of TLRA.

Regardless of the type of application filed, however, a mark will not register (if deemed registrable) until use of the mark in commerce has commenced because the act of using a mark establishes rights in it. "Use in commerce" is defined in the Lanham Act as a "bona fide use of a mark in the ordinary course of trade, and not merely to reserve a right in a mark." In other words, the use must be more than just a token use. The Lanham Act further sets forth two activities that must arise for a mark to be deemed used in commerce: (i) the mark must actually be affixed to the goods or services with which it is associated and (ii) the goods or services must travel in commerce. "Commerce" is likewise defined as that which is regulated by Congress. The power of Congress to regulate commerce is set forth in the Commerce Clause of the Constitution in Article 1, Section 8, Clause 3, which gives Congress the authority to regulate commerce with foreign nations and among the states. For trademark purposes, then, interstate commerce (commerce between two or more states) or commerce between a state and a foreign country constitutes sufficient commercial activity related to a good or a service to support the filing of a federal application for the associated mark.

However, meeting the "use in commerce" requirement is sometimes problematic. For instance, sometimes the mark is not sufficiently associated with a product or service to constitute a trademark use, as owners of domain names have discovered when applying for trademark protection for the name. Furthermore, although a shipment may occur across state lines, sometimes the use is not deemed commercial, particularly with respect to prototypes. In other cases, free samples and promotional gifts shipped across state lines have been found to be sufficient activity to allege use in commerce. The Lanham Act does not, in fact, require that money change hands for the use in commerce requirement to be met as the statute provides for either the sale *or* transport of goods. Sometimes, too, the amount of trade required to show commercial use of a product or service will require flexibility. Indeed, in some of the legislative history surrounding the enactment of TLRA, Congress made clear that "use" will vary from one industry to another and should be interpreted flexibly to encompass less traditional trademark uses or situations. This flexibility is evident in the finding of use in such circumstances as pharmaceutical clinical trials and "seasonal" marks such as those associated with beauty pageants and annual awards shows.

The procedure for filing use-based and ITU-based applications will be discussed in Chapter 3, "The PTO Trademark Application Process," of this Almanac.

Appendix 5, "Definition of "Use in Commerce," of this Almanac provides the full definition of "use in commerce" found in the Lanham Act.

Concurrent Use Applications

Concurrent use applications, provided for under § 2(d) of the Lanham Act, are rarely filed. In such an application, the applicant acknowledges that others are using the mark concurrently and, therefore, the applicant's use of the mark is not exclusive. This acknowledgment is significant because a trademark applicant normally declares in the application, under penalty of perjury, that no other entity has the right to use the mark to the best of the applicant's knowledge and belief and that the applicant's use of the mark will not give rise to confusion with another's mark. Given this non-exclusivity, the applicant in a concurrent-use application requests federal protection of its use of the mark in the geographic area in which the mark is used in commerce. The other users may likewise retain their respective geographic rights. Typically, the decision to make application for registration as a concurrent user arises because the applicant has conducted a comprehensive search of the marketplace and uncovered other parties who have applied for or registered the mark or are using the mark without the benefit of a pending application or registration. Comprehensive searches are discussed in detail in Chapter 3, "The PTO Trademark Application Process," of this Almanac.

It is important to note that a concurrent use proceeding is only available to an applicant (i) whose use either predates any other applicants or registrants; or (ii) in the event a previous registrant has consented to the concurrent use procedure; or (iii) in the event the proceeding is sought following the judgment of a court as to the applicant's concurrent rights to a mark. After the application is properly filed in accordance with one of the first two options, the decision as to concurrent rights will ultimately be decided by the Trademark Trial and Appeal Board (TTAB). If the proceeding is instituted following a court's judgment as to the respective rights of the parties, then generally TTAB action will not be necessary. The TTAB will be discussed in greater detail in Chapter 3, "The PTO Trademark Application Process," of this Almanac.

THE TRADEMARK REGISTERS

The PTO maintains two registries of marks—the Principal Register (a primary register) and the Supplemental Register (a secondary register), and both forms of registration are provided for under the Lanham Act. Unless an application specifies the register desired, the PTO will presume that registration is sought on the Principal Register.

The Principal Register

Trademarks registered on the Principal Register are accorded the highest degree of protection under the Lanham Act. Therefore, applicants generally desire to acquire such a registration, which is reserved for marks that are distinctive or have acquired secondary meaning. As discussed in Chapter 1, "The Nature and Function of a Trademark," of this Almanac, the strongest marks are those which are fanciful, arbitrary or suggestive. Not surprisingly, these marks often find easy registration on the Principal Register. The basic benefits accorded to marks on the Principal Register are as follows:

(1) the filing date of the application generally gives the registrant nationwide priority as of that date with respect to use of the mark, subject to the rights in certain instances of those who can establish an earlier use of the mark;

(2) the right to sue in federal court for trademark infringement;

(3) the right to seek recovery of profits, damages, costs, and attorneys' fees in an action;

(4) constructive notice of a claim of ownership, thereby cutting off any claims of third parties adopting the mark subsequent to the registration;

(5) the right to register with U.S. Customs to stop counterfeiters;

(6) evidentiary presumptions of the ownership and validity of the mark and the right of the registrant to use it exclusively;

(7) the opportunity to make the mark incontestable, which disallows many attacks by third parties against the owner's use of the registered mark;

(8) criminal penalties and treble damages in an action regarding counterfeiting;

(9) a basis for filing trademark applications in foreign countries; and

(10) use of the ® symbol in connection with the mark on labels, packaging, advertising, and the like.

The Supplemental Register

Supplemental registrations lack many of the benefits accorded to principal registrations because marks so registered lack distinctiveness and have not acquired secondary meaning. To be registrable at all, however, marks destined for the Supplemental Register must be capable of acquiring secondary meaning. Therefore, marks found on the Supplemental Register are those defined in Chapter 1, "The Nature and Function of a Trademark," of this Almanac as merely descriptive, deceptively misdescriptive, or primarily merely a surname. In some instances, a supplemental registration may arise after a determination by the PTO that an application on the Principal Register does not meet the requirements of distinctiveness or secondary meaning, and the application is then amended for registration on the Supplemental Register. In other circumstances, the trademark owner may decide in the first instance to file on the Supplemental Register, recognizing that the mark is unlikely to meet the requirements for registration on the Principal Register.

Of all the benefits available to owners of principal registrations, only the right to use the ® symbol, the right to sue and seek recovery of damages, fees and costs in federal court for infringement and substantially related claims, and the right to file applications in foreign countries are available to owners of supplemental registrations. Furthermore, there are certain procedural differences between supplemental and principal registrations. For example, applications made on the Supplemental Register are not published for opposition (publication is discussed in detail in Chapter 3, "The PTO Trademark Application Process," of this Almanac), and these applications must be use-based rather than ITU-based.

Given all the benefits of a principal registration, the owner of a supplemental registration may re-file an application for registration of its mark on the Principal Register following at least five years of registration on the Supplemental Register, provided that the mark has acquired secondary meaning.

Appendix 6, "Statutory References to the Supplemental Register," of this Almanac sets forth those sections of the Lanham Act dealing specifically with marks on the Supplemental Register.

CHAPTER 3:
THE PTO TRADEMARK
APPLICATION PROCESS

CONDUCTING TRADEMARK SEARCHES

Before submitting a trademark application with the PTO, many applicants will choose to undertake a search of various registers to determine whether anyone else is using their mark, or a close proximation of it, to distinguish the same or similar goods and services. The purpose of a search is to inform the prospective trademark owner whether the proposed mark is likely to be confused with a mark already being used in the marketplace—that is, whether the mark is available for use and perhaps registration. Depending on the needs of the trademark applicant, the search may include one or more of the following: (i) marks registered at the PTO; (ii) state-registered marks; (iii) common law rights as may be found in commercial trade directories and the like; and (iv) domain names incorporating the proposed trademark. In considering the depth of the search to be conducted, the prospective trademark owner should be aware that some courts have held that the failure to conduct a thorough trademark search, prior to adoption of a mark, to be a sign of bad faith when deciding upon an award of damages for trademark infringement.

The PTO Search

The PTO's online searchable database (known as TESS), located at http://www.uspto.gov/main/trademarks.htm, provides information on marks existing at the federal level. These marks include those that are pending, registered, and renewed ("live" marks) and those that are expired, abandoned, or cancelled ("dead" marks). Searches may be conducted by using the PTO's basic search function to search for the exact word or phrase of a word mark or by using the PTO's advanced or free form search features to undergo additional searches for marks that are phonetically equivalent or have the same general meaning in the same or related classes of goods or services. Designs can also be searched by visiting http://tess2.uspto.gov/tmdb/dscm/index.htm.

It should be noted that the PTO only looks for pending and registered marks in its registers that are potentially confusingly similar to the applied-for mark in making a determination whether an applicant's mark is registrable on the Principal or Supplemental Register. The PTO does, however, use commonly available references from the Internet to support a determination whether the mark is descriptive or even generic.

When conducting a search, it is particularly prudent to examine dead marks. In some cases, an owner may have inadvertently lost rights to a mark by failing to file a timely post-registration form (discussed in more detail later in this chapter) but is nonetheless still using the mark and able to enforce that use. Similarly, an applicant who abandons an application may still continue to use the mark without benefit of a federal registration or may revive the application if the abandonment resulted from a ministerial error.

State Searches

State trademark registers likewise contain valuable information on the rights of holders of trademarks at the local level. Although not considered by the PTO to determine registrability at the federal level, the findings of a state search are nonetheless instructive to alert a potential trademark owner to potential rights and remedies of senior users of a mark in a geographical area.

Common Law Use

There is no requirement at the state level that a trademark be registered to secure rights to it, but registration is an easy and effective way to put third parties on notice of a claim of trademark rights. Furthermore, local marks are often protected under state laws concerning unfair competition irrespective of registration. Therefore, an additional means of locating potentially problematic uses of a proposed mark is a common law search compiled from telephone directories, trade journals, buyers' guides, trade associations, and other trade sources in a range of industries.

Domain Name Searches

Proposed trademarks are sometimes found to be adopted by others as a domain name. Such adoption does not always indicate that the mark will be unavailable for use, however. If the domain name is not associated with a good or service, then the domain name is not being used in a trademark sense and does not necessarily bar a third party from using, or registering, the domain name as a mark.

SEARCH FACILITIES

Patent and Trademark Depository Libraries

Throughout the United States, qualified libraries serve as Patent and Trademark Depository Libraries (PTDLs), housing text and image data related to pending and registered marks at the PTO. A list of libraries and other information related to the PTDL system can be found at http://www.uspto.gov/web/offices/ac/ido/ptdl/index.html.

Public Search Facility

The public records room of the PTO contains data on registered trademarks since 1870 in a variety of media, such as microfilm, bound volumes, and online access. These records also include dead marks and pending marks. The facility is open to the public on weekdays (excluding public holidays) and is located at 600 Dulany Street, Alexandria, Virginia 22314, (Tel): 571–272–3275.

Professional Services

Because it could be quite timely for a merchant to conduct any or all of the above searches, trademark owners often rely on companies specializing in the production of search reports to compile the data set forth above or engage the services of an attorney to compile or analyze the information.

A GENERAL OVERVIEW OF THE TRADEMARK APPLICATION PROCESS

The PTO strongly encourages applicants to file all required forms and communications electronically. This chapter will illustrate the steps in an electronic filing for registration on the Principal Register unless indicated otherwise. Appendix 7, "Trademark/Service Mark Application," Appendix 8, "Collective Membership Mark Application," Appendix 9, "Certification Mark Application," and Appendix 10, "Collective Mark Application," of this Almanac provide the reader with the PTO's forms for filing applications via mail. The information requested in these forms can be used as a guide for filing electronically.

Here are seven steps in the U.S. trademark application process to use as a reference guide for monitoring the progress of a filing:

    1. Upon receipt by the PTO, the application will receive a filing date (if the minimal filing requirements discussed below are met) as well

as a serial number that should be used in all correspondence with the PTO.

2. The application will be forwarded to an examining attorney in the PTO in a number of months (the length depending on the staffing of the PTO at the time). The examiner will review the application for compliance with the Lanham Act. Notwithstanding any conclusion by the applicant or its counsel that the mark is registrable, the application is ultimately subject to a determination by the examiner whether he or she believes that the mark can be registered. If the examiner refuses registration of the proposed mark, a communication will be sent to the correspondent listed in the application requesting a response to the examiner's conclusions within a six-month period, during which time a response should be filed unless the application will be abandoned. If the application is not refused, or any objections to it are resolved, then the application will be approved for publication for opposition.

3. All trademark applications are published in the *Trademark Official Gazette.* A searchable database of *Gazette* entries is located at http://www.uspto.gov/web/trademarks/tmog. Otherwise, a subscription can be made for paper editions. This publication serves to put third parties on notice of the rights being claimed, and many parties, or their representatives, search the *Gazette* frequently for potentially infringing marks. During the thirty days following publication of the application, anyone who believes that they may be harmed by registration of the mark may file a proceeding at the TTAB to oppose registration of the mark.

4. After the mark has been published in the *Gazette*, and if no opposition has been filed, then the application continues to be pending until the mark is actually used in interstate commerce.

5. For ITU applications, the PTO will, upon publication without opposition, issue a Notice of Allowance (also known as an NOA). The Notice of Allowance will contain a description of all the goods or services subject to the ITU and therefore should be reviewed (like all other notices from the PTO) for accuracy. Any errors should be reported immediately to the PTO or the examiner in charge of the application. The notice also gives the applicant six months to begin using the mark in commerce, during which time a Statement of Use (also known as an SOU and discussed later in the section entitled "Pre-Registration Administrative Procedures" of this chapter) is filed. If the applicant has not yet made use of the mark in commerce prior to the expiration of the six-month period, then the application

will become abandoned unless the applicant files a request for extension of time to file a Statement of Use. Applications based on actual use of the mark (as opposed to an application based on a bona fide intent to use the mark) are not subject to a Notice of Allowance and a Statement of Use (unless the application is converted to an ITU) because the required specimen of use of the mark is filed with the application or thereafter by amendment. Once published for opposition, use-based marks proceed to registration if there is no opposition lodged against the mark or any such opposition is resolved successfully.

6. A successful application will register in a matter of months through the issuance of a Certificate of Registration. Registrations are published in the *Gazette*.

7. After successful registration of a mark, there is a possibility that a party objecting to its registration will file an action at the TTAB to have the mark cancelled. Provided that a mark is not cancelled, its registration will last ten years, at which time the mark can be renewed for an additional ten-year term (and subsequent ten-year terms thereafter) so long as the mark is in use. During the registration of a mark, it is necessary, in most cases, to file certain affidavits stating that the mark is still being used. Trademark owners should be mindful of due dates for post-registration filings. The PTO does not send out reminder notices for actions required to be taken to maintain a registration.

Applicants should also note that Eastern Time controls filing dates. Regardless of PTO business hours, any filing made electronically before midnight, Eastern Time, will receive a filing date as of that date.

ELEMENTS OF A TRADEMARK APPLICATION

A complete trademark application contains the following elements:

(1) the mark, including a drawing (where feasible);

(2) the applicant's name and address;

(3) name and address for correspondence related to the application;

(4) the filing basis;

(5) the description of goods and/or services;

(6) dates of first use (not applicable for ITU applications);

(7) a specimen showing use of the mark (except when the application is initially filed as an ITU);

(8) the declaration and an identification of the signatory to the application; and

(9) the filing fee.

In some instances, additional statements may be made in support of the application, such as a claim of distinctiveness, a disclaimer of one or more words that are too commonplace to be appropriated by a single merchant, a translation of foreign words, a transliteration of non-Latin characters, or the identification in a mark of a name, portrait, or signature of a living individual, whose consent is made of record.

For purposes of receiving a filing date from the PTO, an application must contain at least the following minimal elements of a complete trademark application or else the application will be refused: (i) identification of the applicant; (ii) a name and address for correspondence; (iii) a drawing; (iv) a list of goods or services (which can be left unclassified); and (v) the filing fee for at least one class.

Each of the elements for a complete application will be discussed below.

The Mark and Its Drawing

The proposed mark indicated in the application and also depicted via a "drawing" is either in standard characters (formerly known as a "typed" drawing) or in special (stylized) form. A standard character mark is comprised of word(s), letter(s), or number(s), alone or in any combination, with no design element and no particular font, style, size, or color. A mark rendered in standard characters means the owner can depict the mark very broadly—that is, the owner can use the mark in upper case letters, lower case, a combination of lower case and upper case, bold, italicized, and in any font size. To be eligible for a claim of standard characters, the entered character(s) must appear in the PTO's accepted standard character set, provided in Appendix 11, "Standard Character Set," of this Almanac.

A mark should be depicted in special form if the applicant's desire is to use the mark in a particular style, including the use of stylized words (such as an image forming all or part of a letter comprising the mark), letters, or numbers. Marks that include a logo are filed using this format, as are marks including color. Current rules specify that a mark shown in color must be rendered in color on the drawing page. Moreover, these colors must be claimed in the application as a feature of the mark and their locations within the mark described. If color is not intended to be claimed as a feature, then the drawing of the mark should be rendered in black on a white background or *vice versa*. A design may appear by itself, or combined with words, letters, or numbers.

Of course, some marks cannot be rendered in a drawing, such as those encompassing sound, scent, and other non-visual elements. For such marks, the application should clearly indicate that the mark is non-visual— either in the standard character box of an electronic application or clearly indicated in a paper filing.

Electronic applications greatly simplify the drawing requirement. If the mark is in standard characters, then that option is selected on the form, which will generate a statement that "the mark consists of standard characters, without claim to any particular font, style, size, or color." The standard character elements are then entered into the text box. If the special form option is selected, then the drawing is attached as a digital image in .jpg format. The accompanying text box is used to describe the mark and claim color, if required.

Only one mark may be filed per application. Therefore, if an applicant uses a mark comprised of both words and a design, it may be advisable to file two separate applications—one to protect the word(s) and one to protect the combination of word(s) and design. The decision to apply for two separate applications will depend, in part, on how strong a commercial impression the words alone generate as part of the mark.

Regardless of the type of drawing required, it should not contain any extraneous information such as the "tm" or "sm" designations or the ® symbol if representative of a mark registered in another country.

Paper filers should follow the drawing requirements provided for in the Code of Federal Regulations (CFR), the federal rules implementing trademark practice and procedure, as reproduced in Appendix 12, "Drawing Requirements for Paper Submission," of this Almanac.

The Applicant

A wide range of applicants are entitled to file for trademark registration, identified on the electronic form as the "entity type." Entity types include individuals, corporations, limited liability companies, partnerships, limited partnerships, joint ventures, sole proprietorships, trusts, and estates. In each case, it is important that the applicant be that individual or entity owning or controlling the use of the mark in commerce. In some cases, a mark may be owned by more than one individual applicant. In such a case, the application is deemed to have joint applicants. Minors may also be applicants if the law of domicile permits such an activity.

Depending on the entity type, additional information will be required to properly identify the applicant. For instance, corporations or limited liability companies should use the company name as reflected in the articles of incorporation or organization. Other entities should be reflected as set out in the Trademark Manual of Examining Procedure (TMEP), a manual which sets forth trademark procedures followed by the PTO.

Appendix 13, "Identification of the Applicant," of this Almanac provides an extract of TMEP rules on the proper identification of various applicants, including foreign entities.

Name and Address of Correspondent

In addition to properly naming the applicant, a name and correspondence address to which communications may be sent is also required. If the applicant chooses to retain counsel for the filing process, the correspondence address will be the attorney's address.

The Filing Basis

Of the five filing bases listed in Chapter 2, "Types of Applications and Registrations," of this Almanac, this chapter focuses on use-based and intent-to-use based filings.

A use-based application is also known as a §1(a) application, and an ITU is known as a § 1(b) application. A single application may contain a combination of § 1(a) and § 1(b) claims. For instance, a company manufacturing or planning to produce a wide range of goods may already have affixed the sought-after mark to some goods in commerce and have other goods still in production. For the goods already produced to which the mark is affixed, a § 1(a) claim could be made, and the balance of goods to which the mark has yet to be affixed could be designated under a § 1(b) claim.

In a § 1(a) application, the applicant verifies that (i) the applicant is using the mark in commerce; or (ii) the applicant's related company or licensee is using the mark in commerce; or (iii) the applicant's predecessor in interest used the mark in commerce on or in connection with the identified goods or services.

In a § 1(b) application, the applicant verifies a bona fide (or good faith) intention to use the mark in commerce. It is important to note that the PTO does not evaluate the good faith intent of the applicant to make use of the mark. The PTO will, however, examine a § 1(b) application for registrability as it would any other application. As a result, if there are statutory grounds to refuse registration of the mark, such as a finding that it is merely descriptive, then the application may fail. Moreover, unlike a § 1(a) application, a § 1(b) application cannot be amended to the Supplemental Register if refused registration based on its descriptive nature because only use-based marks can be registered on the Supplemental Register. Thus, a trademark applicant with a fairly descriptive mark not yet in use must consider whether the application should await actual use of the mark in commerce or whether use is likely to arise during the pendency of the application in the event that amendment of the mark to the Supplemental Register becomes necessary. Also, unlike use-based applications, ITU applications are subject to a request by the PTO for more information related to the intended use of the mark, such as samples of advertisements or promotional materials for the goods at issue or goods of the same type. Sometimes, an applicant may not have any such information pending further development of the goods or services to be associated with the mark. In such cases, the applicant should describe the contemplated use and purposes of goods or services to be associated with the mark to the best of the applicant's ability.

A Description of Goods and/or Services

A description of available goods and services to which a mark can be applied (together with their classification numbers) is found in the International Classification of Goods and Services for the Purposes of Registration of Marks (the Nice Classification), currently in its 9th edition as of this printing. The Nice Classification, largely adopted worldwide, was established by an agreement concluded at the Nice Diplomatic Conference on June 15, 1957. When selecting the goods or services applicable to the mark from the Nice Classification, applicants should choose as broad a description of goods as possible. Later amendments to a classification, particularly if requested by an examiner, can only clarify or limit the descriptions; no new items are allowed. Applicants should also note that if the numerical class is in doubt or is otherwise not specified in the application, the examiner assigned to the application will designate the proper class(es). However, as noted previously, the applicant is required to pay for at least one class when filing the application.

Applicants composing their own description of the goods or services related to the mark should refrain from using open-ended phrases like "including" or "such as." Such phrases are too indefinite to accurately describe the goods or services to which the mark relates. Instead, phrases such as "namely" and "consisting of" should be used, together with a precise description of the goods or services. One exception to this rule of thumb, however, relates to house marks. House marks generally refer to "a full of line of" goods. This phrase is therefore generally permissible so long as the goods are all capable of being classified in the same class and provided that the applicant can produce a catalogue or other evidence to show broad usage of the mark.

Appendix 14, "Nice Classification," of this Almanac contains a link to a searchable database of the 9th edition of the Nice Classification on the PTO's website as well as information on the history of the Nice Agreement and the countries that follow it.

Dates of First Use

For § 1(a) applications, two dates of use are supplied: the date of first use of the mark anywhere and the date of first use of the mark in commerce. Use of the mark anywhere means the applicant's first introduction of the mark in ordinary trading channels. This type of use need not be interstate in nature as that is a type of use regulated by Congress and which triggers the means to file a federal trademark application. Thus, use anywhere can be local or intrastate. In some instances, the first introduction of the mark may have occurred in interstate commerce and, therefore, the date of use anywhere and the date of use in commerce will be the same. Furthermore, if more than one item of goods or services is specified in a § 1(a) application, the dates of use need only be for one item specified in each class, provided that the item to which the dates apply is indicated.

Dates of first use do not apply to the initial filing of an ITU application; the dates are supplied later when the mark is put into use in commerce.

Specimens

The purpose of a specimen is to show how the mark is seen by the public relative to the goods or services to which it attaches. A satisfactory specimen, therefore, shows that the mark is being used in commerce on or in connection with the applied-for goods and services. Examples of satisfactory goods-related specimens include hang tags; packaging; labels; instruction manuals; catalogs that prominently display the mark; point-of-sale displays, such as banners, window displays, menus and similar devices; package inserts that do not constitute advertising; and screen displays for certain kinds of software-related marks. Impermissible specimens include a copy of the drawing of the mark and any information that does not serve as a source identifier. Examples of the latter include bills of lading, advertising, certain package inserts, business cards and stationery, printer's proofs, and publicity releases. In some cases, the nature of the material associated with the mark is not capable of production as a standard specimen, such as liquid materials transported in tanker cars. In such cases, an alternative form of specimen may be acceptable if adequate proof is presented to the PTO that a traditional specimen is impractical.

Service mark specimens show that the mark is actually used in the sale or advertising of the services. Therefore, acceptable specimens include newspaper and magazine advertisements, brochures, pamphlets, billboards, direct-mail leaflets, and the like. Business documents, such as letterhead and invoices, may be acceptable service mark specimens if they show the mark and refer to the relevant services. Moreover, live-action events, such as entertainment services, may be adequately depicted using photographs of performances or radio or television listings associated with the mark. Like trademark specimens, proofs and publicity releases are not adequate specimens to show use of a service mark as a source indicator.

For use-based applications (or allegations of use following the filing of an ITU application), one specimen of the mark is required for each class of goods or services claimed in the application unless the range of goods or services included in each class is so disparate that additional specimens are necessary to effectively demonstrate use of the mark. Also, specimens for color marks must adequately represent the colors claimed in the application. Unlike the drawing of the mark indicated in the standard character box or special form attachment, specimens may include use of the "sm" or "tm" designations as well as the ® symbol in instances where it clearly reflects a registration secured abroad.

Specimens filed in connection with electronic applications must be in .jpg or .pdf format. In a paper-filed application, the specimen(s) must be flat and no larger than 8½ inches wide by 11.69 inches long. If the actual specimen (such as a bag used to transport goods in bulk) exceeds the size requirements, then generally an alternative specimen such as a photograph will suffice provided that it clearly shows how the mark is used on or in connection with the goods or in the sale or advertising of the services.

Appendix 15, "Specimen Requirements for Collective Marks, Collective Membership Marks, and Certification Marks," of this Almanac highlights the specimen requirements for collective marks, collective membership marks, and certification marks.

Declaration and Indication of Signatory

The declaration following the end of the trademark application sets forth certain statements concerning the right of the applicant to claim rights to the trademark in question. The signatory to the application is warned that these statements, if willfully false, subject the declarant to a fine or imprisonment, and the application, or any resulting registration, may be declared void. Following are the elements of the declaration:

(1) the signatory is properly authorized to execute the application on behalf of the applicant. Generally, the PTO does not question the authority of the signer unless there is evidence in the record to suggest that the signer is unauthorized;

(2) the signatory believes the applicant to be the owner of the trademark sought to be registered;

(3) the signatory believes the foreign applicant (if applicable) to be entitled to use the mark in commerce;

(4) to the best of the signatory's knowledge and belief, no other person, firm, corporation, or association has the right to use the mark in commerce, either in the identical form thereof or in such near resemblance thereto as to be likely, when used on or in connection with the goods/services of such other person, to cause confusion, or to cause mistake, or to deceive. Note that the mark must not be confusingly similar to either an identical mark or one that resembles the mark in the same or related classes of goods or services. Likelihood of confusion is subject to wide interpretation, as the reader will learn in the section entitled "Pre-Registration Administrative Procedures," below; and

(5) all statements made of the applicant's knowledge are true, and all statements made on information and belief are believed to be true.

Electronic filers have the option of submitting a signature to the application by various methods, unless the application is initially filed without a signature because the appropriate signatory is unavailable. One such method is to electronically sign the application, thus: /john doe/. The other options are to e-mail a text form of the application to a second party for signature or to scan a pen-and-ink obtained signature into the application and then file it electronically. Applicants represented by counsel may permit them to sign applications on their behalf. In fact, electronic filers will indicate on the first screen of their TEAS-related application whether the form is being filed by an attorney. Regardless whether the form is signed electronically or submitted in the mail, the signer, if not an attorney representing the applicant, should be a person with legal authority to bind the applicant or a person with firsthand knowledge of the facts and actual or implied authority to act on behalf of the applicant.

Filing Fees

The initial filing fees are based on the number of classes set forth in the application. If no specific class is specified, the minimum filing fee is for one class. Electronic applications can be filed using the TEAS (Trademark Electronic Application System) form or TEAS Plus form. TEAS applicants pay a higher fee for each class delineated in an application because of the ability to write a free-form definition of the goods or services to which the mark attaches and reserve the right to file subsequent correspondence with the PTO via mail. TEAS Plus applicants pay a lower fee in exchange for agreeing to use electronic filings during the course of the entire application and to use exact descriptions of goods and services as found in the PTO's online manual rather than free-form definitions. A current fee schedule for PTO filings and methods of payment is located at http://www.uspto.gov/main/howtofees.htm.

PRE-REGISTRATION ADMINISTRATIVE PROCEDURES

In General

Several activities can occur during the pendency of an application. This chapter will address the following actions: (i) filing such documents as one or more types of amendment; an allegation of use; request for extension of time; request to delete an ITU basis; request to divide an application; petition to revive an abandoned application; express abandonment; and appointment and revocation of power of attorney or appointment of domestic representative; (ii) responding to office actions; and (iii) opposition proceedings.

Amendments Generally

Amendments can take many forms. One type of an amendment is an assignment of the application, which can be done both pre- (except as noted below) and post-registration. An applicant may also amend its address or change the correspondence address to which PTO notices are sent. Other examples include a preliminary amendment, an amendment after a final office action, and an amendment after publication.

Assignments

A mark may be assigned for several reasons. Some common examples include a change in ownership, a change in the owner's name or the granting of a security interest in a trademark (e.g., as collateral for a bank loan). However, only use-based marks may be assigned, unless the proposed assignee is a successor to the owner's business or to that part of the business to which the mark pertains, and the business is ongoing.

Applicants must file a recordation form cover sheet with the PTO's Assignments Division indicating the nature of the assignment, the party giving the assignment (the conveying party) and the party receiving the assignment (the receiving party), together with the application number(s) or registration number(s) affected by the assignment. This cover sheet must be accompanied by documentation showing the assignment or proving the mark owner's change in name (such as an amendment to a corporate applicant's certificate of incorporation showing a change in name).

Assignments can be filed online at http://etas.uspto.gov. Paper filers must complete the trademark assignment recordation form cover sheet attached as Appendix 16, "Trademark Assignment Recordation Form Cover Sheet," of this Almanac.

Change of Address or Correspondence Address

A trademark owner's address and correspondence address are not necessarily the same. The owner's address is that used for business or residence purposes; whereas, the correspondence address is that address to which PTO notices are sent, which may be the address of the applicant's attorney, if any. Moreover, neither form should be used to effectuate an assignment as discussed above. A change of address or correspondence address may be filed pre- or post-registration as circumstances warrant, either electronically or via mail.

Preliminary Amendment

A preliminary amendment—that is, an amendment preliminary to the examination of a mark—is filed prior to the assignment of an examiner to the application. A common scenario giving rise to the amendment involves some clerical error in the application. For instance, a corporate entity may have been incorrectly referred to as "ABX Vacuums, LLC" instead of "ABC Vacuums, LLC." Other acceptable changes include correction of an address or place of incorporation or formation. Note, however, that a change affecting the applicant must be merely a misidentification and not a substitution of a new applicant. An application that purports to change the applicant is void.

Several other actions are permitted via preliminary amendment. For instance, an applicant may change, delete, or add goods or services or classification numbers, add or modify dates of first use, add or substitute a specimen, submit a foreign registration certificate under a § 44 application, or change the filing basis (e.g., from an ITU to a use-based application). Also, such an amendment may provide a disclaimer or claim a prior registration of the applicant or move the application from the Principal Register to the Supplemental Register. Moreover, an applicant may submit a better quality image to support a specimen, particularly if the original image did not reproduce correctly or was outside the size parameters accepted by the PTO. In some instances, an applicant may even change the mark, including, for instance, the correction of a typographical error. However, a change to a mark will not be permitted if it would amount to a material alteration. A material alteration means that the original essence of the mark has not been retained. Therefore, any change to a mark should be approached with caution.

Changes to be effected by preliminary amendment should generally be undertaken no less than fifteen to thirty days following the initial filing of the application by mail or seven to ten days following an electronic filing so that the PTO has an opportunity to enter the initial application into its TARR (Trademark Applications and Registrations Retrieval) database. To ensure the timely filing of a preliminary amendment, an applicant may access TARR at http://tarr.uspto.gov using the assigned serial number of the application to ensure that it has been fully loaded into the system or else check for the mark using the PTO's public search database.

Amendment After Final Office Action

Sometimes, an amendment of an application may be necessitated by an examiner's final action in examining a mark. For instance, if an examiner finds that the specimen submitted to support a use-based application does not show use of the mark in commerce (e.g., the specimen is a printer's proof of an advertisement), and the applicant cannot submit a proper specimen in response to office actions, then the application may be amended to an ITU application.

Amendment After Publication

Certain amendments are permitted even after an application has been published in the *Gazette* for opposition by third parties. These include restricting or deleting identifications of goods or services, amending classifications, amending drawings (provided the amendment is not a material alteration and the specimens support the amendment), and to add a disclaimer. In some instances, a republication of the mark in the *Gazette* will be required to protect the public's right to notice, as in the case of amending a first use date to a different date that nonetheless precedes the application filing date.

Allegation of Use

An allegation of use is a statement of the dates of first use of the mark anywhere and use of the mark in commerce. The term "allegation of use" is a general term referring to an amendment of an application to allege use prior to publication (also referred to as an amendment to allege use, or AAU) as well as the Statement of Use filed after issuance of a Notice of Allowance. As of January 16, 2009, the PTO issued a rule indicating its preference that the term "allegation of use" be used in lieu of "amendment to allege use" or "statement of use." However, this is not a mandatory requirement and, for purposes of this text, an allegation of use following a notice of allowance will be referred to as a Statement of Use.

Appendix 17, "Trademark/Service Mark Allegation of Use," of this Almanac contains the PTO's form for mailing an allegation of use.

Regardless of the circumstances dictating the filing of an allegation of use, unless the application is going to be divided between goods or services in use with the mark and those that are not (discussed below in the section entitled "Request to Divide the Application"), or the goods or services are deleted from the application, then the statement or allegation of use must apply to all of the goods or services delineated in the application. Also, in each case, the use-based allegation is supported with a specimen (as discussed above in the section entitled "Specimens" in this chapter) and a declaration that the mark is in use in commerce. The specimens will be examined by an examiner to ensure that the materials submitted comply with the Lanham Act—in other words, the specimens must show use of the mark in commerce. Note also that there is a "blackout" period from the publication date until the issuance of a Notice of Allowance during which time no declaration of use may be filed.

Request for Extension of Time to File a Statement of Use

A request for extension of time to file a Statement of Use gives the applicant an additional six-month window to make use of the mark in commerce and file a Statement of Use. The first extension request may be filed as of right without a showing of good cause for the extension, but the applicant must still affirm that it has a continued bona fide intention to use the mark in commerce. Up to four additional extensions can be granted, together with the required declaration, thus giving the applicant up to 36 months following the issue date of the Notice of Allowance to demonstrate use of the mark in commerce. These four additional extensions must be supported with a showing of good cause for the PTO to grant the extension. In other words, the extensions are not as of right. Examples of good cause include product or service research or development, market research, manufacturing activities, promotional activities, steps to acquire distributors, and steps to obtain required governmental approval. Online filers will find that the PTO has provided a field for the applicant to select among a variety of good cause reasons for the extension.

Appendix 18, "Request for Extension of Time to File a Statement of Use," of this Almanac contains the PTO form for mailing a request for extension of time to file a Statement of Use.

In some cases, an applicant may find it prudent to file an extension together with a Statement of Use, often called an "insurance" extension request. This is done because the Statement of Use will be examined by an examining attorney, who may accept it or request additional information, clarification, or response. In fact, once the mark is re-examined in connection with the specimens filed to support its use, the examiner may determine that the mark is being used in a descriptive manner or, in some other respect, warranting a refusal to register it. If the Statement of Use is found to have any deficiencies, they can be remedied only if there is time remaining in the period in which the applicant could file a Statement of Use. Thus an "insurance" extension request is filed to preserve the applicant's ability to file a corrective Statement of Use if required. If the extension is not filed and the PTO refuses the Statement of Use outside the applicable six-month period, the applicant will lose its filing date and the application will be deemed abandoned.

Request to Delete a § 1(b) Basis

In some instances, a § 1(b) basis can be deleted from an application. The basis is deleted for an entire application or an entire class of goods or services when an alternative, previously-declared basis exists in the application. For example, if an application is "mixed" (i.e., some goods or services are subject to a § 1(a) claim and others subject to an ITU basis) or a separate basis for registration under § 44(e) exists, then the § 1(b) basis may be deleted. The § 1(b) basis should not be deleted if it is the only basis supporting the application or where a preliminary amendment would be the appropriate vehicle to effect the change.

Request to Divide the Application

A request to divide the application is often made with respect to a "mixed" application to proceed to publication with the goods or services already used with the mark. The effect of a divided application is the physical separation of a single application into two or more separate applications upon the payment of a fee for each new application created by the division. Such a request can be filed at various phases of the pendency of an application, such as (i) at any time between the filing of the application and the publication date; (ii) during the period between the issuance of a notice of allowance and the time for filing a Statement of Use; or (iii) contemporaneously with an allegation or statement of use. Requests to divide cannot be filed electronically as of this writing. Therefore, a mailed request must be filed with the caption "Request to divide the application" appearing at the top of the first page of the request.

Revival of an Application

The PTO permits the filing of a petition to revive an application either as a result of (i) failing to respond to an office action; (ii) failing to file a Statement of Use or extension within the prescribed time periods; or (iii) failing to receive an office action or a notice of allowance, in which case the applicant's required action will have failed to occur. Any of these failures will cause the issuance of a notice of abandonment, which means that the application is no longer pending and therefore cannot mature into a registration. After receipt of the notice, a petition must be filed within two months, stating that the failure was unintentional. If the notice of abandonment was not received, then an applicant may file the petition within two months following knowledge of the abandonment, provided that the applicant can show a diligent pursuit of the application. An application is deemed diligently pursued if its status is checked with the PTO at least every six months. The status can be checked online via the TARR database or by calling the Trademark Assistance Center at 800–786–9199. If the petition is granted, the application will be restored to "active" status. In some cases, an application is also restored because the abandonment was the result of PTO error.

The PTO encourages electronic filings of petitions to revive to expedite the handling of the application. Applicants filing on paper should observe the PTO's requirements which can be found in Appendix 19, "Petition Information Sheet for Mailed Petitions to Revive an Application," of this Almanac.

Express Abandonment of Application

In some cases, an applicant may intentionally abandon (i.e., withdraw) an application, and an online form exists for this purpose. Such an action may be taken as a result of a dispute with a third party regarding rights to the mark. In that case, an applicant may agree, or be ordered, in the settlement of the case to expressly abandon rights to the mark. An express abandonment might also be filed if it becomes clear that an

ITU application will not mature into a use-based application by the filing of a Statement of Use within the 36-month period allotted. Regardless of the circumstances (unless ordered or decreed otherwise), it should be noted that an owner may still use a withdrawn mark without the benefit of federal registration. Application filing fees are not, in any case, refundable.

Power of Attorney and Revocation

An applicant may represent its own interests in the pursuit of a trademark registration, and an applicant wishing to be represented by an attorney designates that representative in the course of filing an application. In either event, the party engaging in tasks in pursuit of the registration of a mark is said to be *prosecuting* the application. Additionally, although not required, a foreign applicant may designate a domestic representative to receive service of process on its behalf and otherwise bring the foreign applicant within the jurisdiction of the U.S. legal system. Domestic representatives do not fulfill the role of prosecuting the trademark application on the applicant's behalf. At the applicant's election, an attorney may fulfill both the role of the attorney prosecuting the application and the role of domestic representative. The PTO will only communicate with the party of record if a power or appointment is in effect.

Powers and appointments can likewise be withdrawn by the applicant or its representative. If an applicant chooses to revoke a power or appointment, it may elect a replacement to take over the affected role or represent its own interests. A revocation can be filed at any time during the pendency of the application. A representative can likewise request permission from the PTO to withdraw from representation of an applicant so long as the applicant has been properly notified of the request and provided with the information required to continue to prosecute the application. It should be noted that once a mark registers, the PTO considers the power or appointment to have ended. However, a representative can still be appointed post-registration or the PTO will update its records to show a representative if someone other than the applicant files post-registration forms on the applicant's behalf. A post-registration representative can likewise choose to withdraw at some point.

RESPONDING TO OFFICE ACTIONS

Office Actions Generally

An office action, also referred to as an official action, is a written communication from an examiner at the PTO requesting a response from the applicant concerning a procedural or substantive matter related to the application. Office actions may issue pre- or post-registration and are usually responded to in writing by the applicant or its representative unless the examiner invites a resolution by telephone. Many times an office action contains language stating the examiner's refusal to register a mark (discussed in detail below). Unfortunately, many applicants misconstrue this refusal as an indication that the application is fatally flawed and therefore will not mature into a registration. Consequently, the application may be abandoned. However, many refusals can be overcome with arguments supporting the applicant's position. Thus, an applicant should carefully read and consider the examiner's position in the office action and decide upon a course of action rather than simply allow the application to abandon.

The number of office actions issued by an examiner does not generally exceed two, unless additional issues are raised upon the applicant's response to a first office action. Otherwise, a second action is generally a final action, and if issues have not been resolved between the examiner and the applicant once an action is made final, the applicant can take an appeal (discussed below).

This text will discuss (i) common scenarios giving rise to an office action following the initial filing of an application as well as potential responses; (ii) the timing of responses; and (iii) appeals.

COMMON OFFICE ACTIONS

Functional or Generic Findings

In an office action raising issues of functionality or genericness, the examiner refuses registration of the mark on grounds that it simply does not function as a trademark. In other words, the proposed mark neither identifies and distinguishes the goods or services of the applicant nor indicates their source. In a typical functionality refusal, the examiner determines that the proposed mark consists of a design feature of the identified goods that serves a utilitarian purpose. However, a mark may be functional in two respects. If the mark embodies a design feature that is competitively superior, then the mark is deemed *de jure* functional and therefore unregistrable on the Principal or Supplemental Register. On the other hand, if the mark embodies a design feature that is just as readily replaced with other alternatives, the mark is deemed *de facto* functional and may be registrable on either register. Accordingly, the trademark owner must determine the uniqueness of the design features of the mark and when possible, argue that the mark is *de facto* functional. Evidence to support such a conclusion may include any available advertising, promotional or explanatory material concerning the goods, particularly any material specifically related to the feature embodied in the mark.

Genericness is likewise a bar to registration of a mark within the context of the goods or services involved. The examining attorney bears the burden of proving by clear evidence that the proposed mark is generic—that is, that the public primarily uses or understands the term sought to be protected to refer to the genus of goods or services in question. Evidence of the public's understanding of a term can be obtained from any competent source, including dictionary definitions, research databases, newspapers, and other publications. The key to resolving a refusal based on genericness, then, is to show that the mark in question is actually used in a fanciful or arbitrary sense. For instance, the mark ORANGE would be a generic term for fruit but something else entirely if referring to a savings bank. Similarly, another consideration is whether the mark is descriptive and at least capable of registration on the Supplemental Register.

Disclaimer

An examiner issues a disclaimer requirement when one or more words in an application are so commonplace that none of them should be capable of exclusive appropriation by any single trader in the marketplace. Examples of such words include *entertainment, bank, food, shop* and *hospital*, corporate indicators such as *company, inc.,* or *LLC,* or Internet designations such as *www*. A disclaimer does not remove the word(s), indicator or designation from the mark; rather, it indicates that they have no trademark significance separate and apart from the mark as a whole. Generally speaking, disclaimers are not objectionable so long as the breadth of the disclaimer does not undermine the ability of the mark as a whole to function distinctively. Therefore, any disclaimer requirement should be examined with care before agreed.

Unacceptable Specimens

An office action refusing the specimens commonly indicates that they do not show actual trademark or service mark use. The best course of action is to submit substitute specimens. A substituted specimen must be supported by a declaration that (i) in the case of a use-based application, the substitute specimen was in use in commerce at least as early as the filing date of the application; or (ii) in the case of substituted specimens provided upon review of those initially supplied with a Statement of Use, the specimens must have been in use in commerce prior to the expiration of the time allowed the applicant for filing an SOU. If an applicant cannot ultimately submit an acceptable specimen for a use-based application, then the application may need to be amended to an ITU application, at which point additional specimens can be produced when a Statement of Use is later due.

Indefinite Goods or Services

Although goods or services may be classified broadly in the first instance so that the potential items to be associated with the mark are not unduly restricted, in some cases an examiner may find that the identification or goods or recitation of services is unacceptable as indefinite. For instance, "computer programs" is indefinite and contains goods that may be classified in more than one class. In certain cases, the examiner is likely to propose one or more revised descriptions of goods or services that the applicant may adopt in its response as appropriate. In some instances, the applicant may be required to provide more information on the exact nature of the goods or services so that the appropriate descriptions and classifications may be made. These revisions may result in the payment of additional fees if the number of classes in the application is increased.

Mark is Merely Descriptive

It is very common for marks to be refused registration on grounds that they are merely descriptive. As set forth in Chapter 1, "The Nature and Function of a Trademark," of this Almanac, a merely descriptive mark is not entitled to registration on the Principal Register unless it has acquired secondary meaning. The examining attorney must consider whether the mark is merely descriptive—that is, whether it describes the purposes, functions, characteristics or features of the goods or services—in relation to the identified goods or services, not in the abstract. Moreover, the proposed mark need only describe one attribute of the goods or services to be descriptive rather than all of its features, functions, characteristics, or purposes. Generally, if no imagination, thought, or perception is required to determine the nature of the goods or services from the wording in the mark, then the mark will be deemed descriptive. It is instructive to note as well that the foreign language equivalent of a merely descriptive English word is likewise unregistrable.

The applicant may respond to this refusal by submitting evidence and arguments in support of the registration. For instance, the applicant may argue that the mark is suggestive rather than descriptive or include extensive evidence of Web site activity, marketing, and sales dollars to support a claim of acquired distinctiveness. Alternatively, the applicant for a use-based application on the Principal Register may consider amending it to the Supplemental Register.

Likelihood of Confusion

Perhaps the most vexing of all office actions is a refusal to register the mark based on the examiner's conclusion that, upon searching the PTO records, the examiner has found that the applicant's mark, when used on or in connection with the identified goods or services, so resembles the registered or pending mark of another as to be likely to cause confusion, or to cause mistake, or to deceive. Significantly, the goods or services of the parties need not be identical or directly competitive to find a likelihood of confusion. They need only be related in some manner, including their marketing, that they could be encountered by the same purchasers and give rise to a mistaken belief that the goods or services emanate from a common source.

An applicant should consider several factors to determine whether grounds exist to dispute the examiner's refusal to register. These factors include (i) the similarity or dissimilarity of the marks in their entireties as to appearance, sound, connotation, and commercial impression; (ii) the similarity or dissimilarity, and nature, of the goods or services as described in each application; (iii) the similarity or dissimilarity of established trading channels; (iv) the fame of the prior mark (e.g., sales, advertising, and length of use); (v) the nature and extent of any actual confusion; and (vi) the sophistication of the buying public. Another option is to consider obtaining written consent from the cited registrant or applicant. Consent agreements between two parties allowing for one party's use and registration of a mark by another party are accorded great weight by the PTO. However, the possibility exists that the pursued party may not only object to the mark in terms of its registration but also to its use even without the benefit of registration. Therefore, the option to approach a third party for consent should be carefully weighed.

TIMING OF RESPONSES

The time for response to an office action is set forth in the office action. Generally, a response to the office action must be made within six months from its mailing date to avoid abandonment of the application. In some instances, an examiner may expedite the handling of an application. This can be accomplished by issuing a "priority action" to address relatively minor issues such as the authority of the signer to sign the application's declaration, a disclaimer, or an amended description of goods or recitation of services in a single class. In a priority action, the examiner first discusses all of the outstanding issues with the application by phone, e-mail, or personal interview with the applicant or a representative, suggesting in certain instances the desired action. The examiner then follows up with the issuance of a priority action, which must be officially responded to in the six-month period. In other instances, the examiner and the applicant may resolve all outstanding issues together by phone, e-mail, or interview. In such a case, the examiner will confirm the changes to the application by way of an Examiner's Amendment, eliminating the need for the applicant to submit a formal written response to the office action. However, the applicant should carefully read the Examiner's Amendment to ensure that all changes are accurately presented.

APPEALS

Once an examiner has made an action final as to all outstanding requirements, an applicant who cannot comply with those requirements may choose to appeal one or more of the examiner's decisions. Before the formal appellate procedure begins, however, an applicant may choose to file a request for reconsideration in response to the final office action. Any such request should raise new issues or evidence in support of the applicant's arguments against the office action to increase the likelihood of it being considered by an examiner. It should also be noted that a request for reconsideration does not extend the time period for filing a notice of appeal, and an applicant may file both a request for reconsideration and a notice of appeal contemporaneously.

A notice of appeal must be filed with the TTAB (discussed in greater detail in the section entitled "Opposition Proceedings," below) in any case within six months of the mailing date of the final office action. If a request for reconsideration is contemporaneously being considered by the examiner, then the time for filing a brief to accompany the notice of appeal will be suspended pending the outcome of the reconsideration request. Ordinarily, the brief is due within 60 days of the appeal date.

There is no prescribed form for filing a notice of appeal. A sample form provided in the TTAB manual of procedure can be found in Appendix 20, "Notice of Appeal of Examiner's Refusal to Register a Mark," of this Almanac.

If a TTAB outcome is unfavorable to the applicant, then the case may be appealed to the United States Court of Appeals for the Federal Circuit (Federal Circuit). The Federal Circuit is one of thirteen circuit appellate courts in the country. In addition to hearing appeals from the TTAB, it hears appeals related to patents, international trade, and veterans' benefits, among other things.

OPPOSITION PROCEEDINGS

As referred to in the section "A General Overview of the Trademark Application Process," of this chapter, once a mark is published in the *Gazette*, a notice of opposition may be lodged with the TTAB by a party who believes that he or she will be damaged by its registration. The TTAB is an administrative tribunal of the PTO. Its jurisdiction in trademark cases is limited to deciding upon the propriety of registration of a mark. Consequently, the TTAB has no authority over questions concerning an applicant's ongoing right to use the mark independently of registration, nor does the TTAB decide questions of infringement or unfair competition. An opposition must be filed, online or via mail, within 30 days following the publication of a disputed mark unless an extension is granted for a longer period. A person or entity claiming to be damaged by an application may file a first request for either a 30-day extension of time or a 90-day extension of time. A 30-day extension will be granted upon request; whereas, a 90-day extension will granted only for good cause shown. A claimant who was granted an initial 30-day extension of time may file a request for an additional 60-day extension of time, provided that good cause can be shown for the further extension. If a 90-day extension period has been met, then one final request for an extension of time for an additional 60 days may be requested, and the TTAB will grant the request only upon consent of the applicant or upon a showing of extraordinary circumstances.

An opposition is similar to a court proceeding: there is a complaint (the Notice of Opposition) and an answer by the defending party, requests for discovery (such as requests for production of documents related to the dispute) are served, testimony is taken, and briefs are filed. Like appeals of TTAB decisions regarding office actions, a litigant may appeal an outcome to the Federal Circuit.

Appendix 21, "Notice of Opposition," of this Almanac contains a sample format for a notice of opposition.

REGISTRATION AND POST-REGISTRATION PROCEDURES

The Registration Certificate

If an application is deemed to be in condition for issuance of a registration, the application will be sent to the Publication and Issue Unit of the PTO for the processing of a registration certificate. Both principal and supplemental registrations are delivered in a jacket bearing the words "CERTIFICATE OF REGISTRATION" and either the words "Principal Register" or "Supplemental Register," together with an embossed seal of the PTO and a facsimile signature of its director. Inside the jacket, the registration data will include a representation of the mark, its registration number, the owner's name and address as reflected in the PTO's records at the time of issuance of the registration, the classes and descriptions of goods or services, the use dates, a description of the mark (i.e., either the standard character claim or special form claim), the original serial number and filing date, and the name of the examining attorney. The certificate for a principal registration should also contain an informational sheet on the filing of the mark with U.S. Customs (which is discussed in Chapter 6, "Infringement Issues," of this Almanac).

Registrants may request a copy of the registration certificate within one year of failing to receive the original by contacting the Trademark Assistance Center. Also, certified copies of the certificate (which may be required in connection with foreign filings) can be obtained by contacting the Document Services Branch of the Public Records Division of the PTO. As an original document, a registration certificate should be kept in a safe place along with other valuable papers.

Post-Registration Procedures

Unless a trademark is maintained and renewed at the appropriate intervals (and provided no reason exists to terminate it such as a court order or other proceeding), under current law a trademark's duration will be ten years from the date of registration. Marks registered prior to November 16, 1989 were in force for 20 years provided that the appropriate formalities for maintenance and renewal were met. This section will focus on registrations obtained under current law and will discuss the following post-registration procedures at the PTO: (i) amending a registration; (ii) a declaration of continued use or excusable non-use; (iii) a declaration of incontestability; (iv) renewals; and (v) cancellation proceedings. Post-registration matters are handled by the Post Registration Section of the PTO. As is the case in pre-registration matters, a deficiency in meeting the PTO's post-registration filing requirements may result in an office action that is subject to a response, taking into account the general considerations for replying to office actions discussed earlier in this chapter.

Amending a Registration

A registration could require amendment for several reasons. In the case of a change in the owner's address, this type of amendment can easily be filed as discussed above in the section entitled "Change of Address or Correspondence Address" of this chapter. In many other cases, amendments are governed by § 7(e) of the Lanham Act, which allows amendments to registrations on good cause provided that the amendment does not materially alter the character of the mark. The reader will recall that amendments contemplated during the application process are subject to the same material alteration standard. Thus in post-registration cases, the mark must likewise retain its original essence following an amendment to avoid it being deemed a material alteration. This requirement is applicable in particular to amendments affecting a change in the mark itself, such as the addition of color or stylistic elements. Generally, a change that would alter the character of the original drawing from a standard character format to a special form would be a material alteration. If the change is immaterial, then a new drawing of the mark and a new specimen supporting the drawing will be required, together with a declaration that the new specimen was in use in commerce at least as early as the filing date of the amendment.

Another potential amendment is a change in the international classification, particularly if the change reflects one or more updated classes following a change in the Nice Classification. In other instances, a disclaimer of one or more words in the mark may be desired, particularly if a dispute is likely to arise as to the propriety of a claim of exclusivity over commonplace language. Also, in some instances, a date of use may be changed, but only if the amendment would have been permissible if it had been made during the examination of the application. For example, a registration could not be amended to claim a date of use in interstate commerce that is earlier than use of the mark anywhere as the first use anywhere will always be earlier than, or equal to, the date of first use in commerce.

Declaration of Continued Use or Excusable Non-Use

To avoid cancellation of the registration, § 8 of the Lanham Act provides that each owner of a mark on the Principal or Supplemental Register file a declaration of continued use (or excusable non-use) between (i) the fifth and sixth years following the registration date during the initial ten-year period; (ii) the ninth and tenth year following the registration date during the initial ten-year period; and (iii) the ninth and tenth year of each successive ten-year registration period. These dates are included on the jacket of every certificate of registration, and owners should note that the PTO provides no other reminders regarding post-registration filings required to maintain a registration. A grace period of six months is granted following the expiration of the above filing periods, subject to an additional filing fee. The practical effect of the § 8 filing is to keep only those marks which are still active on the registers.

To prove use, a current specimen showing use of the mark in commerce is provided with the declaration. The declaration also supports only those goods or services recited in the registration, unless use is ceasing with respect to one or more of those goods or services. However, in some cases, use of the mark may have been suspended with the intent to resume use in the future. In such instances, the declaration is one of excusable non-use and must state the date on which use was suspended and when it is due to resume, together with a statement of special circumstances showing that such non-use is not intended as an abandonment of the mark. The Lanham Act provides that lack of use of a mark, with no evidence of an intent to resume use, for a consecutive three-year period is presumptive evidence of abandonment of a mark.

Appendix 22, "Excusable and Non-excusable Lack of Use of a Mark," of this Almanac sets forth examples from the TMEP of excusable and non-excusable lack of use of a mark.

Appendix 23, "Declaration of Use of Mark in Commerce," of this Almanac contains the PTO form for mailing a § 8 declaration.

Declaration of Incontestability

Section 15 of the Lanham Act allows owners of marks on the Principal Register to file a declaration of incontestability, which is an optional filing. A declaration of incontestability provides third parties with conclusive proof that the mark is validly registered and owned as reported and that the trademark owner has the right to use the mark to the exclusion of all others. Incontestability, therefore, has obvious benefits to the owner of a mark on the Principal Register. The reader should note that the declaration is unavailable to owners of supplemental registrations, who enjoy lesser rights as can be found in the section entitled "The Supplemental Register" in Chapter 2, "Types of Applications and Registrations," of this Almanac.

The declaration cannot be filed any earlier than following the expiration of five years of continuous use of the mark in connection with the goods or services identified in the application following the registration. If a trademark owner elects to make the declaration, it is due within one year following any such five-year period of continuous use. Therefore, if there are no interruptions in use of the mark for the first five years following registration, the declaration can be filed by the end of the sixth year. Given that this time period coincides with the filing of a required § 8 declaration, a trademark owner may file a combined § 8 and § 15 declaration, a form for which is found in Appendix 24, "Combined Declaration of Use and Incontestability," of this Almanac. The § 15 declaration, either alone or in combination with a § 8 filing, will affirm the continuous use of the mark in commerce with respect to the goods or services identified in the registration and also verify that there has been no decision adverse to the claim of ownership or right to register the mark or maintain the registration and that no proceeding is pending and not disposed of regarding the mark at the PTO or in the courts.

An incontestable mark is not immune from all attacks, however. In other words, the incontestable rights of *use* set out in a proper declaration have no effect on the rights of third parties to attack the *registration* of a mark pursuant to certain grounds in a cancellation proceeding. Cancellation proceedings are discussed below.

Renewals

Section 9 of the Lanham Act provides for renewal of registrations on both registers between the ninth and tenth year period following registration and between each successive ninth and tenth year period or within a grace period of six months thereafter. Because this due date timeframe coincides with the due date for a § 8 filing, a trademark owner may file a form combining both the § 8 and § 9 required filings.

Appendix 25, "Combined Declaration of Use in Commerce/Application for Renewal of Registration of Mark," of this Almanac contains the PTO form for mailing a combined § 8 and § 9 declaration.

Cancellation Proceedings

A party believing that he, she, or it will be damaged by a registration on the Principal or Supplemental Register may file a cancellation proceeding to void the registration. Like opposition proceedings, such a procedure is initiated at the TTAB. Unlike oppositions, though, cancellation proceedings are filed after a registration has occurred rather than prior to that event. A party claiming damage, therefore, has potentially two opportunities to lodge a complaint with the PTO against the existence of a mark for registration: following its publication or following its registration. In the case of marks on the Supplemental Register, however, the filing of a petition for cancellation is the only method of dispute resolution at the PTO because those marks are not published for opposition. Moreover, unlike principal registrations, a petition to cancel a supplemental registration can be filed at any time regardless of the grounds for cancellation.

With respect to a § 15 filing, an incontestable mark is not immune from all attacks concerning its registration. In some instances, a cancellation proceeding can be initiated at any time during the life of a principal registration—even if the owner's rights to use the mark are incontestable—based on certain grounds. Those grounds commonly include abandonment of the mark; genericness or functionality; geographical deceptiveness; and fraud in the procurement of the registration. For some other grounds, a petition to cancel a principal registration must be filed within five years from the date of registration of the mark or else the claim is barred. Grounds that must be filed within the five-year initial registration period are those involving likelihood of confusion and descriptiveness, and claims involving ownership or bona fide use of the mark. Also, it should be noted that the owner of a registration can always voluntarily surrender it for cancellation, and the PTO can cancel a registration pursuant to a court order.

CHAPTER 4:
INTERNATIONAL APPLICATIONS

INTERNATIONAL CONSIDERATIONS GENERALLY

Trademarks can be protected worldwide. As any user of the Internet knows, the reach of trademarks does, indeed, extend globally. Although it is possible to file a trademark application in each individual country of interest, systems are available to protect a trademark in several countries at once. This text will provide general information on two commonly-used systems for international protection: the Madrid Protocol and the Community trademark.

THE MADRID PROTOCOL

A General Overview

The Madrid Protocol is derived from the Madrid Agreement Concerning the International Registration of Marks (the Madrid Agreement). In 1891, the Madrid Agreement was enacted among its member nations to harmonize the trademark application process by allowing trademark owners to file one application covering several countries with a single filing authority—the World Intellectual Property Organization (WIPO). However, many nations chose not to contract with the Madrid Agreement because of several requirements deemed too onerous. For instance, centralized filings under the Madrid Agreement were required to be set forth in the French language, and the fee apportionment among nations was perceived as insufficient for those countries with exacting examination standards. Moreover, international applications could be based only on an existing registration and not on a pending application.

These deficiencies were addressed in 1989 with the adoption of the Protocol Relating to the Madrid Agreement (the Madrid Protocol), allowing for centralized English or French filings of an international application based on a registration or pending application. Both treaties continue to coexist and are collectively referred to as the Madrid System. A member nation of the Madrid System is known as a "contracting party."

The United States acceded to the Madrid Protocol (but not the Madrid Agreement) as of November 2, 2003. As a result, foreign owners of trademarks in member countries can utilize the Madrid Protocol to extend protection of their marks into the United States, and U.S. nationals and domiciliaries can file an application for international registration in reciprocating countries through the PTO. The PTO submits a copy of the international application to the International Bureau (IB) of WIPO, in Geneva, Switzerland. The IB administers filings through the Madrid System.

As of this writing, 77 countries have joined the Madrid Protocol, and 56 countries adhere to the Madrid Agreement. A current list of members of the Madrid System is attached as Appendix 26, "The Madrid System," of this Almanac.

Extension of Protection into the United States

Section 66(a) of the Lanham Act governs requests of foreign trademark owners to extend protection of their rights into the United States. Any such requests are submitted in an application to the PTO from the IB (where the underlying foreign registration originates) and are assigned an examiner to ensure that the foreign applications comply with PTO filing requirements. An application filed in this manner is known as a "66(a) application."

One significant feature of a 66(a) application is the applicant's declaration of a bona fide intent to use the mark in commerce, provided for on a document known as Form MM18. The IB retains Form MM18 as part of the international file but must ensure that it has been signed by an authorized signatory as provided for by PTO rules. Although actual use of the mark in commerce is not required prior to registration under § 66(a), the affidavits of use or excusable non-use and renewals are likewise applicable to marks for which protection is extended into the United States.

Other requirements incidental to the filing of U.S.-originating marks are also applicable to 66(a) applications. For instance, an examiner will review the drawing submitted with the application to ensure that it meets the requirements applicable to any other application. Therefore, the drawing must be legible and free of any extraneous information (such as the ® symbol) and contain the appropriate claims of color, if color is evident. If the application contains any deficiencies, the examiner will likewise issue an office action. Moreover, similar to U.S. applications, a successful 66(a) application will mature into a "66(a) registration" and be issued a registration certificate if the mark is not opposed or an opposition resolves in favor of the applicant.

Despite the similarities in examination, there are some notable differences. For example, the Nice Classification of goods and services in a 66(a) application cannot be amended, even though they might be classified differently under PTO examination standards in a U.S.-originating application, because the 66(a) application is governed by the underlying IB registration. Also, the mark cannot be amended in any way, regardless whether the change would be immaterial. Furthermore, only marks registrable on the Principal Register are eligible for an extension of protection and, therefore, any mark meeting principal registration requirements will be eligible for all the benefits accorded those marks, including the opportunity to declare incontestability. However, if the mark does not qualify for principal registration, it will be refused. Similarly, if the underlying IB registration is cancelled or a portion of it fails for any reason, the 66(a) application or resulting registration will likewise fail. In such an event, the application or registration may be eligible for transformation into a § 1 or § 44 application filed directly with the PTO.

Protection of U.S. Marks Internationally Through the Protocol

U.S. trademark owners can file through the PTO's Madrid Processing Unit either (i) an application for international registration or (ii) a subsequent designation. An application for international registration is an initial filing designating at least one contracting party to the Madrid Protocol. The holder of an international registration can request an extension of protection to additional contracting parties by filing a "subsequent designation." In either case, the PTO will transmit the filing to the IB, together with the international fees set by each country for the examination of the application. Like most documents, the forms may be filed online via TEAS. Applicants filing via mail must use an official WIPO form.

WIPO provides applicants with an international application simulator, which is an instructive tool illustrating use of the Madrid System. Applicants can use the tool to determine eligibility for filing through the Madrid Protocol, locate countries to designate in a filing, and estimate fees for registering a mark. The simulator is located at http://www.wipo.int/madrid/en/madrid_simulator.

Both Appendix 27, "Application for International Registration Under the Madrid Protocol," of this Almanac and Appendix 28, "Application for Designation Subsequent to the International Registration," of this Almanac contain the official WIPO forms for filing an international application and for making subsequent designations, respectively.

Application for International Registration

Trademark owners seeking international protection of a pending application or registration through the PTO must be a U.S. national, a domiciliary, or an entity having an established industrial presence in the United States. The PTO in this instance is deemed the "office of origin" for the international application. Moreover, the application must be based on an active application or registration; expired, cancelled, or abandoned applications or registrations cannot serve as the basis for an international registration.

In addition to the requirements set forth above, the elements required in an international application are as follows:

(1) the filing date and serial number of the application for which international rights are being claimed (known as the "basic application") or the registration date and registration number of the registration (called the "basic registration");

(2) the name of the applicant (which must be identical to that found in the basic application or registration) and a current address;

(3) an exact reproduction of the mark and a description, including color claims where appropriate;

(4) a list of goods and services as found in the basic application or registration and their classifications, which may be narrowed, if necessary, or deleted as appropriate if not the same for all countries;

(5) a list of contracting parties in which protection is sought; and

(6) payment of PTO fees and the fees of each contracting party.

A form or electronic submission containing the required elements will be certified as such and sent to the IB for a determination of the completeness of the application as the IB is the arbiter of the sufficiency of Madrid System filings. In addition to the PTO's application elements, the IB requires a declaration of a bona fide intention to use the mark in commerce on or in connection with the goods or services (as required in ITU applications) if such a declaration is required under the laws of a contracting party.

Similar to the PTO, the IB can issue one or more notices of deficiencies in an application, called a notice of irregularity. Like office actions, these notices must be addressed within the time period set forth in the notice or else the international application will fail. If the application meets the IB's requirements or any outstanding issues are successfully resolved, then the IB issues an international registration and publishes notice of it in the *WIPO Gazette of International Marks*. Thereafter, the application is sent to the contracting parties for a determination under their own trademark laws whether the mark is registrable. Such a review must be completed prior to 18 months after receipt of the application for protection; otherwise, the mark will be automatically protected by that contracting party.

International registrations are vulnerable during the first five years if the underlying basic application or registration fails for some reason, including abandonment, cancellation, or expiration. In such an event, the international registration will be amended (or cancelled entirely) in accordance with the action taken against the basic application or registration. This vulnerability is sometimes referred to as the "central attack." If the international registration is cancelled by the IB due to an action by the PTO against the mark (as opposed to an owner's action such as surrendering the registration or allowing an application to abandon), then the owner may elect to transform the international registration into individual applications with the member nations so long as the transformation occurs within three months following the IB's action against the international registration.

Subsequent Designation

A designation made subsequent to the issuance of an international registration to cover additional contracting parties can be filed with the PTO (if the nationality requirements set out above are met) or directly with the IB. An eligible PTO filing must contain the following elements:

(1) the international registration number;

(2) the name and address of the holder of the registration and an e-mail address for the receipt of notices if filed via TEAS;

(3) the goods and services;

(4) the additional contracting parties; and

(5) the fees.

Like the international application, the subsequent designation will be reviewed by the IB and the contracting parties designated in it for completeness, and any deficiencies must be satisfactorily resolved before the IB will record it in the International Register.

COMMUNITY TRADEMARK

A General Overview

A Community trademark application (known as a CTM and referring to the European Community, or European Union) provides an applicant with the opportunity to acquire trademark rights in all of the countries (known as "member states") comprising the European Union with a single filing. Similar to the Madrid System, a centralized agency known as the Office for Harmonization in the Internal Market (OHIM) in Alicante, Spain, administers Community trademark filings and registrations. The Community trademark system was initiated on April 1, 1996 and complements the individual trademark systems of the member states. As a result, an applicant can maintain its national registration and at the same time claim seniority as to its national rights in a CTM application.

Appendix 29, "Member States of the European Union," of this Almanac contains a list of member states of the European Union as of this writing. Updated information can be obtained on the country page of Europa, the portal website of the European Union, located at http://europa.eu/abc/european_countries/eu_members/index_en.htm.

Appendix 30, "Community Trademark Application," of this Almanac contains a CTM application form.

Following is a discussion of the CTM process:

Searches

As with the U.S. application process, it is good practice to undertake a preliminary search for marks that may be confusingly similar to the desired CTM before filing the application. Applicants may conduct such a search online at http://oami.europa.eu/CTMOline/RequestManager/en_SearchBasic or engage the services of a company or legal professional to do so. The OHIM will, however, undertake its own search after the application has been filed. This post-filing search will be discussed below.

The CTM Application

An eligible applicant must meet one of the four following criteria: (i) the applicant is a national of a member state; (ii) the applicant is a national of a member of the Paris Convention or a member of WIPO; (iii) the applicant is domiciled or has a commercial presence in a member state or Paris

Convention country; or (iv) the applicant is a national of a state that gives reciprocal protection to member states and recognizes CTM registrations as proof of country of origin. U.S. applicants, therefore, meet the criteria for applying for CTM registration at the very least on the basis of U.S. adherence to the Paris Convention and may also apply for priority (as discussed in Chapter 2, "Types of Applications and Registrations," of this Almanac) based on the filing of an earlier application.

The CTM application requires much of the same information as a U.S. application: the designation of the applicant, the type of mark and description, and the goods or services and classification number(s). Moreover, the mark may, like the U.S. rules, consist of elements such as a word(s), a slogan, stylistic elements, color or sound, and a disclaimer may be made as to commonplace terms. Also, an applicant may file the application without aid of a legal representative (although other actions, such as oppositions, will require the appointment of a qualified representative). Finally, the application, together with the fees, may be filed via mail (using the form provided in Appendix 30, "Community Trademark Application," of this Almanac) or electronically (in this case, at http://oami.europa.eu/ows/rw/pages/QPLUS/forms/forms.en.do).

Unlike the U.S. procedure, a CTM application must designate two languages. The first language choice is made at the discretion of the filer. The second language, however, must be one of the five official languages of OHIM: Spanish, German, English, French or Italian. Any of these languages may be further designated as the language to be used in all official correspondence related to the application. The application may be filed at OHIM or at the trademark office of a member state.

The applicant may also claim seniority based on an earlier registration in a member state. Furthermore, an applicant has the ability to use the CTM application to transform a failed Madrid Protocol registration—that is, convert a failed Madrid Protocol registration designating the European Union into a CTM registration. These methodologies of seniority and conversion give CTM applicants unique additional opportunities to preserve and enforce trademark rights.

Examination

Once filed, the application will be examined to ensure that the application requirements have been met. Like a U.S. application, it will also be examined to ensure that the mark is capable of distinguishing goods or services; in other words, the mark must not be generic, descriptive, or deceptive. If a deficiency is found in the application, the applicant will have two months to correct it following notification from OHIM or else the application will fail.

OHIM Searches

If the preliminary examination is successful, then the OHIM will conduct a search of the mark in its own database and submit a report to the applicant listing possibly confusing trademarks as located in the national registers of the member states. A response to this search report is neither required nor expected by the OHIM or any national office as it is merely advisory of potential older rights of third parties in the respective states of the European Union.

Publication for Opposition

Following the submission of the search report to the applicant, the mark is published in the *Community Trademarks Bulletin*. An opposition term of three months starts from the publication date during which third parties may lodge an opposition to the registration based upon older trademark rights. This three-month term cannot be extended. Therefore, if no opposition ensues, then the mark will be registered upon payment of the registration fee.

If an opposition ensues and is successful, then the application will be rejected even if the mark would be registrable in individual countries of the European Union. In that event, the CTM applicant may file applications in any country where the opponent does not have prior rights.

Revocation and Invalidity of a CTM Registration

Like U.S. law, the Community Trademark Act provides that the validity of a mark depends on its actual use for the registered goods or services, which use must commence within five years following the registration date or for a period of five consecutive years. As a result, lack of use can result in revocation of the mark at the instance of a third party. Revocation proceedings can also be instituted on grounds that the mark is generic or because it misleads the public.

Invalidity proceedings, on the other hand, attack other aspects of the mark besides non-use, such as its confusing similarity to another mark or the applicant's bad faith in the filing of the application. Revocation and invalidity proceedings are often collectively referred to as cancellation proceedings.

Renewals

Unless nullified on any of the bases set forth above, a CTM registration will last for a ten-year period calculated from the filing date of the application, renewable for successive ten-year periods thereafter. The registrant has the option of converting its CTM registration to one or more registrations in member states if renewal is not intended to apply to all member states.

CHAPTER 5:
MONETIZING TRADEMARKS

A GENERAL OVERVIEW

Like other forms of intellectual property such as copyrights and patents, trademarks are assets capable of producing value for their owners. For example, colleges license their names and logos in the production of outerwear. Other trademark owners establish a value for their brand and sell it. Both selling and licensing are forms of monetization. This chapter will address some basic issues surrounding these methods of extracting value from a mark and also discuss the ongoing need to police a mark to protect its economic viability.

SELLING A MARK

Under U.S. trademark law, the assignee of a trademark must also acquire the underlying goodwill associated with the mark for the transfer to be valid. Goodwill generally refers to (i) those items needed to carry on the business associated with the trademark, such as customer lists, equipment, clothing, or other tangible items and (ii) intangible items such as the likelihood of consumers and potential consumers to purchase whatever is associated with the mark. A purported transfer of title to a mark without its associated goodwill is referred to as an assignment in gross, or a naked transfer, and is null and void. Consequently, the buyer receives no title to the mark and will be unable to defend it against infringement by third parties.

Assuming the proper identification and attachment of goodwill, the next step is to undertake a valuation of the mark. Indeed, not all marks have great value such as that accorded highly distinctive marks such as Coca-Cola® and other iconic brands. Valuation helps mark owners determine their relative position in the marketplace and is used in a variety of contexts besides the outright sale or licensing of a mark, such as in collateralizing a mark for bank financing, determining damages in an infringement proceeding, and determining licensing fees for a franchise involving the mark.

There are three primary trademark valuation methods: (i) the market approach; (ii) the cost approach; and (iii) the income approach. The market approach addresses a mark's value in relation to other comparable brands in the marketplace. This approach presupposes the owner's knowledge of these comparable values, which may be unlikely unless the owner has access to a wide array of resources. The second approach investigates the cost of replacing or re-creating a mark. However, these costs, particularly the substantial goodwill associated with a famous mark, are often hard to quantify. Finally, the income approach can take many forms, one being a consideration of which portion of key earnings is attributable to the brand and then projecting a discounted present cash flow based on the risks the brand faces in sustaining earnings in the future.

Regardless of the valuation method used to arrive at a value for a salable mark, the benefit of the sale to a buyer could be lost without a proper recordation of the transfer at the PTO. As discussed in the section entitled "Assignments" of Chapter 3, "The PTO Trademark Application Process," of this Almanac, various means of conveying a mark to another party, such as by way of assignments and company mergers, are recorded with the PTO. Section 10 of the Lanham Act provides that a written document evidencing the assignment should be recorded with the PTO within 90 days of its execution. Otherwise, a buyer will have no recourse against a subsequent party claiming to have rights in the mark if that party had no notice of the transfer.

LICENSING

Unlike an assignment, which transfers all rights of ownership to the assignee, a license simply grants another party (the licensee) certain rights to use the mark, such as to manufacture, market, and sell a product branded with a mark owned by the licensor. In the direct-to-retail licensing context, consider such combinations as Kmart and Disney or Eddie Bauer and Ford Motor Company. Licensing arrangements can be domestic or international. Regardless of the geographic scope of the license, many provisions common to any license are particularly noteworthy for their ability to significantly affect licensing revenue. These provisions include exclusivity, termination, royalty rates, and quality control.

An exclusive license is one in which the licensor grants a single licensee the exclusive right and license to use the trademark for the purpose(s) set forth in the agreement. Unless an exception is carved out of such an agreement, this exclusivity means the licensor is likewise excluded from using its own licensed property for its own purposes. Thus a trademark owner should carefully consider the grant of exclusivity and its scope in determining whether the deal is likely to yield the desired economic result.

Another potential impact on economic viability of the licensing arrangement is the ability of the licensor to terminate the agreement. For instance, a poorly performing licensee or one who refuses to make royalty payments on a timely basis will disrupt the licensor's cash flow unless the agreement provides for termination. On the other hand, a licensor may simply find a better licensee and want the ability to transact business with that licensee, which is problematic if the license grant is exclusive. In the former scenario, a provision allowing for termination based on breach of the licensee's obligations will help the licensor mitigate its damages. In the latter scenario, a termination based on convenience—that is, for no particular reason—will give the licensor an opportunity to pursue other opportunities. An agreement may also provide for both forms of termination but with varying notice periods provided to the licensee to wrap up its existing obligations.

Royalty provisions likewise have an impact on the trademark owner's revenue stream. As a result, a licensor should evaluate the impact of such potential royalty provisions as a running royalty, fixed percentage, sliding scale (adjusted royalty based on units sold), a guaranteed minimum, or a ceiling on payments. The owner of a highly distinctive brand is likely to have greater control over the calculation to be used.

Finally, the absence of quality control provisions in a license can wreak havoc on the economic viability of a mark by causing its abandonment. Quality control provisions in a licensing agreement provide, as the words imply, that the mark owner will monitor the quality of the products produced under the mark. There is no general standard, however, for assessing effective quality control; the sufficiency or lack of such control is dependent on the circumstances. In some instances, quality control may involve the submission to a licensee of safety standards relevant to the manufacture of a product. In other cases, a licensor may require a designated number of samples of the product bearing the mark for the licensor's inspection prior to distribution.

The lack of quality control provisions has been linked by the courts with abandonment under § 45 of the Lanham Act on grounds that a lack of quality control risks that consumers will not experience consistency in the nature or quality of the product being offered and, as a result, the ability of the mark to function as an indicator of source or origin is impaired. In fact, § 45 of the Lanham Act specifically provides that any act of omission or commission by a trademark owner that causes a mark to lose its significance as a mark will result in its abandonment. The absence of quality control provisions—and the ultimate determination that the failure has caused the mark to lose its distinctiveness (and therefore its ability to function as a mark)—is known as "naked licensing." Naked licensing can also arise if existing quality control procedures are not applied equally to all licensees. Thus, a trademark owner should ensure that every license agreement (even one between a parent and subsidiary or other allied arrangement) contains a quality control provision and that quality control measures are likewise exercised consistently with all licensees.

POLICING A MARK

In addition to the proper use of a mark and the post-registration maintenance obligations set out in both Chapters 1, "The Nature and Function of a Trademark," and 3, "The PTO Trademark Application Process," of this Almanac, it is equally vital that trademark owners engage resources to monitor the use of their trademarks for instances of infringement that could damage a mark's value. For individual owners, this effort is likely to include the use of third-party monitoring services. For corporate owners, monitoring should include a mix of third-party services and company initiatives.

Third-party monitoring companies often provide the preliminary trademark searches discussed in Chapter 3, "The PTO Trademark Application Process," of this Almanac. Monitoring services can encompass a "watch" of a mark for potential infringement over a wide range of areas, such as a federal watch, a world watch, individual country watch, a state watch, a common law watch, and an Internet watch (for Web-related uses of a mark and domain name registrations incorporating a mark). For competitive intelligence, many service providers offer a watch on trademark filings and assignments for a given applicant or registrant and monitor the application of certain goods and services to applications filed by competitors. It is also important to monitor how one's own mark may violate the rights of others or be contrary to law. For instance, a coined term may actually have a meaning in a foreign language that is contrary to local law. If a mark is to be expanded into a foreign jurisdiction, a search should be performed to address any potential vulnerabilities.

Likewise, for the corporate trademark owner, a teamwork approach to trademark protection and brand management is key to preserving a mark's strength and goodwill.

A team approach to trademark enforcement can encompass several initiatives. First, employees need to be educated about trademarks to understand their importance. Educational efforts can take many forms, such as seminars for marketing personnel with internal or external speakers, newsletters, intranets, and the dissemination of books and other pre-existing materials. Another educational tool is a policy and procedures document discussing the basic principles of trademark law, including the definition of a mark, the types of marks, clearing a mark for usage, applying for a mark, and maintaining a mark. This document, or manual, may also include a summary of the company's existing trademark portfolio, an identification of those responsible for the selection and clearance of marks and receipt of reports on infringement, a list of licensors and others authorized to use a mark, and a guide to the proper usage of pending and registered marks in advertising and other collateral.

Second, employees should be encouraged to make scouting a part of the job and instructed on the collection of evidence showing an infringing use of a mark, whether encountered in business or in private life. If an employee cannot collect the evidence initially, then a report should be submitted indicating a description of the infringing article and the time and place where it was seen. Employees should also be instructed to report any suspected incidences of infringement immediately so that the ability to obtain an injunction or collect damages is uncompromised.

Third, employees in direct contact with customers and potential customers should be especially coached to recognize instances where infringement may be occurring. These employees include salespersons, customer service representatives, purchasing agents, and receptionists. Some common scenarios they should be instructed to note are attempts to return the merchandise of others to the company and misdirected communications such as purchase requests or complaints for an unrelated product or service.

CHAPTER 6:
INFRINGEMENT ISSUES

A GENERAL OVERVIEW

Disputes regarding the use of a mark can be resolved in either state court or federal court. However, given that most questions concerning a mark's unauthorized use by a third party involve a federal law such as the Lanham Act, controversies are most often brought in, or transferred to, a federal forum. This chapter will discuss the following potential causes of action under the Lanham Act in federal trademark litigation relating to the alleged misuse of a mark: (i) infringement; (ii) unfair competition; (iii) dilution; and (iv) counterfeiting.

PRE-LITIGATION INVESTIGATION AND ACTION

Aggrieved trademark owners contemplating litigation need to under-stand their position relative to the defending party, which requires the consideration of several elements such as (i) the market significance of the owner's mark compared with the defendant's mark; (ii) the similari-ties of the marks and their respective goods or services; (iii) previous disputes between the parties; (iv) licensing potential or other possible synergies; and (v) the desired outcome of the dispute. These elements form the basis of pre-litigation investigation. In formulating an action plan, a plaintiff should undertake a review of the PTO file history of the defending party's mark and investigate the defendant's use of its mark in commerce through a combination of outside investigators and a review of publicly-available information on the defendant's goods or services involving the disputed mark.

Once the relevant information is obtained on the activity giving rise to the dispute, a trademark owner should consider the appropriate meas-ures to take to inform the defendant of the conduct giving rise to the complaint. In some cases, informal measures may be employed in an attempt to achieve the desired outcome. For example, if a distributor-ship relationship exists between the parties, a simple phone call or let-ter may suffice in bringing about the desired conduct. In less familiar circumstances, a formal letter to quit the alleged infringing activity, known as a cease and desist letter—or a demand letter—may be more appropriate.

A demand letter should be drafted with certain considerations in mind. First, the tone of the letter should be adjusted to reflect the recipient's relationship to the trademark owner or the scope of the allegedly infring-ing activity. For instance, a zealous fan who creates jewelry based on the trade dress of the complainant's product is unlikely to require a harshly-worded letter to understand that the activity constitutes an infringement, particularly if the activity has not been complained of in an ongoing manner. In other cases, more competitively-driven uses of an owner's mark or one that is substantially similar on goods or serv-ices likely to confuse the public as to source or origin might dictate a harsher letter. Regardless of the circumstances, any letter should address the action required by the complainant and the time period for doing so. The required actions may include immediate cessation of the use of the mark, the addition of a disclaimer (e.g., PETE'S PET SHOP is not affiliated with nor sponsored by PETE'S PET EMPORIUM), a modi-fication of the offending mark, or, in the case of a pending trademark application, an express abandonment of the application and no further use of the mark.

Sometimes a demand letter may be unwarranted or unlikely to produce the desired result, particularly if the conduct is ongoing, willful, or in bad faith. In such cases, it may be advisable to proceed with filing a complaint in federal court, alleging one or more of the following causes of action:

INFRINGEMENT

Section 32 of the Lanham Act provides that a party who, without per-mission, copies, reproduces, or imitates the registered mark of another in commerce as part of the distribution of goods or services in a way that is *likely to cause confusion* between the two marks will be liable in a civil suit for infringement. "Likelihood of confusion" is the standard of proof for infringement that a plaintiff must meet, together with prov-ing ownership of the mark in question.

The courts analyze a number of variables to determine whether likeli-hood of confusion has occurred. In Federal Circuit appeals, these vari-ables are referred to as the "DuPont factors" after the case involving

E.I. DuPont DeNemours & Co. Many other courts (including appellate courts hearing cases on appeal from the various federal district courts) refer to the "Polaroid factors" after a case involving Polaroid Corp. Regardless of the factors used, they are not always entirely dispositive, and other circumstances may be considered. As a guide to understanding the breadth of issues that may be addressed in assessing likelihood of confusion, following are the 13 DuPont factors:

(1) the similarity or dissimilarity of the marks in their entireties as to appearance, sound, connotation, and commercial impression;

(2) the similarity or dissimilarity and nature of the goods or services as described in an application or registration or in connection with which a prior mark is in use;

(3) the similarity or dissimilarity of established, likely-to-continue trade channels;

(4) the conditions under which and buyers to whom sales are made, i.e., "impulse" buyers vs. careful, sophisticated purchasers;

(5) the fame of the prior mark (sales, advertising, length of use);

(6) the number and nature of similar marks in use on similar goods or services;

(7) the nature and extent of any actual confusion;

(8) the length of time during and conditions under which there has been concurrent use without evidence of actual confusion;

(9) the variety of goods or services on which a mark is or is not used;

(10) the market interface between the parties;

(11) the extent to which one party has a right to exclude others from use of its mark on the goods or services of interest;

(12) the extent of potential confusion, i.e., whether *de minimis* or substantial; and

(13) any other established fact probative of the effect of use.

The above factors illustrate that the goods or services of the parties need not be identical or even directly competitive to result in likelihood of confusion. They need only move in commerce in such a way that consumers encountering the goods or services mistakenly believe that they come from a common source. If the parties' marks are identical, however, the relationship between the goods or services of the parties may be examined less closely in finding that likelihood of confusion exists.

Of primary importance to the plaintiff seeking to prove one or more of the DuPont factors or any other factor test is to secure evidence of the consuming public's state of mind when encountering the marks at issue. This evidence is obtained in many instances through market surveys, which can range widely in price from $25,000 to $75,000 or more depending on the nature and extent of testing required in the marketplace to support the claims made in the legal proceeding.

UNFAIR COMPETITION

Consumer confusion as to the source of goods or services as set out under § 32 of the Lanham Act is not the only type of confusion that may give rise to litigation. The Lanham Act also provides for liability under § 43(a) arising from confusion as to sponsorship or affiliation. This section of the Act also addresses the requirements for false advertising claims. A particular difference between § 32 and § 43(a) is that § 43(a) does not require that the plaintiff's mark be registered. As a result, § 43(a) has become a vehicle that expansively addresses the concept of unfair competition and is frequently referred to as the federal unfair competition statute. States also have their own laws against unfair competition, and federal lawsuits often contain claims involving a violation of both federal and state unfair competition laws.

Perhaps unsurprisingly, a claim of infringement for likelihood of confusion under § 32 is likely to be accompanied by a claim under § 43(a) that a defendant's confusingly similar use of another mark suggests that the plaintiff is affiliated with, sponsors, or endorses the products or services of the defendant. Section 43(a) has also been popularly used by celebrities seeking redress for association of their name or likeness with products they have not endorsed. Moreover, this section addresses claims of false designation of origin, such as a false statement by a competitor that its goods are "made in the U.S.A." when in fact they are not. Other proscribed conduct includes making false or misleading descriptions of fact (e.g., passing off another party's product as one's own) or false or misleading representations (e.g., suggesting, without substantiating data, an attribute of one's product that is false). Further, the protections of § 43(a) have evolved to protect trade dress, provided that the trade dress is not functional and is distinctive or has acquired secondary meaning and therefore capable of serving as a source identifier.

The other conduct proscribed by § 43(a), false advertising, applies equally to making false claims about one's own product or service and about a competitor's product or service. A false advertising claim requires proof that the contested statement is either literally false (i.e., false on its face) *or* likely to confuse consumers. Proof of consumer confusion is not required when the statement is literally false, but evidence is required (in the form of consumer surveys, for instance) when the claim is literally true but still alleged to be deceptive in some way. Section 43(a) covers a wide range of advertising, both comparative (e.g., those comparing consumer preferences between brand X and brand Y in taste tests) and non-comparative advertising on a national or local level, as well as product labeling, letters, and oral representations. Not every form of advertising qualifies for redress under the Lanham Act, however. In one case, for instance, an employee's disparaging remarks about a competitor's products did not qualify as commercial advertising or promotion; in another case, dissemination of a list of a competitor's dissatisfied customers to only two people was likewise held insufficient to qualify as advertising under the Lanham Act. In summary, the context of each case is unique, and thus not all forms of commercial speech automatically qualify for redress under federal law.

DILUTION

Not all instances of alleged trademark misuse rise to the level of infringement. In other words, it cannot always be proved that consumers are likely to be confused by a conflicting mark. If the mark is sufficiently well known, however, the complained-of action may dilute the plaintiff's mark. The concept of dilution is governed by federal law as well as by those states that have adopted their own anti-dilution statutes.

The federal law of dilution initially became effective in 1996 as The Federal Trademark Dilution Act. The purpose of the law was to give trademark owners of "famous" marks the right to protect those marks against impairment of their distinctiveness regardless whether the conflicting mark is associated with the same goods or services as the famous mark. Thus the act was designed to protect against third-party uses such as NIKE computers or IBM sneakers. However, the act had its limitations. For instance, the standard of proof required by courts to determine whether dilution was proved was variously applied as either a showing of actual dilution of the mark or the mere likelihood that the third-party usage would cause dilution. That conflict was subsequently addressed in a highly-publicized 2003 decision of the U.S. Supreme Court involving the retailer Victoria's Secret, which held that the proper standard was a showing that actual dilution of the famous mark occurred. Also, given that the legislation protected against impairment of the distinctiveness of a mark, it was unclear whether relief was likewise available if the mark's reputation, rather than its distinctiveness, was harmed by the alleged conduct. Moreover, the requirement that the mark be "famous" was variously construed to mean that fame in a niche market was sufficient.

In an effort to resolve the conflicts inherent in the original law and to address the controversy related to the Supreme Court's holding that actual dilution must be proved, Congress passed the Trademark Dilution Revision Act of 2006. The new act overturns the Supreme Court's ruling that actual dilution is required to prove harm in favor of a "likelihood of dilution" standard that had been employed by many courts in the past. Therefore, plaintiffs need not prove actual harm to the economic value of a mark before relief can be granted; the mere likelihood of such harm will suffice. The act also provides relief against two forms of dilution: dilution by blurring (i.e., third-party actions that impair the value of the famous mark) and dilution by tarnishment (i.e., third-party actions that injure the reputation of the famous mark). Finally, the law clarifies that a "famous" mark is one that is generally recognized by the consuming public rather than a niche market.

COUNTERFEITING

Counterfeiting is commonly understood in the context of the sale of fakes or knock offs. As a matter of trademark law, section 45 of the Lanham Act defines a counterfeit as "a spurious mark which is identical with, or substantially indistinguishable from, a registered mark." In other words, counterfeiting is the unauthorized placement of a mark on goods or services that are manufactured, distributed, and sold to consumers as if those goods or services were the genuine article, which is likely to cause confusion, to cause mistake, or to deceive. Trafficking in counterfeit goods or services is a criminal offense subject to fines or imprisonment under the Trademark Counterfeiting Act of 1984. The government will prosecute an alleged counterfeiter provided that the affected mark is registered on the Principal Register and is used in such a way by a third party as to be indistinguishable from the authentic mark when placed in use on the same goods or services used in connection with the authentic mark. In addition to fines and imprisonment, the government may obtain an order to destroy the counterfeit articles.

In addition, civil actions for counterfeiting are provided for under § 32 of the Lanham Act, and the damages for such actions are found in § 35(c).

Section 35 originally provided that damages would be no less than $500 or more than $100,000 per counterfeit mark for each good or service infringed. If the counterfeiting was found to be willful, the damages could rise to $1 million. These amounts were recently increased with the enactment of the PRO-IP Act of 2008, providing for new figures of $1000, $200,000, and $2 million, respectively.

The economic impact of counterfeiting is staggering. According to the International Anti-Counterfeiting Coalition, a group of brand-owning companies, over $500 billion in counterfeited articles are traded internationally. Considering the economic consequences, not to mention the potential health and safety issues arising from counterfeit drugs, foods, and toys, trademark owners should avail themselves of anti-counterfeiting measures. These measures include recordation of marks on the Principal Register with U.S. Customs and the availability of trademark rights enforcement services offered by other countries.

U.S. Customs & Border Protection (CBP), a bureau of the Department of Homeland Security, maintains a trademark recordation system to assist in the global effort to prevent the importation of goods that infringe marks on the Principal Register. CBP officers monitor imports at over 300 U.S. ports of entry to prevent the importation of goods bearing counterfeit marks and can detain potentially counterfeit goods for five days upon reasonable suspicion. Filings with the CBP can be effectuated online using the Intellectual Property Rights e-Recordation (IPRR) system, located at https://apps.cbp.gov/e-recordations. Unlike electronic filings, paper filings will require the submission of a certified copy of each registration sought to be protected (available for a fee from the PTO), along with copies of supporting documents. Thus, electronic filings provide a cost savings and reduce the time from filing to enforcement by field personnel.

Other countries participating in enforcement strategies include the European Union. Specifically, customs recordation and seizure of counterfeit goods bearing recorded marks are available on a national or multi-national basis under EU legislation known as "Council Regulation (EC) No 1383/2003 concerning customs action against goods suspected of infringing certain intellectual property rights and the measures to be taken against goods found to have infringed such rights." Furthermore, China and Thailand have adopted systems of recordal of intellectual property rights with their customs authorities. Trademark owners are advised to check with local agencies of interest to determine whether an enforcement program exists to combat counterfeiting.

REMEDIES

Various remedies are available to an aggrieved trademark owner, but fundamentally, injunctive relief (provided for in § 34 of the Lanham Act) is the desired outcome for any litigation. An injunction can either order that a certain conduct stop (e.g., an order to cease the use of a mark) or order that a certain conduct be initiated (e.g., the placement of a disclaimer of sponsorship or affiliation). Injunctions can also be granted temporarily during the conduct of the litigation and permanently following a decision on the case. Section 35 of the Act provides for additional remedies such as damages, profits, costs, and, in exceptional cases, attorneys' fees to the prevailing party. However, an award of damages or profits is not guaranteed. For instance, a court may find it inequitable to award a defendant's profits to a plaintiff if the award of a permanent injunction adequately remedies the complained-of conduct. Moreover, as a practical matter it may be difficult for a plaintiff to establish monetary damages arising from the defendant's conduct, and in some districts the award of actual damages may require proof of actual confusion rather than the mere likelihood of confusion. In no event are punitive damages for infringement awarded under the Lanham Act.

DEFENSES

As in other contested proceedings such as oppositions and cancellations, defendants in civil proceedings may avail themselves of any number of defenses to their conduct. These defenses include an allegation of genericness of the mark at issue, functionality, mere descriptiveness, abandonment, fraud, laches (a legal term meaning that the plaintiff acquiesced in the complained-of conduct, such as by delaying any action), or fair use.

Fair use is a particularly notable defense because of its intersection with an individual's First Amendment right to free expression. This defense is set out at § 33(b)(4) of the Lanham Act, which indicates that a use of a mark which is charged to be an infringement is a fair use if made in a non-trademark sense in good faith. The defense typically arises in circumstances where the defendant seeks to make reference to a trademark for purposes of reporting, commentary, criticism, parody, and comparative advertising. In some cases, the use will be defensible on fair use grounds if the mark at issue is used in the context of its ordinary English meaning. For example, a radio station's use in reportage of the trademarked term BOSTON MARATHON was deemed a fair use in the context of simply covering the event. However, the success of this defense is highly dependent on the facts and circumstances of each particular case, including whether the defendant has taken the appropriate action to minimize any potential for confusion as to source, origin, sponsorship, or endorsement.

INSURANCE

Trademark litigation can reach into the hundreds of thousands of dollars. As a result, a prudent trademark owner should consider obtaining insurance coverage for intellectual property disputes. Coverage can include defense and indemnification for damages and legal expenses incurred with respect to alleged infringement of a third party's rights. Traditionally, the insurer's duty, if any, to defend or indemnify was covered under an "advertising injury" endorsement of an insured's comprehensive general liability (CGL) policy. Advertising injury is typically enumerated as that arising out of libel, slander, defamation, violation of privacy rights, copyright infringement, and misappropriation of advertising ideas. Whether misappropriation of advertising ideas encompasses claims of unfair competition, trade dress or trademark infringement triggering coverage under a CGL policy is itself a common matter of contention, and insurers are increasingly amending coverage under CGL policies to exclude infringement claims altogether. Therefore, potential insureds should read a CGL policy carefully to determine whether it refers to these claims either in defining advertising injury or in stating exclusions from coverage.

In recent years, a new type of policy known as a "cyber policy" has emerged. As the name implies, these policies address cyber risks such as those arising from a security breach that compromises the storage of sensitive information. However, this coverage is not limited to computer-related loss or failure; many policies explicitly cover infringement claims and can be crafted to suit the buyer's needs. As a result, insureds have greater opportunities to find adequate cover against trademark-related disputes.

CHAPTER 7:
INTERNET ISSUES REGARDING
TRADEMARKS

TRADEMARKS ON THE INTERNET

The advent of the Internet gave rise to several trademark-related issues, particularly the registrability of domain names as trademarks. According to PTO policy, so long as the domain name functions as an indication of source (rather than strictly as an Internet address), then the domain name is registrable as a trademark. In this regard, the registrable matter is the second-level domain. For instance, in the example www.abc.com, "abc" is the second level domain, "www" refers to the World Wide Web, and ".com" is known as a top-level domain (TLD). Of course, second-level domains are subject to the same procedural requirements and scrutiny as any other mark with regard to their registrability and will be subject to refusal for mere descriptiveness, primarily, merely a surname, likelihood of confusion, genericness, or any other ground for refusal as discussed in Chapter 3, "The PTO Trademark Application Process," of this Almanac.

POLICING TRADEMARKS ON THE INTERNET

It is not uncommon for a registered domain name to be at odds with pre-existing trademark rights. As a consequence, it is incumbent on trademark owners to monitor the Internet for any instances of potential confusion. Such monitoring can be accomplished by engaging the services of a professional search company (as addressed in Chapter 3, "The PTO Trademark Application Process," of this Almanac) to scour the Internet for any use of the trademarked terms under watch or by using a common search engine such as Google to search for terms that are being used in an unauthorized manner. Trademark owners who place trademarked goods or services for sale on e-commerce sites should be especially vigilant. In fact, a federal district court in New York recently concluded that trademark owners cannot delegate their burden of ensuring that trademark rights are not being violated to e-commerce service providers. However, in recognition of their own duties to merchants who choose to do business with them, many e-commerce providers (such as eBay) have adopted extensive intellectual property rights policies and mechanisms for reporting suspected infringements.

Many trademark owners fulfill the duty to protect their rights by undertaking a program of domain name registration to thwart infringing uses of trademarks. Such a program typically includes filing a domain name registration for relevant marks under one or more of the following TLDs, to name a few: *.com*, *.biz*, *.net*, *.us*, or. *info*. Generally, a trademark owner is well advised to register key marks with TLDs likely to be used by consumers in seeking out the goods or services of the owner. These registrations may also include misspelled versions of key marks, plural or singular versions as appropriate, and registration in other countries (using the country's TLD, such as. *uk* for the United Kingdom) where the trademark owner has interests. However, potential registrants should note that some countries, such as Portugal, allow domain names to be registered and owned only by local entities. In other cases, such as France, only the company name can be registered as a domain for purposes of using the country extension "*.fr*." Trademark owners are advised to consult with local counsel in countries of interest for current domain name registration requirements.

ENFORCEMENT ACTIONS FOR TRADEMARKS ON THE INTERNET

In General

Internet-related trademark disputes can arise from several scenarios. For instance, a third party may use a trademark in the text of a Web site page, or in a link, or in a frame (appearing as a screen within a screen) in an unauthorized manner. Also, the complained-of conduct may involve use of a trademark in a metatag. A metatag refers to information embedded into the source code underlying a Web site that is designed to allow search engines such as Google to find and index the site on the Internet. Web site owners using metatags will saturate the code of their site with trademarks in an effort to have search engines list their sites first with respect to those terms. Sometimes, unscrupulous Web site owners may adopt third-party marks in their own metatags in an effort to get a higher listing than a competitor with respect to the relevant goods or services offered by the merchant. Of all the circumstances giving rise to Internet-related disputes, however, one scenario that is increasingly common is cybersquatting, or the use of a domain name designed to mimic that of a trademark owner. Cybersquatters often use misspellings of trademarks as their domain name in an effort to attract site visitors for purposes of counterfeiting or to gain advertising revenue from visitors who click through the bogus site. One recent report indicates that cybersquatting activity is the most perpetrated form of abuse against brand owners.

Given its prevalence, this chapter will address the following actions that may be taken with respect to cybersquatting: (i) self-help measures such as offers to purchase offending domain names or the issuance of a demand letter; (ii) arbitration; and (iii) litigation.

Self-Help Measures to Deal with Domain Name Disputes

As discussed in Chapter 6, "Infringement Issues," of this Almanac, at times a trademark owner may determine that the best method of dealing with an infringer is to proceed initially with a demand letter. Another self-help alternative is to negotiate a sale of the offending domain name. However, cybersquatters often demand large sums for the transfer of a domain name, particularly if it is related to a trademark having widespread fame or notoriety in a niche market. In lesser circumstances, the cost of adjudicating a dispute in arbitration or in court may far exceed the price demanded by the cybersquatter. Trademark owners seeking to use self-help measures to address cybersquatting should weigh the costs and benefits of this approach against the other measures discussed below.

Arbitration Proceedings Generally

Domain name disputes may be resolved through arbitration by qualifying agencies. A qualifying agency is one that subscribes to the Uniform Domain Name Dispute Resolution Policy (UDRP), a set of procedures administered by ICANN. ICANN (Internet Corporation for Assigned Names and Numbers) is a not-for-profit public-benefit corporation responsible for coordinating various activities concerning the overall operation of the Internet. ICANN's activities include the consideration and adoption of new TLDs, the accreditation of domain name registrars, and the administration of its UDRP. WIPO is an example of a qualifying agency. Like other agencies, WIPO also has its own supplemental rules to the UDRP to be observed in the course of an arbitration.

Arguably, WIPO is the world leader in resolving domain name disputes under the UDRP, and its procedures for arbitrating these disputes will be discussed in this chapter. Appendix 31, "Uniform Dispute Resolution

Policy," Appendix 32, "Rules Implementing Domain Name Dispute Resolution Policy," and Appendix 33, "Supplemental Rules of WIPO for Uniform Domain Name Dispute Resolution Policy," of this Almanac contain the UDRP, the rules implementing the UDRP, and the supplemental rules administered by WIPO, respectively.

WIPO Domain Name Dispute Resolution

The first step in addressing a cybersquatting issue before WIPO is to file a complaint, which can be filed online via http://www.wipo.int/amc/en/domains/filing/udrp/complaint.html. Complainants wishing to file via mail, and defendants (respondents) wishing to respond via mail will find sample forms on WIPO's site as well. Those samples are likewise annexed in Appendices 34, "Domain Name Complaint," and 35, "Response to Domain Name Complaint," of this Almanac.

The complainant is required to serve the complaint on the respondent as well as on the domain name registrar responsible for registering the domain name. In each case, the Complaint Transmittal Coversheet accompanying the sample complaint must be attached.

The complainant is also required to select the number of arbitrators that will hear the case—either a single arbitrator or a panel of three—from the list of qualified arbitrators maintained by ICANN. The fees of a single arbitrator are payable by the complainant; if a panel is selected by the respondent, then the fees will be split between the parties. In all other instances, the complainant is responsible for transmitting the appropriate fees to WIPO. A current list of fees is located at http://www.wipo.int/amc/en/arbitration/fees/index.html.

A successful outcome depends on the complainant's ability to prove three factors: (i) the domain name is identical or confusingly similar to a trademark or service mark in which the complainant has rights; (ii) the respondent has no rights or legitimate interests in the domain name; and (iii) the domain name has been registered and is being used in bad faith. Some of the factors that may indicate bad faith in the use of the domain name include registering the name for the purpose of selling or leasing it back to the trademark holder, registration with the intent of preventing the holder of trademark rights to the name from obtaining it, disrupting a competitor's business, or attempting to divert customers of another business. In some cases, WIPO panels have found bad faith if the owner of the domain name failed to conduct a proper trademark search of the term prior to registering it.

Conversely, the respondent will need to demonstrate a lack of evidence with respect to the above factors in its response, which is due within

20 days following receipt of the complaint. Specifically, some of the factors that may indicate a legitimate interest in the domain name include a bona fide offering of goods or services under the domain name, the respondent's notoriety in connection with the domain name, or a genuine noncommercial use of the domain name without an intent to disrupt the financial gain of others.

If the complainant is successful in proving its case, then WIPO is empowered to order the registrar to transfer the domain name at issue or to cancel it. It should be noted that proceedings under the UDRP do not result in an award of monetary damages or other remedies other than the transfer or cancellation of the domain name. In the event that such other remedies are desired, the complainant should proceed to file a complaint in federal court as provided for in the subsection below. In any event, the UDRP process does not prohibit one party or the other from litigating the domain name dispute in court, particularly if a losing respondent seeks a declaration that the respondent is not in violation of federal trademark law or seeks a reinstatement of the domain name.

Domain Name Litigation

As indicated above, domain names can be contested in federal court in lieu of, or in addition to, a UDRP proceeding. Claims made in federal court may include any of the grounds discussed in Chapter 6, "Infringement Issues," of this Almanac—namely, infringement, dilution, or § 43(a) violations. Moreover, a domain name registrant may be found liable as a result of an action brought by the Federal Trade Commission for unfair and deceptive trade practices. Trademark owners may also have the option to file an action under the Anticybersquatting Consumer Protection Act (ACPA), signed into law on November 29, 1999 by President Clinton. The features of this popular vehicle for redress of cybersquatting are discussed below.

The Anticybersquatting Consumer Protection Act

The ACPA is embodied in § 43(d) of the Lanham Act. It creates a cause of action against a domain name registrant who, in bad faith, intends to profit from a distinctive or famous mark or the name of a living person by registering a domain name that is identical or confusingly similar and, in the case of a famous mark, dilutive.

Similar to UDRP proceedings, a plaintiff must show defendant's bad faith intent with respect to the domain name, and the factors considered in UDRP proceedings to determine bad faith are likewise applicable to ACPA actions. Also, like UDRP proceedings, the domain name at issue can be either identical or similar to the conflicting mark.

Dissimilar to UDRP actions, the mere act of registering the domain name is cause for relief as the ACPA provides a civil remedy against a person who *"registers*, traffics in, *or* uses " a domain name. Therefore, bad faith need only be proved in the registration rather than in the use of the domain name at issue. Also, remedies under the ACPA include damages that would normally be available in trademark disputes as well as the forfeiture, cancellation, or transfer of the disputed domain name. Additionally, the ACPA allows the plaintiff to select statutory damages in lieu of actual damages per domain name at issue. Those amounts, as determined in the court's discretion, can range from an amount no less than $1000 and no more than $100,000.

Two distinctive features of the ACPA are the ability to proceed against the domain name itself and the ability to sue for use of one's own name as a domain name. In some instances, a plaintiff may have no choice but to proceed against the domain name rather than the person(s) committing the act of registering, trafficking in, or using it. This scenario is particularly common in cases where the registrant cannot be located or the true identity of the domain name owner has been secreted. In such an event, the ACPA provides that a plaintiff may bring suit against the property at issue—the domain name—rather than the person. Such an action is known as an *in rem* proceeding. However, in such actions, the remedy is limited to forfeiture, cancellation, or transfer of the domain name. The other feature of the ACPA, bringing action against use of an identical or confusingly similar personal name, is a means for individuals to seek redress for attempted profiteering related to a personal name although the statutory damages mentioned above are not available.

In any action taken under the ACPA, the defendant is not precluded from asserting defenses such as fair use. In fact, the law provides that bad faith will not be inferred in the event that the defendant believed and had reasonable grounds to believe that the use was a fair use or otherwise lawful (e.g., permitted under the First Amendment).

Appendix 36, "Anticybersquatting Consumer Protection Act," of this Almanac sets forth the ACPA and provisions concerning statutory damages.

APPENDIX 1:
DEFINITION OF TRADEMARK, SERVICE MARK, CERTIFICATION MARK, AND COLLECTIVE MARK

Excerpt from § 45 of the Lanham Act [15 U.S.C. § 1127]:

The term "trademark" includes any word, name, symbol, or device, or any combination thereof—

(1) used by a person, or

(2) which a person has a bona fide intention to use in commerce and applies to register on the principal register established by this chapter,

to identify and distinguish his or her goods, including a unique product, from those manufactured or sold by others and to indicate the source of the goods, even if that source is unknown.

The term "service mark" means any word, name, symbol, or device, or any combination thereof—

(1) used by a person, or

(2) which a person has a bona fide intention to use in commerce and applies to register on the principal register established by this chapter,

to identify and distinguish the services of one person, including a unique service, from the services of others and to indicate the source of the services, even if that source is unknown. Titles, character names, and other distinctive features of radio or television programs may be registered as service marks notwithstanding that they, or the programs, may advertise the goods of the sponsor.

The term "certification mark" means any word, name, symbol, or device, or any combination thereof—

(1) used by a person other than its owner, or

(2) which its owner has a bona fide intention to permit a person other than the owner to use in commerce and files an application to register on the principal register established by this chapter,

to certify regional or other origin, material, mode of manufacture, quality, accuracy, or other characteristics of such person's goods or services or that the work or labor on the goods or services was performed by members of a union or other organization.

The term "collective mark" means a trademark or service mark—

(1) used by the members of a cooperative, an association, or other collective group or organization, or

(2) which such cooperative, association, or other collective group or organization has a bona fide intention to use in commerce and applies to register on the principal register established by this chapter,

and includes marks indicating membership in a union, an association, or other organization.

APPENDIX 2:
STATE TRADEMARK OFFICES

Alabama
Secretary of State
Land & Trademarks Division
P.O. Box 5616
Montgomery AL 36103-5616
Phone: (334) 242-5325

Alaska
Secretary of State
Division of Banking
Securities & Corporations
P.O. Box 110808
Juneau AK 918891
Phone: (907) 465-2530

Arizona
Secretary of State
1700 W. Washington, 7th Floor
Phoenix AZ 85007
Phone: (602) 542-6187

Arkansas
Secretary of State
Aegon Building
501 Woodlane, Suite 310
Little Rock AR 72201
Phone: (501) 682-3409

California
Secretary of State
Trademarks/Service Marks
1500 11th St.
Sacramento CA 95814

Colorado
Secretary of State
Business Division
1560 Broadway, Suite 200
Denver CO 80202
Phone: (303) 894-2251

Connecticut
Secretary of State
30 Trinity St.
P.O. Box 150470
Hartford CT 06106
Phone: (860) 509-6004

Delaware
Secretary of State
Division of Corporations
P.O. Box 898
Dover DE 19903
Phone: (302) 739-3073

Florida
Secretary of State
Division of Corporations
P.O. Box 6327
Tallahassee FL 32314
Phone: (850) 487-6051

Georgia
Secretary of State
Corporations Division
315 West Tower
#2 Martin Luther King, Jr. Drive
Atlanta GA 30334
Phone: (404) 656-2861

Hawaii
Secretary of State
Business Registration
P.O. Box 40
Honolulu HI 96810
Phone: (808) 586-2727

Idaho
Secretary of State
700 W. Jefferson St., Room 203
Boise ID 83720-0080
Phone: (208) 334-2300

Illinois
Secretary of State
Business Services
69 W. Washington, Suite 1240
Chicago IL 60602
Phone: 1-800-252-8980

Indiana
Secretary of State
Business Services
302 W. Washington, Room E-108
Indianapolis IN 46204
Phone: (317) 232-6540

Iowa
Secretary of State
State House
Des Moines IA 50319
Phone: (515) 281-5865

Kansas
Secretary of State
Memorial Hall
120 S.W. 10th Ave.
Topeka KS 66612-1594
Phone: (785) 296-4564

Kentucky
Secretary of State
Trademarks/Service Marks
Room 86
State Capitol
Frankfort KY 40601
Phone: (502) 564-2848

Louisiana
Secretary of State
Corporations Division
P.O. Box 94125
Baton Rouge LA 70804-9125
Phone: (225) 925-4704

Maine
Secretary of State
Bureau of Corporations,
Elections & Commissions
101 State House Station
Augusta ME 04333-0101
Phone: (207) 624-7740

Massachusetts
Secretary of The Commonwealth
Corporations Division
1 Ashburton Place, 17th Floor
Boston MA 02108
Phone: (617) 727-9640

Michigan
Bureau of Commercial
Services
Corporations Division
7510 Harris Drive
Lansing MI 48910
Phone: (517) 241-6400

Minnesota
Secretary of State
180 State Office Building
St. Paul MN 55155
Phone: (651) 296-2803

Mississippi
Secretary of State
P.O. Box 136
Jackson MS 39205
Phone: (601) 359-1633

Missouri
Secretary of State
600 W. Main and 208
State Capitol
P.O. Box 778
Jefferson City MO 65102
Phone: (573) 751-4936

Montana
Secretary of State
P.O. Box 202801
Helena MT 59620-2801
Phone: (406) 444-2034

Nebraska
Secretary of State
Corporations Division
Room 1305
State Capitol
P.O. Box 94608
Lincoln NE 68509-4608
Phone: (402) 471-4079

Nevada
Secretary of State-Annex
Commercial Recordings
202 North Carson St.
Carson City NV 89701-4271
Phone: (775) 684-5708

New Hampshire
Department of State
Corporation Division
State House, Room 204
Concord NH 03301
Phone: (603) 271-3244

New Jersey
Division of Revenue
TM/SM Unit
P.O. Box 453
Trenton NJ 08625
Phone: (609) 292-9292

New Mexico
Secretary of State
Operations Division
State Capitol North Annex,
Suite 300
Santa FE NM 87503
Phone: (505) 827-3600

New York
Secretary of State
Division of Corporations
State Records & Uniform
Commercial Code
41 State St.
Albany NY 12231-0001
Phone: (518) 473-2492

North Carolina
Secretary of State
Trademarks Section
P.O. Box 29622
Raleigh NC 27626-0622
Phone: (919) 807-2162

North Dakota

Secretary of State
600 E. Boulevard Ave., Dept. 108
Bismarck ND 58505-0500
Phone: (701) 328-4284

Ohio

Secretary of State
P.O. Box 1028
Columbus OH 43216

Oklahoma

Secretary of State
Business Services Division
2300 N. Lincoln Blvd., Room 101
Oklahoma City OK 73105-4897
Phone: (405) 522-3043

Oregon

Secretary of State
Corporation Division
Business Registry Section
Public Service Building
255 Capitol St. NE
Salem OR 97310-1327
Phone: (503) 986-2200

Pennsylvania

Department of State
P.O. Box 8721
Harrisburg PA 17105-8722
Phone: (717) 787-1057

Rhode Island

Secretary of State
Trademark Section
100 North Main St.
Providence RI 02903-1335
Phone: (401) 222-1487

South Carolina

Secretary of State
P.O. Box 11350
Columbia SC 29211
Phone: (803) 734-1728

South Dakota

Secretary of State
Capitol Building
500 East Capitol Avenue,
Suite 204
Pierre SD 57501-5070
Phone: (605) 773-5666

Tennessee

Department of State
Division of Business Services
312 Eighth Avenue North,
6th Floor
William R. Snodgrass Tower
Nashville TN 37243
Phone: (615) 741-0531

Texas

Secretary of State
Corporations Division
P.O. Box 13697
Austin TX 78711

Utah

Department of Commerce
Division of Corporations &
Commercial Code
160 E. 300 S
Salt Lake City UT 84111
Phone: (801) 530-4849

Vermont
Secretary of State
Corporations Division
81 River St., Drawer 09
Montipelier VT 05609-1104
Phone: (802) 828-2386

Virginia
State Corporation Commission
Virginia Securities Division
P.O. Box 1197
Richmond VA 23218
Phone: (804) 371-9187

Washington
Secretary of State
Corporations Division
801 Capitol Way S.
P.O. Box 40234
Olympia WA 98504-0234
Phone: (360) 753-7115

West Virginia
Secretary of State
Corporations Division
Building 1 Suite 157-k
1900 Kanawha Blvd. East
Charleston WV 25305-0770
Phone: (304) 558-8000

Wisconsin
Secretary of State
P.O. Box 7848
Madison WI 53707-7848
Phone: (608) 266-5653

Wyoming
Secretary of State
State Capitol Building
Cheyenne WY 82002
Phone: (307) 777-7378

APPENDIX 3:
IMPERMISSIBLE MARKS

Excerpt from § *2 of the Lanham Act* [15 U.S.C. § 1052]:

No trademark by which the goods of the applicant may be distinguished from the goods of others shall be refused registration on the principal register on account of its nature unless it—

(a) Consists of or comprises immoral, deceptive, or scandalous matter; or matter which may disparage or falsely suggest a connection with persons, living or dead, institutions, beliefs, or national symbols, or bring them into contempt, or disrepute; or a geographical indication which, when used on or in connection with wines or spirits, identifies a place other than the origin of the goods and is first used on or in connection with wines or spirits by the applicant on or after one year after the date on which the WTO Agreement enters into force with respect to the United States.

(b) Consists of or comprises the flag or coat of arms or other insignia of the United States, or of any State or municipality, or of any foreign nation, or any simulation thereof.

(c) Consists of or comprises a name, portrait, or signature identifying a particular living individual except by his written consent, or the name, signature, or portrait of a deceased President of the United States during the life of his widow, if any, except by the written consent of the widow.

(d) Consists of or comprises a mark which so resembles a mark registered in the Patent and Trademark Office, or a mark or trade name previously used in the United States by another and not abandoned, as to be likely, when used on or in connection with the goods of the applicant, to cause confusion, or to cause mistake, or to deceive: Provided, That if the Director determines that confusion, mistake, or deception is not likely to result from the continued use by more than one person of the same or similar marks under conditions and limitations as to the mode or place of use of the marks or the goods on or in connection with which such marks are used, concurrent registrations may be issued to such persons when they have become entitled to use such marks as a result of their concurrent lawful use in commerce prior to

(1) the earliest of the filing dates of the applications pending or of any registration issued under this chapter;

(2) July 5, 1947, in the case of registrations previously issued under the Act of March 3, 1881, or February 20, 1905, and continuing in full force and effect on that date; or

(3) July 5, 1947, in the case of applications filed under the Act of February 20, 1905, and registered after July 5, 1947. Use prior to the filing date of any pending application or a registration shall not be required when the owner of such application or registration consents to the grant of a concurrent registration to the applicant. Concurrent registrations may also be issued by the Director when a court of competent jurisdiction has finally determined that more than one person is entitled to use the same or similar marks in commerce. In issuing concurrent registrations, the Director shall prescribe conditions and limitations as to the mode or place of use of the mark or the goods on or in connection with which such mark is registered to the respective persons.

(e) Consists of a mark which

. . .

(3) when used on or in connection with the goods of the applicant is primarily geographically deceptively misdescriptive of them,

. . . or

(5) comprises any matter that, as a whole, is functional.

APPENDIX 4:
SIGNATORIES TO THE PARIS CONVENTION

CONTRACTING PARTY	TREATY	STATUS	ENTRY INTO FORCE
Albania	Paris Convention	In Force	October 4, 1995
Algeria	Paris Convention	In Force	March 1, 1966
Andorra	Paris Convention	In Force	June 2, 2004
Angola	Paris Convention	In Force	December 27, 2007
Antigua and Barbuda	Paris Convention	In Force	March 17, 2000
Argentina	Paris Convention	In Force	February 10, 1967
Armenia	Paris Convention	In Force	December 25, 1991
Australia	Paris Convention	In Force	October 10, 1925
Austria	Paris Convention	In Force	January 1, 1909
Azerbaijan	Paris Convention	In Force	December 25, 1995
Bahamas	Paris Convention	In Force	July 10, 1973
Bahrain	Paris Convention	In Force	October 29, 1997
Bangladesh	Paris Convention	In Force	March 3, 1991
Barbados	Paris Convention	In Force	March 12, 1985
Belarus	Paris Convention	In Force	December 25, 1991
Belgium	Paris Convention	In Force	July 7, 1884
Belize	Paris Convention	In Force	June 17, 2000
Benin	Paris Convention	In Force	January 10, 1967
Bhutan	Paris Convention	In Force	August 4, 2000
Bolivia	Paris Convention	In Force	November 4, 1993
Bosnia and Herzegovina	Paris Convention	In Force	March 1, 1992
Botswana	Paris Convention	In Force	April 15, 1998

CONTRACTING PARTY	TREATY	STATUS	ENTRY INTO FORCE
Brazil	Paris Convention	In Force	July 7, 1884
Bulgaria	Paris Convention	In Force	June 13, 1921
Burkina Faso	Paris Convention	In Force	November 19, 1963
Burundi	Paris Convention	In Force	September 3, 1977
Cambodia	Paris Convention	In Force	September 22, 1998
Cameroon	Paris Convention	In Force	May 10, 1964
Canada	Paris Convention	In Force	June 12, 1925
Central African Republic	Paris Convention	In Force	November 19, 1963
Chad	Paris Convention	In Force	November 19, 1963
Chile	Paris Convention	In Force	June 14, 1991
China	Paris Convention	In Force	March 19, 1985
Colombia	Paris Convention	In Force	September 3, 1996
Comoros	Paris Convention	In Force	April 3, 2005
Congo	Paris Convention	In Force	September 2, 1963
Costa Rica	Paris Convention	In Force	October 31, 1995
Côte d'Ivoire	Paris Convention	In Force	October 23, 1963
Croatia	Paris Convention	In Force	October 8, 1991
Cuba	Paris Convention	In Force	November 17, 1904
Cyprus	Paris Convention	In Force	January 17, 1966
Czech Republic	Paris Convention	In Force	January 1, 1993
Democratic People's Republic of Korea	Paris Convention	In Force	June 10, 1980
Democratic Republic of the Congo	Paris Convention	In Force	January 31, 1975
Denmark	Paris Convention	In Force	October 1, 1894
Djibouti	Paris Convention	In Force	May 13, 2002
Dominica	Paris Convention	In Force	August 7, 1999
Dominican Republic	Paris Convention	In Force	July 11, 1890
Ecuador	Paris Convention	In Force	June 22, 1999
Egypt	Paris Convention	In Force	July 1, 1951
El Salvador	Paris Convention	In Force	February 19, 1994
Equatorial Guinea	Paris Convention	In Force	June 26, 1997
Estonia	Paris Convention	In Force	August 24, 1994
Finland	Paris Convention	In Force	September 20, 1921
France	Paris Convention	In Force	July 7, 1884
Gabon	Paris Convention	In Force	February 29, 1964
Gambia	Paris Convention	In Force	January 21, 1992

CONTRACTING PARTY	TREATY	STATUS	ENTRY INTO FORCE
Georgia	Paris Convention	In Force	December 25, 1991
Germany	Paris Convention	In Force	May 1, 1903
Ghana	Paris Convention	In Force	September 28, 1976
Greece	Paris Convention	In Force	October 2, 1924
Grenada	Paris Convention	In Force	September 22, 1998
Guatemala	Paris Convention	In Force	August 18, 1998
Guinea	Paris Convention	In Force	February 5, 1982
Guinea-Bissau	Paris Convention	In Force	June 28, 1988
Guyana	Paris Convention	In Force	October 25, 1994
Haiti	Paris Convention	In Force	July 1, 1958
Holy See	Paris Convention	In Force	September 29, 1960
Honduras	Paris Convention	In Force	February 4, 1994
Hungary	Paris Convention	In Force	January 1, 1909
Iceland	Paris Convention	In Force	May 5, 1962
India	Paris Convention	In Force	December 7, 1998
Indonesia	Paris Convention	In Force	December 24, 1950
Iran (Islamic Republic of)	Paris Convention	In Force	December 16, 1959
Iraq	Paris Convention	In Force	January 24, 1976
Ireland	Paris Convention	In Force	December 4, 1925
Israel	Paris Convention	In Force	March 24, 1950
Italy	Paris Convention	In Force	July 7, 1884
Jamaica	Paris Convention	In Force	December 24, 1999
Japan	Paris Convention	In Force	July 15, 1899
Jordan	Paris Convention	In Force	July 17, 1972
Kazakhstan	Paris Convention	In Force	December 25, 1991
Kenya	Paris Convention	In Force	June 14, 1965
Kyrgyzstan	Paris Convention	In Force	December 25, 1991
Lao People's Democratic Republic	Paris Convention	In Force	October 8, 1998
Latvia	Paris Convention	In Force	September 7, 1993
Lebanon	Paris Convention	In Force	September 1, 1924
Lesotho	Paris Convention	In Force	September 28, 1989
Liberia	Paris Convention	In Force	August 27, 1994
Libyan Arab Jamahiriya	Paris Convention	In Force	September 28, 1976
Liechtenstein	Paris Convention	In Force	July 14, 1933
Lithuania	Paris Convention	In Force	May 22, 1994
Luxembourg	Paris Convention	In Force	June 30, 1922

CONTRACTING PARTY	TREATY	STATUS	ENTRY INTO FORCE
Madagascar	Paris Convention	In Force	December 21, 1963
Malawi	Paris Convention	In Force	July 6, 1964
Malaysia	Paris Convention	In Force	January 1, 1989
Mali	Paris Convention	In Force	March 1, 1983
Malta	Paris Convention	In Force	October 20, 1967
Mauritania	Paris Convention	In Force	April 11, 1965
Mauritius	Paris Convention	In Force	September 24, 1976
Mexico	Paris Convention	In Force	September 7, 1903
Monaco	Paris Convention	In Force	April 29, 1956
Mongolia	Paris Convention	In Force	April 21, 1985
Montenegro	Paris Convention	In Force	June 3, 2006
Morocco	Paris Convention	In Force	July 30, 1917
Mozambique	Paris Convention	In Force	July 9, 1998
Namibia	Paris Convention	In Force	January 1, 2004
Nepal	Paris Convention	In Force	June 22, 2001
Netherlands	Paris Convention	In Force	July 7, 1884
New Zealand	Paris Convention	In Force	July 29, 1931
Nicaragua	Paris Convention	In Force	July 3, 1996
Niger	Paris Convention	In Force	July 5, 1964
Nigeria	Paris Convention	In Force	September 2, 1963
Norway	Paris Convention	In Force	July 1, 1885
Oman	Paris Convention	In Force	July 14, 1999
Pakistan	Paris Convention	In Force	July 22, 2004
Panama	Paris Convention	In Force	October 19, 1996
Papua New Guinea	Paris Convention	In Force	June 15, 1999
Paraguay	Paris Convention	In Force	May 28, 1994
Peru	Paris Convention	In Force	April 11, 1995
Philippines	Paris Convention	In Force	September 27, 1965
Poland	Paris Convention	In Force	November 10, 1919
Portugal	Paris Convention	In Force	July 7, 1884
Qatar	Paris Convention	In Force	July 5, 2000
Republic of Korea	Paris Convention	In Force	May 4, 1980
Republic of Moldova	Paris Convention	In Force	December 25, 1991
Romania	Paris Convention	In Force	October 6, 1920
Russian Federation	Paris Convention	In Force	July 1, 1965
Rwanda	Paris Convention	In Force	March 1, 1984
Saint Kitts and Nevis	Paris Convention	In Force	April 9, 1995
Saint Lucia	Paris Convention	In Force	June 9, 1995

CONTRACTING PARTY	TREATY	STATUS	ENTRY INTO FORCE
Saint Vincent and the Grenadines	Paris Convention	In Force	August 29, 1995
San Marino	Paris Convention	In Force	March 4, 1960
Sao Tome and Principe	Paris Convention	In Force	May 12, 1998
Saudi Arabia	Paris Convention	In Force	March 11, 2004
Senegal	Paris Convention	In Force	December 21, 1963
Serbia	Paris Convention	In Force	April 27, 1992
Seychelles	Paris Convention	In Force	November 7, 2002
Sierra Leone	Paris Convention	In Force	June 17, 1997
Singapore	Paris Convention	In Force	February 23, 1995
Slovakia	Paris Convention	In Force	January 1, 1993
Slovenia	Paris Convention	In Force	June 25, 1991
South Africa	Paris Convention	In Force	December 1, 1947
Spain	Paris Convention	In Force	July 7, 1884
Sri Lanka	Paris Convention	In Force	December 29, 1952
Sudan	Paris Convention	In Force	April 16, 1984
Suriname	Paris Convention	In Force	November 25, 1975
Swaziland	Paris Convention	In Force	May 12, 1991
Sweden	Paris Convention	In Force	July 1, 1885
Switzerland	Paris Convention	In Force	July 7, 1884
Syrian Arab Republic	Paris Convention	In Force	September 1, 1924
Tajikistan	Paris Convention	In Force	December 25, 1991
Thailand	Paris Convention	In Force	August 2, 2008
The former Yugoslav Republic of Macedonia	Paris Convention	In Force	September 8, 1991
Togo	Paris Convention	In Force	September 10, 1967
Tonga	Paris Convention	In Force	June 14, 2001
Trinidad and Tobago	Paris Convention	In Force	August 1, 1964
Tunisia	Paris Convention	In Force	July 7, 1884
Turkey	Paris Convention	In Force	October 10, 1925
Turkmenistan	Paris Convention	In Force	December 25, 1991
Uganda	Paris Convention	In Force	June 14, 1965
Ukraine	Paris Convention	In Force	December 25, 1991
United Arab Emirates	Paris Convention	In Force	September 19, 1996
United Kingdom	Paris Convention	In Force	July 7, 1884
United Republic of Tanzania	Paris Convention	In Force	June 16, 1963

CONTRACTING PARTY	TREATY	STATUS	ENTRY INTO FORCE
United States of America	Paris Convention	In Force	May 30, 1887
Uruguay	Paris Convention	In Force	March 18, 1967
Uzbekistan	Paris Convention	In Force	December 25, 1991
Venezuela (Bolivarian Republic of)	Paris Convention	In Force	September 12, 1995
Viet Nam	Paris Convention	In Force	March 8, 1949
Yemen	Paris Convention	In Force	February 15, 2007
Zambia	Paris Convention	In Force	April 6, 1965
Zimbabwe	Paris Convention	In Force	April 18, 1980

APPENDIX 5:
DEFINITION OF "USE IN COMMERCE"

Excerpt from § *45 of the Lanham Act* [15 U.S.C. § 1127]:

The term "use in commerce" means the bona fide use of a mark in the ordinary course of trade, and not made merely to reserve a right in a mark. For purposes of this chapter, a mark shall be deemed to be in use in commerce—

(1) on goods when—

(A) it is placed in any manner on the goods or their containers or the displays associated therewith or on the tags or labels affixed thereto, or if the nature of the goods makes such placement impracticable, then on documents associated with the goods or their sale, and

(B) the goods are sold or transported in commerce, and

(2) on services when it is used or displayed in the sale or advertising of services and the services are rendered in commerce, or the services are rendered in more than one State or in the United States and a foreign country and the person rendering the services is engaged in commerce in connection with the services.

APPENDIX 6:
STATUTORY REFERENCES TO THE
SUPPLEMENTAL REGISTER

Excerpt from §§ *23 to 28 of the Lanham Act* [15 U.S.C. §§ 1091–1096]:

Section 23:

(a) Marks registerable

In addition to the principal register, the Director shall keep a continuation of the register provided in paragraph (b) of section 1 of the Act of March 19, 1920, entitled "An Act to give effect to certain provisions of the convention for the protection of trademarks and commercial names, made and signed in the city of Buenos Aires, in the Argentine Republic, August 20, 1910, and for other purposes," to be called the supplemental register. All marks capable of distinguishing applicant's goods o r services and not registrable on the principal register provided in this chapter, except those declared to be unregistrable under subsections (a), (b), (c), (d), and (e)(3) of section 1052 of this title, which are in law ful use in commerce by the owner thereof, on or in connection with any goods or services may be registered on the supplemental register upon the payment of the prescribed fee and compliance with the provisions of subsections (a) and (e) of section 1051 of this title so far as they are applicable. Nothing in this section shall prevent the registration on the supplemental register of a mark, capable of distinguishing the applicant's goods or services and not registrable on the principal register under this chapter, that is declared to be unregistrable under section 1052 (e)(3) of this title, if such mark has been in lawful use in commerce by the owner thereof, on or in connection with any goods or services, since before December 8, 1993.

(b) Application and proceedings for registration

Upon the filing of an application for registration on the supplemental register and payment of the prescribed fee the Director shall refer the application to the examiner in charge of the registration of marks, who shall cause an examination to be made and if on such examination it shall appear that the applicant is entitled to registration, the registration shall be granted. If the applicant is found not entitled to registration the provisions of subsection (b) of section 1062 of this title shall apply.

(c) Nature of mark

For the purposes of registration on the supplemental register, a mark may consist of any trademark, symbol, label, package, configuration of goods, name, word, slogan, phrase, surname, geographical name, numeral, device, any matter that as a whole is not functional, or any combination of any of the foregoing, but such mark must be capable of distinguishing the applicant's goods or services.

Section 24:

Marks for the supplemental register shall not be published for or be subject to opposition, but shall be published on registration in the Official Gazette of the Patent and Trademark Office. Whenever any person believes that such person is or will be damaged by the registration of a mark on the supplemental register—

(1) for which the effective filing date is after the date on which such person's mark became famous and which would be likely to cause dilution by blurring or dilution by tarnishment under section 1125 (c) of this title; or

(2) on grounds other than dilution by blurring or dilution by tarnishment,

such person may at any time, upon payment of the prescribed fee and the filing of a petition stating the ground therefor, apply to the Director to cancel such registration. The Director shall refer such application to the Trademark Trial and Appeal Board which shall give notice thereof to the registrant. If it is found after a hearing before the Board that the registrant is not entitled to registration, or that the mark has been abandoned, the registration shall be canceled by the Director. However, no final judgment shall be entered in favor of an applicant under section 1051 (b) of this title before the mark is registered, if such applicant cannot prevail without establishing constructive use pursuant to section 1057 (c) of this title.

Section 25:

The certificates of registration for marks registered on the supplemental register shall be conspicuously different from certificates issued for marks registered on the principal register.

Section 26:

The provisions of this chapter shall govern so far as applicable applications for registration and registrations on the supplemental register as well as those on the principal register, but applications for and registrations on the supplemental register shall not be subject to or receive the advantages of sections 1051 (b), 1052 (e), 1052 (f), 1057 (b), 1057 (c), 1062 (a), 1063 to 1068, inclusive, 1072, 1115 and 1124 of this title.

Section 27:

Registration of a mark on the supplemental register, or under the Act of March 19, 1920, shall not preclude registration by the registrant on the principal register established by this chapter. Registration of a mark on the supplemental register shall not constitute an admission that the mark has not acquired distinctiveness.

Section 28:

Registration on the supplemental register or under the Act of March 19, 1920, shall not be filed in the Department of the Treasury or be used to stop importations.

APPENDIX 7:
TRADEMARK/SERVICE MARK
APPLICATION

~TRADEMARK/SERVICE MARK APPLICATION (15 U.S.C. §§ 1051, 1126(d)&(e))~

BASIC INSTRUCTIONS

The following form is written in a "scannable" format that will enable the U.S. Patent and Trademark Office (USPTO) to scan paper filings and capture application data automatically using optical character recognition (OCR) technology. Information is to be entered next to identifying data tags, such as <DATE OF FIRST USE IN COMMERCE>. OCR software can be programmed to identify these tags, capture the corresponding data, and transmit this data to the appropriate data fields in the Trademark databases, largely bypassing manual data entry processes.

Please enter the requested information in the blank space that appears to the right of each tagged (< >) element. However, do not enter any information immediately after the section headers (the bolded wording appearing in all capital letters). If you need additional space, first, in the space provided on the form, enter "See attached." Then, please use a separate piece of paper on which you first list the data tag (e.g., <LISTING OF GOODS AND/OR SERVICES>), followed by the relevant information. Some of the information requested *must* be provided. Other information is either required only in certain circumstances, or provided only at your discretion. **Please consult the "Help" section following the form for detailed explanations as to what information should be entered in each blank space.**

To increase the effectiveness of the USPTO scanners, it is recommended that you use a typewriter to complete the form.

For additional information, please see the *Basic Facts about Trademarks* booklet, available at *http://www.uspto.gov/web/offices/tac/doc/basic/*, or by calling the Trademark Assistance Center, at 1-800-786-9199. You may also wish to file electronically, from *http://www.uspto.gov/teas/index.html*.

MAILING INFORMATION

Send the completed form, appropriate fee(s) (made payable to the "Commissioner of Patents and Trademarks"), and any other required materials to:

> Commissioner for Trademarks
> P.O. Box 1451
> Alexandria, VA 22313-1451

The filing fee for this application is $375.00 *per class* of goods and/or services. You must include at least $375.00 with this application; otherwise the papers and money will be returned to you. Once your application meets the minimum filing date requirements, this processing fee becomes **non-refundable**. This is true even if the USPTO does not issue a registration certificate for this mark.

You may also wish to include a self-addressed stamped postcard with your submission, on which you identify the mark and list each item being submitted (e.g., application, fee, specimen, etc.). We will return this postcard to you, stamped with your assigned serial number, to confirm receipt of your submission.

~TRADEMARK/SERVICE MARK APPLICATION (15 U.S.C. §§ 1051, 1126(d)&(e))~

~To the Commissioner for Trademarks~

<APPLICANT INFORMATION>

<Name>
<Street>
<City>
<State>
<Country>
<Zip/Postal Code>
<Telephone Number>
<Fax Number>
<e-Mail Address>

<APPLICANT ENTITY INFORMATION>~Select only ONE~

<Individual: Country of Citizenship>
<Corporation: State/Country of Incorporation>
<Partnership: State/Country under which Organized>
    <Name(s) of General Partner(s) & Citizenship/Incorporation>

<Other Entity Type: Specific Nature of Entity>
    <State/Country under which Organized>

<TRADEMARK/SERVICE MARK INFORMATION>

<Mark>

The mark may be registered in standard character format or in special form. Applicant must specify whether registration is sought for the mark in standard character format or in a special form by entering "YES" in the appropriate space below.

<Standard Character Format> The mark is presented in standard character format without claim to any particular font style, size or color.
Enter YES, if appropriate _____

<Special Form Drawing> *Enter YES, if appropriate* _____

ATTACH a separate piece of paper that displays the mark you want to register (a "drawing" page), even if the mark is simply a word or words. Display only the exact mark you want to register on the additional piece of paper. Do not display advertising material or other matter that is not part of the mark. Please see additional HELP instructions.

PTO Form 1478 (REV 01/05)
OMB Control No. 0651-0009 (Exp. 8/31/2001)

U.S. DEPARTMENT OF COMMERCE/Patent and Trademark Office
There is no requirement to respond to this collection of information
unless a currently valid OMB number is displayed.

<BASIS FOR FILING AND GOODS/SERVICES INFORMATION>

<Use in Commerce: Section 1(a)>~*Applicant is using or is using through a related company the mark in commerce on or in connection with the below-identified goods and/or services (15 U.S.C. § 1051(a)).~*

<International Class Number(s)>

<Listing of Goods and/or Services>~*List in ascending numerical class order. Please see sample in HELP instructions.~*

<Date of First Use Anywhere>

<Date of First Use in Commerce>
~*Submit one (1) SPECIMEN for each international class showing the mark as used in commerce.~*

<Intent to Use: Section 1(b)>~*Applicant has a bona fide intention to use or use through a related company the mark in commerce on or in connection with the below-identified goods and/or services (15 U.S.C. § 1051(b)).~*

<International Class Number(s)>

<Listing of Goods and/or Services>~*List in ascending numerical class order. Please see sample in HELP instructions.~*

<Foreign Priority: Section 44(d)>~*Applicant has a bona fide intention to use the mark in commerce on or in connection with the below-identified goods/services, and asserts a claim of priority based upon a foreign application in accordance with 15 U.S.C. § 1126(d).~*

<International Class Number(s)>

<Listing of Goods and/or Services>~*List in ascending numerical class order. Please see sample in HELP instructions.~*

<Country of Foreign Filing>

<Foreign Application Number>

<Date of Foreign Filing>

<Foreign Registration: Section 44(e)>~*Applicant has a bona fide intention to use the mark in commerce on or in connection with the below-identified goods/services based on registration of the mark in applicant's country of origin.~*

<International Class Number(s)>

<Listing of Goods and/or Services>~*List in ascending numerical class order. Please see sample in HELP instructions.~*

<Country of Foreign Registration>

<Foreign Registration Number>

<Foreign Registration Date>

<Foreign Registration Renewal Date>

<Foreign Registration Expiration Date>
~*Submit foreign registration certificate or a certified copy of the foreign registration, in accordance with 15 U.S.C. § 1126(e).~*

TRADEMARK/SERVICE MARK APPLICATION

<FEE INFORMATION>

$375.00 x <Number of Classes>	= <Total Filing Fee Paid>

<SIGNATURE INFORMATION>

~ Applicant requests registration of the above-identified mark in the United States Patent and Trademark Office on the Principal Register established by Act of July 5, 1946 (15 U.S.C. § 1051 et seq.) for the above-identified goods and/or services.

The undersigned, being hereby warned that willful false statements and the like so made are punishable by fine or imprisonment, or both, under 18 U.S.C. § 1001, and that such willful false statements may jeopardize the validity of the application or any resulting registration, declares that he/she is properly authorized to execute this application on behalf of the applicant; he/she believes the applicant to be the owner of the trademark/service mark sought to be registered, or, if the application is being filed under 15 U.S.C. § 1051(b), he/she believes applicant to be entitled to use such mark in commerce; to the best of his/her knowledge and belief no other person, firm, corporation, or association has the right to use the mark in commerce, either in the identical form thereof or in such near resemblance thereto as to be likely, when used on or in connection with the goods and/or services of such other person, to cause confusion, or to cause mistake, or to deceive; and that all statements made of his/her own knowledge are true; and that all statements made on information and belief are believed to be true.~

~Signature~ _____

<Date>

<Name>

<Title>

<CONTACT INFORMATION>

<Name>

<Company/Firm Name>

<Street>

<City>

<State>

<Country>

<Zip/Postal Code>

<Telephone Number>

<Fax Number>

<e-Mail Address>

The information collected on this form allows the PTO to determine whether a mark may be registered on the Principal or Supplemental Register, and provides notice of an applicant's claim of ownership of the mark, or bona fide intent to use the mark in commerce. Responses to the request for information are required to obtain the benefit of a registration on the Principal or Supplemental Register. 15 U.S.C. §§1051 et seq. and 37 C.F.R. Part 2. All information collected will be made public. Gathering and providing the information will require an estimated seventeen to twenty-three minutes. Please direct comments on the time needed to complete this form, and/or suggestions for reducing this burden to the Chief Information Officer, U.S. Patent and Trademark Office, U.S. Department of Commerce, Washington D.C. 20231. Please note that the PTO may not conduct or sponsor a collection of information using a form that does not display a valid OMB control number. (See bottom left side of this form)

LINE-BY-LINE HELP INSTRUCTIONS

APPLICANT INFORMATION

Name: Enter the full name of the applicant, i.e., the name of the individual, corporation, partnership, or other entity that is seeking registration. If a joint venture organized under a particular business name, enter that name. If joint or multiple applicants, enter the name of each. If a trust, enter the name of the trustee(s). If an estate, enter the name of the executor(s).
Street: Enter the street address or rural delivery route where the applicant is located.
City: Enter the city and/or foreign area designation where the applicant's address is located.
State: Enter the U.S. state or foreign province in which the applicant's address is located.
Country: Enter the country of the applicant's address. If the address is outside the United States, the applicant may appoint a "Domestic Representative" on whom notices or process in proceedings affecting the mark may be served.
Zip/Postal Code: Enter the applicant's U.S. zip code or foreign country postal identification code.
Telephone Number: Enter the applicant's telephone number.
Fax Number: Enter the applicant's fax number.
e-Mail Address: Enter the applicant's e-mail address.

APPLICANT ENTITY INFORMATION

Indicate the applicant's entity type by entering the appropriate information in the space to the right of the correct entity type. Please note that only one entity type may be selected.
Individual: Enter the applicant's country of citizenship.
Corporation: Enter the applicant's state of incorporation (or the applicant's country of incorporation if the applicant is a foreign corporation).
Partnership: Enter the state under whose laws the partnership is organized (or the country under whose laws the partnership is organized if the partnership is a foreign partnership).
Name(s) of General Partner(s) & Citizenship/incorporation: Enter the names and citizenship of any general partners who are individuals, and/or the names and state or (foreign) country of incorporation of any general partners that are corporations, and/or the names and states or (foreign) countries of organization of any general partners that are themselves partnerships. If the applicant is a limited partnership, then only the names and citizenship or state or country of organization or incorporation of the general partners need be provided.
Other Entity Type: Enter a brief description of the applicant's entity type (e.g., joint or multiple applicants, joint venture, limited liability company, association, Indian Nation, state or local agency, trust, estate). The following sets forth the information required with respect to the most common types of "other" entities:

For *joint or multiple applicants,* enter the name and entity type of each joint applicant. Also, enter the citizenship of those joint applicants who are individuals, and/or the state or (foreign) country of incorporation of those joint applicants that are corporations, and/or the state or (foreign) country of organization (and the names and citizenship of the partners) of those joint applicants that are partnerships. The information regarding each applicant should be preceded by a separate heading tag (<APPLICANT INFORMATION>).

For *sole proprietorship,* enter the name and citizenship of the sole proprietor, and indicate the state where the sole proprietorship is organized.

For *joint venture,* enter the name and entity type of each entity participating in the joint venture. Also, enter the citizenship of those joint venture participants who are individuals, and/or the state or (foreign) country of incorporation of those joint venture participants that are corporations, and/or the state or (foreign) country of organization (and the names and citizenship of the partners) of those joint venture participants that are partnerships. The information regarding each entity should be preceded by a separate heading tag (<APPLICANT INFORMATION>).

For *limited liability company or association*, enter the state or (foreign) country under whose laws the entity is established.

For *state or local agency*, enter the name of the agency and the state and/or locale of the agency (e.g., Maryland State Lottery Agency, an agency of the State of Maryland).

For *trusts*, identify the trustees and the trust itself, using the following format: The Trustees of the XYZ Trust, a California trust, the trustees comprising John Doe, a U.S. citizen, and the ABC Corp., a Delaware corporation. (Please note that the trustees, and not the trust itself, must be identified as the applicant in the portion of the application designated for naming the applicant).

For *estates*, identify the executors and the estate itself using the following format: The Executors of the John Smith estate, a New York estate, the executors comprising Mary Smith and John Smith, U.S. citizens. (Please note that the executors, and not the estate itself, must be identified as the applicant in the portion of the application designated for naming the applicant).

State/Country under Which Organized: Enter the state or country under whose laws the entity is organized.

TRADEMARK/SERVICE MARK INFORMATION

Standard Character Format: Use this mark format to register word(s), letter(s), number(s), or any combination thereof, without claim to any particular font style, size, or color, and absent any design element. The application must also include the following statement:

> "The mark is presented in standard character format without claim to any particular font style, size or color.

Registration of a mark in the standard character format will provide broad rights, namely use in any manner of presentation. A mark is eligible for a claim of the standard character format if, (1) The mark does not include a design element; (2) All letters and words in the mark are depicted in Latin characters; (3) All numerals in the mark are depicted in Roman or Arabic numerals; and (4) The mark includes only common punctuation or diacritical marks.

Stylized or Design Format: Use this mark format if (1) you wish to register a mark with a design element or word(s) or letters(s) having a particular stylized appearance that you wish to protect; otherwise, choose the Standard Character Format, above.

Requirements for DISPLAY of mark on a separate piece of paper:
(a) Use non-shiny white paper that is separate from the application;

(b) Use paper that is 8 to 8.5 inches wide and 11 to 11.69 inches long. One of the shorter sides of the sheet should be regarded as its top edge. The image must be no larger than 3.15 inches high by 3.15 inches wide;

(c) Include the caption "DRAWING PAGE" at the top of the drawing beginning one inch from the top edge; and

(d) Depict the mark in black ink, or in color if color is claimed as a feature of the mark.

(e) Drawings must be typed or made with a pen or by a process that will provide high definition when copied. A photolithographic, printer's proof copy, or other high quality reproduction of the mark may be used. All lines must be clean, sharp and solid, and must not be fine or crowded.

BASIS FOR FILING AND GOODS/SERVICES INFORMATION

Use in Commerce: Section 1(a): Use this section only if you have actually used the mark in commerce on or in connection with *all* of the goods and/or services listed.

International Class Number(s): Enter the international class number(s) of the goods and/or services associated with the mark; e.g., 14; 24; 25. If unknown, leave blank and the USPTO will assign the number(s).

Listing of Goods and/or Services: Enter the *specific* goods and/or services associated with the mark. Do NOT enter the broad class number here, such as 9 or 42 (this information belongs in the field above, namely International Class Number(s)). If the goods and/or services are classified in more than one class, the goods and/or services should be listed in ascending numerical class order, with both the class number and the specific goods and/or services. For example, 14: jewelry

        24: towels

        25: pants, shirts, jackets, shoes

For more information about acceptable wording for the goods/services, see USPTO's on-line *Acceptable Identification of Goods and Services Manual*, at *http://www.uspto.gov/web/offices/tac/doc/gsmanual/*.

Date of First Use Anywhere: Enter the date on which the goods were first sold or transported or the services first rendered under the mark if such use was in the ordinary course of trade. For every applicant (foreign or domestic), the date of first use is the date of the first such use *anywhere,* in the United States or elsewhere. Please note this date may be earlier than, or the same as, the date of the first use of the mark in commerce.

Date of First Use in Commerce: Enter the date on which the applicant first used the mark in commerce, i.e., in interstate commerce, territorial commerce, or commerce between the United States and a foreign country.

Specimen: You must submit one (1) specimen showing the mark as used in commerce on or in connection with any item listed in the description of goods and/or services; e.g., tags or labels for goods, and/or advertisements for services. If the goods and/or services are classified in more than one international class, a specimen must be provided showing the mark used on or in connection with at least one item from each of these classes. The specimen must be flat and no larger than 8 ½ inches (21.6 cm.) wide by 11.69 inches (29.7 cm.) long.

Intent to Use: Section 1(b): Use this section if the applicant only has a bona fide intention to use the mark in commerce in the future as to all or some of the goods and/or services, rather than having actually already made use of the mark in commerce as to *all* of the goods and/or services.

International Class Number(s): Enter the international class number(s) of the goods and/or services associated with the mark; e.g., 14; 24; 25. If unknown, leave blank and the USPTO will assign the number(s).

Listing of Goods and/or Services: Enter the *specific* goods and/or services associated with the mark. Do NOT enter the broad class number here, such as 9 or 42 (this information belongs in the field above, namely International Class Number(s)). If the goods and/or services are classified in more than one class, the goods and/or services should be listed in ascending numerical class order, with both the class number and the specific goods and/or services. For example, 14: jewelry

        24: towels

        25: pants, shirts, jackets, shoes

For more information about acceptable wording for the goods/services, see USPTO's on-line *Acceptable Identification of Goods and Services Manual*, at *http://www.uspto.gov/web/offices/tac/doc/gsmanual/*.

Foreign Priority: Section 44(d): Use this section if you are filing the application within six (6) months of filing the first foreign application to register the mark in a defined treaty country.

International Class Number(s): Enter the international class number(s) of the goods and/or services associated with the mark; e.g., 14; 24; 25. If unknown, leave blank and the USPTO will assign the number(s).

Listing of Goods and/or Services: Enter the *specific* goods and/or services associated with the mark. Do NOT enter the broad class number here, such as 9 or 42 (this information belongs in the field above, namely International Class Number(s)). If the goods and/or services are classified in more than one class, the goods and/or services should be listed in ascending numerical class order, with both the class number and the specific goods and/or services. For example, 14: jewelry

        24: towels

        25: pants, shirts, jackets, shoes

For more information about acceptable wording for the goods/services, see USPTO's on-line *Acceptable Identification of Goods and Services Manual*, at *http://www.uspto.gov/web/offices/tac/doc/gsmanual/*.
Country of Foreign Filing: Enter the country where the foreign application upon which the applicant is asserting a claim of priority has been filed.
Foreign Application Number: Enter the foreign application serial number, if available.
Filing Date of Foreign Application: Enter the date (two digits each for both the month and day, and four digits for the year) on which the foreign application was filed. To receive a priority filing date, you must file the U.S. application within six (6) months of filing the first foreign application in a defined treaty country.

Foreign Registration: Section 44(e): Use this section if applicant is relying on a foreign registration certificate or a certified copy of a foreign registration currently in force. You must submit this foreign registration certificate or a certified copy of the foreign registration.
International Class Number(s): Enter the international class number(s) of the goods and/or services associated with the mark; e.g., 14; 24; 25. If unknown, leave blank and the USPTO will assign the number(s).
Listing of Goods and/or Services: Enter the *specific* goods and/or services associated with the mark. Do NOT enter the broad class number here, such as 9 or 42 (this information belongs in the field above, namely International Class Number(s)). If the goods and/or services are classified in more than one class, the goods and/or services should be listed in ascending numerical class order, with both the class number and the specific goods and/or services. For example, 14: jewelry
24: towels
25: pants, shirts, jackets, shoes
For more information about acceptable wording for the goods/services, see USPTO's on-line *Acceptable Identification of Goods and Services Manual*, at *http://www.uspto.gov/web/offices/tac/doc/gsmanual/*.
Country of Foreign Registration: Enter the country of the foreign registration.
Foreign Registration Number: Enter the number of the foreign registration.
Foreign Registration Date: Enter the date (two digits each for both the month and day, and four digits for the year) of the foreign registration.
Foreign Registration Renewal Date: Enter the date (two digits each for both the month and day, and four digits for the year) of the foreign registration renewal.
Foreign Registration Date: Enter the expiration date (two digits each for both the month and day, and four digits for the year) of the foreign registration.

FEE INFORMATION

The filing fee for this application is $375.00 *per class* of goods and/or services. You must include at least $375.00 with this application; otherwise the papers and money will be returned to you. Once your application meets the minimum filing date requirements, this processing fee becomes **non-refundable**. This is true even if the USPTO does not issue a registration certificate for this mark.
Number of Classes: Enter the total number of classes (*not* the international class number(s)) for which the applicant is seeking registration. For example, if the application covers Classes 1, 5 and 25, then enter the number "3."
Total Filing Fee Paid: Enter the fee amount that is enclosed (either in the form of a check or money order in U.S. currency, made payable to "Commissioner of Patents and Trademarks"), or to be charged to an already-existing USPTO deposit account.

SIGNATURE INFORMATION

Signature: The appropriate person must sign the form. A person who is properly authorized to sign on behalf of the applicant is: (1) a person with legal authority to bind the applicant; or (2) a person with firsthand knowledge of the facts and actual or implied authority to act on behalf of the applicant; or (3) an attorney who has an actual or implied written or verbal power of attorney from the applicant.

Date Signed: Enter the date the form is signed.

Name: Enter the name of the person signing the form.

Title: Enter the signatory's title, if applicable, e.g., Vice President, General Partner, etc.

CONTACT INFORMATION

Although this may be the same as provided elsewhere in the document, please enter the following required information for where the USPTO should mail correspondence.

Name: Enter the full name of the contact person.

Company/Firm Name: Enter the name of the contact person's company or firm.

Street: Enter the street address or rural delivery route where the contact person is located.

City: Enter the city and/or foreign area designation where the contact person's address is located.

State: Enter the U.S. state or Canadian province in which the contact person's address is located.

Country: Enter the country of the contact person's address.

Zip Code: Enter the U.S. zip code or Canadian postal code.

Telephone Number: Enter the appropriate telephone number.

Fax Number: Enter the appropriate fax number, if available.

e-Mail Address: Enter the appropriate e-mail address, if available.

APPENDIX 8:
COLLECTIVE MEMBERSHIP MARK APPLICATION

~COLLECTIVE MEMBERSHIP MARK APPLICATION (15 U.S.C. §§ 1051, 1126(d)&(e))~

Note: The following form complies with the provisions of the Trademark Law Treaty Implementation Act (TLTIA) and the fee increase effective January 10, 2000.

BASIC INSTRUCTIONS

The following form is written in a "scannable" format that will enable the U.S. Patent and Trademark Office (USPTO) to scan paper filings and capture application data automatically using optical character recognition (OCR) technology. Information is to be entered next to identifying data tags, such as <DATE OF FIRST USE IN COMMERCE>. OCR software can be programmed to identify these tags, capture the corresponding data, and transmit this data to the appropriate data fields in the Trademark databases, largely bypassing manual data entry processes.

Please enter the requested information in the blank space that appears to the right of each tagged (< >) element. However, do not enter any information immediately after the section headers (the bolded wording appearing in all capital letters). If you need additional space, first, in the space provided on the form, enter "See attached." Then, please use a separate piece of paper on which you first list the data tag (e.g., <LISTING OF GOODS AND/OR SERVICES>), followed by the relevant information. Some of the information requested must be provided. Other information is either required only in certain circumstances, or provided only at your discretion. **Please consult the "Help" section following the form for detailed explanations as to what information should be entered in each blank space.**

To increase the effectiveness of the USPTO scanners, it is recommended that you use a typewriter to complete the form.

For additional information, please see the Basic Facts about Trademarks booklet, available at *http://www.uspto.gov/web/offices/tac/doc/basic/*, or by calling the Trademark Assistance Center, at 1-800-786-9199. You may also wish to file electronically, from *http://www.uspto.gov/teas/index.html*.

MAILING INFORMATION

Send the completed form, appropriate fee(s) (made payable to the "Commissioner of Patents and Trademarks"), and any other required materials to:

> Commissioner for Trademarks
> P.O. Box 1451
> Alexandria, VA 22313-1451

The filing fee for this application is $375.00 *per class* of goods and/or services. You must include at least $375.00 with this application; otherwise the papers and money will be returned to you. Once your application meets the minimum filing date requirements, this processing fee becomes **non-refundable**. This is true even if the USPTO does not issue a registration certificate for this mark.

You may also wish to include a self-addressed stamped postcard with your submission, on which you identify the mark and list each item being submitted (e.g., application, fee, specimen, etc.). We will return this postcard to you, stamped with your assigned serial number, to confirm receipt of your submission.

~COLLECTIVE MEMBERSHIP MARK APPLICATION (15 U.S.C. §§ 1051, 1126(d)&(e))~

~To the Commissioner for Trademarks~

<APPLICANT INFORMATION>

<Name>
<Street>
<City>
<State>
<Country>
<Zip/Postal Code>
<Telephone Number>
<Fax Number>
<e-Mail Address>

<APPLICANT ENTITY INFORMATION>~Select only ONE~

<Individual: Country of Citizenship>

<Corporation: State/Country of Incorporation>

<Partnership: State/Country under which Organized>

   <Name(s) of General Partner(s) & Citizenship/Incorporation>

<Other Entity Type: Specific Nature of Entity>

   <State/Country under which Organized>

<COLLECTIVE MEMBERSHIP MARK INFORMATION>

<Mark>
<Typed Form>   ~Enter YES, if appropriate~

<MEMBERSHIP INFORMATION>

~Applicant requests registration of the above-identified collective membership mark in the United States Patent and Trademark Office on the Principal Register established by Act of July 5, 1946 (15 U.S.C. § 1051 et seq.) to indicate Membership in a(n):

<TYPE OF ORGANIZATION>~Specify the type or nature of the organization; for example, a social club, labor union, association of real estate brokers.~

<INTERNATIONAL CLASS NUMBER> 200

<FEE INFORMATION>

$375.00 x <Number of Classes>   = <Total Filing Fee Paid>

<FILING BASIS INFORMATION>

<Intent to Use: Section 1(b)>   ~Enter YES, if appropriate~
~Applicant has a bona fide intention to exercise legitimate control over the use of the mark in commerce by its members to indicate membership (15 U.S.C. §§ 1051(b) and 1054).~

PTO Form 4.8 (REV 01/05)
OMB Control No. 0651-0009 (Exp. 8/31/2001)

U.S. DEPARTMENT OF COMMERCE/Patent and Trademark Office
There is no requirement to respond to this collection of information
unless a currently valid OMB number is displayed.

<Use in Commerce: Section 1(a)>   ~Enter YES, if appropriate~
~Applicant is exercising legitimate control over the use of the mark in commerce by its members to indicate membership
(15 U.S.C. §§ 1051(a) and 1054). Applicant submits one (1) SPECIMEN showing the mark as used by members in commerce.~

<Date of First Use Anywhere>

<Date of First Use in Commerce>

<Foreign Priority: Section 44(d)>   ~Enter YES, if appropriate~
~Applicant has a bona fide intention to exercise legitimate control over the use of the mark in commerce by its members on or in
connection with the above-identified goods/services (15 U.S.C. §1054), and asserts a claim of priority based upon a foreign
application in accordance with 15 U.S.C. § 1126(d). ~

<Country of Foreign Filing>

<Foreign Application Number>

<Date of Foreign Filing>

<Foreign Registration: Section 44(e)>   ~Enter YES, if appropriate~
~Applicant has a bona fide intention to exercise legitimate control over the use of the mark in commerce by its members on or in
connection with the above-identified goods/services (15 U.S.C. §1054). Applicant must submit the foreign registration certificate or
a certified copy of the foreign registration, in accordance with 15 U.S.C. §1126(e). ~

<Country of Foreign Registration>

<Foreign Registration Number>

<Foreign Registration Date>

<Foreign Registration Renewal Date>

<Foreign Registration Expiration Date>

<METHOD OF CONTROL>
~Applicant controls, or intends to control (if filing under 15 U.S.C. 1051(b)), the use of the mark by members as follows:~
<Method of Control>

<SIGNATURE AND OTHER INFORMATION>
~DECLARATION: The undersigned, being hereby warned that willful false statements and the like so made are punishable by
fine or imprisonment, or both, under 18 U.S.C. § 1001, and that such willful false statements may jeopardize the validity of the
application or any resulting registration, declares that he/she is properly authorized to execute this application on behalf of the
applicant; he/she believes the applicant to be the owner of the collective membership mark sought to be registered, or, if the
application is being filed under 15 U.S.C. § 1051(b), he/she believes applicant to be entitled to exercise legitimate control over the
use of such mark in commerce; to the best of his/her knowledge and belief no other person, firm, corporation, or association has the
right to use the mark in commerce, either in the identical form thereof or in such near resemblance thereto as to be likely, when used
on or in connection with the goods/services of such other person, to cause confusion, or to cause mistake, or to deceive; and that all
statements made of his/her own knowledge are true; and that all statements made on information and belief are believed to be true.~

~Signature~ _____

<Date Signed>

<Name>

<Title>

<CONTACT INFORMATION>

<Name>
<Company/Firm Name>
<Street>
<City>
<State>
<Country>
<Zip/Postal Code>
<Telephone Number>
<Fax Number>
<e-Mail Address>

The information collected on this form allows the PTO to determine whether a mark may be registered on the Principal or Supplemental Register, and provides notice of an applicant's claim of ownership of the mark or a bona fide intent to use the mark in commerce. Responses to the request for information are required to obtain the benefit of a registration on the Principal or Supplemental Register. 15 U.S.C. §§1051 et seq. and 37 C.F.R. Part 2. All information collected will be made public. Gathering and providing the information will require an estimated seventeen to twenty-three minutes. Please direct comments on the time needed to complete this form, and/or suggestions for reducing this burden to the Chief Information Officer, U.S. Patent and Trademark Office, U.S. Department of Commerce, Washington D.C. 20231. Please note that the PTO may not conduct or sponsor a collection of information using a form that does not display a valid OMB control number. (See bottom left side of this form).

LINE-BY-LINE HELP INSTRUCTIONS FOR COLLECTIVE MEMBERSHIP MARK APPLICATION

In order for the U.S. Patent and Trademark Office ("USPTO") to accept this Application for filing, all the information requested must be entered in the space provided, unless otherwise indicated. **Note:** *If filing pursuant to §1(a)*, please attach one (1) specimen *for each class* showing the mark as used in commerce on or in connection with any item in the class of listed goods and/or services.

APPLICANT INFORMATION

Name: Enter the full name of the applicant, i.e., the name of the individual, corporation, partnership, or other entity that owns the mark. If a joint venture organized under a particular business name, enter that name. If joint or multiple applicants, enter the name of each of these applicants. If a trust, enter the name of the trustee(s). If an estate, enter the name of the executor(s).

Street: Enter the street address or rural delivery route where the applicant is located.

City: Enter the city and/or foreign area designation where the applicant's address is located.

State: For an applicant residing in the United States, enter the U.S. state in which the applicant's address is located.

Country: Enter the country of the applicant's address. If the address is outside the United States, the owner may appoint a "Domestic Representative" on whom notices or process in proceedings affecting the mark may be served.

Zip/Postal Code: Enter the U.S. zip code or foreign country postal identification code.

Telephone Number: Enter the applicant's telephone number.

Fax Number: Enter the applicant's fax number.

e-Mail Address: Enter the applicant's e-mail address.

APPLICANT ENTITY INFORMATION

Indicate the applicant's entity type by entering the appropriate information in the space to the right of the correct entity type. Please note that only one entity type may be selected.

Individual: Enter the applicant's country of citizenship.

Corporation: Enter the applicant's state of incorporation (or the applicant's country of incorporation if the applicant is a foreign corporation).

Partnership: Enter the state under whose laws the partnership is organized (or the country under whose laws the partnership is organized if the partnership is a foreign partnership).

Name(s) of General Partner(s) & Citizenship/Incorporation: Enter the names and citizenship of any general partners who are individuals, and/or the names and state or (foreign) country of incorporation of any general partners which are corporations, and/or the names and states or (foreign) countries of organization of any general partners which are themselves partnerships. If the applicant is a limited partnership, then only the names and citizenship or state or country of organization or incorporation of the general partners need be provided.

Other Entity Type: Enter a brief description of the applicant's entity type (e.g., joint or multiple applicants, joint venture, limited liability company, association, Indian Nation, state or local agency, trust, estate). The following sets forth the information required with respect to the most common types of "other" entities:

> For *joint or multiple applicants*, enter the name and entity type of each joint applicant. Also, enter the citizenship of those joint applicants who are individuals, and/or the state or (foreign) country of incorporation of those joint applicants that are corporations, and/or the state or (foreign) country of organization- and the names and citizenship of the partners- of those joint applicants which are partnerships. The information regarding each applicant should be preceded by a separate heading tag (<APPLICANT INFORMATION>).

For *joint venture*, enter the name and entity type of each entity participating in the joint venture. Also, enter the citizenship of those joint venture participants who are individuals, and/or the state or (foreign) country of incorporation of those joint venture participants that are corporations, and/or the state or (foreign) country of organization- and the names and citizenship of the partners- of those joint venture participants that are partnerships. The information regarding each entity should be preceded by a separate heading tag (<APPLICANT INFORMATION>).

For *limited liability company or association*, enter the state or (foreign) country under whose laws the entity is established.

For *state or local agency*, enter the name of the agency and the state and/or locale of the agency (e.g., Maryland State Lottery Agency, an agency of the State of Maryland).

For *trusts*, identify the trustees and the trust itself, using the following format: The Trustees of the XYZ Trust, a California trust, the trustees comprising John Doe, a U.S. citizen, and the ABC Corp., a Delaware corporation. (Please note that the trustees, and not the trust itself, must be identified as the applicant in the portion of the application designated for naming the applicant).

For *estates*, identify the executors and the estate itself using the following format: The Executors of the John Smith estate, a New York estate, the executors comprising Mary Smith and John Smith, U.S. citizens. (Please note that the executors, and not the estate itself, must be identified as the applicant in the portion of the application designated for naming the applicant).

State/Country under Which Organized: Enter the state or country under whose laws the entity is organized.

COLLECTIVE MEMBERSHIP MARK INFORMATION

Mark: A mark may consist of words alone, a design or logo, or a combination of words and a design or logo. However, an application may consist of only one mark; separate marks must be filed in separate applications. In this space, enter the word mark in typed form (e.g., THE CAT'S MEOW); or, in the case of a non-word mark or a combination mark, a brief description of the mark (e.g., Design of a fanciful cat or Design of a fanciful cat combined with THE CAT'S MEOW). Do NOT include quotation marks around the mark itself, unless the mark actually features these quotation marks. Also, do NOT include any information related to a "pseudo mark" in this field. The "pseudo mark" field is controlled by the USPTO, and is not something that you should try to enter. If the USPTO determines that a pseudo mark is necessary for your particular mark, it will enter this information in the search system.

Typed Form: Enter "YES" if the collective membership mark applied for is in a "typed" format (i.e., if the mark consists of only typed words, letters or numbers, and does not include any special stylization or design element(s)). Please note that a registration for a mark based on a typed drawing affords protection not only for the typed version of the mark, but for all other renderings of the mark as long as those renderings do not contain any design elements. For a drawing in stylized form or design, a special form drawing must be submitted. The drawing should be in black and white.

Display the Mark: Regardless of whether the mark consists of words alone; a design or logo; or a combination of words and a design or logo, submit on a separate piece of paper a display of what the mark is. At the top of the page, include a heading consisting of (1) the applicant's name and address; (2) a listing of the goods and/or services on which on in connection with which the mark is used; and (3) a listing of the basis for filing (and any relevant information related thereto). Then, in the middle of the page, show the mark: If the mark is to be in a "typed" form, simply type the mark in the middle of the page *in all capital letters*. For a mark in stylized form or design, in the middle of the page display an image of the mark in black and white, in an area no greater than 4x4 inches.

MEMBERSHIP INFORMATION

Type of Organization: Enter the specific type or nature of the organization; for example, a social club, labor union, political party, or association of real estate brokers.

International Class Number(s): All collective membership marks are properly classified in Class 200.

FEE INFORMATION

Number of Classes: Enter the number of classes (e.g., "1" or "3") for which applicant seeks registration.

Total Filing Fee Paid: Enter the fee amount that is enclosed (either in the form of a check or money order in U.S. currency, made payable to "Commissioner of Patents and Trademarks"), or that is to be charged to a USPTO deposit account. Please note that the filing fee is $375.00 per class of goods or services listed, and at least $375.00 must accompany the application in order for a filing date to be assigned.

FILING BASIS INFORMATION

Intent to Use: Section 1(b): Enter "YES" if the applicant does not yet exercise control over its members' use of the mark in commerce but has a bona fide intention to exercise such control.

Use in Commerce: Section 1(a): Enter "YES" if the applicant is actually exercising legitimate control over its members' use of the mark in commerce.

Specimens: The applicant must submit one (1) specimen showing the mark as used by the members in commerce on or in connection with any item listed in the description of goods and/or services. Examples of acceptable specimens are membership cards and membership certificates. The specimen must be flat and no larger than 8½ inches (21.6 cm.) wide by 11.69 inches (29.7 cm.) long.

Date of First Use Anywhere: Enter the date on which the mark was first used to indicate membership. For every applicant, whether foreign or domestic, the date of first use of a mark is the date of the first such use *anywhere*, in the United States or elsewhere. Please note this date may be earlier than, or the same as, the date of the first use of the mark in commerce.

Date of First Use in Commerce: Enter date on which the mark was first used to indicate membership in commerce, i.e., in interstate commerce, territorial commerce, or commerce between the United States and a foreign country.

Foreign Priority: Section 44(d): Enter "YES" if applicant is filing the application within six months of filing the first foreign application to register the mark in a defined treaty country.

Country of Foreign Filing: Enter the country where the foreign application upon which the applicant is asserting a claim of priority has been filed.

Foreign Application Number: Enter the foreign application serial number, if available.

Filing Date of Foreign Application: Enter the date (two digits each for both the month and day, and four digits for the year) on which the foreign application was filed. To receive a priority filing date, the applicant must file the United States application within six months of filing the first foreign application in a defined treaty country.

Foreign Registration: Section 44(e): Enter "YES" if applicant is relying on a foreign registration certificate or a certified copy of a foreign registration currently in force. Applicant must submit this foreign registration certificate or a certified copy of the foreign registration.

Country of Foreign Registration: Enter the country of the foreign registration.

Foreign Registration Number: Enter the number of the foreign registration.

Foreign Registration Date: Enter the date (two digits each for both the month and day, and four digits for the year) of the foreign registration.

Foreign Registration Renewal Date: Enter the date (two digits each for both the month and day, and four digits for the year) of the foreign registration renewal.

Foreign Registration Expiration Date: Enter the expiration date (two digits each for both the month and day, and four digits for the year) of the foreign registration.

METHOD OF CONTROL

Method of Control: The applicant must specify how it controls, or intends to control (if filing under Section 1(b)), the use of the mark by members. If the applicant's bylaws or other written provisions specify the manner of control, or intended manner of control, it will be sufficient to so state.

SIGNATURE AND OTHER INFORMATION

Signature: The appropriate person must sign the form. A person who is properly authorized to sign on behalf of the applicant includes a person with legal authority to bind the applicant and/or a person with firsthand knowledge and actual or implied authority to act on behalf of the applicant.

Date Signed: Enter the date (two digits each for both the month and day, and four digits for the year) on which the application is signed.

Name: Enter the name of the person signing the application.

Title: Enter the signatory's position, if applicable, e.g., Vice President, General Partner. Or, if appropriate, enter the language "Duly Authorized Officer."

CONTACT INFORMATION

Although this may be the same as provided elsewhere in the document, please enter the following required information for where the USPTO should mail correspondence.

Name: Enter the full name of the contact person.

Company/Firm Name: Enter the name of the contact person's company or firm.

Street: Enter the street address or rural delivery route where the contact person is located.

City: Enter the city and/or foreign area designation where the contact person's address is located.

State: Enter the U.S. state or Canadian province in which the contact person's address is located.

Country: Enter the country of the contact person's address.

Zip Code: Enter the U.S. zip code or Canadian postal code.

Telephone Number: Enter the appropriate telephone number.

Fax Number: Enter the appropriate fax number, if available.

e-Mail Address: Enter the appropriate e-mail address, if available.

APPENDIX 9:
CERTIFICATION MARK APPLICATION

~CERTIFICATION MARK APPLICATION (15 U.S.C. §§ 1051, 1126(d)&(e))~

Note: The following form complies with the provisions of the Trademark Law Treaty Implementation Act (TLTIA) and the fee increase effective January 10, 2000.

BASIC INSTRUCTIONS

The following form is written in a "scannable" format that will enable the U.S. Patent and Trademark Office (USPTO) to scan paper filings and capture application data automatically using optical character recognition (OCR) technology. Information is to be entered next to identifying data tags, such as <DATE OF FIRST USE IN COMMERCE>. OCR software can be programmed to identify these tags, capture the corresponding data, and transmit this data to the appropriate data fields in the Trademark databases, largely bypassing manual data entry processes.

Please enter the requested information in the blank space that appears to the right of each tagged (< >) element. However, do not enter any information immediately after the section headers (the bolded wording appearing in all capital letters). If you need additional space, first, in the space provided on the form, enter "See attached." Then, please use a separate piece of paper on which you first list the data tag (e.g., <LISTING OF GOODS AND/OR SERVICES>), followed by the relevant information. Some of the information requested must be provided. Other information is either required only in certain circumstances, or provided only at your discretion. **Please consult the "Help" section following the form for detailed explanations as to what information should be entered in each blank space.**

To increase the effectiveness of the USPTO scanners, it is recommended that you use a typewriter to complete the form.

For additional information, please see the Basic Facts about Trademarks booklet, available at http://www.uspto.gov/web/offices/tac/doc/basic/, or by calling the Trademark Assistance Center, at 1-800-786-9199. You may also wish to file electronically, from http://www.uspto.gov/teas/index.html.

MAILING INFORMATION

Send the completed form, appropriate fee(s) (made payable to the "Commissioner of Patents and Trademarks"), and any other required materials to:

> Commissioner for Trademarks
> P.O. Box 1451
> Alexandria, VA 22313-1451

The filing fee for this application is $375.00 *per class* of goods and/or services. You must include at least $375.00 with this application; otherwise the papers and money will be returned to you. Once your application meets the minimum filing date requirements, this processing fee becomes **non-refundable**. This is true even if the USPTO does not issue a registration certificate for this mark.

You may also wish to include a self-addressed stamped postcard with your submission, on which you identify the mark and list each item being submitted (e.g., application, fee, specimen, etc.). We will return this postcard to you, stamped with your assigned serial number, to confirm receipt of your submission.

~CERTIFICATION MARK APPLICATION (15 U.S.C. §§ 1051, 1126(d)&(e))~

~To the Commissioner for Trademarks~

<APPLICANT INFORMATION>

<Name>
<Street>
<City>
<State>
<Country>
<Zip/Postal Code>
<Telephone Number>
<Fax Number>
<e-Mail Address>

<APPLICANT ENTITY INFORMATION>~Select only ONE~

<Individual: Country of Citizenship>
<Corporation: State/Country of Incorporation>
<Partnership: State/Country under which Organized>
    <Name(s) of General Partner(s) & Citizenship/Incorporation>

<Other Entity Type: Specific Nature of Entity>
    <State/Country under which Organized>

<CERTIFICATION MARK INFORMATION>

<Mark>
<Typed Form>   ~Enter YES, if appropriate~

<GOODS AND/OR SERVICES>

~Applicant requests registration of the above-identified certification mark in the United States Patent and Trademark Office on the Principal Register established by Act of July 5, 1946 (15 U.S.C. § 1051 et seq.) for the following goods and/or services:~
<International Class Number(s)> ~"A" if Goods, "B" if Services~
<Listing of Goods and/or Services> ~List by ascending class and filing basis~

<CERTIFICATION>

~The certification mark, as used (or, if filing under 15 U.S.C. §1051(b), intended to be used) by authorized persons, certifies (or, if filing under 15 U.S.C. §1051(b) is intended to certify) ~

<Certification Statement>

PTO Form 1478 (REV 01/05)
OMB Control No. 0651-0009 (Exp. 8/31/2001)

U.S. DEPARTMENT OF COMMERCE/Patent and Trademark Office
There is no requirement to respond to this collection of information
unless a currently valid OMB number is displayed.

\<FEE INFORMATION\>

$375.00 x \<Number of Classes\>	= \<Total Filing Fee Paid\>

\<FILING BASIS INFORMATION\>~*May enter more than one*~

\<Intent to Use: Section 1(b)\>   ~*Enter YES, if appropriate*~

~*Applicant has a bona fide intention to exercise legitimate control over the use of the certification mark in commerce by authorized persons on or in connection with the above-identified goods/services (15 U.S.C. §§ 1051(b) and 1054). Applicant will not engage in the production or marketing of the goods/services to which the mark is applied. Applicant will later provide with the filing of an Allegation of Use (Amendment to Allege Use/Statement of Use) a* **COPY OF STANDARDS** *the applicant will use to determine whether goods or services will be certified.* ~

\<Use in Commerce: Section 1(a)\>   ~*Enter YES, if appropriate*~

~*Applicant is exercising legitimate control over the use of the certification mark in commerce on or in connection with the above-identified goods/services. (15 U.S.C. §§ 1051(a) and 1054). Applicant is not engaged in the production or marketing of the goods or services to which the mark is applied. Applicant submits one (1)* **SPECIMEN** *with this application showing the mark as used by authorized persons in commerce. Applicant also provides with this application a* **COPY OF STANDARDS** *the applicant uses to determine whether goods or services will be certified.*~

\<Date of First Use Anywhere\>

\<Date of First Use in Commerce\>

\<Foreign Priority: Section 44(d)\>   ~*Enter YES, if appropriate*~

~*Applicant has a bona fide intention to exercise legitimate control over the use of the certification mark in commerce by authorized persons on or in connection with the above-identified goods/services (15 U.S.C. §1054), and asserts a claim of priority based upon a foreign application in accordance with 15 U.S.C. § 1126(d). Applicant will not engage in the production or marketing of the goods/ services to which the mark is applied.* ~

\<Country of Foreign Filing\>

\<Foreign Application Number\>

\<Date of Foreign Filing\>

\<Foreign Registration: Section 44(e)\>   ~*Enter YES, if appropriate*~

~*Applicant has a bona fide intention to exercise legitimate control over the use of the certification mark in commerce by authorized persons on or in connection with the above-identified goods/services (15 U.S.C. §1054). Applicant must submit the foreign registration certificate or a certified copy of the foreign registration, in accordance with 15 U.S.C. §1126(e). Applicant will not engage in the production or marketing of the goods/services to which the mark is applied.* ~

\<Country of Foreign Registration\>

\<Foreign Registration Number\>

\<Foreign Registration Date\>

\<Foreign Registration Renewal Date\>

\<Foreign Registration Expiration Date\>

<SIGNATURE AND OTHER INFORMATION>

~DECLARATION: The undersigned, being hereby warned that willful false statements and the like so made are punishable by fine or imprisonment, or both, under 18 U.S.C. § 1001, and that such willful false statements may jeopardize the validity of the application or any resulting registration, declares that he/she is properly authorized to execute this application on behalf of the applicant; he/she believes the applicant to be the owner of the certification mark sought to be registered, or, if the application is being filed under 15 U.S.C. § 1051(b), he/she believes applicant to be entitled to exercise legitimate control over use of the mark in commerce; to the best of his/her knowledge and belief no other person, firm, corporation, or association has the right to use the mark in commerce, either in the identical form thereof or in such near resemblance thereto as to be likely, when used on or in connection with the goods and/or services of such other person, to cause confusion, or to cause mistake, or to deceive; and that all statements made of his/her own knowledge are true; and that all statements made on information and belief are believed to be true.~

~Signature~ _____

<Date Signed>

<Name>

<Title>

<CONTACT INFORMATION>

<Name>

<Company/Firm Name>

<Street>

<City>

<State>

<Country>

<Zip/Postal Code>

<Telephone Number>

<Fax Number>

<e-Mail Address>

The information collected on this form allows the PTO to determine whether a mark may be registered on the Principal or Supplemental Register, and provides notice of an applicant's claim of ownership of the mark, or bona fide intent to use the mark in commerce. Responses to the request for information are required to obtain the benefit of a registration on the Principal or Supplemental Register. 15 U.S.C. §§1051 et seq. and 37 C.F.R. Part 2. All information collected will be made public. Gathering and providing the information will require an estimated seventeen to twenty-three minutes. Please direct comments on the time needed to complete this form, and/or suggestions for reducing this burden to the Chief Information Officer, U.S. Patent and Trademark Office, U.S. Department of Commerce, Washington D.C. 20231. Please note that the PTO may not conduct or sponsor a collection of information using a form that does not display a valid OMB control number. (See bottom left side of this form).

LINE-BY-LINE HELP INSTRUCTIONS FOR CERTIFICATION MARK APPLICATION

In order for the U.S. Patent and Trademark Office ("USPTO") to accept this Application for filing, all the information requested must be entered in the space provided, unless otherwise indicated. **Note:** If filing pursuant to §1(a), please attach one (1) specimen for each class showing the mark as used in commerce on or in connection with any item in the class of listed goods and/or services.

APPLICANT INFORMATION

Name: Enter the full name of the applicant, i.e., the name of the individual, corporation, partnership, or other entity that owns the mark. If a joint venture organized under a particular business name, enter that name. If joint or multiple applicants, enter the name of each of these applicants. If a trust, enter the name of the trustee(s). If an estate, enter the name of the executor(s).

Street: Enter the street address or rural delivery route where the applicant is located.

City: Enter the city and/or foreign area designation where the applicant's address is located.

State: For an applicant residing in the United States, enter the U.S. state in which the applicant's address is located.

Country: Enter the country of the applicant's address. If the address is outside the United States, the owner may appoint a "Domestic Representative" on whom notices or process in proceedings affecting the mark may be served.

Zip/Postal Code: Enter the U.S. zip code or foreign country postal identification code.

Telephone Number: Enter the applicant's telephone number.

Fax Number: Enter the applicant's fax number.

e-Mail Address: Enter the applicant's e-mail address.

APPLICANT ENTITY INFORMATION

Indicate the applicant's entity type by entering the appropriate information in the space to the right of the correct entity type. Please note that only one entity type may be selected.

Individual: Enter the applicant's country of citizenship.

Corporation: Enter the applicant's state of incorporation (or the applicant's country of incorporation if the applicant is a foreign corporation).

Partnership: Enter the state under whose laws the partnership is organized (or the country under whose laws the partnership is organized if the partnership is a foreign partnership).

Name(s) of General Partner(s) & Citizenship/Incorporation: Enter the names and citizenship of any general partners who are individuals, and/or the names and state or (foreign) country of incorporation of any general partners which are corporations, and/or the names and states or (foreign) countries of organization of any general partners which are themselves partnerships. If the applicant is a limited partnership, then only the names and citizenship or state or country of organization or incorporation of the general partners need be provided.

Other Entity Type: Enter a brief description of the applicant's entity type (e.g., joint or multiple applicants, joint venture, limited liability company, association, Indian Nation, state or local agency, trust, estate). The following sets forth the information required with respect to the most common types of "other" entities:

For *joint or multiple applicants*, enter the name and entity type of each joint applicant. Also, enter the citizenship of those joint applicants who are individuals, and/or the state or (foreign) country of incorporation of those joint applicants that are corporations, and/or the state or (foreign) country of organization- and the names and citizenship of the partners- of those joint applicants which are partnerships. The information regarding each applicant should be preceded by a separate heading tag (<APPLICANT INFORMATION>).

CERTIFICATION MARK APPLICATION

For *joint venture*, enter the name and entity type of each entity participating in the joint venture. Also, enter the citizenship of those joint venture participants who are individuals, and/or the state or (foreign) country of incorporation of those joint venture participants that are corporations, and/or the state or (foreign) country of organization- and the names and citizenship of the partners- of those joint venture participants that are partnerships. The information regarding each entity should be preceded by a separate heading tag (<APPLICANT INFORMATION>).

For *limited liability company or association*, enter the state or (foreign) country under whose laws the entity is established.

For *state or local agency*, enter the name of the agency and the state and/or locale of the agency (e.g., Maryland State Lottery Agency, an agency of the State of Maryland).

For *trusts*, identify the trustees and the trust itself, using the following format: The Trustees of the XYZ Trust, a California trust, the trustees comprising John Doe, a U.S. citizen, and the ABC Corp., a Delaware corporation. (Please note that the trustees, and not the trust itself, must be identified as the applicant in the portion of the application designated for naming the applicant).

For *estates*, identify the executors and the estate itself using the following format: The Executors of the John Smith estate, a New York estate, the executors comprising Mary Smith and John Smith, U.S. citizens. (Please note that the executors, and not the estate itself, must be identified as the applicant in the portion of the application designated for naming the applicant).

State/Country under Which Organized: Enter the state or country under whose laws the entity is organized.

CERTIFICATION MARK INFORMATION

Mark: A mark may consist of words alone, a design or logo, or a combination of words and a design or logo. However, an application may consist of only one mark; separate marks must be filed in separate applications. In this space, enter the word mark in typed form (e.g., THE CAT'S MEOW); or, in the case of a non-word mark or a combination mark, a brief description of the mark (e.g., Design of a fanciful cat or Design of a fanciful cat combined with THE CAT'S MEOW). Do NOT include quotation marks around the mark itself, unless the mark actually features these quotation marks. Also, do NOT include any information related to a "pseudo mark" in this field. The "pseudo mark" field is controlled by the USPTO, and is not something that you should try to enter. If the USPTO determines that a pseudo mark is necessary for your particular mark, it will enter this information in the search system.

Typed Form: Enter "YES" if the certification mark is in a "typed" format (i.e., if the mark consists of only typed words, letters or numbers, and does not include any special stylization or design element(s)). Please note that a registration for a mark based on a typed drawing affords protection not only for the typed version of the mark, but for all other renderings of the mark as long as those renderings do not contain any design elements. For a drawing in stylized form or design, a special form drawing must be submitted. The drawing should be in black and white.

GOODS AND/OR SERVICES

International Class Number(s): Enter the appropriate international class number(s): for goods, "A" and for services, "B."

Listing of Goods and/or Services, by Class: Enter the specific goods and/or services associated with the mark. If the applicant is relying on more than one filing basis, the specific basis should be set forth, followed by the goods and/or services that the particular basis covers.

CERTIFICATION

Certification statement: Enter, for example, a particular regional origin of the goods; a characteristic of the goods or services; or that labor was performed by a particular group.

FEE INFORMATION

Number of Classes: Enter the number of classes (e.g., "1" or "3") for which applicant seeks registration.
Total Filing Fee Paid: Enter the fee amount that is enclosed (either in the form of a check or money order in U.S. currency, made payable to "Commissioner of Patents and Trademarks"), or that is to be charged to a USPTO deposit account. Please note that the filing fee is $375.00 per class of goods or services listed, and at least $375.00 must accompany the application in order for a filing date to be assigned.

FILING BASIS INFORMATION

Intent to Use: Section 1(b): Enter "YES" if the applicant does not yet exercise control over use of the mark in commerce but has a bona fide intention to exercise such control.

Use in Commerce: Section 1(a): Enter "YES" if the applicant is actually exercising legitimate control over use of the mark in commerce.
Specimens: The applicant must submit one (1) specimen showing the mark as used by authorized persons in commerce on or in connection with any item listed in the description of goods and/or services. Examples of acceptable specimens are tags or labels for goods, and advertisements for services. If the goods and/or services are classified in more than one international class, a specimen must be provided showing the mark used on or in connection with at least one item from each of these classes. The specimen must be flat and no larger than 8½ inches (21.6 cm.) wide by 11.69 inches (29.7 cm.) long.
Copy of Standards: The applicant must submit with the application the standards that the applicant uses to determine whether particular goods or services will, in fact, be certified. (In an application filed based on an intent to use in commerce, this should be provided with the Allegation of Use (Amendment to Allege Use/Statement of Use).
Date of First Use Anywhere: Enter the date on which the goods were first sold or transported or the services first rendered under the mark if such use was in the ordinary course of trade. For every applicant, whether foreign or domestic, the date of first use of a mark is the date of the first such use *anywhere*, in the United States or elsewhere. Please note this date may be earlier than, or the same as, the date of the first use of the mark in commerce.
Date of First Use in Commerce: Enter the date on which authorized persons first used the mark in commerce, i.e., in interstate commerce, territorial commerce, or commerce between the United States and a foreign country.

Foreign Priority: Section 44(d): Enter "YES" if applicant is filing the application within six months of filing the first foreign application to register the mark in a defined treaty country.
Country of Foreign Filing: Enter the country where the foreign application upon which the applicant is asserting a claim of priority has been filed.
Foreign Application Number: Enter the foreign application serial number, if available.
Filing Date of Foreign Application: Enter the date (two digits each for both the month and day, and four digits for the year) on which the foreign application was filed. To receive a priority filing date, the applicant must file the United States application within six months of filing the first foreign application in a defined treaty country.

Foreign Registration: Section 44(e): Enter "YES" if applicant is relying on a foreign registration certificate or a certified copy of a foreign registration currently in force. Applicant must submit this foreign registration certificate or a certified copy of the foreign registration.
Country of Foreign Registration: Enter the country of the foreign registration.
Foreign Registration Number: Enter the number of the foreign registration.
Foreign Registration Date: Enter the date (two digits each for both the month and day, and four digits for the year) of the foreign registration.

Foreign Registration Renewal Date: Enter the date (two digits each for both the month and day, and four digits for the year) of the foreign registration renewal.

Foreign Registration Expiration Date: Enter the expiration date (two digits each for both the month and day, and four digits for the year) of the foreign registration.

SIGNATURE AND OTHER INFORMATION

Signature: The appropriate person must sign the form. A person who is properly authorized to sign on behalf of the applicant includes a person with legal authority to bind the applicant and/or a person with firsthand knowledge and actual or implied authority to act on behalf of the applicant.

Date Signed: Enter the date (two digits each for both the month and day, and four digits for the year) on which the application is signed.

Name: Enter the name of the person signing the application.

Title: Enter the signatory's position, if applicable, e.g., Vice President, General Partner. Or, if appropriate, enter the language "Duly Authorized Officer."

CONTACT INFORMATION

Although this may be the same as provided elsewhere in the document, please enter the following required information for where the USPTO should mail correspondence.

Name: Enter the full name of the contact person.

Company/Firm Name: Enter the name of the contact person's company or firm.

Street: Enter the street address or rural delivery route where the contact person is located.

City: Enter the city and/or foreign area designation where the contact person's address is located.

State: Enter the U.S. state or Canadian province in which the contact person's address is located.

Country: Enter the country of the contact person's address.

Zip Code: Enter the U.S. zip code or Canadian postal code.

Telephone Number: Enter the appropriate telephone number.

Fax Number: Enter the appropriate fax number, if available.

e-Mail Address: Enter the appropriate e-mail address, if available.

APPENDIX 10:
COLLECTIVE MARK APPLICATION

~COLLECTIVE TRADEMARK/SERVICE MARK APPLICATION
(15 U.S.C. §§ 1051, 1126(d)&(e))~

Note: The following form complies with the provisions of the Trademark Law Treaty Implementation Act (TLTIA) and the fee increase effective January 10, 2000.

BASIC INSTRUCTIONS

The following form is written in a "scannable" format that will enable the U.S. Patent and Trademark Office (USPTO) to scan paper filings and capture application data automatically using optical character recognition (OCR) technology. Information is to be entered next to identifying data tags, such as <DATE OF FIRST USE IN COMMERCE>. OCR software can be programmed to identify these tags, capture the corresponding data, and transmit this data to the appropriate data fields in the Trademark databases, largely bypassing manual data entry processes.

Please enter the requested information in the blank space that appears to the right of each tagged (< >) element. However, do not enter any information immediately after the section headers (the bolded wording appearing in all capital letters). If you need additional space, first, in the space provided on the form, enter "See attached." Then, please use a separate piece of paper on which you first list the data tag (e.g., <LISTING OF GOODS AND/OR SERVICES>), followed by the relevant information. Some of the information requested must be provided. Other information is either required only in certain circumstances, or provided only at your discretion. **Please consult the "Help" section following the form for detailed explanations as to what information should be entered in each blank space.**

To increase the effectiveness of the USPTO scanners, it is recommended that you use a typewriter to complete the form.

For additional information, please see the Basic Facts about Trademarks booklet, available at *http://www.uspto.gov/web/offices/tac/doc/basic/*, or by calling the Trademark Assistance Center, at 1-800-786-9199. You may also wish to file electronically, from *http://www.uspto.gov/teas/index.html*.

MAILING INFORMATION

Send the completed form, appropriate fee(s) (made payable to the "Commissioner of Patents and Trademarks"), and any other required materials to:

> Commissioner for Trademarks
> P.O. Box 1451
> Alexandria, VA 22313-1451

The filing fee for this application is $375.00 *per class* of goods and/or services. You must include at least $375.00 with this application; otherwise the papers and money will be returned to you. Once your application meets the minimum filing date requirements, this processing fee becomes **non-refundable**. This is true even if the USPTO does not issue a registration certificate for this mark.

You may also wish to include a self-addressed stamped postcard with your submission, on which you identify the mark and list each item being submitted (e.g., application, fee, specimen, etc.). We will return this postcard to you, stamped with your assigned serial number, to confirm receipt of your submission.

~COLLECTIVE TRADEMARK/SERVICE MARK APPLICATION
(15 U.S.C. §§ 1051, 1126(d)&(e))~

~To the Commissioner for Trademarks~

<APPLICANT INFORMATION>

<Name>

<Street>

<City>

<State>

<Country>

<Zip/Postal Code>

<Telephone Number>

<Fax Number>

<e-Mail Address>

<APPLICANT ENTITY INFORMATION>~Select only ONE~

<Individual: Country of Citizenship>

<Corporation: State/Country of Incorporation>

<Partnership: State/Country under which Organized>

   <Name(s) of General Partner(s) & Citizenship/Incorporation>

<Other Entity Type: Specific Nature of Entity>

   <State/Country under which Organized>

<COLLECTIVE TRADEMARK/SERVICE MARK INFORMATION>

<Mark>

<Typed Form>   *~Enter YES, if appropriate~*

<GOODS AND/OR SERVICES>

~Applicant requests registration of the above-identified collective mark in the United States Patent and Trademark Office on the Principal Register established by Act of July 5, 1946 (15 U.S.C. § 1051 et seq.) for the following goods/services:~

<International Class Number(s)>

<Listing of Goods and/or Services> *~List by ascending class and filing basis~*

PTO Form 1963 (REV 01/05)
OMB Control No. 0651-0009 (Exp. 8/31/2001)

U.S. DEPARTMENT OF COMMERCE/Patent and Trademark Office
There is no requirement to respond to this collection of information
unless a currently valid OMB number is displayed.

<FEE INFORMATION>

$375.00 x <Number of Classes>   = <Total Filing Fee Paid>

<FILING BASIS INFORMATION>

<Intent to Use: Section 1(b)>   *~Enter YES, if appropriate~*
~Applicant has a bona fide intention to exercise legitimate control over the use of the mark in commerce by its members on or in connection with the above-identified goods/services (15 U.S.C. §§ 1051(b) and 1054).~

<Use in Commerce: Section 1(a)>   *~Enter YES, if appropriate~*
~Applicant is exercising legitimate control over the use of the mark in commerce by its members on or in connection with the above-identified goods/services. (15 U.S.C. §§ 1051(a) and 1054). The applicant submits one (1) SPECIMEN with this application showing the mark as used by the members in commerce.~

<Date of First Use Anywhere>

<Date of First Use in Commerce

<Foreign Priority: Section 44(d)>   *~Enter YES, if appropriate~*
~Applicant has a bona fide intention to exercise legitimate control over the use of the mark in commerce by its members on or in connection with the above-identified goods/services (15 U.S.C. §1054), and asserts a claim of priority based upon a foreign application in accordance with 15 U.S.C. § 1126(d). ~

<Country of Foreign Filing>

<Foreign Application Number>

<Date of Foreign Filing>

<Foreign Registration: Section 44(e)>   *~Enter YES, if appropriate~*
~Applicant has a bona fide intention to exercise legitimate control over the use of the mark in commerce by its members on or in connection with the above-identified goods/services (15 U.S.C. §1054). Applicant must submit the foreign registration certificate or a certified copy of the foreign registration, in accordance with 15 U.S.C. §1126(e).~

<Country of Foreign Registration>

<Foreign Registration Number>

<Foreign Registration Date>

<Foreign Registration Renewal Date>

<Foreign Registration Expiration Date>

<METHOD OF CONTROL>

~Applicant controls, or intends to control (if filing under 15 U.S.C. §1051(b)), the use of the mark by members as follows:~
<Method of Control>

<SIGNATURE AND OTHER INFORMATION>

~DECLARATION: The undersigned, being hereby warned that willful false statements and the like so made are punishable by fine or imprisonment, or both, under 18 U.S.C. § 1001, and that such willful false statements may jeopardize the validity of the application or any resulting registration, declares that he/she is properly authorized to execute this application on behalf of the applicant; he/she believes the applicant to be the owner of the collective trademark/service mark sought to be registered, or, if the application is being filed under 15 U.S.C. § 1051(b), he/she believes applicant to be entitled to exercise legitimate control over use of the mark in commerce; to the best of his/her knowledge and belief no other person, firm, corporation, or association has the right to use the mark in commerce, either in the identical form thereof or in such near resemblance thereto as to be likely, when used on or in connection with the goods/services of such other person, to cause confusion, or to cause mistake, or to deceive; and that all statements made of his/her own knowledge are true; and that all statements made on information and belief are believed to be true.~

~Signature~_____

<Date Signed>

<Name>

<Title>

<CONTACT INFORMATION>

<Name>

<Company/Firm Name>

<Street>

<City>

<State>

<Country>

<Zip/Postal Code>

<Telephone Number>

<Fax Number>

<e-Mail Address>

The information collected on this form allows the PTO to determine whether a mark may be registered on the Principal or Supplemental Register, and provides notice of an applicant's claim of ownership of the mark or a bona fide intention to use the mark in commerce. Responses to the request for information are required to obtain the benefit of a registration on the Principal or Supplemental Register. 15 U.S.C. §§1051 et seq. and 37 C.F.R. Part 2. All information collected will be made public. Gathering and providing the information will require an estimated seventeen to twenty-three minutes. Please direct comments on the time needed to complete this form, and/or suggestions for reducing this burden to the Chief Information Officer, U.S. Patent and Trademark Office, U.S. Department of Commerce, Washington D.C. 20231. Please note that the PTO may not conduct or sponsor a collection of information using a form that does not display a valid OMB control number. (See bottom left side of this form).

LINE-BY-LINE HELP INSTRUCTIONS

In order for the U.S. Patent and Trademark Office ("USPTO") to accept this Application for filing, all the information requested must be entered in the space provided, unless otherwise indicated. **Note:** *If filing pursuant to §1(a)*, please attach one (1) specimen *for each class* showing the mark as used in commerce on or in connection with any item in the class of listed goods and/or services.

APPLICANT INFORMATION

Name: Enter the full name of the applicant, i.e., the name of the individual, corporation, partnership, or other entity that owns the mark. If a joint venture organized under a particular business name, enter that name. If joint or multiple applicants, enter the name of each of these applicants. If a trust, enter the name of the trustee(s). If an estate, enter the name of the executor(s).

Street: Enter the street address or rural delivery route where the applicant is located.

City: Enter the city and/or foreign area designation where the applicant's address is located.

State: For an applicant residing in the United States, enter the U.S. state in which the applicant's address is located.

Country: Enter the country of the applicant's address. If the address is outside the United States, the owner may appoint a "Domestic Representative" on whom notices or process in proceedings affecting the mark may be served.

Zip/Postal Code: Enter the U.S. zip code or foreign country postal identification code.

Telephone Number: Enter the applicant's telephone number.

Fax Number: Enter the applicant's fax number.

e-Mail Address: Enter the applicant's e-mail address.

APPLICANT ENTITY INFORMATION

Indicate the applicant's entity type by entering the appropriate information in the space to the right of the correct entity type. Please note that only one entity type may be selected.

Individual: Enter the applicant's country of citizenship.

Corporation: Enter the applicant's state of incorporation (or the applicant's country of incorporation if the applicant is a foreign corporation).

Partnership: Enter the state under whose laws the partnership is organized (or the country under whose laws the partnership is organized if the partnership is a foreign partnership).

Name(s) of General Partner(s) & Citizenship/Incorporation: Enter the names and citizenship of any general partners who are individuals, and/or the names and state or (foreign) country of incorporation of any general partners which are corporations, and/or the names and states or (foreign) countries of organization of any general partners which are themselves partnerships. If the applicant is a limited partnership, then only the names and citizenship or state or country of organization or incorporation of the general partners need be provided.

Other Entity Type: Enter a brief description of the applicant's entity type (e.g., joint or multiple applicants, joint venture, limited liability company, association, Indian Nation, state or local agency, trust, estate). The following sets forth the information required with respect to the most common types of "other" entities:

For *joint or multiple applicants*, enter the name and entity type of each joint applicant. Also, enter the citizenship of those joint applicants who are individuals, and/or the state or (foreign) country of incorporation of those joint applicants that are corporations, and/or the state or (foreign) country of organization- and the names and citizenship of the partners- of those joint applicants which are partnerships. The information regarding each applicant should be preceded by a separate heading tag (<APPLICANT INFORMATION>).

For *joint venture*, enter the name and entity type of each entity participating in the joint venture. Also, enter the citizenship of those joint venture participants who are individuals, and/or the state or (foreign) country of incorporation of those joint venture participants that are corporations, and/or the state or (foreign) country of organization- and the names and citizenship of the partners- of those joint venture participants that are partnerships. The information regarding each entity should be preceded by a separate heading tag (<APPLICANT INFORMATION>).

For *limited liability company or association*, enter the state or (foreign) country under whose laws the entity is established.

For *state or local agency*, enter the name of the agency and the state and/or locale of the agency (e.g., Maryland State Lottery Agency, an agency of the State of Maryland).

For *trusts*, identify the trustees and the trust itself, using the following format: The Trustees of the XYZ Trust, a California trust, the trustees comprising John Doe, a U.S. citizen, and the ABC Corp., a Delaware corporation. (Please note that the trustees, and not the trust itself, must be identified as the applicant in the portion of the application designated for naming the applicant).

For *estates*, identify the executors and the estate itself using the following format: The Executors of the John Smith estate, a New York estate, the executors comprising Mary Smith and John Smith, U.S. citizens. (Please note that the executors, and not the estate itself, must be identified as the applicant in the portion of the application designated for naming the applicant).

State/Country under Which Organized: Enter the state or country under whose laws the entity is organized.

COLLECTIVE TRADEMARK/SERVICE MARK INFORMATION

Mark: A mark may consist of words alone, a design or logo, or a combination of words and a design or logo. However, an application may consist of only one mark; separate marks must be filed in separate applications. In this space, enter the word mark in typed form (e.g., THE CAT'S MEOW); or, in the case of a non-word mark or a combination mark, a brief description of the mark (e.g., Design of a fanciful cat or Design of a fanciful cat combined with THE CAT'S MEOW). Do NOT include quotation marks around the mark itself, unless the mark actually features these quotation marks. Also, do NOT include any information related to a "pseudo mark" in this field. The "pseudo mark" field is controlled by the USPTO, and is not something that you should try to enter. If the USPTO determines that a pseudo mark is necessary for your particular mark, it will enter this information in the search system.

Typed Form: Enter "YES" if the collective mark applied for is shown in a typed drawing format (i.e., if the mark consists of only typed words, letters or numbers, and does not include a design). Please note that a registration for a mark based on a typed drawing affords protection not only for the typed version of the mark, but for all other renderings of the mark as long as those renderings do not contain any design elements. For a drawing in stylized form or design, a special form drawing must be submitted. The drawing should be in black and white.

GOODS AND/OR SERVICES

International Class Number(s): Enter the international class number(s) of the goods and/or services associated with the mark.

Listing of Goods and/or Services, by Class: Enter the specific goods and/or services associated with the mark. For multiple-class applications, the goods and/or services should be listed in ascending numerical class order. If the applicant is relying on more than one filing basis, the specific basis should be set forth, followed by the goods and/or services that the particular basis covers. For example:

Class 25: 1(b): shirts, pants; 1(a): shoes; Class 30: 1(b): cookies; 1(a): ice cream

FEE INFORMATION

Number of Classes: Enter the number of classes (e.g., "1" or "3") for which applicant seeks registration. **Total Filing Fee Paid:** Enter the fee amount that is enclosed (either in the form of a check or money order in U.S. currency, made payable to "Commissioner of Patents and Trademarks"), or that is to be charged to a USPTO deposit account. Please note that the filing fee is $375.00 per class of goods or services listed, and at least $375.00 must accompany the application in order for a filing date to be assigned.

FILING BASIS INFORMATION

Intent to Use: Section 1(b): Enter "YES" if the applicant does not yet exercise control over its members' use of the mark in commerce but has a bona fide intention to exercise such control.

Use in Commerce: Section 1(a): Enter "YES" if the applicant is actually exercising legitimate control over its members' use of the mark in commerce.

Specimens: The applicant must submit one (1) specimen showing the mark as used by the members in commerce on or in connection with any item listed in the description of goods and/or services. Examples of acceptable specimens are tags or labels for goods, and advertisements for services. If the goods and/or services are classified in more than one international class, a specimen must be provided showing the mark used on or in connection with at least one item from each of these classes. The specimen must be flat and no larger than 8½ inches (21.6 cm.) wide by 11.69 inches (29.7 cm.) long.

Date of First Use Anywhere: Enter the date on which the goods were first sold or transported or the services first rendered under the mark if such use was in the ordinary course of trade. For every applicant, whether foreign or domestic, the date of first use of a mark is the date of the first such use *anywhere*, in the United States or elsewhere. Please note this date may be earlier than, or the same as, the date of the first use of the mark in commerce.

Date of First Use in Commerce: Enter the date on which members of the applicant first used the mark in commerce, i.e., in interstate commerce, territorial commerce, or commerce between the United States and a foreign country.

Foreign Priority: Section 44(d): Enter "YES" if applicant is filing the application within six months of filing the first foreign application to register the mark in a defined treaty country. **Country of Foreign Filing:** Enter the country in which the foreign application upon which the applicant is asserting a claim of priority has been filed. **Foreign Application Number:** Enter the foreign application serial number, if available. **Filing Date of Foreign Application:** Enter the date (two digits each for both the month and day, and four digits for the year) on which the foreign application was filed. To receive a priority filing date, the applicant must file the United States application within six months of filing the first foreign application in a defined treaty country.

Foreign Registration: Section 44(e): Enter "YES" if applicant is relying on a foreign registration certificate or a certified copy of a foreign registration currently in force. Applicant must submit this foreign registration certificate or a certified copy of the foreign registration. **Country of Foreign Registration:** Enter the country of the foreign registration. **Foreign Registration Number:** Enter the number of the foreign registration. **Foreign Registration Date:** Enter the date (two digits each for both the month and day, and four digits for the year) of the foreign registration. **Foreign Registration Renewal Date:** Enter the date (two digits each for both the month and day, and four digits for the year) of the foreign registration renewal. **Foreign Registration Expiration Date:** Enter the expiration date (two digits each for both the month and day, and four digits for the year) of the foreign registration.

METHOD OF CONTROL

Method of Control: The applicant must specify how it controls, or intends to control (if filing under Section 1(b)), the use of the mark by members. If the applicant's bylaws or other written provisions specify the manner of control, or intended manner of control, it will be sufficient to so state.

SIGNATURE AND OTHER INFORMATION

Signature: The appropriate person must personally sign the form. A person who is properly authorized to sign on behalf of the applicant includes a person with legal authority to bind the applicant and/or a person with firsthand knowledge and actual or implied authority to act on behalf of the applicant.

Date Signed: Enter the date (two digits each for both the month and day, and four digits for the year) on which the application is signed.

Name: Enter the name of the person signing the application.

Title: Enter the signatory's position, if applicable, e.g., Vice President, General Partner. Or, if appropriate, enter the language "Duly Authorized Officer."

CONTACT INFORMATION

Although this may be the same as provided elsewhere in the document, please enter the following required information for where the USPTO should mail correspondence.

Name: Enter the full name of the contact person.

Company/Firm Name: Enter the name of the contact person's company or firm.

Street: Enter the street address or rural delivery route where the contact person is located.

City: Enter the city and/or foreign area designation where the contact person's address is located.

State: Enter the U.S. state or Canadian province in which the contact person's address is located.

Country: Enter the country of the contact person's address.

Zip Code: Enter the U.S. zip code or Canadian postal code.

Telephone Number: Enter the appropriate telephone number.

Fax Number: Enter the appropriate fax number, if available.

e-Mail Address: Enter the appropriate e-mail address, if available.

APPENDIX 11:
STANDARD CHARACTER SET

STANDARD CHARACTER	DESCRIPTION	DECIMAL	HEX	NUMERIC ENTITY
	space	32	20	&#032;
!	exclamation mark	33	21	&#033;
"	(double) quotation mark	34	22	&#034;
#	number sign	35	23	&#035;
$	dollar sign	36	24	&#036;
%	percent sign	37	25	&#037;
&	ampersand	38	26	&#038;
'	apostrophe	39	27	&#039;
(	left parenthesis	40	28	&#040;
)	right parenthesis	41	29	&#041;
*	asterisk	42	2A	&#042;
+	plus sign	43	2B	&#043;
,	comma	44	2C	&#044;
−	minus sign, hyphen	45	2D	&#045;
.	period, decimal point,	46	2E	&#046;
/	slash, virgule, solidus	47	2F	&#047;
0	digit 0	48	30	&#048;
1	digit 1	49	31	&#049;
2	digit 2	50	32	&#050;
3	digit 3	51	33	&#051;

STANDARD CHARACTER	DESCRIPTION	DECIMAL	HEX	NUMERIC ENTITY
4	digit 4	52	34	&#052;
5	digit 5	53	35	&#053;
6	digit 6	54	36	&#054;
7	digit 7	55	37	&#055;
8	digit 8	56	38	&#056;
9	digit 9	57	39	&#057;
:	colon	58	3A	&#058;
;	semicolon	59	3B	&#059;
<	less-than sign	60	3C	&#060;
=	equal sign	61	3D	&#061;
>	greater-than sign	62	3E	&#062;
?	question mark	63	3F	&#063;
@	commercial at sign	64	40	&#064;
A	capital A	65	41	&#065;
B	capital B	66	42	&#066;
C	capital C	67	43	&#067;
D	capital D	68	44	&#068;
E	capital E	69	45	&#069;
F	capital F	70	46	&#070;
G	capital G	71	47	&#071;
H	capital H	72	48	&#072;
I	capital I	73	49	&#073;
J	capital J	74	4A	&#074;
K	capital K	75	4B	&#075;
L	capital L	76	4C	&#076;
M	capital M	77	4D	&#077;
N	capital N	78	4E	&#078;
O	capital O	79	4F	&#079;
P	capital P	80	50	&#080;
Q	capital Q	81	51	&#081;

STANDARD CHARACTER	DESCRIPTION	DECIMAL	HEX	NUMERIC ENTITY
R	capital R	82	52	&#082;
S	capital S	83	53	&#083;
T	capital T	84	54	&#084;
U	capital U	85	55	&#085;
V	capital V	86	56	&#086;
W	capital W	87	57	&#087;
X	capital X	88	58	&#088;
Y	capital Y	89	59	&#089;
Z	capital Z	90	5A	&#090;
[	left square bracket	91	5B	&#091;
\	backslash, reverse solidus	92	5C	&#092;
]	right square bracket	93	5D	&#093;
^	spacing circumflex accent	94	5E	&#094;
_	spacing underscore, low line,	95	5F	&#095;
`	grave accent	96	60	&#096;
a	small a	97	61	&#097;
b	small b	98	62	&#098;
c	small c	99	63	&#099;
d	small d	100	64	&#100;
e	small e	101	65	&#101;
f	small f	102	66	&#102;
g	small g	103	67	&#103;
h	small h	104	68	&#104;
i	small i	105	69	&#105;
j	small j	106	6A	&#106;
k	small k	107	6B	&#107;
l	small l	108	6C	&#108;
m	small m	109	6D	&#109;
n	small n	110	6E	&#110;
o	small o	111	6F	&#111;

STANDARD CHARACTER	DESCRIPTION	DECIMAL	HEX	NUMERIC ENTITY
p	small p	112	70	&#112;
q	small q	113	71	&#113;
r	small r	114	72	&#114;
s	small s	115	73	&#115;
t	small t	116	74	&#116;
u	small u	117	75	&#117;
v	small v	118	76	&#118;
w	small w	119	77	&#119;
x	small x	120	78	&#120;
y	small y	121	79	&#121;
z	small z	122	7A	&#122;
{	left brace (curly bracket)	123	7B	&#123;
|	vertical line	124	7C	|
}	right brace (curly bracket)	125	7D	&#125;
~	tilde accent	126	7E	&#126;
€	Euro	128	80	&#128;
‚	low left rising single quote	130	82	&#130;
f	small italic f, function of,	131	83	&#131;
„	low left rising double quote	132	84	&#132;
. . .	low horizontal ellipsis	133	85	&#133;
‰	per thousand (mille) sign	137	89	&#137;
Š	capital S caron or hacek	138	8A	&#138;
‹	left single angle quote mark	139	8B	&#139;
Œ	capital OE ligature	140	8C	&#140;
Ž	latin capital letter Z with caron	142	8E	&#142;
'	left single quotation mark,	145	91	&#145;
'	right single quote mark	146	92	&#146;
"	left double quotation mark,	147	93	&#147

STANDARD CHARACTER	DESCRIPTION	DECIMAL	HEX	NUMERIC ENTITY
"	right double quote mark	148	94	&#148;
–	en dash	150	96	&#150;
—	em dash	151	97	&#151;
~	small spacing tilde accent	152	98	&#152;
š	small s caron or hacek	154	9A	&#154;
›	right single angle quote mark	155	9B	&#155;
œ	small oe ligature	156	9C	&#156;
ž	latin small letter Z with caron	158	9E	&#158;
Ÿ	capital Y dieresis or umlaut	159	9F	&#159;
¡	inverted exclamation mark	161	A1	&#161;
¢	cent sign	162	A2	&#162;
£	pound sterling sign	163	A3	&#163;
¤	general currency sign	164	A4	&#164;
¥	yen sign	165	A5	&#165;
§	section sign	167	A7	&#167;
¨	spacing dieresis or umlaut	168	A8	&#168;
a	feminine ordinal indicator	170	AA	&#170;
<<	left (double) angle quote	171	AB	&#171;
°	degree sign	176	B0	&#176;
±	plus-or-minus sign	177	B1	&#177;
´	spacing acute accent	180	B4	&#180;
µ	micro sign	181	B5	&#181;
·	middle dot, centered dot	183	B7	&#183;
¸	spacing cedilla	184	B8	&#184;
º	masculine ordinal indicator	186	BA	&#186;
>>	right (double) angle quote	187	BB	&#187;
¿	inverted question mark	191	BF	&#191;
À	capital A grave	192	C0	&#192;

STANDARD CHARACTER	DESCRIPTION	DECIMAL	HEX	NUMERIC ENTITY
Á	capital A acute	193	C1	&#193;
Â	capital A circumflex	194	C2	&#194;
Ã	capital A tilde	195	C3	&#195;
Ä	capital A dieresis or umlaut	196	C4	&#196;
Å	capital A ring	197	C5	&#197;
Æ	capital AE ligature	198	C6	&#198;
Ç	capital C cedilla	199	C7	&#199;
È	capital E grave	200	C8	&#200;
É	capital E acute	201	C9	&#201;
Ê	capital E circumflex	202	CA	&#202;
Ë	capital E dieresis or umlaut	203	CB	&#203;
Ì	capital I grave	204	CC	&#204;
Í	capital I acute	205	CD	&#205;
Î	capital I circumflex	206	CE	&#206;
Ï	capital I dieresis or umlaut	207	CF	&#207;
Ð	capital ETH	208	D0	&#208;
Ñ	capital N tilde	209	D1	&#209;
Ò	capital O grave	210	D2	&#210;
Ó	capital O acute	211	D3	&#211;
Ô	capital O circumflex	212	D4	&#212;
Õ	capital O tilde	213	D5	&#213;
Ö	capital O dieresis or umlaut	214	D6	&#214;
×	multiplication sign	215	D7	&#215;
Ø	capital O slash	216	D8	&#216;
Ù	capital U grave	217	D9	&#217;
Ú	capital U acute	218	DA	&#218;
Û	capital U circumflex	219	DB	&#219;
Ü	capital U dieresis or umlaut	220	DC	&#220;

STANDARD CHARACTER	DESCRIPTION	DECIMAL	HEX	NUMERIC ENTITY
Ý	capital Y acute	221	DD	&#221;
Þ	capital THORN	222	DE	&#222;
ß	small sharp s, sz ligature	223	DF	&#223;
à	small a grave	224	E0	&#224;
á	small a acute	225	E1	&#225;
â	small a circumflex	226	E2	&#226;
ã	small a tilde	227	E3	&#227;
ä	small a dieresis or umlaut	228	E4	&#228;
å	small a ring	229	E5	&#229;
æ	small ae ligature	230	E6	&#230;
ç	small c cedilla	231	E7	&#231;
è	small e grave	232	E8	&#232;
é	small e acute	233	E9	&#233;
ê	small e circumflex	234	EA	&#234;
ë	small e dieresis or umlaut	235	EB	&#235;
ì	small i grave	236	EC	&#236;
í	small i acute	237	ED	&#237;
î	small i circumflex	238	EE	&#238;
ï	small i dieresis or umlaut	239	EF	&#239;
ð	small eth	240	F0	&#240;
ñ	small n tilde	241	F1	&#241;
ò	small o grave	242	F2	&#242;
ó	small o acute	243	F3	&#243;
ô	small o circumflex	244	F4	&#244;
õ	small o tilde	245	F5	&#245;
ö	small o dieresis or umlaut	246	F6	&#246;
÷	division sign	247	F7	&#247;
ø	small o slash	248	F8	&#248;
ù	small u grave	249	F9	&#249;
ú	small u acute	250	FA	&#250;

STANDARD CHARACTER	DESCRIPTION	DECIMAL	HEX	NUMERIC ENTITY
û	small u circumflex	251	FB	&#251;
ü	small u dieresis or umlaut	252	FC	&#252;
ý	small y acute	253	FD	&#253;
þ	small thorn	254	FE	&#254;
ÿ	small y dieresis or umlaut	255	FF	&#255;
Ā	Amacr—latin capital letter A with macron	256	100	&#256;
ā	amacr—latin small letter a with macron	257	101	&#257;
Ă	Acaron—latin capital letter A with caron (breve)	258	102	&#258;
ă	acaron—latin small letter a with caron (breve)	259	103	&#259;
Ą	Acedil—latin capital letter A with cedilla	260	104	&#260;
ą	acedil—latin small letter a with cedilla	261	105	&#261;
Ć	Cacute—latin capital letter C with acute	262	106	&#262;
ć	cacute—latin small letter c with acute	263	107	&#263;
Č	Ccaron—latin capital letter C with caron	268	10C	&#268;
č	ccaron—latin small letter c with caron	269	10D	&#269;
Ď	Dcaron—latin capital letter D with caron	270	10E	&#270;
Đ	Dstrok—latin capital letter D with stroke	272	110	&#272;
đ	dstrok—latin small letter d with stroke	273	111	&#273;
Ē	Emacr—latin capital letter E with macron	274	112	&#274;
ē	emacr—latin small letter e with macron	275	113	&#275;
Ė	Edot—latin capital letter E with dot above	278	116	&#278;

STANDARD CHARACTER	DESCRIPTION	DECIMAL	HEX	NUMERIC ENTITY
ė	edot—latin small letter e with dot above	279	117	&#279;
Ę	Ecedil—latin capital letter E with cedilla	280	118	&#280;
ę	ecedil—latin small letter e with cedilla	281	119	&#281;
Ě	Ecaron—latin capital letter E with caron	282	11A	&#282;
ě	ecaron—latin small letter e with caron	283	11B	&#283;
Ğ	Gcaron—latin capital letter G with caron (breve)	286	11E	&#286;
ğ	gcaron—latin small letter e with caron (breve)	287	11F	&#287;
Ç	Gcedil—latin capital letter G with cedilla	290	122	&#290;
ġ	gapos—latin small letter g with cedilla above	291	123	&#291;
Ī	Imacr—latin capital letter I with macron	298	12A	&#298;
ī	imacr—latin small letter i with macron	299	12B	&#299;
Į	Iogon—latin capital letter I with ogonek	302	12E	&#302;
į	iogon—latin small letter i with ogonek	303	12F	&#303;
İ	Idot—latin capital letter I with dot	304	130	&#304;
ı	nodot—latin small letter i with no dot	305	131	&#305;
Ķ	Kcedil—latin capital letter K with cedilla	310	136	&#310;
ķ	kcedil—latin small letter k with cedilla	311	137	&#311;
Ĺ	Lacute—latin capital letter L with acute	313	139	&#313;
ĺ	lacute—latin small letter l with acute	314	13A	&#314;
Ļ	Lcedil—latin capital letter L with cedilla	315	13B	&#315;

STANDARD CHARACTER	DESCRIPTION	DECIMAL	HEX	NUMERIC ENTITY
Ļ	lcedil—latin small letter l with cedilla	316	13C	&#316;
Ľ	Lcaron—latin capital letter L with caron	317	13D	&#317;
ľ	lcaron—latin small letter l with caron	318	13E	&#318;
Ł	Lstrok—latin capital letter L with stroke	321	141	&#321;
ł	lstrok—latin small letter l with stroke	322	142	&#322;
Ń	Nacute—latin capital letter N with acute	323	143	&#323;
ń	nacute—latin small letter n with acute	324	144	&#324;
Ņ	Ncedil—latin capital letter N with cedilla	325	145	&#325;
ņ	ncedil—latin small letter n with cedilla	326	146	&#326;
Ň	Ncaron—latin capital letter N with caron	327	147	&#327;
ň	ncaron—latin small letter n with caron	328	148	&#328;
Ō	Omacr—latin capital letter O with macron	332	14C	&#332;
ō	omacr—latin small letter o with macron	333	14D	&#333;
Ő	Odblac—latin capital letter O with double acute	336	150	&#336;
ő	odblac—latin small letter o with double acute	337	151	&#337;
Ŗ	Rcedil—latin capital letter R with cedilla	342	156	&#342;
ŗ	rcedil—latin small letter r with cedilla	343	157	&#343;
Ř	Rcaron—latin capital letter R with caron	344	158	&#344;
ř	rcaron—latin small letter r with caron	345	159	&#345;
Ś	Sacute—latin capital letter S with acute	346	15A	&#346;

STANDARD CHARACTER	DESCRIPTION	DECIMAL	HEX	NUMERIC ENTITY
ś	sacute—latin small letter s with acute	347	15B	&#347;
Ş	Scedil—latin capital letter S with cedilla	350	15E	&#350;
ş	scedil—latin small letter s with cedilla	351	15F	&#351;
Š	Scaron—latin capital letter S with caron	352	160	&#352;
š	scaron—latin small letter s with caron	353	161	&#353;
Ţ	Tcedil—latin capital letter T with cedilla	354	162	&#354;
ţ	tcedil—latin small letter t with cedilla	355	163	&#355;
Ť	Tcaron—latin capital letter T with caron	356	164	&#356;
ť	tcaron—latin small letter t with caron	357	165	&#357;
Ū	Umacr—latin capital letter U with macron	362	16A	&#362;
ū	umacr—latin small letter u with macron	363	16B	&#363;
Ů	Uring—latin capital letter U with ring above	366	16E	&#366;
ů	uring—latin small letter u with ring above	367	16F	&#367;
Ű	Udblac—latin capital letter U with double acute	368	170	&#368;
ű	udblac—latin small letter u with double acute	369	171	&#369;
Ų	Uogon—latin capital letter U with ogonek	370	172	&#370;
ų	uogon—latin small letter u with ogonek	371	173	&#371;
Ź	Zacute—latin capital letter Z with acute	377	179	&#377;
ź	zacute—latin small letter z with acute	378	17A	&#378;
Ż	Zdot—latin capital letter Z with dot above	379	17B	&#379;

STANDARD CHARACTER	DESCRIPTION	DECIMAL	HEX	NUMERIC ENTITY
ż	zdot—latin small letter z with dot above	380	17C	&#380;
Ž	Zcaron—latin capital letter Z with caron	381	17D	&#381;
ž	zcaron—latin small letter z with caron	382	17E	&#382;

APPENDIX 12:
DRAWING REQUIREMENTS FOR PAPER SUBMISSIONS

Excerpted from Trademark Manual of Examining Procedure:

807.06 Paper Drawings

In a paper submission, the drawing should:

(a) Be on non-shiny white paper that is separate from the application;

(b) Be on paper that is 8 to 8.5 inches (20.3 to 21.6 cm.) wide and 11 to 11.69 inches (27.9 to 29.7 cm.) long. One of the shorter sides of the sheet should be regarded as its top edge. The image must be no larger than 3.15 inches (8 cm) high by 3.15 inches (8 cm) wide;

(c) Include the caption "DRAWING PAGE" at the top of the drawing beginning one inch (2.5 cm.) from the top edge; and

(d) Depict the mark in black ink, or in color if color is claimed as a feature of the mark.

(e) Drawings must be typed or made with a pen or by a process that will provide high definition when copied. A photolithographic, printer's proof copy, or other high quality reproduction of the mark may be used. All lines must be clean, sharp and solid, and must not be fine or crowded.

Paper drawings may be filed by mail or hand delivery. Drawings may not be submitted by facsimile transmission.

***

Further requirements (from 37 C.F.R. 2.52):

(d) Heading. Across the top of the drawing, beginning one inch (2.5 cm.) from the top edge and not exceeding one third of the sheet, there must be placed a heading, listing in separate lines, applicant's complete name; applicant's post office address; the dates of first use of the mark and first use of the mark in commerce in an application under section 1(a) of the Act; the priority filing date of the relevant foreign application in an application claiming the benefit of a prior foreign application in accordance with section 44(d) of the Act; and the goods or services recited in the application or a typical item of the goods or services if a number of items are recited in the application. This heading should be typewritten. If the drawing is in special form, the heading should include a description of the essential elements of the mark.

APPENDIX 13:
IDENTIFICATION OF THE APPLICANT

Excerpted from Trademark Manual of Examining Procedure:

803.01 (related to minors)

The question of whether an application can be filed in the name of a minor depends on state law. If the minor can validly enter into binding legal obligations, and can sue or be sued, in the state in which he or she is domiciled, the application may be filed in the name of the minor. Otherwise, the application should be filed in the name of a parent or legal guardian, clearly setting forth his or her status as a parent or legal guardian. An example of the manner in which the applicant should be identified in such cases is:

> John Smith, United States citizen, (parent/legal guardian) of Mary Smith.

803.02 Name of Applicant

The name of the applicant should be set out in its correct legal form. For example, a corporate applicant should be identified by the name set forth in the articles of incorporation.

If the applicant's legal name includes the assumed name under which it does business, an assumed name designation should be used to connect the actual name with the assumed name. Assumed name designations include "d.b.a." (doing business as), "a.k.a." (also known as), and "t.a." (trading as). The particular assumed name designation used is optional. Only the abbreviation of the assumed name designation will be printed in the *Official Gazette* and on the certificate of registration. If an applicant gives the assumed name designation in full, the abbreviation will automatically be used for printing purposes.

803.02(a) Individual

If the applicant is an individual person who is doing business under an assumed business name, the individual's name should be set forth, followed by an assumed name designation (*e.g.,* d.b.a., a.k.a., or t.a.) and by the assumed business name.

803.02(b) Partnership, Joint Venture, or Other "Firm"

If a partnership, joint venture, or other "firm" has been organized under a particular business name, the application should be filed in that name. If the partnership or firm has not been organized under a business name, the names of the members should be listed as though they composed a company name. If a partnership or joint venture is doing business under an assumed name, this may be indicated, using an assumed name designation.

803.02(c) Corporation and Association

If the applicant is a corporation, the official corporate name must be set out as the applicant's name. Listing an assumed business name is optional. The name of a division of the applicant should *not* be included in or along with the applicant's name. If the applicant wishes to indicate in the application that actual use of the mark is being made by a division of the applicant, the applicant may provide a statement that "the applicant, *through its division* [specify name of division], is using the mark in commerce." This statement should not appear in conjunction with the listing of the applicant's name, and will not be printed on the registration certificate.

Associations should be identified by the full, official name of the association.

803.03 Legal Entity of Applicant

Immediately after the applicant's name, the application should set out the applicant's form of business, or legal entity, such as partnership, joint venture, corporation, or association. The words "company" and "firm" are indefinite for purposes of designating a domestic applicant's legal entity, because those words do not identify a particular type of legal entity in the United States. (However, the word "company" is acceptable to identify entities organized under the laws of foreign countries that are equivalent or analogous to United States corporations or associations.

803.03(a) Individual or Sole Proprietorship

For an individual, it is not necessary to specify "individual," but it is acceptable to do so. The applicant may state that he or she is doing business under a specified assumed company name.

An applicant may identify itself as a sole proprietorship. If an applicant does so, the applicant must also indicate the state where the sole proprietorship is organized, in addition to the name and national citizenship of the sole proprietor.

803.03(b) Partnership, Joint Venture or Other "Firm"

The application of a partnership or a joint venture should specify the state or country under whose laws the partnership or joint venture is organized.

In addition, domestic partnerships must set forth the names, legal entities, and national citizenship (for individuals), or state or country of organization (for businesses) of all general partners or active members that compose the partnership or joint venture.

These requirements apply to both general and limited partnerships. They also apply to a partnership that is a general partner in a larger partnership. Limited partners or silent or inactive partners need not be listed. The following format should be used:

"_____, a (partnership, joint venture) organized under the laws of _____, composed of _____ (name and citizenship)."

In the case of a domestic partnership consisting of ten or more general partners, if the partnership agreement provides for the continuing existence of the partnership in the event of the addition or departure of specific partners, the Office will require that the applicant provide the names, legal entities, and national citizenship (or the state or country of organization) of the principal partners only. If there are more than ten principal partners, the applicant need list only the first ten principal partners. If there is no class of principal partners, the applicant may list any ten general partners.

***

803.03(e) Trusts, Conservatorships, and Estates

If a trust is the owner of a mark in an application, the examining attorney must ensure that the trustee(s) is identified as the applicant. Thus, the examining attorney should require that the trust's application be captioned as follows:

> The Trustees of the XYZ Trust, a California trust, the trustees comprising John Doe, a United States citizen, and the ABC Corporation, a Delaware corporation.

The application must first refer to the trustee(s) as the applicant and indicate the name of the trust, if any. Then the state under whose laws the trust exists must be set forth. Finally, the names and citizenship of the individual trustees must be listed.

The same format generally applies to conservatorships and estates as follows:

> The Conservator of Mary Jones, a New York conservatorship, the conservator comprising James Abel, a United States citizen.

> The Executors of the John Smith estate, a New York estate, the executors comprising Mary Smith and James Smith, United States citizens.

803.03(e)(i) Business Trusts

Most states recognize an entity commonly identified as a "business trust," "Massachusetts trust," or "common-law trust." A business trust has attributes of both a corporation and a partnership. Many states have codified laws recognizing and regulating business trusts; other states apply common law. The Office must accept the entity designation "business trust," or any appropriate variation provided for under relevant state law.

The business trust is created under the instructions of the instrument of trust. Generally, the "trustee" has authority equivalent to an officer in a corporation. Laws vary to some extent as to the authority conferred on various individuals associated with the business trust.

The application must first refer to the trustee(s) as the applicant and indicate the name of the trust, if any. The state under whose laws the trust exists, and the names and citizenship (or state of incorporation or organization) of the individual trustees, must also be set forth. Accordingly, the examining attorney should require that the business trust's application be captioned as follows:

> The Trustees of the DDT Trust, a California business trust, the trustees comprising Sue Smith, a United States citizen, and the PDQ Corporation, a Delaware corporation.

803.03(f) Governmental Bodies and Universities

It is difficult to establish any rigid guidelines for designating the entity of a governmental body. Due to the variety in the form of these entities, the examining attorney must consider each case on an individual basis. The following are just a few examples of acceptable governmental entities:

Department of the Air Force, an agency of the United States.

Maryland State Lottery Agency, an agency of the State of Maryland.

City of Richmond, Virginia, a municipal corporation organized under the laws of the Commonwealth of Virginia.

These examples are not exhaustive of the entity designations that are acceptable.

The structure of educational institutions varies significantly. The following are examples of acceptable university entities:

Board of Regents, University of Texas System, a Texas governing body.

University of New Hampshire, a nonprofit corporation of New Hampshire.

Auburn University, State University, Alabama.

These examples are not exhaustive of the entity designations that are acceptable.

803.03(g) Banking Institutions

The nature of banking institutions is strictly regulated and, thus, there are a limited number of types of banking entities. Some banking institutions are federally chartered while others are organized under state law. The following are examples of acceptable descriptions of banking institutions:

First American Bank of Virginia, a Virginia corporation.

Pathway Financial, a federally chartered savings and loan association.

This is not an exhaustive listing of acceptable entity designations.

***

803.03(i) Common Terms Designating Entity of Foreign Applicants

In designating the legal entity of foreign applicants, acceptable terminology is not always the same as for United States applicants. The word "corporation" as used in the United States is not necessarily equivalent to juristic entities of foreign countries; the word "company" is, sometimes, more accurate. If the applicant is from the United Kingdom or another commonwealth country (*e.g.,* Canada or Australia) and the term "company" is used, no inquiry is needed. "Limited company" is also acceptable in commonwealth countries.

Foreign Entities

This table lists common terms and abbreviations used by various foreign countries to identify legal commercial entities. If a designation or its abbreviation appears in the table below, the examining attorney may accept the entity designation without further inquiry.

Abbr.	COUNTRY	DESCRIPTION
A. en P.	Mexico	*Asociación en Participación.* Joint venture.
AB	Sweden	*Aktiebolag.* Joint Stock Company, equivalent to a corporation.
A.C.	Mexico	*Asociación Civil.* Civil Association of a non-commercial nature.
ACE	Portugal	*Agrupamento Complementar de Empresas.* Association of businesses.
AD	Bulgaria	*Aktzionero Druzhestvo.* Limited Liability Company.
AE	Greece	*Anonymos Etairia.* Joint Stock Company, equivalent to a corporation.
AG	Austria	*Aktiengesellschaft.* Joint Stock Company, equivalent to a corporation.
AG	Germany	*Aktiengesellschaft.* Joint Stock Company, equivalent to a corporation.
AG	Switzerland	*Aktiengesellschaft.* Joint Stock Company, equivalent to a corporation.
AL	Norway	*Andelslag.* Cooperative society.
AmbA	Denmark	*Andelsselskab.* Limited Liability Cooperative.
ANS	Norway	*Ansvarlig selskap.* Trading partnership.
Apb	Sweden	*Publikt Aktiebolag.* Public Stock Corporation.
ApS	Denmark	*Anpartsselskab.* Private Limited Company.
ApS & Co. K/S	Denmark	Similar to a general partnership, but the entity with unlimited liability is a company (ApS) instead of an individual.

Abbr.	COUNTRY	DESCRIPTION
AS	Norway	*Aksjeselskap.* Stock Company, equivalent to a corporation.
A/S	Denmark	*Aktieselskap.* Stock Company, equivalent to a corporation.
A.S.	Czech Republic	*Akciova Spolecnost.* Joint Stock Company, equivalent to a corporation.
A.S.	Estonia	*Aktsiaselts.* Joint Stock Company, equivalent to a corporation.
A.S.	Slovakia	*Akciova Spolecnost.* Joint Stock Company, equivalent to a corporation.
A.S.	Turkey	*Anonim Sirketi.* Joint Stock Company, equivalent to a corporation.
ASA	Norway	*Allmennaksjeselskap.* Public stock corporation.
Association/ Associazione	Switzerland/ France/Italy	*Association.*
AVV	France/Switzerland	*Aruba Vrijgestelde Vennootschap.* Aruba Exempt Company.
BM or B.M.	Israel	*Be'eravon Mugbal.* Limited Company.
BK or CC	South Africa	*Beslote Korporasie.* Close Corporation.
Bt	Hungary	*Betiti társaság.* Limited Liability Partnership.
B.V.	Belgium	*Besloten Vennootschap.* Limited Liability Company.
B.V.	Netherlands	*Besloten Vennootschap.* Limited Liability Company.
B.V.	Netherlands Antilles	*Besloten Vennootschap.* Limited Liability Company.
BVBA	Belgium	*Besloten Vennootschap met Beperkte Aansprakelijkheid.* Flemish language equivalent of the SPRL—means that the company is a private limited company.
CA	Ecuador	*Compania Anonima.* Public Limited Company.
c.c.c.	Wales	*Cwmni Cyfyngedig Cyhoeddus.* Public Limited Company, Welsh language equivalent to PLC.
C.V.	Netherlands	*Commanditaire Vennootschap.* Limited Partnership.

Abbr.	COUNTRY	DESCRIPTION
CVA	Belgium	*Commanditaire Vennootschap op Aandelen.* Limited partnership, with shares. Flemish language equivalent to the French language SCA.
CVoA	Netherlands	*Commanditaire Vennootschap op Andelen.* Limited Partnership, with shares.
Cyf.	Wales	*Cyfyngedig.* Private Limited Company, Welsh language equivalent to Ltd.
DA	Norway	*Selskap med delt ansar.* Limited Partnership.
d.d.	Croatia	*Dionicko Drustvo.* Joint stock company.
d.d.	Slovenia	*Delniska Druzba.* Stock company
DI	Italy/Switzerland	*Ditta individuale.* Sole Proprietorship.
d.n.o.	Slovenia	*Druzba z neomejeno odgovornostjo.* Partnership, all partners have unlimited liability.
d.o.o.	Croatia	*Drustvo s Ogranicenom Odgovornoscu.* Limited Liability Company.
d.o.o.	Slovenia	*Druzba z Omejeno Odgovornostjo.* Limited Liability Company.
EE	Greece	*Eterrorrythmos.* Limited liability partnership.
EEG	Austria	*Eingetragene Erwerbsgesellschaft.* Professional Partnership.
EIRL	Peru	*Empresa Individual de Responsabilidad Limitada.* Personal business with limited liability.
EG	Switzerland	*Einfache Gesellschaft.* Simple Partnership.
ELP	Bahamas	*Exempted Limited Partnership.* Has one or more limited partners, and one general partner, which must be a resident of the Bahamas or a company incorporated in the Bahamas.
EOOD	Bulgaria	*Ednolichno Druzhestvo s Ogranichena Otgovornost.* Limited liability company.
EPE	Greece	*Etairia periorismenis efthinis.* Limited liability company.
EURL	France	*Enterprise Unipersonnelle à Responsabilité Limitée.* Incorporated sole proprietorship with limited liability.

Abbr.	COUNTRY	DESCRIPTION
e.V.	Germany	*Eingetragener Verein.* Non-profit society/ association.
Einzelfirma	Germany/Swiss	*Einzelfirma.* Sole Proprietorship.
Fondation/ Fondazione	Switzerland/ France/Italy	*Foundation.* Foundation having some attributes of a corporation.
GbR	Germany	*Gesellschaft burgerlichen Rechts.* Partnership without a legal name.
GCV	Belgium	*Gewone Commanditaire Vennootschap.* Limited Partnership. Flemish language equivalent to the French language SCS.
G.K.	Japan	*Godo kaisha* or *Godokaisha. A* variant of the American limited liability company.
Gen	Switzerland	*Genossenschaft.* Cooperative Society.
GesmbH	Austria	*Limited Liability Company.* This abbreviation is only used in Austria (not Germany or Switzerland).
GIE	France	*Groupement d'intérét économique.* Economic Grouping of Interest. Two or more persons or entities form an alliance with the goal of facilitating or developing economic activity of the members.
GmbH & Co. KG	Germany	Like a *KG*, but the entity with unlimited liability is a *GmbH* instead of a person. (See the *KG* entry for more information).
GmbH	Austria	*Gesellschaft mit beschränkter Haftung.* Limited Liability Company.
GmbH	Germany	*Gesellschaft mit beschränkter Haftung.* Limited Liability Company.
GmbH	Switzerland	*Gesellschaft mit beschränkter Haftung.* Limited Liability Company.
Gomei Kaisha	Japan	*Gomei Kaisha.* Similar to an American general partnership.
Goshi Kaisha	Japan	*Goshi Kaisha* or *Goshikaisha.* Similar to an American limited partnership.
HB	Sweden	*Handelsbolag.* Trading Partnership.
hf	Iceland	*Hlutafelag.* Limited liability company.
I/S	Denmark	*Interessentskab.* General partnership.
j.t.d.	Croatia	*Javno Trgovacko Drustvo.* Unlimited liability company.
KA/S	Denmark	*Kommanditaktieselskab.* Limited partnership with share capital.

Abbr.	COUNTRY	DESCRIPTION
KAG	Switzerland	*Kommandit-Aktiengesellschaft. Limited partnership with shares.*
Kb	Sweden	*Kommanditbolag.* Limited partnership.
KD	Bulgaria	*Komanditno Drushestwo.* Partnership.
k.d.	Croatia	*Komanditno Drustvo.* Limited Partnership.
k.d.	Slovenia	*Komanditna Druzba.* Limited Partnership
KDA	Bulgaria	*Komanditno drushestwo s akzii.* Partnership with shares.
k.d.d.	Slovenia	*Komanditna delniska druzba.* Limited Partnership with shares.
Kft	Hungary	*Korlátolt Felelösségû Társaság.* Limited liability company.
KG	Austria	*Kommanditgesellschaft.* A limited partnership under a legal name whose entity survives even though the partners might change.
KG	Germany	*Kommanditgesellschaft.* A limited partnership under a legal name whose entity survives even though the partners might change.
KG	Switzerland	*Kommanditgesellschaft.* A limited partnership under a legal name whose entity survives even though the partners might change.
KGaA	Germany	*Kommanditgesellschaft auf Aktien.* A limited partnership with shares.
K.K.	Japan	*Kabushiki Kaishi.* Joint Stock Company.
Kkt	Hungary	*Közkereseti Társaság*, General Partnership.
KolG	Switzerland	*Kollektivgesellschaft.* General Partnership.
Kol. SrK	Turkey	*Kollektiv Sirket.* Unlimited liability partnership.
Kom. SrK	Turkey	*Komandit Sirket.* Limited liability partnership.
k.s.	Czech Republic	*Komanditni Spolecnost.* Limited partnership.
K/S	Denmark	*Kommanditselskab.* Limited partnership.
KS	Norway	*Kommandittselskap.* Limited partnership.
Kv	Hungary	*Közös vállalat.* Joint Venture.

Abbr.	COUNTRY	DESCRIPTION
Ky	Finland	*Kommandiittiyhtiö*. Limited Partnership.
Lda	Portugal	*Sociedade por Quotas Limitada*. Similar to an American Limited Liability Company.
LDC	Bahamas	*Limited Duration Company*. A company, but it has a life of 30 years or less.
Ltd.	Commonwealth countries; China	*Limited Company*. Indicates that a company is incorporated and that the owners have limited liability
Ltda	Brazil	*Sociedade por Quotas de Responsabiliadade Limitada*. Similar to a limited liability company.
NV	Netherlands	*Naamloze Vennootschap*. Public limited liability company, equivalent to a corporation.
NV	Belgium	*Naamloze Vennootschap*. Public limited liability company, equivalent to a corporation.
NV	Netherlands Antilles	*Naamloze Vennootschap*. Public limited liability company, equivalent to a corporation.
NV	Suriname	*Naamloze Vennootschap*. Public limited liability company, equivalent to a corporation.
OE	Greece	*Omorrythmos*. Partnership.
OHG	Austria	*Offene Handelsgesellschaft*. Partnership.
OHG	Germany	*Offene Handelsgesellschaft*. Partnership.
OOD	Bulgaria	*Druzhestvo s Ogranichena Otgovornost*. Limited Liability Company.
OAO	Russian Federation	*Otkrytoe Aktsionernoe Obshchestvo*. Joint Stock Company.
OOO	Russian Federation	*Obschestvo s ogranichennoy otveststvennostyu*. Limited Liability Company.
OÜ	Estonia	*Osaühing*. Private limited liability company.
Oy	Finland	*Osakeyhtiö*. Corporation.
OYJ	Finland	*Julkinen Osakeyhtiö*. Public limited company.
P/L or Pty. Ltd.	Australia	Proprietary Limited Company.

Abbr.	COUNTRY	DESCRIPTION
PC Ltd	Australia	Public Company Limited by Shares.
PLC	UK & Ireland	Public Limited Company.
PMA	Indonesia	*Penenaman Modal Asing.* Foreign joint venture company.
PMDN	Indonesia	*Penanaman Modal Dalam Negeri.* Domestic Capital investment company.
PrC	Ireland	Private Company limited by shares.
Prp. Ltd.	Botswana	Private company limited by shares.
PT	Indonesia	*Perseroan Terbuka.* Limited company.
PT Tbk	Indonesia	*Perseroan Terbatas, Terbuka.* Stock corporation.
Pty.	Australia	Proprietary Company.
RI	Switzerland	*Raison individuelle.* Sole Proprietorship.
RAS	Estonia	*Riiklik Aktsiaselts.* State (owned) Joint Stock company.
Rt	Hungary	*Részvénytársaság.* Stock Company.
S. de R.L.	Mexico	*Sociedad de Responsabilidad Limitada.* Limited Liability Company.
S. en C.	Colombia & Peru	*Sociedad en Comandita.* Limited Partnership.
S.N.C.	Mexico	*Sociedad en Nombre Colectivo.* General Partnership.
S/A	Brazil	*Sociedades Anônimas.* Joint stock company, equivalent to a corporation.
SA	Argentina	*Sociedad Anonima.* Joint stock company, equivalent to a corporation.
SA	Belgium	*Société Anonyme.* Joint stock company, equivalent to a corporation.
SA	France/Switzerland	*Société Anonyme.* Joint stock company, equivalent to a corporation.
SA	Ivory Coast	*Société Anonyme.* Joint stock company, equivalent to a corporation.
SA	Luxembourg	*Société Anonyme.* Joint stock company, equivalent to a corporation.
SA	Mexico	*Sociedad Anónima.* Joint stock company, equivalent to a corporation.
SA	Morocco	*Société Anonyme.* Joint stock company, equivalent to a corporation.

Abbr.	COUNTRY	DESCRIPTION
SA	Poland	*Spolka Akcyjna*. Joint stock company, equivalent to a corporation.
SA	Portugal	*Sociedad Anónima*. Joint stock company, equivalent to a corporation.
SA	Romania	*Societate pe actiuni*. Joint stock company, equivalent to a corporation.
SA	Spain	*Sociedad Anonima*. Joint stock company, equivalent to a corporation.
S.A.	Brazil	*Sociedade por Ações*. Privately-held company.
SA de CV	Mexico	*Sociedad Anonima*, Joint stock company, with variable capital
SAFI	Uruguay	*Sociedad Anonima Financiera de Inversion*. Offshore company.
Sagl	Switzerland	*Società a garanzia limitata*. Limited Liability Company.
S.A.I.C.A.	Venezuela	*Sociedad Anónima Inscrita de Capital Abierto*. Open Capital Company.
SApA	Italy/Switzerland	*Societa in Accomandita per Azioni*. Limited partnership with shares.
Sarl	France & Other	*Société à responsabilité limitée*. Limited Liability Company. Used in France and other French speaking countries.
Sarl	Luxembourg	*Société à Responsabilité Limitée*. Limited Liability Company.
SAS	France	*Société par Actions Simplifiée*. Simplified Stock Corporation which has the legal status of a corporation. Note, however, that "*societe par action*" by itself is not an official French entity designation.
SAS	Italy	*Societá in Accomandita Semplice*. Limited Partnership.
SC	France/Switzerland	*Société en commandite*. Partnership with limited and general partners.
SC	France	*Société civile*. Partnership with full liability.
SC	Poland	*Spólka prawa cywilnego*. Partnership with all partners having unlimited liability.
SC	Italy/Switzerland	*Societa cooperativa*. Cooperative society. This type of entity may be incorporated with either limited or unlimited liability.

Abbr.	COUNTRY	DESCRIPTION
SCOP	France/Switzerland	*Société Coopérative.* Cooperative society. This type of entity may be incorporated with either limited or unlimited liability.
S.C.	Spain	*Sociedad en Commandita.* General Partnership.
SCA	France/Belgium/ Switzerland	*Société en commandite par actions.* Limited partnership with share capital, occupies a position between a limited partnership and a corporation.
SCA	Romania	*Societate in còmandita pe actiuni.* Limited liability partnership with shares.
SCP	Brazil	*Sociedade em Conta de Participacão.* Partnership where there is one partner assumed responsible for running the business.
SCS	Belgium & France	*Société en Commandite Simple.* A special partnership very similar to an American limited partnership
S.C.S.	Brazil	*Sociedade em Comandita Simples.* Limited Partnership.
SCS	Mexico	*Sociedad en Comandita Simple.* Limited Partnership.
SCS	Romania	*Societate in comandita simpla.* Limited liability partnership.
Sdn Bhd	Malaysia	*Sendirian Berhad.* Limited Liability Company.
SE	European Union	*Societas Europae.* European Company. A Public Limited Company, equivalent to a corporation.
SENC	Luxembourg	*Société en Nom Collectif.* General Partnership.
SGPS	Portugal	*Sociedade gestora de participações socialis.* Holding Enterprise.
SK	Poland	*Spólka komandytowa.* Limited liability partnership.
SL	Spain	*Sociedad de Responsabilidad Limitada.* Limited liability company, may be identified as a joint stock company with limited liability.
SLNE	Spain	*Sociedad Limitada Nueva Empresa.* Limited Liability New Business, a modified Limited Liability Company.

Abbr.	COUNTRY	DESCRIPTION
SNC	France/Switzerland	*Société en nom collectif.* General Partnership.
SNC	Italy/Switzerland	*Società in Nome Collettivo.* General Partnership.
SNC	Romania	*Societate in Nume Colectiv.* General Partnership.
SNC	Spain	*Sociedad en Nombre Colectivo.* General Partnership.
SOPARFI	Luxembourg	*Société de Participation Financiére.* Holding company.
SP	France	*Société en participation.* Undisclosed partnership.
SpA	Italy	*Società per Azioni.* Limited share company, equivalent to a corporation.
spol s.r.o.	Czech Republic	*Spolecnost S Rucenim Omezenym.* Limited Liability Company.
SPRL	Belgium	*Société Privée à Responsabilité Limitée.* French language equivalent to a private limited liability company.
SRC	Spain	*Sociedad Regular Colectiva.* A regular collective company, similar to a partnership.
Sp. z.o.o.	Poland	*Spólka z ograniczona odpowiedzialnoscia.* Limited liability company, privately-held.
Srl	Chile	*Sociedad de responsabilidad limitada.* Limited Liability company.
Srl	Italy	*Società a Responsabilità Limitata.* Limited liability (joint stock) company.
Srl	Romania	*Societate cu Raspondere Limitata.* Limited-liability company, privately-held.
SS	Italy/Switzerland	*Società Semplice.* Simple Partnership.
SS	Switzerland	*Société Simple.* Simple Partnership
Stiftung	Germany/Swiss	*Stiftung.* Foundation having some attributes of a corporation.
td	Slovenia	*Tiha druzba.* Sole proprietorship.
TLS	Turkey	*Türk Limited Sirket.* Private Limited Liability Company.
Verein	Switzerland	*Verein.* Association.
VOF	Netherlands	*Vennootschap onder firma.* General partnership.

Abbr.	COUNTRY	DESCRIPTION
v.o.s.	Czech Rep	*Verejna Obchodni Spolecnost*. General partnership.
YK	Japan	*Yugen Kaisha*. Limited company, similar to an American closely held corporation. Abolished in 2006 and replaced with the *Godo Kaisha*.

APPENDIX 14:
NICE CLASSIFICATION

The Nice Classification is located on the PTO website at the following address:

http://tess2.uspto.gov/netahtml/tidm.html.

Following is additional information on the Nice Agreement:

The *International (Nice) Classification of Goods and Services for the Purposes of the Registration of Marks* was established by an Agreement concluded at the Nice Diplomatic Conference, on June 15, 1957, was revised at Stockholm, in 1967, and at Geneva, in 1977, and was amended in 1979.

The countries party to the Nice Agreement constitute a Special Union within the framework of the *Paris Union for the Protection of Industrial Property*. They have adopted and apply the Nice Classification for the purposes of the registration of marks.

Each of the countries party to the Nice Agreement is obliged to apply the Nice Classification in connection with the registration of marks, either as the principal classification or as a subsidiary classification, and has to include in the official documents and publications relating to its registrations of marks the numbers of the classes of the Classification to which the goods or services for which the marks are registered belong

Use of the Nice Classification is mandatory not only for the national registration of marks in countries party to the Nice Agreement, but also for the international registration of marks effected by the International Bureau of WIPO, under the *Madrid Agreement Concerning the International Registration of Marks* and under the *Protocol Relating to the Madrid Agreement Concerning the International*

Registration of Marks, and for the registration of marks by the African Intellectual Property Organization (OAPI), by the African Regional Intellectual Property Organization (ARIPO), by the Benelux Trademark Office (BBM) and by the Office for Harmonization in the Internal Market (Trade Marks and Designs) (OHIM).

The Nice Classification is also applied in a number of countries not party to the Nice Agreement

REVISIONS OF THE NICE CLASSIFICATION

The Nice Classification is based on the Classification prepared by the *United International Bureaux for the Protection of Intellectual Property* (BIRPI)—predecessor of WIPO—in 1935. It was that Classification, consisting of a list of 34 classes and an alphabetical list of goods, that was adopted under the Nice Agreement and later expanded to embrace also eleven classes covering services and an alphabetical list of those services.

The Nice Agreement provides for the setting up of a Committee of Experts in which all countries party to the Agreement are represented. The Committee of Experts decides on all changes in the Classification, in particular the transfer of goods and services between various classes, the updating of the alphabetical list and the introduction of necessary explanatory notes.

The Committee of Experts has, since the entry into force of the Nice Agreement, on April 8, 1961, held 20 sessions and has, amongst its most noticeable achievements, undertaken a general review of the Alphabetical List of goods and services from the point of view of form (in the late 1970s); substantially modified the General Remarks, the Class Headings and the Explanatory Notes (in 1982); introduced a "basic number" for each single product or service in the Alphabetical List (in 1990), which number enables the user to find the equivalent product or service in the alphabetical lists of other language versions of the Classification; and revised Class 42 with the creation of Classes 43 to 45 (in 2000).

At its twentieth session, held in October 2005, the Committee of Experts adopted changes to the eighth edition of the Nice Classification.

EDITIONS OF THE NICE CLASSIFICATION

The first edition of the Nice Classification was published in 1963, the second in 1971, the third in 1981, the fourth in 1983, the fifth in 1987, the sixth in 1992, the seventh in 1996 and the eighth in 2001. This edition (the ninth), published in June 2006, will enter into force on January 1, 2007.

* * *

The authentic versions of the Nice Classification (English and French) are published in two parts. Part I (this volume) lists, in alphabetical order, all the goods in one list and all the services in another list. Part II lists, in alphabetical order for each class, the goods or services belonging to that class. There is also a version with a bilingual (English/French) alphabetical list.

The ninth edition of the Nice Classification may be ordered from the World Intellectual Property Organization (WIPO), 34, chemin des Colombettes, P.O. Box 18, CH-1211 Geneva 20 or from the Electronic Bookshop on the website of WIPO at the following address: http://www.wipo.int/ebookshop.

Geneva, June 2006

COUNTRIES PARTY TO THE NICE AGREEMENT

(January 2006)

Albania	Estonia
Algeria	Finland
Armenia	France
Australia	Georgia
Austria	Germany
Azerbaijan	Greece
Bahrain	Guinea
Barbados	Hungary
Belarus	Iceland
Belgium	Ireland
Benin	Israel
Bosnia and Herzegovina	Italy
Bulgaria	Jamaica
China	Japan
Croatia	Kazakhstan
Cuba	Kyrgyzstan
Czech Republic	Latvia
Democratic People's Republic of Korea	Lebanon
	Liechtenstein
Denmark	Lithuania
Dominica	Luxembourg
Egypt	Malawi

Mexico
Monaco
Mongolia
Morocco
Mozambique
Netherlands
Norway
Poland
Portugal
Republic of Korea
Republic of Moldova
Romania
Russian Federation
Saint Kitts and Nevis
Saint Lucia
Serbia and Montenegro
Singapore
Slovakia

Slovenia
Spain
Suriname
Sweden
Switzerland
Syrian Arab Republic
Tajikistan
The former Yugoslav
Republic of Macedonia
Trinidad and Tobago
Tunisia
Turkey
Ukraine
United Kingdom
United Republic of Tanzania
United States of America
Uruguay
Uzbekistan

Total: 78 countries)

OTHER COUNTRIES AND ORGANIZATIONS USING THE NICE CLASSIFICATION

(January 2006)

In addition to the 78 countries party to the Nice Agreement, listed on the previous page, the following 68 countries and four organizations also use the Nice Classification: [1] [2]

Angola
Argentina
Bangladesh
Bolivia
Botswana
Brazil
Burundi
Cambodia
Chile
Colombia
Costa Rica
Cyprus

Democratic Republic of the Congo
Djibouti
Ecuador
El Salvador
Ethiopia
Ghana
Guatemala
Guyana
Haiti
Honduras
India
Indonesia

Iran (Islamic Republic of)
Iraq
Jordan
Kenya
Kuwait
Lesotho
Libya
Madagascar
Malaysia
Malta
Mauritius
Namibia
Nepal
Netherlands Antilles
New Zealand
Nicaragua
Nigeria
Pakistan
Panama
Paraguay
Peru
Philippines
Qatar
Rwanda
Saint Vincent and the
    Grenadines

Samoa
San Marino
Saudi Arabia
Seychelles
Sierra Leone
Solomon Islands
South Africa
Sri Lanka
Sudan
Swaziland
Thailand
Tonga
Uganda
United Arab Emirates
Venezuela
Viet Nam
Yemen
Zambia
Zimbabwe
African Intellectual Property
    Organization (OAPI)[1]
African Regional Intellectual
    Property Organization (ARIPO)[2]
Benelux Trademark Office (BBM)
Office for Harmonization in the
    Internal Market (OHIM)

[1] The following States are members of the African Intellectual Property Organization (OAPI) (January 2006): Benin (also party to the Nice Agreement), Burkina Faso, Cameroon, Central African Republic, Chad, Congo, Côte d'Ivoire, Equatorial Guinea, Gabon, Guinea (also party to the Nice Agreement), Guinea-Bissau, Mali, Mauritania, Niger, Senegal, Togo (16).

[2] The following States are members of the African Regional Intellectual Property Organization (ARIPO) (January 2006): Botswana, Gambia, Ghana, Kenya, Lesotho, Malawi (also party to the Nice Agreement), Mozambique (also party to the Nice Agreement), Namibia, Sierra Leone, Somalia, Sudan, Swaziland, Tanzania, Uganda, Zambia, Zimbabwe (16).

APPENDIX 15:
SPECIMEN REQUIREMENTS FOR COLLECTIVE MARKS, COLLECTIVE MEMBERSHIP MARKS, AND CERTIFICATION MARKS

Excerpted from Trademark Manual of Examining Procedure:

1303.02(b) Specimens of Use for Collective Trademark and Collective Service Mark Applications

The specimen should show use of the mark to indicate that the party providing the goods or services is a member of a certain group. The manner of use required is similar to trademark or service mark use. For example, collective trademark specimens should show the mark used on the goods, or packaging for the goods; collective service mark specimens should show the mark used in advertising for the services, or in the rendering of the services.

The purpose of the mark must be to indicate that the product or service is provided by a member of a collective group. However, the specimen itself does not have to state that purpose explicitly. The examining attorney should accept the specimen if the mark is used on the specimen to indicate the source of the product or service, and there is no information in the record that is inconsistent with the applicant's averments that the mark is a collective mark owned by a collective group and used by members of the group to indicate membership.

***

1304.09(c) Specimens of Use for Membership Marks

The most common type of specimen is a membership card. Membership certificates are also acceptable. The applicant may submit a blank or voided membership card or certificate.

For trade or professional associations, decals bearing the mark for use by members on doors or windows in their establishments, wall plaques bearing the mark, or decals or plates for use, *e.g.*, on members' vehicles, are satisfactory specimens. If the members are in business and place the mark on their business stationery to show their membership, pieces of such stationery are acceptable. Flags, pennants, and banners of various types used in connection with political parties, club groups, or the like could be satisfactory specimens.

Many associations, particularly fraternal societies, use jewelry such as pins, rings or charms to indicate membership. However, not every ornamental design on jewelry is necessarily an indication of membership. The record must show that the design on a piece of jewelry is actually an indication of membership before the jewelry can be accepted as a specimen of use. Shoulder, sleeve, pocket, or similar patches, whose design constitutes a membership mark and which are authorized by the parent organization for use by members on garments to indicate membership, are normally acceptable as specimens. Clothing authorized by the parent organization to be worn by members may also be an acceptable specimen.

A specimen that shows use of the mark by the collective organization itself, rather than by a member, is not acceptable. Collective organizations often publish various kinds of printed material, such as catalogs, directories, bulletins, newsletters, magazines, programs, and the like. Placing the mark on these items by the collective organization represents use of the mark as a trademark or service mark to indicate that the collective organization is the source of the material. The mark is not placed on these items by the parent organization to indicate membership of a person in the organization.

***

1306.06(c) Specimens of Use for Certification Marks

A certification mark specimen must show how a person other than the owner uses the mark to certify regional or other origin, quality, or other characteristics of that person's goods or services; or that members of a union or other organization performed the work or labor on the goods or services. Materials that bear the mark, and are actually attached or applied to the goods or used in relation to the services by the persons authorized to use the mark, constitute proper specimens.

Sometimes, the owner/certifier prepares tags or labels that bear the certification mark that are supplied to the authorized users to attach to their goods or use in relation to their services. These tags or labels are acceptable specimens.

APPENDIX 16:
TRADEMARK ASSIGNMENT
RECORDATION FORM COVER SHEET

Form **PTO-1594** (Rev. 11-08)
OMB Collection 0651-0027 (exp. 12/31/2008)

U.S. DEPARTMENT OF COMMERCE
United States Patent and Trademark Office

RECORDATION FORM COVER SHEET
TRADEMARKS ONLY

To the Director of the U. S. Patent and Trademark Office: Please record the attached documents or the new address(es) below.

1. Name of conveying party(ies):

☐ Individual(s)　　☐ Association
☐ General Partnership　　☐ Limited Partnership
☐ Corporation- State:_____
☐ Other_____

Citizenship (see guidelines)_____

Additional names of conveying parties attached? ☐ Yes ☐ No

3. Nature of conveyance)/Execution Date(s) :

Execution Date(s)_____

☐ Assignment　　☐ Merger
☐ Security Agreement　　☐ Change of Name
☐ Other_____

2. Name and address of receiving party(ies)

Additional names, addresses, or citizenship attached? ☐ Yes ☐ No

Name:_____

Internal Address:_____

Street Address:_____

City:_____

State:_____

Country:_____ Zip:_____

☐ Association　Citizenship_____
☐ General Partnership　Citizenship_____
☐ Limited Partnership　Citizenship_____
☐ Corporation　Citizenship_____
☐ Other_____　Citizenship_____

If assignee is not domiciled in the United States, a domestic representative designation is attached: ☐ Yes ☐ No
(Designations must be a separate document from assignment)

4. Application number(s) or registration number(s) and identification or description of the Trademark.

A. Trademark Application No.(s)

B. Trademark Registration No.(s)

Additional sheet(s) attached? ☐ Yes ☐ No

C. Identification or Description of Trademark(s) (and Filing Date if Application or Registration Number is unknown):

TRADEMARK ASSIGNMENT RECORDATION FORM COVER SHEET

5. Name & address of party to whom correspondence concerning document should be mailed: Name:_____ Internal Address:_____ _____ Street Address: _____ _____ City:_____ State:_____ Zip:_____ Phone Number: _____ Fax Number: _____ Email Address:_____	**6. Total number of applications and** registrations involved: [ ] **7. Total fee** (37 CFR 2.6(b)(6) & 3.41) $_____ ☐ Authorized to be charged to deposit account ☐ Enclosed **8. Payment Information:** Deposit Account Number _____ Authorized User Name _____

9. Signature:

_____   _____
Signature   Date

_____   Total number of pages including cover
Name of Person Signing   sheet, attachments, and document: [   ]

Documents to be recorded (including cover sheet) should be faxed to (571) 273-0140, or mailed to:
Mail Stop Assignment Recordation Services, Director of the USPTO, P.O. Box 1450, Alexandria, VA 22313-1450

Guidelines for Completing Trademarks Cover Sheets (PTO-1594)

Cover Sheet information must be submitted with each document to be recorded. If the document to be recorded concerns both patents and trademarks, separate patent and trademark cover sheets, including any attached pages for continuing information, must accompany the document. All pages of the cover sheet should be numbered consecutively for example, if both a patent and trademark cover sheet is used, and information is continued on one additional page for both patents and trademarks, the pages of the cover sheet would be numbered from 1 to 4.

Item 1. Name of Conveying Party(ies).
Enter the full name of the party(ies) conveying the interest. If there is more than one conveying party, enter a check mark in the "Yes" box to indicate that additional information is attached. The name of the second and any subsequent conveying party(ies) should be placed on an attached page clearly identified as a continuation of the information in Item 1. Enter a check mark in the "No" box, if no information is contained on an attached page.

Item 2. Name and Address of Receiving Party(ies).
Enter the name and full address of the first party receiving the interest. If there is more than one party receiving the interest, enter a check mark in the "Yes" box to indicate that additional information is attached. If the receiving party is an individual, check the "other" box, place the word "individual" in the following line, and enter the citizenship of the receiving individual. If the receiving party is a legal entity, designate the legal entity of the receiving party by checking the appropriate box. If the receiving party has more than one citizenship, then the citizenship of **each** partner should be specified on an additional sheet, and "See additional sheet" should be written on the line for citizenship. A corporation must set forth the state, if applicable, or country of incorporation. An association must set forth the state, if applicable, or country under which they are organized. If the receiving party is not domiciled in the United States, a designation of domestic representative is encouraged. Place a check mark in the appropriate box to indicate whether or not a designation of domestic representative is attached. Enter a check mark in the "No" box if no information is contained on an attached page.

Item 3. Nature of Conveyance/Execution Date(s).
Enter the execution date(s) of the document. It is preferable to use the name of the month, or an abbreviation of that name, to minimize confusion over dates. In addition, place a check mark in the appropriate box describing the nature of the conveying document. If the "Other" box is checked, specify the nature of the conveyance. The "Other" box should be checked if the conveying/receiving party is correcting a previously filed document.

Item 4. Application Number(s) or Registration Number(s).
Indicate the application number(s) including series code and serial number, and/or registration number(s) against which the document is to be recorded. The identification of the trademark should be provided for all properties to avoid recordation against the wrong property. A filing date should be provided only when the application or registration number is unknown. Enter a check mark in the appropriate box: "Yes" or "No" if additional numbers appear on attached pages. Be sure to identify numbers included on attached pages as the continuation of Item 4.

Item 5. Name and Address of Party to whom correspondence concerning document should be mailed.
Enter the name and full address of the party to whom correspondence is to be mailed.

Item 6. Total Applications and Trademarks Involved.
Enter the total number of applications and trademarks identified for recordation. Be sure to include all applications and registrations identified on the cover sheet and on additional pages.

Block 7. Total Fee Enclosed.
Enter the total fee enclosed or authorized to be charged. A fee is required for each application and registration against which the document is recorded.

Item 8. Payment Information.
Enter the deposit account number and authorized user name to authorize charges.

Item 9. Signature.
Enter the name of the person submitting the document. The submitter must sign and date the cover sheet. Enter the total number of pages including the cover sheet, attachments, and document.

Privacy Act Statement for Patent Assignment Recordation Form Cover Sheet

The Privacy Act of 1974 (P.L. 93-579) requires that you be given certain information in connection with the above request for information. This collection of information is authorized by 35 U.S.C. 1, 2, 261 and E.O. 9424. This information will primarily be used by the USPTO for the recordation of assignments related to patents and patent applications. Submission of this information is voluntary but is required in order for the USPTO to record the requested assignment. If you do not provide the information required on the cover sheet, the assignment will not be recorded, and all documents will be returned to you.

After the information is recorded, the records and associated documents can be inspected by the public and are not confidential, except for documents that are sealed under secrecy orders or related to unpublished patent applications. Assignment records relating to unpublished patent applications are maintained in confidence in accordance with 35 U.S.C. 122. Records open to the public are searched by users for the purpose of determining ownership for other property rights with respect to patents and trademarks.

Routine uses of the information you provide may also include disclosure to appropriate Federal, state, local, or foreign agencies in support of their enforcement duties and statutory or regulatory missions, including investigating potential violations of law or contract and awarding contracts or other benefits; to a court, magistrate, or administrative tribunal in the course of presenting evidence; to members of Congress responding to requests for assistance from their constituents; to the Office of Management and Budget in connection with the review of private relief legislation; to the Department of Justice in connection with a Freedom of Information Act request; to a contractor in the performance of their duties; to the Office of Personnel Management for personnel studies; and to the General Services Administration (GSA) as part of their records management responsibilities under the authority of 44 U.S.C. 2904 and 2906. Such disclosure to GSA shall not be used to make determinations about individuals.

APPENDIX 17:
TRADEMARK/SERVICE MARK
ALLEGATION OF USE

~TRADEMARK/SERVICE MARK ALLEGATION OF USE (Statement of Use/ Amendment to Allege Use) (15 U.S.C. § 1051(c) or (d))~

WHEN TO FILE: Before the USPTO will register a mark that was based upon applicant's bona fide intention to use the mark in commerce, the owner must (1) use the mark in commerce; and (2) file an Allegation of Use. The Allegation of Use can only be filed either **on or before** the day the examining attorney approves the mark for publication in the *Official Gazette*; or **on or after** the day the Notice of Allowance is issued. If the Allegation of Use is filed *between* those periods, it will be returned. To avoid return of an untimely Allegation of Use, you can check the status of your application by calling 1-800-786-9199, or using *http://tarr.uspto.gov/*.

BASIC INSTRUCTIONS

The following form is written in a "scannable" format that will enable the U.S. Patent and Trademark Office (USPTO) to scan paper filings and capture application data automatically using optical character recognition (OCR) technology. Information is to be entered next to identifying data tags, such as <MARK>. OCR software can be programmed to identify these tags, capture the corresponding data, and transmit this data to the appropriate data fields in the Trademark databases, largely bypassing manual data entry processes.

Please enter the requested information in the blank space that appears to the right of each tagged (<   >) element. However, do not enter any information immediately after the section headers (the bolded wording appearing in all capital letters). If you need additional space, first, in the space provided on the form, enter "See attached." Then, please use a separate piece of paper on which you first list the data tag (e.g., <Goods and/or Services Not in Use to be **Deleted**>), followed by the relevant information. Some of the information requested *must* be provided. Other information is either required only in certain circumstances, or provided only at your discretion. **Please consult the "Help" section following the form for detailed explanations as to what information should be entered in each blank space.**

To increase the effectiveness of the USPTO scanners, it is recommended that you use a typewriter to complete the form.

For additional information, please see the *Basic Facts about Trademarks* booklet, available at *http://www.uspto.gov/web/offices/tac/doc/basic/*, or by calling the Trademark Assistance Center at 1-800-786-9199.

MAILING INFORMATION

Send the completed form; appropriate fee (the filing fee for the Allegation of Use is $100.00 *per class* of goods and/or services, made payable to the "Commissioner of Patents and Trademarks"); and one (1) SPECIMEN, showing the mark as currently used in commerce for at least one product or service in each international class covered, to:

> Commissioner for Trademarks
> P.O. Box 1451
> Alexandria, VA 22313-1451

You may also wish to include a self-addressed stamped postcard with your submission, on which you identify the mark and serial number, and list each item being submitted (e.g., allegation of use, fee, specimen, etc.). We will return this postcard to confirm receipt of your submission.

~TRADEMARK/SERVICE MARK ALLEGATION OF USE (Statement of Use/ Amendment to Allege Use) (15 U.S.C. § 1051(c) or (d))~

~To the Commissioner for Trademarks~

\<TRADEMARK/SERVICEMARK INFORMATION>

\<Mark>

\<Serial Number>

\<APPLICANT INFORMATION>

\<Name>

\<Street>

\<City>

\<State>

\<Country>

\<Zip/Postal Code>

\<NOTICE OF ALLOWANCE INFORMATION>

\<Notice of Allowance> *~Enter YES if you are filing the Allegation of Use after a Notice of Allowance has issued. If not, enter NO.~*

\<GOODS AND/OR SERVICES INFORMATION>

\<All Goods and/or Services in Application/Notice of Allowance>*~The owner is using or using through a related company the mark in commerce on or in connection with all goods and/or services listed in the application or Notice of Allowance. If not, list in the next section the goods and/or services not in use to be deleted.~*

\<Goods and/or Services Not in Use to be **Deleted**>*~In the following space, list only those goods and/or services (and/or entire class(es)) appearing in the application or Notice of Allowance for which the owner is not using the mark in commerce.* **LEAVE THIS SPACE BLANK IF THE OWNER IS USING THE MARK ON OR IN CONNECTION WITH ALL THE GOODS AND/OR SERVICES LISTED IN THE APPLICATION OR NOTICE OF ALLOWANCE.~**

\<USE INFORMATION>

\<Date of First Use Anywhere>

\<Date of First Use in Commerce>

\<OPTIONAL - REQUEST TO DIVIDE INFORMATION>

\<Request to Divide> *~Enter YES if you are submitting a request to divide with this document. If not, enter NO.~*

PTO Form 1553 (REV 01/05)
OMB Control No. 0651-0009 (Exp. 8/31/2001)

U.S. DEPARTMENT OF COMMERCE/Patent and Trademark Office
There is no requirement to respond to this collection of information
unless a currently valid OMB number is displayed.

\<FEE INFORMATION\>

$100.00 x \<Number of Classes\>	= \<Total Fees Paid\>

\<SPECIMEN AND SIGNATURE INFORMATION\>

~Applicant requests registration of the above-identified trademark/service mark in the United States Patent and Trademark Office on the Principal Register established by the Act of July 5, 1946 (15 U.S.C. §1051 et seq., as amended). Applicant is the owner of the mark sought to be registered, and is using the mark in commerce on or in connection with the goods/services identified above, as evidenced by the attached specimen(s) showing the mark as used in commerce.

(You MUST ATTACH A SPECIMEN showing the mark as used in commerce for at least one product or service in each international class covered.)

The undersigned being hereby warned that willful false statements and the like are punishable by fine or imprisonment, or both, under 18 U.S.C. § 1001, and that such willful false statements and the like may jeopardize the validity of this document, declares that he/she is properly authorized to execute this document on behalf of the Owner; and all statements made of his/her own knowledge are true and that all statements made on information and belief are believed to be true.~

~Signature~ _____

\<Date Signed\>

\<Name\>

\<Title\>

\<CONTACT INFORMATION\>

\<Name\>

\<Company/Firm Name\>

\<Street\>

\<City\>

\<State\>

\<Country\>

\<Zip/Postal Code\>

\<Telephone Number\>

\<Fax Number\>

\<e-Mail Address\>

\<CERTIFICATE OF MAILING\> *~Recommended to avoid lateness due to mail delay.~*

~I certify that the foregoing is being deposited with the United States Postal Service as first class mail, postage prepaid, in an envelope addressed to the Commissioner for Trademarks, P.O. Box 1451, Alexandria, VA 22313-1451, on~

\<Date of Deposit\>

~Signature~ _____

\<Name\>

LINE-BY-LINE HELP INSTRUCTIONS

TRADEMARK/SERVICE MARK INFORMATION

Mark: Enter the word mark in typed form; or, in the case of a design or stylized mark, a brief description of the mark (e.g., "Design of a fanciful cat").

Serial Number: Enter the eight-digit USPTO serial number (e.g., 75/457392).

APPLICANT INFORMATION

Name: Only the owner of the mark may file the Allegation of Use. Enter the full name of the owner of the mark, i.e., the name of the individual, corporation, partnership, or other entity that is seeking registration. If a joint venture organized under a particular business name, enter that name. If joint or multiple applicants, enter the name of each applicant. If a trust, enter the name of the trustee(s). If an estate, enter the name of the executor(s).

Street: Enter the street address or rural delivery route where the owner is located.

City: Enter the city and/or foreign area designation where the owner's address is located.

State: Enter the U.S. state or foreign province in which the owner's address is located.

Country: Enter the country of the owner's address.

Zip/Postal Code: Enter the owner's U.S. zip code or foreign country postal identification code.

NOTICE OF ALLOWANCE INFORMATION

Notice of Allowance: Enter YES or NO as to whether the mark has been published for opposition in the Official Gazette and a Notice of Allowance has been issued in connection with the application. Before the USPTO will register a mark that was based upon applicant's bona fide intention to use the mark in commerce, the owner must (1) use the mark in commerce; and (2) file an Allegation of Use. The Allegation of Use can only be filed either on or before the day the examining attorney approves the mark for publication in the Official Gazette; or on or after the day the Notice of Allowance is issued. If the Allegation of Use is filed between those periods, it will be returned. To avoid return of an untimely Allegation of Use, you can check the status of your application by calling 703-305-8747, or using *http://tarr.uspto.gov/*.

GOODS AND/OR SERVICES INFORMATION

All Goods and/or Services in Application/Notice of Allowance: If the owner is NOT using the mark in commerce on or in connection with all of the goods and/or services listed in the application or Notice of Allowance, complete the next section. Otherwise, we will presume such use on or in connection with all goods and/or services.

Goods and/or Services Not in Use to be Deleted: List the goods and/or services (if any) identified in the application or Notice of Allowance with which the owner is NOT using the mark in commerce; or, specify an entire international class(es), as appropriate (e.g., Classes 9 & 42).

USE INFORMATION

Date of First Use Anywhere: Enter the date on which the goods were first sold or transported or the services first rendered under the mark if such use was in the ordinary course of trade. For every applicant, whether foreign or domestic, the date of first use of a mark is the date of the first such use anywhere, in the United States or elsewhere. Please note this date may be earlier than, or the same as, the date of the first use of the mark in commerce.

Date of First Use in Commerce: Enter the date on which the applicant first used the mark in commerce, i.e., in interstate commerce, territorial commerce, or commerce between the U.S. and a foreign country.

OPTIONAL - REQUEST TO DIVIDE INFORMATION

Request to Divide: Enter YES or NO as to whether you are submitting a Request to Divide with this document. Specifically, if the applicant chooses to include only some of the originally identified goods and/or services in this Allegation of Use, and to designate the remaining goods/services as part of a separate application for registration, then a divisional application and fee are required. 37 C.F.R. §2.87.

FEE INFORMATION

The filing fee for the Allegation of Use is $100.00 per class of goods and/or services.

Number of Classes: Enter the number of classes (not the international class number(s)) to which the Allegation of Use applies. For example, if the Allegation of Use applies to Classes 1, 5 and 25, then the number of classes entered would be "3."

Total Filing Fee Paid: Enter the fee amount that is enclosed (either in the form of a check or money order in U.S. currency, made payable to "Commissioner of Patents and Trademarks"), or that is to be charged to an already-existing USPTO deposit account.

SPECIMEN AND SIGNATURE INFORMATION

Specimen: A specimen showing use of the mark for at least one product or service in each class to which the Allegation of Use applies must be submitted with this form. Examples of acceptable specimens are tags or labels for goods, and advertisements for services. The specimen must be flat and no larger than 8½ inches (21.6 cm.) wide by 11.69 inches (29.7 cm.) long.

Signature: The appropriate person must sign the form. A person who is properly authorized to sign on behalf of the owner is: (1) a person with legal authority to bind the owner; or (2) a person with firsthand knowledge of the facts and actual or implied authority to act on behalf of the owner; or (3) an attorney who has an actual or implied written or verbal power of attorney from the owner.

Date Signed: Enter the date the form is signed.

Name: Enter the name of the person signing the form.

Title: Enter the signatory's title, if applicable, e.g., Vice President, General Partner, etc.

CONTACT INFORMATION

Although this may be the same as provided elsewhere in the document, please enter the following required information for where the USPTO should mail correspondence.

Name: Enter the full name of the contact person.

Company/Firm Name: Enter the name of the contact person's company or firm.

Street: Enter the street address or rural delivery route where the contact person is located.

City: Enter the city and/or foreign area designation where the contact person's address is located.

State: Enter the U.S. state or Canadian province in which the contact person's address is located.

Country: Enter the country of the contact person's address.

Zip Code: Enter the U.S. zip code or Canadian postal code.

Telephone Number: Enter the appropriate telephone number.

Fax Number: Enter the appropriate fax number, if available.

e-Mail Address: Enter the appropriate e-mail address, if available.

CERTIFICATE OF MAILING

Although optional, use of this section is recommended to avoid lateness due to mail delay. Papers are considered timely filed if deposited with the United States Postal Service with sufficient postage as first class mail on or before the due date, and accompanied by a signed Certificate of Mailing attesting to timely deposit. The USPTO will look to the date shown on the Certificate of Mailing, rather than the date of actual receipt, to determine the timeliness of this document.

Date of Deposit: Enter the date of deposit with the United States Postal Service as first class mail.

Signature: The person signing the certificate should have a reasonable basis to expect that the correspondence will be mailed on or before the indicated date.

Name: Enter the name of the person signing the Certificate of Mailing.

APPENDIX 18:
REQUEST FOR EXTENSION OF TIME TO FILE A STATEMENT OF USE

~REQUEST FOR EXTENSION OF TIME TO FILE A STATEMENT OF USE (15 U.S.C. § 1058(d))~

WHEN TO FILE: You must file a Statement of Use within six (6) months after the mailing of the Notice of Allowance, UNLESS, within that same period, you submit a request for a six-month extension of time to file the Statement of Use. The request for an extension must:
- be filed in the USPTO within six (6) months after the issue date of the Notice of Allowance, or previously-granted extension period;
- include a verified statement of the applicant's continued bona fide intention to use the mark in commerce;
- specify the goods/services to which the request pertains as they are identified in the Notice of Allowance; and
- include a fee of $150.00 for each class of goods/services.

You may request five (5) extensions of time. No extensions may extend beyond thirty-six (36) months from the issue date of the Notice of Allowance. The USPTO must receive the second (2⁺), third (3⁺), fourth (4⁺), and fifth (5⁺) extensions within the previously-granted extension period. Do NOT wait until the request for extension has been granted before filing the next request. In addition to the requirements described above, the second (2⁺) and subsequent requests must specify applicant's ongoing efforts to use the mark in commerce.

You may submit one (1) extension request during the six-month period in which you file the Statement of Use, unless the granting of this request would extend the period beyond thirty-six (36) months from the issue date of the Notice of Allowance. Instead of specifying ongoing efforts, for this request you should state the belief that the applicant has made valid use of the mark in commerce, as evidenced by the Statement of Use, but that if the USPTO finds the Statement defective, the applicant will require additional time to file a new Statement of Use.

If the original application were based on both Section 1(a) (Use in Commerce) and 1(b) (Intent to Use), this extension request is necessary only for those goods that were based on Section 1(b). You should NOT file an Extension Request (or Statement of Use) for those goods that were filed based on use in commerce.

BASIC INSTRUCTIONS

The following form is written in a "scannable" format that will enable the U.S. Patent and Trademark Office (USPTO) to scan paper filings and capture application data automatically using optical character recognition (OCR) technology. Information is to be entered next to identifying data tags, such as <MARK>. OCR software can be programmed to identify these tags, capture the corresponding data, and transmit this data to the appropriate data fields in the Trademark databases, largely bypassing manual data entry processes.

Please enter the requested information in the blank space that appears to the right of each tagged (< >) element. However, do not enter any information immediately after the section headers (the bolded wording appearing in all capital letters). Some of the information requested *must* be provided. Other information is either required only in certain circumstances, or provided only at your discretion. **Please consult the "Help" section following the form for detailed explanations as to what information should be entered in each blank space.**

To increase effectiveness of the USPTO scanners, it is recommended that you use a typewriter to complete the form.

For additional information, please see the *Basic Facts about Trademarks* booklet, available at *http://www.uspto.gov/web/offices/tac/doc/basic/*, or by calling the Trademark Assistance Center, at 1-800-786-9199.

MAILING INFORMATION

Send the completed form and appropriate fee (the filing fee for the Extension Request is $150.00 *per class* of goods and/or services, made payable to the "Commissioner of Patents and Trademarks") to:

> Commissioner for Trademarks
> P.O. Box 1451
> Alexandria, VA 22313-1451

You may also wish to include a self-addressed stamped postcard with your submission, on which you identify the mark and serial number, and list each item being submitted (e.g., extension request, fee, etc.). We will return this postcard to confirm receipt of your submission.

~REQUEST FOR EXTENSION OF TIME TO FILE A STATEMENT OF USE (15 U.S.C. § 1051(d))~

~To the Commissioner for Trademarks~

<TRADEMARK/SERVICEMARK INFORMATION>

<Mark>

<Serial Number>

<APPLICANT INFORMATION>

<Name>

<Street>

<City>

<State>

<Country>

<Zip/Postal Code>

<NOTICE OF ALLOWANCE INFORMATION>

<Notice of Allowance Mailing Date>   ~Enter date in the format MM/DD/YYYY.~

<GOODS AND/OR SERVICES INFORMATION>

<All Goods and/or Services in Notice of Allowance>~*The applicant has a continued bona fide intention to use or use through a related company the mark in commerce on or in connection with all the goods and/or services listed in the Notice of Allowance. If not, list in the next section the goods and/or services to be deleted.~*

<Goods and/or Services to be **Deleted**>~*In the following space, list only those goods/services (or entire class(es)) appearing in the Notice of Allowance for which the applicant does not have a continued bona fide intention to use the mark in commerce. LEAVE THIS SPACE BLANK IF THE APPLICANT DOES HAVE A CONTINUED BONA FIDE INTENTION TO USE THE MARK IN COMMERCE ON OR IN CONNECTION WITH ALL GOODS/ SERVICES LISTED IN THE NOTICE OF ALLOWANCE.~*

<EXTENSION REQUEST INFORMATION>~

<Number of Extension Request>   ~*Enter which request (1", 2", 3", 4' or 5') this is following the mailing of the Notice of Allowance.~*

<ONGOING EFFORTS TO USE MARK IN COMMERCE>~*Applies to 2", 3", 4' & 5' extension requests only.~*

~*The applicant has made the following ongoing efforts to use the mark in commerce on or in connection with those goods and/or services for which use of the mark in commerce has not yet been made.~*
<Explanation>

PTO Form 1581 (REV 01/05)
OMB Control No. 0651-0009 (Exp. 8/31/2001)

U.S. DEPARTMENT OF COMMERCE/Patent and Trademark Office
There is no requirement to respond to this collection of information
unless a currently valid OMB number is displayed.

184   Understanding Trademark Law: A Beginner's Guide

<STATEMENT OF USE SUBMITTED>~*if applicable*~

<Additional Time Requested>~*Enter YES if you believe the applicant has made valid use of the mark in commerce, as evidenced by the Statement of Use submitted with this request. If the Statement of Use does not meet the requirements of 37 C.F.R. 2.88, you request additional time to correct the Statement of Use. If not, enter NO.*~

<FEE INFORMATION>

$150.00 x <Number of Classes>   = <Total Filing Fee Paid>

<SIGNATURE INFORMATION>

~*Applicant is entitled to use the mark sought to be registered and has a continued bona fide intention to use the mark in commerce on or in connection with all the goods and/or services listed in the Notice of Allowance. Applicant requests a six-month extension of time to file the Statement of Use under 37 CFR 2.89.*~

The undersigned, being hereby warned that willful false statements and the like are punishable by fine or imprisonment, or both, under 18 U.S.C. § 1001, and that such willful false statements and the like may jeopardize the validity of this document, declares that he/she is properly authorized to execute this document on behalf of the Applicant; and all statements made of his/her own knowledge are true and that all statements made on information and belief are believed to be true.~

~Signature~ _____

<Date Signed>

<Name>

<Title>

<CONTACT INFORMATION>

<Name>

<Company/Firm Name>

<Street>

<City>

<State>

<Country>

<Zip/Postal Code>

<Telephone Number>

<Fax Number>

<e-Mail Address>

<CERTIFICATE OF MAILING>~*Recommended to avoid lateness due to mail delay.*~

~I certify that the foregoing is being deposited with the United States Postal Service as first class mail, postage prepaid, in an envelope addressed to the Commissioner for Trademarks, P.O. Box 1451, Alexandria, VA 22313-1451, on~

<Date of Deposit>

~Signature~ _____

<Name>

The information collected on this form allows an applicant to demonstrate that it has commenced use of the mark in commerce regulable by Congress. With respect to applications filed on the basis of an intent to use the mark, responses to the request for information are required to obtain the benefit of a registration on the Principal or Supplemental Register. 15 U.S.C. §§1051 et seq. and 37 C.F.R. Part 2. All information collected will be made public. Gathering and providing the information will require an estimated thirteen minutes. Please direct comments on the time needed to complete this form, and/or suggestions for reducing this burden to the Chief Information Officer, U.S. Patent and Trademark Office, U.S. Department of Commerce, Washington D.C. 20231. Please note that the PTO may not conduct or sponsor a collection of information using a form that does not display a valid OMB control number. (See bottom left side of this form).

LINE-BY-LINE HELP INSTRUCTIONS

TRADEMARK/SERVICE MARK INFORMATION

Mark: Enter the word mark in typed form; or, in the case of a design or stylized mark, a brief description of the mark (e.g., "Design of a fanciful cat").

Serial Number: Enter the eight-digit USPTO serial number (e.g., 75/453687).

APPLICANT INFORMATION

Name: Enter the full name of the applicant, i.e., the name of the individual, corporation, partnership, or other entity that is seeking registration. If a joint venture organized under a particular business name, enter that name. If joint or multiple applicants, enter the name of each of these applicants. If a trust, enter the name of the trustee or trustees. If an estate, enter the name of the executor or executors.

Note: If title of the application has changed, you should establish current title, either by (1) recording the appropriate document(s) with the USPTO Assignment Branch; or (2) submitting evidence with this declaration, such as a copy of a document transferring title from one party to another. To have the USPTO databases reflect the current applicant, you must choose option (1).

Street: Enter the street address or rural delivery route where the applicant is located.

City: Enter the city and/or foreign area designation where the applicant's address is located.

State: Enter the U.S. state or foreign province in which the applicant's address is located.

Country: Enter the country of the applicant's address.

Zip/Postal Code: Enter the applicant's U.S. zip code or foreign country postal identification code.

NOTICE OF ALLOWANCE INFORMATION

Notice of Allowance Mailing Date: Enter the date when the USPTO mailed the Notice of Allowance. Please enter the date in the format of MM/DD/YYYY; e.g., 12/03/1999.

GOODS AND/OR SERVICES INFORMATION

All Goods and/or Services in Notice of Allowance: If the applicant does NOT have a continued bona fide intention to use the mark in commerce on or in connection with *all* of the goods and/or services listed in the Notice of Allowance, complete the next section. Otherwise, we will presume such bona fide intention to use the mark in commerce on or in connection with all of the goods and/or services listed in the Notice of Allowance.

Goods and/or Services to be Deleted: List all goods and/or services (if any) identified in the Notice of Allowance with which the applicant does NOT have a continued bona fide intention to use the mark in commerce; or, specify an entire international class(es), as appropriate (e.g., Classes 9 & 42).

EXTENSION REQUEST INFORMATION

Number of Extension Request: Indicate whether this is the 1st, 2nd, 3rd, 4th or 5th Request for an Extension of Time to File a Statement of Use that you are submitting.

ONGOING EFFORTS TO USE MARK IN COMMERCE

Explanation: For 2nd, 3rd, 4th and 5th Extension Requests only, provide information regarding ongoing efforts the applicant is making to use the mark in commerce with the identified goods and/or services, such as (1) product or service research or development; (2) market research; (3) promotional activities; (4) steps to acquire distributors; and/or (5) steps to obtain required governmental approval, or similar specified activity.

STATEMENT OF USE SUBMITTED

Additional Time Requested: Enter YES if you believe applicant has made valid use of the mark in commerce, as evidenced by the Statement of Use submitted with this request. If the Statement of Use does not meet the requirements of 37 C.F.R. 2.88, you request additional time to correct the Statement of Use. If not, enter NO.

FEE INFORMATION

The filing fee for the Request for Extension of Time to file a Statement of Use is $150.00 *per class*.
Number of Classes: Enter the number of classes (*not* the international class number(s)) to which the Extension Request applies. For example, if the Extension Request applies to Classes 1, 5 and 25, then the number of classes entered would be "3."
Total Filing Fee Paid: Enter fee amount enclosed (either in form of check or money order in U.S. currency, made payable to "Commissioner of Patents and Trademarks"), or to be charged to an already-existing USPTO deposit account.

SIGNATURE INFORMATION

Signature: The appropriate person must sign the form. A person who is properly authorized to sign on behalf of the applicant is: (1) a person with legal authority to bind the applicant; or (2) a person with firsthand knowledge of the facts and actual or implied authority to act on behalf of the applicant; or (3) an attorney who has an actual or implied written or verbal power of attorney from the applicant.
Date Signed: Enter the date the form is signed.
Name: Enter the name of the person signing the form.
Title: Enter the signatory's title, if applicable, e.g., Vice President, General Partner, etc.

CONTACT INFORMATION

Although this may be the same as provided elsewhere in the document, please enter the following required information for where the USPTO should mail correspondence.
Name: Enter the full name of the contact person.
Company/Firm Name: Enter the name of the contact person's company or firm.
Street: Enter the street address or rural delivery route where the contact person is located.
City: Enter the city and/or foreign area designation where the contact person's address is located.
State: Enter the U.S. state or Canadian province in which the contact person's address is located.
Country: Enter the country of the contact person's address.
Zip Code: Enter the U.S. zip code or Canadian postal code.
Telephone Number: Enter the appropriate telephone number.
Fax Number: Enter the appropriate fax number, if available.
e-Mail Address: Enter the appropriate e-mail address, if available.

CERTIFICATE OF MAILING

Although optional, use of this section is recommended to avoid lateness due to mail delay. The USPTO considers papers timely filed if deposited with the U.S. States Postal Service with sufficient postage as first class mail on or before the due date, *and* accompanied by a signed Certificate of Mailing attesting to timely deposit. The USPTO will look to the date shown on the Certificate of Mailing, rather than date of actual receipt, to determine timeliness.
Date of Deposit: Enter the date of deposit with the United States Postal Service as first class mail.
Signature: The person signing the certificate should have a reasonable basis to expect that the correspondence will be mailed on or before the indicated date.
Name: Enter the name of the person signing the Certificate of Mailing.

APPENDIX 19:
PETITION INFORMATION SHEET FOR MAILED PETITIONS TO REVIVE AN APPLICATION

Sending Petition Papers

The filing date of a document in the USPTO is the date of receipt in the Office, not the date of deposit in the mail. However, a petition that is mailed to the USPTO before the expiration of the deadline will be considered to have been timely filed if (1) it is properly addressed and deposited with the U.S. Postal Service with postage sufficient for first class mail, and (2) the petition includes a certificate of mailing that identifies the date the petition was mailed, and the address to which it was mailed. You are encouraged to use a certificate of mailing (see sample below) to ensure the timeliness of the petition. Please keep a photocopy of the petition and the signed certificate. If the petition is filed and then lost, a photocopy of the petition and the certificate of mailing may help to establish that the petition was timely filed. The following is a sample certificate if mailing:

Certificate of Mailing

I hereby certify that this correspondence is being deposited with the United States Postal Service as first class mail with postage prepaid in an envelope addressed to: Commissioner for Trademarks, P.O. Box 1451, Alexandria, VA 22313–1451 on the date shown below:

_____

Signature

_____

Print Name of Signatory

_____

Date

Three Types of Petitions—Requirements

PETITION TYPE 1—Office Action Received (No Response Filed or Untimely Response Filed)

1. $100 petition fee per application.

2. A statement that the delay in filing a response was unintentional, signed by someone with firsthand knowledge of the facts.

3. A proposed response to the outstanding Office action.

PETITION TYPE 2—Notice of Allowance Received (No SOU or Extension Request Filed or Untimely SOU or Extension Request Filed)

1. $100 petition fee per application.

2. A statement that the delay in filing an SOU or extension request was unintentional, signed by someone with firsthand knowledge of the facts.

3. The required fees for all extension requests that became due since the NOA issued.

4. Either an SOU or the last extension request that was due.

Advisory: Filing a petition to revive an abandoned application does not stay or suspend the time for filing an SOU. During the pendency of the petition, you should file an SOU or any further extension requests that come due. Also, a petition will not be granted if it results in an SOU being filed more than 36 months after the issuance date of the NOA.

PETITION TYPE 3—Office Action or NOA Not Received

1. $100 petition fee per application.

2. A statement that the delay in filing a response, or SOU or extension request, was unintentional because the Office action or NOA was not received by applicant or the attorney of record, signed by someone with firsthand knowledge of the facts.

APPENDIX 20:
NOTICE OF APPEAL OF EXAMINER'S
REFUSAL TO REGISTER A MARK

Notice of Appeal – Suggested Format

IN THE UNITED STATES PATENT AND TRADEMARK OFFICE
BEFORE THE TRADEMARK TRIAL AND APPEAL BOARD

....
(Name of applicant)

....
(Serial Number of application)

....
(Filing date of application)

....
(Mark)

<u>NOTICE OF APPEAL</u>

Applicant hereby appeals to the Trademark Trial and Appeal Board from the decision of the Trademark Examining Attorney refusing registration.[1]

By..
        (Signature)[2]

....
(Identification of person signing)[3]

FOOTNOTES

[1] The required fee must be submitted for each class for which an appeal is taken. If an appeal is taken for fewer than the total number of classes in the application, the classes in which the appeal is taken should be specified.

[2] The notice of appeal may be signed by the applicant or by the applicant's attorney or other authorized representative. If an applicant signing for itself is a partnership, the signature must be made by a partner; if an applicant signing for itself is a corporation or similar juristic entity, the signature must be made by an officer of the corporation or other juristic entity who has authority to sign for the entity and whose title is given.

[3] State the capacity in which the signing individual signs, e.g., attorney for applicant, applicant (if applicant is an individual), partner of applicant (if applicant is a partnership), officer of applicant identified by title (if applicant is a corporation), etc.

Appendix of Forms - 18

APPENDIX 21:
NOTICE OF OPPOSITION

Suggested Format for Notice of Opposition

(This is a suggested format for preparing a Notice of Opposition. This document is not meant to be used as a form to be filled in and returned to the Board. Rather, it is a suggested format, which shows how the Notice of Opposition should be set up. Opposers may follow this format in preparing their own Notice of Opposition but need not copy those portions of the suggested format which are not relevant.)

IN THE UNITED STATES PATENT AND TRADEMARK OFFICE
BEFORE THE TRADEMARK TRIAL AND APPEAL BOARD

In the matter of trademark application Serial No............................
For the mark..
Published in the Official Gazette on..........(Date)............................

(Name of opposer)
v.
(Name of applicant)

NOTICE OF OPPOSITION

State opposer's name, address, and entity information as follows:[1]

(Name of individual as opposer, and business trade name, if any;
Business address)

OR   (Name of partnership as opposer; Names of partners;
Business address of partnership)

OR   (Name of corporation as opposer; State or country of incorporation;
Business address of corporation)

The above-identified opposer believes that it/he/she will be damaged by registration of the mark shown in the above-identified application, and hereby opposes the same.[2]

The grounds for opposition are as follows:

[Please set forth, in separately numbered paragraphs,
the allegations of opposer's standing and grounds for opposition.][3]

By _____ (Signature)[4] _____   Date_____
    (Identification of person signing)[5]

OMB No. 0651-0040 (Exp. 5/31/04)

FOOTNOTES

[1] If opposer is an individual, state the opposer's name, business trade name, if any, and business address. If opposer is a partnership, state the name of the partnership, the names of the partners, and the business address of the partnership. If opposer is a corporation, state the name of the corporation, the state (or country, if opposer is a foreign corporation) of incorporation, and the business address of the corporation. If opposer is an association or other similar type of juristic entity, state the information required for a corporation, changing the term "corporation" throughout to an appropriate designation.

[2] The required fee must be submitted for each party joined as opposer for each class opposed, and if fewer than the total number of classes in the application are opposed, the classes opposed should be specified.

[3] Set forth a short and plain statement here showing why the opposer believes it/he/she would be damaged by the registration of the opposed mark, and state the grounds for opposing. Each numbered paragraph should be limited, as far as practicable, to a statement of a single set of circumstances. See Rules 8(a) and 10(b) of the Federal Rules of Civil Procedure.

[4] The opposition need not be verified, and may be signed by the opposer or by the opposer's attorney or other authorized representative. If an opposer signing for itself is a partnership, the signature must be made by a partner; if an opposer signing for itself is a corporation or similar juristic entity, the signature must be made by an officer of the corporation or other juristic entity who has authority to sign for the entity and whose title is given.

[5] State the capacity in which the signing individual signs, e.g., attorney for opposer, opposer (if opposer is an individual), partner of opposer (if opposer is a partnership), officer of opposer identified by title (if opposer is a corporation), etc.

REPRESENTATION INFORMATION

If the opposer is not domiciled in the United States, and is not represented by an attorney or other authorized representative located in the United States, a domestic representative must be designated.

If the opposer wishes to furnish a power of attorney, it may do so, but an attorney at law is not required to furnish a power.

APPENDIX 22:
EXCUSABLE AND NON-EXCUSABLE LACK
OF USE OF A MARK

In addition to a showing that there is no intention to abandon the mark, the owner must show that nonuse is due to special circumstances beyond the owner's control that excuse nonuse. The following examples provide general guidelines as to what is considered to be a special circumstance that excuses nonuse:

• *Decreased Demand*. Decreased demand for the product sold under the mark, resulting in its discontinuance for an indefinite period, does not excuse nonuse. The purpose of the affidavit requirement is to eliminate registrations of marks that are in nonuse due to ordinary changes in social or economic conditions.

• *Trade Embargo or Other Circumstance Beyond Owner's Control*. Nonuse may be considered excusable where the owner of the registration is willing and able to continue use of the mark in commerce, but is unable to do so due to a trade embargo.

• *Sale of a Business*. Temporary nonuse due to the sale of a business might be considered excusable.

• *Retooling*. The mark might be out of use temporarily because of an interruption of production for retooling of a plant or equipment, with production possible again at a scheduled time. However, nonuse due to retooling is excusable only if the owner shows that the plant or equipment being retooled was essential to the production of the goods and that alternative equipment was unavailable on the market.

• *Orders on Hand*. If the product is of a type that cannot be produced quickly or in large numbers (*e.g.*, airplanes), yet there are orders on hand and activity toward filling them, nonuse might be considered excusable.

• *Illness, Fire and Other Catastrophes*. Illness, fire and other catastrophes may create situations of temporary nonuse, with the owner being able to outline arrangements and plans for resumption of use. Such nonuse is often excusable. However, a mere statement that the owner is ill and cannot conduct his or her business will not in itself excuse nonuse; the owner must show that the business is an operation that could not continue without his or her presence.

• *Negotiations with Distributors*. A recitation of efforts to negotiate agreements that would allow for resumption of use of the mark, or a statement that samples of the goods have been shipped to potential distributors, may establish lack of intention to abandon the mark, but does not establish the existence of special circumstances that excuse the nonuse.

• *Use in Foreign Country*. Use of the mark in a foreign country has no bearing on excusable nonuse of a mark in commerce that can be regulated by the United States Congress.

• *Use of Mark on Different Goods/Services*. Use of the mark on goods/services other than those recited in the registration does not establish either special circumstances or lack of intention to abandon the mark.

• *Use of Mark in Another Form*. Use of a mark as an essential part of a materially different composite mark does not excuse the failure to use the mark at issue.

APPEDIX 23:
DECLARATION OF USE OF MARK
IN COMMERCE

~DECLARATION OF USE OF MARK IN COMMERCE UNDER § 8 (15 U.S.C. § 1058)~

WHEN TO FILE: You must file a Section 8 declaration, specimen, and fee on a date that falls on or between the fifth (5") and sixth (6") anniversaries of the registration (or, for an extra fee of $100.00 per class, you may file within the six-month grace period following the sixth (6") anniversary date). You must subsequently file a Section 8 declaration, specimen, and fee on a date that falls on or between the ninth (9") and tenth (10") anniversaries of the registration, and each successive ten-year period thereafter (or, for an extra fee of $100.00 per class, you may file within the six-month grace period). *FAILURE TO FILE A SECTION 8 DECLARATION WILL RESULT IN CANCELLATION OF THE REGISTRATION.*
Note: Because the time for filing a ten-year Section 8 declaration coincides with the time for filing a Section 9 renewal request, a combined §§ 8 & 9 form exists. For more information, please see *Basic Facts about Maintaining a Trademark Registration* (for a copy, call the Trademark Assistance Center, at 1-800-786-9199).

BASIC INSTRUCTIONS

The following form is written in a "scannable" format that will enable the U.S. Patent and Trademark Office (USPTO) to scan paper filings and capture application data automatically using optical character recognition (OCR) technology. Information is to be entered next to identifying data tags, such as <MARK>. OCR software can be programmed to identify these tags, capture the corresponding data, and transmit this data to the appropriate data fields in the Trademark databases, largely bypassing manual data entry processes.

Please enter the requested information in the blank space that appears to the right of each tagged (< >) element. However, do not enter any information immediately after the section headers (the bolded wording appearing in all capital letters). Some of the information requested *must* be provided. Other information is either required only in certain circumstances, or provided only at your discretion. **Please consult the "Help" section following the form for detailed explanations as to what information should be entered in each blank space.**

To increase the effectiveness of the USPTO scanners, it is recommended that you use a typewriter to complete the form.

MAILING INFORMATION

Send the completed form; appropriate fee (The filing fee for the § 8 Declaration is $100.00 per class, made payable to the "Commissioner of Patents and Trademarks"); and any other required materials to:

Commissioner for Trademarks
P.O. Box 1451
Alexandria, VA 22313-1451

You may also wish to include a self-addressed stamped postcard with your submission, on which you identify the mark and registration number, and list each item being submitted (e.g., declaration, fee, specimen, etc.). We will return this postcard to you to confirm receipt of your submission.

~DECLARATION OF USE OF MARK IN COMMERCE UNDER § 8 (15 U.S.C. § 1058)~

~To the Commissioner for Trademarks~

<TRADEMARK/SERVICE MARK INFORMATION>

<Mark>

<Registration Number>

<Registration Date>

<OWNER INFORMATION>

<Name>

<Street>

<City>

<State>

<Country>

<Zip/Postal Code>

<DOMESTIC REPRESENTATIVE>~Required ONLY if the owner's address is outside the United States.~

<Name>   ~is hereby appointed the owner's representative
upon whom notice or process in the proceedings affecting the mark may be served.~
<Street>

<City>

<State>

<Zip Code>

<GOODS AND/OR SERVICES INFORMATION>

<All Goods and/or Services in Existing Registration>~The owner is using the mark in commerce on or in connection with all goods and/or services listed in the existing registration. If not, list in the next section the goods and/or services to be deleted.~

<Goods and/or Services Not in Use to be **Deleted**>~In the following space, list only those goods and/or services (or entire class(es)) appearing in the registration for which the owner is **no longer** using the mark in commerce. LEAVE THIS SPACE BLANK IF THE OWNER IS USING THE MARK ON OR IN CONNECTION WITH ALL GOODS AND/OR SERVICES LISTED IN THE REGISTRATION.~

<FEE INFORMATION>

~Section 8 Filing Fee~
$100.00 x <Number of Classes>   = <Filing Fee Due>
~Grace Period Fee: If filing during the six-month grace period, enter § 8 Grace Period Fee~
$100.00 x <Number of Classes>   = <Grace Period Fee Due>
~Filing Fee Due + Grace Period Fee Due~ = <Total Fees Paid>

PTO Form 1583 (REV 01/05)
OMB Control No. 0651-0009 (Exp. 8/31/2001)

U.S. DEPARTMENT OF COMMERCE/Patent and Trademark Office
There is no requirement to respond to this collection of information
unless a currently valid OMB number is displayed.

<SPECIMEN AND SIGNATURE INFORMATION>

~The owner is using the mark in commerce on or in connection with the goods/services identified above, as evidenced by the attached specimen(s) showing the mark as currently used in commerce.

(You MUST ATTACH A SPECIMEN showing the mark as currently used in commerce for at least one product or service in each international class covered.)

The undersigned, being hereby warned that willful false statements and the like are punishable by fine or imprisonment, or both, under 18 U.S.C. § 1001, and that such willful false statements and the like may jeopardize the validity of this document, declares that he/she is properly authorized to execute this document on behalf of the Owner; and all statements made of his/her own knowledge are true and that all statements made on information and belief are believed to be true.~

~Signature~ _____

<Date Signed>

<Name>

<Title>

<CONTACT INFORMATION>

<Name>

<Company/Firm Name>

<Street>

<City>

<State>

<Country>

<Zip/Postal Code>

<Telephone Number>

<Fax Number>

<e-Mail Address>

<CERTIFICATE OF MAILING>~*Recommended to avoid lateness due to mail delay.~*

~I certify that the foregoing is being deposited with the United States Postal Service as first class mail, postage prepaid, in an envelope addressed to the Commissioner for Trademarks, P.O. Box 1451, Alexandria, VA 22313-1451, on~

<Date of Deposit>

~Signature~ _____

<Name>

LINE-BY-LINE HELP INSTRUCTIONS

TRADEMARK/SERVICE MARK INFORMATION

Mark: Enter the word mark in typed form; or, in the case of a design or stylized mark, a brief description of the mark (e.g., "Design of a fanciful cat").
Registration Number: Enter the USPTO registration number.
Registration Date: Enter the date on which the registration was issued.

OWNER INFORMATION

Name: Enter the full name of the **current** owner of the registration, i.e., the name of the individual, corporation, partnership, or other entity that owns the registration. If joint or multiple owners, enter the name of each of these owners.
Note: If ownership of the registration has changed, you must establish current ownership, either by (1) recording the appropriate document(s) with the USPTO Assignment Branch; or (2) submitting evidence with this declaration, such as a copy of a document transferring ownership from one party to another. To have the USPTO databases reflect the current owner, you must choose option (1).
Street: Enter the street address or rural delivery route where the owner is located.
City: Enter the city and/or foreign area designation where the owner's address is located.
State: Enter the U.S. state or foreign province in which the owner's address is located.
Country: Enter the country of the owner's address. If the address is outside the United States, the owner may appoint a "Domestic Representative" on whom notices or process in proceedings affecting the mark may be served. *See* "Domestic Representative" section, below.
Zip/Postal Code: Enter the owner's U.S. zip code or foreign country postal identification code.

DOMESTIC REPRESENTATIVE

Complete this section **only** if the address of the current owner is outside the U.S. or one of its territories.
Name: Enter the name of the domestic representative.
Street: Enter the street address or rural delivery route where the domestic representative is located.
City: Enter the city where the domestic representative's address is located.
State: Enter the U.S. state in which the domestic representative's address is located.
Zip Code: Enter the U.S. zip code.

GOODS AND/OR SERVICES INFORMATION

All Goods and/or Services in Existing Registration: If the owner is NOT using the mark in commerce on or in connection with all of the goods/services listed in the registration, complete the next section. Otherwise, we will presume such use on or in connection with ALL goods and/or services.
Goods and/or Services Not In Use to be Deleted: List the goods and/or services (if any) identified in the registration with which the owner is NO LONGER using the mark in commerce; or, specify an entire international class(es), as appropriate (e.g., Classes 9 & 42).
Note: If the owner is not currently using the mark in commerce on or in connection with some or all of the identified goods and/or services, but expects to resume use, *and* the nonuse is due to special circumstances that excuse the nonuse, you must submit a Declaration of Excusable Nonuse under § 8. For an information sheet on the requirements for a claim of excusable nonuse, contact the Trademarks Assistance Center, at 1-800-786-9199.

FEE INFORMATION

Section 8 Filing Fee: The filing fee for the § 8 Declaration is $100.00 per class.
Number of Classes: Enter the total number of classes (*not* the international class number(s)) to which the § 8 Declaration applies; e.g., if the § 8 Declaration applies to Classes 1, 5 & 25, then enter the number "3."
Filing Fee Due: Enter total of $100.00 multiplied by the number of classes; e.g., $100.00 x 3 = $300.00.
Grace Period Fee: If filed during six-month grace period, a late fee of $100.00 per class must be submitted.
Number of Classes: See above.

Grace Period Fee Due: Enter total of $100.00 multiplied by number of classes; e.g., $100.00 x 3 = $300.00. **Total Fee Paid:** Enter the total of the Filing Fee Due plus the Grace Period Fee Due; e.g., $300.00 + $300.00 = $600.00. This amount must either be enclosed (in the form of a check or money order in U.S. currency, made payable to "Commissioner of Patents and Trademarks"), or charged to an already-existing USPTO deposit account.

Note: If the filing is deficient, additional fees may be required.

SPECIMEN AND SIGNATURE INFORMATION

Specimen(s): Attach a specimen showing current use of the registered mark in commerce for at least one product or service in each class that the § 8 Declaration covers; e.g., tags or labels for goods, and advertisements for services. Please print the registration number directly on the specimen (or on a label attached thereto). Specimens must be flat, no larger than 8½ inches (21.6 cm.) wide by 11.69 inches (29.7 cm.) long.

Signature: The appropriate person must sign the form. A person who is properly authorized to sign on behalf of the owner is: (1) a person with legal authority to bind the owner; or (2) a person with firsthand knowledge of the facts and actual or implied authority to act on behalf of the owner; or (3) an attorney who has an actual or implied written or verbal power of attorney from the owner.

Date Signed: Enter the date the form is signed.

Name: Enter the name of the person signing the form.

Title: Enter the signatory's title, if applicable, e.g., Vice President, General Partner, etc.

CONTACT INFORMATION

Although this may be the same as provided elsewhere in the document, please enter the following required information for where the USPTO should mail correspondence.

Name: Enter the full name of the contact person.

Company/Firm Name: Enter the name of the contact person's company or firm.

Street: Enter the street address or rural delivery route where the contact person is located.

City: Enter the city and/or foreign area designation where the contact person's address is located.

State: Enter the U.S. state or Canadian province in which the contact person's address is located.

Country: Enter the country of the contact person's address.

Zip Code: Enter the U.S. zip code or Canadian postal code.

Telephone Number: Enter the appropriate telephone number.

Fax Number: Enter the appropriate fax number, if available.

e-Mail Address: Enter the appropriate e-mail address, if available.

CERTIFICATE OF MAILING

Although optional, use of this section is recommended to avoid lateness due to mail delay. Papers are considered timely filed if deposited with the United States Postal Service with sufficient postage as first class mail on or before the due date and accompanied by a signed Certificate of Mailing attesting to timely deposit. The USPTO will look to the date shown on the Certificate of Mailing, rather than the date of actual receipt, to determine the timeliness of this document.

Date of Deposit: Enter the date of deposit with the United States Postal Service as first class mail.

Signature: The person signing the certificate should have a reasonable basis to expect that the correspondence will be mailed on or before the indicated date.

Name: Enter the name of the person signing the Certificate of Mailing.

APPENDIX 24:
COMBINED DECLARATION OF USE AND INCONTESTABILITY

~COMBINED DECLARATION OF USE & INCONTESTIBILITY UNDER §§ 8 & 15 (15 U.S.C. §§ 1058 & 1065)~

WHEN TO FILE: You may file a Combined Declaration of Use & Incontestability under Sections 8 & 15 only if you have continuously used a mark registered on the Principal (*not* Supplemental) Register in commerce for five (5) consecutive years. You must file the Combined Declaration, specimen, and fee on a date that falls on or between the fifth and sixth anniversaries of the registration (or, for an extra fee of $100.00 per class, you may file within the six-month grace period following the sixth-anniversary date). If you have NOT continuously used the mark in commerce for five (5) consecutive years, you must *still* file a Section 8 Declaration. You must subsequently file a Section 8 declaration, specimen, and fee on a date that falls on or between the ninth (9°) and tenth (10°) anniversaries of the registration, and each successive ten-year period thereafter (or, for an extra fee of $100.00 per class, you may file within the six-month grace period). *FAILURE TO FILE THE SECTION 8 DECLARATION WILL RESULT IN CANCELLATION OF THE REGISTRATION.* **Note**: Because the time for filing a ten-year Section 8 declaration coincides with the time for filing a Section 9 renewal application, a combined §§ 8 & 9 form exists. For more information, please see *Basic Facts About Maintaining a Trademark Registration* (for a copy, call the Trademark Assistance Center, at 1-800-786-9199).

BASIC INSTRUCTIONS

The following form is written in a "scannable" format that will enable the U.S. Patent and Trademark Office (USPTO) to scan paper filings and capture application data automatically using optical character recognition (OCR) technology. Information is to be entered next to identifying data tags, such as <MARK>. OCR software can be programmed to identify these tags, capture the corresponding data, and transmit this data to the appropriate data fields in the Trademark databases, largely bypassing manual data entry processes.

Please enter the requested information in the blank space that appears to the right of each tagged (< >) element. However, do not enter any information immediately after the section headers (the bolded wording appearing in all capital letters). Some of the information requested *must* be provided. Other information is either required only in certain circumstances, or provided only at your discretion. **Please consult the "Help" section following the form for detailed explanations as to what information should be entered in each blank space.**

To increase the effectiveness of the USPTO scanners, it is recommended that you use a typewriter to complete the form.

MAILING INFORMATION

Send the completed form; appropriate fee (The filing fee for Combined Declaration of Use & Incontestability under §§ 8 & 15 is $300.00 per class, made payable to the "Commissioner of Patents and Trademarks"); and any other required materials to:

> Commissioner for Trademarks
> P.O. Box 1451
> Alexandria, VA 22313-1451

You may also wish to include a self-addressed stamped postcard with your submission, on which you list each item being submitted (e.g., declaration, fee, specimen, etc.). We will return this postcard to you to confirm receipt of your submission.

~COMBINED DECLARATION OF USE & INCONTESTIBILITY UNDER §§ 8 & 15 (15 U.S.C. §§ 1058 & 1065)~

~To the Commissioner for Trademarks~

<TRADEMARK/SERVICE MARK INFORMATION>

<Mark>

<Registration Number>

<Registration Date>

<OWNER INFORMATION>

<Name>

<Street>

<City>

<State>

<Country>

<Zip/Postal Code>

<DOMESTIC REPRESENTATIVE>~*Required ONLY if the owner's address is outside the United States.*~

<Name>   ~is hereby appointed the owner's
representative upon whom notice or process in the proceedings affecting the mark may be served.~
<Street>

<City>

<State>

<Zip Code>

<GOODS AND/OR SERVICES INFORMATION>

<All Goods and/or Services in Existing Registration>~*The owner has used the mark in commerce for five (5) consecutive years after the date of registration, or the date of publication under § 12(c), and is still using the mark in commerce on or in connection with all goods and/or services listed in the existing registration. If the owner is not using the mark in commerce on or in connection with all the goods and/or services, list in the next section the goods and/or services to be deleted.*~

<Goods and/or Services Not in Use to be **Deleted**>~*In the following space, list only those goods and/or services (or entire class(es)) appearing in the registration for which the owner is no longer using the mark in commerce. **LEAVE THIS SPACE BLANK IF THE OWNER IS USING THE MARK ON OR IN CONNECTION WITH ALL GOODS AND/OR SERVICES LISTED IN THE REGISTRATION.***~

PTO Form 1583 (REV 01/05)
OMB Control No. 0651-0009 (Exp. 8/31/2001)

U.S. DEPARTMENT OF COMMERCE/Patent and Trademark Office
There is no requirement to respond to this collection of information
unless a currently valid OMB number is displayed.

204   Understanding Trademark Law: A Beginner's Guide

<FEE INFORMATION>

~Combined §§ 8 & 15 Filing Fee~
$300.00 x <Number of Classes>   = <Filing Fee Due>

~Grace Period Fee: If filing during the six-month grace period, enter § 8 Grace Period Fee~
$100.00 x <Number of Classes>   = <Grace Period Fee Due>

~Filing Fee Due + Grace Period Fee Due = <Total Fees Paid>

<SPECIMEN AND SIGNATURE INFORMATION>

~The owner is using the mark in commerce on or in connection with the goods/services identified above, as evidenced by the attached specimen(s) showing the mark as currently used in commerce. The mark has been in continuous use in commerce for five (5) consecutive years after the date of registration, or the date of publication under § 12(c), and is still in use in commerce on or in connection with all goods and/or services listed in the existing registration. There has been no final decision adverse to the owner's claim of ownership of such mark for such goods and/or services, or to the owner's right to register the same or to keep the same on the register; and there is no proceeding involving said rights pending and not disposed of either in the Patent and Trademark Office or in the courts. **(You MUST ATTACH A SPECIMEN showing the mark as currently used in commerce for at least one product or service in each international class covered.)**

The undersigned, being hereby warned that willful false statements and the like are punishable by fine or imprisonment, or both, under 18 U.S.C. § 1001, and that such willful false statements and the like may jeopardize the validity of this document, declares that he/she is properly authorized to execute this document on behalf of the Owner; and all statements made of his/her own knowledge are true and that all statements made on information and belief are believed to be true.

~Signature~ _____

<Date Signed>

<Name>

<Title>

<CONTACT INFORMATION>

<Name>

<Company/Firm Name>

<Street>

<City>

<State>

<Country>

<Zip/Postal Code>

<Telephone Number>

<Fax Number>

<e-Mail Address>

<CERTIFICATE OF MAILING> *~Recommended to avoid lateness due to mail delay.~*

~I certify that the foregoing is being deposited with the United States Postal Service as first class mail, postage prepaid, in an envelope addressed to the Commissioner for Trademarks, P.O. Box 1451, Alexandria, VA 22313-1451, on~

<Date of Deposit>

~Signature~ _____

<Name>

The information collected on this form allows the PTO to determine whether a mark for which a registration was issued is still in use in commerce in connection with some or all of the goods identified in the registration. Responses to the request for information are required in order to retain the benefit of a registration on the Principal or Supplemental Register. 15 U.S.C. §§1051 et seq. and 37 C.F.R. Part 2. All information collected will be made public. Gathering and providing the information will require an estimated eleven minutes. Please direct comments on the time needed to complete this form, and/or suggestions for reducing this burden to the Chief Information Officer, U.S. Patent and Trademark Office, U.S. Department of Commerce, Washington D.C. 20231. Please note that the PTO may not conduct or sponsor a collection of information using a form that does not display a valid OMB control number. (See bottom left side of this form).

LINE-BY-LINE HELP INSTRUCTIONS

TRADEMARK/SERVICE MARK INFORMATION

Mark: Enter the word mark in typed form; or, in the case of a design or stylized mark, a brief description of the mark (e.g., "Design of a fanciful cat").
Registration Number: Enter the USPTO registration number.
Registration Date: Enter the date on which the registration was issued.

OWNER INFORMATION

Name: Enter the full name of the **current** owner of registration, i.e., the name of the individual, corporation, partnership, or other entity that owns the registration. If joint or multiple owners, enter the name of each of these owners. **Note:** If ownership of the registration has changed, you must establish current ownership, either by (1) recording the appropriate document(s) with the USPTO Assignment Branch; or (2) submitting evidence with this declaration, such as a copy of a document transferring ownership from one party to another. To have the USPTO databases reflect the current owner, you must choose option (1).
Street: Enter the street address or rural delivery route where the owner is located.
City: Enter the city or foreign area designation where the owner's address is located.
State: Enter the U.S. state or foreign province in which the owner's address is located.
Country: Enter the country of the owner's address. If the address is outside the United States, the owner may appoint a "Domestic Representative" on whom notices or process in proceedings affecting the mark may be served. *See* "Domestic Representative" section, below.
Zip/Postal Code: Enter the owner's U.S. zip code or foreign country postal identification code.

DOMESTIC REPRESENTATIVE

Complete this section **only** if the address of the current owner is outside the U.S. or one of its territories.
Name: Enter the name of the domestic representative.
Street: Enter the street address or rural delivery route where the domestic representative is located.
City: Enter the city where the domestic representative's address is located.
State: Enter the U.S. state in which the domestic representative's address is located.
Zip Code: Enter the U.S. zip code.

GOODS AND/OR SERVICES INFORMATION

All Goods and/or Services in Existing Registration: If the owner has NOT used the mark in commerce for five (5) consecutive years after the date of registration, or the date of publication under § 12(c), or the owner is NOT still using the mark in commerce on all goods/services identified in the registration, complete the next section. Otherwise, we will presume such use on or in connection with ALL goods and/or services.
Goods and/or Services Not In Use to be Deleted: List the goods or services (if any) identified in the registration with which the owner is NO LONGER using the mark in commerce; or, specify an entire international class(es), as appropriate (e.g., Classes 9 & 42).
Note: If the owner is not currently using the mark in commerce on or in connection with some or all of the identified goods and/or services, but expects to resume use, *and* the nonuse is due to special circumstances that excuse the nonuse, you must submit a Declaration of Excusable Nonuse under § 8. For an information sheet on the requirements for a claim of excusable nonuse, contact the Trademark Assistance Center, at 1-800-786-9199. **Note:** If the owner is still using the mark on or in connection with some goods and/or services, but does not wish to claim incontestability with respect to those goods and/ or services, the owner should file a separate "Declaration under § 8" (PTO Form 1583) for the goods and/ or services on or in connection with which the mark is still in use, and a "Declaration of Incontestability of Mark under § 15" (PTO Form 4.16) for the goods and/or services for which incontestability is claimed, rather than a Combined Declaration Under §§ 8 and 15.

FEE INFORMATION

Combined Sections 8 & 15 Filing Fee: Filing fee for Combined §§ 8 & 15 Declaration is $300.00 per class ($100.00 per class for the Section 8 Declaration and $200.00 per class for the Section 15 Declaration.)
Number of Classes: Enter the total number of classes (*not* the international class number(s)) to which the §§ 8 & 15 Declaration applies. E.g., if the §§ 8 & 15 Declaration applies to Classes 1, 5 and 25, enter the number "3."
Filing Fee Due: Enter the total of $300.00 multiplied by the number of classes; e.g., $300.00 x 3 = $900.00.
Grace Period Fee: If filed during six-month grace period, a late fee of $100.00 per class must be submitted.
Number of Classes: See above.
Grace Period Fee Due: Enter the total of $100.00 multiplied by number of classes; e.g., $100.00 x 3 = $300.00.
Total Fee Paid: Enter the total of the Filing Fee Due plus the Grace Period Fee Due; e.g., $900.00 + $300.00 = $1200.00. This amount must either be enclosed (in the form of a check or money order in U.S. currency, made payable to "Commissioner of Patents and Trademarks"), or charged to an already-existing USPTO deposit account.
Note: If the filing is deficient, additional fees may be required.

SPECIMEN AND SIGNATURE INFORMATION

Specimen(s): Attach a specimen showing current use of the registered mark in commerce for at least one product or service in each class that the § 8 Declaration covers; e.g., tags or labels for goods, and advertisements for services. Please print the registration number directly on the specimen (or on a label attached thereto). Specimens must be flat and no larger than 8½ inches (21.6 cm.) wide by 11.69 inches (29.7 cm.) long.
Signature: The appropriate person must sign the form. A person who is properly authorized to sign on behalf of the owner is: (1) a person with legal authority to bind the owner; or (2) a person with firsthand knowledge of the facts and actual or implied authority to act on behalf of the owner; or (3) an attorney who has an actual or implied written or verbal power of attorney from the owner.
Date Signed: Enter the date the form is signed.
Name: Enter the name of the person signing the form.
Title: Enter the signatory's title, if applicable, e.g., Vice President, General Partner, etc.

CONTACT INFORMATION

Although this may be the same as provided elsewhere in the document, please enter the following required information for where the USPTO should mail correspondence.
Name: Enter the full name of the contact person.
Company/Firm Name: Enter the name of the contact person's company or firm.
Street: Enter the street address or rural delivery route where the contact person is located.
City: Enter the city and/or foreign area designation where the contact person's address is located.
State: Enter the U.S. state or Canadian province in which the contact person's address is located.
Country: Enter the country of the contact person's address.
Zip Code: Enter the U.S. zip code or Canadian postal code.
Telephone Number: Enter the appropriate telephone number.
Fax Number: Enter the appropriate fax number, if available.
e-Mail Address: Enter the appropriate e-mail address, if available.

CERTIFICATE OF MAILING

Although optional, use is recommended to avoid lateness due to mail delay. Papers are considered timely filed if deposited with the U.S. Postal Service with sufficient postage as first class mail on or before the due date and accompanied by a signed Certificate of Mailing attesting to timely deposit. The USPTO will look to the date shown on the Certificate of Mailing, rather than the date of actual receipt, to determine timeliness.

Date of Deposit: Enter the date of deposit with the United States Postal Service as first class mail.

Signature: The person signing the certificate should have a reasonable basis to expect that the correspondence will be mailed on or before the indicated date.

Name: Enter the name of the person signing the Certificate of Mailing.

APPENDIX 25:
COMBINED DECLARATION OF USE IN
COMMERCE/APPLICATION FOR RENEWAL
OF REGISTRATION OF MARK

~COMBINED DECLARATION OF USE IN COMMERCE/APPLICATION FOR
RENEWAL OF REGISTRATION OF MARK UNDER §§ 8 & 9 (15 U.S.C. §§ 1058 & 1059)~

WHEN TO FILE: You must file a Section 8 declaration, specimen, and fee on a date that falls on or between the ninth (9ᵗʰ) and tenth (10ᵗʰ) anniversaries of the registration, and each successive ten-year period thereafter (or, for an extra fee of $100.00 per class, you may file within the six-month grace period). Also, you must file a renewal application within the same period (or, for an extra fee of $100.00 per class, you may file within the six-month grace period following the registration expiration date). *FAILURE TO FILE THIS DOCUMENT WILL RESULT IN CANCELLATION/EXPIRATION OF THE REGISTRATION.* **Note**: Because the time for filing a ten-year Section 8 declaration coincides with the time for filing a Section 9 renewal application, you may use this combined §§ 8 & 9 form. For more information, please see *Basic Facts about Maintaining a Trademark Registration* (for a copy, call the Trademark Assistance Center, at 1-800-786-9199).

BASIC INSTRUCTIONS

The following form is written in a "scannable" format that will enable the U.S. Patent and Trademark Office (USPTO) to scan paper filings and capture application data automatically using optical character recognition (OCR) technology. Information is to be entered next to identifying data tags, such as <MARK>. OCR software can be programmed to identify these tags, capture the corresponding data, and transmit this data to the appropriate data fields in the Trademark databases, largely bypassing manual data entry processes.

Please enter the requested information in the blank space that appears to the right of each tagged (<   >) element. However, do not enter any information immediately after the section headers (the bolded wording appearing in all capital letters). *Some* of the information requested *must* be provided. Other information is either required only in certain circumstances, or provided only at your discretion. **Please consult the "Help" section following the form for detailed explanations as to what information should be entered in each blank space.**

To increase the effectiveness of the USPTO scanners, it is recommended that you use a typewriter to complete the form.

MAILING INFORMATION

Send the completed form; appropriate fee (The filing fee for the Combined §§ 8 & 9 Declaration/Application is $500.00, $100.00 per class for the Section 8 Declaration and $400.00 per class for the renewal application, made payable to the "Commissioner of Patents and Trademarks"); and any other required materials to:

> Commissioner for Trademarks
> P.O. Box 1451
> Alexandria, VA 22313-1451

You may also wish to include a self-addressed stamped postcard with your submission, on which you identify the mark and registration number, and list each item being submitted (e.g., declaration, fee, specimen, etc.). We will return this postcard to confirm receipt of your submission.

~COMBINED DECLARATION OF USE IN COMMERCE/APPLICATION FOR RENEWAL OF REGISTRATION OF MARK UNDER §§ 8 & 9 (15 U.S.C. §§ 1058 & 1059)~

~To the Commissioner for Trademarks~

\<TRADEMARK/SERVICE MARK INFORMATION\>

\<Mark\>

\<Registration Number\>

\<Registration Date\>

\<OWNER INFORMATION\>

\<Name\>

\<Street\>

\<City\>

\<State\>

\<Country\>

\<Zip/Postal Code\>

\<DOMESTIC REPRESENTATIVE\>~*Required ONLY if the owner's address is outside the United States.*~

\<Name\>   ~is hereby appointed the owner's representative upon whom notice or process in the proceedings affecting the mark may be served.~

\<Street\>

\<City\>

\<State\>

\<Zip Code\>

\<GOODS AND/OR SERVICES INFORMATION\>

\<All Goods and/or Services in Existing Registration\>~*The owner is using mark in commerce on or in connection with all goods and/or services listed in the existing registration. If not, list in the next section the goods and/or services to be deleted.*~

\<Goods and/or Services Not in Use to be **Deleted**\>~*In the following space, list only those goods and/or services (or entire class(es)) appearing in the registration for which the owner is no longer using the mark in commerce. LEAVE THIS SPACE BLANK IF THE OWNER IS USING THE MARK ON OR IN CONNECTION WITH ALL GOODS AND/OR SERVICES LISTED IN THE REGISTRATION).*~

\<FEE INFORMATION\>

~*Combined §§ 8 & 9 Filing Fee*~

$500.00 x \<Number of Classes\>   ` = \<Filing Fee Due\>

~*Grace Period Fee: If filing during the six-month grace period, enter Combined §§ 8 & 9 Grace Period Fee.*~

$200.00 x \<Number of Classes\>   = \<Grace Fee Due\>

~*Filing Fee Due + Grace Period Fee Due*~ = \<Total Fees Paid\>

PTO Form 1963 (REV 01/05)
OMB Control No. 0651-0009 (Exp. 8/31/2001)

U.S. DEPARTMENT OF COMMERCE/Patent and Trademark Office
There is no requirement to respond to this collection of information
unless a currently valid OMB number is displayed.

<SPECIMEN AND SIGNATURE INFORMATION>

~Section 8: Declaration of Use in Commerce

The owner is using the mark in commerce on or in connection with the goods/services identified above, as evidenced by the attached specimen(s) showing the mark as currently used in commerce.

(You MUST ATTACH A SPECIMEN showing the mark as currently used in commerce for at least one product or service in each international class covered.)

The undersigned being hereby warned that willful false statements and the like are punishable by fine or imprisonment, or both, under 18 U.S.C. § 1001, and that such willful false statements and the like may jeopardize the validity of this document, declares that he/she is properly authorized to execute this document on behalf of the Owner; and all statements made of his/her own knowledge are true and that all statements made on information and belief are believed to be true.

Section 9: Application for Renewal

The registrant requests that the registration be renewed for the goods and/or services identified above.~

~Signature~ _____

<Date Signed>

<Name>

<Title>

<CONTACT INFORMATION>

<Name>

<Company/Firm Name>

<Street>

<City>

<State>

<Country>

<Zip/Postal Code>

<Telephone Number>

<Fax Number>

<e-Mail Address>

<CERTIFICATE OF MAILING>~Recommended to avoid lateness due to mail delay.~

~I certify that the foregoing is being deposited with the United States Postal Service as first class mail, postage prepaid, in an envelope addressed to the Commissioner for Trademarks, P.O. Box 1451, Alexandria, VA 22313-1451, on~

<Date of Deposit>

~Signature~ _____

<Name>

LINE-BY-LINE HELP INSTRUCTIONS

TRADEMARK/SERVICE MARK INFORMATION

Mark: Enter the word mark in typed form; or, in the case of a design or stylized mark, a brief description of the mark (e.g., "Design of a fanciful cat").
Registration Number: Enter the USPTO registration number.
Registration Date: Enter the date on which the registration was issued.

OWNER INFORMATION

Name: Enter the full name of the **current** owner of the registration, i.e., the name of the individual, corporation, partnership, or other entity that owns the registration. If joint or multiple owners, enter the name of each of these owners. **Note:** If ownership of the registration has changed, you must establish current ownership, either by (1) recording the appropriate document(s) with the USPTO Assignment Branch; or (2) submitting evidence with this declaration, such as a copy of a document transferring ownership from one party to another. To have the USPTO databases reflect the current owner, you must choose option (1).
Street: Enter the street address or rural delivery route where the owner is located.
City: Enter the city and/or foreign area designation where the owner's address is located.
State: Enter the U.S. state or foreign province in which the owner's address is located.
Country: Enter the country of the owner's address. If the address is outside the United States, the owner may appoint a "Domestic Representative" on whom notices or process in proceedings affecting the mark may be served. *See* "Domestic Representative" section, below.
Zip/Postal Code: Enter the owner's U.S. zip code or foreign country postal identification code.

DOMESTIC REPRESENTATIVE

Complete this section **only** if the address of the current owner is outside the U.S. or one of its territories.
Name: Enter the name of the domestic representative.
Street: Enter the street address or rural delivery route where the domestic representative is located.
City: Enter the city where the domestic representative's address is located.
State: Enter the U.S. state in which the domestic representative's address is located.
Zip Code: Enter the U.S. zip code.

GOODS AND/OR SERVICES INFORMATION

All Goods and/or Services in Existing Registration: If the owner is NOT using the mark in commerce on or in connection with all of the goods/services identified in the registration, complete the next section. Otherwise, we will presume such use on or in connection with ALL goods and/or services.
Goods and/or Services to be Deleted: List the goods and/or services (if any) identified in the registration with which the owner is NO LONGER using the mark in commerce; or, specify an entire international class(es), as appropriate (e.g., Classes 9 & 42). **Note:** If the owner is not currently using the mark in commerce on or in connection with some or all of the identified goods and/or services, but expects to resume use, *and* the nonuse is due to special circumstances that excuse the nonuse, you must submit a Declaration of Excusable Nonuse under § 8.

FEE INFORMATION

Combined Sections 8 & 9 Filing Fee: The filing fee for the Combined §§ 8 & 9 is $500.00 per class ($100.00 per class for the Section 8 Declaration and $400.00 per class for the renewal application).
Number of Classes: Enter the total number of classes (*not* the international class number(s)) to which the Combined §§ 8 & 9 applies. For example, if the Combined §§ 8 & 9 applies to Classes 1, 5 and 25, then enter the number "3."
Filing Fee Due: Enter total of $500.00 multiplied by the number of classes; e.g., $500.00 x 3 = $1500.00.
Grace Period Fee: If filed during the six-month grace period, a late fee of $200.00 per class must be submitted ($100.00 for the Section 8 declaration and $100.00 for the renewal application).
Number of Classes: See above.

Grace Period Fee Due: Enter total of $200.00 multiplied by number of classes; e.g., $200.00 x 3 = $600.00.
Total Fee Paid: Enter the total of the Filing Fee Due plus the Grace Period Fee Due; e.g., $1500.00 + $600.00 = $2100.00. This amount must either be enclosed (in the form of a check or money order in U.S. currency, made payable to "Commissioner of Patents and Trademarks"), or charged to an already-existing USPTO deposit account.
Note: If the filing is deficient, additional fees may be required.

SPECIMEN AND SIGNATURE INFORMATION

Specimen(s): Attach a specimen showing current use of the registered mark in commerce for at least one product or service in each class that the § 8 Declaration covers; e.g., tags or labels for goods, and advertisements for services. Please print registration number directly on the specimen (or on a label attached thereto). Specimens must be flat and no larger than 8½ inches (21.6 cm.) wide by 11.69 inches (29.7 cm.) long.
Signature: The appropriate person must sign the form. A person who is properly authorized to sign on behalf of the owner is: (1) a person with legal authority to bind the owner; or (2) a person with firsthand knowledge of the facts and actual or implied authority to act on behalf of the owner; or (3) an attorney who has an actual or implied written or verbal power of attorney from the owner.
Date Signed: Enter the date the form is signed.
Name: Enter the name of the person signing the form.
Title: Enter the signatory's title, if applicable, e.g., Vice President, General Partner, etc.

CONTACT INFORMATION

Although this may be the same as provided elsewhere in the document, please enter the following required information for where the USPTO should mail correspondence.
Name: Enter the full name of the contact person.
Company/Firm Name: Enter the name of the contact person's company or firm.
Street: Enter the street address or rural delivery route where the contact person is located.
City: Enter the city and/or foreign area designation where the contact person's address is located.
State: Enter the U.S. state or Canadian province in which the contact person's address is located.
Country: Enter the country of the contact person's address.
Zip Code: Enter the U.S. zip code or Canadian postal code.
Telephone Number: Enter the appropriate telephone number.
Fax Number: Enter the appropriate fax number, if available.
e-Mail Address: Enter the appropriate e-mail address, if available.

CERTIFICATE OF MAILING

Although optional, use of this section is recommended to avoid lateness due to mail delay. Papers are considered timely filed if deposited with the United States Postal Service with sufficient postage as first class mail on or before the due date and accompanied by a signed Certificate of Mailing attesting to timely deposit. The USPTO will look to the date shown on the Certificate of Mailing, rather than the date of actual receipt, to determine the timeliness of this document.
Date of Deposit: Enter the date of deposit with the United States Postal Service as first class mail.
Signature: The person signing the certificate should have a reasonable basis to expect that the correspondence will be mailed on or before the indicated date.
Name: Enter the name of the person signing the Certificate of Mailing.

APPENDIX 26:
THE MADRID SYSTEM

5. Madrid Agreement Concerning the International Registration of Marks

Madrid Agreement (Marks) (1891), revised at Brussels (1900), at Washington (1911),
at The Hague (1925), at London (1934), Nice (1957) and at Stockholm (1967), and amended in 1979

and

6. Protocol Relating to the Madrid Agreement Concerning the International Registration of Marks

Madrid Protocol (1989), amended in 2006

(Madrid Union)[1]

Status on October 27, 2008

State/IGO	Date on which State became party to the Madrid Agreement[2]	Date on which State/IGO became party to the Madrid Protocol (1989)
Albania	October 4, 1995	July 30, 2003
Algeria	July 5, 1972	–
Antigua and Barbuda	–	March 17, 2000
Armenia	December 25, 1991	October 19, 2000[6,10]
Australia	–	July 11, 2001[5,6]
Austria	January 1, 1909	April 13, 1999
Azerbaijan	December 25, 1995	April 15, 2007
Bahrain	–	December 15, 2005[10]
Belarus	December 25, 1991	January 18, 2002[6,10]
Belgium	July 15, 1892[3]	April 1, 1998[3,6]
Bhutan	August 4, 2000	August 4, 2000
Bosnia and Herzegovina	March 1, 1992	January 27, 2009
Botswana	–	December 5, 2006
Bulgaria	August 1, 1985	October 2, 2001[6,10]
China	October 4, 1989[4]	December 1, 1995[4,5,6]
Croatia	October 8, 1991	January 23, 2004
Cuba	December 6, 1989	December 26, 1995
Cyprus	November 4, 2003	November 4, 2003[5]
Czech Republic	January 1, 1993	September 25, 1996
Democratic People's Republic of Korea	June 10, 1980	October 3, 1996
Denmark	–	February 13, 1996[5,6,7]
Egypt	July 1, 1952	–
Estonia	–	November 18, 1998[5,6,8]
European Community	–	October 1, 2004[6,10]
Finland	–	April 1, 1996[5,6]
France	July 15, 1892[9]	November 7, 1997[9]
Georgia	–	August 20, 1998[6,10]
Germany	December 1, 1922	March 20, 1996
Ghana	–	September 16, 2008[5,6]
Greece	–	August 10, 2000[5,6]
Hungary	January 1, 1909	October 3, 1997
Iceland	–	April 15, 1997[6,10]
Iran (Islamic Republic of)	December 25, 2003	December 25, 2003[5]
Ireland	–	October 19, 2001[5,6]
Italy	October 15, 1894	April 17, 2000[5,6]

(continuation)

State/IGO	Date on which State became party to the Madrid Agreement[2]	Date on which State/IGO became party to the Madrid Protocol (1989)
Japan	–	March 14, 2000[6,10]
Kazakhstan	December 25, 1991	–
Kenya	June 26, 1998	June 26, 1998[5]
Kyrgyzstan	December 25, 1991	June 17, 2004[6]
Latvia	January 1, 1995	January 5, 2000
Lesotho	February 12, 1999	February 12, 1999
Liberia	December 25, 1995	
Liechtenstein	July 14, 1933	March 17, 1998
Lithuania	–	November 15, 1997[5]
Luxembourg	September 1, 1924[3]	April 1, 1998[3,6]
Madagascar	–	April 28, 2008[10]
Monaco	April 29, 1956	September 27, 1996
Mongolia	April 21, 1985	June 16, 2001
Montenegro	June 3, 2006	June 3, 2006
Morocco	July 30, 1917	October 8, 1999
Mozambique	October 7, 1998	October 7, 1998
Namibia	June 30, 2004[2]	June 30, 2004[8]
Netherlands	March 1, 1893[3,11]	April 1, 1998[3,6,11]
Norway	–	March 29, 1996[5,6]
Oman	–	October 16, 2007
Poland	March 18, 1991	March 4, 1997[10]
Portugal	October 31, 1893	March 20, 1997
Republic of Korea	–	April 10, 2003[5,6]
Republic of Moldova	December 25, 1991	December 1, 1997[6]
Romania	October 6, 1920	July 28, 1998
Russian Federation	July 1, 1976[12]	June 10, 1997
San Marino	September 25, 1960	September 12, 2007[6,10]
Sao Tome and Principe	-	December 8, 2008
Serbia[13]	April 27, 1992	February 17, 1998
Sierra Leone	June 17, 1997	December 28, 1999
Singapore	–	October 31, 2000[5,6]
Slovakia	January 1, 1993	September 13, 1997[10]
Slovenia	June 25, 1991	March 12, 1998
Spain	July 15, 1892	December 1, 1995
Sudan	May 16, 1984	
Swaziland	December 14, 1998	December 14, 1998
Sweden	–	December 1, 1995[5,6]
Switzerland	July 15, 1892	May 1, 1997[6,10]
Syrian Arab Republic	August 5, 2004	August 5, 2004
Tajikistan	December 25, 1991	
The former Yugoslav Republic of Macedonia	September 8, 1991	August 30, 2002
Turkey	–	January 1, 1999[5,6,8]
Turkmenistan	–	September 28, 1999[6,10]
Ukraine	December 25, 1991	December 29, 2000[5,6]
United Kingdom	–	December 1, 1995[5,6,14]
United States of America	–	November 2, 2003[5,6]
Uzbekistan	–	December 27, 2006[6,10]
Viet Nam	March 8, 1949	July 11, 2006[6]
Zambia	–	November 15, 2001
Total: (84)	(56)	(78)

---

[1] The Madrid Union is composed of the States party to the Madrid Agreement and the Contracting Parties to the Madrid Protocol.

[2] All the States party to the Madrid Agreement have declared, under Article 3*bis* of the Nice or Stockholm Act, that the protection arising from international registration shall not extend to them unless the proprietor of the mark so requests.

(continuation)

---

[3] The territories of Belgium, Luxembourg and the Kingdom of the Netherlands in Europe are to be deemed a single country, for the application of the Madrid Agreement as from January 1, 1971, and for the application of the Protocol as from April 1, 1998.

[4] Not applicable to either the Hong Kong Special Administrative Region or the Macau Special Administrative Region.

[5] In accordance with Article 5(2)(b) and (c) of the Protocol, this Contracting Party has declared that the time limit to notify a refusal of protection shall be 18 months and that, where a refusal of protection results from an opposition to the granting of protection, such refusal may be notified after the expiry of the 18–month time limit.

[6] In accordance with Article 8(7)(a) of the Protocol, this Contracting Party has declared that, in connection with each request for territorial extension to it of the protection of an international registration and the renewal of any such international registration, it wants to receive, instead of a share in the revenue produced by the supplementary and complementary fee, an individual fee.

[7] Not applicable to the Faroe Islands and to Greenland.

[8] In accordance with Article 14(5) of the Protocol, this Contracting Party has declared that the protection resulting from any international registration effected under this Protocol before the date of entry into force of this Protocol with respect to it cannot be extended to it.

[9] Including all Overseas Departments and Territories.

[10] In accordance with Article 5(2)(b) of the Protocol, this Contracting Party has declared that the time limit to notify a refusal of protection shall be 18 months.

[11] The instrument of ratification of the Stockholm Act and the instrument of acceptance of the Protocol were deposited for the Kingdom in Europe. The Netherlands extended the application of the Madrid Protocol to the Netherlands Antilles with effect from April 28, 2003.

[12] Date of accession by the Soviet Union, continued by the Russian Federation as from December 25, 1991.

[13] Serbia is the continuing State from Serbia and Montenegro as from June 3, 2006.

[14] Ratification in respect of the United Kingdom and the Isle of Man.

APPENDIX 27:
APPLICATION FOR INTERNATIONAL REGISTRATION UNDER THE MADRID PROTOCOL

MM2(E)

MADRID AGREEMENT AND PROTOCOL CONCERNING THE

INTERNATIONAL REGISTRATION OF MARKS

APPLICATION FOR INTERNATIONAL REGISTRATION

GOVERNED EXCLUSIVELY BY THE MADRID PROTOCOL

(Rule 9 of the Common Regulations)

World Intellectual Property Organization
34, chemin des Colombettes, P.O. Box 18,
1211 Geneva 20, Switzerland
Tel.: (41-22) 338 9111
Fax (International Trademark Registry): (41-22) 740 1429
e-mail: intreg.mail@wipo.int – Internet: *http://www.wipo.int*

MM2(E) – December 2008

MM2(E)

APPLICATION FOR INTERNATIONAL REGISTRATION
GOVERNED EXCLUSIVELY BY THE MADRID PROTOCOL

For use by the applicant	For use by the applicant/Office
This international application includes the following number of: — continuation sheet(s): .... — MM17 form(s):	Applicant's reference: .... Office's reference: ....

1 CONTRACTING PARTY WHOSE OFFICE IS THE OFFICE OF ORIGIN

....

2 APPLICANT

(a) Name: ....

....

(b) Address: ....

....

(c) Address for correspondence: ....

....

(d) Telephone : .... Fax: ....

E-mail address: ....

(e) Preferred language for correspondence: ☐ English   ☐ French   ☐ Spanish

(f) Other indications (as may be required by certain designated Contracting Parties; for example, if the **United States of America** is designated, it is necessary to include these indications):

(i) if the applicant is a natural person, nationality of applicant: ....

(ii) if the applicant is a legal entity:

— legal nature of the legal entity: ....

— State and, where applicable, territorial unit within that State, under the law of which the legal entity is organized:

....

3 ENTITLEMENT TO FILE

(a) Check the appropriate box:

(i) ☐ where the Contracting Party mentioned in item 1 is a State, the applicant is a national of that State; or

(ii) ☐ where the Contracting Party mentioned in item 1 is an organization, the name of the State of which the applicant is a national: ....; or

(iii) ☐ the applicant is domiciled in the territory of the Contracting Party mentioned in item 1; or

(iv) ☐ the applicant has a real and effective industrial or commercial establishment in the territory of the Contracting Party mentioned in item 1.

(b) Where the address of the applicant, given in item 2(b), is not in the territory of the Contracting Party mentioned in item 1, indicate in the space provided below:

(i) if the box in paragraph (a)(iii) of the present item has been checked, the domicile of the applicant in the territory of that Contracting Party, or,

(ii) if the box in paragraph (a)(iv) of the present item has been checked, the address of the applicant's industrial or commercial establishment in the territory of that Contracting Party.

....

....

MM2(E) – December 2008

4 APPOINTMENT OF A REPRESENTATIVE (if any)

Name: ....

Address: ....

....

Telephone: .... Fax: ....

E-mail address: ....

5 BASIC APPLICATION OR BASIC REGISTRATION

Basic application number: .... Date of the basic application: .... (dd/mm/yyyy)

Basic registration number: .... Date of the basic registration: .... (dd/mm/yyyy)

6 PRIORITY CLAIMED

☐ The applicant claims the priority of the earlier filing mentioned below:

Office of earlier filing: ....

Number of earlier filing (if available): ....

Date of earlier filing: .... (dd/mm/yyyy)

If the earlier filing does not relate to all the goods and services listed in item 10 of this form, indicate in the space provided below the goods and services to which it does relate:

....

....

☐ If several priorities are claimed, check box and use a continuation sheet giving the above required information for each priority claimed.

7 THE MARK

(a) Place the reproduction of the mark, as it appears in the basic application or basic registration, in the square below.

(b) Where the reproduction in item (a) is in black and white and color is claimed in item 8, place a color reproduction of the mark in the square below.

(c) ☐ The applicant declares that he wishes the mark to be considered as a mark in standard characters.

(d) ☐ The mark consists of a color or a combination of colors as such.

Where the Office of origin has addressed this form by facsimile, the present space must be completed before addressing the original of this page to the International Bureau.

Number of basic registration or Office reference as shown on the first page of this form: ....

Signature by the Office of origin: ....

MM2(E) – December 2008

8 COLOR(S) CLAIMED

(a) ☐ The applicant claims color as a distinctive feature of the mark.

Color or combination of colors claimed: ....

....

....

(b) Indication, for each color, of the principal parts of the mark that are in that color (as may be required by certain designated Contracting Parties):

....

....

....

9 MISCELLANEOUS INDICATIONS

(a) Transliteration of the mark (this information is compulsory where the mark consists of or contains matter in characters other than Latin characters, or numerals other than Arabic or Roman numerals):

....

....

(b) Translation of the mark (as may be required by certain designated Contracting Parties):

(i) into English: ....

(ii) into French: ....

(iii) into Spanish: ....

(c) ☐ The words contained in the mark have no meaning (and therefore cannot be translated).

(d) Where applicable, check the relevant box or boxes below:

☐ Three-dimensional mark

☐ Sound mark

☐ Collective mark, certification mark, or guarantee mark

(e) Description of the mark (where applicable):

....

....

(f) Verbal elements of the mark (where applicable):

....

....

(g) The applicant declares that he wishes to disclaim protection for the following element(s) of the mark:

....

....

....

MM2(E) – December 2008

10 GOODS AND SERVICES

(a) Indicate below the goods and services for which the international registration is sought:

Please use font "Courier New" or "Times New Roman", size 12 pt, or above

Class   Goods and services

(b) ☐ The applicant wishes to **limit** the list of goods and services in respect of one or more designated Contracting Parties, as follows:

Please use font "Courier New" or "Times New Roman", size 12 pt, or above

Contracting Party   Class(es) or list of goods and services for which
                                            protection is sought in this Contracting Party

☐ If the space provided is not sufficient, check the box and use a **continuation sheet**

MM2(E) – December 2008

11 DESIGNATED CONTRACTING PARTIES

(Information concerning national or regional procedures for each Contracting Party designated may be found at the following website: *http://www.wipo.int/madrid/en/members/ipoffices_info.html*. Additional information may be found in the information notices available at: *http://www.wipo.int/madrid/en/notices/*.)

Check the corresponding boxes:

AG Antigua and Barbuda	DK Denmark	KP Democratic People's Republic of Korea	PT Portugal
AL Albania	EM European Community[1]	KR Republic of Korea	RO Romania
AM Armenia	EE Estonia	LI Liechtenstein	RS Serbia
AN Netherlands Antilles	ES Spain	LS Lesotho	RU Russian Federation
AT Austria	FI Finland	LT Lithuania	SE Sweden
AU Australia	FR France	LV Latvia	SG Singapore[2]
AZ Azerbaijan	GB United Kingdom[2]	MA Morocco	SI Slovenia
BG Bulgaria	GE Georgia	MC Monaco	SK Slovakia
BH Bahrain	GH Ghana[4]	MD Republic of Moldova	SL Sierra Leone
BT Bhutan	GR Greece	ME Montenegro	SM San Marino
BW Botswana	HR Croatia	MG Madagascar	ST Sao Tome and Principe
BX Benelux	HU Hungary	MK The former Yugoslav Rep. of Macedonia	SY Syrian Arab Republic
BY Belarus	IE Ireland[2]	MN Mongolia	SZ Swaziland
CH Switzerland	IR Iran (Islamic Republic of)	MZ Mozambique	TM Turkmenistan
CN China	IS Iceland	NA Namibia	TR Turkey
CU Cuba[4]	IT Italy	NO Norway	UA Ukraine
CY Cyprus	JP Japan[4]	OM Oman	US United States of America[3]
CZ Czech Republic	KE Kenya	PL Poland	UZ Uzbekistan
DE Germany	KG Kyrgyzstan		VN Viet Nam
			ZM Zambia

Others: ....

[1] If the **European Community** is designated, it is compulsory to indicate a second language before the Office of the European Community, among the following (check one box only): ☐ French   ☐ German   ☐ Italian   ☐ Spanish

Moreover, if the applicant wishes to claim the seniority of an earlier mark registered in, or for, a Member State of the European Community, the official form MM17 must be annexed to the present international application.

[2] By designating **Ireland**, **Singapore** or the **United Kingdom**, the applicant declares that he has the intention that the mark will be used by him or with his consent in that country in connection with the goods and services identified in this application.

[3] If the **United States of America** is designated, it is compulsory to annex to the present international application the official form (MM18) containing the declaration of intention to use the mark required by this Contracting Party. Item 2(f) of the present form should also be completed.

[4] **Cuba**, **Ghana** and **Japan** have made a notification under Rule 34(3)(a) of the Common Regulations. Their respective **individual fees are payable in two parts**. Therefore, if **Cuba**, **Ghana** or **Japan** is designated, only the first part of the applicable individual fee is payable at the time of filing the present international application. The second part will have to be paid only if the Office of the Contracting Party concerned is satisfied that the mark which is the subject of the international registration qualifies for protection. The date by which the second part must be paid, and the amount due, will be notified to the holder of the international registration at a later stage.

12 SIGNATURE BY THE APPLICANT OR HIS REPRESENTATIVE
(if required or allowed by the Office of origin)

.... (dd/mm/yyyy)

13 CERTIFICATION AND SIGNATURE OF THE INTERNATIONAL APPLICATION BY THE OFFICE OF ORIGIN

(a) Certification

The Office of origin certifies

(i) that the request to present this application was received on .... (dd/mm/yyyy).

(ii) that the applicant named in item 2 is the same as the applicant named in the basic application or the holder named in the basic registration mentioned in item 5, as the case may be,

that any indication given in item 7(d), 9(d) or 9(e) appears also in the basic application or the basic registration, as the case may be,

that the mark in item 7(a) is the same as in the basic application or the basic registration, as the case may be,

that, if color is claimed as a distinctive feature of the mark in the basic application or the basic registration, the same claim is included in item 8 or that, if color is claimed in item 8 without having being claimed in the basic application or basic registration, the mark in the basic application or basic registration is in fact in the color or combination of colors claimed, and

that the goods and services listed in item 10 are covered by the list of goods and services appearing in the basic application or basic registration, as the case may be.

Where the international application is based on two or more basic applications or basic registrations, the above declaration shall be deemed to apply to all those basic applications or basic registrations.

(b) Office's signature: ....

Date of signature: .... (dd/mm/yyyy)

MM2(E) – December 2008

FEE CALCULATION SHEET

(a) INSTRUCTIONS TO DEBIT FROM A CURRENT ACCOUNT

☐ The International Bureau is hereby instructed to debit the required amount of fees from a current account opened with the International Bureau (if this box is checked, it is not necessary to complete (b)).

Holder of the account: .... Account number: ....

Identity of the party giving the instructions: ....

(b) AMOUNT OF FEES (see Fee Calculator: **www.wipo.int/madrid/en/fees/calculator.jsp**)

Basic fee: 653 Swiss francs if the reproduction of the mark is in black and white only and 903 Swiss francs if there is a reproduction in color. (*For international applications filed by applicants whose country of origin is a Least Developed Country, in accordance with the list established by the United Nations* (**www.wipo.int/ldcs/en/country**), *65 Swiss francs if the reproduction is in black and white only and 90 Swiss francs if there is a reproduction in color.*)   ....

Complementary and supplementary fees:

Number of designations for which complementary fee is applicable		Complementary fee		Total amount of the complementary fees		
....	x	100 Swiss francs	=	....	=>	....

Number of classes of goods and services beyond three		Supplementary fee		Total amount of the supplementary fees		
....	x	100 Swiss francs	=	....	=>	....

Individual fees (Swiss francs):

Designated Contracting Parties	Individual fee	Designated Contracting Parties	Individual fee
....	....	....	....
....	....	....	....
....	....	....	....
....	....	....	....
....	....	....	....

Total individual fees => ....

GRAND TOTAL (Swiss francs) ....

(c) METHOD OF PAYMENT

Identity of the party effecting the payment: ....

Payment received and acknowledged by WIPO ☐   WIPO receipt number ....

Payment made to WIPO bank account
IBAN No. CH51 0483 5048 7080 8100 0
Credit Suisse, CH-1211 Geneva 70
Swift/BIC: CRESCHZZ80A   ☐   Payment identification ....   dd/mm/yyyy ....

Payment made to WIPO postal account
IBAN No. CH03 0900 0000 1200 5000 8
Swift/BIC: POFICHBE   ☐   Payment identification ....   dd/mm/yyyy ....

MM2(E) – December 2008

Understanding Trademark Law: A Beginner's Guide

MM2(E) – December 2008

APPENDIX 28:
APPLICATION FOR DESIGNATION SUBSEQUENT TO THE INTERNATIONAL REGISTRATION

MM4(E)

MADRID AGREEMENT AND PROTOCOL CONCERNING THE

INTERNATIONAL REGISTRATION OF MARKS

DESIGNATION SUBSEQUENT TO THE INTERNATIONAL REGISTRATION

(Rule 24 of the Common Regulations)

IMPORTANT

1. This subsequent designation must be presented to the International Bureau:

    (a) through the Office of the Contracting Party of the holder where any Contracting Party is designated under the Madrid Agreement;

    (b) through the Office of origin where Rule 7(1) (as in force before October 4, 2001) applies;

    (c) in all other cases, either directly by the holder or by the Office of the Contracting Party of the holder.

2. The period of protection of a subsequent designation expires on the same date as the international registration to which it relates.

World Intellectual Property Organization
34, chemin des Colombettes, P.O. Box 18,
1211 Geneva 20, Switzerland
Tel.: (41-22) 338 9111
Fax (International Trademark Registry): (41-22) 740 1429
e-mail: intreg.mail@wipo.int – Internet: *http://www.wipo.int*

MM4(E) – December 2008

MM4(E)

DESIGNATION SUBSEQUENT TO THE INTERNATIONAL REGISTRATION

For use by the holder	For use by the holder/Office
This subsequent designation includes the following number of: – continuation sheet(s): .... – MM17 form(s):	Holder's reference: .... Office's reference: ....

1 INTERNATIONAL REGISTRATION NUMBER ....

2 HOLDER OF THE INTERNATIONAL REGISTRATION (as recorded in the International Register)

Name: ....

Address: ....

....

....

3 APPOINTMENT OF A REPRESENTATIVE

(**do not complete this item** if there is no change in the representative already recorded in the International Register)

Name: ....

Address: ....

....

Telephone: .... Fax: ....

E-mail address: ....

SIGNATURE OF THE HOLDER APPOINTING THE ABOVE (NEW) REPRESENTATIVE

....

MM4(E) – December 2008

4 CONTRACTING PARTIES DESIGNATED SUBSEQUENTLY

(Information concerning national or regional procedures for each Contracting Party designated may be found at the following website: http://www.wipo.int/madrid/en/members/ipoffices_info.html. Additional information may be found in the information notices available at: http://www.wipo.int/madrid/en/notices/)

Check the corresponding boxes:

☐ **AG** Antigua and Barbuda
☐ **AL** Albania
☐ **AM** Armenia
☐ **AN** Netherlands Antilles
☐ **AT** Austria
☐ **AU** Australia
☐ **AZ** Azerbaijan
☐ **BA** Bosnia and Herzegovina
☐ **BG** Bulgaria
☐ **BH** Bahrain
☐ **BT** Bhutan
☐ **BW** Botswana
☐ **BX** Benelux
☐ **BY** Belarus
☐ **CH** Switzerland
☐ **CN** China
☐ **CU** Cuba[4]
☐ **CY** Cyprus
☐ **CZ** Czech Republic
☐ **DE** Germany
☐ **DK** Denmark

☐ **DZ** Algeria
☐ **EE** Estonia
☐ **EG** Egypt
☐ **EM** European Community[1]
☐ **ES** Spain
☐ **FI** Finland
☐ **FR** France
☐ **GB** United Kingdom[2]
☐ **GE** Georgia
☐ **GH** Ghana[4]
☐ **GR** Greece
☐ **HR** Croatia
☐ **HU** Hungary
☐ **IE** Ireland[2]
☐ **IR** Iran (Islamic Republic of)
☐ **IS** Iceland
☐ **IT** Italy
☐ **JP** Japan[4]
☐ **KE** Kenya
☐ **KG** Kyrgyzstan
☐ **KP** Democratic People's Republic of Korea

☐ **KR** Republic of Korea
☐ **KZ** Kazakhstan
☐ **LI** Liechtenstein
☐ **LR** Liberia
☐ **LS** Lesotho
☐ **LT** Lithuania
☐ **LV** Latvia
☐ **MA** Morocco
☐ **MC** Monaco
☐ **MD** Republic of Moldova
☐ **ME** Montenegro
☐ **MG** Madagascar
☐ **MK** The former Yugoslav Rep. of Macedonia
☐ **MN** Mongolia
☐ **MZ** Mozambique
☐ **NA** Namibia
☐ **NO** Norway
☐ **OM** Oman
☐ **PL** Poland
☐ **PT** Portugal

☐ **RO** Romania
☐ **RS** Serbia
☐ **RU** Russian Federation
☐ **SD** Sudan
☐ **SE** Sweden
☐ **SG** Singapore[2]
☐ **SI** Slovenia
☐ **SK** Slovakia
☐ **SL** Sierra Leone
☐ **SM** San Marino
☐ **ST** Sao Tome and Principe
☐ **SY** Syrian Arab Republic
☐ **SZ** Swaziland
☐ **TJ** Tajikistan
☐ **TM** Turkmenistan
☐ **TR** Turkey
☐ **UA** Ukraine
☐ **US** United States of America[3]
☐ **UZ** Uzbekistan
☐ **VN** Viet Nam
☐ **ZM** Zambia

Others: ....

[1] If the **European Community** is designated, it is compulsory to indicate a second language before the Office of the European Community. The second language must be chosen from among the following five languages, but may not be the language of the international application from which the international registration indicated in item 1 resulted, regardless of the language of the present subsequent designation. Thus, for example, if the international application was filed in French and this subsequent designation is in English, French may not be selected as the second language (check one box only):

☐ English   ☐ French   ☐ German   ☐ Italian   ☐ Spanish

Moreover, if the holder wishes to claim the seniority of an earlier mark registered in, or for, a Member State of the European Community, the official form MM17 must be annexed to the present subsequent designation.

[2] By designating **Ireland**, **Singapore** or the **United Kingdom**, the holder declares that he has the intention that the mark will be used by him or with his consent in that country in connection with the goods and services identified in the present subsequent designation.

[3] If the **United States of America** is designated, it is compulsory to annex to the present subsequent designation the official form (MM18) containing the declaration of intention to use the mark required by this Contracting Party. Item 6(a) of the present form should also be completed.

[4] **Cuba, Ghana** and **Japan** have made a notification under Rule 34(3)(a) of the Common Regulations. Their respective **individual fees are payable in two parts**. Therefore, if **Cuba, Ghana** or **Japan** is designated, only the first part of the applicable individual fee is payable at the time of filing the present international application. The second part will have to be paid only if the Office of the Contracting Party concerned is satisfied that the mark which is the subject of the international registration qualifies for protection. The date by which the second part must be paid, and the amount due, will be notified to the holder of the international registration at a later stage.

5 GOODS AND SERVICES CONCERNED BY THE SUBSEQUENT DESIGNATION (**check only one box**)

(a) ☐ the subsequent designation is made, in respect of **all** the Contracting Parties designated in item 4, for **all** the goods and services listed in the international registration indicated in item 1; or

(b) ☐ the subsequent designation is made, in respect of **all** the Contracting Parties designated in item 4, only for those goods and services listed in the continuation sheet (which must be grouped in the appropriate class(es)); or

(c) ☐ the subsequent designation is only for those goods and services listed in the continuation sheet in respect of the Contracting Parties identified in the said continuation sheet; in respect of the other Contracting Parties designated in item 4, the subsequent designation is for all the goods and services listed in the international registration identified in item 1.

MM4(E) – December 2008

6 MISCELLANEOUS INDICATIONS

(a) Indications concerning the holder (as may be required by certain designated Contracting Parties; for example, if the **United States of America** is designated, it is necessary to include these indications):

(i) if the holder is a natural person, nationality of the holder: ....

(ii) if the holder is a legal entity:

– legal nature of the legal entity: ....

– State and, where applicable, territorial unit within that State, under the law of which the legal entity is organized:

....

(b) Indication, for each color, of the principal parts of the mark that are in that color (as may be required by certain designated Contracting Parties):

....

....

....

....

(c) Translation of the mark (as may be required by certain designated Contracting Parties):

(i) into English: ....

(ii) into French: ....

(iii) into Spanish: ....

(d) If the words contained in the mark have no meaning (and therefore cannot be translated), check this box ☐

7 DATE OF EFFECT OF THE SUBSEQUENT DESIGNATION
(if neither of these boxes is checked, the date of this subsequent designation will be the date of its receipt by the International Bureau or, if it has been presented through the intermediary of an Office, the date of receipt by that Office)

(a) ☐ this subsequent designation shall take effect immediately after the renewal of the international registration indicated in item 1;

(b) ☐ this subsequent designation shall take effect immediately after the recording in the International Register of the following change concerning the international registration indicated in item 1 (specify the change):

....

....

....

8 SIGNATURE BY THE HOLDER OR HIS REPRESENTATIVE

Holder (as recorded in the International Register)	Representative of the holder (as recorded in the International Register)
Name:	Name: ....
Signature:	Signature: ....

MM4(E) – December 2008

Understanding Trademark Law: A Beginner's Guide

Page 4

9 DATE OF RECEIPT AND DECLARATION BY THE OFFICE
(where the subsequent designation is presented through an Office)

(a) Date of receipt of the subsequent designation by the Office: .... (dd/mm/yyyy)

(b) Declaration that the <u>basic application</u> has matured to registration:

Only applicable where:
- the subsequent designation relates to an international registration which was based on a basic application;
- the present subsequent designation is the first designating a Contracting Party under the Agreement, and
- it is presented through the Office of origin.

(i) Date of the registration resulting from the basic application: .... (dd/mm/yyyy)

(ii) Number of the registration resulting from the basic application: ....

10 OFFICE PRESENTING THE SUBSEQUENT DESIGNATION
(if applicable)

Name of the Office: ....

Signature and/or stamp of the Office: ....

MM4(E) – December 2008

FEE CALCULATION SHEET

(a) INSTRUCTIONS TO DEBIT FROM A CURRENT ACCOUNT

☐ The International Bureau is hereby instructed to debit the required amount of fees from a current account opened with the International Bureau (if this box is checked, it is not necessary to complete (b)).

Holder of the account: .... Account number: ....

Identity of the party giving the instructions: ....

(b) AMOUNT OF FEES; METHOD OF PAYMENT

Basic fee (Swiss francs)   300.--

Complementary fees:

Number of designations for which complementary fee is applicable		Complementary fee		Total amount of the complementary fees	
....	x	100 Swiss francs	=	....	=> ....

Individual fees (Swiss francs):

Designated Contracting Parties	Individual fee	Designated Contracting Parties	Individual fee
....	....	....	....
....	....	....	....
....	....	....	....
....	....	....	....
....	....	....	....

Total individual fees   =>   ....

GRAND TOTAL (Swiss francs)   ....

Identity of the party effecting the payment: ....

Payment received and acknowledged by WIPO	☐	WIPO receipt number ....
Payment made to WIPO bank account IBAN No. CH51 0483 5048 7080 8100 0 Credit Suisse, CH-1211 Geneva 70 Swift/BIC: CRESCHZZ80A	☐	Payment identification dd/mm/yyyy ....
Payment made to WIPO postal account IBAN No. CH03 0900 0000 1200 5000 8 Swift/BIC: POFICHBE	☐	Payment identification dd/mm/yyyy ....

MM4(E) – December 2008

CONTINUATION SHEET

No: .... of ....

MM4(E) – December 2008

APPENDIX 29:
MEMBER STATES OF THE
EUROPEAN UNION

Austria	Latvia
Belgium	Lithuania
Bulgaria	Luxembourg
Cyprus	Malta
Czech Republic	Netherlands
Denmark	Poland
Estonia	Portugal
Finland	Romania
France	Slovakia
Germany	Slovenia
Greece	Spain
Hungary	Sweden
Ireland	United Kingdom
Italy	

APPENDIX 30:
COMMUNITY TRADEMARK
APPLICATION

OFFICE FOR HARMONIZATION IN THE INTERNAL MARKET (OHIM)
APPLICATION FOR A COMMUNITY TRADE MARK

For receiving office	Date of receipt (DD/MM/YYYY)	Number of pages (including this one)	Mod. 009
	/ /		

*Languages			
Language of the application or ISO code		**Your reference** (not more than 20 characters)	
Second language	ES DE EN FR IT		
Use second language for all correspondence related to this CTM application	☐		

*Applicant — ID number ☐ multiple applicants on continuation sheet   ☐ legal entity   ☐ natural

Name of legal entity or first name and surname	
Legal form of the entity	
Tel, fax, e-mail	
Address Street and number	
City and postal code	
Country	
Postal address (if different)	
Nationality	

* Mark   ☐ attached

☐ Word mark

☐ Figurative mark   ☐ Colour per se   ☐ Other (specify)

☐ Three-dimensional mark ☐ Sound mark

Indication of colour(s)		☐ attached
Description of the mark		☐ attached
Disclaimer		☐ attached

☐ Collective mark   Regulation governing use of collective mark ☐ attached ☐ to follow
☐ National search reports requested (subject to payment of an additional fee)

---

*List of goods and services

Same list as in previous CTM No. [   ]

Class No.	Goods and services

☐ continuation sheet attached

Signature

Name		*Signature

#TM009FEN

page number

| 1 | of | |

* Mandatory details

APPLICATION FOR A COMMUNITY TRADE MARK

Representative	ID number	
Name		
Tel, fax, e-mail		
Address Street and number		
City and postal code		
Country		
Postal address (if different)		
Type of representative	☐ legal practitioner ☐ professional representative ☐ association of representatives ☐ employee	

Priority claimed ☐ The applicant claims the priority of the earlier filing(s) mentioned below Certificate(s) ☐ attached ☐ to follow

Country of first filing	Number	Filing date*
		/ /

☐ Continuation sheet(s)

Seniority claimed ☐ The applicant claims the seniority of the earlier registration(s) mentioned below Certificate(s) ☐ attached ☐ to follow

Member State	Nature (national / international)	Number	Filing date*
			/ /
			/ /
			/ /
			/ /
			/ /
			/ /

☐ Continuation sheet(s)

Transformation under Madrid Protocol

IR number	
Date of cancellation of the IR	/ /
Date of the IR	/ /
Date of priority of the IR	/ /

Translation of

List of goods/ services ☐ attached

Colours ☐ attached

Description of the mark ☐ attached

Disclaimer ☐ attached

Payment of fees

Basic application fee	€	
Classes exceeding three	€	
Fee for national search reports	€	
Total fees	€	

Transfer to account of OHIM

☐ Banco Bilbao Vizcaya Argentaria

☐ La Caixa

Date of transfer (DD/MM/YYYY) / /

Current account with OHIM

☐ Account No.

☐ Do not use my current account with OHIM

Basic application fee and, if applicable, the fee for the national search reports

to be withdrawn from current account of applicant / representative with OHIM

☐ immediately

☐ one month after the filing date

☐ together with the class fee

#TM009EN

* DD/MM/YYYY

RESET FORM

page number
[ ] of [ ]

APPENDIX 31:
UNIFORM DISPUTE RESOLUTION POLICY

Notes:

1. This policy is now in effect. See **www.icann.org/udrp/udrp-schedule.htm** for the implementation schedule.

2. This policy has been adopted by all ICANN-accredited registrars. It has also been adopted by certain managers of country-code top-level domains (*e.g.,*.nu,.tv,.ws).

3. The policy is between the registrar (or other registration authority in the case of a country-code top-level domain) and its customer (the domain-name holder or registrant). Thus, the policy uses "we" and "our" to refer to the registrar and it uses "you" and "your" to refer to the domain-name holder.

UNIFORM DOMAIN NAME DISPUTE RESOLUTION POLICY

(As Approved by ICANN on October 24, 1999)

1. *Purpose*. This Uniform Domain Name Dispute Resolution Policy (the "Policy") has been adopted by the Internet Corporation for Assigned Names and Numbers ("ICANN"), is incorporated by reference into your Registration Agreement, and sets forth the terms and conditions in connection with a dispute between you and any party other than us (the registrar) over the registration and use of an Internet domain name registered by you. Proceedings under *Paragraph 4* of this Policy will be conducted according to the Rules for Uniform Domain Name Dispute Resolution Policy (the "Rules of Procedure"), which are available at www.icann.org/udrp/udrp-rules-24oct99.htm, and the selected administrative-dispute-resolution service provider's supplemental rules.

2. *Your Representations*. By applying to register a domain name, or by asking us to maintain or renew a domain name registration, you hereby represent and warrant to us that (a) the statements that you made in your Registration Agreement are complete and accurate; (b) to your knowledge, the registration of the domain name will not infringe upon or otherwise violate the rights of any third party; (c) you are not registering the domain name for an unlawful purpose; and (d) you will not knowingly use the domain name in violation of any applicable laws or regulations. It is your responsibility to determine whether your domain name registration infringes or violates someone else's rights.

3. *Cancellations, Transfers, and Changes*. We will cancel, transfer or otherwise make changes to domain name registrations under the following circumstances:

a. subject to the provisions of *Paragraph 8*, our receipt of written or appropriate electronic instructions from you or your authorized agent to take such action;

b. our receipt of an order from a court or arbitral tribunal, in each case of competent jurisdiction, requiring such action; and/or

c. our receipt of a decision of an Administrative Panel requiring such action in any administrative proceeding to which you were a party and which was conducted under this Policy or a later version of this Policy adopted by ICANN. (See *Paragraph 4(i)* and *(k)* below.)

We may also cancel, transfer or otherwise make changes to a domain name registration in accordance with the terms of your Registration Agreement or other legal requirements.

4. *Mandatory Administrative Proceeding*.

This Paragraph sets forth the type of disputes for which you are required to submit to a mandatory administrative proceeding. These proceedings will be conducted before one of the administrative-dispute-resolution service providers listed at www.icann.org/udrp/approved-providers.htm (each, a "Provider").

a. **Applicable Disputes.** You are required to submit to a mandatory administrative proceeding in the event that a third party (a "complainant") asserts to the applicable Provider, in compliance with the Rules of Procedure, that

(i) your domain name is identical or confusingly similar to a trademark or service mark in which the complainant has rights; and

(ii) you have no rights or legitimate interests in respect of the domain name; and

(iii) your domain name has been registered and is being used in bad faith.

In the administrative proceeding, the complainant must prove that each of these three elements are present.

b. Evidence of Registration and Use in Bad Faith. For the purposes of *Paragraph 4(a)(iii)*, the following circumstances, in particular but without limitation, if found by the Panel to be present, shall be evidence of the registration and use of a domain name in bad faith:

(i) circumstances indicating that you have registered or you have acquired the domain name primarily for the purpose of selling, renting, or otherwise transferring the domain name registration to the complainant who is the owner of the trademark or service mark or to a competitor of that complainant, for valuable consideration in excess of your documented out-of-pocket costs directly related to the domain name; or

(ii) you have registered the domain name in order to prevent the owner of the trademark or service mark from reflecting the mark in a corresponding domain name, provided that you have engaged in a pattern of such conduct; or

(iii) you have registered the domain name primarily for the purpose of disrupting the business of a competitor; or

(iv) by using the domain name, you have intentionally attempted to attract, for commercial gain, Internet users to your web site or other on-line location, by creating a likelihood of confusion with the complainant's mark as to the source, sponsorship, affiliation, or endorsement of your web site or location or of a product or service on your web site or location.

c. How to Demonstrate Your Rights to and Legitimate Interests in the Domain Name in Responding to a Complaint. When you receive a complaint, you should refer to *Paragraph 5* of the Rules of Procedure in determining how your response should be prepared. Any of the following circumstances, in particular but without limitation, if found by the Panel to be proved based on its evaluation of all evidence presented, shall demonstrate your rights or legitimate interests to the domain name for purposes of *Paragraph 4(a)(ii)*:

(i) before any notice to you of the dispute, your use of, or demonstrable preparations to use, the domain name or a name corresponding to the domain name in connection with a bona fide offering of goods or services; or

(ii) you (as an individual, business, or other organization) have been commonly known by the domain name, even if you have acquired no trademark or service mark rights; or

(iii) you are making a legitimate noncommercial or fair use of the domain name, without intent for commercial gain to misleadingly divert consumers or to tarnish the trademark or service mark at issue.

d. Selection of Provider. The complainant shall select the Provider from among those approved by ICANN by submitting the complaint to that Provider. The selected Provider will administer the proceeding, except in cases of consolidation as described in *Paragraph 4(f)*.

e. Initiation of Proceeding and Process and Appointment of Administrative Panel. The Rules of Procedure state the process for initiating and conducting a proceeding and for appointing the panel that will decide the dispute (the "Administrative Panel").

f. Consolidation. In the event of multiple disputes between you and a complainant, either you or the complainant may petition to consolidate the disputes before a single Administrative Panel. This petition shall be made to the first Administrative Panel appointed to hear a pending dispute between the parties. This Administrative Panel may consolidate before it any or all such disputes in its sole discretion, provided that the disputes being consolidated are governed by this Policy or a later version of this Policy adopted by ICANN.

g. Fees. All fees charged by a Provider in connection with any dispute before an Administrative Panel pursuant to this Policy shall be paid by the complainant, except in cases where you elect to expand the Administrative Panel from one to three panelists as provided in *Paragraph 5(b)(iv)* of the Rules of Procedure, in which case all fees will be split evenly by you and the complainant.

h. Our Involvement in Administrative Proceedings. We do not, and will not, participate in the administration or conduct of any proceeding before an Administrative Panel. In addition, we will not be liable as a result of any decisions rendered by the Administrative Panel.

i. Remedies. The remedies available to a complainant pursuant to any proceeding before an Administrative Panel shall be limited to requiring the cancellation of your domain name or the transfer of your domain name registration to the complainant.

j. Notification and Publication. The Provider shall notify us of any decision made by an Administrative Panel with respect to a domain name you have registered with us. All decisions under this Policy will be published in full over the Internet, except when an Administrative Panel determines in an exceptional case to redact portions of its decision.

k. Availability of Court Proceedings. The mandatory administrative proceeding requirements set forth in *Paragraph 4* shall not prevent either you or the complainant from submitting the dispute to a court of competent jurisdiction for independent resolution before such mandatory administrative proceeding is commenced or after such proceeding is concluded. If an Administrative Panel decides that your domain name registration should be canceled or transferred, we will wait ten (10) business days (as observed in the location of our principal office) after we are informed by the applicable Provider of the Administrative Panel's decision before implementing that decision. We will then implement the decision unless we have received from you during that ten (10) business day period official documentation (such as a copy of a complaint, file-stamped by the clerk of the court) that you have commenced a lawsuit against the complainant in a jurisdiction to which the complainant has submitted under *Paragraph 3(b)(xiii)* of the Rules of Procedure. (In general, that jurisdiction is either the location of our principal office or of your address as shown in our Whois database. See *Paragraphs 1* and *3(b)(xiii)* of the Rules of Procedure for details.) If we receive such documentation within the ten (10) business day period, we will not implement the Administrative Panel's decision, and we will take no further action, until we receive (i) evidence satisfactory to us of a resolution between the parties; (ii) evidence satisfactory to us that your lawsuit has been dismissed or withdrawn; or (iii) a copy of an order from such court dismissing your lawsuit or ordering that you do not have the right to continue to use your domain name.

5. *All Other Disputes and Litigation*. All other disputes between you and any party other than us regarding your domain name registration that are not brought pursuant to the mandatory administrative proceeding provisions of *Paragraph 4* shall be resolved between you and such other party through any court, arbitration or other proceeding that may be available.

6. *Our Involvement in Disputes*. We will not participate in any way in any dispute between you and any party other than us regarding the registration and use of your domain name. You shall not name us as a party or otherwise include us in any such proceeding. In the event that we are named as a party in any such proceeding, we reserve the right to raise any and all defenses deemed appropriate, and to take any other action necessary to defend ourselves.

7. *Maintaining the Status Quo*. We will not cancel, transfer, activate, deactivate, or otherwise change the status of any domain name registration under this Policy except as provided in *Paragraph 3* above.

8. *Transfers During a Dispute*.

a. Transfers of a Domain Name to a New Holder. You may not transfer your domain name registration to another holder (i) during a pending administrative proceeding brought pursuant to *Paragraph 4* or for a period of fifteen (15) business days (as observed in the location of our principal place of business) after such proceeding is concluded; or (ii) during a pending court proceeding or arbitration commenced regarding your domain name unless the party to whom the domain name registration is being transferred agrees, in writing, to be bound by the decision of the court or arbitrator. We reserve the right to cancel any transfer of a domain name registration to another holder that is made in violation of this subparagraph.

b. Changing Registrars. You may not transfer your domain name registration to another registrar during a pending administrative proceeding brought pursuant to *Paragraph 4* or for a period of fifteen (15) business days (as observed in the location of our principal place of business) after such proceeding is concluded. You may transfer administration of your domain name registration to another registrar during a pending court action or arbitration, provided that the domain name you have registered with us shall continue to be subject to the proceedings commenced against you in accordance with the terms of this Policy. In the event that you transfer a domain name registration to us during the pendency of a court action or arbitration, such dispute shall remain subject to the domain name dispute policy of the registrar from which the domain name registration was transferred.

9. *Policy Modifications*. We reserve the right to modify this Policy at any time with the permission of ICANN. We will post our revised Policy at <URL> at least thirty (30) calendar days before it becomes effective. Unless this Policy has already been invoked by the submission of a complaint to a Provider, in which event the version of the Policy in effect at the time it was invoked will apply to you until the dispute is over, all such changes will be binding upon you with respect to any domain name registration dispute, whether the dispute arose before, on or after the effective date of our change. In the event that you object to a change in this Policy, your sole remedy is to cancel your domain name registration with us, provided that you will not be entitled to a refund of any fees you paid to us. The revised Policy will apply to you until you cancel your domain name registration.

APPENDIX 32:
RULES IMPLEMENTING DOMAIN NAME
DISPUTE RESOLUTION POLICY

Note: These rules are now in effect. See **www.icann.org/udrp/udrp-schedule.htm** for the implementation schedule.

RULES FOR UNIFORM DOMAIN NAME DISPUTE RESOLUTION POLICY (THE "RULES")

(As Approved by ICANN on October 24, 1999)

Administrative proceedings for the resolution of disputes under the Uniform Dispute Resolution Policy adopted by ICANN shall be governed by these Rules and also the Supplemental Rules of the Provider administering the proceedings, as posted on its web site.

1. *Definitions*

In these Rules:

Complainant means the party initiating a complaint concerning a domain-name registration.

ICANN refers to the Internet Corporation for Assigned Names and Numbers.

Mutual Jurisdiction means a court jurisdiction at the location of either (a) the principal office of the Registrar (provided the domain-name holder has submitted in its Registration Agreement to that jurisdiction for court adjudication of disputes concerning or arising from the use of the domain name) or (b) the domain-name holder's address as shown for the registration of the domain name in

---

Registrar's Whois database at the time the complaint is submitted to the Provider.

Panel means an administrative panel appointed by a Provider to decide a complaint concerning a domain-name registration.

Panelist means an individual appointed by a Provider to be a member of a Panel.

Party means a Complainant or a Respondent.

Policy means the *Uniform Domain Name Dispute Resolution Policy* that is incorporated by reference and made a part of the Registration Agreement.

Provider means a dispute-resolution service provider approved by ICANN. A list of such Providers appears at www.icann.org/udrp/approved-providers.htm.

Registrar means the entity with which the Respondent has registered a domain name that is the subject of a complaint.

Registration Agreement means the agreement between a Registrar and a domain-name holder.

Respondent means the holder of a domain-name registration against which a complaint is initiated.

Reverse Domain Name Hijacking means using the Policy in bad faith to attempt to deprive a registered domain-name holder of a domain name.

Supplemental Rules means the rules adopted by the Provider administering a proceeding to supplement these Rules. Supplemental Rules shall not be inconsistent with the Policy or these Rules and shall cover such topics as fees, word and page limits and guidelines, the means for communicating with the Provider and the Panel, and the form of cover sheets.

2. *Communications*

(a) When forwarding a complaint to the Respondent, it shall be the Provider's responsibility to employ reasonably available means calculated to achieve actual notice to Respondent. Achieving actual notice, or employing the following measures to do so, shall discharge this responsibility:

(i) sending the complaint to all postal-mail and facsimile addresses (A) shown in the domain name's registration data in Registrar's Whois database for the registered domain-name holder, the technical contact, and the administrative contact and (B) supplied by Registrar to the Provider for the registration's billing contact; and

(ii) sending the complaint in electronic form (including annexes to the extent available in that form) by e-mail to:

(A) the e-mail addresses for those technical, administrative, and billing contacts;

(B) postmaster@<the contested domain name>; and

(C) if the domain name (or "www." followed by the domain name) resolves to an active web page (other than a generic page the Provider concludes is maintained by a registrar or ISP for parking domain-names registered by multiple domain-name holders), any e-mail address shown or e-mail links on that web page; and

(iii) sending the complaint to any address the Respondent has notified the Provider it prefers and, to the extent practicable, to all other addresses provided to the Provider by Complainant under *Paragraph 3(b)(v)*.

(b) Except as provided in *Paragraph 2(a)*, any written communication to Complainant or Respondent provided for under these Rules shall be made by the preferred means stated by the Complainant or Respondent, respectively (see *Paragraphs 3(b)(iii)* and *5(b)(iii))*, or in the absence of such specification

(i) by telecopy or facsimile transmission, with a confirmation of transmission; or

(ii) by postal or courier service, postage pre-paid and return receipt requested; or

(iii) electronically via the Internet, provided a record of its transmission is available.

(c) Any communication to the Provider or the Panel shall be made by the means and in the manner (including number of copies) stated in the Provider's Supplemental Rules.

(d) Communications shall be made in the language prescribed in *Paragraph 11*. E-mail communications should, if practicable, be sent in plaintext.

(e) Either Party may update its contact details by notifying the Provider and the Registrar.

(f) Except as otherwise provided in these Rules, or decided by a Panel, all communications provided for under these Rules shall be deemed to have been made:

(i) if delivered by telecopy or facsimile transmission, on the date shown on the confirmation of transmission; or

(ii) if by postal or courier service, on the date marked on the receipt; or

(iii) if via the Internet, on the date that the communication was transmitted, provided that the date of transmission is verifiable.

(g) Except as otherwise provided in these Rules, all time periods calculated under these Rules to begin when a communication is made shall begin to run on the earliest date that the communication is deemed to have been made in accordance with *Paragraph 2(f)*.

(h) Any communication by

(i) a Panel to any Party shall be copied to the Provider and to the other Party;

(ii) the Provider to any Party shall be copied to the other Party; and

(iii) a Party shall be copied to the other Party, the Panel and the Provider, as the case may be.

(i) It shall be the responsibility of the sender to retain records of the fact and circumstances of sending, which shall be available for inspection by affected parties and for reporting purposes.

(j) In the event a Party sending a communication receives notification of non-delivery of the communication, the Party shall promptly notify the Panel (or, if no Panel is yet appointed, the Provider) of the circumstances of the notification. Further proceedings concerning the communication and any response shall be as directed by the Panel (or the Provider).

3. *The Complaint*

(a) Any person or entity may initiate an administrative proceeding by submitting a complaint in accordance with the Policy and these Rules to any Provider approved by ICANN. (Due to capacity constraints or for other reasons, a Provider's ability to accept complaints may be suspended at times. In that event, the Provider shall refuse the submission. The person or entity may submit the complaint to another Provider.)

(b) The complaint shall be submitted in hard copy and (except to the extent not available for annexes) in electronic form and shall:

(i) Request that the complaint be submitted for decision in accordance with the Policy and these Rules;

(ii) Provide the name, postal and e-mail addresses, and the telephone and telefax numbers of the Complainant and of any representative authorized to act for the Complainant in the administrative proceeding;

(iii) Specify a preferred method for communications directed to the Complainant in the administrative proceeding (including person to be contacted, medium, and address information) for each of (A) electronic-only material and (B) material including hard copy;

(iv) Designate whether Complainant elects to have the dispute decided by a single-member or a three-member Panel and, in the event Complainant elects a three-member Panel, provide the names and contact details of three candidates to serve as one of the Panelists (these candidates may be drawn from any ICANN-approved Provider's list of panelists);

(v) Provide the name of the Respondent (domain-name holder) and all information (including any postal and e-mail addresses and telephone and telefax numbers) known to Complainant regarding how to contact Respondent or any representative of Respondent, including contact information based on pre-complaint dealings, in sufficient detail to allow the Provider to send the complaint as described in *Paragraph 2(a)*;

(vi) Specify the domain name(s) that is/are the subject of the complaint;

(vii) Identify the Registrar(s) with whom the domain name(s) is/are registered at the time the complaint is filed;

(viii) Specify the trademark(s) or service mark(s) on which the complaint is based and, for each mark, describe the goods or services, if any, with which the mark is used (Complainant may also separately describe other goods and services with which it intends, at the time the complaint is submitted, to use the mark in the future.);

(ix) Describe, in accordance with the Policy, the grounds on which the complaint is made including, in particular,

(1) the manner in which the domain name(s) is/are identical or confusingly similar to a trademark or service mark in which the Complainant has rights; and

(2) why the Respondent (domain-name holder) should be considered as having no rights or legitimate interests in respect of the domain name(s) that is/are the subject of the complaint; and

(3) why the domain name(s) should be considered as having been registered and being used in bad faith

(The description should, for elements (2) and (3), discuss any aspects of *Paragraphs 4(b)* and *4c* of the Policy that are applicable. The description shall comply with any word or page limit set forth in the Provider's Supplemental Rules.);

(x) Specify, in accordance with the Policy, the remedies sought;

(xi) Identify any other legal proceedings that have been commenced or terminated in connection with or relating to any of the domain name(s) that are the subject of the complaint;

(xii) State that a copy of the complaint, together with the cover sheet as prescribed by the Provider's Supplemental Rules, has been sent or transmitted to the Respondent (domain-name holder), in accordance with *Paragraph 2(b)*;

(xiii) State that Complainant will submit, with respect to any challenges to a decision in the administrative proceeding canceling or transferring the domain name, to the jurisdiction of the courts in at least one specified Mutual Jurisdiction;

(xiv) Conclude with the following statement followed by the signature of the Complainant or its authorized representative:

"Complainant agrees that its claims and remedies concerning the registration of the domain name, the dispute, or the dispute's resolution shall be solely against the domain-name holder and waives all such claims and remedies against (a) the dispute-resolution provider and panelists, except in the case of deliberate wrongdoing, (b) the registrar, (c) the registry administrator, and (d) the Internet Corporation for Assigned Names and Numbers, as well as their directors, officers, employees, and agents."

"Complainant certifies that the information contained in this Complaint is to the best of Complainant's knowledge complete and accurate, that this Complaint is not being presented for any improper purpose, such as to harass, and that the assertions in this Complaint are warranted under these Rules and under applicable law, as it now exists or as it may be extended by a good-faith and reasonable argument."; and

(xv) Annex any documentary or other evidence, including a copy of the Policy applicable to the domain name(s) in dispute and any trademark or service mark registration upon which the complaint relies, together with a schedule indexing such evidence.

(c) The complaint may relate to more than one domain name, provided that the domain names are registered by the same domain-name holder.

4. *Notification of Complaint*

(a) The Provider shall review the complaint for administrative compliance with the Policy and these Rules and, if in compliance, shall forward the complaint (together with the explanatory cover sheet prescribed by the Provider's Supplemental Rules) to the Respondent, in the manner prescribed by *Paragraph 2(a)*, within three (3) calendar days following receipt of the fees to be paid by the Complainant in accordance with *Paragraph 19*.

(b) If the Provider finds the complaint to be administratively deficient, it shall promptly notify the Complainant and the Respondent of the nature of the deficiencies identified. The Complainant shall have five (5) calendar days within which to correct any such deficiencies, after which the administrative proceeding will be deemed withdrawn without prejudice to submission of a different complaint by Complainant.

(c) The date of commencement of the administrative proceeding shall be the date on which the Provider completes its responsibilities under *Paragraph 2(a)* in connection with forwarding the Complaint to the Respondent.

(d) The Provider shall immediately notify the Complainant, the Respondent, the concerned Registrar(s), and ICANN of the date of commencement of the administrative proceeding.

5. *The Response*

(a) Within twenty (20) days of the date of commencement of the administrative proceeding the Respondent shall submit a response to the Provider.

(b) The response shall be submitted in hard copy and (except to the extent not available for annexes) in electronic form and shall:

(i) Respond specifically to the statements and allegations contained in the complaint and include any and all bases for the Respondent (domain-name holder) to retain registration and use of the disputed domain name (This portion of the response shall comply with any word or page limit set forth in the Provider's Supplemental Rules.);

(ii) Provide the name, postal and e-mail addresses, and the telephone and telefax numbers of the Respondent (domain-name holder) and of any representative authorized to act for the Respondent in the administrative proceeding;

(iii) Specify a preferred method for communications directed to the Respondent in the administrative proceeding (including person to be contacted, medium, and address information) for each of (A) electronic-only material and (B) material including hard copy;

(iv) If Complainant has elected a single-member panel in the Complaint (see *Paragraph 3(b)(iv))*, state whether Respondent elects instead to have the dispute decided by a three-member panel;

(v) If either Complainant or Respondent elects a three-member Panel, provide the names and contact details of three candidates to serve as one of the Panelists (these candidates may be drawn from any ICANN-approved Provider's list of panelists);

(vi) Identify any other legal proceedings that have been commenced or terminated in connection with or relating to any of the domain name(s) that are the subject of the complaint;

(vii) State that a copy of the response has been sent or transmitted to the Complainant, in accordance with *Paragraph 2(b)*;

(viii) Conclude with the following statement followed by the signature of the Respondent or its authorized representative:

> "Respondent certifies that the information contained in this Response is to the best of Respondent's knowledge complete and accurate, that this Response is not being presented for any improper purpose, such as to harass, and that the assertions in this Response are warranted under these Rules and under applicable law, as it now exists or as it may be extended by a good-faith and reasonable argument."; and

(ix) Annex any documentary or other evidence upon which the Respondent relies, together with a schedule indexing such documents.

(c) If Complainant has elected to have the dispute decided by a single-member Panel and Respondent elects a three-member Panel, Respondent shall be required to pay one-half of the applicable fee for a three-member Panel as set forth in the Provider's Supplemental Rules. This payment shall be made together with the submission of the response to the Provider. In the event that the required payment is not made, the dispute shall be decided by a single-member Panel.

(d) At the request of the Respondent, the Provider may, in exceptional cases, extend the period of time for the filing of the response.

The period may also be extended by written stipulation between the Parties, provided the stipulation is approved by the Provider.

(e) If a Respondent does not submit a response, in the absence of exceptional circumstances, the Panel shall decide the dispute based upon the complaint.

6. *Appointment of the Panel and Timing of Decision*

(a) Each Provider shall maintain and publish a publicly available list of panelists and their qualifications.

(b) If neither the Complainant nor the Respondent has elected a three-member Panel (*Paragraphs 3(b)(iv)* and *5(b)(iv)*), the Provider shall appoint, within five (5) calendar days following receipt of the response by the Provider, or the lapse of the time period for the submission thereof, a single Panelist from its list of panelists. The fees for a single-member Panel shall be paid entirely by the Complainant.

(c) If either the Complainant or the Respondent elects to have the dispute decided by a three-member Panel, the Provider shall appoint three Panelists in accordance with the procedures identified in *Paragraph 6(e)*. The fees for a three-member Panel shall be paid in their entirety by the Complainant, except where the election for a three-member Panel was made by the Respondent, in which case the applicable fees shall be shared equally between the Parties.

(d) Unless it has already elected a three-member Panel, the Complainant shall submit to the Provider, within five (5) calendar days of communication of a response in which the Respondent elects a three-member Panel, the names and contact details of three candidates to serve as one of the Panelists. These candidates may be drawn from any ICANN-approved Provider's list of panelists.

(e) In the event that either the Complainant or the Respondent elects a three-member Panel, the Provider shall endeavor to appoint one Panelist from the list of candidates provided by each of the Complainant and the Respondent. In the event the Provider is unable within five (5) calendar days to secure the appointment of a Panelist on its customary terms from either Party's list of candidates, the Provider shall make that appointment from its list of panelists. The third Panelist shall be appointed by the Provider from a list of five candidates submitted by the Provider to the Parties, the Provider's selection from among the five being made in a manner that reasonably balances the preferences of both Parties, as they may specify to the Provider within five (5) calendar days of the Provider's submission of the five-candidate list to the Parties.

(f) Once the entire Panel is appointed, the Provider shall notify the Parties of the Panelists appointed and the date by which, absent exceptional circumstances, the Panel shall forward its decision on the complaint to the Provider.

7. *Impartiality and Independence*

A Panelist shall be impartial and independent and shall have, before accepting appointment, disclosed to the Provider any circumstances giving rise to justifiable doubt as to the Panelist's impartiality or independence. If, at any stage during the administrative proceeding, new circumstances arise that could give rise to justifiable doubt as to the impartiality or independence of the Panelist, that Panelist shall promptly disclose such circumstances to the Provider. In such event, the Provider shall have the discretion to appoint a substitute Panelist.

8. *Communication Between Parties and the Panel*

No Party or anyone acting on its behalf may have any unilateral communication with the Panel. All communications between a Party and the Panel or the Provider shall be made to a case administrator appointed by the Provider in the manner prescribed in the Provider's Supplemental Rules.

9. *Transmission of the File to the Panel*

The Provider shall forward the file to the Panel as soon as the Panelist is appointed in the case of a Panel consisting of a single member, or as soon as the last Panelist is appointed in the case of a three-member Panel.

10. *General Powers of the Panel*

(a) The Panel shall conduct the administrative proceeding in such manner as it considers appropriate in accordance with the Policy and these Rules.

(b) In all cases, the Panel shall ensure that the Parties are treated with equality and that each Party is given a fair opportunity to present its case.

(c) The Panel shall ensure that the administrative proceeding takes place with due expedition. It may, at the request of a Party or on its own motion, extend, in exceptional cases, a period of time fixed by these Rules or by the Panel.

(d) The Panel shall determine the admissibility, relevance, materiality and weight of the evidence.

(e) A Panel shall decide a request by a Party to consolidate multiple domain name disputes in accordance with the Policy and these Rules.

11. *Language of Proceedings*

(a) Unless otherwise agreed by the Parties, or specified otherwise in the Registration Agreement, the language of the administrative proceeding shall be the language of the Registration Agreement, subject to the authority of the Panel to determine otherwise, having regard to the circumstances of the administrative proceeding.

(b) The Panel may order that any documents submitted in languages other than the language of the administrative proceeding be accompanied by a translation in whole or in part into the language of the administrative proceeding.

12. *Further Statements*

In addition to the complaint and the response, the Panel may request, in its sole discretion, further statements or documents from either of the Parties.

13. *In-Person Hearings*

There shall be no in-person hearings (including hearings by teleconference, videoconference, and web conference), unless the Panel determines, in its sole discretion and as an exceptional matter, that such a hearing is necessary for deciding the complaint.

14. *Default*

(a) In the event that a Party, in the absence of exceptional circumstances, does not comply with any of the time periods established by these Rules or the Panel, the Panel shall proceed to a decision on the complaint.

(b) If a Party, in the absence of exceptional circumstances, does not comply with any provision of, or requirement under, these Rules or any request from the Panel, the Panel shall draw such inferences therefrom as it considers appropriate.

15. *Panel Decisions*

(a) A Panel shall decide a complaint on the basis of the statements and documents submitted and in accordance with the Policy, these Rules and any rules and principles of law that it deems applicable.

(b) In the absence of exceptional circumstances, the Panel shall forward its decision on the complaint to the Provider within fourteen (14) days of its appointment pursuant to Paragraph 6.

(c) In the case of a three-member Panel, the Panel's decision shall be made by a majority.

(d) The Panel's decision shall be in writing, provide the reasons on which it is based, indicate the date on which it was rendered and identify the name(s) of the Panelist(s).

(e) Panel decisions and dissenting opinions shall normally comply with the guidelines as to length set forth in the Provider's Supplemental Rules. Any dissenting opinion shall accompany the majority decision. If the Panel concludes that the dispute is not within the scope of *Paragraph 4(a)* of the Policy, it shall so state. If after considering the submissions the Panel finds that the complaint was brought in bad faith, for example in an attempt at Reverse Domain Name Hijacking or was brought primarily to harass the domain-name holder, the Panel shall declare in its decision that the complaint was brought in bad faith and constitutes an abuse of the administrative proceeding.

16. *Communication of Decision to Parties*

(a) Within three (3) calendar days after receiving the decision from the Panel, the Provider shall communicate the full text of the decision to each Party, the concerned Registrar(s), and ICANN. The concerned Registrar(s) shall immediately communicate to each Party, the Provider, and ICANN the date for the implementation of the decision in accordance with the Policy.

(b) Except if the Panel determines otherwise (see *Paragraph 4(j)* of the Policy), the Provider shall publish the full decision and the date of its implementation on a publicly accessible web site. In any event, the portion of any decision determining a complaint to have been brought in bad faith (see *Paragraph 15(e)* of these Rules) shall be published.

17. *Settlement or Other Grounds for Termination*

(a) If, before the Panel's decision, the Parties agree on a settlement, the Panel shall terminate the administrative proceeding.

(b) If, before the Panel's decision is made, it becomes unnecessary or impossible to continue the administrative proceeding for any reason, the Panel shall terminate the administrative proceeding, unless a Party raises justifiable grounds for objection within a period of time to be determined by the Panel.

18. *Effect of Court Proceedings*

(a) In the event of any legal proceedings initiated prior to or during an administrative proceeding in respect of a domain-name dispute that is the subject of the complaint, the Panel shall have the discretion to decide whether to suspend or terminate the administrative proceeding, or to proceed to a decision.

(b) In the event that a Party initiates any legal proceedings during the pendency of an administrative proceeding in respect of a domain-name dispute that is the subject of the complaint, it shall promptly notify the Panel and the Provider. See *Paragraph 8* above.

19. *Fees*

(a) The Complainant shall pay to the Provider an initial fixed fee, in accordance with the Provider's Supplemental Rules, within the time and in the amount required. A Respondent electing under *Paragraph 5(b)(iv)* to have the dispute decided by a three-member Panel, rather than the single-member Panel elected by the Complainant, shall pay the Provider one-half the fixed fee for a three-member Panel. See *Paragraph 5(c)*. In all other cases, the Complainant shall bear all of the Provider's fees, except as prescribed under Paragraph 19(d). Upon appointment of the Panel, the Provider shall refund the appropriate portion, if any, of the initial fee to the Complainant, as specified in the Provider's Supplemental Rules.

(b) No action shall be taken by the Provider on a complaint until it has received from Complainant the initial fee in accordance with *Paragraph 19(a)*.

(c) If the Provider has not received the fee within ten (10) calendar days of receiving the complaint, the complaint shall be deemed withdrawn and the administrative proceeding terminated.

(d) In exceptional circumstances, for example in the event an in-person hearing is held, the Provider shall request the Parties for the payment of additional fees, which shall be established in agreement with the Parties and the Panel.

20. *Exclusion of Liability*

Except in the case of deliberate wrongdoing, neither the Provider nor a Panelist shall be liable to a Party for any act or omission in connection with any administrative proceeding under these Rules.

21. *Amendments*

The version of these Rules in effect at the time of the submission of the complaint to the Provider shall apply to the administrative proceeding commenced thereby. These Rules may not be amended without the express written approval of ICANN.

APPENDIX 33:
SUPPLEMENTAL RULES OF WIPO FOR UNIFORM DOMAIN NAME DISPUTE RESOLUTION POLICY

WORLD INTELLECTUAL PROPERTY ORGANIZATION SUPPLEMENTAL RULES FOR UNIFORM DOMAIN NAME DISPUTE RESOLUTION POLICY

(the WIPO "Supplemental Rules")

(In effect as of December 1, 1999)

1. *Scope*
2. *Definitions*
3. *Communications*
4. *Submission of Complaint*
5. *Formalities Compliance Review*
6. *Appointment of Case Administrator*
7. *Panelist Appointment Procedures*
8. *Declaration*
9. *Fees*
10. *Word Limits*
11. *Amendments*
12. *Exclusion of Liability*

1. Scope

(a) **Relationship to Rules**. These Supplemental Rules are to be read and used in connection with the *Rules for Uniform Domain Name Dispute Resolution Policy*, approved by the Internet Corporation for Assigned Names and Numbers (ICANN) on October 24, 1999 (the "Rules").

(b) **Version of Supplemental Rules**. The version of these Supplemental Rules as in effect on the date of the submission of the complaint shall apply to the administrative proceeding commenced thereby.

2. Definitions

Any term defined in the Rules shall have the same meaning in these Supplemental Rules.

3. Communications

(a) **Modalities**. Subject to Paragraphs 3(b) and 5(b) of the Rules, except where otherwise agreed beforehand with the Center, any submission that may or is required to be made to the Center or to an Administrative Panel pursuant to these Rules, may be made:

(i) by telecopy or facsimile transmission, with a confirmation of transmission;

(ii) by electronic mail (e-mail) using the address specified by the Center; or

(iii) where both parties agree, through the Center's Internet-based case filing and administration system.

(b) **E-Mail Address**. For the purposes of any communications by electronic mail to the Center, including those required under Paragraphs 3(b) and 5(b) of the Rules, the following address should be used: domain.disputes@wipo.int.

(c) **Copies**. When a paper submission is to be made to the Center by a Party, it shall be submitted in four (4) sets together with the original of such submission.

(d) **Archive**. The Center shall maintain an archive of all communications received or required to be made under the Rules.

4. Submission of Complaint

(a) **Complaint Transmittal Coversheet**. In accordance with Paragraph 3(b)(xii) of the Rules, the Complainant shall be required to send or transmit its complaint under cover of the Complaint

Transmittal Coversheet set out in *Annex A* hereto and posted on the Center's web site. Where available, the Complainant shall use the version that is in the same language(s) as the registration agreement(s) for the domain name(s) that is/are the subject of the complaint.

(b) **Registrar Notification**. The Complainant shall provide a copy of the complaint to the concerned Registrar(s) at the same time as it submits its complaint to the Center.

(c) **Complaint Notification Instructions**. In accordance with Paragraph 4(a) of the Rules, the Center shall forward the complaint to the Respondent together with the instructions set out in Annex B hereto and posted on the Center's website.

5. Formalities Compliance Review

(a) **Deficiency Notification**. The Center shall, within five (5) calendar days of receiving the complaint, review the complaint for compliance with the formal requirements of the Policy, Rules and Supplemental Rules and notify the Complainant and Respondent of any deficiencies therein.

(b) **Withdrawal**. If the Complainant fails to remedy any deficiencies identified by the Center within the time period provided for in Paragraph 4 of the Rules (i.e., five (5) calendar days), the Center shall notify the Complainant, the Respondent and the concerned Registrar(s) of the deemed withdrawal of the complaint.

(c) **Fee Refunds**. Unless the Complainant confirms its intention to re-submit a complaint to the Center following a deemed withdrawal, the Center shall refund the fee paid by the Complainant pursuant to Paragraph 19 of the Rules, less a processing fee as set forth in *Annex D*.

6. Appointment of Case Administrator

(a) **Notification**. The Center shall advise the Parties of the name and contact details of a member of its staff who shall be the Case Administrator and who shall be responsible for all administrative matters relating to the dispute and communications to the Administrative Panel.

(b) **Responsibilities**. The Case Administrator may provide administrative assistance to the Administrative Panel or a Panelist, but shall have no authority to decide matters of a substantive nature concerning the dispute.

7. Panelist Appointment Procedures

(a) **Party Candidates**. Where a Party is required to submit the names of three (3) candidates for consideration for appointment by the Center as a Panelist (i.e., in accordance with paragraphs 3(b)(iv), 5(b)(v) and 6(d) of the Rules), that Party shall provide the names and contact details of its three candidates in the order of its preference. In appointing a Panelist, the Center shall, subject to availability, respect the order of preference indicated by a Party.

(b) **Presiding Panelist**

(i) The third Panelist appointed in accordance with Paragraph 6(e) of the Rules shall be the Presiding Panelist.

(ii) Where, under Paragraph 6(e) of the Rules, a Party fails to indicate its order of preference for the Presiding Panelist to the Center, the Center shall nevertheless proceed to appoint the Presiding Panelist.

(iii) Notwithstanding the procedure provided for in Paragraph 6(e) of the Rules, the Parties may jointly agree on the identity of the Presiding Panelist, in which case they shall notify the Center in writing of such agreement no later than five (5) calendar days after receiving the list of candidates provided for in Paragraph 6(e).

(c) **Respondent Default**

Where the Respondent does not submit a response or does not submit the payment provided for in Paragraph 5(c) of the Rules by the deadline specified by the Center, the Center shall proceed to appoint the Administrative Panel, as follows:

(i) If the Complainant has designated a single member Administrative Panel, the Center shall appoint the Panelist from its published list;

(ii) If the Complainant has designated a three member Administrative Panel, the Center shall, subject to availability, appoint one Panelist from the names submitted by the Complainant and shall appoint the second Panelist and the Presiding Panelist from its published list.

8. Declaration

In accordance with Paragraph 7 of the Rules, prior to appointment as a Panelist, a candidate shall be required to submit to the Center a Declaration of Independence and Impartiality using the form set out in Annex C hereto and posted on the Center's web site.

9. Fees

The applicable fees for the administrative procedure are specified in Annex D hereto and posted on the Center's web site.

10. Word Limits

(a) The word limit under Paragraph 3(b)(ix) of the Rules shall be 5,000 words.

(b) The word limit under Paragraph 5(b)(i) of the Rules shall be 5,000 words.

(c) For the purposes of Paragraph 15(e) of the Rules, there shall be no word limits.

11. Amendments

Subject to the Policy and Rules, the Center may amend these Supplemental Rules in its sole discretion.

12. Exclusion of Liability

Except in respect of deliberate wrongdoing, an Administrative Panel, the World Intellectual Property Organization and the Center shall not be liable to a party, a concerned registrar or ICANN for any act or omission in connection with the administrative proceeding.

APPENDIX 34:
DOMAIN NAME COMPLAINT

COMPLAINT TRANSMITTAL COVERSHEET

Attached is a Complaint that has been filed against you with the World Intellectual Property Organization (**WIPO**) Arbitration and Mediation Center (the **Center**) pursuant to the Uniform Domain Name Dispute Resolution Policy (the **Policy**) approved by the Internet Corporation for Assigned Names and Numbers (**ICANN**) on October 24, 1999, the Rules for Uniform Domain Name Dispute Resolution Policy (the **Rules**), and the WIPO Supplemental Rules for Uniform Domain Name Dispute Resolution Policy (the **Supplemental Rules**).

The Policy is incorporated by reference into your Registration Agreement with the Registrar(s) of your domain name(s), in accordance with which you are required to submit to a mandatory administrative proceeding in the event that a third party (a **Complainant**) submits a complaint to a dispute resolution service provider, such as the Center, concerning a domain name that you have registered. You will find the name and contact details of the Complainant, as well as the domain name(s) that is/are the subject of the Complaint in the document that accompanies this Coversheet.

You have no duty to act at this time. Once the Center has checked the Complaint to determine that it satisfies the formal requirements of the Policy, the Rules and the Supplemental Rules, it will forward an official copy of the Complaint to you. You will then have 20 calendar days within which to submit a Response to the Complaint in accordance with the Rules and Supplemental Rules to the Center and the Complainant. You may represent yourself or seek the assistance of legal counsel to represent you in the administrative proceeding.

- The **Policy** can be found at http://www.wipo.int/amc/en/domains/rules/

- The **Rules** can be found at http://www.wipo.int/amc/en/domains/rules/

- The **Supplemental Rules**, as well as other information concerning the resolution of domain name disputes can be found at http://www.wipo.int/amc/en/domains/rules/

- A **model Response** can be found at http://www.wipo.int/amc/en/domains/respondent/index.html

Alternatively, you may contact the Center to obtain any of the above documents. The Center can be contacted in Geneva, Switzerland by telephone at +41 22 338 8247, by fax at +41 22 740 3700 or by e-mail at domain.disputes@wipo.int.

You are kindly requested to contact the Center to provide the contact details to which you would like (a) the official version of the Complaint and (b) other communications in the administrative proceeding to be sent.

A copy of this Complaint has also been sent to the Registrar(s) with which the domain name(s) that is/are the subject of the Complaint is/are registered.

By submitting this Complaint to the Center the Complainant hereby agrees to abide and be bound by the provisions of the Policy, Rules and Supplemental Rules.

Before the:

WORLD INTELLECTUAL PROPERTY ORGANIZATION ARBITRATION AND MEDIATION CENTER

[NAME AND ADDRESS OF COMPLAINANT]
(Complainant)

-v-   **Disputed Domain Name*[s]*:**

[NAME AND ADDRESS OF RESPONDENT]   *[<the contested domain name(s)>]*
(Respondent)

COMPLAINT

(Rules, para. 3(b))

I. Introduction

[1.] This Complaint is hereby submitted for decision in accordance with the Uniform Domain Name Dispute Resolution Policy (the Policy), approved by the Internet Corporation for Assigned Names and Numbers (ICANN) on October 24, 1999, the Rules for Uniform Domain Name Dispute Resolution Policy (the Rules), approved by ICANN on October 24, 1999 and the WIPO Supplemental Rules for Uniform Domain Name Dispute Resolution Policy (the Supplemental Rules).

II. The Parties

A. *The Complainant*

(Rules, para. 3(b)(ii) and (iii))

[2.] The Complainant in this administrative proceeding is *[provide full name and, if relevant, legal status, place of incorporation and principal place of business]*.

[3.] The Complainant's contact details are:

Address: *[Specify mailing address]*
Telephone: *[Specify telephone number]*
Fax: *[Specify fax number]*
E-mail: *[Specify e-mail address]*

---

*[If there is more than one Complainant, provide the above informa-
tion for each, describe the relationship between the Complainants
and why each Complainant has a sufficient common interest in the
domain name(s) in issue for a joinder to be permissible.]*

[4.] The Complainant's authorized representative in this administrative proceeding is:

*[If relevant, identify authorized representative and provide all
contact details, including postal address, telephone number, fax
number, e-mail address; if there is more than one authorized
representative, provide contact details for each.]*

[5.] The Complainant's preferred method of communications directed
to the Complainant in this administrative proceeding is:

Electronic-only material

Method: e-mail
Address: *[Specify one e-mail address]*
Contact: *[Identify name of one contact person]*

Material including hardcopy

Method: *[Specify one: fax, post/courier]*
Address: *[Specify one address, if applicable]*
Fax: *[Specify one fax number]*
Contact: *[Identify name of one contact person]*

B. *The Respondent*

(Rules, para. 3(b)(v))

[6.] According to *[indicate why the person/entity identified in the
Complaint has been identified as the Respondent, e.g., the concerned
registrar's Whois database. (Information about the concerned registrar can be found on the Internic database at http://www.internic.
net/whois.html)]*, the Respondent in this administrative proceeding
is *[identify Respondent (the domain name holder), including full
name, and if relevant, legal status, place of incorporation and
principal place of business, or residence)]*. Copies of the printout of
the database search*[es]* conducted on *[date]* are provided as Annex
[Annex number].

[7.] All information known to the Complainant regarding how to contact the Respondent is as follows:

*[Provide all contact details (postal address, telephone number, fax
number, email addresses) for the Respondent, including those that*

may have been used successfully in the course of pre-complaint dealings and those available from any Whois look-up service.]

[If there is more than one Respondent, provide the contact details for each Respondent and describe the relationship between them, which justifies them being named in a common complaint.]

III. The Domain Name[s] and Registrar[s]

(Rules, para. 3(b)(vi) and (vii))

[8.]   This dispute concerns the domain name*[s]* identified below:

[Identify precisely the domain name(s) in issue.]

[9.]   The registrar*[s]* with which the domain name*[s] [is/are]* registered *[is/are]*:

[Provide the name and full contact details of the registrar(s) with which the domain name(s) (is/are) registered.]

IV. Jurisdictional Basis for the Administrative Proceeding

(Rules, paras. 3(a), 3(b)(xv)

[10.] This dispute is properly within the scope of the Policy and the Administrative Panel has jurisdiction to decide the dispute. The registration agreement, pursuant to which the domain name*[s]* that *[is/are]* the subject of this Complaint *[is/are]* registered, incorporates the Policy. *[If relevant, indicate when the domain name(s) (was/were) registered and specify the provision of the registration agreement that makes the Policy applicable to the domain names(s).]* A true and correct copy of the domain name dispute policy that applies to the domain name*[s]* in question is provided as Annex *[Annex number]* to this Complaint.

V. Factual and Legal Grounds

(Policy, paras. 4(a), (b), (c); Rules, para. 3)

[In completing this Section V., do not exceed the 5000 word limit: Supplemental Rules, para. 10(a). Relevant documentation in support of the Complaint should be submitted as Annexes, with a schedule indexing such Annexes. Copies of case precedents or commentaries that are referred to for support should be referred to with complete citations and, if not voluminous, submitted as Annexes.]

[11.] This Complaint is based on the following grounds:

A. *The domain name[s] [is/are] identical or confusingly similar to a trademark or service mark in which the Complainant has rights;*

(Policy, para. 4(a)(i), Rules, paras. 3(b)(viii), (b)(ix)(1))

• *[In accordance with Rules, para. 3(b)(viii), specify the trademark(s) or service mark(s) on which the Complaint is based and, for each mark, describe the goods or services, if any, in connection with which the mark is used. A separate description may also be given of the goods or services with which the Complainant intends to use the mark in the future. If applicable, attach copies of the registration certificates for the relevant marks.]*

• *[In accordance with Rules, para. 3(b)(ix)(1), describe the manner in which the domain name(s) (is/are) identical or confusingly similar to a trademark or service mark in which the Complainant has rights.]*

B. *The Respondent has no rights or legitimate interests in respect of the domain name[s];*

(Policy, para. 4(a)(ii), Rules, para. 3(b)(ix)(2))

• [In accordance with Rules, para. 3(b)(ix)(2), describe why the Respondent should be considered as having no rights or legitimate interests in respect of the domain name(s) that (is/are) the subject of the Complaint. Attention should be paid to any relevant aspects of the Policy, para. 4(c), including:

– *Whether before any notice to the Respondent of the dispute, there is any evidence of the Respondent's use of, or demonstrable preparations to use, the domain name(s) or a name corresponding to the domain name(s) in connection with a bona fide offering of goods or services;*

– *Whether the Respondent (as an individual, business, or other organization) has been commonly known by the domain name, even if the Respondent has acquired no trademark or service mark rights;*

– *Whether the Respondent is making a legitimate non-commercial or fair use of the domain name(s), without intent for commercial gain misleadingly to divert consumers or to tarnish the trademark or service mark at issue.]*

C. *The domain name[s] [was/were] registered and [is/are] being used in bad faith.*

(Policy, paras. 4(a)(iii), 4(b); Rules, para. 3(b)(ix)(3))

- [In accordance with Rules, para. 3(b)(ix)(3), describe why the domain name(s) should be considered as having been registered and used in bad faith by the Respondent. Attention should be paid to any relevant aspects of the Policy, para. 4(b), including:

  – *Circumstances indicating that the domain name(s) (was/were) registered or acquired primarily for the purpose of selling, renting, or otherwise transferring the domain name registration(s) to the owner of the trademark or service mark (normally the Complainant) or to a competitor of that Complainant, for valuable consideration in excess of the Respondent's out-of-pocket costs directly related to the domain name(s); or*

  – *Whether the domain name(s) (was/were) registered in order to prevent the owner of the trademark or service mark from reflecting the mark in a corresponding domain name, provided that the Respondent has engaged in a pattern of such conduct; or*

  – *Whether the domain name(s) (was/were) registered primarily for the purpose of disrupting the business of a competitor; or*

  – *Whether by using the domain name(s), the Respondent intentionally attempted to attract for commercial gain, Internet users to the Respondent's web site or other on-line location, by creating a likelihood of confusion with the Complainant's mark as to the source, sponsorship, affiliation, or endorsement of the Respondent's web site or location or of a product or service on the Respondent's web site or location.]*

VI. Remedies Requested

(Rules, para. 3(b)(x))

[12.] In accordance with Paragraph 4(i) of the Policy, for the reasons described in Section V above, the Complainant requests the Administrative Panel appointed in this administrative proceeding *[choose **one** per domain name: "issue a decision that <the contested domain name(s)> be transferred to the Complainant"/"be cancelled."]*

VII. Administrative Panel

(Rules, para. 3(b)(iv))

[13.] The Complainant elects to have the dispute decided by a *[choose one: "single-member Administrative Panel"/"three-member Administrative Panel"].*

[ ] *[If a three-member Administrative Panel is designated, the names of three persons must be provided, one of whom the Center shall attempt to appoint to the Administrative Panel in accordance with Para. 6 of the Rules and Para. 7 of the Supplemental Rules. The names of the nominees may be taken from the Center's published list of panelists at http://arbiter.wipo.int/domains/ panel/panelists.html, or that of any other ICANN-accredited dispute resolution service provider.]*

VIII. Mutual Jurisdiction

(Rules, para. 3(b)(xiii))

[14.] In accordance with Paragraph 3(b)(xiii) of the Rules, the Complainant will submit, with respect to any challenges that may be made by the Respondent to a decision by the Administrative Panel to transfer or cancel the domain name*[s]* that *[is/are]* the subject of this Complaint, to the jurisdiction of the courts at *[choose* **one** *of the following:*

(a) "the location of the principal office of the concerned registrar." (or)

(b) "the location of the domain name holder's address, as shown for the registration of the domain name(s) in the concerned regis- trar's Whois database at the time of the submission of the Complaint to the Center." (or)

(c) "the location of the principal office of the concerned registrar AND the domain name holder's address, as shown for the regis- tration of the domain name(s) in the concerned registrar's Whois database at the time of the submission of the Complaint to the Center."

A Mutual Jurisdiction election must be made for each domain name that is the subject of the Complaint.]

IX. Other Legal Proceedings

(Rules, para. 3(b)(xi))

[15.] *[If any, identify other legal proceedings that have been commenced or terminated in connection with or relating to the domain name(s) that (is/are) the subject of the Complaint and summarize the issues that are the subject of (that/those) proceeding(s).]*

X. Communications

(Rules, paras. 2(b), 3(b)(xii); Supplemental Rules, paras. 3, 4)

[16.] A copy of this Complaint, together with the cover sheet as pre-scribed by the Supplemental Rules, has been sent or transmitted to the Respondent on *[date]* by *[indicate method(s) of communication and contact details used, with reference to Rules, para. 2(b)]*.

[17.] A copy of this Complaint, has been sent or transmitted to the concerned registrar*[s]* on *[date]* by *[indicate method(s) of communication and contact details used]*.

[18.] This Complaint is submitted to the Center in electronic form (except to the extent not available for annexes), and in four (4) sets together with the original.

XI. Payment

[19.] As required by the Rules and Supplemental Rules, payment in the amount of USD *[amount]* has been made by *[method]*.

XII. Certification

(Rules, para. 3(b)(xiv))

[20.] The Complainant agrees that its claims and remedies concerning the registration of the domain name*[s]*, the dispute, or the dispute's resolution shall be solely against the domain name holder and waives all such claims and remedies against (a) the WIPO Arbitration and Mediation Center and Panelists, except in the case of deliberate wrongdoing, (b) the concerned registrar*[s]*, (c) the registry administrator, (d) the Internet Corporation for Assigned Names and Numbers, as well as their directors, officers, employees, and agents.

[21.] The Complainant certifies that the information contained in this Complaint is to the best of the Complainant's knowledge complete and accurate, that this Complaint is not being presented for any improper purpose, such as to harass, and that the assertions in this Complaint are warranted under the Rules and under applicable law, as it now exists or as it may be extended by a good-faith and reasonable argument.

Respectfully submitted,

Date: _____

_____

[Name/Signature]

APPENDIX 35:
RESPONSE TO DOMAIN NAME COMPLAINT

Before the:

**WORLD INTELLECTUAL PROPERTY ORGANIZATION
ARBITRATION AND MEDIATION CENTER**

[NAME AND ADDRESS OF COMPLAINANT AS STATED IN COMPLAINT] (**Complainant**)	**Case No:** *[Indicate assigned case number]*
-v-	**Disputed Domain Name*[s]*:**
[NAME AND ADDRESS OF RESPONDENT] (**Respondent**)	*[<the contested domain name(s)>]*

RESPONSE

(Rules, para. 5(b))

I. Introduction

[1.] On *[indicate date on which the Notification of Complaint and Commencement of Administrative Proceeding was received]*, the Respondent received a Notification of Complaint and Commencement of Administrative Proceeding from the WIPO Arbitration and Mediation Center (the **Center**) by *[e-mail/fax/post/courier]* informing the Respondent that an administrative proceeding had been commenced by the Complainant in accordance with the Uniform Domain Name Dispute Resolution Policy (the **Policy**), approved by the Internet Corporation for Assigned Names and Numbers (**ICANN**) on October 24, 1999, the Rules for Uniform Domain Name Dispute Resolution Policy (the **Rules**), approved by ICANN on October 24, 1999, and the WIPO Supplemental Rules for Uniform Domain Name Dispute Resolution Policy (the **Supplemental Rules**). The Center set *[insert date]* as the last day for the submission of a Response by the Respondent.

II. Respondent's Contact Details

(Rules, para. 5(b)(ii) and (iii))

[2.] The Respondent's contact details are:

Name: *[Specify full name]*
Address: *[Specify mailing address]*
Telephone: *[Specify telephone number]*
Fax: *[Specify fax number]*
E-mail: *[Specify e-mail address]*
[If there is more than one Respondent, provide the above information for each.]

[3.] The Respondent's authorized representative in this administrative proceeding is:

[If relevant, identify authorized representative and provide all contact details, including postal address, telephone number, fax number, e-mail address; if there is more than one authorized representative, provide contact details for each.]

[4.] The Respondent's preferred method of communications directed to the Respondent in this administrative proceeding is:

Electronic-only material

Method: e-mail
Address: *[Specify one e-mail address]*
Contact: *[Identify name of one contact person]*

Material including hardcopy

Method: *[Specify one: fax, post/courier]*
Address: *[Specify one address, if applicable]*
Fax: *[Specify one fax number]*
Contact: *[Identify name of one contact person]*

III. Response to Statements and Allegations Made in Complaint

(Policy, paras. 4(a), (b), (c); Rules, para. 5)

[In completing this Section III., do not exceed the 5000 word limit: Supplemental Rules, para. 10(b). Relevant documentation in support of the Response, should be submitted as Annexes, with a schedule indexing such documents. Case precedents or commentaries that are referred to for support should be referred to with complete citations and, if not voluminous, submitted as Annexes.]

[5.] The Respondent hereby responds to the statements and allegations in the Complaint and respectfully requests the Administrative Panel to deny the remedies requested by the Complainant.

[The Rules, para. 5(b)(i) instruct the Respondent in its Response to "Respond specifically to the statements and allegations contained in the complaint and include any and all bases for the Respondent (domain name holder) to retain registration and use of the disputed domain name...." For a complainant to succeed, it must establish that each of the three conditions under the Policy, paras. 4(a)(i), (ii), (iii) are satisfied. With reference to that para. 4(a), in this section the Respondent may wish to discuss some or all of the following, to the extent relevant and supported by evidence:]

A. Whether the domain name[s] [is/are] identical or confusingly similar to a trademark or service mark in which the Complainant has rights;

(Policy, para. 4(a)(i))

[In this connection, consideration may, for example, be given to the following:]

• *[Any challenges to the trade or service mark rights asserted by the Complainant.]*

• *[A refutation of the arguments made by the Complainant concerning the manner in which the domain name(s) (is/are) allegedly identical or confusingly similar to a trademark or service mark in which the Complainant claims it has rights.]*

B. *Whether the Respondent has rights or legitimate interests in respect of the domain name[s];*

(Policy, para. 4(a)(ii))

[In this connection, consideration may, for example, be given to the following:]

• *[A refutation of the arguments made by the Complainant as to why the Respondent should be considered as having no rights or legitimate interests in respect of the domain name(s) that (is/are) the subject of the Complaint. Evidence should be submitted in support of any claims made by the Respondent concerning its alleged rights or legitimate interests in the domain name(s).]*

• *[The Policy, para. 4(c) sets out examples of circumstances demonstrating the Respondent's rights to or legitimate interests in the domain name(s) for the purposes of the Policy, para. 4(a)(ii). With reference to that para. 4(c), to the extent argued by the Complainant, the Respondent should discuss and show that:*

– before the Respondent received any notice of the dispute, there is evidence of the Respondent's use of, or demonstrable preparations to use, the domain name(s) or a name corresponding to the domain name(s) in connection with a bona fide offering of goods or services;

– the Respondent (as an individual, business, or other organization) has been or is commonly known by the domain name(s) in issue, even if the Respondent has acquired no trademark or service mark rights;

– the Respondent is making a legitimate non-commercial or fair use of the domain name(s), without intent for commercial gain misleadingly to divert consumers or to tarnish the trademark(s) or service mark(s) at issue.]

C. *Whether the domain name[s] [has/have] been registered and [is/are] being used in bad faith.*

(Policy, para. 4(a)(iii))

[In this connection, consideration may, for example, be given to the following:]

• *[A refutation of the arguments made by the Complainant as to why the domain name(s) should be considered as registered and used in bad faith.]*

• *[The Policy, para. 4(b) identifies several examples of circumstances that an Administrative Panel could consider as constituting bad faith. With reference to that para. 4(b), to the extent argued by the Complainant, the Respondent should discuss and show that:*

– the domain name(s) (was/were) not registered or acquired primarily for the purpose of selling, renting, or otherwise transferring the domain name registration(s) to the Complainant, as the alleged owner of the trademark or service mark, or to a competitor of the Complainant, for valuable consideration in excess of the Respondent's out-of-pocket costs directly related to the domain name(s);

– the domain name(s) (was/were) not registered in order to prevent the Complainant from reflecting the mark in a corresponding domain name and, in connection therewith, the Respondent has not engaged in a pattern of such conduct;

– the Complainant and the Respondent are not competitors and/or the domain name(s) (was/were) not registered by the Respondent primarily to disrupt the Complainant's business;

– the domain name(s) (was/were) not registered by the Respondent in an intentional attempt to attract for commercial gain, Internet users to the Respondent's web site or other on-line location, by creating a likelihood of confusion with the Complainant's mark as to the source, sponsorship, affiliation, or endorsement of the Respondent's web site or location or of a product or service on the Respondent's web site or location.]

[D. If appropriate and the allegation can be substantiated with evidence, the Rules provide that a Respondent may ask the Panel to make a finding of reverse domain name hijacking. (Rules, para. 15(e))]

IV. Administrative Panel

(Rules, paras. 5(b)(iv) and (b)(v) and para. 6;
Supplemental Rules, para. 7)

[6.] The Respondent elects to have the dispute decided by a *[state "single-member Administrative Panel" if the Complainant has asked for a single-member Administrative Panel and the Respondent agrees with that election. If the Respondent does not agree and wants a three-member Administrative Panel instead, state "three-member Administrative Panel." Note that in the latter case the Respondent must pay half of the Center's fee for a three-member*

Administrative Panel, as set out in Supplemental Rules, Annex D. If the Complainant has indicated it wants a three-member Administrative Panel, then the Respondent does not have the option of choosing a single-member Administrative Panel].

[ ] *[If the Respondent designates a three-member Administrative Panel, or if the Complainant has designated a three-member Panel, the Respondent must provide the names of three persons, one of whom the Center will endeavor to appoint to the Administrative Panel in accordance with Para. 6 of the Rules and Para. 7 of the Supplemental Rules. The names of these three nominees may be taken from the Center's published list of panelists at http://arbiter. wipo.int/domains/panel/panelists.html, or that of any other ICANN-accredited dispute resolution service provider.]*

V. Other Legal Proceedings

(Rules, para. 5(b)(vi))

[ ] *[If any, identify other legal proceedings that have been commenced or terminated in connection with or relating to the domain name(s) that (is/are) the subject of the Complaint and summarize the issues that are the subject of (that/those) proceeding(s).]*

VI. Communications

(Rules, paras. 2(b), 5(b)(vii); Supplemental Rules, para. 3)

[7.] A copy of this Response has been sent or transmitted to the Complainant on *[date]* by *[indicate methods of communication and contact details used, with reference to Rules, para. 2(b)].*

[8.] This Response is submitted to the Center in electronic form (except to the extent not available for annexes), and in four (4) sets together with the original.

VII. Payment

(Rules, para. 5(c); Supplemental Rules, Annex D)

[ ] *[If relevant, state: "In view of the Complainant's designation of a single-member Panel and the Respondent's designation of a three-member Panel, the Respondent hereby submits payment in the amount of USD (amount) by (method)."]*

VIII. Certification

(Rules, para. 5(b)(viii), Supplemental Rules, para. 12)

[9.] The Respondent agrees that, except in respect of deliberate wrong-doing, an Administrative Panel, the World Intellectual Property

Organization and the Center shall not be liable for any act or omission in connection with the administrative proceeding.

[10.] The Respondent certifies that the information contained in this Response is to the best of the Respondent's knowledge complete and accurate, that this Response is not being presented for any improper purpose, such as to harass, and that the assertions in this Response are warranted under the Rules and under applicable law, as it now exists or as it may be extended by a good-faith and reasonable argument.

Respectfully submitted,

Date: _____

_____

[Name/Signature]

APPENDIX 36:
ANTICYBERSQUATTING
CONSUMER PROTECTION ACT
[PUB. L. NO. 106-113, 11/29/99]

Section 43(d) of the Lanham Act:

(d) Cyberpiracy prevention

(1)(A) A person shall be liable in a civil action by the owner of a mark, including a personal name which is protected as a mark under this section, if, without regard to the goods or services of the parties, that person —

(i) has a bad faith intent to profit from that mark, including a personal name which is protected as a mark under this section; and

(ii) registers, traffics in, or uses a domain name that —

(I) in the case of a mark that is distinctive at the time of registration of the domain name, is identical or confusingly similar to that mark;

(II) in the case of a famous mark that is famous at the time of registration of the domain name, is identical or confusingly similar to or dilutive of that mark; or

(III) is a trademark, word, or name protected by reason of section 706 of title 18 or section 220506 of title 36.

(B)(i) In determining whether a person has a bad faith intent described under subparagraph (A), a court may consider factors such as, but not limited to —

(I) the trademark or other intellectual property rights of the person, if any, in the domain name;

(II) the extent to which the domain name consists of the legal name of the person or a name that is otherwise commonly used to identify that person;

(III) the person's prior use, if any, of the domain name in connection with the bona fide offering of any goods or services;

(IV) the person's bona fide noncommercial or fair use of the mark in a site accessible under the domain name;

(V) the person's intent to divert consumers from the mark owner's online location to a site accessible under the domain name that could harm the goodwill represented by the mark, either for commercial gain or with the intent to tarnish or disparage the mark, by creating a likelihood of confusion as to the source, sponsorship, affiliation, or endorsement of the site;

(VI) the person's offer to transfer, sell, or otherwise assign the domain name to the mark owner or any third party for financial gain without having used, or having an intent to use, the domain name in the bona fide offering of any goods or services, or the person's prior conduct indicating a pattern of such conduct;

(VII) the person's provision of material and misleading false contact information when applying for the registration of the domain name, the person's intentional failure to maintain accurate contact information, or the person's prior conduct indicating a pattern of such conduct;

(VIII) the person's registration or acquisition of multiple domain names which the person knows are identical or confusingly similar to marks of others that are distinctive at the time of registration of such domain names, or dilutive of famous marks of others that are famous at the time of registration of such domain names, without regard to the goods or services of the parties; and

(IX) the extent to which the mark incorporated in the person's domain name registration is or is not distinctive and famous within the meaning of subsection (c).

(ii) Bad faith intent described under subparagraph (A) shall not be found in any case in which the court determines that the person believed and had reasonable grounds to believe that the use of the domain name was a fair use or otherwise lawful.

(C) In any civil action involving the registration, trafficking, or use of a domain name under this paragraph, a court may order the forfeiture or cancellation of the domain name or the transfer of the domain name to the owner of the mark.

(D) A person shall be liable for using a domain name under subparagraph (A) only if that person is the domain name registrant or that registrant's authorized licensee.

(E) As used in this paragraph, the term "traffics in" refers to transactions that include, but are not limited to, sales, purchases, loans, pledges, licenses, exchanges of currency, and any other transfer for consideration or receipt in exchange for consideration.

(2)(A) The owner of a mark may file an in rem civil action against a domain name in the judicial district in which the domain name registrar, domain name registry, or other domain name authority that registered or assigned the domain name is located if—

(i) the domain name violates any right of the owner of a mark registered in the Patent and Trademark Office, or protected under subsection (a) or (c) of this section; and

(ii) the court finds that the owner —

(I) is not able to obtain in personam jurisdiction over a person who would have been a defendant in a civil action under paragraph (1); or

(II) through due diligence was not able to find a person who would have been a defendant in a civil action under paragraph

(1) by —

(aa) sending a notice of the alleged violation and intent to proceed under this paragraph to the registrant of the domain name at the postal and e-mail address provided by the registrant to the registrar; and

(bb) publishing notice of the action as the court may direct promptly after filing the action.

(B) The actions under subparagraph (A)(ii) shall constitute service of process.

(C) In an in rem action under this paragraph, a domain name shall be deemed to have its situs in the judicial district in which —

(i) the domain name registrar, registry, or other domain name authority that registered or assigned the domain name is located;

or

(ii) documents sufficient to establish control and authority regarding the disposition of the registration and use of the domain name are deposited with the court.

(D)(i) The remedies in an in rem action under this paragraph shall be limited to a court order for the forfeiture or cancellation of the domain name or the transfer of the domain name to the owner of the mark. Upon receipt of written notification of a filed, stamped copy of a complaint filed by the owner of a mark in a United States district court under this paragraph, the domain name registrar, domain name registry, or other domain name authority shall —

(I) expeditiously deposit with the court documents sufficient to establish the court's control and authority regarding the disposition of the registration and use of the domain name to the court; and

(II) not transfer, suspend, or otherwise modify the domain name during the pendency of the action, except upon order of the court.

(ii) The domain name registrar or registry or other domain name authority shall not be liable for injunctive or monetary relief under this paragraph except in the case of bad faith or reckless disregard, which includes a willful failure to comply with any such court order.

(3) The civil action established under paragraph (1) and the in rem action established under paragraph (2), and any remedy available under either such action, shall be in addition to any other civil action or remedy otherwise applicable.

(4) The in rem jurisdiction established under paragraph (2) shall be in addition to any other jurisdiction that otherwise exists, whether in rem or in personam.

***

Section 35(d) of the Lanham Act:

(d) Statutory damages for violation of section 1125(d)(1)

In a case involving a violation of section 1125(d)(1) of this title, the plaintiff may elect, at any time before final judgment is rendered by the trial court, to recover, instead of actual damages and profits, an award of statutory damages in the amount of not less than $1,000 and not more than $100,000 per domain name, as the court considers just.

GLOSSARY

ACPA—Anticybersquatting Consumer Protection Act, creating redress against a domain name registrant who intends, in bad faith, to profit from a distinctive or famous mark by registering a domain name that is confusingly similar or identical to the mark.

Allegation of use/amendment to allege use—A document filed to allege use of a mark in commerce following the filing of an application (see also **SOU**). Following a final PTO rulemaking effective January 16, 2009, the PTO prefers that a document entitled "Amendment to Allege Use" be titled "Allegation of Use" instead.

Blackout period—The period of time between a mark's approval for publication for opposition and the date of issuance of the Notice of Allowance, during which time an application cannot be amended to file an allegation of use.

Cancellation proceeding—An action brought in the TTAB by a party who believes it will be damaged by the continuation of a registration that has already issued for a mark.

Central attack—Refers to the vulnerability of an international registration during its first five years if the underlying application or registration fails for some reason.

Certification mark—A mark used by third parties to certify a mode of manufacture, quality, or some other characteristic of a good or service.

CFR—Code of Federal Regulations, title 37 of which includes the rules of practice governing trademarks, often incorporated into the TMEP.

Collective mark—A mark owned by a parent organization and used by its members to apply to their own goods or services.

Collective membership mark—A mark used by members of a group to denote their membership in that group.

Conveying party—The person or entity conveying, or transferring, ownership of a trademark application or registration to another party. The conveying party is also known as an assignor.

Court of Appeals for the Federal Circuit—The federal appellate court hearing, among other things, appeals related to PTO proceedings.

CTM—Refers to a Community Trademark application, which is an application covering the member states of the European Union.

Disclaimer—A statement made a part of a trademark application and resulting registration that the owner does not claim exclusive rights to one or more elements of the mark separate and apart from the mark as a whole.

Examiner's amendment—An amendment to a trademark application issued by an examiner following a communication with a trademark owner or the owner's authorized representative, typically resolving outstanding issues related to an application and placing it in condition for publication.

Filing basis—Refers to one of the five bases available for filing a trademark application: use-based, intent-to-use, foreign priority, foreign registration or Madrid Protocol.

ICANN—Internet Corporation for Assigned Names and Numbers, a public benefit corporation responsible for coordinating various activities concerning the overall operation of the Internet.

Incontestability—The status accorded a trademark registered on the Principal Register upon the filing of an affidavit of incontestability after the mark has been in continuous use in commerce for at least five consecutive years, verifying the owner's valid registration and right to use the mark to the exclusion of all others.

Inherently distinctive—Refers to a mark that is capable of identifying and distinguishing one merchant's goods or services from others immediately upon its use.

International Bureau—Known as the IB, the agency within WIPO responsible for administering applications made through the Madrid Protocol.

International registration—Also known as an IR, a trademark registration covering several countries.

ITU—Common acronym for an intent-to-use based trademark application.

Lanham Act—The federal law governing trademarks, also known as the Trademark Act.

Likelihood of confusion—The standard of proof to be met by a plaintiff in a trademark infringement suit.

Madrid Protocol—An international treaty allowing trademark owners to file one application covering several countries with a single filing authority.

Naked licensing—The act of licensing a trademark to a third party without effective quality control, resulting in the mark's loss of distinctiveness.

Nice classification—Refers to the International (Nice) Classification of Goods and Services for the Purpose of Registration of Marks, containing a series of numerical classifications of goods and services for use in trademark applications.

NOA—Common acronym for a Notice of Allowance, a document that issues following publication of, and lack of opposition against, an intent-to-use based application.

Notice of abandonment—A written notice issued by the PTO stating that an application is no longer pending and therefore cannot mature into a registration.

Notice of irregularity—A written notice of deficiency in an application for international registration issued by the International Bureau in a Madrid Protocol application.

Notice of publication—A written notice issued by the PTO notifying an applicant that its mark will be published in the Official Gazette.

Office action—A written communication from an examiner at the PTO requesting a response from the trademark applicant concerning a matter related to the application.

Office of origin—The filing authority through which an application for international registration originates.

OG—Official Gazette, also known as TMOG (Trademark Official Gazette), a weekly publication of the PTO in which marks approved by examining attorneys for registration as well as registered marks are published for public viewing.

Opposition proceeding—An action brought in the TTAB by a party who believes it will be injured by an applicant's registration of the applied-for mark.

Paris Convention—Refers to the Paris Convention for the Protection of Industrial Property, an international treaty offering reciprocal rights of intellectual property protection to nations that adhere to the treaty.

Power of attorney—A trademark owner's grant of authorization to a third party to act on behalf of the trademark owner.

Principal Register—The highest level of trademark registration, reserved for marks that are inherently distinctive or that have acquired secondary meaning.

Prosecution—A term encompassing the full range of tasks involved in pursuing the registration of a trademark with the PTO.

PTO—The United States Patent and Trademark Office.

Receiving party—The person or entity receiving a transfer of a trademark application or registration from its current owner. The receiving party is also known as an assignee.

Request for extension of time to file a statement of use—A request made by or on behalf of a trademark applicant to the PTO for a six-month extension of time to file the statement of use that is due following the issuance of a notice of allowance with respect to an intent-to-use based application.

Request for reconsideration—An applicant's petition to an examiner to reconsider a final refusal to register a mark.

Secondary meaning—Refers to evidence that a mark has acquired distinctiveness through use and is therefore capable of functioning as a trademark.

Service mark—A word(s), name, symbol (such as a logo), or device (or a combination of these elements) that identifies and distinguishes one merchant's services from those of another.

SOU—Common acronym for a Statement of Use, a document typically filed following the issuance of a Notice of Allowance to declare use of a mark in commerce (see also **Allegation of Use**). Following a final PTO rulemaking effective January 16, 2009, the PTO prefers that an SOU be titled "Allegation of Use."

Standard character mark—A depiction of a mark using Latin characters, Roman or Arabic numerals, common punctuation or diacritical marks, and no design element.

Stylized/special form mark—A depiction of a mark in a particular style of lettering, including a design or logo.

Subsequent designation—A filing made subsequent to the issuance of an international registration to cover additional countries.

Supplemental Register—A level of trademark registration for marks that lack distinctiveness but are capable of acquiring secondary meaning through continued use.

TARR—Trademark Applications and Registrations Retrieval, a PTO database of applications and registrations searchable by serial or registration number.

TEAS—The PTO's online filing system for trademark applications and other documents related to the application and registration of a mark.

TESS—Trademark Electronic Search System, the PTO's online searchable database.

TMEP—Trademark Manual of Examining Procedure, a guide used by examiners in addressing issues related to trademark applications and post-registration matters.

Trade dress—A term originating from the packaging, or dressing, of a product and now generally referring to the overall assembly of elements such as product appearance, design and packaging, the overall impact of which is to distinguish that product from other products.

Trademark—A word(s), name, symbol (such as a logo), or device (or a combination of these elements) that identifies and distinguishes one merchant's goods from those of another.

Trademark Dilution Revision Act—A 2006 federal act revising The Federal Trademark Dilution Act of 1996 by amending, among other things, the standard of proof in trademark dilution cases.

TTAB—Trademark Trial and Appeal Board. The TTAB is an administrative tribunal of the PTO that hears appeals of refusals to register a mark and maintains jurisdiction over cancellation and opposition proceedings.

UDRP—Common acronym for the Uniform Domain Name Dispute Resolution Policy administered by ICANN.

WIPO—World Intellectual Property Organization.